THE RELUCTANT WELFARE STATE
American Social Welfare Policies—
Past, Present, and Future

E   D   I   T   I   O   N

3

THE RELUCTANT WELFARE STATE
American Social Welfare Policies—
Past, Present, and Future

Bruce S. Jansson
University of Southern California

Brooks/Cole Publishing Company

I(**T**)**P**® *An International Thomson Publishing Company*

Pacific Grove • Albany • Bonn • Boston • Cincinnati • Detroit
London • Madrid • Melbourne • Mexico City • New York • Paris
San Francisco • Singapore • Tokyo • Toronto • Washington

Sponsoring Editor: *Lisa Gebo*
Marketing Team: *Jean Vevers Thompson and Margaret Parks*
Editorial Assistant: *Terry Thomas*
Production Editor: *Laurel Jackson*
Production Assistant: *Dorothy Bell*
Manuscript Editor: *Bernard Gilbert*
Permissions Editor: *Mary Kay Hancharick*
Interior and Cover Design: *Sharon L. Kinghan*
Interior Illustration: *Lisa Torri*

Cover Photos: *© Bob Daemmrich / Stock Boston, © Stock Montage, Inc., © Katherine McGlynn / The Image Works*
Art Editor: *Lisa Torri*
Photo Editor: *Robert J. Western*
Photo Researcher: *Susan Kaprov*
Indexer: *James Minkin*
Typesetting: *TBH Typecast, Inc.*
Cover Printing: *Phoenix Color Corporation*
Printing and Binding: *Quebecor Printing Fairfield*

For more information, contact:

BROOKS/COLE PUBLISHING COMPANY
511 Forest Lodge Road
Pacific Grove, CA 93950
USA

International Thomson Publishing Europe
Berkshire House 168-173
High Holborn
London WC1V 7AA
England

Thomas Nelson Australia
102 Dodds Street
South Melbourne, 3205
Victoria, Australia

Nelson Canada
1120 Birchmount Road
Scarborough, Ontario
Canada M1K 5G4

International Thomson Editores
Seneca 53
Col. Polanco
C.P. 11560 México, D. F., México

International Thomson Publishing GmbH
Königswinterer Strasse 418
53227 Bonn
Germany

International Thomson Publishing Asia
221 Henderson Road
#05-10 Henderson Building
Singapore 0315

International Thomson Publishing Japan
Hirakawacho Kyowa Building, 3F
2-2-1 Hirakawacho
Chiyoda-ku, Tokyo 102
Japan

Printed in the United States of America

10 9 8 7 6 5 4

Library of Congress Cataloging-in-Publication Data

Jansson, Bruce S.
    The reluctant welfare state : American social welfare policies—
past, present, and future / Bruce S. Jansson.—3rd ed.
        p.   cm.
    Includes bibliographical references and index.
    ISBN 0-534-34141-1
    1. United States—Social policy.   2. United States—Social
conditions.   3. Public welfare—United States—History.   I. Title.
HN57.J25   1997
361.6'1'0973—dc20   96-12028
                                                    CIP

To Betty Ann

Contents

Preface

Before I undertook this revision, I asked myself whether social policy history is still relevant to students who are entering the social work profession. Viewed merely as a descriptive enterprise that focuses on the memorization of events and facts, it clearly is not. Nor is it relevant if history, interesting as it may be, is seen as an end in itself. Social policy history is powerfully relevant to social workers, however, if it is used to stimulate critical thinking about issues, developments, and policies in prior eras and in contemporary society. It can encourage the following:

1. Ethical reasoning about a range of issues, including controversial policies and social reform
2. Analysis of limitations and strengths of the American welfare state, including the role of the federal government and entitlements
3. Analysis of the evolution and structure of the American welfare state—and comparisons with the welfare states of other nations
4. Analysis of specific policies
5. Awareness of the evolution and direction of the social work profession
6. Knowledge of the oppression of diverse outgroups—including women, African Americans, Latinos, Native Americans, gay men and lesbians, older Americans, children, and people with physical disabilities—and of policies that might help them better their condition
7. Understanding of the need to include policy practice and social reform work in professional careers in order to help outgroups and others improve their lot
8. Understanding of how the lives of ordinary people and social work clients are deeply affected by social policies of local, state, and federal governments, as well as by agency policies

All these purposes are even more compelling today in the United States, where basic values and commitments are questioned more extensively than in any recent period and where the central theme of this book—the reluctance of the American welfare state—has never been more acutely demonstrated.

To focus the teaching of social policy history so that it promotes critical thinking about these kinds of issues, I have added 33 inserts to this edition. Some are titled "Critical Analysis"; others are titled "Ethical Analysis of Key Issues and Policies." They cover a range of topics relevant not only to specific historical periods, but to contemporary society. When discussing poorhouses in the 19th century, for example, students are asked to analyze when people are "deserving" and when, if ever, they are "undeserving." When discussing conservatives' efforts to curtail AFDC in the 1990s, students are asked to analyze whether denial or curtailment of benefits to single mothers would diminish out-of-wedlock births.

To promote critical thinking, I discuss competing radical, liberal, libertarian, and conservative ideologies in the new first chapter and identify their premises, core values, and perspectives. I argue that social workers can develop their policy identities by examining issues that have arisen in prior eras and the contemporary period.

I introduce readers to analytic and ethical-reasoning skills in the new second chapter. I provide a framework for ethical reasoning that links ethical principles, analysis of policy outcomes, and practical considerations. To help students understand how the American welfare state evolved, the chapter also discusses contextual and political factors that have shaped social policies in the United States.

Two concluding chapters have been rewritten to stimulate critical thinking about the direction of the

American welfare state. Chapter 13 discusses six dimensions that make the American welfare state more reluctant than most European ones and identifies a number of factors that have contributed to this reluctance. Drawing on examples from prior chapters, I critically examine key assumptions and panaceas of conservatives in Chapter 14 and dispute conservatives' contention that many social problems are primarily caused by the welfare state. I also discuss the limitations of public policies and suggest that they often cannot solve a range of problems, even if they provide many positive benefits. By discussing reform projects of social workers in prior eras, I discuss how students can include policy practice in their professional careers.

I include an extended chapter on the Clinton presidency that analyzes the conflict among Newt Gingrich, "New Democrats" like Bill Clinton, and Democratic liberals in Congress.

I retain the previous edition's emphasis on the oppression of various outgroups during American history. Drawing on the rapidly expanding research of many historians, I have supplemented these materials with more emphasis on empowerment strategies. Although these groups have often been subjected to punitive policies and discrimination, they have developed ingenious survival strategies, such as self-help, advocacy, and political action.

I have merged the chapters on the medieval and colonial periods. This revision allows me to place colonial Americans in their European context and also to examine how they evolved unique institutions by the end of the 18th century.

I have made some interpretive changes in this edition. Prompted by the work of such historians as Gordon Wood and Joyce Appleby, I have substantially modified my interpretation of the colonial period. Whereas the previous edition emphasized the lack of competing perspectives in this period, the current edition emphasizes political conflicts within American society from the 1750s through the early part of the 19th century. Influenced by Charles Sellers, I place even more emphasis on economic inequality in my discussion of the 19th century. I have used Theda Skocpol's inventive insights in my discussion of the 19th century and the progressive period, though I argue that she overreaches when she contends that Americans constructed a significant welfare state in these periods.

To help instructors teach social policy history so that it encourages creative thinking, I have developed a compendium of innovative approaches that emphasize the relevance of social welfare history to professional education. Titled *Creative Ways to Teach Social Policy History and to Link It to Contemporary Society and the Profession,* it draws on contributions from faculty from around the country.

I have benefitted from the comments of many reviewers. Paul Harris and Kenneth Smemo, both from the Department of History at Moorhead State University, helped to refine my discussion on several historical points. Professor Charles Atherton, professor emeritus of the University of Alabama, saved me from a number of errors with his extended comments. Many helpful suggestions were provided by other reviewers, who include Janice Adams, Indiana Wesleyan University; Joel Blau; William Hershey, University of Washington; Robert Hudson, Boston University; David E. Pollio, Washington University; John McNutt, Indiana University East; Tom Roy, University of Montana; and Martin B. Tracy, Southern Illinois University. I received first-rate research assistance from Eugene Alper on Chapter 12. Jeanette Cambra provided invaluable assistance in locating fugitive materials, drafting the chapter on Clinton, and co-authoring the compendium of innovative teaching approaches. Three colleagues—Professors Ramon Salcido, Essie Seck, and Madeline Stoner—steered me toward important materials on outgroups.

Lisa Gebo, the sponsoring editor for this book, encouraged me to undertake this revision and brainstormed ways of introducing critical thinking. The production editor, Laurie Jackson, skillfully shepherded the book through production, and the copy editor, Bernard Gilbert, made many good editing suggestions. All errors of omission or commission rest on my shoulders alone.

Many thanks to Betty Ann, who tolerated the piles of books and papers that littered the household as this revision was in progress, not to mention other encouragement that she provided.

Bruce S. Jansson

1

Social Reform in a Society with Conflicting Tendencies

Like other societies, the United States has experienced social problems throughout its existence. In the colonial period, released indentured servants often experienced poverty as they tried to eke out an existence on the American frontier. Poor immigrants encountered poverty, discrimination, and disease in the rough American cities of the 19th and early 20th centuries. Native Americans, African Americans, and Latinos encountered hostility from the broader society as they endeavored to improve their economic conditions or merely to retain their traditional lands and customs. Homeless persons in the 20th century had their counterparts in the 19th century, who were commonly called vagabonds. The predicament of people with AIDS in the 1980s and 1990s, in which a desperate medical condition is compounded by unfavorable health and social policies, was foreshadowed by the treatment of those with malaria, typhoid fever, cholera, and syphilis in earlier eras.

Throughout this nation's history, those who must bear the brunt of social problems—individuals contending with poverty, discrimination, and disease—have depended in considerable measure not only on their personal and familial tenacity and on community supports, but also on the policies of public and nonpublic agencies and of federal, state, and local governments. At various times, these policies, singly and in combination, have provided assistance to some, have left others with no assistance, and have worsened the plight of many.

This is a book about the evolution of American social policies from colonial times to the present. It chronicles and analyzes conflicting tendencies in American attitudes to social problems. Sometimes Americans have developed positive strategies to address specific problems; at others, they have chosen not to act or to develop punitive policies.

At many points in this book, we consider American policies directed to specific populations that have often experienced a disproportionate burden of social problems. These groups include African Americans, women, Native Americans, Latinos, gay men and lesbians, children, persons with chronic physical disabilities, persons with psychiatric disorders, and persons accused of violating laws. Moreover, we often discuss problems of those in the lower economic strata of society. Our focus here is not exclusively on the hardships these groups have endured; we also acknowledge their resilience and strength in forging survival strategies.

However, this book is not *only* about the social problems of specific subgroups

1

within the population. Most Americans confront social problems and needs at some time in their life. In the absence of national health insurance, for example, middle-class Americans may experience catastrophic illnesses that can bankrupt them. The economic losses experienced by middle-class Americans in the 1980s and 1990s have spawned problems such as family violence, crime, and substance abuse.

A RELUCTANT WELFARE STATE

Profound ambivalence toward the victims of social problems has existed in American society since the colonial period. On the one hand, Americans have exhibited compassion toward those who are hungry, destitute, ill, and transient, as illustrated by a host of ameliorative public policies and a rich tradition of private philanthropy. On the other, they have demonstrated a callous disregard for persons in need. Assistance has often been coupled with punitive and demeaning regulations; federal programs were not developed until relatively late in the nation's history; and racial and other groups have been subjected to consistently oppressive treatment. The term *reluctant welfare state* expresses this paradox of punitiveness and generosity.

In the 19th century, the nation developed a set of poorhouses, mental and children's institutions, and sectarian welfare agencies, but these policies were grievously insufficient to deal with the serious economic and social problems of immigrants, factory workers, displaced Native Americans and Spanish-speaking persons, and urban residents. A federal welfare state was fashioned belatedly in the 20th century, during the New Deal, to supplement various social policies at local and state levels. However, it was limited and harsh in comparison to its counterparts in Western Europe. Portions of this American welfare state have often been attacked by conservatives, who question its cost, its centralization of power in the nation's capital, and its effectiveness, as illustrated by arguments espoused by Newt Gingrich and other Republicans in the 1990s. Conservatives fought funding of relief programs in the New Deal, blocked national health insurance after World War II, sought to cut funding of social programs created during the Great Society of the 1960s, made large cuts in programs helping poor people during the administration of Ronald Reagan in the 1980s, and sought to end many social programs funded or administered by the federal government in the wake of Republicans' electoral triumphs in 1994, when they gained control of both houses of Congress.

While their responses to social problems or to the specific needs of various groups in the broader society were often belated or inadequate, Americans did develop a variety of regulations, institutions, and social programs that helped people cope with poverty, illness, and many other problems. In the colonial period and in the 19th century, local and state governments constructed an array of institutions, albeit sometimes inadequate or punitive, to help individuals who were poor, older, or mentally ill. Just after the turn of the 20th century, progressive reformers developed many regulations, such as housing codes and child-labor laws, that helped to protect people against victimization by landlords and corporations. Under the leadership of Franklin Roosevelt, New Deal reformers helped millions of Americans who had been cast into unemployment by the Great Depression. In the 1960s, during the era of the Great Society, Congress passed a wide range of reforms, such as Head Start, Medicare and Medicaid, and the Older Americans Act. Despite concerted efforts by conservatives to cut social spending by the federal government in the 1970s, 1980s, and 1990s, domestic expenditures (excluding interest on the national debt and defense spending) had reached approximately $1.3 trillion by 1996.

Finally, we should note that groups confronted with harsh economic and social conditions have not passively awaited assistance from outside agencies; over the years, they have fashioned an array of ingenious survival strategies for themselves, whether by founding self-help organizations, community groups, and advocacy groups, or by pursuing redress in the courts.

THE CONTROVERSIAL NATURE OF SOCIAL POLICY

Throughout history, social policies have been aswsociated with political controversy and conflict. Some people (we often label them conservatives today) opposed the development of policy initiatives to address the social needs of citizens—the use of federal funds to build mental institutions in the 1840s, the development of civil rights legislation in the 1960s, and the development of major initiatives to help homeless people in the 1990s. Contemporary conservatives view themselves as ideological descendants of the founding fathers, 19th-century capitalism, and Presidents Coolidge, Hoover, Eisenhower, and Reagan. Libertarians have sought to curtail government control or regulation of citizens. Emphasizing the Bill of Rights, they oppose laws that outlaw the use of drugs like cocaine, that prohibit abortion, or that censor publications. As the term *libertarian* suggests, they want to enhance the freedom of citizens to the extent possible, in contrast to conservatives, who support the criminalization of specific drugs and abortion. Social reformers (today, we often refer to those who seek incremental reforms as liberals), including Dorothea Dix, Jane Addams, Franklin Roosevelt, and Lyndon Johnson, obtained enactment of a range of policy reforms despite the concerted opposition of conservatives and many interest groups. Contemporary liberals perceive themselves as ideological descendants of Presidents Theodore and Franklin Roosevelt, Wilson, Kennedy, and Lyndon Johnson, as well as such professional leaders as Jane Addams. These individuals were in the vanguard of the movement to build an American welfare state, even if their limited vision and the political opposition that they encountered meant that it was a reluctant welfare state. American radicals, including union organizers, socialists, and communists, have periodically pressured liberals and conservatives to consider major expansions of the welfare state, just as various social movements have sought reforms for specific causes. American radicals trace their heritage to union organizers and legendary radical figures of the 19th and 20th centuries, such as Eugene Debs and Norman Thomas, as well as the socialists and communists of the 1930s. They often identify with grass-roots social movements, including movements to abolish imprisonment for debt and to end slavery prior to the Civil War, the Industrial Workers of the World in the progressive era, the Southern Tenant Farmers Association, the unemployed workers movement, the industrial workers movement in the New Deal, the civil rights and welfare rights movements of the 1960s, and organizations representing homeless persons in the 1980s.

Citizens in societies with conflicting policies

FIGURE 1.1   (*left*) An American conservative: Ronald Reagan; (*center*) an American liberal: Franklin Delano Roosevelt; (*right*) an American radical: Jesse Jackson

SOURCE: (*left*) © Scott Stewart /UPI/Bettmann; (*center*) UPI/Bettmann; (*right*) © Gutierrez/UPI/Bettmann

and relatively harsh traditions must at some point shape their personal values. Do they share the values of contemporary American conservatives, libertarians, liberals, or radicals? Do they favor the expansion of the federal government's social welfare role, advocate the status quo, or want reductions in existing programs? Citizens must decide what policies they advocate with respect to contemporary social problems such as homelessness and the provision of medical care to those who cannot afford insurance.

While recognizing that they are not homogeneous groups, we can compare conservatives, libertarians, liberals, and radicals with respect to ten dimensions, as illustrated in Table 1.1: They differ in their attitudes toward the federal government and state and local government; in their beliefs about the causes of social problems; in their views of capitalism, human nature, the safety net, abortion, nongovernmental associations and agencies, and subgroups; and in the core value they consider most important.

For conservatives, freedom is fundamental; they value the freedom to retain personal wealth and to conduct enterprises with minimal public regulation. Conservatives are optimistic that unfettered capitalism will produce prosperity if government does not place excessive regulations upon it. Rather than favoring government programs or tax policies that redistribute wealth, they believe that economic growth will "trickle down" to persons in the lower economic strata. Many conservatives believe, as well, that communities, families, churches, and nongovernmental organizations can meet most needs of citizens and that these nongovernmental entities can even replace many public programs—for example, by encouraging individuals and communities to care for homeless persons. To the extent that social programs *are* developed, many conservatives prefer to have them vested not with the federal government but with local and state governments, which would bear their full funding and implementation. If local resources are unavailable to implement specific programs, conservatives often favor policies such as block grants, where state and local units of government receive fixed annual allowances from the federal authority and are free to decide precisely how to use them.

Conservatives are relatively pessimistic about the fundamental nature of human beings, particularly those of limited means. They tend to believe that people in need can be corrupted by social programs, that is, that those who receive benefits will rely on them *instead of* seeking gainful employment. To counter what they regard as the "perverse incentives" provided by welfare and other social programs, many conservatives want to make social benefits less munificent and to set time limits and other conditions to their receipt. To prevent large numbers in the population from using social programs, conservatives usually want to tighten eligibility requirements. In contrast to their pessimism about persons in the lower economic strata, conservatives tend to be relatively optimistic about persons in the upper economic strata. Far from contending that wealth or inheritances might corrupt those individuals, conservatives want them to retain much of their wealth, on the assumption that they will place it in job-creating investments that will ultimately spur economic growth. In seeking the causes of social problems, conservatives generally emphasize personal or cultural factors. They contend that many people use social programs because they do not want to work or because American culture fails to emphasize "personal responsibility."

Conservatives do not emphasize disparities in economic and social status between subgroups (such as African Americans or women) and the general population and often dispute data suggesting that these disparities are wide or growing. Conservatives such as Ronald Reagan opposed civil rights legislation in the 1960s. Conservatives tend to oppose affirmative action, as well as redistributive policies such as increasing the tax rates on affluent Americans. They often question whether widespread discrimination exists or discount its importance.

Conservatives are not a homogeneous group, as an examination of the contemporary Republican Party makes clear. Persons from the "religious

TABLE 1.1 Comparison of different ideologies

	Conservatives	Libertarians	Liberals	Radicals
Views of federal government	Negative, except in military and international policy and as source of subsidies for business	Negative	Relatively positive	Positive, unless it is under control of monied interests
Views of state and local government	Relatively positive	Negative	Divided, but federal government is often preferred	Less positive than views of federal government
Views of causes of social problems	Emphasis on personal and cultural factors	Unclear	More emphasis than conservatives on environmental factors	Environmental factors generated by monied interests
Views of capitalism	Positive	Positive	Positive, but regulations are favored	Negative, unless workers are empowered
Views of human nature	Relatively optimistic about affluent people, less optimistic about poor people	Favor policies that maximize the liberty of all people	Relatively optimistic about poor people but less optimistic about rich people	Pessimistic about monied interests, but optimistic about other people
Views of safety net	Want relatively meager safety net	Unclear	Want relatively generous safety net	Favor generous safety net
Attitudes to abortion and other moral issues	Divided, but a significant faction favors government controls	Dislike government regulation of social matters	Usually oppose restrictions on abortion but favor restrictions on drugs	Often oppose restriction of social matters
Core value	Liberty, though some government incentives and regulations are favored	Liberty	Liberty, but social justice is also important	Social justice
Views of nongovernmental and governmental programs	Favor nongovernmental initiatives	Favor nongovernmental initiatives	Favor a mixture of both	Favor governmental programs, but often recommend worker or citizen inclusion in government decisions
Views of subgroups who lag behind others in economic status or who experience discrimination	Tend to deny their existence or minimize discrimination	Unclear	Favor some redistribution and strong civil rights	Emphasize oppression of outgroups and seek major corrective action

right," who constitute a large proportion of the contemporary conservative movement, strongly believe the government should act to restrict abortion, censor pornographic literature, outlaw certain drugs, and allow prayer in the public schools. They have often clashed with other conservatives who oppose some of these policies. Some conservatives, such as Newt Gingrich, carry an antigovernmental ethos far further than do moderate Republicans, who are more supportive of government programs, less inclined to cut domestic spending deeply, and more inclined to retain many government regulations. Nor do conservatives always act in a manner that is consistent with their stated principles. Many Republican legislators, for example, oppose new reform initiatives such as Medicare when they are first proposed, only to vote for their funding and expansion after their enactment; in part, this is because these lawmakers realize that their constituents often like—and use—such government programs.

Libertarians agree with conservatives about the primacy of freedom but, unlike conservatives, they oppose policies that enforce a single standard of public morality. For example, they oppose laws that restrict abortions, criminalize drugs, or impose censorship of journalism or art. Because libertarians tend not to like taxes, which they regard as infringing on the economic independence of citizens, they do not emphasize public expenditures or redistribution.

While liberals want to keep government powers more limited than do radicals, they are less sanguine than conservatives about unfettered capitalism. Left to its own devices, capitalism often produces considerable inequality, as is apparent from the disparities between wages, salaries, and private wealth that exist in the United States today. Moreover, many capitalists victimize people; examples include avaricious landlords, entrepreneurs who pay low wages, and purveyors of tainted food and drugs. Believing that many people are subjected to discrimination in employment, education, use of public places, and accommodations, liberals have often favored the enactment of civil rights legislation. Placing somewhat more emphasis upon equality than do conservatives and wanting to restrict the victimization of people, liberals favor an array of government regulations and programs, such as: minimum-wage legislation; regulation of working conditions; subsidies for persons of low income, through welfare programs, Medicare, Medicaid, and Food Stamps; and job-training and Head Start programs to provide individuals with the skills and knowledge necessary to be productive citizens. Liberals are less inclined than are conservatives to believe that nongovernmental associations, not-for-profit agencies, churches, or civic groups can solve or address major social problems without government assistance; however, they often support partnerships between government and these entities. Liberals are more optimistic about government's ability to ameliorate major social problems such as poverty and homelessness. Whereas conservatives view government cynically and emphasize the negative qualities of bureaucracy and regulations, liberals are more inclined to believe that government officials can implement strategies to assist those in need.

Liberals recognize disparities in economic and social status between subgroups (such as women or African Americans) and the general population. They favor redistributive policies, such as the progressive income tax, and redistributive programs like Medicaid. Liberals like Hubert Humphrey and Lyndon Johnson were in the forefront of the civil rights movement, just as many liberals have supported policies that affirm the employment and social rights of women, gay men and lesbians, and persons with physical disabilities.

Just as conservatives are not a homogeneous group, varieties of liberals exist. Some liberals favor a relatively expansive welfare state that attempts both to equalize opportunity and to decrease economic inequality (stalwart liberals); others are content to equalize opportunity through Head Start and similar programs and a minimal set of safety-net programs such as Food Stamps (traditional liberals). Stalwart liberals favor relatively generous welfare programs, tax policies that redistribute resources to people in the lower economic strata, and affirmative action programs that provide special assistance to groups who lag behind the rest of the population. Hubert Humphrey, Claude Pepper, Robert Kennedy, and Martin Luther King exemplify stalwart liberals. Traditional liberals, such as John Kennedy and Lyndon Johnson, emphasize educational, medical, and job-training supports for citizens but do not favor tax or welfare policies that substantially redistribute resources to poor persons. Stalwart liberals seek to temper freedom with social justice by supporting a wide range of social programs and some redistribution of resources to low-income persons, while traditional liberals, more cautious in seeking reforms that address economic inequality, prefer to equalize opportunity through the expansion of educational, medical, and social services. In the 1990s, a number of Democrats sought to evolve a centrist position that emphasized the roles of local and state government and personal responsibility. They sought to enlist Bill Clinton in their efforts to define "new Democrats," but later complained that he emphasized traditional liberalism in the first two years of his administration.[1]

Many kinds of radical positions exist. Emphasizing equality, radicals are deeply pessimistic about the efficacy of unfettered capitalism in advancing social justice. Some radicals, such as socialists, want to transform capitalistic institutions into publicly run industries or favor worker ownership of corporations. Realizing that these policies are difficult to achieve because of the sheer power of corporations, radicals favor the major redistribution of wealth through tax policies, as well as far-reaching government programs that both provide services and benefits to all citizens and target them to less affluent citizens. Whereas liberals favor government programs and progressive taxes but usually want to keep them within certain limits, radicals have fewer inhibitions about far-reaching government interventions. While also advocating broader reforms, some radicals emphasize far-reaching reforms to help specific groups, such as African Americans and women. Feminists favor far-reaching policies to equalize conditions between women and men—for example, children's allowances, remuneration for raising families, affirmation action, aggressive collection of child support from former spouses, and a constitutional amendment to guarantee equal rights for women.

Radicals are often critical of existing social programs, which, they argue, reflect the interests of corporate and conservative groups; for example, they might contend that programs like Aid to Families with Dependent Children (AFDC) are structured so as to provide a source of cheap labor. Others view government programs as a conspiracy to defuse pressure for social change by making relatively small concessions to working-class persons. They often advocate grass-roots organizing to develop constituencies for radical policies; for example, radicals would support projects to unionize workers in low-wage service industries.

Radicals believe that the social and economic problems of subgroups stem from their oppression by the broader society and corporate interests. They strongly support civil rights and redistributive policies to restore equal status and opportunity for oppressed groups. More than liberals, they link the oppression of subgroups to the economic and political subjugation of the working class, which includes many of their members. To upgrade the economic and political status of women and African Americans, for example, they would favor sweeping economic reforms, such as curtailing the ability of corporations to move their operations to low-wage nations or to underpay their employees.

USING SOCIAL POLICY HISTORY TO DEVELOP A POLICY IDENTITY

The hundreds of thousands of professionals who deliver the services and resources of the welfare state to consumers include physicians, nurses, psychologists, and social workers, who work in a variety of public, not-for-profit, and for-profit agencies. The social work profession illustrates dilemmas and choices that confront intermediaries between the welfare state and consumers. Because the agencies for which they work typically receive public or private funding, and such funds are rarely given without accompanying policies, regulations, and demands for accountability, social workers must interact frequently with funders, legislators, and government officials.

Social workers work with relatively controversial persons and populations—with individuals who are mentally ill, poor, aging, addicted, delinquent, violent, or unemployed, with gay men and lesbians, or with people who have disabilities. In their work with racial and ethnic communities, they have to contend with barriers to ethnic-sensitive practice such as policies to control or regulate poor people and institutional resistance to change. The force of tradition may express itself as failure to recruit bilingual staff in an area to which non–English-speaking persons have recently moved. Disinclination to provide different services to specific ethnic groups may arise from a misconceived notion that all clients should receive the same services. Some agencies may fear loss of professional prestige if they serve predominantly low-income ethnic-group clients. Agencies may fail to provide rewards and incentives to staff to provide ethnic-sensitive services, may fail to give ethnic clients and groups authentic inputs to agency decision making, and may believe that hiring token ethnic-minority staff is a valid alternative to agency-wide ethnic-sensitive practice.[2]

Social workers work with complex problems. Drug addiction, alcoholism, serious mental disorders, juvenile delinquency, child abuse, and other social problems are caused by a variety of personal, familial, genetic, community, economic, cultural, and other factors. This complexity invites controversy about how best to address the problems and often makes it difficult for social workers to achieve tangible success.

Because of the difficulties intrinsic to their work, social workers may encounter suspicion, indifference, or hostility from funders, evaluators, taxpayers, and consumers. If they work for publicly funded programs, social workers must bear the consequences of low funding in their professional work; for example, many social workers have large caseloads. Because they work with controversial populations and issues, social workers are more subject to social policies that control, restrict, and regulate their practice. Funders and legislators tend to insist on careful documentation of their work, to place limits on the intensity or duration of their work with consumers, and to resist policies that stipulate advanced training to perform specific kinds of tasks.

In light of these external pressures on them, social workers need to develop positions on policy issues in their work. Using their knowledge of human behavior, research about effective interventions, and ethical judgments about the rights and needs of their clients, social workers must be proactive participants in the shaping of policies. We discuss in Chapter 14 the emerging intervention in social work known as *policy practice* that articulates skills that social workers need in order to shape policies in organizational, community, and legislative settings.

Social workers sometimes need to grapple with ethical dilemmas. Their intermediary position between government, society, and consumers, for example, sometimes leads to tension between obedience and reform. When policies are punitive, misdirected, or simplistic—or when social programs are underfunded—social workers have to decide whether and when to assume professional and personal risks. When should they question policies? When should they encourage others to oppose disliked policies? When should they refuse to implement specific policies? These issues are difficult to resolve, because they involve not only distant policy authorities but also colleagues and administrators in social agencies, with whom the social worker has frequent contact.

Even when they do not encounter tensions between societal policies and expectations and their own professional values, social workers must be alert to the subtle influence of societal prejudice on their own work. A social worker who believes that alcoholics should be able to control their condition may, in consequence, act in a punitive fashion toward this group. A social worker may unwittingly refer women to one set of job listings and men to other, more challenging positions. Or a social worker in a hospital emergency room may give more immediate and responsive treatment to children than to elderly persons. As these examples suggest, prejudices are not necessarily conscious. It is equally important for social workers to address covert or institutional expressions of prejudice, such as agency or community practices that give ethnic groups inferior or fewer services or less access to opportunities. Perhaps a social agency, desirous of increasing its revenues, decides to emphasize fee-paying clients to the detriment of low-income ones.[3] Perhaps a local school deemphasizes vocational programs that impoverished students particularly use and need. Perhaps no halfway houses for persons with mental disorders exist in a certain jurisdiction because residents object to them, so that recovering mental patients are forced into facilities in blighted and crime-ridden areas.

Social workers have to decide whether, when, and how to support political candidates or social movements that address policy issues in the broader society. Do Democrats, Republicans, Socialists, Libertarians, or other political parties offer the best platforms for addressing social problems in the nation? What are the merits of specific reforms to help welfare, gay and lesbian, African American, Latino, female, and other populations? Is it appropriate to mobilize the clients or consumers of an agency to protest specific policies and, if so, under what circumstances?

Social policy history provides an ideal means of evolving our personal *policy identities,* which consist of a set of explicit values and positions that shape our selection or rejection of policy choices. By providing us with many examples of social reform and of opposition to it, such history encourages us to make moral judgments about the choices and actions of specific people or factions. Did conservative opposition to social reforms represent principled opposition or merely a self-interested defense of vested interests? When are libertarians correct in their insistence that government not regulate citizens' moral choices or their use of certain drugs? Were the positions of liberal reformers meritorious or flawed in specific historical eras? Did radicals, such as communists and socialists in the New Deal era, propose ill-advised or sensible policies? Are the centrist or conservative policies of contemporary American leaders sufficient to address the social and economic needs of the nation?

History encourages us to ponder the identity of the social work profession (or other professions), because it provides many examples of the positions of the profession's leaders and members on controversial topics. Social workers have often championed the needs of poor people, persons of color, and other groups, as well as policies to serve the broader population, such as Social Security pensions. Yet social workers sometimes demurred from supporting policies that were meant to help these populations or even supported punitive policies. While some professionals have wanted social work to include social reform in its arsenal of interventions, others want to emphasize only counseling.[4]

When we evaluate the actions and choices of people in prior eras, we must, of course, beware of ignoring differences between the contemporary period and those eras. In the 19th century, for example, governmental institutions were more primitive and the nation lacked a federal income tax, so that citizens and officials of that era could not contemplate, much less finance and implement, the kinds of major social programs that we take for granted today. Indeed, we have to approach distant eras in somewhat the way that anthropologists analyze different societies and culture; that is, we must suspend judgments in an effort to understand how people perceived their world and the problems in it. Even with these caveats, however, we can and should make evaluative judgments about the actions and choices of our predecessors. For example, we can note that the founding fathers were convinced they *had* to legitimize slavery by mentioning it in the Constitution in order to keep Southerners from bolting the Union, but also make the moral judgment that they were insensitive to the brutality and inhumanity of the institution of slavery. In similar fashion, we can criticize the use of workhouses in the 19th century, even though many people at that time believed them to be humane institutions.

POLICY ERAS IN U.S. HISTORY

The history of American social policy can be divided into a series of policy eras—specific periods that have an identifiable policy direction, substance, and intensity. The *policy direction* of an era

TABLE 1.2 Social welfare policy eras
in U.S. history

Policy	Era
Initial policy inheritance	Medieval and Colonial Eras
Americanizing of the policy inheritance	1800–1902
First urban reform movement	1902–1917
Development of initial federal programs	1932–1941
Development of federal roles in services	1960–1968
Conflicting policy tendencies	1945–1952
	1961–1963
	1969–1980
	1992–1996
Conservative policies	1868–1902
	1917–1932
	1952–1960
	1980–1992

describes the general nature of the policies enacted then. In relatively conservative periods, the emphasis of policy makers is on maintaining the status quo, eliminating reforms established in a preceding era, or making major amendments of prior enactments. In relatively liberal eras, policy makers enact major new reforms that redistribute services and resources or that increase the role of the federal government. The *substance* of policy refers to the general strategies favored by decision makers in a specific era. For example, between roughly 1905 and 1917, legislators enacted regulatory reforms that established minimum public health, housing, and work-safety standards. Decision makers in the 1930s placed far more emphasis on legislation that redistributed resources and jobs to unemployed and poor persons. Reformers in the early 1970s emphasized provision of cash benefits to people rather than social services, which received more attention in the 1960s. The *intensity* of reform describes the rate of policy activity. Relatively few policy changes occurred in the 1920s and 1950s, for example, but many changes were initiated in the 1930s, 1960s, and 1980s.

American social welfare policy has evolved in a series of phases (Table 1.2). Some eras are sufficiently similar to others that they can be grouped together; in Table 1.2, various conservative eras are presented together because each is characterized by lack of interest in social reforms.

Let's briefly review the policy trends in U.S. history. During the 17th and 18th centuries, American colonists brought with them from Europe a cultural inheritance that powerfully influenced the early development of American social welfare policy. As we discuss in Chapter 3, these early Americans were children of sweeping religious, political, and cultural movements in Europe, such as the Protestant Reformation and the Enlightenment. The ideas of these original settlers influenced the course of American social policy development in the 19th and 20th centuries, and many of their assumptions and beliefs persist in contemporary America.

The social welfare institutions developed during the 19th century were consonant with the realities of an agricultural, dispersed, and entrepreneurial nation. Social welfare policy was dominated by municipal and county programs and by local philanthropic efforts. (States began to assume significant welfare functions only in the latter part of the 19th century.) The inability of Americans to develop major social welfare programs in this period is illustrated by their failure to assist the freed slaves in the aftermath of the Civil War or to regulate the emerging industrial order.

Americans developed their first sustained urban reform movement between 1905 and 1917, during the progressive era. Reformers emphasized a regulatory and local response to the many social problems in the burgeoning cities; they enacted regulations to improve working conditions, public health, and housing.

During the Great Depression of the 1930s, or about 150 years after the founding of the republic, Americans developed their first set of national social welfare programs, which assisted those who were poor or unemployed; these efforts culminated in the passage of the Social Security Act in 1935. Programs established during the 1930s represented a remarkable policy breakthrough for the United

States, but reforms were still deeply conditioned by traditional American beliefs that limited the size and scope of federal social programs.

Many social programs were enacted during the administrations of John Kennedy and Lyndon Johnson in the 1960s, when the federal government assumed major roles in medical care, education, mental health, and job training for the first time. Programs were established for specific populations, such as children and elderly people, and civil rights laws and regulations were passed. The emphasis was on reforms that enlarged national funding of service-oriented programs, rather than on the redistribution of economic resources to citizens living in poverty.

At various points in American history, conflicting policy tendencies have existed. While a Democrat (Harry Truman) led the nation following World War II and proposed some liberal reforms, he confronted a conservative Congress. Similarly, a Democratic president, Jack Kennedy, was unable to pass liberal legislation between 1961 and his death in late 1963, because of opposition in Congress. The period encompassing the presidencies of Richard Nixon, Gerald Ford, and Jimmy Carter from 1969 to 1980 appears at first glance to be profoundly conservative, but this appearance is deceiving, because many major reforms were enacted. Democrat Bill Clinton pledged himself to a relatively liberal agenda in his campaign of 1992 but was unable to get most of it enacted, especially after 1994, when Congress was dominated by Republicans such as House Speaker Newt Gingrich.

Conservative eras often interrupted the evolution of social reforms. In the period between the Civil War and 1902, for example, national discourse was dominated by Social Darwinism, which emphasized individualism and deterrent policies. The decade of the 1920s was characterized by preoccupation with material success, rather than with social reform to address the needs of women, factory workers, and African Americans in the South.

President Dwight Eisenhower presided over the conservative decade of the 1950s, when cold-war rhetoric and suburbanization of the nation drew attention away from the social needs of many urban and rural citizens. The administrations of Ronald Reagan and George Bush (1980–1992) were profoundly conservative.

This book analyzes policies in the different eras presented in Table 1.2, beginning with the colonial period and ending with the presidency of Bill Clinton. In Chapter 13, drawing on the discussion of preceding chapters, we examine why the American response to social needs has been reluctant. In Chapter 14, we discuss tactics for expanding the American response to social needs.

At various points, readers will be asked to engage in critical thinking—to ponder the ethical merits of specific policies, to examine continuities and change in the American response to social needs, and to examine obstacles to social reforms in specific eras.

NOTES

1. For a discussion of varieties of liberals and conservatives, see James Riechley, *Conservatives in an Age of Change: the Nixon and Ford Administrations* (Washington, D.C.: Brookings Institution, 1981), pp. 22–41.

2. Alfreda Iglehrt and Rosina Becerra, *Social Services and the Ethnic Community* (Boston: Allyn and Bacon, 1995), pp. 208–217.

3. See issues posed by Lester Salamon, "The Marketization of Welfare: Changing Nonprofit and For-Profit Roles in the American Welfare State," *Social Service Review* (March 1993), 16–39.

4. See the debate between Mimi Abramovitz (who favors a social reform perspective) and D. Ray Bardill (who opposes a social reform perspective) in the *Journal of Social Work Education*, 29 (Winter 1993), 6–18.

2

C H A P T E R

A Framework for Understanding the Evolution of the Reluctant Welfare State

If it simply listed the various policies that Americans have chosen, social work history would be boring indeed. Our interest lies not merely in describing the social policies selected in specific eras but in analyzing *why* Americans chose certain policies while ignoring others. We cannot determine why certain policies were selected, however, without broadening our inquiry to include those cultural, political, economic, and other contextual factors that shaped the actions of Americans in specific eras. Why did Americans develop their welfare state so belatedly, as compared with most European societies? Why are Americans willing to tolerate higher rates of economic inequality, unemployment, and poverty than many Europeans are? Why do Americans often emphasize opportunity-enhancing policies, like education, while deemphasizing policies that redistribute resources from persons with wealth to those in need?

A systems framework helps us understand why Americans developed a reluctant welfare state (Figure 2.1). This framework describes contextual factors that shape choices of decision makers and advocates; the political or deliberative processes where divergent groups and persons advance their proposals or oppose proposals of others; the social policy choices that are made; and the effects of policies on consumers and the nation.

THE TWO-SIDED CONTEXT

An array of contextual factors influence citizens and legislators as they consider and select social policies in specific eras. They include cultural, economic, institutional, social, and legal factors, as well as the sequencing or timing of key events. In the succeeding chapters, we discuss these factors as they have shaped policy selection in various eras.

1. *Cultural factors* include the way Americans perceived the importance and causes of specific social problems, the extent they believed that those in need were responsible for the problems, and the extent they thought that society has an obligation to assist those in need with ameliorative programs. We discuss how perceptions of various subgroups within the population, such as women and racial groups, shaped social policies.

FIGURE 2.1   A systems approach to policy making

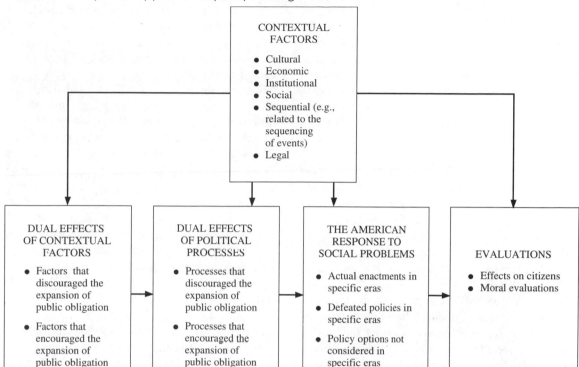

2. *Economic factors* include the extent the government possessed resources, such as tax revenues, to fund social programs; the extent corporations provided social benefits to employees; and the budgetary priorities of governments.

3. *Institutional factors* include the extent governments possessed administrative capabilities to develop and implement social programs and the balance between federal, state, and local jurisdictions in social policy.

4. *Social factors* include wars, migrations of populations, demographic changes, industrialization, global economic competition, and urbanization—that is, changes in the social environment that shape the selection of policies.

5. The *sequencing of events* describes the effects of the *timing* of important developments on the evolution of the U.S. welfare state. Unlike many European nations, for example, the United States did not evolve major *federal* social programs, aside from veterans' programs, until relatively late in its national history—that is, the 1930s. Because Americans were unfamiliar with the merits of programs funded by the federal government, they were probably more suspicious of them than were European nations accustomed to a considerable social policy role of the central government.

6. *Legal factors* include the influence of constitutional provisions on the evolution of the welfare state. Since the U.S. Constitution did not explicitly mention social policy, for example, many people assumed, until well into the 1930s, that it was unconstitutional to develop major social programs at the federal level.

As we examine the impact of contextual factors on social policy, we will discover that, in every era, some contextual factors inhibited the development of ameliorating policies but others promoted such policies. Take the example of culture. From the nation's inception in the 1780s, many Americans believed that they could create a utopian society that would serve as a beacon to the rest of the world. Jefferson thought that democratic institutions and the predominance of small farms would spare Americans the maladies of poverty and crime that bedeviled the large cities of Europe. Believing that they could avoid social problems, Americans in the 19th century were ill prepared to recognize—much less cope with—the severe unemployment, begging, and homelessness that existed in the growing urban areas. Another cultural factor that impeded the development of social policies in the 19th century was widespread racism, which disposed many Americans to support harsh policies toward Native Americans, African Americans, Latinos, and Asian Americans.

Other cultural beliefs supported the development of ameliorative policies. From the inception of the republic, Americans stressed individual rights, as reflected by the swift insertion of a Bill of Rights into the Constitution. Eventually, albeit after several centuries of conflict, this emphasis on rights promoted the enactment of civil rights statutes, in the 1960s and succeeding decades, that provided protections to persons of color, persons with disabilities, and women.

Likewise, economic, institutional, social, sequential, and legal factors have sometimes discouraged and sometimes encouraged the evolution of ameliorating policies in particular eras. We shall discuss many of these factors in specific chapters; then, in Chapter 13, we review their cumulative effects in shaping the reluctant welfare state.

THE ROLE OF POLITICAL PROCESSES IN CREATING A RELUCTANT WELFARE STATE

Contextual factors help to shape the actions of decision makers, but they do not tell us *how* choices are actually made in the push and pull of political processes. In the real world, policy proposals must undergo the hardships of political maneuvering and conflict before they receive the approval of legislators, Supreme Court justices, or other decision makers.

In trying to understand the origins of the reluctant welfare state, we need to analyze why American political processes are structured in a way that tends to favor opponents of social legislation and also why these processes have sometimes facilitated the enactment of such legislation.

Let's begin by discussing some factors that have discouraged social reforms in the United States. Political theorists such as C. Wright Mills have contended that the political process discriminates against social reformers because of the power and resources of corporations, special interests, and conservatives. Nor do they lack evidence that social reforms have been defeated or diluted by such opposition. The foes of ameliorating policies have usually had ample resources to hire lobbyists, rally local opposition, and give campaign funds to legislators. Corporations have often defeated measures to regulate them; for example, in the latter part of the 19th century they defeated attempts to curtail child labor and to limit the working hours of women. Using their extensive resources, the American Medical Association repeatedly defeated efforts to enact national health insurance through most of the 20th century.

Conservatives have often mobilized powerful national constituencies to oppose social reforms. A succession of Republican presidents from Richard Nixon onward persuaded white, ethnic males to leave the Democratic Party by appealing to their opposition to affirmative action, taxes, and crime—and by suggesting that Democrats were unduly beholden to persons of color and women. They were also able to draw millions of Southern Baptists and other religious fundamentalists into their conservative coalition, partly through televangelism and grass-roots organizing. These tactics enabled Republicans to control the presidency for most of the past 30 years and to take control of both Houses of Congress by 1994; they used their power to seek conservative appointments to the courts and cuts in the funding of social programs.

Even when Republicans lacked a numerical majority in Congress, they were often able to form coalitions with conservative Southern Democrats opposed to social reforms. They coupled this formidable power with parliamentary tactics, such as the filibuster, to block social legislation. In addition, conservatives have often enhanced their power by controlling key positions in Congress, for example, by chairing Congressional committees. Prior to the mid-1970s, committee chairs were appointed on the basis of seniority—a policy that favored long-serving conservative Southern Democrats, who rarely encountered opposition in local primaries or elections.

Conservatives' power was often bolstered, too, by the advantages that accrue to the *opponents* of legislation in the complicated American system of governance. Legislation must wend its way through a number of committees, two chambers, and a conference committee in the Congress before the incumbent president signs (or vetoes) it. Opponents can stop it at many points in this trajectory.

Moreover, conservatives—usually with some support from liberals—have often been able to block social reforms by denying them resources: by cutting taxes, so as to deplete the funds available for social programs; by supporting costly ventures, such as military programs, that divert resources from the domestic agenda; and by seeking cuts in social programs in the annual appropriations process.

At the same time, however, social reformers have often had considerable successes; as we know, a large proportion of the federal budget is devoted to domestic programs. Drawing on broad support from the public, reformers helped elect such liberal presidents as Theodore Roosevelt, Woodrow Wilson, Franklin Roosevelt, Harry Truman, John Kennedy, and Lyndon Johnson, each of whom used the powers of office to enact hundreds of social reforms. Reformers have often built broad coalitions to support reforms. For example, in the Great Depression, Franklin Roosevelt drew together a coalition of persons of color, intellectuals, ethnic minorities, and trade unions. Civil rights and liberal religious groups obtained broad public support for civil rights legislation in the 1960s. By linking liberal groups and agricultural interests, reformers secured the passage of the Food Stamps program, as well as numerous expansions of it.

Just as conservatives have blocked reforms by appealing to popular beliefs—for example, the widespread belief that most welfare recipients cheat—liberals have often obtained public support for reforms by appealing to widely held values. While many Americans do not want to help those they regard as undeserving—for example, those whose ill fortune can be linked to immoral behavior—they are generally sympathetic to the needs of those whom they see as innocent victims of adversity, such as unemployed people, persons with medical conditions, retirees who need pensions, widows, and children. Americans tend to like programs that equip people to find opportunities, for example, educational and preschool programs. While Americans have often enacted punitive programs, they have shown their unwillingness to allow persons in poverty to starve, by supporting a "safety net" that protects individuals' basic needs. Americans have also supported laws that protect citizens from capricious discrimination in such areas as employment, housing, voting, and nursing homes.

Liberals have had some surprising successes not just in passing laws, but in securing funding for them in subsequent years. Such interest groups as the Child Welfare League of America, the American Association of Retired Persons, the National Association of Social Workers, and advocacy groups for special populations like persons with disabilities have lobbied legislators to fund social programs. In many cases, lobbyists have persuaded conservatives to support these policies by pointing out that many of their constituents benefit from such programs. (We examine some tactics that reformers have used in Chapter 14.)

As we discuss social policy in different eras, then, we will often discuss the political processes that facilitated or hindered social reforms.

POLICY CHOICES

As we have seen, contextual factors and political processes have shaped the selection of specific policies in each historical era. Some American social policies—for example, the reliance on workhouses in the 19th century—have been restrictive or punitive, while others—for example, the Food

Stamps program—have offered genuine assistance to citizens.

In its broadest sense, social policy represents a collective strategy to address social problems. This collective strategy is fashioned by laws, rules, regulations, and budgets of government—that is, enactments that affect or bind the actions of citizens, government officials, professionals, and the staff of social agencies. Let's consider these aspects of social policy in more detail.

Constitutions define the social policy powers of government at the federal and state levels. As we have already noted, the failure of the federal Constitution to enumerate social welfare functions for the federal government was interpreted to mean that such functions should be left to state and local governments. As a result, the development of social welfare policies in this country was seriously delayed.

Some social welfare strategies involve *public policies*, laws enacted in local, state, or federal legislatures. The Chinese Exclusion Act of 1882, the Social Security Act of 1935, the Adoption Assistance and Child Welfare Act of 1980, and the Americans with Disabilities Act of 1991 are examples of public laws, as are the state and local laws that established poorhouses and mental institutions in the 19th century.

Court decisions play important roles in American social policy. By overruling, upholding, and interpreting statutes of legislatures, courts establish policies that significantly influence the American response to social needs. For example, in the 1980s, the courts required the Reagan administration to award disability benefits to many disabled persons even though many administration officials opposed this policy.

Budget and spending programs are also an expression of policy, since society cannot respond adequately to social problems if resources are not allocated to the relevant programs and institutions. For example, Americans chose not to expend a major share of the gross national product on social programs prior to the 1930s but greatly increased levels of spending in the Great Depression and succeeding decades. Despite the large increases in spending on social programs in the 1960s, the 1970s, and even the 1980s, the nation chose to devote a significant portion of its federal budget to military spending during the cold war and also to make successive tax cuts— policies that much reduced the resources available for social programs.

Stated or implied objectives also constitute a form of policy. For example, the preambles and titles of social legislation suggest broad purposes or goals. Thus, as its title suggests, the Family Support Act of 1988 emphasized the provision of services and training to those in need rather than the provision of economic resources or food. Politicians' public pronouncements often suggest their broad strategies; for example, compare the state of the union messages of relatively liberal presidents to those of conservative presidents.

Rules, procedures, and regulations define the way in which policies are to be implemented. Legislation often prescribes, for example, the rules or procedures to be used by agency staff in determining applicants' eligibility for specific programs. Courts often prescribe procedures that the staff of social agencies must employ to safeguard the rights of clients, patients, and consumers; the protections afforded to people who are involuntarily committed to mental institutions provide an example here. Government agencies issue administrative regulations to guide the implementation of policies.

Nongovernmental entities such as social agencies must conform to the policies enunciated by courts and the various levels of government. In addition, every social agency develops internal policies of its own. For example, agency staff members determine their distinctive approaches to providing services. Social policy historians try to determine how the staff of poorhouses and mental institutions shaped their eligibility policies in the 19th century. In similar fashion, contemporary policy analysts gauge how different social agencies implement specific policies—for example, whether staff in a child welfare agency believe that their task is to provide a range of preventive services to families (such as referrals to job-training, medical, and educational programs) or, more narrowly, to rescue children from abusive situations.

EVALUATING SOCIAL POLICIES IN THE PAST AND IN THE PRESENT

When evaluating social policies, we ask whether a specific policy choice was well or ill advised given the social problems of that era. Could officials have chosen alternative policies? Did practical resources and technical realities preclude a different policy response? Did the founding fathers err in legitimating slavery in the Constitution? Was the reliance on poorhouses and orphanages in the 19th century meritorious or ill considered? Did public officials fail to give freed slaves sufficient assistance to enter the economic mainstream? Were Republicans' proposals to reform welfare legislation in 1995 ill advised?

When we evaluate specific policies, we enter the realm of ethical reasoning, because we are making normative judgments that involve value-laden terms like *right, wrong,* and *duty.* We can contrast these normative statements with purely (or mostly) objective or descriptive statements, such as a recitation of the actual laws that were enacted in a specific era.

We reach these normative judgments in different ways. Sometimes, we decide a policy is right or wrong on the basis of specific information or data—for example, a study that found that the Food Stamps program markedly reduced malnutrition in the population. In such cases, we focus on the actual effects or outcomes of policies. In other cases, we use a reasoning process that involves ethical principles such as social justice or fairness. While we may use information as part of our reasoning process—for example, data about the effects of a policy in helping African Americans improve their economic condition—we emphasize ethical principles.

Indeed, numerous philosophical approaches to ethical reasoning have emerged over the centuries. We briefly summarize three of them here, along with some practical considerations. Our contention is that we often combine various approaches when deciding whether a specific policy is right or wrong—or whether it is right or wrong *on balance,* in comparison with alternative policy options.

Evaluating Specific Policies with Reference to Outcomes

First, in the program-outcome approach, we ask if a specific policy effectively addresses a social problem. (Theorists who emphasize outcomes when reaching ethical judgments about the merits of specific policies are known as utilitarians.) We can make our evaluative judgments by referring to actual data about the effects of policies on people, if such data are available. In the case of the Food Stamps program, for example, we might cite research data suggesting that the recipients of Food Stamps often improve their nutritional well-being because they receive financial subsidies to help them purchase food.[1]

When we lack data, we can still make informed judgments about the *likely* effects of specific policies on the well-being of people, even though we cannot claim scientific certainty. For example, what were the likely effects of workhouses in the 19th century on people who were destitute? Supporters of workhouses thought that these institutions helped people, by making dependency so unsavory that they would return to work quickly. Our knowledge of human behavior and labor markets suggests that incarceration in workhouses probably conferred many negative effects on residents; while they received sustenance and lodging, they were provided with no job training and treated in a demeaning fashion, to the detriment of their self-esteem. Likewise, we can infer that the absence of unemployment insurance prior to its enactment in 1935 caused extraordinary hardship among the victims of the recessions that have occurred with great regularity in American history. In similar fashion, we can conclude that many persons have been harmed by lack of health insurance, as suggested by data indicating that rates of illness and death are generally higher among uninsured Americans than among insured Americans.

When we examine the merits of a policy by looking at outcomes, we must also ask whether its benefits are worth the cost. We might oppose government funding for a medical treatment that cost $1 million per patient, even if it helped some patients, on the grounds that society could not afford it—or that those funds could better be used on relatively inexpensive programs, such as prenatal health care. Utilitarians often compare the cost-to-benefit ratios of social programs to determine their relative merit. A program with a high cost-to-benefit ratio, such as the expensive medical treatment, would be regarded as inferior to a program with a low cost-to-benefit ratio, such as prenatal health care.

If we use a utilitarian approach, then, we assign ethical merit to programs or policies with:

- positive program outcomes, as shown by evaluative research;
- probable positive outcomes, as judged on the basis of our knowledge of human behavior and economics;
- a relatively low cost-to-benefit ratio.

Ethical Reasoning from First Principles

We often lack good data about the effects of a policy. Even when we have data, people may disagree about what it means or about whether a program with a positive outcome is too costly to be justified. Furthermore, preoccupation with outcomes can sometimes lead us toward flawed ethical positions, as in the infamous Tuskegee experiment, in which African Americans with syphilis were deliberately not treated, so that researchers could study the unchecked course of the disease. We sometimes support policies that do not yield low cost-to-benefit ratios, such as providing expensive medical interventions to elderly persons or persons with AIDS even when we doubt that these interventions will significantly extend their lives. A group of moral philosophers known as deontologists have often made these kinds of criticisms of utilitarians; this group seeks to ground ethical reasoning in certain first-order or basic moral rules that provide guiding principles for society.[2]

But how do deontologists derive these kinds of principles? Some consult the precepts of major religions or religious writings such as the Koran or Bible. Others cite the work of philosophers such as Immanuel Kant, who identified a number of first-order principles. Still others, such as contemporary philosopher John Rawls, obtain first principles by a process of reasoning. To illustrate his approach, let's take the example of health care in the United States, where wide discrepancies exist in access to health care. In his seminal work, *A Theory of Justice,* Rawls argues that we can best construct our moral vision of a good society by trying to imagine its internal arrangements from behind a veil of ignorance—that is, in a state where we are unaware of our personal status (such as our income) or our personal access to opportunities.[3] Rawls says that, if we are aware of our current status and are, for example, relatively well off, we would likely want a society that perpetuated our economic well-being, even if others did not share it. However, if we retreat behind a veil of ignorance, where our personal income and opportunities are not known to us, we would likely conclude that society should only allow those inequalities that would preserve or further the common good of society. Not knowing in advance where we would be placed in society, we would not want to take the risk that we would be stuck in the lower strata. Thus, we would prefer an egalitarian society, in which most people have similar statuses and opportunities, to an inegalitarian society, where most people are in the lower strata (Figure 2.2). Of course, we could decide to be gamblers—to take the chance, as in a lottery, that we would end up in the higher reaches of an inegalitarian society—but the odds would not be in our favor. The rational person would, Rawls concludes, opt for an egalitarian society. We would accept some inequalities, such as relatively high salaries for brain surgeons and others with particular expertise and training, in order to attract the most skilled and dedicated persons.

We can place Rawls's argument in simpler form by asking, "If you had the choice at the start of your existence, before you knew what position in society you would obtain, would you choose to live in the United States (with its relatively inegalitarian arrangements in health care and elsewhere) or in a more egalitarian society like Sweden, where discrepancies between affluent and less affluent classes are less marked, and access to health care and to education is relatively equal?" (Remember when performing this mental exercise that you possess no

FIGURE 2.2   (*left*) Affluent Americans in an era of growing inequality; (*right*) inner-city Americans outside the economic mainstream

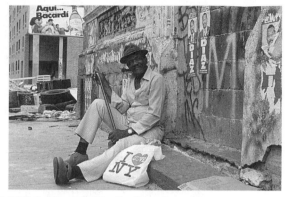

SOURCE: (*left*) © David Weintraub/Photo Researchers, Inc.; (*right*) © Gerd Ludwig/Woodfin Camp & Associates

affiliation to any specific society, including its language and customs.) Rawls asserts that you would likely select Sweden because, on balance, you would not want to risk that you might end up at the bottom of the American social system, in a blighted inner-city neighborhood with no health care.

Rawls's argument can be recast as a restatement of the Golden Rule, a tenet central to Christianity that has parallels in other religions and in secular philosophies. The Golden Rule says: "Do unto others as you would have them do unto you." If you are not willing to share the impoverished experiences of many persons in the inner city, for example, you should not support inegalitarian policies that contribute to such experiences. This argument suggests that failure to engage in *any* social reform, whether as a private citizen or as a responsible professional, is tantamount to violation of the Golden Rule. If we do not want to live without adequate health care and other amenities, we have a moral duty to try to improve the lot of those persons who do live in such conditions.

Alternatively, we could use the ethical principle of *fairness* to seek policies that equalize conditions between citizens. Fairness is a simple concept that is related to equality, but somewhat more limited. When we focus on fairness, we primarily want persons to have the same chance of obtaining positive things (such as income, services, and opportunities). If society is unwilling to support equality, why not, at least, develop social arrangements that

give each of us equal chances at prized things? Of course, our seeking fairness does not mean that we cannot also work for general equality, so that no one experiences poverty.

Considerable evidence suggests that neither prized things nor inequalities are randomly distributed in the population. American society has a variety of *outgroups*—that is, subgroups who possess a disproportionate share of social malaise. We can usefully distinguish among varieties of outgroups. The lower echelons of society constitute an *economic* outgroup, whose members are subject to class-based prejudice. African Americans, Latinos, and Native Americans are examples of *racial* outgroups, whose members have often been subject to racial prejudice. Certain groups, notably women and older people, have often been kept out of the economic and social mainstream by virtue of the specialized roles ascribed to them; we can call these groups *sociological* outgroups. As one example, women were traditionally expected to limit themselves to child-rearing and homemaking functions; indeed, middle-class married women did not enter the labor force in large numbers until World War II. *Nonconformist* outgroups include persons widely perceived to have different lifestyle preferences (for example, gay men and lesbians), to have violated social norms (for example, criminal offenders and juvenile delinquents), or to possess stigmatizing social problems (for example, those diagnosed with mental illness). Widely perceived to be outside prevailing norms, members of these groups have often experienced discrimination. Some groups, such as Asian Americans, Jewish Americans, and certain white ethnic groups, have found it difficult to obtain assistance from policy makers, because they are widely perceived to be problem-free, *model* outgroups. While many members of these groups have made remarkable progress in entering the economic mainstream, this progress has tended to impede awareness of the major social problems that many of their members still experience; for example, many members of white ethnic groups lack health insurance. Finally, we can identify *dependent* outgroups, such as children, who occupy an unusual status. Generally lacking political clout, children depend on the goodwill of adults for requisite services, housing, and resources.

In specific historical periods, controversy has enveloped various outgroups, whose members experienced numerous social problems, and also those persons who sought to be their advocates. Did outgroup members cause their own problems and thus not deserve the assistance of society, or were their problems caused by the discrimination that they experienced? What strategies would have best improved their economic and social condition? To what extent *should* society have sought to raise them to a more equal standing with others? Should they have been encouraged to use self-help strategies, or was governmental assistance needed?

While some outgroups found themselves engulfed in controversy, others were subject to the indifference of the broader population. Until the abolitionists succeeded in publicizing their needs, for example, the slaves in the South suffered from benign neglect from government officials; indeed, the founding fathers legitimized slavery in the Constitution. Although some courageous feminists championed the needs of women in the 19th century, most Americans were indifferent to their economic and social needs. Gay men and lesbians, who were subject to extraordinary discrimination, found few advocates in American history until the last few decades. Children in the 1990s experience high rates of poverty and often lack access to medical care.

Professionals, and social workers in particular, should work to ameliorate such inequalities, both by getting these outgroups better and more services in specific agencies and by seeking changes in local, state, and federal policies. Take the suggestion that the Head Start program should be expanded to serve all low-income African American children. We can support this proposal as a method of enhancing fairness, because it would provide African American children with the kinds of educational, health, and child development services long taken for granted by many white families, who send their children to nursery schools, have easy access to family doctors, and purchase computers and other educational aides for their children. While such expansion of Head Start hardly leads to a societal reduction of inequality on a grand scale, as implied by Rawls's framework, it would reduce inequalities between African American children and many white children, for example.

As our discussion of social justice and fairness suggests, deontologists seek to establish moral principles that take precedence over calculations of the consequences of specific choices. While differences exist among them, deontologists have variously derived a range of first-order ethical principles that include honesty, freedom, self-determination, confidence-keeping, not-killing, due process, beneficence, equality, and social justice. In addition, some ethicists contend that society and subparts of it, such as organizations, possess certain rights, including the right to public order. Some first-order principles are listed in Box 2.1. Note that considerable controversy about how to define the various terms exists within the philosophical literature.

Like utilitarian reasoning, reasoning from first principles such as those in Box 2.1 has particular shortcomings. When ethical principles conflict, it is difficult to make choices. Consider policies regarding euthanasia, for example. On the one hand, supporters of laws that allow physicians to end the lives of people with terminal illnesses contend that their policy furthers the ethical principle of self-determination or autonomy. Foes of euthanasia contend, however, that it undermines the principle of not-killing. When first principles con-

BOX 2.1 Various First-Order Ethical Principles

Not killing people: The right to life and health

Autonomy: The right to make critical decisions about one's own destiny

Freedom: The right to hold and express personal opinions and take personal actions

Honesty: The right to correct and accurate information

Confidentiality: The right to privacy

Equality: The right of individuals to receive the same services, resources, opportunities, or rights as other persons

Social justice: The right to live in an egalitarian society where economic and social differences between social classes and groups are markedly reduced.

Fairness: The right of equal access by citizens, regardless of their personal characteristics, to specific social resources and opportunities, as well as to equal treatment by the staff of major institutions

Due process: The right to procedural safeguards when accused of crimes or when benefits are withdrawn

Beneficence: The right to receive those treatments, services, or benefits that allow one to establish or maintain a decent standard of well-being

flict, ethicists must somehow prioritize one of them or find a compromise solution that balances the competing principles.

Relativism

Some philosophers criticize both utilitarians and deontologists; they contend that most people make ethical choices *not* through an extended process of reasoning, but by resorting to norms that they derive from their particular culture. When people in the colonial period placed wrongdoers on public display, they accepted a widely held norm that this punishment was morally acceptable. When people in the 19th century placed children in orphanages, they believed they were acting ethically, whereas most contemporary Americans would cringe at a policy of taking children away from parents who lack the resources to support them.

Some relativists also contend that ethical choices are often shaped by self-interest. When important policy issues come before legislatures, for example, representatives of different interest groups often develop opposing positions. In 1994, when the Congress considered national health insurance, many health care providers wanted patients to be able to choose their physicians and hospitals freely, but some corporations sought to reduce their health-care expenditures by lobbying for managed care policies that would require patients to use low-cost physicians and hospitals chosen by employers.

It seems at first glance that choices based on self-interest must be morally flawed. In fact, however, moral people *often* couple their personal interests with ethical choices. Take the case of social workers who support expanded funding for mental-health programs. While they take this position partly to advance the well-being of persons with mental conditions, they also realize that the enhanced funding would provide employment for social workers. Likewise, advocates for specific populations, such as women, African Americans, or Latinos, try to advance the collective interests of these groups. Were we to contend that self-interested choices were immoral, we would wrongly call into question an array of meritorious policies.[4]

Relativism usefully advances our knowledge about the way people often make ethical choices, but it has its own shortcomings. Absent *any* first-order principles or *any* consideration of consequences, ethical choices would have no parameters. We could even justify slavery in 19th-century America on the grounds that it was consonant with the culture of the South, without regard for widely accepted ethical principles or its harmful consequences for the slaves.

BOX 2.2   Some Sensitizing Approaches for Evaluating Social Policies

Some Considerations Drawn from Deontologists
- Identify first-order principles that are relevant to an ethical dilemma and decide, on balance, which choices or actions best satisfy them.
- When first-order principles conflict—that is, point to different choices—seek a compromise solution that satisfies each to some degree.

Some Considerations Drawn from Utilitarians
- Conduct research to identify the likely consequences of specific options or actions (or, when data are lacking, use knowledge about human behavior to infer the likely effects of specific policies).

- Select the option or choice that maximizes positive consequences for society or for one (or more) of its subunits.

Some Considerations Drawn from Relativists
- Analyze cultural factors that shape the ethical choices of people in specific historical periods, as well as other factors, such as institutional and fiscal realities.
- Analyze how the interests of people—including ourselves—shape policy choices.

Practical Considerations
- Consider the practical implications of specific policies, such as their political feasibility and their cost, as well as administrative aspects.

TOWARD ETHICAL REASONING: AN ECLECTIC APPROACH

Whether examining ethical issues in contemporary society or making ethical judgments about policy choices in historical eras, we should ask a *variety* of questions that reflect all of the philosophical schools considered here. We should consider first-order principles that have obtained a wide following in Western societies, whether derived from a reasoning process, as in the case of Rawls, or from religious sources. Even when we subscribe to first-order principles, we often cannot rigidly follow their dictates without examining some possible consequences of a specific course of action. Finally, relativists usefully note that most people do not make ethical choices in an extended process of deliberations; rather, they tend to rely on the norms and traditions of their society or their specific community, as well as their personal interests.

Not all of the considerations that shape ethical choices can be easily classified under the headings of deontologism, utilitarianism, and relativism, however. Our choices may also be shaped by *practical considerations,* such as the availability of

resources or political calculations (Box 2.2). A certain policy might meet our moral scrutiny, but we might ultimately reject it (or seek an amended version of it) on grounds that it could not realistically be enacted or funded. We might prefer a government-run system of health insurance, as in Canada, but decide reluctantly to support a modified system, on the grounds that Americans would not accept our preferred version.

Ethical reasoning, then, forces us to consider many kinds of information when making ethical choices. It requires us to integrate or synthesize the information during a *process of reasoning.* In this process, we look for points of convergence and divergence. If deontologic and utilitarian perspectives *converge* to suggest that a specific course of action or a specific policy choice is more meritorious than others, we can be fairly certain about our resulting decision. If these different considerations lead us in *diverging* paths—that is, suggest different actions or choices—we have to devote time and thought to seeking some resolution. Perhaps we will decide to give priority to one of the perspectives, or perhaps we will seek a compromise solution that draws on a range of considerations. Whatever our ultimate choice, we engage in a

INSERT 2.1   ETHICAL ANALYSIS OF KEY ISSUES AND POLICIES: SETTING POLICY ABOUT ABORTIONS

The Supreme Court's *Roe v. Wade* ruling (1973), which prohibits states from banning abortions in the first trimester of pregnancy, illustrates the joining of different ethical considerations. The Court found *first-order principles* of not-killing (the fetus) and self-determination (for the pregnant woman) to be relevant to the case. It also considered the fact that many women, when denied abortions, obtained illegal ones under dubious medical circumstances, and sometimes died or suffered serious injury as a result (a *utilitarian consideration*). The Court struck an *ethical balance* between the two first-order principles: it guaranteed that women's self-determination would be prioritized in the first trimester, while granting states the right to prioritize the not-killing of fetuses in the second and third trimesters. And the justices paid attention to *practical considerations* when they acknowledged that it is not possible to prevent many women from seeking abortions, even if government wants to stop the practice. (Many women will seek illegal abortions.)

This ruling illustrates, as well, how *cultural norms* shape our policy choices. While many Americans still believed that abortions should never be legalized in 1973, public opinion had shifted profoundly toward freedom of choice in the wake of the feminist movement of the 1960s and early 1970s, which emphasized women's rights. Even a decade earlier than 1973, the Court would probably not have made this ruling. Of course, if we prioritize women's right to choose, we might criticize Supreme Court justices for not reaching a similar conclusion earlier, though our knowledge of the culture of the 1950s would help us to understand why this was so.

Whether or not we agree with the Court's decision, it reflects the *balancing process* that often occurs in ethical reasoning. In this case, several first-order principles are considered and balanced against one another. These principles, in turn, are balanced against utilitarian considerations, as well as practical considerations. Ethical reasoning is often influenced by the political and cultural context, as reflected by the growing importance of women's rights in the early 1970s.

At numerous places in this text, ethical issues are posed. No single right solution exists, since alternative resolutions are often possible. In each case, however, a *deliberative process* should be undertaken to weigh alternative resolutions and to work toward a preferred solution.

process of *ethical analysis* as we use a variety of considerations to decide whether a policy is (or was) meritorious.

We use ethical reasoning not only to develop positions on specific issues, such as abortions and euthanasia, but to develop broader perspectives on the kinds of issues that distinguish conservatives, libertarians, liberals, and radicals (review Table 1.1). We shape our positions about the role of the federal government, the nature of the safety net, and the extent that the federal government should redress inequalities by examining first principles and outcomes, as well as on the basis of pragmatic considerations.

Social policy history is filled with examples of social reform movements, as well as the determined efforts of individuals to make American society more humane. Of course, having decided that certain policies are ethically flawed, whether because they violate first-order principles or have adverse outcomes, we would be ethically remiss if we did not try to change them. Consider social policy history, then, as a kind of laboratory that illustrates how advocates have moved beyond ethical analysis into the realm of policy practice; that is, they have made efforts to develop policy proposals and to seek their enactment in local, state, and federal legislatures, as well as specific agencies. (We return to policy practice in Chapter 14.)

▋ NOTES

1. The classic statement of utilitarianism is found in Jeremy Bentham, *An Introduction to the Principles of Morals and Legislation* (London: Athlone Press, 1970). For a critique of this approach, see J. L. Mackie, *Ethics: Inventing Right from Wrong* (London: Penguin Books, 1977), pp. 126–134.

2. For an excellent discussion of various moral rules, see Tom Beauchamp and James Childress, *Principles of Biomedical Ethics,* 4th ed. (New York: Oxford University Press, 1994).

3. John Rawls, *A Theory of Justice* (Cambridge, Mass.: Harvard University Press, 1971).

4. A sophisticated advocacy of relativism (he calls it "intuitivism") is made by Mackie, *Ethics.*

C H A P T E R

Fashioning a New Society in the Wilderness

Selected Orienting Events

1100s–1400s	Peak of feudal society
1492	Columbus's first voyage to the New World
1500s–1700s	Policy of mercantilism developed
1517	Reformation begins when Luther posts his 95 theses
1534	Henry VIII separates Church of England from Roman Catholicism
1600s	English Enlightenment (see John Locke's publication of *Two Treatises of Government* in 1689)
1601	English Poor Law Act
1607–1733	England establishes 13 permanent colonies on the Atlantic Coast
1676	Bacon's Rebellion in colonial Virginia
Late 1600s	Establishment of laws in southern colonies reducing blacks to chattel
1680	House of Burgesses in Virginia recommends that every county build a workhouse
1700s	Scottish and Continental Enlightenment (see Adam Smith's publication of *The Wealth of Nations* in 1776)
1763	Proclamation Line established to separate settlers' lands from Native American lands
1775–1783	American Revolution
1787	Constitutional Convention held in Philadelphia
1788	Constitution is ratified by the states
1789	George Washington elected to first of two terms
1791	Bill of Rights ratified as first ten amendments to the Constitution
1800	Thomas Jefferson elected to first of two terms

It was a diverse group of white settlers that came to the New World in the 17th and 18th centuries, predominantly from England but also in surprising numbers from Germany, the Netherlands, and Africa. In New England, Puritans and Protestants from the European Continent, fleeing religious persecution, wanted to establish spiritual communities based on their brand of Protestantism. Many Catholics came to Maryland to seek freedom from persecution in England. Many settlers hoped to better their economic condition in the New World, particularly as population growth in Europe limited access to the land and to economic opportunities. A large percentage of white immigrants became indentured servants, in the hope that they could better their lot once their term of service was completed. Many slaves were brought forcibly to the New World from Africa, primarily to work on tobacco and cotton farms and plantations. Because these people were so disparate and had such different motives for coming to the New World, it was unclear what ideas and institutions, much less what kinds of social policies, they would fashion—and how they would relate to the Native American population.

Deeply influenced by European institutions and ideas, the colonists rapidly created a new society in the wilderness. By 1800, they had fashioned institutions and a political culture that differed dramatically from those in the European nations from which they had come. To understand the colonists, as well as the society they fashioned, we need to understand the Old World that shaped them. After discussing their heritage, we discuss the unique set of institutions and culture that they devised in the New World.

THE FEUDAL INHERITANCE

With the decline of the Roman Empire after the fourth century, marauding bands of outlaws pillaged local villages and took land from local farmers in England and other European countries. Local populations gradually ceded title of their lands to powerful noblemen and monarchs, who allowed them to remain on the land but required them to render services in return for protection. By the 12th century, most of Europe had become splintered into a series of fiefdoms, which had developed localistic, hierarchical, communalistic, and traditional social institutions.[1]

Medieval society was hierarchical. Land was held by monarchs, noblemen, and the Catholic Church. Noblemen paid taxes to monarchs and helped obtain recruits for their armies. In return for protection, rights, and assistance, serfs worked the land for noblemen, monarchs, and the Church, paid taxes to them, and gave them a share of the produce from the land. Citizens also paid mandatory taxes to the Church in return for its religious, social, and legal assistance.

Medieval society was not capitalistic. Commodities were bartered in markets and in private transactions. Land was not bought and sold in the modern sense but was transferred through inheritance to successive generations of noblemen, so that it remained within specific families for centuries. (Noblemen were forbidden to sell their property outside their families by prohibitions known as *entail,* which reflected the prominence of tradition and family.) Serfs were bound to the land; that is, they were required to work it. While bound to the land, they also possessed rights to work specific amounts of land, which prevented noblemen from summarily evicting them; their children often inherited those rights. The serfs received no money for farming the land, but could sometimes sell surplus goods in local farmers' markets when coinage appeared. Some pastures and woodlands were reserved for the common use of a village so that peasants could graze cattle in them and gather fuel.[2]

Serfs did not live in dispersed housing but within small villages. Villagers elected members who negotiated with the nobleman's representative (the bailiff) to decide which fields would lie fallow, who would tend animals in common pastures, and which members of the villages would serve in the king's armies to meet the monarch's manpower levy.

The work ethic in the modern sense did not exist

in this subsistence-oriented society. Serfs worked to meet basic obligations and subsistence needs—and no more. Numerous religious, seasonal, and traditional holidays were observed each year. Noblemen did not expect more than this minimal labor from serfs because they, too, were oriented to a subsistence and bartering economy. Little work was performed in the fall and winter owing to inclement weather.

Though noblemen, crusaders, and traders accumulated vast wealth, the acquisition of wealth by exploiting market mechanisms—for example, charging interest on loaned money or raising the prices of food or commodities—was regarded with considerable suspicion. Early merchants who sought to accumulate money, or who tried to increase prices—and profits—by withholding grain from the market, were often persecuted. Some medieval theorists even developed the notion that wealth should be shared, since it belonged to the society in which it was developed; however, this idea was not carried to the logical conclusion that society should take lands or resources from noblemen, the Church, or kings and redistribute them to serfs.

Medieval society emphasized conformity with tradition. People were born into a position or status in society and usually remained within it. Rarely did people move their places of residence. Rights to the use of land as well as attendant obligations to noblemen were inherited. Persons who violated traditions—for example, those who failed to honor obligations or to maintain deference to social superiors—were subject not only to peer pressure but to various courts. Noblemen who tried to evict serfs from the land and serfs who refused to provide required service to noblemen were subject to sanctions.

The Catholic Church was the only recognized church in the medieval period and was intimately associated with governmental institutions. It was, in effect, a government paralleling secular jurisdictions, with its own taxes, laws, and courts. In addition, many ecclesiastical officials served in secular government and in the monarch's inner circle of counselors. Those who wished to establish a separate church—or to urge reforms in the existing one—met with strenuous persecution from Church or governmental officials and were sometimes sentenced to death. Just as noblemen did, the Catholic Church used serfs to farm its vast amounts of land. (In England, King Henry VIII declared the English branch of the Catholic Church to be a state church in 1534, and succeeded in wresting control of it from the Vatican.)

 ## SOCIAL POLICY IN MEDIEVAL SOCIETY

In this localistic, traditional, and hierarchical society, social problems were usually addressed through family and peer relationships and by mutual obligation. Noblemen provided food to serfs in return for labor and maintained stocks of food as reserves for famine. Villagers shared oxen and helped one another plant and harvest crops, as they moved together from field to field. Families and villagers were expected to assist elderly persons, children, and those who were mentally ill.[3]

The medieval Church assumed social welfare functions by providing food and lodging to people who were hungry, sick, or transient. Such individuals approached monasteries and requested food or lodging, which was given without any inquiry as to the reasons for their destitution. It was the Church's canon law that established principles about vagrancy and poverty during the Middle Ages, long before secular governments had developed policies. Viewing involuntary poverty as its own deterrent because few people *want* to live in poverty, Church leaders saw no need for punitive policies. As Tierney notes, Church officials "no more thought of punishing a man for being afflicted with poverty than we would think of punishing a man for being afflicted with tuberculosis."[4] Even by the 12th century, the Church supervised the care of the poor through the use of tithes, which local parishes collected and used to help fund poor relief. This positive belief about the rights of people who were poor, and the duty of society to afford relief to them, was eventually transferred from the Church to government, as we will discuss in due course, but the initial and primary impetus for poor relief came from the Church. Monasteries' welfare functions were usually limited in extent, however, so that only a small proportion of their resources was expended on aid and services.[5] Unemployment hardly existed, because most persons worked the land or engaged in hunting. The massive problems, such as plagues and famines, that often overwhelmed local helping institutions were viewed fatalistically as problems that society could not avoid.

The relatively small size of formal social programs should not obscure the fact that medieval society was organized to provide economic and social security. Most people had rights and obligations to farm land, use common pastures and woods, and occupy housing in local villages; these rights and obligations were protected and enforced by tradition, courts, and the Church. Entry into trades was strictly regulated to prevent excessive enrollments and to guarantee life membership to incumbents.[6]

Feudal society should not be glamorized, however. Extraordinary social and economic disparities existed between noblemen and serfs. Serfs were bound to the land, could not hunt without scrutiny of gameskeepers, had no chance for upward mobility, often could not own land, could not migrate, and could be conscripted into armies to fight battles that were often based on monarchs' petty territorial and religious objectives. One legacy of feudal society, then, was a social and economic conservatism that discouraged basic changes in land ownership and participation in political affairs by ordinary people.[7]

THE GRADUAL UNRAVELING OF FEUDALISM

The early American settlers immigrated from European societies that were in the throes of transition from feudal institutions to individualistic, democratic, and capitalist societies. To understand the perspectives of the early settlers, we need to examine how the roles, sanctions, and controls that existed in feudal society gradually weakened during the 16th, 17th, and 18th centuries, as manifested by the emergence of capitalism, the displacement of serfs from the land, the development of new classes, the rise of restrictive notions of the proper roles of government, the Protestant Reformation, changing conceptions of the meaning of human existence, and the Enlightenment. Historians do not understand the precise relationships between these developments—for example, whether capitalism, religion, or cultural changes assumed the primary role in unraveling feudalism. Despite its complex origins, the unraveling was vitally important to the origins of American society, whose early immigrants came from societies in which older ideas were widely criticized as new ideas and institutions emerged.

The barter and subsistence economy of medieval society was gradually replaced by a capitalistic economy; this development had profound social and political consequences throughout Europe. (Our examples below are drawn from the experiences of England.) Paper money, coins, and precious metals were increasingly used as mediums of exchange as bartering diminished. Buyers and sellers of commodities and land, instead of charging or paying a traditional fee, increasingly made economic decisions according to dictates of the market. A merchant might successively raise the price of bread, for example, until demand for it diminished, just as noblemen who wanted to raise cash would sell their land at the highest possible price. People became commodities themselves in labor markets; they worked for wages. While some employers paid a fair wage, others successively lowered wages to levels that labor markets would bear, regardless of their laborers' survival needs. This use of money and markets was complemented by the concepts of saving, investment, and profit. Where they had once merely sought subsistence, people began to hoard money, which they invested in land or other goods to increase their net worth. Indeed, some persons loaned their assets to others at the highest possible rate of interest.[8]

This gradual conversion to capitalism had many consequences. Capitalism fostered widespread economic and social uncertainty among agricultural laborers, who could no longer assume a relatively secure position on the land of their ancestors. Many of them had succeeded in converting their status from serfs to peasants; rather than being bound to the land, they became tenant farmers who rented their land. However, they soon discovered that noblemen, freed from ancient obligations, could now force them off the land. They found themselves buffeted by the uncertainties of inflation, depressions, unemployment, and displacement. Increasingly, they had to seek available work even if it paid a miserly wage. Many of those who had once occupied a secure niche within villages that were affixed to feudal estates now roamed the countryside or sought uncertain lodging in London and other growing cities. Urban dwellers could not raise subsistence crops, collect fuel from forests, or raise animals on common pastures. Thus, unemployment and hunger became major social problems; they brought a good deal of hardship to many persons and increased social tension within England. Peasants resented their loss of economic security, and many middle- and upper-class persons resented and feared dispossessed persons.[9]

The simplicity of feudal society, which facilitated the perpetuation of social power by noblemen, was fractured by the rise of new social classes. Small urban areas began to develop by the 14th century, as domestic commerce and foreign trade expanded. Merchants increasingly disliked efforts by the royal court and by noblemen to tax and regulate them. By the end of the 17th century, a virulent animosity had developed between upper and lower strata in English society. The upper strata feared the increasing numbers of vagabonds and persons without employment. Some gentry and merchants referred to the poor as "savages," "beasts," and "incorrigibles." Many believed that peasants and the urban poor were intrinsically lazy and could learn habits of productivity only when subjected to harsh discipline.[10] Landless persons at the bottom of the social order were less likely to respond with deference to social elites and often rioted to protest enclosures of fields, the raising of rents charged to tenant farmers, and the lack of food during famines. In the 17th and 18th centuries, many people feared that "unruly mobs"

would be aroused by demagogues to seek major changes in society. These fears reached fever pitch at the end of the 18th century with the French Revolution. Riots, mobs, and incidents of violence, though sporadic, were a decided feature of English life in the long transition from feudal to modern institutions and contributed to the decline of feudal patterns of deference and authority.[11]

Many persons in England sought to establish limits on the powers of central government. Many merchants hoped to reduce taxes and regulations. Elected representatives in Parliament, who sought to share decision-making powers with the monarch, had achieved a balance of power by 1700. Parliament obtained the power to veto tax initiatives while ceding trade policy to the crown. Monarchs, who had previously been able to dominate national politics, increasingly had to exercise power by rewarding persons through appointments, granting trade and commercial privileges, and distributing other favors. Religious dissenters wanted the ability to worship without interference from the state church. Landowners wanted to be able to enclose or sell their fields without having to honor ancient rights of peasants. All these cases reflect a notion of the self-directing and autonomous individual that was strikingly different from the collective notions of the feudal era. Complementing the notion of individual autonomy were economic concepts of personal initiative and risk taking. Many persons, including Protestants, Catholics, and Anglicans, believed that hard work, frugality, and saving resources were superior to traditional ideas about subsistence and seasonal labor.[12]

This emphasis on freedom, autonomy, and personal initiative in the secular world complemented the religious beliefs of many Protestants. Protestantism can be traced to 1517, when Martin Luther, a Catholic priest who had become disenchanted with the corruption and ritualism of the Church, posted 95 theses on the door of a church in Wittenberg. The theses stated his opposition to the use of "indulgences" (which allowed people to contribute money to a worthy cause so as to receive forgiveness for sins) and other Church practices. After he was excommunicated in 1521, he founded the

Lutheran Church, which became merely one of many sects that were established during the Protestant Reformation. Protestants hoped to increase the personal involvement of parishioners in the church by requiring church members to read and study the scriptures, by placing more emphasis on sermons, and by giving congregations enhanced roles in church governance. In the several centuries after the Protestant Reformation, there emerged an array of sects that drew on some of the ideas developed by Luther, Calvin, and other Protestant leaders; these sects included Anabaptists, Congregationalists, Methodists, Presbyterians, and Quakers. Some Protestants did not object to the concept of an official state church; they hoped to persuade the king to make their faith the established orthodoxy. Others, however, moved inexorably to the notion that all religions should be tolerated in English society, a concept that fundamentally challenged the notion of a single state church. The major religious purpose in life, Protestants believed, was to control such evil passions as pride, greed, lust, laziness, and desire for power by cultivating reason and moral virtue, by working hard, and by avidly reading the scriptures. In this emerging religious perspective, each person was charged with developing a personal quest for a moral existence. The Protestants differed among themselves about whether the individual could actually earn salvation by working hard and suppressing the passions through devotion, but they all emphasized work as a means of controlling the passions. Whatever their precise beliefs, members of Protestant sects were persecuted extensively in England and other countries. When emigration to the New World became an option, in the 17th and 18th centuries, many of them seized the opportunity.

The emerging emphasis on work and careers sometimes fostered suspicion of people living in poverty, on the premise that persons who were truly hard working should have something to show for it; after all, God was likely to bestow good fortune on moral persons. This judgmental orientation, reinforced by a growing class consciousness, resulted in an extraordinarily harsh orientation toward persons in poverty, which contrasted markedly with the nonpunitive relief policies of the medieval monasteries.[13]

In the 17th century, a number of English political theorists, including John Locke, espoused limited government, free speech, secularism, optimism, science, and the use of reason to discover natural laws. Locke contended that government did not exist in the primeval "state of nature," but that citizens developed a "contract" for a limited government when they discovered that some people attacked others and took their property. Thus, the citizens constructed a government that would emphasize preserving law and order. To ensure that despots would not arise, the citizens established a multibranched system of governance with checks and balances. We shall see that, while the American colonists drew on many sources when they constructed their Constitution in the 1780s, ideas of Locke and other writers in this so-called English Enlightenment deeply influenced their work. These writers also fervently questioned monarchical and religious authorities. They were also influenced by such writers as Adam Smith (who questioned excessive governmental intrusion into private matters) and Voltaire (who opposed state religions) in the Scottish and Continental Enlightenment of the 18th century.

 ## POLICY CHOICES IN THE PERIOD OF TRANSITION

Some English social welfare policies during this period of transition from feudal to postfeudal society advocated assistance to persons who were unemployed and poor, within the limits of a society that lacked resources and governmental agencies. Other policies, however, reflected a punitive orientation; these negative policies may be traced both to social elites' fear and anger and to the economic, political, and individualistic ideas that had contributed to the unraveling of feudalism.

Positive Policies

Officials in the small towns of feudal Europe had regulated virtually every facet of economic and social affairs during the 16th and 17th centuries.

INSERT 3.1   CRITICAL ANALYSIS:
WHAT PROMOTED THE MASS EXODUS FROM EUROPE?

Ponder how the fraying of feudal society promoted the emigration of large numbers of citizens from Europe to the American colonies in the 17th and 18th centuries, by considering several questions.

1. In 14th-century, medieval society, why would emigration have been difficult, even had citizens had access to ships? Consider how most people were bound to the land as serfs and unable to leave. Or how entrepreneurial activity was restricted to a relatively few merchants, so that incentive to colonize distant lands was limited. Or how, prior to the Protestant Reformation, relatively few people possessed a religious motive to flee European societies. Or how, absent strains of individualism that appeared during and after the Protestant Reformation, people lacked a worldview that promoted personal risk taking.

2. Consider how each of the factors associated with the fraying of feudalism contributed to emigration by providing motives, as well as people. More people now *wanted* to leave Europe, whether

- descendents of serfs who became tenant farmers with uncertain economic futures
- persons in growing towns who lacked steady work
- persecuted members of Protestant sects

In addition, population growth in Europe, as well as enclosures of land, limited people's access to the land and also their economic opportunities. Finally, with the rise of crime and the appearance of vagabonds and class tensions, members of the upper orders now possessed a motive to force less prosperous individuals to leave England.

3. Consider, as well, how a *demand* for immigrants in the New World was needed to promote a mass exodus. (We will see that many American land owners needed labor, thus providing a vast market for indentured servants.)

Entry into trades, decisions about who could set up businesses, the prices of commodities, wage rates, and locations of new construction were strictly regulated by the monarch and by local officials, partly to protect peasants from economic uncertainties. Local regulations were supplemented by a national policy of the English government to manage the economy so as to conserve food at home and to facilitate the development of foreign trade. A parliamentary act of 1548, for example, required citizens to eat fish on Fridays and Saturdays; the goal was to promote the building of ships and to conserve livestock. (Wednesdays were added by an act in 1563!) The English government encouraged immigration of Flemish experts in cotton and weaving to promote the development of a textile industry, provided government subsidies to various industries, and aggressively sought foreign markets.[14]

A policy called mercantilism had evolved by the 17th century; this policy envisioned the develop-

ment of colonies in the New World so as to obtain raw materials and new markets for England. Mercantilism is a system by which a government regulates its agriculture, industry, and commerce to create a favorable balance of trade. Mercantilism's proponents were convinced that external trade was needed to promote the prosperity of England. The monarch commissioned trading companies to settle lands in the New World, encouraged emigration to these settlements, and hoped that the settlers would both provide markets for English produce and supply England with gold and raw materials. To stimulate the growth of the merchant marine, the Parliament required that trade with these colonies be conducted in English ships.

Mercantilism can be viewed not only as an exercise in economic nationalism but also as a social policy to increase jobs and economic growth in England and thereby to help the large number of persons who had been cast off the land by enclosures and population growth. It was supplemented by other economic measures that were not narrowly constructed to encourage trade; for example, controls were placed on the prices of commodities and foodstuffs, so that everyone could afford basic necessities like bread and corn. Moreover, in an attempt to accommodate the many unemployed persons flooding the countryside, the English government tried to intervene in job markets so as to stimulate employment; landed gentry were sometimes asked, for example, to hire servants even when they did not want them and to extend terms of indentured status for servants and of apprenticeship for workers.[15]

As we have seen, the Catholic Church had required its local parishes to collect taxes and to use part of these proceeds to care for those in need. The Church of England inherited this custom, but did not faithfully put it into practice, largely because of the vast number of those who needed help in the wake of enclosures, population growth, and urbanization, but also partly on account of corruption within the church bureaucracy. Government authorities decided to supplant this local system of welfare by requiring the parishes to appoint unpaid overseers, who were charged with collecting taxes and distributing relief to those in need. In the landmark Elizabethan Poor Law Act of 1601, the national government consolidated various laws that had assigned welfare roles to local parishes. When parishes could not meet their responsibilities, counties were required to assume relief-giving functions. In effect, then, government became the chief enforcer of poor relief by 1601, thus supplanting the Church of England.

The Elizabethan Poor Law Act of 1601
Be it enacted . . . that the Churchwardens of every Parish, and foure, three, or two substantial Householders there . . . to bee nominated yeerely . . . under the hande and seale of two or more Justices of the Peace in the same Countie . . . shall be called Overseers of the poore of the same Parish, and they . . . shall take order from time to time . . . for setting to worke of the children of all such whose parents shall not . . . bee thought able to keepe and maintaine their children; and also for setting to worke all such persons maried, or unmaried, having no meanes to maintaine them, use no ordinary and dayly trade of life to get their living by, and also to rayse weekely or otherwise (by taxation of every inhabitant . . . in the said Parish) a convenient stocke of Flaxe, Hempe, Wool, Threed, Iron and other necessary ware to set the poore on worke, and also competent summes of money for, and towards the necessary reliefe of the lame, impotent, old, blinde, and such other among them being poore, and not able to worke, and also for the putting out of such children to bee apprentices . . . it shall and may be lawfull for the saide Churchwardens and Overseers . . . to errect, build . . . convenient houses of dwelling for the said impotent poor, and also to place Inmates or more families than one in one cottage, or house.

The Father and Grandfather, and the Mother and Grandmother, and the children of every poore, old, blinde, lame, and impotent person . . . not able to worke, being of sufficient ability, shall at their owne charges relieve and maintaine every such poore person . . .

Local parishes fulfilled their welfare responsibilities in several ways. They could provide "outdoor relief" to persons in their homes; provide "indoor relief" to persons in special institutions that came to be variously known as almshouses, poorhouses, or workhouses; or require persons to become indentured servants or apprentices. These latter two options were more punitive than outdoor relief, since they conditioned relief on residence within an institution or assumption of a specific labor status.

The Elizabethan Poor Law represented, on balance, a positive policy, even though it required that some able-bodied persons should be made to work in poorhouses and urged relatives to care for their own, impoverished relatives. (We shall see, however, that in many local jurisdictions it was administered in a punitive fashion during the next several centuries.) Research on poor law institutions of southern England suggests that poor law officials undertook a range of welfare roles that sometimes approached those of modern welfare states: They provided unemployment relief; initiated public works; regulated local prices to help poor persons; gave such in-kind assistance as food, clothing, and wood; gave health care; removed children from abusive households; and gave legal protections to apprentices. More than 50% of the people in southern England used outdoor relief in specific years. Many local jurisdictions possessed "laws of settlement" that entitled people to local poor law relief after a year's residence. Often used in punitive fashion to force people to leave if they became destitute before a year's residence had elapsed, laws of settlement could also be viewed more positively, as guarantors of poor relief for new agricultural migrants once they had lived for a year in a new location.[16]

Since the poor law did not outline in detail how local overseers were to implement their local programs, considerable local variation ensued. Some overseers placed more emphasis on indoor relief than others. Controversy regarding the relative merits of indoor and outdoor relief developed in the nation. In certain periods, advocates of a harsh policy enacted national policies to promote construction of workhouses; however, this punitive policy also provoked widespread revulsion, which sometimes took the form of riots by poor people in periods of high unemployment. In southern England, a relatively benevolent interpretation of the poor laws was dominant until well into the 18th century.[17]

Whether motivated by the feudal Catholic tradition of sharing wealth or the Protestant emphasis on giving as a moral duty, affluent persons gave money to many charities, including 800 hospitals in England by the 16th century. These hospitals served persons of limited means; some specialized in such groups as orphans. Local governments often shared in the costs of construction and implementation of these institutions, but most charity in 17th-century England was provided by private philanthropy. Charitable trusts and bequests were so common that the 1601 Statute of Charitable Uses was enacted to regulate them.

Punitive Policies

Punitive policies of the time included restrictive interpretations of the Elizabethan Poor Law, denial of civil liberties to the poor, and harsh use of laws of settlement. The Elizabethan Poor Law assigned responsibility for the poor to local public officials. Those in poverty could be assisted in their homes, but some could be placed in poorhouses and set to work on a "stocke of Flaxe, Hempe, Wool, Threed, Iron, and other necessary ware." When those living in poverty were regarded as "undeserving," policies tended to be punitive; in 1723, for example, Parliament enacted a law that mandated the use of poorhouses by local parishes rather than the continuation of the less stigmatizing policy of outdoor relief.[18]

Some theorists were so critical of people in poverty that they proposed enslaving them, in order to teach them discipline and moral virtues— with heavy reliance on corporal punishment. Parliament at one point enacted a law requiring those who were indigent to wear a sign marked with a P! (It was later rescinded.) Those in need were exposed to harsh discipline, back-breaking work, and moral teaching in the many workhouses that were constructed in the 17th and 18th centuries. The harshness of the workhouse strategy was offset, however, by the fact that few counties constructed them until the 18th and 19th centuries— and by the leniency of some local officials, who chose to provide outdoor relief instead.[19]

Laws of settlement, which required persons to remain in their native counties, were enacted during the long transition from feudal to postfeudal society and remained in effect until the 1870s in parts of England. In the 16th and 17th centuries, laws of settlement were sometimes viewed as protections for transient persons, since they entitled them to local relief after a year of residence. By the late 18th century, however, local officials began to urge local landowners not to hire laborers for more than a year, so as to limit parish and county welfare costs.[20] Vast numbers of peasants found themselves carted home after brief stints of labor.

Children were often subjected to treatment that would be regarded as harsh by modern standards. A common belief was that the central task in childrearing was to break the will of children, so that they could become right-living persons. Regarded as little adults, children were often apprenticed or indentured at an early age and subjected to rigorous working conditions. Free education was not widely available until well into the 18th century, and then only at the primary school level.

 ## THE AMERICAN COLONISTS

Recent historical research—by Gordon Wood and Joyce Appleby, for example—emphasizes the extent to which the culture and institutions of the American colonists resembled those of European nations.[21] Indeed, American society in 1750 was similar in many respects to England. By 1800, however, the Americans had created a political culture and institutions that departed markedly from their counterparts in England; they had, indeed, founded a new society in the New World. To understand the evolution of American social policy in the colonial period, and to obtain clues about its likely direction in the 19th century, we need to understand this process of transformation at the inception of the Republic.

Patterns of Continuity

The earliest American settlers in the early part of the 17th century created communal, hierarchical, and regulated enclaves that conformed to older traditions. Settlers in the Massachusetts Bay Colony in the 17th century worked fields together, much as their feudal ancestors did, on land given to trading companies by the crown. The farmers were expected to give a large share of their produce to the company, in exchange for the right to work company lands. They lived in villages that were surrounded by company fields, rather than in the dispersed patterns characteristic of American agriculture in the 18th and 19th centuries. Similar patterns were observed in the settlements in Virginia in the early 17th century.[22]

The social structure in these earliest colonies was also hierarchical in the feudal sense. A few wealthy investors received rights to large tracts of land and were served by a landless class of indentured servants. A variety of artisans and craftsmen occupied an intermediary position in the social structure. Since participation in the process of governance was conditioned on both holding land and meeting specific religious requirements, many persons were disenfranchised.

Early life was tightly regulated. In Virginia, for example, each settler was required to plant a certain amount of corn, in order to ensure adequate food crops. The colonists decided who could and who could not trap certain kinds of animals, where common pasturage was to be, the maximum levels of wages that could be paid, and the maximum prices that could be charged for specific products. Regulations were also promulgated that established apprenticeship requirements for entry into the various trades.[23] The individual colonies created official churches—Protestant churches in New England and a Church of England in Virginia. They also divided the countryside into parishes and imposed on all citizens, including those who worshipped in different churches, a tax to support the official church. Officials in these early churches, who were accorded extraordinary deference, often assumed roles in secular governance.

Wood contends that the politics and culture of Americans in the different colonies mirrored England even in 1750, long after the earliest settlements—and that both the colonies and England retained many ideas and institutions from medieval Europe. Most English-speaking Americans, for example, remained loyal to the English monarchy. State religions still existed in many colonies. While not as well established or affluent as its English counterpart, an American aristocracy existed; this aristocracy was deeply prejudiced against ordinary people, from whom it demanded considerable deference. Like the royal court in England, this aristocracy freely obtained favors from legislatures and royal governors in the various colonies. Many colonies required parents to pass their land onto their oldest son or their children, rather than selling it.[24]

While people in England and America did not think in terms of social classes until well into the 19th century, they conceptualized society as a series of vertical ranks or titles, ascending from indentured servants and tenant farmers at the lowest ranks to a landed aristocracy. Marked inequalities existed in England and America; at the lowest ranks, indentured servants, tenant farmers, and common laborers possessed scant resources and no land. Furthermore, between one-half and two-thirds of white immigrants in the 18th century entered indentured service before or after arriving in the colonies. (Evidence suggests that many who became indentured servants were driven from England, Scotland, and Wales as unemployment increased markedly during the 17th century; but a considerable number were also felons who were deported to the colonies as indentured servants.[25]) Local courts provided protection for some indentured servants who were beaten or whose term of service, typically four to seven years, was not honored by their masters, but their legal rights were not as complete as in England. Servants were beholden to their masters, who had paid their transportation costs to this country. Owners could try to extend the period of indentured service by appealing to local courts if their servants ran away, swore at them, or committed other petty offenses. Female indentured servants were often denied permission to marry, because their masters feared the women would leave their service.[26]

Indentured servants who had completed their terms often had difficulty in finding an economic niche for themselves. Lacking funds to purchase land, many became tenant farmers and worked at low wages for landowners. Some became part of the relatively poor and landless population in the small cities of colonial America. Those who purchased land often had to go to relatively cheap land on the frontier, where they encountered danger from Native Americans. Those servants who chose to become apprentices in hopes of entering a trade had to serve an additional seven years of service to tradesmen and were often mistreated by their masters.[27]

Although the early cities were small, the sizable numbers of unskilled and semiskilled persons who came to reside in them were subject to the numerous recessions that bedeviled the fragile American economy. In a credit-hungry economy, many Americans became overextended, could not pay debts, and were imprisoned. Produce was often plentiful, but grain exports to Europe were some-times so great that shortages occurred in American cities. Consumer goods were often scarce in a nation that imported most of its manufactured goods. Nash argues that these urban, white, and landless people often became increasingly aware of differences in wealth, and thus the likelihood of urban unrest in hard times increased.[28]

Riots were common in both England and the American colonies. Sometimes they were provoked by frustration at the slow workings of cumbersome bureaucracies. Periodic food shortages or rising prices of food prompted riots in local jurisdictions, even in the colonies. American squatters—people who inhabited land without obtained legal title—often rioted to persuade local officials to give them titles or to allow them to purchase their land at reasonable fees. A series of nine major rebellions, each lasting a year or more, erupted in rural areas in the 17th and 18th centuries. These rebellions were waged by persons with a homestead ethic who believed that their land titles had been unfairly seized by trading companies or that their land was excessively taxed by legislatures. Thus, Bacon's Rebellion in 17th-century Virginia involved a number of landless freedmen and indentured servants who protested against the monopoly of land by large owners.[29]

American colonists in 1750, then, had not developed a distinctive culture or set of political institutions. They often thought of themselves as Europeans rather than as occupying an independent status in the New World. English emigres primarily read literature from England, conversed about English politics, and often intended to return to England once they had obtained sufficient funds.

Patterns of Change

Between 1750 and 1800, a dramatically new society was created. To understand how this came about, we need to analyze the forces and events that powerfully transformed the American colonies. The first enclaves in the early 17th century were semifeudal in nature, with villages and state churches, but that pattern soon changed. Realizing that landless persons could settle freely on open land at the frontier, trading companies decided it was in their interests to sell land to immigrants, who eagerly bought what was offered. When governments were established in the different colonies, they also sold large amounts of land to individuals.

Access to land was the most powerful transforming factor in the New World. Whereas two-thirds of colonists owned land in 1750, only one-fifth of English citizens owned land. As they obtained property, many Americans came to perceive themselves not as common laborers, but as stakeholders in the emerging society. They increasingly demanded to participate in local and colonial politics; as landholders, they often were able to vote. They placed greater emphasis on work and initiative than landless people in England, because they realized that their personal economic fate hinged on their ability to produce and sell crops and other commodities, such as candles or garments. The colonies lacked a large, landless, and destitute population, such as that existing in London and other English cities by 1750. This new society was a *landed* one, mostly composed of persons with holdings of between 90 and 160 acres.[30]

Nor did these colonists live in the localistic and static world that had existed in Europe for centuries. As indentured servants finished their terms of service, they often moved onto small plots of land at the frontier, where they were joined by new immigrants from Europe. As land became more scarce on the Eastern seaboard, they moved to new areas. In a relatively brief period, huge areas of Pennsylvania, New York State, and the Carolinas became flooded with immigrants. The dynamic and changing nature of this new society was fostered not only by mobility, but by population growth due to the relatively high birth rate and to continuing immigration. The white population in the colonies practically doubled every twenty years, increasing from one to two million between 1750 and 1770 and from two to four million from 1770 to 1790.

In a society with such mobility, the semifeudal norms and traditions of the early colonies quickly eroded. Many observers noted that frontier people were a raucous lot; they were often violent, they lacked governmental institutions, and they possessed a fierce individualism.

Maintenance of an official church became increasingly problematic in the various colonies. America soon became a sanctuary for numerous Protestant sects, who, despite various "toleration acts" in England, were still subject to widespread persecution; their children were excluded from English universities, their suffrage was subjected to numerous restrictions, and they were forced to tithe to the Church of England. As members of the various sects became representatives in local and colonial government, they urged separation of church and state and termination of the requirement in a number of colonies that citizens pay taxes to support the state church. Separation of church and state, which was made explicit in the Constitution, was inevitable in a country with so many religious sects.

While England was the birthplace of capitalism and its attendant class of merchants, many English people, especially the landed aristocrats, still viewed it with suspicion. Americans came to embrace it with a fervor and a completeness unknown to the English. In 1750, American society was still largely rural; only 5% of the population lived in cities. However, most Americans were small capitalists on their farms, where they labored to produce crops and commodities for export to Europe, which provided a vast market during a period of rapid population growth. While factories had hardly emerged in the New World, many farmers supplemented their income by producing a wide array of goods—including hats, candles, clothing, and tools—in their homes and barns.[31]

The conflicts of colonial politics further eroded the communal and hierarchical nature of the early settlements. Settlers in the western sections of the colonies demanded funds for a militia to protect them from Native Americans and for the construction of roads and other improvements. These demands were often resisted by easterners, and intense competition for the limited public funds ensued. Many colonists soon came to oppose the royal governors appointed by the crown, who, they believed, sought to advance the trade and financial interests of the monarchy by exploiting them—for example, by taxing them excessively; by demanding excessive exportation of agricultural products even at the risk of food shortages; by forbidding them from establishing manufacturing that would compete with English goods; and by demanding that trade with England be transmitted in English ships.

Conflict also increased between ordinary people and the American aristocracy. Unlike the long-established and wealthy aristocracy of England, American aristocrats tended to be self-made men who lacked lineage to centuries of noblemen. They were poorer than their English counterparts; few had huge houses and manorial estates. Lacking the trappings of the English aristocracy and enveloped in a society where most people owned land, they commanded less respect from Americans than did the English aristocracy from the English.

The American settlers entered a New World where ancient rights to land, an entrenched aristocracy, and a monarchy did not exist. The absence of these practices, classes, and institutions contributed to an indigenous culture that was increasingly antithetical to them. Had these practices, classes, and institutions already existed in the New World, colonists would not only have been reminded of them, but would have encountered sanctions for not honoring them.

THE AMERICAN REVOLUTION AS CATALYST

An array of economic, social, and religious factors were antithetical to the hierarchy, social controls, and deference that the American colonists brought with them from Europe, but the colonists had not yet decisively overthrown the old order, even if they constantly squabbled with Royal Governors of the colonies, chafed at various taxes and regulations that the Crown imposed on them, and established legislatures or assemblies in the various colonies. According to the historian Gordon Wood, the American Revolution was the catalyst that moved Americans to define their differences from the Old World and to forge a distinctive set of institutions.[32]

What were the events leading up to the Revolution? King George was worried about the costs incurred by the Crown in seeking to protect the colonies from Native Americans. Partly to offset these costs, the Crown exacted new taxes on a wide range of goods. Already resentful of the various controls and taxes that the Crown imposed on the colonies, many colonial leaders were outraged by this new burden.

Many colonists were familiar with the arguments of English parliamentary leaders who had sought to eclipse the power of the monarchy for decades and had obtained from it many concessions that increased the power of the Parliament. Some of these leaders even wanted to end the monarchy in favor of a republic. Drawing on the arguments of these parliamentary leaders, colonial leaders like Thomas Jefferson and James Madison developed a rationale for making the colonies independent from the Crown; these efforts culminated in the Declaration of Independence of 1776.

The demand for independence and the associated attack on the monarchy drew a wide and favorable response, because large numbers of colonists, ensconced on their own plots of land and wanting to participate more fully in their own governance, had no wish to return to an old regime that might rescind their economic and political gains. The imposition of taxes on their goods by the Crown in the 1760s was a symbol of a different (and English) society that was not consonant with the New World. Were they to relent to the Crown, might not they endanger not merely their political right to resist taxes imposed on them in London, but their landholding, entrepreneurial, and individualistic culture? Might not those American aristocrats who still fancied themselves as possessing the prerogatives of English aristocrats try to repress the political freedom and power that ordinary people were obtaining in the New World? When viewed narrowly, the American Revolution was simply a rebellion against an overreaching Crown that insisted on its right to impose taxes without consulting the colonies' elected assemblies. When viewed more broadly, however, the Revolution was the catalyst for colonists to define their new society in terms markedly different from the customs of the Old World.[33]

When King George agreed to rescind only some of his new taxes and when he did not honor the Americans' insistence on independence, war ensued; it lasted seven years. By the time it had ended, about one-tenth of white males had joined the militia. The sheer length of the conflict dramatized the formal separation from England and encouraged widespread acceptance of a new ideology of Republicanism that deemphasized hierarchy, lauded individualism, favored the toil of ordinary people, and sought democracy. The battle against the Crown was supplemented, moreover, by intensive conflict *within* the colonies. Many Loyalists (or Tories), often drawn from the ranks of the large landowners and the aristocratic class, did not participate in the Revolution; some resettled in Canada and elsewhere.

While it fostered widespread acceptance of an ideology that extolled individualism, the leveling of distinctions between people, and freedom, the American Revolution may be contrasted to the French or Russian Revolutions, in which social classes were pitted against one another and revolutionaries sought to redistribute wealth. A host of research strongly suggests that the American Revolution, though accompanied by a surge in idealism and sacrifice, had relatively limited effects on social reform. It did not help to obtain legal parity for women, to provide just treatment to Native Americans, to end slavery, or to reduce the marked inequality between social classes.[34] Our purpose is not to question the legitimacy of the colonial grievances but merely to underscore their limited and focused nature, which did not include the grist of true revolutions: the questioning of social relations *within* a society and between its social classes. Since most Americans possessed land, no large class of landless and urbanized people existed (as in the French Revolution) and no large class of landless peasants existed (as in the Russian Revolution). These American revolutionaries fought both for independence *and* to establish a society grounded on individualism and freedom, but not to effect dramatic changes in the nation's social structure.

The achievement of independence enhanced the self-image of the colonists, who had managed to outwit and outduel a major world power. They confidently believed they could create a utopia of yeoman farmers by embracing capitalism and democratic institutions. Europeans such as Locke, by contrast, knew that their ideas could be only partially realized in societies encumbered by centuries of tradition as well as by classes and institutions that resisted change. As Commager put it, the Europeans imagined the Enlightenment while the Americans created it.[35]

It is fitting that land ownership figured prominently in the ideology of colonial leaders like Thomas Jefferson. We have noted how the widespread ownership of land promoted individualism and a leveling of class distinctions. The importance that colonial leaders attached to land ownership is illustrated by a portion of a letter that Jefferson wrote from France to James Madison in 1785. In the letter, Jefferson contrasted social conditions in France and in the colonies.

> The property of this country is absolutely cocentered in a very few hands, having revenues of from half a million of guineas a year downwards. These employ the flower of the country as servants, some of them having as many as 200 domestics, not labouring. They employ also a great number of manufacturers, and tradesmen, and lastly the class of labouring husbandmen. But after all these comes the most numerous of all the classes, that is, the poor who cannot find work. I asked myself what could be the reason that so many should be permitted to beg who are willing to work, in a country where there is very considerable proportion of uncultivated lands? . . . The earth is given as common stock for man to labour and live on . . . it is too soon yet in our country to say that every man who cannot find employment but who can find uncultivated land, shall be at liberty to cultivate it, paying a moderate rent. But it is not too soon to provide by every possible means that as few as possible shall be without a little portion of land. The small landowners are the most precious part of a state.[36]

 ## FROM REVOLUTION TO LIMITED GOVERNMENT

If the Revolution brought independence and the rejection of many ideas and institutions drawn from England, it also ushered in an era of limited government, in which the federal government's responsibility for social policy would be stifled.

When they finally achieved their independence in 1783, the Americans confronted a dilemma. If the 13 colonies became separate nations, they would confront many problems. Trade would be difficult with 13 separate currencies. They could not easily fashion treaties with foreign nations that had designs on frontier lands—especially Spain, France, and England—if they lacked a common foreign policy and navy. They could not easily fend off Native Americans on the frontier without a shared militia. Nor could they easily plan and build roads and canals across their boundaries if they remained independent. At the same time, each of the colonies jealously guarded its prerogatives; none wanted to yield excessive authority to a central government that might usurp its freedom in a manner akin to King George and the English Parliament.

They turned to the difficult task of constructing a Constitution in 1787. Meeting in Philadelphia, 55 delegates from all states except Rhode Island commenced their work in May 1787 and approved a document in September. It became the law of the land in June 1788 when the ninth colony, New Hampshire, ratified it.

Although they realized that they needed their government to have *some* powers, the framers of the Constitution were also obsessed with the dangers of an oppressive central government. To avoid this possibility, they created a complex system of checks and balances, including a popularly elected House of Representatives, Senators elected by legislatures in their states, a president elected by an electoral college rather than by direct election, and an independent judiciary. To further circumscribe the federal government, the framers enumerated its specific powers; the list included the right to issue currency, to form a militia, and to make treaties. (Furthermore, as we note subsequently, they specifically reserved to the states all powers not given to the federal government when they added the Tenth Amendment to the Constitution as part of the Bill of Rights.)[37]

The Constitution had momentous implications for the development of social policies in the new Republic. By not enumerating social policy as one of the federal government's powers, the framers intended that it fall entirely within the province of state and local government. Until well into the 20th century, many presidents and legislators, as well as justices, assumed that it was unconstitutional for the Congress to enact social policies.

Because the founders realized that the government would need to evolve in order to meet the changing needs of the nation, they inserted four provisions that *eventually* provided a legal rationale for the development of federal social policy.

1. They gave the federal government the power to regulate interstate commerce, which was used in the 20th century to regulate the work conditions of workers whose companies shipped goods to other states.
2. They included a clause that allowed the federal government to enact laws that furthered the nation's "general welfare." This ill-defined clause was later used by social reformers to justify a range of social interventions.
3. The founders stipulated that the federal government could "make all laws that shall be necessary and proper for carrying into execution the foregoing [enumerated] powers." Like the general welfare clause, this phrase was sufficiently broad to justify a broad range of legislation.
4. By allowing the Constitution to be amended, the founders provided a mechanism for change. Constitutional amendments protected the rights of African Americans and other groups in the wake of the Civil War.

As originally written, however, the Constitution must be viewed as retarding the development of federal social programs, because it did not mention social welfare policies and appeared to restrict the federal government to specific and relatively limited powers. By contrast, the French Constitution, which was written a few years later, outlawed slavery, guaranteed all citizens the right to work, urged humane care of the poor, and declared education to be a public obligation.[38]

While the Constitution ceded considerable power to them, local and colonial governments were extraordinarily weak in the colonial era. It is true that they imposed taxes and regulations on local citizens and businesses, (for example, they

INSERT 3.2 CRITICAL ANALYSIS: THE OMISSION OF SOCIAL POLICY FROM THE CONSTITUTION

Speculate why the framers did *not* discuss social policy in the Constitution? Consider such factors as:

- the absence, in a rural society with small towns, of the social problems that exist in an urbanized society;
- the legacy of local poor law traditions and private philanthropy, which led the framers to assume that local institutions would suffice;
- the widespread assumption that the federal government would possess relatively scant resources. While the Constitution empowered the federal government to "raise revenue," many framers opposed the imposition of large federal taxes.

often established prices and wages), required males to work certain numbers of days on roads and other public improvements, and constructed many roads and bridges (sometimes with tolls). But these local governments existed in an environment that was not conducive to the development of major powers, as Greene makes clear:

> With only a tiny bureaucracy and no police, a localized judiciary system that rarely met more than fifteen to thirty days in any given year, and legislators that in peacetime were rarely in session for more than a month in any given year, government was small, intermittent, and inexpensive. Except during wartime, taxes were low, and the only public activities that engaged most men were infrequent militia or jury service and some more frequent participation in vital public works such as building and repairing bridges and roads . . . [W]hile they wanted enough government to secure peace and to maintain . . . civil order, most Americans were . . . in favor of just so much government as will do justice, protect property, and defend the country.[39]

LEGITIMATING LIMITED GOVERNMENT

The framers wanted to put strict limits on the power of the federal government, but they did not agree about *how* limited the new government would be. During the two terms of President George Washington, a heated battle developed between two factions led, respectively, by Thomas Jefferson, Washington's Secretary of State, and Alexander Hamilton, his Secretary of the Treasury. A self-made man with aristocratic inclinations, Hamilton wanted a relatively strong central government that would pursue mercantilist policies akin to the Crown. He wanted the federal government to invest resources in roads, canals, and bridges; to establish a national bank to oversee the economy; to fund promising new economic projects; to impose considerable taxes in order to fund these projects and pay off debts that remained from fighting the Revolutionary War; and to develop a strong navy and militia. Hamilton favored a relatively loose interpretation of the Constitution. While acknowledging that the Constitution only mentioned certain powers, Hamilton believed that it implied other powers, such as the power to establish a National Bank. By contrast, Jefferson favored a limited federal government; he supported "strict constructionism," according to which the government would be limited to the powers enumerated in the Constitution. He wanted the American economy to center upon agriculture; opposed a National Bank on the grounds that it was not mentioned in the Constitution; opposed mercantilist policies; wanted low federal taxes; and opposed a standing army.[40]

Jefferson's view of a limited government was shared not merely by many federal legislators, but by many people in the various states. So-called antifederalists had even sought to prevent ratification of the Constitution, which they believed conferred excessive powers on the federal government. Partly at their insistence, the first ten amendments to the Constitution (the so-called Bill of Rights) were added in 1791, so as to protect citizens' rights from capricious actions of the federal government.

Often caught between the forces of Jefferson and Hamilton, President Washington tried to define the powers of the central government; usually, he sided with Hamilton. His patience was tested on many occasions. One such incident was the so-called Whiskey Rebellion. Needing funds to retire the national debt and to fund the government, the Congress enacted an excise tax on distilled liquor at Hamilton's request. However, in Western Pennsylvania, local insurgents questioned the federal government's right to impose these taxes. This tax revolt was quelled only after Washington personally accompanied troops into Pennsylvania.[41]

The battle between the Hamiltonians and the Jeffersonians persisted during Washington's tenure and during the presidency of John Adams. Then, in 1800, Jefferson narrowly defeated Adams in a tumultuous presidential contest. In his two terms, Jefferson implemented his limited-government vision; he sharply reduced expenditures and slashed taxes.

Defeated by Jefferson, the federalists soon disappeared as a viable force. With few exceptions, all the presidents of the 19th century subscribed to Jefferson's views of limited government. As we shall see when discussing the Gilded Age in the decades after the Civil War, however, they frequently used federal resources and powers to help corporations and the railroads. Using Jefferson's doctrine of strict constructionism, none of them supported the use of federal resources to fund major social programs other than war pensions.

Some readers may wonder why a text on social policy devotes so much time to distant constitutional developments and to these early disputes about federal power. However, this examination of the founders' philosophies clarifies an important aspect of social policy in the United States: that a strong defense of the central government's role in social welfare is relatively recent in American history. By contrast, in England and other European countries, extensive central government policy and regulatory roles have existed since (at least) the 18th century. Not until the 1930s, or almost 150 years after the founding of the republic, did Americans develop strong social policy roles for the federal government.

POSITIVE RESPONSES TO SOCIAL NEED

Americans inherited the same combination of positive and punitive social policies that existed in England in the 17th and 18th centuries, but they often did not enforce negative policies, on the assumption that pauperism and even poverty would not become widespread in their land-owning utopia. Furthermore, most early settlers brought with them the tradition of regulation of local economic affairs that had been so pervasive in Europe. Strange as it seems to contemporary Americans, cities, counties, and colonial assemblies limited wages and prices, granted business licenses to merchants, controlled the exportation of grain and other commodities, and regulated the rights and obligations of indentured servants and apprentices. These various regulations did not necessarily benefit poor persons, since they could be devised in a manner that assisted those with wealth or those masters who had indentured or apprenticed labor. Nonetheless, colonists believed that government should assume a wide range of functions to further economic development and to assist persons in the lower economic strata. From England, the colonists also brought with them the mercantile tradition, which gave government major roles in promoting job development and economic growth through the building of roads and bridges and other capital improvement projects. The development of regulatory policies at the local and state levels must be regarded as a positive social welfare response to social and economic needs.[42]

A tradition of private philanthropy developed with remarkable rapidity and often led to projects that were jointly funded by government and private donors. Benjamin Franklin participated in many partnerships between the public and private sectors —for example, to develop libraries, fire-fighting services, orphanages, and educational programs. The prevalence of Protestantism in the New World promoted the ethic of charitable giving. Wealth was often perceived by early Protestants as a mixed blessing; although it was the proper reward for a life of hard work, it could also promote laziness, pride, and greed—traits that were viewed by many colonists as sinful. Donation to charity became a way of easing this guilt about material possessions. Many of the earliest Puritan settlers believed that good works were morally correct but could not in themselves influence the Lord to grant salvation; however, by the middle of the 18th century, a growing number of clergy and citizens believed that moral living could increase the likelihood of achieving salvation. The sermons of preachers of the Great Awakening, a grassroots movement to revitalize and personalize Protestant religion during the 18th century, denied that good works can merit salvation but emphasized the importance of benevolence as a *sign* that one was saved.[43]

As in England, church parishes were a major source of charity. The Puritan churches of Massachusetts Bay, for example, elected officers whose major responsibility was to oversee sick and impoverished members of the congregation. Many American Protestants likened church organizations to extended families that cared for their members in times of adversity.[44]

Officials in colonial and local governments also continued the tradition of the English Poor Law by requiring the election or appointment of officials in local parishes who would collect taxes to pay for poor relief. Colonial assemblies were particularly generous in assisting persons who had been wounded or disabled in battles with Native Americans on the frontier. They often funded direct assistance to those individuals, without relying on local jurisdictions and without imposing the punitive policies that characterized other forms of assistance. Thomas Jefferson's portrayal of assistance to the poor in Virginia in the 18th century underscores generosity to those persons perceived to be capable of working, even though he notes that vagabonds were sometimes placed in workhouses.

> The poor, unable to support themselves, are maintained by an assessment on the tytheable persons in their parish. This assessment is levied and administered by twelve persons in each parish, called vestrymen, originally chosen by the housekeepers of the parish, but afterwards filling vacancies in their own body by their own choice. These are usually the most discreet farmers, so distributed through their parish, that every part of it may be under the immediate eye of some one of them. They are well acquainted with the details and economy of private life, and they find sufficient inducements to execute their charge well, in their philanthropy, in the approbation of their neighbours, and the distinction which that gives them. The poor who have neither property, friends, nor strength to labour, are boarded in the houses of good farmers, to whom a stipulated sum is annually paid. To those who are able to help themselves a little, or have friends from whom they derive some succours, inadequate however to their full maintenance, supplementary aids are given, which enable them to live comfortably in their own houses, or in the houses of their friends. Vagabonds, without visible property or vocation, are placed in workhouses, where they are well cloathed, fed, lodged, and made to labour. Nearly the same method of providing for the poor prevails through all our states; and from Savannah to Portsmouth you will seldom meet a beggar.[45]

In some jurisdictions, such as Boston, widowed or divorced women with children successfully resisted the tendency to place all dependent persons in poorhouses and received outdoor relief.[46] Of course, these benign interpretations of the workings of poor law institutions are balanced by harsher interpretations, which we note later.

Colonial courts also assumed a range of social welfare functions. Many children became orphans in colonial society because of their parents' early deaths from plagues, accidents, and childbirth. Local courts oversaw the economic affairs of these orphans, to ensure that they received funds granted to them by their deceased parents' wills which were often given in the form of proceeds over a period of years from the sale of livestock in the estate.[47]

Early Americans often supported the development of policies to equalize opportunity precisely because they favored self-improvement. Americans emphasized some opportunity-enhancing policies even before the American Revolution, which expanded options for many citizens. Some favored universal and public education, though universal education was not developed until the 19th century. Suffrage was generally tied to a property qualification, but it was already granted to more persons than in England. Perhaps the largest social welfare program of the colonial period and the early republic, however, was land distribution. Although wealthy people bought large amounts of land in early Virginia, many smaller farmers were able to acquire land from the Crown, trading companies chartered by the Crown, and colonial governments.[48] Americans also developed private philanthropic institutions, which tended to support opportunity-enhancing educational, health, and self-help projects that reflected the new society's preoccupation with self-improvement.

PUNITIVE POLICIES

Just as the English had done, many Americans viewed persons who were unemployed as undeserving and, hence, favored punitive treatment—in other words, indoor relief. In Massachusetts in 1780, vagabonds, paupers, and indentured servants were not granted the vote. The institution of the workhouse gained considerable popularity in colonial America. As early as 1688, for example, the House of Burgesses in Virginia recommended that every county build a workhouse. A frenzied period of construction occurred in New York State in the

early and middle 18th century. Jurisdictions that lacked the funds to build workhouses adopted other punitive devices. A poor person or family could be auctioned to a low bidder, who would take care of them in return for payments from local officials; a child could be placed as an indentured servant under a willing master; and persons without means could find themselves summarily escorted to the boundaries of a jurisdiction, since the American colonies had enacted laws of settlement similar to those in England.

Americans also took a dim view of "moral crimes." Many jurisdictions enacted laws prohibiting adultery and fornication, swearing, or even malicious gossiping. In colonial Virginia, persons found guilty of these crimes were generally made to devote a certain number of hours to public works— for example, the construction of a local bridge. Alcoholism was a major problem in the American colonies and sometimes led to imprisonment. Major crimes were similarly met with harsh treatment. Debtors were often imprisoned, even when they had no means of paying debts that were due to disability or health problems. As in England, capital punishment was extensively employed, sometimes even for petty theft, and executions were often public events attended by throngs of people.

Social welfare institutions did not extend assistance to African Americans, who were defined to be outside the social compact; this policy prevented slaveowners from freeing their slaves when they could no longer work or were sick—actions that would have raised the poor law costs of local jurisdictions. Various colonies enacted laws that made slaves ineligible for assistance from poor law institutions and that forbade their owners from releasing them when they were ill or aged.[49]

The settlers lived in a violent world. Most of them possessed firearms to hunt, to fend off Native Americans, and to obviate the creation of standing armies. They waged several major wars, fought Native Americans, engaged in various sectarian and sectional battles, fought in taverns, participated in various rural and urban riots, and witnessed public executions and lashings.[50]

HARSH TREATMENT OF OUTGROUPS

If the colonists were sometimes punitive or harsh in their treatment of white citizens, such as indigent people, they were often brutal in their treatment of Native Americans and African slaves. Nor did women enjoy many legal rights in this period.

The Native Americans

In medieval Europe, most people lived in relatively homogenous societies of white persons, and had little or no contact with persons of other races. As Sanders suggests, the idea of race was only "dim and sporadic" for most Europeans during the Middle Ages.[51] But race assumed fateful dimensions in the minds of many Europeans by the late 15th century, as explorers like Columbus made contact with native peoples in the Caribbean and in Central and South America—and as Europeans, desperate for labor, sought to import African slaves into these regions.

Depicted in older history books as a heroic figure (Figure 3.1), Columbus has been portrayed less flatteringly by modern historians. After a first voyage in 1492 that was primarily a trip of discovery, Columbus set sail on a second voyage—complete with 17 ships and 1,200 men—intending to colonize the New World.[52] When he discovered that a small settlement called Navidad, left from the first voyage, had been burned and its inhabitants murdered, Columbus's dream of concord between the indigenous people and the Spanish ended. Dor-Ner suggests that

> the Navidad incident would set a pattern of violence and mistrust between Europeans and Native Americans that would be played out in blood as successive waves of Spanish, English, and French colonialists swept through the Americas . . . this poisonous attitude would in time . . . echo at the Little Big Horn, where Sitting Bull took no prisoners [and] would be brutally distilled in the infamous remark of General

FIGURE 3.1   The clash of cultures in the New World

SOURCE: Bettmann Archive

Philip Sheridan: "The only good Indians I ever saw were dead."[53]

Columbus and his Spanish successors quickly devised a method of controlling the indigenous people by placing them in a position akin to feudal serfs. Though indigenous people in their villages were allowed to keep their property, they were forced to give most of their produce to the conquerors in return for "protection." Moreover, tens of thousands of them were conscripted for forced labor in mining and other endeavors. The Pope and also Queen Isabella of Spain often tried to place moral constraints on Columbus and other conquistadors, but they had scant success in stopping the brutalization of the indigenous population, despite the protests of a handful of courageous priests.

The early forays into the Caribbean were soon followed by the pillaging of native settlements in Central and South America. Far more deadly to the indigenous people than the violence and servitude imposed on them by the conquerors were the diseases brought by the Europeans; they had no natural resistance to smallpox, measles, diphtheria, whooping cough, the bubonic plague, typhoid fever, cholera, scarlet fever, and influenza and died by the millions from these various diseases. In Central Mexico, the native population declined from 11 million in 1519 to 2.5 million in 1597—a staggering loss that was repeated throughout Central and South America and in the Caribbean.[54]

Medieval culture did not prepare the Europeans to resist exploitation of the native populations or to outlaw the use of slaves in the New World. As Christians, for example, the Europeans were prone to divide humankind into two groups: Christians and heathens. The Church had long held the notion that heathens could be placed in servitude once they had "rejected" Christianity; on this principle, the Crusades had sought to conquer Moslem peoples in the Middle East. Feudalism provided the notion that native villages could be controlled by recreating the feudal equivalent of serfdom; in the New World, far removed from the ancient protections that had provided some assistance to European serfs, the indigenous population and then the slaves could be exploited with little interference from European courts, the Church, or the Crown.

Nor should we forget racism. Placed in contact with people of different racial background, the Europeans were quick to interpret differences in skin color and costume as signs of primitive, heathen, savage, and lazy dispositions. As native peoples and slaves physically resisted exploitation, the Europeans could seize on this behavior as proof of their savagery. Nor did the Europeans develop racist ideas only during the conquest of the New World; they had long imagined that cannibalistic and savage people lived in undiscovered territories.[55]

Historians' early estimates placed the Native American population of North America (excluding Mexico) at only one million persons, but recent research suggests that, in fact, this area was densely populated by Native Americans, who numbered some ten million persons in 1490. Every portion of North America was occupied. This huge and disperse population—including coastal tribes on the Pacific and Atlantic, tribes inhabiting the forests east of the Mississippi, the Plains tribes that hunted buffalo, tribes that occupied the Rocky Mountains, and tribes that lived in the deserts of the southwestern and western portions of the continent—represented a major barrier for the white settlers, because these tribes occupied the land, the most valuable resource in the New World.[56]

The early colonists quickly encountered two groups of Native Americans: a string of coastal tribes that occupied coastal areas from New England to Florida and a group of inland tribes that inhabited areas like the Appalachian Mountains. Colonists in the earliest settlements in Virginia and Massachusetts took the view that Native Americans in the coastal tribes could be converted to Christianity and, in the meantime, could help settlers by familiarizing them with native crops and hunting techniques. Early settlements in Massachusetts established "praying colonies," where converted Native Americans lived as part of the community. The settlers were certain that the Native Americans would choose Western culture not only so as to gain salvation but also to obtain its technological benefits; how could they, the colonists reasoned, retain their nomadic, un-Christian, and primitive existence when offered the benefits of civilization and Christianity?[57] This expectation was naive on many counts. Native Americans valued their own culture, which differed markedly from the settlers'. The Native Americans worshipped their own deities, did not collect or value property, led a nomadic life, and were content with a subsistence existence that required only as much work as was needed for survival.

As the numbers of white settlers increased, it became obvious that Native American culture was endangered. Once they had given up feudal strip farming and communal property, many of the earliest settlers began to develop and enclose fields, much as the English landowners had done; this practice quickly depleted the Native Americans' lands. If Native Americans resisted, colonists cited their violence as evidence that they were savages beyond any hope of conversion to Christianity. If they did *not* resist, the relentless expansion of white settlements continued unabated. The settlers also conducted their share of unprovoked violence—for example, because some group within their settlement enjoyed slaughtering Indians, because they were overcome with fear as they heard of other violence, or because they wished to retaliate for some earlier violence. Petty theft by a Native American led in one case to the massacre of an entire tribe.[58]

As in the Caribbean, the spread of diseases, such as smallpox, cholera, and diphtheria, was even more devastating to Native Americans than was warfare. Since these diseases were wholly new to the Native Americans, they lacked biological resistance to them. By roughly 1675, the coastal tribes extending from New England to the Carolinas had been virtually eliminated; the few survivors pushed westward to join with still-powerful inland tribes.

The inland tribes in and around the Appalachian Mountains proved able to resist the white settlers until the mid-18th century. Their remarkable resilience was made possible by their geographic remoteness from the coastal settlements and by their ingenuity in developing alliances with the French and adapting their hunting practices to provide furs to the white settlers' commercial markets.

The white settlers could have agreed to permanently cede large portions of lands on the frontier to the Native Americans, but did not, for several reasons. England and the trading companies, who had established the white settlements in the first instance to provide raw materials and markets for the English mercantile system, supported continuing migration inland for furs and other commodities that could be used in England. Moreover, the colonists believed that land was created by God to be farmed and that forest and other unfarmed land occupied by nonfarming Native Americans was wasted land that should be given to (or taken by) the white settlers.[59]

The settlers attempted to wrest the land from the Native Americans in a manner that would make their exploitation appear to be compatible with moral codes. They successfully used the seemingly legal device of the treaty; by this means, they created the impression that Native Americans had voluntarily and legally ceded land to the colonists. Native Americans were made to sign under threat of coercion, while intoxicated, or in exchange for money or gifts. When the Native Americans stopped teaching their children to use bows, they could no longer obtain food without guns, and so white settlers could entice them to sign treaties by offering them guns and other commodities. To decrease their dependence on the settlers, one tribe tried to revive ancient hunting skills in the mid-18th century, but few of them had the patience to undergo the years of practice required to use arrows when guns were available.[60]

However, the settlers were not so successful in obtaining lands from the inland tribes. Tribes in an area extending from New York State to the Ohio Valley joined in a common negotiating alliance; their shrewd bargaining led the British Crown to draw a line, known as the Proclamation Line of 1763, that separated settlers' lands from Native Americans' lands on the western frontier. (The Crown was willing to make this concession in order to thwart alliances between the Native Americans and the French, who vigorously contested the English for possession of portions of the New World.) The Crown had difficulty enforcing this line, however, because individual settlers, trading companies, and colonies relentlessly sought lands beyond it. After the American Revolution, the Americans displayed far less resolve in enforcing the line than had the English.[61]

Inland tribes such as the Iroquois in the North and the Cherokees in the South were doomed, however. As the frequency of their contact with white settlers increased, they proved as vulnerable to the fatal diseases as their coastal counterparts had been. When they altered their hunting patterns to collect furs, as a means of purchasing guns and other products, they dispersed their tribal settlements, and thus made them more vulnerable to attack. The white settlers soon employed treaties, as well as brute force, to displace them from their traditional lands. The ability of Native Americans to resist the white settlers was further diminished by animosities between tribes, which were sometimes rooted in traditional rivalries and sometimes

INSERT 3.3   ETHICAL ANALYSIS OF KEY ISSUES AND POLICIES: GEORGE WASHINGTON'S SOLUTION FOR NATIVE AMERICANS

When thinking about Native Americans, George Washington toyed with a "solution": why not, he thought, give each Native American a specific amount of land, say 60 acres, on condition that the individual settle on it and engage in agriculture.

1. Discuss this solution from the perspective of ethical principles, such as those discussed in Chapter 2.
2. Even *had* Washington obtained support from the Congress for this policy, how might it have worked in practice:
    a. from the vantage point of Native Americans?
    b. from the vantage point of white settlers?
3. To the extent that Washington's solution would not have been ethical *or* practicable, what more ethical alternative approach might the U.S. government have used? In answering this question, discuss whether the Americans should have honored the Proclamation Line of 1763.

provoked by the increasing scarcity of land as the white settlers advanced. As the 19th century began, Native Americans were in retreat from large areas immediately beyond the Appalachian Mountains and were being pushed into the inner and western recesses of the North American continent.

African Slaves

Slavery had existed in Roman times, and Christians had long enslaved Moslems, but the numbers of slaves involved were relatively small, and slavery had ended in Europe by the end of the 14th century. To fill minor labor shortages, Portugal and Spain began using Africans as slaves in their domestic economies in the 15th century. Even this minor use of slaves might have ended had Columbus and numerous successors not established colonies in the New World, first in the Caribbean and then in Central and South America.[62]

The wholesale deaths of the indigenous populations from disease and overwork created an economic dilemma for the Europeans when they introduced the labor-intensive crops of sugar and then tobacco in the Caribbean and South America. To find laborers for these crops, the Europeans, drawing on their experience with slavery, decided to import vast numbers of Africans to the New World.

By a quirk of biology, these African slaves proved to be relatively resistant to European diseases; thus, not only did they survive but they could be used as a self-replenishing source of labor. Moreover, the huge African population could be regularly raided, for a seemingly endless supply of laborers. By 1670, Portuguese Brazil had at least 200,000 slaves, and the English had at least 20,000 slaves in Barbados.

The New World was a labor-hungry society, because land had to be cleared, roads built, and crops raised in a harsh environment. Labor was particularly needed in Virginia and the Carolinas, where the settlers had decided to stake their economic existence on tobacco, a labor-intensive crop. Native Americans were a potential source of labor, but they were not willing to work in the settlers' fields and could not be easily enslaved because they could escape to the wilderness. White indentured servants became the major source of agricultural labor in the early Southern colonies, but they also proved unsuitable, because many of them objected to the backbreaking work in the intolerable summer heat and had to be replaced when their prescribed term of indentured service was at an end. They posed a political problem as well, since the freed indentured servants roamed the American countryside and agitated against oppressive working conditions when they lacked funds to purchase their own land. When the English economy improved in the mid-17th century, and the harsh working conditions of the tobacco colonies became well known, it was increasingly difficult to recruit the English as indentured servants.[63]

Massive importation of Africans was delayed, however, because the death rate from malaria and other epidemics was so high that planters would have lost most of their slaves. When the death rate declined, the advantages of slaves as a source of labor became obvious. Slaves were kept for life rather than for brief terms and provided a self-replenishing source of labor; the planters would be spared the task of continually recruiting and importing indentured servants. The political and social problems of accommodating freed servants were obviated, since slaves were not released. Slaves could be brutally disciplined without the surveillance of local courts; by contrast, indentured servants could be whipped only with consultation from local courts and could request a hearing if they believed they had been mistreated.

For slavery to exist, however, the Southern plantation owners had to develop laws that circumscribed the rights of slaves and punished those whites who chose *not* to cooperate in maintaining slavery. In the tobacco colonies, that legal task had been accomplished by the beginning of the 18th century. Slaves were not allowed to own property; indeed, their property was confiscated in Virginia and given to local parishes for redistribution to poor whites. Whites were forbidden by law to have sexual relations with Africans, and persons who sheltered or assisted runaway slaves were subjected to harsh treatment. Slaves were thus reduced to the legal status of chattel.[64]

The new laws cemented the white population—including the poor whites—behind the oppression of the slaves. Although subject to punishment if they assisted runaways or engaged in sexual activity with them, all white people obtained the right to discipline slaves, even without permission from their owners. Some historians believe that, by investing even the poor white population with superior legal rights, the large slaveowners decreased the likelihood of alliances between low-income whites and slaves. (Before the enactment of these laws, indentured white servants had often worked in the fields alongside Africans and had even intermarried with them.) Indeed, by the 18th century, many white people in Southern jurisdictions, even those of modest means, saw owning slaves as a sign of respectability and upward mobility.

Although some slaves had reached the New World earlier, the torrent of importation began after 1676, when the Royal African Company's monopoly was shattered and many private companies entered the lucrative slave trade. Shipments from Africa rose from 10,000 individuals per year in the 1690s to 40,000 per year in the 1790s. Roughly one million slaves were imported to the colonies or born in the colonies *before* the American Revolution. So many slaves were imported that they constituted almost 20% of the population in the New World by the time of the American Revolution—and 40–60% of the population of many Southern jurisdictions. The slaves lived on plantations of differing sizes, ranging from huge plantations in rice-growing coastal regions of the deep South to far smaller holdings of fewer than five slaves in Virginia and Maryland, where masters typically were of relatively modest means.[65]

As with Native Americans, a vicious circle of violence developed. Slaves did not enjoy the harsh working conditions associated with tobacco farming and often refused to work as hard as their masters desired. Their resistance confirmed the white settlers' beliefs that they were uncivilized and beyond hope of conversion to English values or religion. Racism—the imputation of negative characteristics to entire groups of persons who share similar physiological characteristics—became pervasive in the white community.

The slaves' working and social conditions were often degrading in the extreme. In the rice-growing areas of the coastal Carolinas, slaves worked in gangs of 50 or more as they planted, cultivated, and harvested rice. Less prosperous farmers used smaller groups of slaves to plant corn and other crops. Available evidence suggests that owners made frequent use of whipping; vicious punishment of runaways; "intrusion, inspection, and harassment" of the minutest aspects of their personal lives; sales of "surplus" slaves in a pattern that disrupted familial relationships; imposition of a class system with preferential treatment given to those slaves who worked in the owners' houses; and a conscious pattern of disrupting families by taking children from them at an early age and often placing husbands and wives in separate sleeping quarters.[66]

By defining African Americans and Native Americans as nonpersons, Southern white settlers did not have to feel guilty about their actions or policies. Violence was often rationalized as serving the broader needs of society or even of the nonpersons themselves. In killing Native Americans, for example, many colonists believed they were promoting the advance of Christianity and civilization, just as many slaveholders believed that harsh treatment of slaves helped teach them discipline and good work habits.

But slavery was not only a Southern institution in the colonial period. Slaves were also held in the Northern colonies, until all but New York and New Jersey eradicated the practice during the period from 1776 to 1783. (New York and New Jersey enacted laws that ended the institution in 1799 and 1804, respectively.) Agitation by Quakers and other religious groups assumed a major role in ending slavery in the North.[67]

Although slavery was largely eliminated in the North, Northern representatives at the Constitutional Convention in the 1780s had to decide whether to accede to Southerners' wishes to retain the institution. Many of the framers of the Constitution eyed slavery uneasily, because they feared that social turmoil from slave rebellions would allow England to conquer the South (for its cotton) or might require the federal government to commit troops to restore tranquility. (These pragmatic fears were more prevalent than moral outrage.) Northerners also feared that Southerners would bolt the Constitutional Convention—and the new nation—if they mentioned abolition, but they did not want slavery transplanted to the frontier. They also did not want Southerners to capture control of the Con-

gress by adding large numbers of slave-favoring congressmen as new states entered the union from frontier areas.

This conflict between Northerners and Southerners became the most contentious division during the Constitutional Convention and led to a series of compromises. The Northerners obtained exclusion of slavery from the frontier north of the Ohio River in the Northwest Ordinance of 1787 and were allowed to place a tax on imported slaves. But Southerners won most of the concessions: Slavery was not limited to those states where it existed; slaves were counted as though they were three-fifths of a person for purposes of apportioning congressional representatives; and Congress was not permitted to interfere with the importation of slaves until 1807. (Legislation to prohibit importation was finally enacted in 1808.) Slavery was legitimized by the Constitution, which referred to it in three places.[68]

In retrospect, both Southerners and Northerners miscalculated during the Constitutional Convention. Southerners assumed that they would soon control the Congress as new slave states were added to the Union and as the population of Southern states increased; thus, they believed no additional interference with the institution would develop. Northerners assumed that slavery would disappear naturally, as the economy grew and as yeomen farmers populated the West. Neither side realized that both regions would obtain new states on the frontier, and a political stalemate would culminate in a civil war. Already, in 1787, the two regions disagreed on other issues as well. Southerners wanted a weak central government that could not impose tariffs or supervise interstate commerce, whereas many Northerners favored a stronger central government.

Appleby argues persuasively that the framers left war as the only means of abolishing slavery when they legitimated it in the Constitution. Once legitimated, slavery could not be abolished without passage of a constitutional amendment, but the necessary two-thirds vote of both houses of Congress or ratification by three-fourths of state legislatures would have been unattainable once the many

Southern states were part of the Union. Had the framers *not* mentioned slavery in the Constitution, it could have been eliminated by a simple majority vote in Congress, in a manner akin to its abolition by a majority vote in the British Parliament.[69]

When considering African slaves and Native Americans, many colonists were afflicted by racism, the imputation of negative characteristics to people of color. Benjamin Franklin feared that African people would "darken" the people of America, who could, by excluding Africans and Native Americans, increase "the lovely White." And Jefferson advocated the removal of Africans from America so that the New World would be a "sanctuary" for European immigrants and their progeny. Moreover, the Congress in 1790 enacted legislation that restricted citizenship to Caucasians —legislation that was used to deny citizenship to Asian immigrants in the 19th century and later.[70]

The Status of Women

Contemporary historians have analyzed the lives of women in medieval society and concluded that, despite notable exceptions such as female royalty, they lived within relatively restrictive boundaries. Virtually without exception, people viewed both society and the family as hierarchies in medieval times—and husbands were seen as the superior member of the family, to which women and children were subordinate. Indeed, as Fraser notes, England was governed by feudal law "where a wife passed from the guardianship of her father to her husband [who] also stood in relation to her as a feudal lord." As the subordinate party, women were expected to be obedient, to confine themselves to household duties (or, in pastoral areas, to those farming duties that were most related to the household, such as milking cows, making cheese, and making clothing).[71]

It was widely assumed that women were "weaker vessels"—that is, inferior to males not just physically but also morally and in intelligence. Prior to the 17th century in England, virtually no women were literate, and educational reformers in that century, who gave some women exposure to education, refrained from allowing them to learn subjects like Latin, a language essential in an era that emphasized classical studies.

The economic roles of women were circumscribed. The guilds and crafts that developed to regulate skilled work in the towns and cities were dominated by men; women were excluded or, at best, allowed to be second-class members. Much of the work that women undertook—as domestic servants, small retailers, spinsters, or midwives— was not organized into guilds or crafts, and thus women were deprived of the kinds of security that guilds and crafts afforded. Though husbands and wives often worked together in the fields in feudal settings, the husbands generally passed the rights to farm strips of land to their sons; consequently, daughters lacked land rights.[72]

Women had few legal protections in the medieval period. The Church of England provided wives some protections against cruelty, lack of support, and desertion. Divorce was not sanctioned, but women could petition the Church for separation; often, though, they made these petitions only after their husbands had left them.[73]

Used to hierarchy in Europe, the colonists also assigned authority in families and in society to men. Men concerned themselves with farming, business, politics, and professions, whereas women were relegated to domestic matters and the raising of children. Although, on occasion, a woman whose husband died might assume management of a business, women generally refrained from seeking expanded economic and social roles.[74]

Feminism, in the modern sense of the word, did not exist in colonial America, even among such articulate women as Abigail Adams, the wife of John Adams. Virtually no one considered the possibility that women might vote. The colonists developed elaborate codes of etiquette that defined patterns of deference among the various members of the family, in a hierarchy extending from the husband to the wife to the children. Women could own property and sign contracts when they were unmarried or widowed, but they did not usually retain property or sign contracts when married. Children were the legal property of husbands after marriages had been officially dissolved, even when the husband had been unfaithful or abusive. Women were not allowed to serve on juries. Except for the Quakers, Protestant sects did not allow women to assume major roles in church governance. Married women were not expected to work, although women in lower-income groups most likely had to work to survive in many cases. Already in the colonial period, the wages of working women, married or unmarried, were far less than those of men who undertook comparable work. Furthermore, the segregation of working women into poorly paid work—as small retailers, seamstresses, laundresses, and domestic servants, for example—suggested that the feminization of poverty, a term used in the contemporary period, had relevance to many women in urban areas in the colonial era. Women were excluded altogether from the professions of law and medicine.[75]

Religious traditions encouraged colonists to believe that women were inferior to men. In medieval times, Catholic doctrine stressed that Eve had brought sin into the world by seducing Adam. Though a number of thinkers in the Renaissance criticized the notion that women were morally or intellectually inferior to men, the Protestantism of the 17th century retained strong misogynist (sexist) tendencies, including the portrayal of women as seducers. However, Protestant sects did support minimal literacy for women, so that they could read the Bible.[76]

Although limited in their roles, women in the colonial period were probably not so restricted as women in the 19th century. The high mortality rate in colonial society meant that many women assumed responsibility for the trades or businesses of their deceased husbands. Because society desperately needed labor, women were able to enter some trades. Midwives delivered children. In agriculture, women not only helped their husbands run farms but also produced candles and cloth in a society that lacked manufacturing industries. Much like Gandhi in 20th-century India, women made homespun cloth during the American Revolution to reduce dependence on English imports. However, we should not exaggerate the economic roles of women in colonial times; as Harris notes, they often assumed economic roles only *after* their husbands had died, and they performed them in a larger context of subordination.[77]

The domestic burdens of women were also less onerous in the 18th century than in the 19th century, because children generally entered trades at the age of 10 or 11. By the mid-19th century, however, children were increasingly seen as needing extended and intensive parenting, and women were required to devote a major portion of their lives to parenting and spousal responsibilities.

Some evidence exists that the economic conditions of women deteriorated toward the end of the 18th century. One contributing factor was that husbands, who often died before their wives, began to leave most of their estates to their children. In addition, although outdoor relief for women who were single heads of households had prevailed in earlier periods, women who could not fend for themselves were increasingly forced into newly constructed poorhouses. Some jurisdictions did allow women entering marriage to construct settlements that retained their rights to the property that was already theirs. However, few women availed themselves of these settlements; in consequence, they lost control of their property, both within the marriage and when their husbands died, divorced, or left them.[78]

Women suffered extraordinary hardship because no adequate method of birth control existed. Aside from abstinence and coitus interruptus, mostly herbal and other folk methods were used; these were of dubious value. Moreover, because procreation was widely regarded as the ultimate purpose of marriage, few women used birth control at all, except to increase the interval between childbirths by means of abstinence. Women tended to marry in their early 20s and to have children every other year; a typical family might have seven children or more. It is estimated that as many as one in five women died during childbirth or from the toll of successive pregnancies. Moreover, many women were pregnant at the point of marriage—probably around 20% in some jurisdictions.[79]

Women in the colonial period gained some benefit from certain Protestant beliefs. In particular, American Protestants' strong belief that families should be "peaceable" and intact led them to support laws that granted divorces on grounds of desertion (the most common reason women sought divorce) and cruelty. (Most divorce petitions were initiated by men, but they were often rejected by local courts.) Laws existed in many colonies, as well, that forbade physical abuse of women and children and that punished rapists, although then (as now) many rapists escaped punishment by alleging that the woman had consented.[80]

■ OMINOUS SIGNS

From the earliest colonial era, ominous signs existed that American society would develop a particularly harsh set of policies toward persons living in poverty, as well as African Americans and Native Americans.

The colonists lived in an agrarian society. They cannot be blamed if their policies and ideas, when inherited by subsequent generations, proved inadequate to the social problems of an urbanized and industrialized nation. Nevertheless, the pervasive influence of certain colonial ideas in the 19th century—and even in the 20th century—served to retard the development of national social programs.

Feudal society was replete with regulations and traditions that stifled upward mobility, changes in residence, sale of land, and changes in occupation, but it also offered many protections to its citizens precisely because it was so regulated. Courts protected the rights of serfs and their successors, whether tenant farmers, indentured servants, or apprentices. The early colonies inherited many of these feudal regulations, but lacked England's rich history of enforcement.[81]

The English landed gentry were descendants of the noblemen of feudal times, if not by direct family lineage then by accepting the prescribed social roles when they purchased large estates. In the transition from feudal to postfeudal society, many of the landed gentry in England resorted to enclosure and other policies that harmed emancipated serfs. Others, however, imbued with a sense of obligation to persons in lower social and economic strata, supported policies of job creation and mercantilism. Conservative philosophers like Edmund Burke contended that English society was an "organic" entity bound together by ancient traditions.

The Americans in the upper social strata had weaker notions of their social obligations than did their English counterparts. Few aristocrats and noblemen came to America; most immigrants were from the lower and middle classes. These self-made individuals—the American version of an aristocracy—sometimes believed, by the 19th century, that *everyone* should be able to obtain economic success. An example of American elites' limited sense of social obligation is provided by colonial Virginia. Although Virginia's landholding aristocracy appeared similar to its English counterpart, available evidence suggests that many powerful landowners possessed scant interest in the needs of the lower strata of society; they expanded their holdings through ruthless exploitation of indentured servants, tenant farmers, and slaves.[82]

Governmental institutions were extraordinarily weak in the colonies and mostly devoted to protecting public order. In the 19th century, the functions of local, state, and federal jurisdictions were curtailed even further, when an ideology of limited government became ascendant.

The early Americans hoped to create a utopia of land-owning, hard-working, moral citizens. Education would allow children to develop their reason and to learn good work habits. Widespread ownership of land, the colonists believed, would inspire settlers to work hard, so as to improve their holdings and increase their personal wealth. Granted democratic institutions, Americans would inform themselves about policy issues, so as to prevent the rise of despots who might try to concentrate property and power in the hands of social elites, appease landless and urban lower classes by taking private property from other citizens, or create an urbanized society. By maintaining an agricultural society, Americans would be able to avoid such social problems as unemployment, alienation, crime, and social disorder; colonists believed that these problems inevitably infested urban areas, where wage-earning and poor residents were more prone to social disorder and the appeals of despots.

Moreover, the early Americans placed extraordinary faith in the family, where moral conduct and the work ethic would be taught and modeled.

To summarize, the colonists believed that virtuous conduct was systematically fostered in America by education, widespread land ownership, the absence of excessive economic and social inequality, a system of governance that prevented the emergence of despots, cohesive families, and an agricultural economy. They were convinced that major social problems could not arise in the New World, precisely because they had masterminded a set of political, educational, familial, and economic institutions that would avert them.[83] Thomas Jefferson waxed ecstatic in a letter to John Adams about the utopian nature of this new nation as compared with Europe.

> With respect to aristocracy, we should further consider, that before the establishment of the American States, nothing was known to history but the man of the old world, crowded within limits either small or overcharged, and steeped in the vices which that situation generates. A government adapted to such men would be one thing; but a very different one, that for the man of these States. Here every one may have land to labor for himself, if he chooses, or, preferring the exercise of any other industry, may exact for it such compensation, as not only to afford a comfortable subsistence, but wherewith to provide for a cessation from labor in old age. Every one, by his property, or by his satisfactory situation, is interested in the support of law and order. And such men may safely and advantageously reserve to themselves a wholesome control over their public affairs, and a degree of freedom, which, in the hands of the *canaille* [the proletarians] of the cities of Europe, would be instantly perverted to the demolition and destruction of everything public and private. The history of the last twenty-five years of France, and of the last forty years in America, nay of its last two hundred years, proves the truth of both parts of this observation.[84]

This belief that Americans had created a utopian society served to retard the development of social programs, by blinding the colonists and succeeding generations of Americans to the existence of social needs in their midst. If America is a utopia, few social programs or regulations are necessary. Even in the 19th century, when the nation began to develop an urban society and poverty and other social needs became relatively widespread, the persistent notion of the American utopia perpetuated a kind of collective denial.

Americans aimed to achieve freedom in their new society by developing state and federal constitutions, elaborating a Bill of Rights, ending taxation without representation, establishing freedom of religion, and expanding suffrage. Liberty is an important social objective, but Americans failed to grapple with another vital objective, that of equality, which would have required them to develop institutions capable of reducing economic and social discrepancies. Whereas the slogan of the French Revolution was liberty *and* equality, the American Revolution emphasized liberty. When the framers anxiously submitted the Constitution to state conventions for ratification, widespread protests erupted against their work, on the grounds that they had not included a Bill of Rights to protect citizens' freedom against capricious acts of government. In response, the first ten amendments were added to the Constitution by the First Congress in 1791.

Although the colonists wanted to limit the power of government, they often supported the regulation of prices, economic planning, and public improvements. With the American Revolution completed and the Constitution written, however, a remarkable political conflict took place in the 1790s between allies of Jefferson, who formed the Republican party (which later became the Democratic party), and allies of Washington, Adams, and Hamilton, who formed the Federalist party. The Federalists, who had favored economic planning and a somewhat stronger federal government, were routed in the election of 1800 by the Jeffersonians, whose beliefs formed an American consensus about drastic reductions in the economic role of government, reductions in various federal taxes, and a strict interpretation of the Constitution so that the government did not exceed its enumerated powers. The American consensus engineered by Jefferson meant that the federal government would remain exceedingly weak for generations.[85]

OVERVIEW: SOCIAL POLICY AT THE NATION'S INCEPTION

American social policy in the colonial era cannot be easily characterized because, like English policy in this period, it reflected conflicting tendencies. On the one hand, mercantile policies, local regulation of prices and wages, and the development of poor law institutions represented positive responses to social problems. Indeed, these policies can be viewed as distant descendants of feudal notions of social obligation, even if they accorded to governments helping roles that, during the feudal era, had been implemented by the Church and noblemen. On the other hand, many American colonists possessed moralistic (and punitive) orientations toward unemployed persons, believed that government should only assist destitute persons, were extremely fearful of the national government, and believed that social problems like unemployment emanated from moral defects. With the victory of Jefferson in 1800, moreover, the nation tilted decisively toward a limited federal government that was not even granted explicit powers to develop and implement social policies by the Constitution.

An array of factors shaped American social welfare policies in the colonial era and led to a reliance on relatively modest local policies. Cultural factors included the emphasis on individualism and limited government. Among political factors, the lack of a large class of landless people and the subjugation of persons of color meant that little pressure was exerted on public officials to develop policies that would redistribute land or resources. Institutional factors included a weak central government as well as relatively weak local jurisdictions. Americans were already displaying an aversion to taxation as reflected by their dislike of British taxes and a Whiskey Rebellion that questioned the authority of the federal government to levy taxes.

Social welfare policy in the colonial period centered on the local poor law institutions, which included a mixture of indoor (institutional) relief and outdoor relief. Local courts assumed relatively minor social welfare functions with respect to orphans, divorce petitions, and prosecutions of persons accused of rape. Nongovernmental social welfare agencies made an appearance in the colonial period; the pattern of relatively weak governmental welfare institutions supplemented by nongovernmental programs was already emerging.

The policies of the Americans toward African slaves and Native Americans, however, appear particularly onerous, even when we note that these white settlers only had the harsh precedent of the Spanish conquests of the Caribbean, Central America, and South America to guide them.

NOTES

1. Gerald Handel, *Social Welfare in Western Society* (New York: Random House, 1982), p. 31.

2. K. D. M. Snell, *Annals of the Laboring Poor: Social Change and Agrarian England, 1660–1900* (Cambridge: Cambridge University Press, 1985), pp. 166–194. For a discussion of the social structure of feudal villages, see George Homans, *English Villagers of the Thirteenth Century* (New York: Russell and Russell, 1960).

3. Homans, *English Villagers,* pp. 353–381.

4. Brian Tierney, *Medieval Poor Law: A Sketch of Canonical Theory and Its Application in England* (Berkeley, Calif.: University of California Press, 1959), p. 12.

5. Gerald Handel, *Social Welfare in Western Society* (New York: Random House, 1982), p. 62.

6. Edmund Morgan, *American Slavery, American Freedom: The Ordeal of Colonial America* (New York: Norton, 1975), pp. 65–66.

7. Joyce Appleby, *Capitalism and a New Social Order: The Republican Vision of the 1790s* (New York: New York University Press, 1984), pp. 1–23.

8. Joyce Appleby, *Economic Thought and Ideology in Seventeenth-Century England* (Princeton, N.J.: Princeton University Press, 1978), pp. 158–198.

9. Margaret James, *Social Problems and Policy during the Puritan Revolution* (London: George Routledge and Sons, 1930), pp. 78–130; Snell, *Annals,* pp. 228–269. Peasants' resentment at the loss of their

ability to raise crops on common pastures and on strips is discussed by Snell, *Annals,* pp. 209–227; and by Louise Tilly, "Food Entitlement, Famine, and Conflict." In Robert Rotberg and Theodore Rabb, eds., *Hunger and History* (Cambridge: Cambridge University Press, 1983), pp. 135–151.

10. James, *Social Problems,* pp. 241–302; Morgan, *American Slavery*, p. 326.

11. Charles Tilly, "Collective Action in England and America." In Richard Brown and Don Fehrenbacher, eds., *Tradition, Conflict, and Modernization: Perspectives on the American Revolution* (New York: Academic Press, 1977), pp. 45–50.

12. For discussion of changing beliefs in the transition from feudalism, see Appleby, *Economic Thought*, pp. 183–184, 190–198, as well as Robert Webb, *Modern England: From the Eighteenth Century to the Present* (New York: Dodd, Mead, 1970), pp. 43–46.

13. James, *Social Problems,* pp. 271–283; Morgan, *American Slavery*, pp. 321–325.

14. Morgan, *American Slavery,* pp. 196–197.

15. Ibid., p. 67.

16. Snell, *Annals,* pp. 104–137.

17. Ibid., p. 105.

18. Daniel Baugh, "Poverty, Protestantism, and Political Economy: English Attitudes Toward the Poor, 1600–1800." In Stephen Baxter, ed., *England's Rise to Greatness* (Berkeley, Calif.: University Press of California, 1983), pp. 84–94.

19. Snell, *Annals,* p. 107.

20. Ibid., pp. 110–114.

21. Gordon Wood, *The Radicalism of the American Revolution* (New York: Alfred A. Knopf, 1992); Joyce Appleby, *Liberalism and Republicanism in the Historical Imagination* (Cambridge, Mass.: Harvard University Press, 1992).

22. Francis Bremer, *The Puritan Experiment* (New York: St. Martin's Press, 1976), pp. 51–52.

23. Ibid., pp. 89–93; Morgan, *American Slavery, American Freedom,* pp. 133–149.

24. Wood, *The Radicalism of the American Revolution,* pp. 11–92.

25. Appleby, *Liberalism and Republicanism*, p. 153.

26. Morgan, *American Slavery,* pp. 126–128.

27. Ibid., pp. 238–239.

28. Gary Nash, "Social Change and the Growth of Pre-Revolutionary Urban Radicalism." In Arthur Young, ed., *The American Revolution: Explorations in the History of American Radicalism* (DeKalb, Ill.: Northern Illinois University Press, 1976), pp. 11–12. Also see Gary Nash, "Social Development." In Greene and Pole, eds., *Colonial British America,* (Baltimore: Johns Hopkins University Press, 1984), p. 247.

29. Richard Brown, "Backcountry Rebellions and the Homestead Ethic." In Richard Brown and Don Fehrenbacher, eds., *Tradition, Conflict, and Modernization: Perspectives on the American Revolution,* pp. 73–95; Edward Countryman, "Out of the Bounds of Law: Northern Land Rioters in the Eighteenth Century." In Young, ed., *The American Revolution,* pp. 37–70.

30. Wood, *Radicalism of the American Revolution,* p. 123.

31. Ibid., pp. 325–347.

32. Ibid., pp. 169–197.

33. Ibid., p. 229.

34. Jack Greene, "The Limits of the American Revolution." In Jack Greene, ed., *The American Revolution: Its Character and Limits* (New York: New York University Press, 1987), p. 12.

35. Henry Commager, *The Empire of Reason: How Europe Imagined and America Realized the Enlightenment* (Garden City, N.Y.: Anchor Press, 1977).

36. Merril Peterson, *Portable Thomas Jefferson* (New York: Viking Press, 1975), pp. 396–397.

37. Christopher Collier and James Collier, *Decision in Philadelphia: the Constitutional Convention of 1787* (New York: Random House, 1986), pp. 181–194.

38. Commager, *The Empire of Reason,* p. 226.

39. Greene, "Limits of the American Revolution," pp. 8–9.

40. Richard Smith, *Patriarch: George Washington and the New American Nation* (Boston: Houghton Mifflin, 1993), pp. 50–51.

41. Ibid., p. 145.

42. Louis Hartz, *Economic Policy and Democratic Thought in Pennsylvania* (Cambridge, Mass.: Harvard University Press, 1948), p. 4; Morgan, *American Slavery,* pp. 134–136.

43. Robert Bremner, *American Philanthropy* (Chicago: University of Chicago Press, 1970), pp. 5–42.

44. Ibid.

45. Peterson, *Portable Jefferson,* pp. 180–181.

46. Alfred Young, "The Women of Boston: 'Persons of Consequence' in the Making of the American Revolution, 1765–76." In Harriet Applewhite and Darline Levy, *Women and Politics in the Age of Democratic Revolution* (Ann Arbor, Mich.: University of Michigan Press, 1990), p. 186.

47. Morgan, *American Slavery,* pp. 165–170.

48. Jack Sosin, *The Revolutionary Frontier, 1763–1783* (New York: Holt, Rinehart & Winston, 1967), pp. 172–192.

49. Young, "The Women of Boston," p. 340.

50. Countryman, "Out of the Bounds of Law," p. 74.

51. Ronald Sanders, *Lost Tribes and Promised Lands* (Boston: Little, Brown, 1978), p. 17.

52. For example, see Zvi Dor-Ner, *Columbus and the Age of Discovery* (New York: William Morrow, 1991), p. 201.

53. Ibid., p. 208.

54. Ibid., pp. 216–217.

55. Sanders, *Lost Tribes,* p. 7.

56. Jim Potter, "Demographic Development and Family Structure." In Greene and Pole, eds., *Colonial British America,* p. 133; Angie Debo, *History of the Indians of the United States* (Norman, Okla.: University of Oklahoma Press, 1970), pp. 53ff.

57. Bremer, *The Puritan Experiment,* pp. 198–204; Morgan, *American Slavery,* pp. 22, 47.

58. Gary Nash, *Red, White, and Black: The Peoples of Early America* (Englewood Cliffs, N.J.: Prentice Hall, 1974), pp. 69–87.

59. Morgan, *American Slavery,* pp. 22–24; John Yolton, *The Locke Reader* (Cambridge: Cambridge University Press, 1977), pp. 289–292.

60. Francis Jennings, "The Indian's Revolution." In Young, ed., *The American Revolution,* pp. 333–336.

61. Ibid.

62. Nash, *Red, White, and Black,* pp. 156, 160.

63. Morgan, *American Slavery,* pp. 295–297.

64. Ibid., pp. 330–337.

65. Ibid., p. 330; Nash, "Social Development," pp. 244, 254; Collier and Collier, *Decision,* p. 16; and Peter Kolchin, *American Slavery, 1619–1877* (New York: Hill and Wang, 1993), pp. 28–34.

66. Richard Dunn, "Servants and Slaves: The Recruitment and Employment of Labor." In Greene and Pole, eds., *Colonial British America,* pp. 179–180.

67. Sylvia Frey, "Liberty, Equality, and Slavery: The Paradox of the American Revolution." In Greene, ed., *The American Revolution,* pp. 235–236.

68. Collier and Collier, *Decision,* pp. 137–179; Harold Hyman, *Equal Justice Under Law: Constitutional Development, 1835-1875* (New York: Harper & Row, 1982), p. 4.

69. Appleby, *Liberalism and Republicanism,* pp. 223–225.

70. Ronald Takaki, *Strangers from a Different Shore* (Boston: Little, Brown, 1989), pp. 16, 207.

71. Susan Amussen, *An Ordered Society: Gender and Class in Early Modern England* (Oxford: Basil Blackwell, 1988), p. 133; Antonia Fraser, *The Weaker Vessel* (New York: Knopf, 1984), p. 5.

72. Maryanne Kowaleski and Judith Bennett, "Crafts, Guilds, and Women in the Middle Ages: Fifty Years After Marian K. Dale." In Judith Bennett et al., eds., *Sisters and Workers in the Middle Ages* (Chicago: University of Chicago Press, 1989), pp. 11–38.

73. Amussen, *Ordered Society,* pp. 95–133.

74. Joan Wilson, "The Illusion of Change: Women and the American Revolution." In Young, ed., *The American Revolution,* pp. 426–431.

75. Nancy Woloch, *Women and the American Experience* (New York: Knopf, 1984), pp. 76–80; Linda Kerber, "'I have Donmuch to Carrey on the Warr': Women and the Shaping of Republican Ideology after the American Revolution." In Applewhite and Levy, *Women and Politics,* p. 233; and Elaine Crane, "Dependence in the Era of Independence: The Role of Women in a Republican Society." In Greene, *The American Revolution,* p. 262.

76. Barbara Harris, *Beyond Her Sphere: Women and the Professions in American History* (Westport, Conn.: Greenwood Press, 1978), pp. 20ff.

77. Ibid., p. 20.

78. Crane, "Dependence in the Era of Independence," pp. 260–266.

79. John D'Emilio and Estelle Freedman, *Intimate Matters: A History of Sexuality in America* (New York: Harper & Row, 1988), pp. 22–23.

80. Ibid., p. 31.

81. Stanley Elkins, *Slavery: A Problem in American Institutional and Intellectual Life* (New York: Grosset & Dunlap, 1963), pp. 27–37.

82. Morgan, *American Slavery,* p. 235.

83. Bernard Bailyn, *The Ideological Origins of the American Revolution* (Cambridge, Mass.: Harvard University Press, 1967), pp. 272–319.

84. Peterson, *Portable Jefferson,* p. 538.

85. Appleby, *Capitalism,* pp. 53–61.

4

Social Welfare Policy in the Early Republic: 1789–1860

Selected Orienting Events

1820s	Speenhamland System introduced in the South of England
1824	First House of Refuge founded in New York; Yates Report issued in New York State
1828	Andrew Jackson elected to first of two terms
1830s	Zenith of Sunday School movement
1830s–1840s	Chartist Movement in England; zenith of antebellum temperance movement
1830s–1850s	Movement to establish public schools
1834	Report of English Poor Law Commission issued
1843	New York Association for Improving the Condition of the Poor established in New York
1845	The term *manifest destiny* coined
1848	Seneca Falls Convention
1845–1849	Irish potato famine
1853	Charles Loring Brace founds Children's Aid Society of New York
1854	President Pierce vetoes a bill, initiated by Dorothea Dix, to fund construction of mental institutions by means of revenues from land sales

Having established their independence from England and written their Constitution, Americans were free to shape their national destiny both geographically (how would they define the boundaries of a nation with seemingly endless expanses of land on their western frontier?) and institutionally (what political and social institutions would they evolve?). Between the inception of the republic in 1789 and the Civil War in 1861, Americans devoted vast energy to problems of poverty, street children and orphans, mental illness, crime, illiteracy, and alcoholism and developed policies concerning Native Americans, Spanish–speaking persons, and African Americans.

Most of the programs and policies were fashioned in local and state legislatures in this period; aside from the use of federal troops on the frontier, the involvement of federal authorities was relatively minor. In these local undertakings against social problems and in local skirmishes with native peoples on the frontier, Americans began to evolve a policy identity—a curious mixture of idealistic, simplistic, and punitive approaches to social policy.

SOCIAL REALITIES IN THE NEW NATION

American society was regionalistic in the early 19th century. The Northeast, the Northern frontier extending from Pennsylvania to Kansas and Nebraska, and the South were characterized by very different social and economic patterns. New Englanders, who had developed some factories and industries by 1860, were concerned with developing their shipping, fishing, and manufacturing industries in the face of efforts by England and other European nations to sabotage the emerging American industry. To make Americans dependent on them for manufactured items—such as steel, shoes, and textiles—the English dumped these items on the American market at artificially low prices, refused to allow the export of machines and technology to America, and discouraged the development of an American shipping industry.

The Northern frontier—the contemporary Mid-

west—produced agricultural staples such as corn, wheat, beef, and pork. Settlers on the Western frontier, who desperately sought cheap land and a ready supply of credit to purchase and develop it, pressured federal authorities and state and territorial legislatures to provide militia to fend off Native Americans. They also sought federal and local funds to build roads and canals, so that they could send their agricultural commodities to the East.

Long before the outbreak of the Civil War, Southerners were intent on ensuring the growth and stability of slavery and their agricultural economy based on tobacco and cotton. They won federal policies that allowed them to expand slavery into frontier areas such as Texas, and they enacted in Southern legislatures, with scant dissent from whites, a series of measures that made it impossible for slaves to marry, to obtain property, or to be educated.

Politicians and political parties often sought to advance the particular economic goals of these regions in battles over tariffs, internal improvements such as canals and roads, and the price of land that was charged by federal authorities to settlers on the frontier. New England wanted relatively high tariffs to protect its growing industry. Frontier areas and the South wanted lower tariffs to minimize the cost of their goods. Frontier areas often wanted public improvements to allow transportation to and from their areas. Southern and frontier interests also wanted cheap land, so that settlers could readily obtain land on the frontier, whereas many New Englanders opposed these policies because they feared loss of their population to Western lands. National politicians often catered to these regional issues in national elections, which were sometimes determined by patterns of regional support. For example, support from frontier and Southern regions was crucial to Thomas Jefferson's presidential victory in 1800 and to Andrew Jackson's election in 1828, whereas Abraham Lincoln became president in 1860 by obtaining support from New England and the Midwest.

The settlement of areas extending from Pennsylvania to Nebraska, from the Carolinas to Texas, and from the East Coast to the gold mines of California occurred with unprecedented speed. This speed and range of settlement was made possible by a number of factors. Continued immigration from Europe and large families in nonfrontier communities provided a plentiful supply of individuals willing to settle new territories; soil and weather conditions were favorable to settlement; and the settlers encountered ineffective resistance from the indigenous population of Native Americans and Spanish-speaking persons, who were outnumbered and technologically outgunned.[1] Settling the frontier may sound romantic to contemporary readers, but realities were often harsh. Much like Mexico or Brazil today, the United States was saddled with extraordinary debt as it tried to build its agriculture and industry from scratch. Enormous debts were amassed as Americans borrowed from banks and wealthy individuals in Europe, who financed the speculative American economy. During much of the century, the American banking and currency system was in chaos; it was characterized by frequent and sharp recessions; fluctuations between inflation and deflation; unregulated banks that would frequently go bankrupt or charge excessive rates of interest; and the inability of authorities to develop a national bank that could, like today's Federal Reserve system, promote or discourage economic expansion to avert the twin perils of recession and inflation. Locally and nationally, considerable effort was expended in debates about banking and currency policies to foster economic growth and to avert recessions. (Americans were inclined to support a variety of economic panaceas —for example, abolishing national banking institutions, using hard rather than paper currency, or issuing more paper currency.)

The debates about the economy were fueled by the economic difficulties of countless Americans. Subject to the vicissitudes of world markets and to frequent recessions, farmers, merchants, and bankers often could not repay loans from local or foreign creditors; many local laws allowed imprisonment of debtors even when small sums were involved. (Local courts often practiced leniency.) There was widespread agitation against imprisonment for debt, as well as against local banks and speculators who charged excessive rates of interest

or profiteered in land speculation prior to the Civil War.[2]

The scant public resources of the debt-ridden nation were largely devoted to internal improvements, so as to allow transportation within and settlement of this frontier empire. Despite the initial appearance of industry in New England, American society was predominantly an agricultural nation prior to the Civil War. In 1830, 91% of Americans lived in towns of less than 2,500 persons. Eastern cities remained small by modern standards; Philadelphia contained only 120,000 persons in 1830, even though it had grown from 40,000 persons in 1785. Many rural Americans were only distantly aware that a growing population of poor persons lived in urban settings. Farmers, after all, were able to obtain a subsistence living even when they experienced hard times, and could not understand that urban Americans lacked this security.[3]

This enormous frontier brought Jefferson's yeoman republic into existence, diverted attention from serious social problems in the nation, and blunted interest in reforms. Indeed, many Americans assumed that anyone could obtain land and fend for themselves; compassion for persons who lacked the physical and financial means to homestead successfully was limited. Preoccupied with personal economic issues, with settling the Western frontier, and with regional issues, relatively few persons were concerned about barbarous working conditions in the new industries of New England, the plight of tenant farmers on the frontier, or the accumulation of massive quantities of land by speculators and railroads in the West.[4]

 ## IMMIGRATION AND URBANIZATION

Jefferson's dream of an agricultural utopia seemed partially realized in the early 19th century, when small landowners, who were often reasonably secure financially, were the dominant social group in the new nation. Together with growing numbers of small businessmen, local officials, and government officials, they formed the American middle class, whose average income was relatively high by English standards. A social and political elite of clergy, businessmen, and large landholders dominated local politics and commanded deference from other citizens.[5]

America had developed a network of cities even before 1860, particularly on the East coast, and these cities grew at fantastic rates as the nation industrialized in the wake of the Civil War. Before and after the war, cities were plagued by many problems. They increasingly became repositories for immigrants from Ireland and Germany. Between 1814 and 1845, nearly one million impoverished Irish citizens—mostly Catholic peasants from southern Ireland, who replaced the predominant immigrant group of the 18th century, the so-called Scotch-Irish from Ulster, who were Protestant—entered the United States. These were followed by another 1.2 million Irish immigrants in a scant seven years after the disastrous potato famine of 1845–1849, which decimated Ireland's population.[6]

Early American cities were rough places. Shanty towns and tenements were hurriedly constructed by speculators in the absence of housing codes. Abundant public health hazards—including open sewers and poor sanitation—gave rise to epidemics. Prostitution, gambling, street begging, and drinking were rampant. Widespread unemployment accompanied the major recessions in 1819, 1833, 1837, and 1857, when as many as one-fifth of the entire populations of New York and other large cities received welfare benefits in almshouses or from outdoor soup kitchens maintained by public and private agencies.[7] When discussing the hardships of the Panic of 1819, the historian Charles Sellers notes:

> Distress was most acute in the cities . . . In Philadelphia, three out of four workers were reported idle . . . philanthropic groups distributed soup to the starving . . . the 8,000 public paupers who alarmed other New Yorkers in 1819 swelled in a year to nearly 13,000 . . . even the smaller towns faced the prospect of families naked—children freezing in the winter's

storm . . . and everywhere the cities and towns lost population as the destitute fled back to kin in the countryside for subsistence.[8]

Those most susceptible to economic straits during recessions were unskilled laborers, such as cartmen, chimneysweeps, woodcutters, and stevedores, who constituted the largest group in the labor force.[9]

When American industry was still in its infancy, employees of shoe, textile, and other enterprises often worked in groups of as many as 12 employees or else in larger groups in the nation's few factories. Working conditions were generally oppressive. A working week of six 12-hour days was typical; income was at subsistence levels; and rates of job-related injury were high. A wave of strikes occurred in the 1820s and 1830s in Eastern cities. Between 1833 and 1836, there were 172 strikes in New England; strikers demanded a ten-hour day and mobilized a brief "general strike" of 20,000 workers in Philadelphia. Unions maintained a precarious existence, however, on account of the newness of American industry, court rulings that were adverse to unions, frequent recessions, and company owners' strong-arm tactics against union organizers.[10]

Census and tax data suggest that, contrary to popular belief, extraordinary differentials in wealth existed in the United States. With the influx of immigrants and the emergence of agricultural, professional, industrial, merchant, and banking elites, economic inequality increased in the cities of New England between the 1820s, when 1% of the population held one-fourth the wealth, and the 1850s, when 1% of the population held one-half the wealth. Both before and after the Civil War, mobility between social classes was limited. Residential segregation of social classes existed in all cities. Less information exists about the extent and nature of poverty in agricultural and frontier communities, but a large class of low-paid agricultural laborers helped landowners clear the land and prepare the soil for cultivation. Work on the frontier was often brutally hard; settlers used hand tools and oxen to clear wooded areas. Immigrants were often conscripted to work for labor-contract companies that skimmed profits from their subsistence wages and intimidated them from seeking private employment.[11]

The extraordinary migration of Americans across the landscape, both on the Western frontiers and to Eastern cities from the countryside, itself caused social problems. Prostitution arose to accommodate the imbalanced sex ratios on the frontier and the trend to delay marriage. As they tried to eke out an existence on the frontier or in the growing cities, people responded to economic uncertainty with suicide and alcoholism. In the absence of governmental institutions, churches, and local leaders, unlawful behavior was widespread in many frontier communities.[12]

A youth crisis developed in the 1840s, when many teenagers, finding themselves without work opportunities at the end of apprenticeship programs, roamed the streets and countryside. However, the crisis eased by the end of the century, with the rise of high school education and increasing numbers of jobs in industry (Figure 4.1). As we shall see, Americans built large numbers of or-

FIGURE 4.1   Street children at about the time of the Civil War

SOURCE: Courtesy of YMCA of the USA Archives, University of Minnesota Libraries

phanages to house youth who left their homes before the age of 16 or those whose parents voluntarily committed them for lack of personal resources to care for them.[13]

Where social institutions existed to address economic and social needs, they were often poorly maintained. Touring America in the 1840s, Charles Dickens, the noted English author, found American prisons and almshouses to be scandalous, even when compared to the inhumane English institutions of that period. Almshouses, which represented the major social strategy to deal with social problems, were typically crowded, unsanitary, and poorly staffed. In these institutions, orphans mingled with those who had been categorized, rightly or wrongly, as mentally ill, delinquent, or senile.[14]

A MORAL CRUSADE

In the first half of the 19th century, a moral crusade was conducted to rid the land of a host of social problems. Most Americans were disturbed not by social and economic inequality but by "willful" violation of the social norms that had characterized village life in earlier periods. Troubled by high levels of drinking, vagrancy, begging, and unemployment, many citizens were determined to battle them by a variety of policy initiatives—for example, building institutions, religious conversion, outreach projects to teach morality to poor people and immigrants, and policies to prohibit consumption of liquor.[15]

Historians have advanced many explanations for this moral crusade. Some implicate the alarm felt by many citizens at the rapid growth of cities and the influence of the frontier; both were widely perceived as causing lawlessness, alcoholism, internal discord, prostitution, and gambling—in short, as ruining the morals of American sons and daughters who migrated to them from the tranquility and social order of villages. Others note widespread popular animus toward the growing legions of Irish and German immigrants, many of whom were Catholic; members of the established Protestant population came to believe that they were being inundated by uncivilized people, who would provide a breeding ground for alcoholism and crime. Still others implicate religious motivations; the 1820s and 1830s witnessed the eruption of a vast religious movement that sought to convert Americans to evangelical Protestantism, complete with fiery sermons, streamside baptisms, and tent revivals. Armed with religious fervor, many Americans sought to convert souls not just to religion, but away from what they perceived as evil habits, such as drinking.

Nor were fears of social problems altogether unfounded. In fact, Americans consumed extraordinary amounts of liquor early in the 19th century as compared to later periods. Many social problems were highly visible; beggars and street children were seen in the growing cities, and vagabonds in the countryside. Still, contemporary historians correctly note that many of these fears were exaggerated. Fears of immigrants were partly based on prejudice against Catholics and foreigners. While possessing social problems, cities were hardly bastions of alcoholism and crime.

But these fears arose in the context of explosive social and economic change. The scale of migration to the frontier is without parallel in world history (except perhaps for the movement of tens of millions of Russians from their western settlements to an eastern frontier to escape the Nazis during World War II). Although most of America remained predominantly agricultural, the large and rapidly expanding Eastern cities were new and strange phenomena. As villages expanded into larger towns and towns became cities with heterogeneous populations that included immigrants, local leaders were less able to use peer pressure to enforce social norms of deference and religious observation. The social reform policies of the early and middle 19th century cannot be understood without placing them in the context of these rapid social changes and the fears they engendered.[16]

In the first half of the 19th century, America had a potpourri of Protestant sects, some Catholic strongholds in Eastern cities, and a small number of Jewish settlers. Local clergy assumed major social and political roles in promulgating social norms, in

INSERT 4.1   CRITICAL ANALYSIS: COMPARING MORAL CRUSADES IN THE 19TH CENTURY AND THE 1990S

With the advantage of hindsight, many historians believe that Americans in the early portion of the 19th century exaggerated the moral ills that Americans possessed.

1. Discuss the various factors that, singly and in combination, led Americans to exaggerate moral ills in their period.

2. In the 1990s, broad concern developed about "illegitimate births" of teenage mothers, with a widespread moralistic judgment that the women had conceived children on account of flaws in their character or because they wanted to get AFDC benefits. Is there a parallel between the moral crusade of the 1990s to diminish illegitimate births and the moral crusades of the early and middle 19th century? What factors in contemporary society lead many Americans to emulate their ancestors in the 19th century?

inveighing against such sins as drinking and swearing, and in urging citizens to be industrious.

Partly because of this religious backdrop, social problems were generally seen in moral terms. Many persons believed that bankruptcy was caused by profligate spending; crime by drinking or lack of deference to social superiors; and insanity by lust. Problems were commonly perceived to be interrelated; thus, persons who ceased to attend church might be expected to become alcoholics and then delinquent or insane.[17]

Social theorists, politicians, and citizens believed that alcoholism, crime, insanity, gambling, prostitution, and vagrancy were caused solely by individual and moral defects—or by immoral special interests like the liquor industry. They stereotyped paupers as the progeny of families with intergenerational poverty, and they equated common social problems with immigrant populations, whose numbers expanded sharply in the last half of the century. This preoccupation with morality blinded Americans to alternative explanations of social problems, such as lack of employment, an undisciplined economy that led to frequent recessions, discrimination against immigrants, and lack of adequate social institutions for urban residents. Furthermore, these moral conceptions of social problems led Americans to embrace equally simplistic solutions, which tended to combine moral, religious, educational, disciplinary, and deterrent policies.[18]

To implement their moral crusade, 19th-century social reformers usually turned to local governments, as well as to nongovernmental organizations like sectarian agencies and churches. The development of national solutions to social problems was impeded by the localistic nature of the new society. As we discussed in Chapter 3, the colonists harbored fears that the newly established federal government would interfere with the autonomy of the states, and a national grass-roots movement nearly sabotaged the approval of the American Constitution, in the belief that it gave the national government excessive authority. Once the republic was established, these fears did not diminish. In the early 19th century, John Calhoun, Henry Clay, and other successors to Hamilton wanted the federal government to subsidize canals, roads, bridges, and other public improvements, but their limited programs were constantly attacked by allies of Jefferson, who believed them to be unconstitutional. Thus, Madison refused in 1817 to fund internal improvements, because the power was not mentioned in the Constitution, and in 1830 Jackson vetoed federal assistance to a local turnpike, on the grounds that it represented favoritism. Indeed, the Jacksonian era (1828–1836) represented a golden age of decentralization and of limited governmental institutions. Critics believed that this preoccupation with localism and limited government severely impeded the nation's ability to cope with pressing economic problems; for example, Jackson's dismantling of the national bank in 1832 meant that federal authorities could not soften the frequent violent swings in the economy. Nor did federal authorities possess sufficient resources from their minimal taxes to fund significant programs even had they desired them; the entire federal government numbered 153 people at the start of Jefferson's administration in 1800, and had increased to only 352 people by 1829.[19]

Localism led not only to attacks on powers of the national government but also to opposition to economic activity by state governments. In the early 19th century, many states provided major funds for internal improvements such as turnpikes and canals, but by mid-century these interventions were increasingly seen as ill-advised use of governmental power that helped certain sections of the population at the expense of others. Many Americans initially resisted assistance to local educational institutions by the states, on the grounds that it represented ill-advised centralization of authority. The major exception to this trend to limit governmental powers was a series of Supreme Court rulings that gave state governments the right to use private land for public purposes (eminent domain) and the right to charter monopolies, as well as rulings that gave the federal government the right to interpret the interstate commerce clause in relatively broad fashion.[20]

Presidents continued to believe that social welfare programs belonged exclusively within the province of local government. Dorothea Dix successfully persuaded the Congress to enact a bill in 1854 to allow the federal government to give the proceeds of some federal land sales to states in order to help them construct mental institutions, but President Franklin Pierce vetoed it with a message that expressed the philosophy of virtually all the presidents of the nineteenth century.

> I can not find any authority in the Constitution for making the Federal Government the great almoner of public charity throughout the United States. To do so would, in my judgment, be contrary to the letter and spirit of the Constitution and subversive of the whole theory upon which the Union of these States is founded. . . . And when the people of the several States had in their State conventions, and thus alone, given force to the Constitution, . . . they ingrafted thereon the explicit declaration that "the powers not delegated to the United States by the Constitution . . . are reserved to the States." . . . Can it be controverted that the great mass of the business of Government— that involved in the social relations . . . the mental and moral culture of men . . . the relief of the needy or otherwise unfortunate members of society—did in practice remain with the States?[21]

SOCIAL REFORM POLICIES

Americans developed three kinds of social policies in the early and middle 19th century. First, many popular policies consisted of "moral treatment" for Americans who had (or might fall into) sinful lifestyles, including crime, alcoholism, mental illness, or neglect of religion. Second, some social policies were initiated to give Americans political, economic, and social opportunities, such as the vote, education, land distribution, and abolition of imprisonment for indebtedness. Finally, a series of policies were devised to control, regulate, and oppress people of color—notably, African Americans and Native Americans—and Spanish-speaking persons. (We discuss the latter policies in Chapter 5 in connection with the frontier and the Civil War.)

Temperance

The temperance movement, which easily exceeded abolitionism in size and political influence, was the largest social reform movement in the several decades preceding the Civil War. In 1833, the American Temperance Society had 6,000 chapters, with a combined membership of one million persons.

The making and selling of alcoholic beverages had been a major business in America since colonial times, when many farmers had derived substantial income from grain sales to distilleries. Alcoholic beverages were sold in a national network of taverns that served local residents in towns and travelers along many stagecoach routes. The tavern was a central social institution in American villages, towns, and cities.

But many Americans perceived even social drinking to represent immoral behavior that had ominous broader implications for individuals and the nation. Temperance reformers believed that someone who sipped alcohol socially moved inexorably toward heavier use, which eventually culminated in alcoholism, crime, insanity, and poverty. They feared that the nation would be led inexorably to debauchery and decline as large numbers of Americans followed this course. Alcoholism was widespread, and scores of inebriates could be found in cities and in many towns, but this catastrophic scenario mainly reflected the reformers' own fantasies and fears.

Temperance crusaders sought to restrict licenses for taverns, to tax alcohol heavily, and to limit retail sales of alcohol to consumers in various localities in the 1820s and 1830s. In some areas they obtained legislation that allowed courts to impose fines or prison sentences on sellers and users of alcoholic beverages. Countless pamphlets were written and distributed to warn Americans of the dangers of alcohol, to link drinking with atheism and immoral living, and to warn that "the very first drink is a long step toward Hell."

When these various remedies still had not eradicated the problem, temperance reformers turned to state legislatures to obtain passage of laws modeled after legislation that had first been enacted in Maine. Local and state temperance societies circulated petitions and presented hundreds of signatures to local and state politicians; scrutinized the positions of candidates of both major parties as a prelude to supporting or opposing them in local elections; and solicited contributions for acceptable candidates. In the 1840s and 1850s, 13 states enacted prohibitions on the sale of alcohol that made it possible to seize and confiscate alcoholic beverages. Court cases involving the illegal sales of alcohol were placed in preferred positions on court calendars to avoid customary delays in litigation.

Despite these ambitious efforts, the temperance movement had only limited success. Most states rescinded their prohibition laws by the 1870s, because of adverse court rulings that declared that governmental interference with the making and selling of liquor was unconstitutional. Although many white Protestant citizens supported prohibition, Irish and German immigrants vehemently opposed it—as did substantial numbers of middle- and working-class Americans—on the grounds that drinking and socializing in taverns were integral to their culture. So divisive was the issue in some areas that politicians sought to avoid it by insisting that decisions be made by voters in popular referenda, where restrictive measures were defeated. Local police were often reluctant to enforce prohibition statutes or were so understaffed that enforcement was impractical. Despite repeated defeats, efforts to limit consumption of alcohol continued, if ineffectually, in the latter part of the 19th century, and resurfaced with the imposition of national prohibition by the Volstead Act of 1919, which was subsequently repealed during Franklin Roosevelt's Administration in 1933.[22]

The temperance crusade illustrates analytic deficiencies that were common to reformers in the antebellum period. Alcoholism is caused by many factors, including culture, the presence of role models in families, genetic predisposition, poverty, psychological and physical factors, advertising, and peer pressure. When they contended that immorality was the primary cause of alcoholism and that prohibition would eradicate the problem, temperance reformers took a simplistic approach to a complex problem. In reality, neither the legal prohibition of alcohol consumption nor horror stories of ruined lives will suffice as deterrents, as our long history of temperance reform proves.

Antipauperism Strategies

Americans had always believed that individuals could be self-sufficient if they worked hard and adhered to moral principles. Armed with this moral perspective, most Americans were not overfearful in the 17th and 18th centuries that lack of work would be a major social problem, because they believed that virtually all Americans could own land. Although some Americans urged a deterrent approach to welfare, including incarceration in hostile and punitive workhouses, it was commonly assumed in the colonial era that local poor relief would be largely used by persons who had a legitimate claim to it, such as those disabled as a result of accidents, wars, disease, or old age.

By the early 19th century, and certainly by the 1830s, many Americans feared pauperism as much as alcoholism. They saw numerous very poor people for the first time, not only within large cities in the East but even in smaller towns. As Americans became part of the world economy, periodic recessions led to massive unemployment, particularly in urban areas. Shortages of food and fuel became so acute during severe winters that large numbers of families risked starvation and death. Disease and work-related accidents left many persons temporarily or permanently disabled; high rates of mortality and social dislocation increased the population of orphans, who sometimes became street beggars. Particularly from the 1840s onward, Eastern cities received waves of immigrants from Europe, who were penniless and without job skills; many vagabonds roamed the American countryside in search of employment. Children who had lost their parents or who had left their homes in their early teens in search of work were often on the streets; some shined shoes or sold newspapers for small change. With the demise of indentured service in the 19th century, new immigrants were cast into the job market and were free to migrate wherever they wished after their arrival. Technically, they could be returned to their first residence if they sought relief in a new location, but laws of settlement were difficult to enforce in a society with extensive migration.[23]

To address the problem of pauperism, American reformers devised three major strategies.

1. They sought to vastly increase the number of almshouses and to modify their internal operations to make them truly deterrent.
2. They tried to establish personal contact with millions of low-income youth to prevent pauperism.
3. They tried to establish systems of surveillance so that charity was not given indiscriminately to destitute persons.

The second and third strategies led to the development of various nongovernmental organizations, which we discuss shortly.

Numerous Americans had advocated the construction of workhouses in the colonial era, but in many areas they had not been built, because of indifference to the plight of the poor, the relatively small numbers of public wards, and the absence of economic resources to build and maintain them. Indeed, some localities resorted extensively to outdoor relief, and laws of settlement were often not vigorously implemented. The antipauperism reformers of the 1820s and 1830s sought to breathe new life into the older deterrent ideas and policies that had not been fully implemented. Before 1820, New York State had allowed localities to decide for themselves whether to use almshouses, apprenticing out, or outdoor relief. In 1824, the Yates Report, which was issued by the secretary of the state, recommended the construction of poorhouses by every county in New York State; an ambitious construction program followed. Subsequent legislation in New York State strengthened laws of settlement and required their vigorous enforcement. New York City, which bore the brunt of the state's welfare costs, succeeded in obtaining state resources to assist it in enlarging its poorhouse and its house of correction.

The work component of the poorhouse and its internal programs were strengthened. Women and children were often put to work weaving garments and making other articles, whereas able-bodied men were made to engage in manual labor, such as working on public roads and chopping wood. Some antipauperism advocates even hoped that the poorhouse might actually cover its expenses through the sale of commodities and the labor of its residents. Residents were increasingly placed under a rigorous regimen that extended beyond work. They were required to follow a strict schedule, which included spartan meals, long hours, lectures on morality, and religious observation. Poorhouses truly became "total institutions" that sought the moral regeneration of residents through techniques that their supporters believed could be applied with scientific precision.[24]

As in the instance of temperance reformers, antipauperism advocates soon found that their ambitious plans were foiled by numerous factors.

Most persons who sought public relief could not be "saved," because the reasons for their pauperism had nothing to do with their moral character. Poorhouses increasingly became places of residence for elderly persons who were sick or disabled and for persons with mental disabilities or disorders. Poorhouse officials had no recourse but to provide outdoor relief when recessions occurred, because the number of nearly starving citizens far exceeded available spaces. Epidemics as well as occupational accidents filled workhouses with persons with disabilities in an era that lacked medical science and work-safety provisions. Many orphans needed assistance because their parents abandoned them or died in epidemics. Immigrants were often forced to seek assistance because they arrived penniless in the new nation.

These crushing realities, which were more significant causes of pauperism than moral character, were generally ignored in an era that was fascinated with personal morality. Antipauperism crusaders joined other reformers who sought to form nongovernmental organizations that could establish personal contact with poor persons in order to elevate them to high moral standards. One of the major crusades to reach the poor was the Sunday School movement, an effort to bring hundreds of thousands of low-income children into Sunday schools. At its zenith around 1835, the American Sunday School Union, which possessed its own administrative staff, independent of existing denominations, had roughly 400,000 recruits. Thousands of middle-class teachers were recruited, trained, and supervised; they provided highly structured religious and moral instruction to low-income youth, in order to help the children internalize such moral principles as honesty and industry. Teachers avoided physical punishment; relied on a system of rewards and punishments; provided structured lectures and exercises; and used extensive peer pressure to discipline recalcitrant children. (Children who did not take moral instruction seriously were given dunce status and, if necessary, expelled.) Leaders in the Sunday School movement were convinced that its success hinged on the instructional skills of the teachers, whose training and supervision was rigorous. Massive parades of the various schools were held

in cities to increase community recognition of the movement and facilitate the recruitment of youth.[25]

As in the case of temperance and antipauperism, however, Sunday school leaders found their hopes dashed by the time of the Civil War. Immigrants were increasingly Catholic and resisted efforts by condescending Protestants to instruct them. Volunteer teachers willing to submit to high standards and intense supervision became more difficult to find. Since the zeal of reformers diminished as the reform momentum declined, many of them turned to other causes. But as with the temperance crusade, it was the intrinsic weakness of the Sunday school reformers' ideology that led to their demise. Poor immigrants often resisted reformers' outreach, because they themselves realized that their poverty was caused by labor markets, poor health, and unemployment rather than by lack of moral character.

Some reformers believed that the rise in pauperism was due to undisciplined and indiscriminate relief giving by charitable and public organizations. Many nongovernmental charitable groups had arisen in the early 19th century; these included organizations that helped specific ethnic groups or occupations, widows or single women, and individuals with specific problems, such as debtors. Local politicians also gave funds to applicants who came to their offices, whether from personal coffers or from the city treasury. Reformers feared that devious applicants could seek aid from multiple sources, feign poverty, or use charity to avoid work.

Their remedy was to tighten the administration of charity institutions. For example, the nongovernmental Association for Improving the Condition of the Poor (AICP), which was active in New York City during the 1840s and 1850s, divided the city into many districts, where agencies were convened regularly to exchange information about recipients and to tighten their giving procedures. Procedures for carefully interrogating applicants were established, so that false stories could be detected. A cadre of middle- and upper-income staff were trained to become skilled interviewers, who would be in a position to deny assistance to undeserving persons and then to initiate an inten-

---

INSERT 4.2   ETHICAL ANALYSIS OF KEY ISSUES AND POLICIES: WHEN ARE PEOPLE DESERVING AND UNDESERVING?

1. Discuss under what circumstances, if any, people in need are undeserving. To ground your analysis in concrete cases, establish a typology of people who cannot support themselves, and analyze why persons in each group do not work:

- persons who become unemployed during recessions
- persons who work, but cannot support themselves (or their families) because their wages are too low
- people who do not work because of mental disorders or disabilities, physical disabilities, or substance abuse
- people who lack the skills to obtain employment
- people who do not want to work (list possible reasons for this choice).

2. If relatively few people become destitute because they have "character defects," discuss the ethical dangers faced by policy makers who devise punitive policies for their relief-giving programs. Specifically, discuss the ethical dangers of poorhouses, by referring both to first-order ethical principles and program-outcome (or utilitarian) considerations.

---

sive personal relationship with them and teach them moral virtues through instruction and by personal example. The AICP also developed the first model tenement and helped to enact a pure milk law—projects that suggest its leaders also sought broader social reforms. (We note in Chapter 5 how charity organization societies, which were similar to—but larger and more bureaucratic than—the antipauper organizations in the antebellum period developed in a number of cities after the Civil War.)[26]

Character-Building Institutions

In the early and middle 19th century, reformers organized the construction of many public institutions, including prisons, mental institutions, houses of correction, orphanages, houses of refuge for youth, and institutions for people who had been diagnosed as deaf, blind, or "feebleminded." An institutional strategy was ideally suited to these reformers, who wanted to change moral behavior by placing persons in an environment where they could be subjected to intensive moral treatment, undiluted by external distractions.

It is difficult for contemporary citizens to understand the mindset of the reformers who established institutions in the 19th century, because we live in an *anti-institutional* era; today, institutions are widely reviled. As Eric Monkkonen argues, reformers in the 19th century were proud of these institutions, which, they believed, rescued unfortunate individuals from unsavory lives and influences in the external world, from incarceration in poorhouses, or from lodging in police stations.[27] Citizens would boast of the institutions in their locale, as local landmarks. Leaders of churches and ethnic groups avidly raised funds for these highly visible institutions, thousands of which dotted the American landscape by the latter part of the 19th century, and invested extraordinary effort in keeping them running. As we shall see, the idealistic origins of these institutions were often subverted when reformers found that they could not secure operating funds sufficient to prevent overcrowding and warehousing of residents in a custodial environment.

In colonial societies, prisons merely held lawbreakers and did not seek to change their behavior. They contained an indiscriminate mixture of people—youth, murderers, burglars, debtors, and others. Children younger than 7 could not be imprisoned, but some jurisdictions allowed children between the ages of 7 and 14 to be imprisoned and even subjected to the death penalty if courts believed they knew the difference between right and wrong. These prisons were often privately owned; the proprietors charged inmates a fee for their residence and would not discharge them until they, or their friends, had paid their bills.

The reformers in the 19th century sought to transform prisons from custodial institutions to ones that systematically instructed their residents. Daily regimens of labor, reflection, and instruction were planned as a method of changing the behavior of inmates. Physical punishment was avoided so far as possible; reformers hoped to create an environment where inmates would voluntarily modify their behavior and adopt moral virtues.[28]

Many reformers became convinced that persons with mental problems should be removed from almshouses and placed in separate institutions for the insane. They, too, wanted to use moral treatment to rehabilitate persons with mental disorders. A cadre of reformers—including many physicians who subsequently became the superintendents of mental institutions—lobbied for the construction of these institutions. The accomplishments of Dorothea Dix were particularly noteworthy. Dix documented problems within states by counting persons with mental disorders in almshouses and describing their brutal treatment; then she obtained signatures on petitions that demanded state legislatures build special mental institutions. By the time she had completed her state-by-state lobbying effort and evidence gathering, which included interviewing more than 10,000 persons with mental disorders in almshouses, 32 institutions had been constructed.

These reformers, like many Americans in this era, believed cities to be unwholesome places that created, or at least exacerbated, mental problems. They wanted relatively small institutions to be located in rural areas, where staff could establish a personal and caring relationship with residents and supervise regimens that included meditation, moral and religious instruction, gardening, recreation, and hard work. Like prison reformers, they opposed the use of physical restraints whenever pos-

sible, because they wanted residents to internalize new moral codes.

Many of these mental institutions probably realized the objectives of their founders and superintendents. Their records show that many residents were discharged after marked improvement. Apart from the moral and religious overlay, their approach to treatment of mental illness had much in common with contemporary efforts to create a supportive and low-stress environment for patients with psychiatric disorders. But these institutions, like prisons, were ultimately sabotaged by political and demographic realities. Funds were provided to construct many institutions but not to foster their maintenance or expansion. After the Civil War, their clientele increasingly consisted of low-income, non-English-speaking, Catholic immigrants, who resisted the moral regimens that were established by middle-class Protestant reformers. The state mental institutions depended on local boards of overseers for referrals from local poorhouses, but they increasingly referred older persons and those with senile dementia, who could not benefit from moral treatment. As low-income and elderly residents moved into the institutions, some middle-class persons began to use private institutions. Consequently, the state mental institutions, now perceived as repositories for destitute persons, were even less likely to receive adequate funding from state legislatures.[29]

New institutions for children were built. Convinced that they possessed scientific knowledge about the idiosyncratic needs of specific groups, reformers set about developing *specialized* services for each group, rather than mixing them together. The dizzying array of specialized institutions for children included houses of refuge, orphanages, homes for "wayward children," and institutions for the "feebleminded."

Houses of refuge were intended for delinquent and neglected children. Colonial laws gave authorities the right to sever parental custody when children were neglected or had become vagabonds, though some authorities only reluctantly removed children from their homes. Roughly one-half the children admitted to the houses of refuge came from court orders, and the remainder were voluntarily placed by parents because they lacked the funds or capacity to care for them. Like prisons and mental institutions, houses of refuge combined lecture, study, and physical labor. Reformers believed that these houses were effective in helping many youths, but many residents fled from them, and considerable turmoil existed within them.[30]

Orphanages were established for poor children, usually of school age, whose parents (or parent) could no longer support them or would not support them. Some came from intact families, while others were "wayward children" who lived on the streets. (Most street children, variously called waifs, ragamuffins, and half-orphans, were poor urban working-class children without intact families.) To understand a common scenario by which children entered orphanages, consider a woman whose husband died and left her with five children to support. What was she to do? Unless her husband left her a business or farm, she often had to resort to taking in laundry or boarders or doing piecework at home—for example, sewing garments. (Other occupations were closed to most women in this period and, with five children, she could hardly become a live-in domestic servant—a primary source of income for unmarried women.) Surveying her bleak economic prospects, the woman might voluntarily send three of her children to an orphanage, where they would remain until the age of 16. In other cases, local justices of the peace committed children to orphanages if they ruled that their parents could not properly meet their needs or if they lived on the streets.

Large numbers of orphanages were constructed in the 19th century by churches, as well as by Irish, German, and other immigrant groups: indeed, Baltimore alone had 28 of them by 1910. While all orphanages provided moral training, they varied widely in their precise programs. In some, children attended public schools, while others provided some of their education within the institution. Some emphasized vocational education, while others provided general education. Some were built in cities, while others were in rural settings. In addition to orphanages, some specialized institutions for wayward children—that is, children who lived on the streets—arose in many cities.[31]

By 1840, "idiocy" was widely seen as a special problem; it was even included on questionnaires of that year's census. No consensus existed about its precise causes; some reformers believed it stemmed from lack of will power, while medical theories implicated physiological factors. Like orphans and neglected children, "feebleminded" people were often housed in poorhouses and mental institutions until reformers determined to wrest them away. Once in a specialized institution, children and adults were placed under a rigorous regimen of training, both to increase their will power and to impart skills that would make them productive laborers. Early reformers hoped that, with careful training, the inmates might eventually leave the institution but, by the latter part of the 19th century, superintendents had lowered their goals merely to training the inmates to perform various duties *within* the institution, where most spent the remainder of their lives.[32]

These various institutional approaches, including prisons, mental institutions, orphanages, homes for wayward children, and houses of refuge, achieved considerable success at first—at least compared to what had preceded them. By placing children in houses of refuge, reformers kept them away from hardened criminals in the prison population; by placing children in orphanages, reformers separated them from destitute adults in poorhouses. Prisons became public institutions that possessed a rehabilitation strategy, and persons with mental disorders were rescued from workhouses. Initially blessed with relatively low staff-to-resident ratios, these institutions could provide individualized and intensive services. Because they existed in a society that was generally indifferent to the fate of criminals, persons with mental disorders, or delinquent youth, however, the institutions did not receive sufficient public funding to sustain these intensive and ameliorative services. Furthermore, politicians were unwilling to divert scarce public resources to institutions when they needed them to fund road construction and other internal improvements in a growing society. Various institutions—particularly workhouses and prisons—were continually engulfed in scandal; superintendents were variously charged with fraud, excessive leniency, or providing contracts to political cronies. Moral reform was often impeded by inadequate funding, which prevented the institutions from hiring enough trained staff. In some cases, superintendents came to see that it was in their professional interest if residents were institutionalized for the remainder of their lives, because the superintendents could then petition for additional funds on the grounds that they lacked sufficient space for their inmate population. Public authorities, desperate for places to put older people who could not survive in independent living arrangements and who lacked relatives to care for them, often placed them in large numbers in mental institutions or even poorhouses; the result was to overwhelm the staff of these organizations.[33]

An articulate if idiosyncratic dissenter from the institutional consensus emerged in the 1850s. Charles Loring Brace founded and then became director of the private Children's Aid Society of New York. Brace believed that street urchins and other vagabond children were intrinsically creative but that their natural virtues became stifled when they were placed in institutions. Contending that low-income and immigrant families were often as oppressive as institutions, he took the dramatic step of sending over 90,000 of these children to live with families on or near the frontier between 1853 and 1895. Brace remains a controversial figure; while some people believed he was rescuing the children from poverty and from oppressive families, critics argued that the children were placed with families who had been inadequately screened and were frequently used as unpaid farm labor. Few Americans in this era joined Brace in arguing against the use of institutions that sought to radically reform their residents through a prescribed and rigorous regimen.[34]

The reformers of the early and middle 19th century can be criticized for believing institutions to be a panacea, but they often responded with compassion to the plight of children begging on the streets, criminal offenders incarcerated in brutish settings, and persons with mental disorders who were bound in chains. In considering alternatives, we should not quickly conclude that deinstitutionalization is a panacea. We see its consequences in contemporary society, where persons with psychiatric disorders are released to the community without adequate housing, income, and medical and social services; children are placed in inferior foster homes; and homeless people are left to lead dangerous and degrading lives on public streets. Like the institutions of the 19th century, community-based programs today are often sabotaged by poor funding and inadequate staffing.

INSERT 4.3   CRITICAL ANALYSIS: WHY DIDN'T THE 19TH-CENTURY REFORMERS SEEK COMMUNITY-BASED SOLUTIONS?

1. In contemporary society, we take for granted such community-based programs as foster care for children, half-way houses for persons with psychiatric disorders, or independent living centers for persons with physical disabilities. We can hardly imagine a society where social services focused on placing people into institutions, whether through voluntary or involuntary commitments. Why didn't reformers in the 19th century seek community-based programs? In answering this question, consider such factors as:

- their views of pathology as compared to ours
- their views of civil rights or liberties as compared to ours
- the extent that their society possessed staff and program expertise to implement community-based programs.

2. While no one would like to return to institutional domination of the human services, discuss what role institutions can legitimately assume even in contemporary society. (Try to be specific; give examples of kinds of persons who might benefit from institutional care for varying lengths of time.)

Opportunity-Enhancing Policies

In the early and middle 19th century, America extended suffrage to most white males, developed public schools, and distributed land to many settlers. Americans in the 20th century take these institutions and policies for granted, but they represented major—even unimaginable—reforms to Europeans. In Europe, during the first half of the 19th century, suffrage was extended only to persons with considerable property; education was restricted to affluent persons who could afford tuition; and land was not widely distributed. Cambridge University refused to fill a position in American studies with an American scholar in the 1840s because its officials feared he would discuss universal suffrage.[35]

No system of public education existed in the United States in 1800, but by 1860 the nation possessed a national network of primary and secondary schools. This massive growth in public education, which extended to girls as well, represented a major policy advance in the 19th century. Four systems of education existed prior to these reforms: private tutors; boarding schools; day schools that were run by various sects; and charity schools that gave free education to the urban poor. Thomas Jefferson and other colonial leaders who had espoused free public education had been staunchly resisted by those who did not want high taxes and who believed that education should be provided by the family or by religious sects. Several rationales for publicly funded education emerged by the 1820s and gathered momentum in succeeding decades. An uneducated citizenry, educational reformers argued, would not be able to participate in American democracy, which could lead to tyranny, mob rule, and other evils. In short, much like founders of other institutions in this period, they defined education as a moral enterprise that would teach youth moral rules and so allow them to avoid poverty, alcoholism, and crime. Many people viewed public education as a method of assimilating Irish immigrants into American culture. Some reformers, noting uneasily the strikes and protest of the period, favored public education as a means of controlling the populace; Ralph Waldo Emerson, the noted author, declared, "You must educate them to keep them from our throats." Some persons also realized that a literate work force was needed if America was to develop an industrial economy. Thanks to the rise of public education in the 19th century, more than one-half of white children, of ages 5–19, had enrolled in schools by 1850.[36]

Crusades to end imprisonment for debt represented one of the major social reform movements of the 19th century. Previously, many Americans who had incurred large debts in order to start farms and businesses had found themselves threatened with imprisonment when they fell behind in their payments. Agitation in various states led to gradual relaxing of these laws and finally to their abolition in most states by the time of the Civil War.

By 1830, all white males were granted the vote in most jurisdictions. Along with suffrage came greater political participation. In presidential contests, for example, opposing candidates were variously called "atheists," "criminals," and "agitators." Interest groups had already assumed prominence in American politics, as persons with similar interests found that they could obtain policies by joining with others, lobbying, assisting friendly legislators, and making campaign contributions (or bribes) to politicians.

Political appearances could be deceiving, however. American interest-group democracy, which seemed to give the common people an unprecedented role in political life, often empowered corporations and privileged persons. Fearing that one faction could dominate American politics, Jefferson and many of the colonial leaders had constructed elaborate checks and balances to prevent this possibility, but these safeguards did not prevent specific interest groups from gaining enormous power. By the latter half of the 19th century, industrial tycoons dominated the politics of the nation, just as land speculators and agricultural interests possessed considerable power in the antebellum period.[37]

RADICAL MOVEMENTS: CONSPICUOUS BY THEIR ABSENCE

Although, as we have seen, Americans pioneered opportunity-enhancing policies, comparisons between England and the United States during the 1830s and 1840s suggest that the United States provided an environment hostile to social reform. England was hardly kind to poor people and those with mental disorders, but a relatively strong (by American standards) political mobilization of the lower class known as chartism developed in the late 1830s. In his classic work on the English working class, G. D. H. Cole contends that chartism arose partly from discontent when advocates of poorhouses insisted on building them even during a marked downturn in the economy, but its leaders quickly embraced universal male suffrage, equal electoral districts, annual Parliaments, payment of legislators, secret ballots, and removal of property qualifications for legislators. To support these working-class demands, 150 local groups were quickly organized. They sent huge petitions to Parliament urging their measures; one was over six miles long and was signed by more than three million people, at a time when the population of Britain numbered only 19 million. While often split by schisms over tactics and their precise program, many chartists broadened their demands in the 1840s to include the repeal of tariffs on corn, demands for a ten-hour day, more humane treatment of people in workhouses, development of free education, factory regulations, and legislation to strengthen unions.[38]

Poor persons and laborers were more organized in England than in the United States for several reasons. First, many American workers, such as Irish Americans, tended to identify with their ethnic groups, and often did not identify with, or organize around, their social class. Second, prejudice often splintered workers; for example, white Protestant workers tended to be suspicious of Irish Catholic workers. Third, partly because the federal government was so weak, Americans focused on such local issues as securing city jobs, garbage collection, and other amenities rather than on national economic and social policies. Fourth, American workers probably regarded poor relief as primarily relevant to paupers (that is, to nonworkers), whereas English workers viewed poor-law institutions as relevant to working-class interests.[39]

Finally, more dissent and argument existed in England about the causes and nature of poverty. Many Englishmen subscribed to the moralistic and individualistic explanations that were widely accepted by Americans, but some English theorists and citizens emphasized economic and social factors that perpetuated pauperism and poverty. However, the former group, led by Edwin Chadwick, controlled an influential commission whose findings in 1834 recommended that indoor relief and punitive policies replace the relatively generous poor relief that existed in many parts of England. Convinced that nonpunitive administration of the Poor Laws harmed the economy and drained the public treasury by enticing many people not to work, Chadwick was determined to enforce a harsh workhouse regimen. (He found particularly abhorrent the Speenhamland system of relief in the 1820s, where local poor relief officials actually supplemented the wages of working people in the community whenever the price of bread rose above a certain amount—a policy that suggested that people ought to have a guaranteed income even if they worked in low-wage jobs.) Chadwick's harsh policies were sharply questioned by those who saw industrialization, recessions, low wages, and inflation as the primary causes of dependency. Some reformers even proposed health insurance and old-age pensions for the poor. Reformers found assistance from some aristocrats and the English Conservative party; Benjamin Disraeli and other conservative leaders assumed attitudes befitting the heirs to the feudal nobles, who had provided assistance to serfs during hard times.[40]

Given this contrast between the United States and England, with its more vital radical traditions, it remained to be seen whether Americans could couple their extraordinary interest in facilitating economic, educational, and political opportunity with compassion for persons who were less successful than others. Compassion existed, but it often took the form of relatively harsh, condescending, or moralistic assistance to poor persons, who were incessantly accused of causing their own plight by insufficient application or virtue. Ominously, the working class in the United States was poorly organized, when contrasted with European nations, and so provided uncertain pressure for the development of social welfare programs.

 ## OUTGROUPS IN THE EARLY REPUBLIC

In the 18th century, as we have seen, the American colonists lived in a triracial society that included white settlers, African Americans, and Native Americans. As the 19th century unfolded, Americans encountered other indigenous populations; in the Southwest of the continent, for example, they met Spanish-speaking people who lived in areas that became part of Mexico after its independence from Spain in 1821. Moreover, Americans imported significant numbers of Asians from China, Japan, Korea, and the Philippines to work in agriculture and construction projects in the latter part of the 19th century. We also need to discuss white ethnic minorities, particularly the Irish, whose Catholicism, as well as their sheer numbers and poverty, exposed them to the ire of the white Protestant population even before the Civil War. And we must extend our analysis of the policies, laws, and culture that affected women in the colonial period to the first seven decades of the new republic.

We discuss Irish immigrants and women in this chapter, as well as some emerging policies toward sexual matters that had important implications for women and persons who deviated from commonly accepted sexual norms. (We save discussion of the plight of African slaves, Native Americans, Asian immigrants, and Spanish-speaking persons for Chapter 5.)

Irish Immigrants

Some contemporary writers wrongly imply that white ethnic populations, such as the Irish immigrants, assimilated to their new land with ease and with minor discrimination from the dominant population. In fact, the Irish, whose numbers in America increased fantastically in the decade after the potato famine that lasted between 1845 and 1849, illustrate the nature and extent of problems that white, low-income, ethnic immigrants encountered in the new nation. (The problems of the Irish were later experienced by millions of Italian, Jewish, and Eastern European immigrants in the period from 1870 to 1924.)

With the advantage of hindsight, we can see that Ireland was a land tempting disaster in the decades before 1845. Its population consisted of millions of impoverished farmers, whose numbers had so greatly increased in the 70 years before the potato famine that Ireland was the most densely populated nation in Europe. Many Irish peasants lived in degrading poverty, often as tenants to absentee landowners or as owners of small plots of less than five acres. This agrarian and impoverished society depended for its survival on the potato—a crop that had been introduced to Europe from South America and that provided extraordinary nourishment for its burgeoning population. Even a few acres of this easily grown crop sufficed to feed a family the bulk of its diet.

Though there had been periodic and small famines, no one was prepared for the widespread potato rot in 1845, which devastated the crop on which the nation depended. Imbued with the doctrines of laissez-faire economics, the British government responded to the catastrophe with sublime confidence that market mechanisms would suffice to make good Ireland's depleted food supply. The government's plan was simply to buy stocks of corn and, by periodically selling some of its reserve, to keep the market price of corn at a level that the Irish peasants could afford. Moreover, the government hoped that relatively modest increases in poor law relief would tide the peasants over until the ensuing year when, it was assumed, the potato harvest would be normal.[41]

Tragically, the plant disease that devastated the harvest in 1845 continued to attack the crops during the next four years. About 750,000 persons, or nearly one-eighth of the population, died of starvation or disease. Cecil Woodham-Smith notes unimaginable horrors:

> At a farm in Caheragh, County Cork, a woman and her two children were found dead and half-eaten by dogs; in a neighboring cottage five more corpses . . . were lying . . . Father John O'Sullivan . . . found a room full of dead people; a man, still living, was lying in bed with a dead wife and two dead children, while a starving cat was eating another dead infant.[42]

People weakened by malnutrition succumbed to mass infections like typhoid fever and dysentery in a nation with only 28 hospitals. A number of factors—crop failures in other parts of Europe; British hatred of the Irish; prevailing notions of limited government; British insistence on financing poor relief from taxes levied on the already impoverished Irish citizens; and punitive responses to widespread riots in the Irish countryside—prevented the use of humane policies to address the emergency.

Roughly one and one-half million Irish peasants sought refuge in the United States from 1845 to 1854, in what was merely the start of a long-term migration from Ireland. Driven by poverty, hatred of landlords, and a desire to join relatives in America, another two and one-half million immigrants had reached the United States by 1900. Of course, this reprieve from starvation and hardship required funds for steamship passage, which were often obtained by selling family heirlooms. Moreover, many people died in passage from various diseases.

Once in the new land, the Irish soon encountered misfortune on a scale just short of the starvation that they had escaped. Ships were sometimes turned away by American authorities, on the grounds that passengers were too diseased. Anti-Catholic, anti-Irish, and anti-immigrant sentiments often sparked riots against the emigres. As unskilled peasants with no capital and no knowledge of the agricultural techniques needed to develop larger farms on the frontier, most of the Irish immigrants moved to Eastern and Midwestern cities, where they lived in appalling poverty in low-income ghettos. They could perform only unskilled tasks such as cleaning stables, unloading boats, and pushing carts; women found work as domestics. In a land with few regulations, they occupied shanty towns built by speculators; as many as nine people lived in a single room, and many were crowded into cellars. Cholera epidemics swept through these low-income areas; indeed, one report suggests that, in some Irish communities, more than half the children died and the average age of persons buried was less than 15. Other Irish became the labor force for companies and governments building railroads, roads, and canals. Still others became the labor force for coal mines.[43]

Soon, considerable numbers of the Irish occupied American poorhouses and jails. Irish immigrants commonly took to whiskey to forget their troubles, and booze as well as poverty led to high rates of crime. Protestant Americans believed they were being overrun and often responded with hatred. (Indeed, in 1847 alone, 37,000 Irish immigrants arrived in Boston, a city that had only 115,000 residents in 1845.) In the 1850s, a potent Know-Nothing movement argued that Catholics represented a menace to American national and Protestant identity and that Catholics would dilute the pure "Anglo-Saxon" racial stock of America. Hatred of Catholics spawned the American Political party, which elected six governors in the 1850s. As Higham notes, nativism was an important ingredient in American public life between 1860 and 1925; always simmering, it boiled over again in the 1890s and in the period from 1905 to 1924.[44]

Subjected to discrimination and encountering dire poverty, the Irish immigrants developed remarkable strategies for coping with their environment. They quickly discovered that they could use politics to enhance their well-being, simply by using their massive voting power in local elections. In cities such as Boston, in the latter part of the 19th century, they were able to elect a succession of Irish mayors, who helped them get jobs, protected them from discrimination and violence, and approved community improvements. The Catholic Church became a prime benefactor, as well, by underwriting charities and helping them form social, athletic, and community groups. Like succeeding waves of immigrants from other nations, the Irish formed tightly knit urban enclaves, both to protect themselves and to evolve community institutions to advance their collective fortunes.[45]

The Status of Women

The doctrine of separate spheres, which had emerged in the colonial period, grew stronger in the early 19th century and led to the cult of domesticity, which consigned women to household and familial functions while reserving the professions and business to males. The economic roles of women were further constrained by the increasing importance attached to child rearing. Whereas children in the colonial period had often been regarded as little adults, who were to begin full-time work at the age of 11, they were increasingly viewed as requiring extended moral education and socialization within the family. Although this child rearing could have been shared equally by both parents, Americans in the early 19th century developed the notion that women were uniquely equipped to perform this function. Sometimes perceived as immoral temptresses in the colonial period, women came to be portrayed as morally superior to men— and consequently as best suited to inculcate moral character into the nation's youth. Married women were urged to devote themselves to raising children and to administering their households; they had few rights to own or manage property, except in those cases where their husbands predeceased them. Almost no married women from the middle or upper classes worked outside their households, and even many working-class women sought to avoid external work. (Female slaves were given no choice.) Widowed women often encountered bleak realities. As in the colonial period, husbands often left the bulk of their estates to children, so that widows were left to fend for themselves; to survive, they might rent out rooms in their homes, which were often occupied, as well, by one or more of their children, who now owned the house. High rates of male mortality meant that 32% of adult

women and 61% of women over the age of 60 were widows in the 1850s.[46]

The prohibition against labor did not extend to single women, who often worked as domestic and live-in servants. Working conditions for servants were hard: low wages, only one day off each week, and often harsh treatment by employers. Partly because they wanted more independence, some single women found work in factories in New England, where they worked long hours at low pay, but factory jobs were not plentiful; the nation did not industrialize in a major way until after the Civil War. Women were virtually excluded from medicine, law, and the clergy, though growing numbers of them became school teachers (as public education became more common) and, after the Civil War, nurses.[47]

But seeds of discontent and protest were finally sown in 1848 at a convention in Seneca Falls, New York, which issued a Declaration of Sentiments modeled after the Declaration of Independence. The 68 women and 32 men who signed it declared: "We hold these truths to be self-evident that all men and women are created equal" and "have the duty to throw off such government" that visits on them "a long train of abuses and usurpation." In this remarkable and prescient document, the signers attacked the cult of domesticity and the prevalent notion that women were intellectually and legally inferior to men; they demanded suffrage, access to the professions, and legal rights—such as the ability to hold property while married. The Seneca Falls Convention was followed by similar conferences, roughly one each year, between 1849 and the outbreak of the Civil War in 1861.

Historians have identified various reasons why feminism arose in this period. The cult of domesticity, which virtually imprisoned women in their homes, subjected them to so much boredom and so many restrictions that a vanguard of women protested. Moreover, many women became leaders in the budding abolitionist movement, which fostered women's rights in several ways. As they worked to end slavery, which represented an incongruity between the equal rights doctrines of the nation and its practices, women came to recognize a similar incongruity between these doctrines and their own limited legal and social roles. Furthermore, many women experienced discrimination in their work for abolition, both from male abolitionists (who sought to limit them to background roles) and from the public (who often objected to *any* woman speaking in public). Also, more women were receiving the rudiments of education in a growing number of high schools and academies for women —and Oberlin became the first college to admit women in 1837.

But we should not imply that the women who subscribed to feminism in this period, such as Susan B. Anthony and Elizabeth Cady Stanton, represented the mainstream of female (or male) thought at the time. Indeed, many avant-garde women were content to seek access to the professions and to positions in teaching *within* the old framework of separate spheres and the cult of domesticity and did not agree with "radical feminists" who sought an array of public and political reforms. (In Chapter 5, we note how male abolitionists mostly abandoned women in the wake of the Civil War, by refusing to include women in constitutional amendments designed to give the freed slaves certain civil and legal rights.)[48]

Women's freedom was also constricted by the lack of effective birth control in the colonial period. In 1800, each married woman had an average of 6.4 children; with so many children, women could not easily pursue their independent interests. Moreover, many women died during childbirth or from the toll of successive pregnancies.

A remarkable decline in the number of children took place in the 19th century. While child births often decline when nations industrialize, birth rates plummeted in the United States in unprecedented fashion for an agricultural society—to 4.9 children per married woman by 1850 and to 2.8 children by 1880. Historians do not fully understand why this came about. Various explanations have been suggested. One incentive for women to limit family size—particularly in the wake of the Civil War, when the nation rapidly industrialized—was that larger investments of effort were required to prepare children for the labor force in an urban society than when they were laborers on family farms. Another factor was that, by the end of the 19th cen-

tury, many Americans viewed sex as a reflection of romantic love, in contrast to the predominant colonial attitude that sex was a utilitarian, procreative enterprise, a means of having children. In addition, Americans' extraordinary emphasis on moral qualities in the 19th century prompted interest in the control of sexual activity. The remarkable reductions in birth rates could not have occurred, however, without greater use of contraception. While women had long resorted to a small range of unreliable techniques—the use of sponges, douches, coitus interruptus, and abstinence during the most fertile portion of the menstrual cycle—they gained access to vulcanized rubber condoms and diaphragms after midcentury. Though available primarily by word of mouth and through vaguely worded advertisements, these techniques probably assumed larger roles in limiting families as the century progressed.[49]

Of course, women's (and men's) freedom to control procreation could be limited by public policies. Named after Anthony Comstock, its sponsor, the Comstock law of 1873 outlawed the circulation of contraceptive information and devices through the U.S. mails, because of fear that the use of contraceptives would excessively limit the growth of the American population. Comstock, who worked for the U.S. Postal Service, devoted the next four decades to prosecuting purveyors of "obscenity," including physicians who openly dispensed contraceptives. (In addition, many local jurisdictions enacted obscenity laws that were used by the early 20th century, along with the Comstock law, to prosecute feminists who sought to openly discuss contraception or to disseminate birth control devices.) Moreover, by the late 19th century, many physicians opposed abortion. Prior to the Civil War, abortion had been used without stigma to limit family size, even if it relied on herbs and other uncertain techniques, but physicians increasingly came to see it as an unnatural curtailing of women's reproductive function.[50]

Nor did public policies only target birth control devices. Homosexuality was not stigmatized in the 19th century, though various localities had laws against sodomy (sexual intercourse between men). But by the end of the century (when the term *homosexuality* was first coined), physicians had declared that same-gender sexual relations represented medical pathology; this development presaged the stigmatizing of such behavior in the 20th century.[51]

THE EVOLUTION OF AMERICAN SOCIAL POLICIES

Many Americans viewed the social problems of the new nation as a pestilence that threatened its moral and social order. Social problems were generally viewed as emanating from the moral defects of citizens—and particularly immigrants in the burgeoning cities. Reformers, correspondingly, tried to develop institutions that could purge these defects from stigmatized groups—people with mental disorders, criminals, paupers, and delinquent youth—or sought preventive strategies, which included temperance and moral instruction through the Sunday School movement or the expanding network of public schools.

In short, the services available to citizens who needed assistance were harsh and controlling. Relatively few reformers acknowledged that structural factors—such as the nation's uncertain economy, the blighted conditions of its cities, or discrimination against its immigrants—assumed a major role in causing social problems. The lack of strong reform and political organizations that represented the policy needs of the lower class, such as were developing in England, deprived the nation of alternative perspectives. Nor did the nation develop expansive notions of social obligation; social programs, most reformers believed, should concentrate only on the provision of institutional and social services to individuals who were truly destitute and ill rather than to a broad range of its citizens. (Public education was an important exception, though even education was conceived primarily as moral instruction.) Most services were, moreover, to be provided by local governments and private philanthropic organizations; Americans accorded the federal government virtually no social welfare roles other than maintenance

of some institutions for the deaf and a small program of pensions for veterans.

In Chapter 5, we discuss how these various beliefs about social policy made the nation ill equipped to cope with the social problems that accompanied industrialization in the wake of the Civil War. Furthermore, when coupled with widespread racism, these beliefs led to particularly harsh treatment of Native Americans, Asian Americans, Spanish-speaking persons, and African Americans.

NOTES

1. James Davis, *Frontier America, 1800–1840: A Comparative Demographic Analysis of the Frontier Process* (Glendale, Calif.: Arthur H. Clark Co., 1977), pp. 19–21; Richard Slotkin, *The Fatal Environment: The Myth of the Frontier in the Age of Industrialization, 1800–1890* (New York: Atheneum, 1985), pp. 3–47.

2. Edward Pessen, *Jacksonian America. Society, Personality, and Politics* (Homewood, Ill.: Dorsey Press, 1978), p. 85; Malcolm Rohrbough, *The Land Office Business: The Settlement and Administration of American Public Lands, 1789–1837* (New York: Oxford University Press, 1968), pp. 137–156.

3. Paul Boyer, *Urban Masses and Moral Order in America, 1820–1920* (Cambridge, Mass.: Harvard University Press, 1978), pp. 3–4; Raymond Mohl, *Poverty in New York, 1783–1825* (New York: Oxford University Press, 1971), pp. 3–13; and Richard Bushman, "Family Security in the Transition from Farm to City, 1750–1850," *Journal of American History*, 6 (Fall 1980), 238–256.

4. Davis, *Frontier America*, pp. 16–17; Slotkin, *The Fatal Environment*, p. 47.

5. Stephan Thernstrom, *Poverty and Progress: Social Mobility in a 19th Century City* (Cambridge, Mass.: Harvard University Press, 1964), pp. 33–57.

6. Charles Sellers, *The Market Revolution: Jacksonian America, 1815–1846* (New York: Oxford University Press, 1991), p. 389.

7. Mohl, *Poverty*, pp. 14–34; Pessen, *Jacksonian America*, pp. 55–58.

8. Sellers, *The Market Revolution*, p. 137.

9. Eric Foner, *History of the Labor Movement in the United States,* Vol. 1 (New York: International Publishers, 1955), pp. 106–143; Mohl, *Poverty,* pp. 20–30.

10. Foner, *History of the Labor Movement,* Vol. 1, pp. 108–120.

11. Pessen, *Jacksonian America,* pp. 77–83.

12. Sellers, *The Market Revolution,* p. 261.

13. Michael Katz, Michael Doucet, and Mark Stern, *The Social Organization of Early Industrial Capitalism* (Cambridge, Mass.: Harvard University Press, 1982), pp. 242–284.

14. Rowland Berthoff, *An Unsettled People: Social Order and Disorder in American History* (New York: Harper & Row, 1971), pp. 148–161; Boyer, *Urban Masses,* p. 68.

15. Boyer, *Urban Masses,* pp. 12–21, 67–75; Thernstrom, *Poverty and Progress,* pp. 42–46, 50–56; and Nathan Huggins, *Protestants Against Poverty* (Westport, Conn.: Greenwood Press, 1971), pp. 3–14.

16. Berthoff, *An Unsettled People,* pp. 288–292.

17. Boyer, *Urban Masses,* pp. 3–64; Mohl, *Poverty,* pp. 159–170.

18. Michael Katz, *Poverty and Policy in American History* (New York: Academic Press, 1983), pp. 134–156; Huggins, *Protestants Against Poverty,* p. 177; and Mohl, *Poverty,* pp. 259–265.

19. Sellers, *The Market Revolution,* pp. 37, 114–124; Bray Hammond, *Banks and Politics in America from the Revolution to the Civil War* (Princeton, N.J.: Princeton University Press, 1957), pp. 451–499; and Pessen, *Jacksonian America,* p. 147.

20. Louis Hartz, *Economic Policy and Democratic Thought in Pennsylvania* (Cambridge, Mass.: Harvard University Press, 1948), pp. 309–320; Carl Kaestle, *Pillars of the Republic: Common Schools and American Society, 1780–1860* (New York: Hill and Wang, 1983), pp. 136–181; Robert Steamer, *The Supreme Court in Crisis: A History of Conflict* (Amherst, Mass.: University of Massachusetts Press, 1971), pp. 41–44, 61–62; and Edward White, *The American Judicial Tradition: Profiles of Leading American Judges* (New York: Oxford University Press, 1976), pp. 49–61.

21. June Axinn and Herman Levin, *Social Welfare: A History of the American Response to Need* (New York: Harper & Row, 1982), pp. 80–84.

22. Ian Tyrrell, *Sobering Up: From Temperance to Prohibition in Antebellum America, 1800–1862* (Westport, Conn.: Greenwood Press, 1979), pp. 3–13, 63–67, 87–115, 235–245, 290–297.

23. Gerald Grob, *Mental Institutions in America: Social Policy to 1875* (New York: Free Press, 1973), p. 168; Merril Peterson, *The Portable Thomas Jefferson* (New York: Viking Press, 1975), pp. 180–181; and Mohl, *Poverty,* pp. 14–34.

24. Katz, *Poverty and Policy,* pp. 90–98, 134–142, 157–165.

25. Boyer, *Urban Masses,* pp. 34–53.

26. Boyer, *Urban Masses,* pp. 86–94; Mohl, *Poverty,* pp. 47, 241–258; and Huggins, *Protestants Against Poverty,* pp. 111–135.

27. Eric Monkkonen, "Nineteenth-Century Institutions, Dealing with the Urban 'Underclass.'" In Michael Katz, ed., *The "Underclass" Debate: Views from History* (Princeton, N.J.: Princeton University Press, 1993), pp. 334–365.

28. Joseph Hawes, *Children in Urban Society: Juvenile Delinquency in Nineteenth-Century America* (New York: Oxford University Press, 1971), pp. 20–24, 45–51; Robert Mennel, *Thorns and Thistles: Juvenile Delinquents in the United States, 1825–1940* (Hanover, N.H.: University Press of New England, 1973), pp. 3–31.

29. Grob, *Mental Institutions,* pp. 103–110, 156–157, 174–220; David Rothman, *The Discovery of the Asylum: Social Order and Disorder in the New Republic* (Boston: Little, Brown and Co.: 1971), pp. 206–236.

30. Hawes, *Children,* pp. 45–51; Mennel, *Thorns,* pp. 12–31.

31. Peter Halloran, *Boston's Wayward Children: Social Services for Homeless Children, 1830–1930* (London: Associated University Presses, 1989); Nurith Zmora, *Orphanages Reconsidered: Child Care Institutions in Progressive Era Baltimore* (Philadelphia: Temple University Press, 1994).

32. James Trent, *Inventing the Feeble Mind: A History of Mental Retardation in the United States* (Berkeley: University of California Press, 1994).

33. Ibid., pp. 60–95; Walter Trattner, *Homer Folks: Pioneer in Social Welfare* (New York: Columbia University Press, 1968), pp. 76–81.

34. Mennel, *Thorns,* pp. 32–40.

35. Joyce Appleby, *Capitalism and a New Social Order: The Republican Vision of the 1790s* (New York: New York University Press, 1984), p. 2.

36. Sellers, *The Market Revolution,* pp. 368–369; Kaestle, *Pillars,* pp. 75–103; Michael Katz, *The Irony of Early School Reform: Educational Innovation in Mid-Nineteenth Century Massachusetts* (Cambridge, Mass.: Harvard University Press, 1968), pp. 124–160.

37. Pessen, *Jacksonian America,* pp. 104–114.

38. G. D. H. Cole and Raymond Postgate, *The British Common People, 1746–1946* (New York: Barnes & Noble Books, 1961), pp. 279–327.

39. Ibid., pp. 279, 315; Ira Katznelson, "Working-Class Formation and the State: Nineteenth Century England in American Perspective." In Peter Evans, Dietrich Rueschemeyer, and Theda Skocpol, eds., *Bringing the State Back In* (Cambridge: Cambridge University Press, 1985), pp. 270–278.

40. Cole and Postgate, pp. 278–280; Michael Barker, *Gladstone and Radicalism: The Reconstruction of Liberal Policy in Britain, 1885–1894* (New York: Harper & Row, 1975), pp. 37–40; and Norman Gash, *Reaction and Reconstruction in English Politics: 1832–1852* (Oxford: Clarendon Press, 1965), pp. 139–140, 149–150.

41. John Ibson, *Will the World Break Your Heart? A Historical Analysis of the Dimensions and Consequences of Irish-American Assimilation.* Doctoral dissertation. Brandeis University, 1976; Cecil Woodham-Smith, *The Great Hunger: Ireland 1845–1849* (New York: Signet Books, 1962), pp. 24–30, 86.

42. Woodham-Smith, *The Great Hunger,* p. 177.

43. Ibid., pp. 224, 248.

44. Ibid., pp. 243–265; John Higham, *Strangers in the Land: Patterns of American Nativism, 1860–1925* (New York: Atheneum, 1972), pp. 3–11.

45. Lawrence Fuchs, *The American Kaleidoscope: Race, Ethnicity, and the Civic Culture* (Hanover, N.H.: University Press of New England, 1990), pp. 35–53.

46. Barbara Harris, *Beyond Her Sphere: Women and the Professions in American History* (Westport, Conn.: Greenwood Press, 1978), pp. 40ff; Katz, Doucet, and Stern, *The Social Organization,* pp. 290–92.

47. Harris, *Beyond Her Sphere,* pp. 60ff.

48. Ibid., pp. 73ff.

49. John D'Emilio and Estelle Freedman, *Intimate Matters: A History of Sexuality in America* (New York: Harper & Row, 1988), pp. 58–60; Sellers, *The Market Revolution,* p. 258.

50. D'Emilio and Freedman, *Intimate Matters,* p. 85.

51. Ibid., pp. 121–130.

5

C H A P T E R

Lost Opportunities: The Frontier, The Civil War, and Industrialization

Selected Orienting Events

1803	Louisiana Purchase
1820	Missouri Compromise
1828	Andrew Jackson elected for first of two terms
1836	Battle of the Alamo
1838–1839	Forced march of the Cherokees
1845	The term *manifest destiny* coined
1846–1848	Mexican-American War
1848	Treaty of Guadalupe Hidalgo; Seneca Falls Convention
1859	Charles Darwin publishes *On the Origin of Species by Means of Natural Selection*
1860	Abraham Lincoln elected for first of two terms
1861–1865	Civil War
1863	Emancipation Proclamation
1865	Lincoln assassinated
1865–1868	Presidency of Andrew Johnson
1865–1872	Freedmen's Bureau in existence
1865–1900	The Gilded Age; the United States industrializes rapidly
1868	Ulysses Grant elected for first of two terms
1873–1878	An extended period of recession
1877	President Hayes uses federal troops to end national railroad strike
1880–1914	Arrival of 21 million immigrants in the United States
1882	Chinese Exclusion Act
1887	Dawes Act
1890	U.S. Census declares frontier to have officially ended; Sherman Antitrust Act
1902	Reclamation Act

In this chapter, we focus on three epic developments that posed enormous challenges to the new nation during the 19th century: the rapid settlement of the frontier (over the first eight decades of the century); the Civil War (in the middle of the century); and the development of an industrial system (primarily during and after the Civil War). Americans' responses to these three events can be understood as a lost opportunity for social reform.

POLICY AT THE FRONTIER

The American frontier has been romanticized in countless films and books. In reality, while many white settlers—along with speculators and railroad companies—became rich, others could not obtain land or were bankrupted in the volatile swings of the frontier economy. The frontier was also the stage for the persecution of Native Americans, Spanish-speaking persons, and other groups.

Land Policy

In the early and middle 19th century, most of the unsettled land was in territories owned by the federal government. Federal authorities had to decide on an appropriate policy: whether to give land to settlers; to allow persons to buy unlimited quantities of land; to sell or give the land to churches and other organizations; or (most radically) to distribute the land to former slaves, Native Americans, impoverished immigrants, urban dwellers, and squatters.

The basic strategy for distributing the land, which was developed by the 1780s, was to sell it in blocks at public auctions to the highest bidders, provided their bids exceeded a prescribed minimum price. The advantages of this strategy, from the government's point of view, were that public auction of vast quantities of unsettled land would most likely keep land prices relatively low; would avoid the large public bureaucracies required if the government were to distribute land directly to individuals; and would conform to the tenets of capitalism, which governed the distribution of American lands almost from the beginning of the national experience. Tens of millions of acres were sold at federal land offices between 1790 and 1890, when the frontier no longer existed.

Far from proving equitable, however, the auctions often enriched relatively affluent Americans, speculators, and railroad companies. Competitive bidding at auctions tended to favor already wealthy persons who had recently sold their farms in settled areas. Believing that railroad lines through the territories would stimulate economic growth, the federal government gave (or sold at minimum prices) vast tracts to the railroad companies, which then sold the land to settlers—at inflated prices. Speculators and land companies soon discovered how to manipulate the auction system. Using scouts and information leaked by officials at federal land offices, they located valuable farm and other lands, made mutual agreements not to engage in competitive bidding, and secured large tracts at the minimum federal price, which they later sold at higher prices to settlers.[1]

It is a myth that the frontier was largely sold to farmhands, poor immigrants, or poor urban dwellers. A large class of squatters settled frontier lands without titles, since they lacked funds to purchase them; they grew several crops on the land before moving westward to renew the process. The federal government periodically tried to help squatters and persons of limited means. Many "preemption laws" allowed squatters to purchase their land at the federal auctions. Furthermore, to help poorer persons buy land, federal authorities successively lowered the minimum sizes of land blocks from 320 to 160 to 40 acres and decreased the required down payment. But these policies were insufficient to make land ownership possible for many squatters and other would-be settlers. Relatively little land was distributed to freed slaves in the wake of the Civil War, and land was not widely used for charitable institutions, aside from land-grant colleges.[2]

Settlers' problems were compounded by inadequate regulation of the frontier banks that financed land purchases. In the absence of sufficient federal currency, notes of local banks were used as currency, but their value fluctuated wildly in periodic recessions or when the banks had to repay their foreign creditors. President Jackson's veto of the United States Bank in 1832 compounded the economic turmoil.

The frontier also provided rich opportunities for deception and fraud. Speculators, railroads, and steamship companies hired salesmen who, with promises of fertile American lands, would persuade European peasants to part with their life savings, in exchange for a plot of barren land in a remote location. By hiring persons to falsely claim squatting rights, speculators were able to buy land at minimum prices. Federal land agents often gave information about choice lands to speculators for a fee—and themselves participated freely in land speculation.[3]

Conquest and Persecution

During the colonial period, prejudice against Native Americans was softened by the condescending belief that the destructive influence of tribal customs made them lazy. In the 19th century, such environmental explanations of the differences between Native Americans and whites were increasingly supplanted by unmitigated racism, which promoted vicious suppression of Native Americans and Spanish-speaking persons on the frontier. American anthropologists became convinced that white persons from England and Germany, whom they called Anglo-Saxons, were biologically superior to other races in intelligence and industriousness. They went on to argue that this supposed superiority had allowed Anglo-Saxons to conquer indigenous persons, develop new technology, and establish democratic and legal institutions. Unlike many colonial theorists, who assumed that Native Americans shared common biological origins with whites, these anthropologists contended that Anglo-Saxons derived from a biological stock different from that of other races.[4]

Scientists have since disproved these theories of biological superiority. They have shown that all human races derived from ancestors in Africa or Asia—something that 19th-century anthropologists would have found disconcerting—and that there is no significant difference in brain size between races.[5] Racist ideas that placed Anglo-Saxons on a biological pedestal were nonetheless widely accepted in the 19th century and were linked to nationalism through the concept of *manifest destiny*, a term coined by Democratic politician John O'Sullivan in 1845. According to the doctrine of manifest destiny, God willed Anglo-Saxons to develop the North American continent as a laboratory, in order to show the world that Americans could build a utopian society that fused capitalism, Protestantism, and democracy. Anthropologists and politicians argued that indigenous peoples who blocked the expansion of the frontier should be violently suppressed and that Anglo-Saxons should not dilute their species by marrying members of other racial groups.[6]

In the colonial period the frontier had been circumscribed by territorial claims of the Spanish and the French; by the determination of the English Crown to limit settlers' advance on some Native American lands (see the discussion of the Proclamation Line in Chapter 3); and by the tenacity of Native American tribes, whose resistance to the advance of white settlers was often effective. By the early 19th century, with the departure of the European powers and with huge increases in the numbers of white settlers, the balance of power at the frontier shifted toward the settlers, who moreover, continued to make use of their advanced weapons, their ability to play tribes off against each other, and their willingness to entice or force tribal leaders to sign treaties. What's more, the unexpected acquisition of the Louisiana Territory from the French in 1803 opened up a frontier extending from the Mississippi to the Pacific, with the exception of huge Spanish territories on the Southwestern and Western parts of the continent. (Those territories became part of Mexico when it gained independence from Spain in 1821.)

When Jefferson negotiated the Louisiana Purchase, he had the notion that Native Americans should live on small tracts of land in their existing territories (with the remaining lands to be sold to white settlers by federal land agents). However, he came to adopt a "removal policy," which would relocate most Native Americans who lived west of the Mississippi to lands far from the existing frontier. This relocation policy was anathema to many Native American leaders, such as the legendary Tecumseh, who tried over some decades to organize an effective resistance by tribes in the Ohio Valley and the South. But the push of the white settlers was inexorable; often under force of arms, tribal leaders (or those cooperative individuals identified as leaders by white officials) ceded vast tracts to the American government. Those few federal officials who sought to protect land granted to Native Americans by these treaties had little success in restraining settlers from occupying the land and brutalizing the Native Americans who lived there.[7]

Even those Native Americans who chose to become farmers were displaced as the frontier moved westward. Consider the Cherokees, who farmed lands in Georgia. Many Cherokees signed treaties with federal authorities that guaranteed tribal jurisdiction over certain lands and declared their statehood independent of Georgia, so as to forestall efforts to take their land. Some politicians resisted their removal and cited treaty obligations, but the Georgia legislators declared the Cherokees to be merely tenants, who could be evicted and removed to Western territories. (Georgia invited its citizens to plunder the Cherokees and enacted legislation that made it illegal for Cherokees to testify in court against white men who took their property!) In desperation, the Cherokees appealed to President Jackson, who promptly ruled that the issue was a state matter; Jackson strongly supported the congressional "removal legislation" that was enacted in 1830. The Cherokees then appealed to the U.S. Supreme Court on the grounds that, as a foreign power, their land claims could not be violated by Georgia. Though showing some sympathy to them, the Supreme Court ruled the Cherokees to be merely a "domestic dependent nation" that could not claim to be a foreign power; as such, the Court argued, the Cherokees lacked jurisdiction. When a subsequent Supreme Court ruling was more favorable, President Andrew Jackson simply ignored it; Cherokees were rounded up into stock-

ades and forcibly marched to territories in an area that later became the state of Oklahoma. It has been estimated that as many as 45% of the tribe died of starvation or disease during this forced exodus. Similar policies were used to evict other, large Southern tribes such as the Chocktaws, the Chickasaws, and the Creeks; the Seminoles in Florida were pushed into swampy and undesirable lands that became their reservations. Tribes in the Ohio, Indiana, and Illinois areas were similarly removed to the West, often under treaties that promised that their Western lands would be kept intact for them for "perpetuity." By the end of the 1830s, then, many displaced tribes existed in territories west of the Mississippi, in areas that later became Kansas, Arkansas, Oklahoma, Nebraska, and Texas. Other tribes were confined to relatively small reservations in scattered locations in Florida, Minnesota, and elsewhere.[8]

Settlers also dealt brutally with Spanish-speaking people on the Western frontier. The Louisiana Purchase gave most lands west of the Mississippi to the Americans but *not* the lands held by Spain, which became part of Mexico in 1821. White settlers found the area that became Texas to be suitable for ranching and for cotton in the 1820s and 1830s. As they pushed west and were resisted by the indigenous population, episodes of violence escalated, but the region was easy to conquer because of the political instability and weakness of Mexico. When a particular battle at the Alamo in San Antonio in 1836 was publicized as the massacre of innocent white settlers by barbaric Mexicans, many Americans supported the efforts of the white settlers to gain independence from Mexico and establish a territorial government, which became an American state in 1845. When the Mexican government refused to recognize this new state constructed from Mexican territory, the United States declared war in 1846 and, in a one-sided affair, routed the Mexicans in a series of battles that culminated in the ransacking of Mexico City in 1847.

The Mexicans ceded territory that is now California, Nevada, New Mexico, Utah, parts of Colorado, Wyoming, and Arizona—and they recognized the independence of Texas. In an attempt to protect the stranded Spanish-speaking persons in the ceded territory, they insisted on a provision in the Treaty of Guadalupe Hidalgo that required Americans to honor the civil liberties and rights of the indigenous and Spanish-speaking population. But the provision had little effect. Spanish-speaking persons were told that their land titles, which existed under Mexican law, had to be converted to American titles; this policy led to the transferral of millions of acres of land to white settlers in Texas and then other areas that had been ceded by Mexico. (The indigenous persons lacked legal resources and access to impartial judges.) White squatters often claimed their land extralegally—and many indigenous Spanish-speaking persons were massacred by land-hungry settlers. Landless, lacking resources, and denied civil rights and civil liberties, the Spanish-speaking population proved a useful source of labor for American ranchers and eventually for growers of vegetable and cotton crops. Large farming operations were made possible by the passage of the Reclamation Act in 1902, which provided federal funds to build an irrigation system that brought water from the Colorado River to California. Isolated from urban populations in labor camps that were organized by large owners and companies, the Spanish-speaking farmworkers were brutally suppressed when they complained about their subsistence wages and harsh working conditions.[9]

In effect, then, the settlers had engaged in three conquests by the mid-1840s: the initial development of the frontier in the colonial period; a massive relocation of Native Americans from the formation of the republic to the late 1830s; and the acquisition from the Mexicans of much of the Western and Southwestern part of the continent in the 1830s and 1840s. These conquests led to the formation of the various states east of the Mississippi, as well as Texas, and paved the way for the establishment of many Southwestern states, as well as California, which became a state in 1850.

But the white settlers had created a problem for themselves when they had forcibly relocated many tribes west of the Mississippi, for Native Americans now occupied vast tracts of land that white

settlers desired—and some of these lands also contained minerals. A fourth conquest was needed to obtain lands that Native Americans held under treaties with the United States in areas that later became the states of Nebraska, Kansas, Arkansas, and Oklahoma, as well as the areas ceded to the United States by Mexico, such as Colorado and California. They also had to dispossess tribes from the Badlands in what later became North and South Dakota, from the areas that became Montana and Idaho, and from their territories in the Pacific Northwest.[10]

This fourth conquest used many of the techniques perfected earlier. Once again, tribes were induced to sign treaties by which they ceded land in exchange for minimal cash and more promises that their (now smaller) reservations would be guaranteed to them for perpetuity. Native Americans' resistance was softened by running railroads through their lands (and thereby allowing both settlers and troops to penetrate their territory more rapidly); by mass killing of the buffalo on which they depended for sustenance; and by threats that Congress would rescind prior treaties if they failed to sign new treaties. The removal policy came to a climactic and tragic conclusion in the wake of the Civil War, when President Grant chose Civil War generals such as Sherman and Sheridan to evict Native Americans from lands west of the Mississippi. They resorted to the usual mixture of unenforced treaties and brutal assaults, but they undertook this policy with a savagery that was unmistakable in its intent: to kill all Native Americans who would not agree to settle on reservations. In 1868, thanks to the skilled tactics of Sitting Bull, Crazy Horse, and other Native American chiefs and warriors, the American government signed a treaty that guaranteed a huge area of the Badlands to the Sioux and Cheyenne. White settlers' discovery of gold on those lands, however, placed enormous pressure on the government to evict the Native Americans. George Custer, a flamboyant Civil War general, was given the task of killing the Native Americans who still occupied this area. Confident that the Native Americans lacked courage to fight, he marched a small contingent directly at Native American forces numbering in the thousands—and he and his forces were killed in a battle popularly known as Custer's Last Stand. Instead of viewing Custer's demise as the result of the government's illegal abrogation of its treaty with the Sioux, most white Americans sympathized with Custer, who was widely perceived as an innocent victim of savages. The Native Americans had won a pyrrhic victory, because they soon encountered the entire army of the United States, which indiscriminately attacked them; the final massacre of women, children, and men took place at Wounded Knee in 1890.

In the 1870s, many public officials began a movement to break up reservations, on the grounds that tribal ownership of land represented an unnatural and communalistic experiment inconsistent with Anglo patterns of individualistic land ownership. The Dawes Act, which Congress enacted in 1887, conditioned Native Americans' continued access to the land on their acceptance of individual plots; each head of family would be given 160 acres. Although some protections were initially established, the new policy meant that whites could take land from Native Americans, one by one, by a variety of tricks—by coercing or enticing them to sell their land for minimal prices; by using devious legal techniques to obtain title to their plots; or by arguing that Native Americans had failed to claim some of their allotments. In this way, speculators and crooks were able to liquidate vast holdings. For example, five major tribes had held an area equivalent to half the size of Oklahoma, but their holdings were reduced from 19.5 million acres in the 1850s to slightly over 300,000 acres by 1956.[11]

Finding Laborers

Americans on the Western frontier often needed to obtain labor to grow crops, to build public improvements such as railroads, and to serve as miners. Many white settlers in Texas imported slaves from other sections of the South to make it a major cotton-growing region. We have already noted that, once dispossessed from the land, the Spanish-speaking population provided the major source of labor for the cultivation of cotton, fruit, and vegetables in California.

Asian immigrants provided another source of labor. About one million Asians arrived between the gold rush of 1849 and the Immigration Act of 1924, in a complex pattern representing migrations from China, Japan, Korea, the Philippines, and India. (Chinese and Japanese constituted the bulk of the migration.) Like European immigrants, most of the Asians came voluntarily in search of a better life but, like slaves and Native Americans, they possessed physiological characteristics that made it easy for the white population to identify them and often to stigmatize and segregate them.

The Asian influx began with Chinese immigrants, who came to America to find gold in the 1840s and to do manual labor for farmers, manufacturers, miners, and the railroads that were extending lines eastward from the Pacific. In 1870, California's 63,000 Chinese constituted almost 10% of the state's population. Chinese laborers were ideally suited to employers' needs: They could be paid minimal wages (coercive tactics were used when they threatened to strike for higher wages) and used to depress the wages of white workers; and they did not constitute a political threat because as "aliens" and persons of color, they were denied legal rights. (The California Supreme Court ruled in 1854 that Chinese people could not testify in court against whites, even if one of their number had been murdered by a white citizen.) They were disallowed from owning mines by tax levies, could not become citizens, were required to attend segregated schools, and could not vote.

Rampant racism and fears by white laborers that they would lose their jobs to Chinese workers led to the enactment of the Chinese Exclusion Act of 1882, which excluded further Chinese immigrants despite their usefulness to employers. Japanese labor soon provided a low-wage substitute, particularly for white landowners who sought to grow fruit and vegetables in California. By 1902, California's 139,000 Japanese residents vastly outnumbered the roughly 70,000 Chinese residents.

Like the Chinese, the Japanese immigrants were often greeted by racist epithets, such as "Jap," and realtors often refused to sell them houses. The Japanese were attacked by white laborers and were denied citizenship and the vote. A sizable network of Japanese businesses developed; some (such as restaurants and boarding houses) catered to Japanese clients. When the use of refrigerated railroad cars created large national markets for fruits and vegetables, the Japanese quickly became major producers of these products; they ingeniously adapted techniques of irrigation used in Japan to American farms. By initially leasing or renting land, they obtained resources to purchase their own land.

But the growing Japanese population soon encountered white racism. Angered by their competition, white laborers demanded that the Chinese Exclusion Act, due for renewal in 1902, include a ban on Japanese immigration. President Theodore Roosevelt, anxious for diplomatic reasons not to antagonize Japan, opposed this policy and at one point used federal troops to protect the Japanese from race riots in San Francisco. However, in the Gentleman's Agreement of 1907, he persuaded Japan not to permit further emigration of laborers to the United States, except by family members of existing residents. (Once he had left office, Roosevelt favored exclusion of the Japanese.) Moreover, angered by the success of the Japanese in agriculture, California enacted legislation in 1913 to disallow Japanese immigrants from obtaining land and to restrict their leases to three years. On discovering that the Japanese were circumventing the law by registering their land in the names of their American-born children, the California legislature further tightened the legislation so as to disallow this practice and even leasing itself. (Similar legislation was enacted in 12 other states.) The Japanese suffered another rebuff in 1922, when the Supreme Court ruled that Japanese Americans could not become citizens, because 1790 federal legislation specified that citizens must be Caucasians. To make matters worse, legislation enacted by Congress in 1924 restricted the number of foreign-born persons admitted each year to 2% of the number of that nationality residing in the United States in 1890—a measure clearly directed at the Japanese population, which had numbered only 2,039 persons in 1890. (The Chinese were still banned from any immigration.)[12]

Appraisal of Frontier Policy

Many persons benefited from the expansion of the frontier. Imagine the euphoria of the descendant of a serf who managed to survive the westward trek and the first penniless years on a small tract in the American Midwest. Despite abuses of the auction system of land disposal, a large class of yeoman farmers developed; they participated vigorously in local politics and helped one another with practical tasks. Civic participation in territorial governments was promoted by a desire to achieve admission to the Union as a state, which conferred tangible benefits—in particular, protection from Native Americans and access to federal funds for internal improvements. A tradition of sectarian and private philanthropy developed in some frontier communities.

But speculation and greed were as much the legacy of the frontier as mutual aid. Americans came to the frontier as individualists and as persons who believed in limited government; accordingly, they fashioned local institutions that emphasized the protection of property rights rather than the development of programs and institutions that would help individuals who were disabled, sick, or poor or Native Americans who had been displaced by the white settlers. As with farm foreclosures of the 1920s and 1980s, the society demonstrated little compassion for persons who were bankrupted by economic forces beyond their control. Assessed in terms of the sheer speed at which the population was dispersed through the countryside and the rate at which the land was cleared and cultivated or ranched, the American frontier was an unqualified success. Measured in terms of the development of social institutions to meet common human needs or the distribution of lands to needy persons, however, the American frontier was a failure, particularly when the crushed lives of the indigenous peoples are entered into the balance.

INSERT 5.1   CRITICAL ANALYSIS: THE HISTORICAL ROOTS OF AMERICAN VIOLENCE

In the latter part of the 20th century, the United States has far higher homicide rates than other industrialized nations. Does the American historical experience cast any light on this phenomenon? In thinking about this issue, consider the American attachment to personal ownership of weapons, relatively unrestricted by government policy, and ask whether this attachment stems from the widespread ownership of weapons on the American frontier. Would restriction of gun ownership dramatically reduce homicides in contemporary America?

Could restrictions on the ownership of guns—for example, handguns—have been enacted even in the 19th century?

The American frontier not only reflected American individualism but also perpetuated and intensified that individualism. As stories of settlement, conquest, and success reached Americans in other sections of the country, prevailing American individualism was reinforced: Frontier success seemed to confirm the idea that anyone could succeed by hard work and taking risks. If unlimited land is available, some Americans asked, why do Americans need to develop other social resources and programs to help the needy?[13]

Arguably, the frontier both reflected and intensified American racism as well. Native Americans and Spanish-speaking residents who attacked white settlers as they moved across the land were portrayed as barbaric and uncivilized peoples. Some commentators viewed the frontier as a laboratory experiment that juxtaposed "advanced" with "lesser" peoples—an experiment that confirmed the racial and genetic superiority of Anglo-Saxons. The pangs of guilt felt by some white settlers were eased by their belief that their conquest would improve the general quality of the human race and the nation.

The development of farms, plantations, and mines in newly developed territories, as well as the construction of roads and railroads to reach these areas, required large amounts of labor. As Southerners had done, entrepreneurs at the frontier used slaves to grow cotton and tobacco and employed Latinos and Asians on farms, in the mines, on the railroads, and in emerging industries. These laborers were often treated brutally by their employers—and they resided in jurisdictions that enacted harsh legislation to deprive them of their basic rights. Nor were federal authorities helpful; indeed, immigration legislation and various court rulings served to buttress and supplement the discrimination and racism rampant in local jurisdictions.

THE CIVIL WAR AND FREED SLAVES: AN EXERCISE IN FUTILITY?

As a percentage of the total population, more American lives were lost during the Civil War than during World War II. However, battlefield casualties reflect only one portion of the human toll. Millions of people were dislocated during and after the war, and freed slaves were cast into a society with few economic or social supports. Of course, slaves *were* freed, an enormous achievement.

Origins of the Civil War

Was the war fought to help the slaves or for other objectives? Controversy exists among historians about the war's precise causes, but research suggests that the war can be attributed to multiple factors, many of which had little to do with improving the condition of freed slaves.[14]

By 1830, the American nation included three societies that were profoundly different from one another. With poor soil and long winters, New England had relatively marginal agriculture, and many of its citizens had begun to envision their region as a center for commerce and industry. Its leading citizens demanded high tariffs to protect its fledgling industry from foreign competitors and demanded federal subsidies for its small shipping industry.

The expanding Northern frontier, which extended into Ohio, Indiana, Illinois, and Missouri, became the breadbasket of the nation; its crops were increasingly transported to New England in exchange for commodities. This area sought federal funds to develop roads, canals, and railroads that were vital to trade with New England. New England and the frontier communities gradually became closely linked, because each depended on the other for goods. When a poor crop occurred on the frontier, New England had to import food, and so there were fewer resources to build industry; likewise, a recession in New England meant that prices for agricultural produce from the frontier plummeted.

The South, which included the Old South (states such as Virginia, the Carolinas, Alabama, and Georgia) and a Southern frontier (territories in states that are now Mississippi, Louisiana, and Texas), depended on tobacco and cotton, which were often cultivated by slaves. Like the agricultural produce of the Northern frontier, cotton and tobacco became part of the world economy thanks to New England shippers, who bought and exported Southern cotton in order to finance the expansion of New England industry. The conditions of the slaves varied, but many historians believe that the American version of slavery was even more repressive than slavery in South America and the West Indies. Reduced to chattel and lacking support from church, government, and legal institutions, slaves were wholly at the mercy of their masters.

Even this cursory discussion points to sectional rivalries that precipitated the Civil War. Most Northern families, who usually knew someone who had gone to the frontier to obtain land, wanted to preserve the frontier for white settlers. But the frontier also appealed to Southerners, who wanted new lands for cotton plantations. Slavery could not easily coexist with free labor, since it required sup-portive laws, local police, courts, and public opinion to keep the slaves in their bondage and to ensure the return of runaways. Northern settlers were not likely to cooperate in the maintenance of slavery because they came from areas dominated by small farmers and free labor, who feared the preemption of land by plantations. While abolitionists in the North were widely reviled in the 1830s because of deep-seated racism, by the 1850s growing numbers of Northerners came to view the institution of slavery as morally flawed.[15]

This rivalry for land was exacerbated by political realities. A delicate balance existed in the Congress among New England, the Northern frontier, and the South. New England wanted high tariffs and subsidies for ships; the frontier areas wanted public money for internal improvements and cheap land; and the South wanted low tariffs and, at least until the 1830s, some internal improvements. In the decades following the 1830s, however, Southern views and institutions became markedly different from those of the North. Its leaders rallied behind an extreme view of limited government; they wanted virtually no taxes, no internal improvements, and low tariffs. Whereas the North already emphasized railroads and public education by the 1840s, the South remained a relatively backward agricultural area dominated by cotton and tobacco. While many Southern leaders prior to the 1830s had not defended slavery but rather contended that its swift elimination would be impractical, they idealized it in succeeding decades as a means of avoiding the chasm between social classes that existed under "wage slavery" in New England's emerging industrial system.

As the cultural and policy views of the North and South diverged, each side came to view with alarm the possibility that the other might dominate the Congress by obtaining new representatives from frontier states. Both Northerners and Southerners realized that the region that controlled Congress could also write legislation to outlaw or condone slavery in the frontier areas.[16]

Because Northerners and Southerners had known since the early 19th century that cohabitation of specific territories was difficult, they had avoided armed conflict by partitioning the frontier into slaveholding and free territories. A series of ingenious compromises from 1787 to 1850 gave sections of the frontier to each side, as illustrated by the Missouri Compromise of 1820 and the Compromise of 1850.

When the Territory of Missouri applied for statehood in 1818, free states and slave states each had 22 senators in the U.S. Senate. To retain this balance, the Missouri Compromise proposed to admit Maine as a free state and Missouri as a slave state—and to avert future discord by prohibiting slavery to the north of a line extending westward from Missouri's Southern boundary through the remainder of the Louisiana Purchase. This outcome seemed to be a draw between slave and free states. However, the Compromise ignored the fact that settlers from *both* the North and South would soon stream into frontier lands, with the hope of eventually claiming them for the North or the South regardless of the Compromise of 1820.

By 1850, an atmosphere of mutual paranoia had developed. Once again, there was a balance between slave and free states (15 of each) in 1848, but the American conquest of Mexico made available a huge territory that would eventually give rise to many new states. Utah and then California sought admission as free states, while Texas, already admitted as a slave state in 1845, claimed half of New Mexico. The Compromise of 1850, which was achieved with considerable difficulty in this tense atmosphere, sought to give both North and South concessions. California was admitted as a free state, while the remainder of the formerly Mexican land was divided into the territories of Utah and New Mexico, which had no federal restrictions on slavery. But the Compromise contained a fatal flaw: It did not specifically address the needs of two new territories that were rapidly filling with settlers from both the North and South—namely, Kansas and Nebraska.

Under the terms of the Missouri Compromise of 1820, these territories should have been free, but increasing numbers of Northerners and Southerners were not in a mood to compromise. Many Southerners were convinced that the Congress did not have the right to declare that they could not bring slaves into *any* territory or state; many

Northerners believed slavery should be outlawed from the start in all territories. In this embattled atmosphere, the Congress decided to allow each territory to choose for itself whether to be free or slaveholding.

When Congress relinquished its role of partitioning the frontier, the battle between the North and South moved to the territories, where determined settlers from each region confronted one another. As battles were waged, dramatic stories of the other side's brutality spread through the North and South. In the 1850s, settlers from both the North and South poured into the Kansas and Nebraska territories. Rival territorial conventions and legislatures convened by slaveholding and Northern settlers declared opposite policies in the territories. Armed conflict between Southerners and Northerners became commonplace, as individuals took the law into their own hands.

Another provision of the Compromise of 1850 further embittered the atmosphere. To appease Southerners, the Compromise included a stronger fugitive-slave law, which denied fugitives the right to trial by jury and permitted their return to slavery merely on the testimony of a claimant. Fugitives who escaped to the North—even those who had lived there in freedom for 30 years or more—were hunted down by Southern slave catchers. Previously, many Northerners had seen slavery as a distant institution, but this law made them realize the extent to which they had cooperated with the South in preserving slavery—and helped abolitionists to dramatize its inhumanity.

Regional polarization was soon reflected in a realignment of the nation's political parties. Two major political parties existed in 1850: the Whigs and the Democrats competed relatively evenly in the South and the states that now comprise the Midwest. With the rapid emergence of the Republican party after the presidential election of 1856, the Republican party (to which Abraham Lincoln tied his fortunes) supplanted the Whig party and quickly became the party of the North; its leaders demanded that slavery be outlawed from the outset in all territories. Leaders of the Democratic party, which became the party of the South, argued that Congress lacked the constitutional authority to outlaw slavery in the territories or anywhere else. Many Southerners believed that they had no recourse but to secede from the Union when Lincoln was elected president in 1860. They were convinced that he would close the territories to slavery and, with Congress controlled by Northerners, eventually try to amend the Constitution so as to end slavery. The South fired the first shot by attacking a federal fort in South Carolina in 1861, but the seeds of the Civil War were sown in the conflict over the rich lands of the Western frontier.

If many Northerners fought the war primarily to secure land and political power for their region, a second cause of the war was nationalism. South Carolinans had threatened to secede from the Union in 1832, but they were intimidated by Andrew Jackson, who believed the Union should be preserved at all costs. Southerners' contemplation of secession in the 1850s exposed them to Northerners' nationalistic wrath. But nationalism did not foster humanitarian proposals to help slaves; indeed, nationalism was often linked to racism, as Americans envisioned the dominion of the Anglo-Saxon race from coast to coast.

The Northern desire to abolish slavery may be cited as a third cause of the war. If *any* group were to fight the war with the interests of slaves at heart, it should have been the abolitionists, who courageously endured the wrath of Northern white audiences when they promoted their cause in the decades preceding the war. However, even the abolitionists had limited notions of the social reforms that freed slaves would need in the wake of emancipation. Most abolitionists were imbued with the prevailing racism of their era. On the one hand, they were attracted by the gentleness commonly ascribed to African Americans in the 19th century, and argued that the laziness attributed to African Americans was not an intrinsic characteristic but rather was due to environmental factors. On the other hand, many abolitionists were also convinced that African Americans had a savage side to their nature, could not be trusted, and were consumed by sexual urges. Some abolitionists even believed that African Americans should not be allowed to inter-

marry with whites and that they should not be given the vote.[17]

Another limitation of abolitionists was that, like their contemporaries, they applied a moral ideology to the social problems of poverty, alcoholism, and crime. Many abolitionists believed that slaves were morally flawed because the plantation environment had encouraged them to be shiftless and promiscuous. To rehabilitate slaves, they urged utilization of the same set of educational and poorhouse institutions that Northern reformers sought for immigrants living in poverty. Their ideology blinded them to the need to distribute land to freed slaves, to provide them with resources with which to purchase their own land, or to help them migrate to Northern cities, where the emerging industrial order offered vast economic opportunities. Furthermore, many abolitionists pointed to the relative poverty of African Americans in the North, where they were concentrated in urban areas such as New York City and Philadelphia, as evidence that African Americans needed a supervised moral regimen after they had obtained their freedom. Some abolitionists even ascribed the widespread discrimination by Northerners against African Americans —who were denied the vote in most Northern states, placed in segregated public schools, and denied access to public transportation and public accommodations—to the poor reputation that African Americans had brought on themselves by not sufficiently improving their economic status.[18]

Those who supported the Civil War out of a genuine desire to help the slaves, then, rarely envisioned the need for reforms such as massive distribution of land or resources to them. The primary motivations for the war were sectional rivalries, nationalism, and the Northerners' moralistic ideology, rather than a desire to help freed slaves by enacting sweeping economic and social reforms. It is ironic that the moral-treatment ideology, which was a simplistic approach to the social needs of poor whites, was applied to the African American population, whose problems were so obviously linked to the oppression they had experienced in both the South and the North.

Once emancipated, Southern slaves were ill prepared to participate in the capitalist economy. They had been systematically denied education by white owners, who feared it might make them rebellious. Some slaves were allowed to attend white Protestant churches, but had to sit in segregated galleries.

We ought not to portray slaves as docile victims, however. Slaves developed complex tactics for coping with their oppression. Couples married and had tightly knit families even within the confines of a plantation. While owners could sell their slaves at any time, many encouraged stable families, in order to encourage their slaves to produce more babies. Slaves often embraced evangelical Protestantism, which they infused with their own rhythmic singing and turned to their own purposes. As Sellers notes, "A gospel subversive of slavery resonated through spirituals and resentment of oppressors through secular songs and tales." They learned to present themselves to whites as compliant and docile, while maintaining "day-to-day resistance of malingering, stealing, tool breaking, and arson." Many ran away, whether singly or in small groups, despite the obvious danger to themselves; a few, like Nat Turner in 1831, even took the suicidal course of open rebellion.[19]

Social Policy During the War

The primary issue to be resolved during the war was the legal status of slaves. In its infamous Dred Scott decision of 1857, the Supreme Court had declared that slaves—and free descendants of slaves—were not persons and thus not entitled to constitutional protections or citizenship, even when they lived in free territories. Known as the Great Emancipator, Lincoln was hardly a militant opponent of slavery; he often infuriated abolitionists, who wanted him to seek an immediate end to slavery. Prior to the war, he had not proposed to terminate slavery; instead, he wanted only to restrict it to existing slave states. Nor did he immediately declare the slaves to be free once the war began, because he hoped Southern states would negotiate an early end to the war if they were allowed to retain slaves in existing states. When he

finally issued the Emancipation Proclamation in 1863, he declared only those slaves to be free who were in areas still in rebellion against the Union, in an obvious effort to get border states, such as Kentucky, to cease hostilities.[20]

In the turmoil of the Civil War, the social welfare issues of dislocated persons received only secondary attention and were addressed improvisationally. The Union (Northern) Army was the major instrument of social welfare, by virtue of its presence in the South. Vast numbers of African Americans had to be supported as they left plantations, either because the Union Army had conquered Southern territory or because slaves fled behind Union lines. The Union Army constructed and maintained many camps where former slaves were placed in barracks or tents and given food and health care. These camps provided harsh surroundings; roughly 25% of their occupants died of disease. Remember, though, that mortality rates were similar for Union troops, because of the lack of modern medical technology to stem epidemics and infection. Some of the military administrators of the camps, like most citizens of the era, believed that the freed slaves were intrinsically lazy, and so they placed many of them on work details on camp fortifications or had them work under contract labor on plantations in conquered territories.

Many Northern philanthropic societies sent legions of volunteers to assist refugees behind Union lines; some were nonsectarian, while others drew assistance from churches. They provided clothing, food, and medical supplies and developed some schools. Various government departments developed programs in the South, though often in isolation from one another. The War Department operated the camps for the freed slaves, and the Treasury Department controlled lands that had been confiscated from Confederate landowners.

The first systematic inquiry into the condition of freed slaves, which was conducted in 1862 when President Lincoln appointed the American Freedmen's Inquiry Commission, recommended the establishment of a federal agency to coordinate the work of federal and private agencies and to develop new programs to meet the needs of freed slaves, which could not be sufficiently addressed by private philanthropy. After extended debate in the Congress, the Bureau of Refugees, Freedmen, and Abandoned Land was established. Though the bureau was informally known as the Freedmen's Bureau, its official name emphasized refugees, because many legislators did not want to show favoritism to African Americans. President Johnson opposed the bureau on the grounds that it would do more for African Americans than had been done for whites. A debate about the proper location of the agency in the federal bureaucracy nearly stalemated the legislation: Abolitionists wanted it to be placed in the Treasury Department, which controlled lands that had been abandoned by, or confiscated from, Confederate supporters, in order to facilitate transfer of these lands to freed slaves; but legislators placed the agency in the War Department.[21]

The Freedmen's Bureau was established in 1865 in a manner that virtually ensured that it would be unable to develop sweeping economic and social programs to help the freedmen. Its position in the War Department reflected its status as a wartime, rather than permanent, agency; indeed, it was terminated in 1872. Virtually no funding was given to the new agency; it was assumed that private philanthropy, largely from the North, could address most of the needs of freed slaves. The legislation was staunchly opposed by Southerners—and some Northerners—on the grounds that it represented unconstitutional delving by federal authorities into welfare matters, which were perceived by many persons to belong to the jurisdiction of state and local governments. The Freedmen's Bureau was given authority to establish courts in the South to help African Americans obtain their freedom, to make certain that terms of contract labor between freed slaves and landowners were clearly written and honored, and to distribute confiscated and abandoned land, but it lacked even a full-time director of legal affairs. Because it was located in the War Department, many army officials were appointed to its staff; some of them were sensitive to the economic and social needs of freed African Americans, but others favored punitive or racist remedies.[22]

Other policy setbacks during the Civil War had ominous implications for the freed slaves. In an agricultural society, freed slaves desperately needed land; without it, they had to work as tenant farmers or sharecroppers. Legislation that established the Freedmen's Bureau promised 40 acres of abandoned or confiscated land to every male refugee, but it could not be implemented unless governmental authorities identified abandoned land, took possession of it, and distributed it to the penniless former slaves. However, confiscation of land ran counter to American veneration of property owners' rights and the belief that government had no right to interfere with it; even many abolitionists did not support land confiscation during the war. Furthermore, Southern landowners were able to use elaborate legal stratagems to prevent the confiscation of their property; one effective tactic was to use local or even federal courts to oppose the rulings of courts operated by the Freedmen's Bureau. Relatively few African Americans were resettled on farms; the Freedmen's Bureau was able to resettle roughly 40,000 freed slaves—out of a total of more than three million—on forty acres of abandoned or confiscated land. The most successful efforts to redistribute land were undertaken by Generals Sherman and Grant, who unilaterally gave land to African Americans in conquered territories in Georgia and Alabama. These policies were foiled after the war, however, when President Andrew Johnson declared that African Americans occupied the lands illegally and required them to surrender their lands to the prior owners.[23]

Reconstruction

As the war neared its conclusion, Lincoln faced difficult choices. He could have supported a policy of guaranteeing freed slaves the right to vote, access to public accommodations, and access to federal courts when they were harassed by local citizens. He also could have excluded former Confederate officials from local, state, or federal government in order to prevent the restoration of racist policies. But he chose the more cautious approach of deferring to the Southern states and restoring

---

**INSERT 5.2   ETHICAL ANALYSIS OF KEY ISSUES AND POLICIES:
THE CASE OF GOVERNMENTAL HELP FOR FREED SLAVES**

Discuss the ethical merit of the government's policies toward freed slaves in the wake of the Civil War.

1. How had slavery ill prepared the slaves for survival in a competitive, capitalistic economy? (Identify an array of personal, economic, and social factors that enable people to compete in a capitalistic economy.)

2. How might the federal government have redressed the obstacles or impediments that the freed slaves encountered? (Identify specific, tangible steps the government might have taken to better help the freed slaves enter the economic mainstream.)

3. What ethical principles did the government violate by *not* helping the freed slaves more assertively in the wake of the war?

---

their power as quickly as possible, partly because he did not want to stiffen the resolve of the South to fight to the bitter end. He appointed military governors in each state and promised a return to civilian and Southern rule, subject only to the requirement that 10% of the white population vote their loyalty to the Union and agree to end slavery. This passive federal role—which allowed Southern states to retain laws that prohibited African Americans from voting as well as other infringements of their civil liberties—was stoutly opposed by many abolitionists, who feared that the South would soon return to a system of quasi-slavery, where African Americans would be nominally free but would lack land, resources, and the vote. The abolitionists' arguments were not heeded by Lincoln, however, who seemed intent on restoring order in the South as soon as possible and on terms that were acceptable to established Southern leaders.[24]

With hindsight, we can see that the war, while emancipating slaves, did not change white racism in the North or the South. Even had Lincoln not been assassinated, it is unlikely that he could have imposed on Southerners enlightened policies toward the freed slaves because most of them—like most Northerners—were antagonistic to African Americans. Indeed, on the eve of his assassination, Lincoln was still uncertain about suffrage for African Americans and was contemplating the vote merely for "the very intelligent, and especially those who have fought gallantly in our ranks."[25] We shall never know what policies Lincoln would

have sought, for he was assassinated and replaced by Vice President Andrew Johnson in 1865. Johnson was an unabashed Southerner who had always detested African Americans and whose dislike of the Southern aristocracy was transformed into a crusade to develop a political base among white monied interests in the postwar South. His term of office (1865–1868) was an unmitigated disaster for freed slaves. He proposed to allow Southern states back into the Union with virtually no requirement that they protect African Americans' civil or voting rights. He pardoned vast numbers of Confederate officials so that they could resume political careers in the South, and he even appointed some of them as officials of the Freedmen's Bureau. He declared the bureau's courts to be exempt from the requirement that their officials pledge loyalty to the Union. He sought to dissolve the Freedmen's Bureau when its officials advocated policies that he disliked.

Southerners who had expected the worst from the North—confiscation of land, restrictions preventing Confederate officials from holding political office, and requirements that they protect the civil liberties of African Americans—were astounded to discover that they had a strong ally in the White House. Johnson's policies emboldened Southern white leaders to develop "Black codes" that limited African Americans' ability to move around the countryside, restricted their rights of assembly and free speech, and subjected them to whipping for discourteous or insubordinate behavior.[26]

Southern actions and President Johnson's open support of white Southern interests outraged many in the North, who wondered whether the Civil War had been worth the carnage if the South continued to oppress freed slaves. Indeed, Lincoln's assassination and Johnson's provocative policies radicalized the North. In quick succession, a number of Northern states rescinded legislation that deprived African Americans of the vote and other civil liberties. Johnson and the Democratic party were resoundingly defeated in the congressional elections of 1866, in which Republicans successfully argued that Johnson was a captive of the South. Northerners demanded passage of a succession of civil rights acts. The Thirteenth Amendment to the Constitution, which abolished slavery, was ratified by Northern states in 1865. The Military Reconstruction Act of 1867 required Southern states to include universal suffrage in their constitutions before they could be readmitted to the Union and allowed the army to serve as protector of civil rights by bypassing local courts.

The Fourteenth Amendment, which was ratified in 1868, rescinded the provision in the Constitution that had counted each African American as only three-fifths a person, required that all citizens be given "equal protection" under the law, and stipulated that all persons be accorded the protection of due process. The Fifteenth Amendment, which was enacted in 1870, established universal suffrage of all adult males, though it did not exclude the use of poll taxes and literacy tests, which Southern jurisdictions eventually utilized to disenfranchise African Americans. Civil Rights Acts enacted in 1870 and 1875, respectively, limited the ability of states to enforce discriminatory legislation and outlawed segregation in public facilities and schools. The Ku Klux Klan Act of 1872 declared infringements of the civil rights of persons to be a federal offense.[27]

Southern behavior was constrained not only by this federal legislation but also by the ongoing presence of federal troops and area offices of the Freedmen's Bureau. Since the South remained an occupied society until 1877, Southern whites were impeded from violating the rights of freed slaves or from attacking Northern liberals who had settled in the South. The Freedmen's Bureau continued to hear cases in its courts, to build schools, and to provide rations to former slaves who were starving or penniless, though its programs reached only a small fraction of them.[28]

The Southern states reeled before this onslaught of federal legislation. The Democratic party, which had dominated the South for decades, was now supplanted by a Republican party that consisted of a range of white and African American voters. The transformed Southern legislatures now contained significant numbers of African American legislators, as well as sympathetic whites who had migrated to the South during and after the war. These bodies enacted many reforms, including the development of schools and mental institutions and public improvements such as roads. Taxes were raised by the Republican legislatures to rebuild Southern institutions that had been devastated by war.[29]

The liberalizing of Southern politics had only been accomplished, however, by the North's imposition of laws and troops. Southern states twice refused to ratify the Fourteenth Amendment, even when the North had required this action as a precondition for the removal of military governors. By so doing, the Southern states indicated that they preferred living under military occupation to acceding to a constitutional amendment that extended equal protection of the laws to all citizens. What would happen, some wondered, if the North lost the desire to allocate resources or troops to the South?

Even before this question could be answered, ominous signs appeared. The Ku Klux Klan, in essence an arm of the Southern Democratic party, began to intimidate African Americans and whites from the North. Northern troops, which numbered only 15,000 soldiers, could not curb the Klan's actions in dispersed rural areas of the South. Civil rights advocates were dismayed by the resurgence of the Democratic party in the South in the 1860s and early 1870s. The Democrats achieved this dramatic comeback by playing on the racial fears of poor whites, with the claim that Republicans represented freed slaves and Northern settlers, popularly known as carpetbaggers. Democrats also argued that Republican governments in the Southern states, which had raised taxes in order to pay for schools and internal improvements, were imposing "big government"; why not return, they asked, to the laissez-faire government and low taxes that had marked the South before the Civil War?

The response of the Republican party in the South to these Democratic attacks was hardly encouraging to freed slaves. Although one wing of the Southern Republican party, which included many African American legislators, had strongly supported civil rights and social programs to help freed slaves and poor whites in the aftermath of the war, the party soon came under the domination of Southern Republicans who softened their advocacy of civil rights legislation and displaced the freed slaves and their allies with moderate and conservative white Southerners.

Northerners' growing indifference to the South was also alarming to the freed slaves, who believed that institutionalized repression of African Americans would reemerge without unrelenting Northern pressure on the South. Many abolitionists, considering their work done, turned to other causes and ceased to pressure the Republican party to support civil rights measures. Other urgent concerns—economic problems, the disastrous recession of 1873, and policies governing the rates of railroads, labor disorders, currency policy, and tariffs—also distracted Northerners from issues in the South. Northern imposition of civil rights legislation had been partly motivated by anger at the South both for precipitating the war and for its defiant postwar passage of codes repressing African Americans, but the desire for revenge was dulled with the passing of years. The costs of maintaining the military occupation of the South made many Northerners disinclined to continue it.[30]

A symbolic event in 1877 illustrated the decline of Northern pressure on the South. In the 1876 presidential contest between Democrat Samuel Tilden and Republican Rutherford Hayes, the vote had been so close that the electoral college was stalemated. To break the stalemate, the Democrats finally agreed to support Hayes, but only if he agreed to withdraw troops from the South. That fateful deal dimmed the hopes of African Ameri-

cans in the South, who were left to the mercy of Southern whites. The Republican party, which had spearheaded federal civil rights legislation after the war, had viewed the Southern question as negotiable in the push and pull of the political process.

Reformers lost an opportunity to improve the lot of freed slaves after the Civil War. The major instrument of reform, the Freedmen's Bureau, was distressingly underfunded and had limited social welfare functions. More than 30% of its scant resources were devoted to educational programs for African Americans, but education could hardly suffice if African Americans had no land, resources, homes, or civil and political rights. The education given by the Freedmen's Bureau focused on moral rules, because it was widely assumed that African Americans, like low-income persons in the North, could succeed in life only if they were instructed in the tenets of honesty, religion, and thrift. Although initially enacted to last only one year after the end of the war, the Freedmen's Bureau did manage to survive until 1872.[31]

Nearly one-fifth of African American families owned land in 1870, but most of them were tenant farmers, who became mired in debt as they borrowed money from white Southerners for seeds, fertilizer, machines, and food. Many African American landowners were forced into foreclosure by their inability to repay debts or to secure loans from white-controlled banks. African Americans who relocated to Southern cities were subject to unrelenting discrimination in job markets and to segregated housing and schools.[32]

There seemed room for optimism even as late as 1877, however. African Americans still voted in most Southern jurisdictions; around 10% of school-age African Americans attended schools that had been established by the Freedmen's Bureau; and a small group of African American landowners and small businessmen existed. These gains were offset by a continuing erosion of civil rights. Civil rights legislation and the Fourteenth Amendment were interpreted so restrictively by the Supreme Court that they afforded few protections for African Americans. The requirement that persons could not be deprived of their civil liberties without due process was ruled by the Supreme

Court to apply only to discrimination against African Americans by individuals; states' discriminatory laws (such as those requiring poll taxes or literacy tests for voters) were thus legitimized.

In the late 19th century, a new generation of political leaders who hardly remembered the Civil War came to power in the North and South. They increasingly assumed that African Americans should not participate in political, social, or economic affairs. Southern states enacted a new wave of laws, so-called Jim Crow legislation, that deprived African Americans of their basic civil rights. These laws were not rescinded until nearly a century after the Civil War.[33]

It is instructive to compare the advantages enjoyed by European immigrants with the condition of freed slaves. White immigrants were given access to cheap land on the frontier—often 160 acres per person. Other white immigrants—or their children—developed small businesses in rural areas or in cities. Often literate even before they came to the United States, white immigrants sent their children to public schools in the North. As factories developed, immigrants obtained jobs in them, albeit at low wages. Enjoying free movement, immigrants and their descendants traveled between cities and regions to better their condition. They formed churches and associations to promote the interests of their groups; powerful political machines in major cities distributed jobs to the Irish, Italians, Germans, and others.

By contrast, freed slaves were mostly mired in isolated rural areas where they could not emulate the white immigrants' economic development. Lacking assets such as land and small businesses, they could not develop capital or borrow funds from banks. Mostly illiterate, they often lacked access to the public schools that could prepare them to compete in the capitalist order. Separated from the industrial centers that dominated the American economy by 1900, they could not find an economic niche in manufacturing that might bring a measure of security to them and their children. Trapped in a sharecropping system, African Americans could not save funds, and so they had no resources—much less land or businesses—to pass

on to their children when they died. Dispersed in remote areas with poor communication, they could not easily organize associations akin to the self-help groups formed by the Irish and Italians. Once the repressive codes were in place and they had been denied suffrage, they could not develop political machines that would distribute jobs and resources to African Americans. Freed slaves, then, were subjected not just to personal discrimination, but to a *structural* discrimination that made it likely that they would fall behind white immigrants in the North—not because African Americans lacked the work ethic or supportive families, but because they were denied access to the assets, economic opportunities, and associations enjoyed by their Northern white counterparts.[34]

Women, Policy, and the War

Curiously, abolitionism and the Civil War were associated with policy issues affecting women. Many women entered the world of politics by participating in temperance, charity, and church movements in the antebellum period, though they often occupied decidedly subordinate positions, in separate women's auxiliaries. The women in the abolitionist movement were more daring. Many of them defied the widespread custom that women could not engage in public speaking to mixed audiences, despite jeers from skeptical audiences, and were so bold as to sign public petitions, despite Congress's consideration of legislation in 1834 to disallow petitions signed by women. Numerous women became leaders in the abolitionist crusade.

These abolitionist leaders, often with support from male abolitionists, applied the logic of emancipation to themselves and began to question traditional marriage vows that required women to pledge obedience, as well as sexist language in the Bible and hymns, discriminatory property laws, and the condescension of males. As we discussed in Chapter 4, a small number of women and men held the first convention devoted to women's rights in 1848 in Seneca Falls, New York, where they issued a declaration of principles that advocated changes in property laws to allow married women to inherit their husband's property and to keep earned wages. They also sought liberalization of divorce laws and universal suffrage. These women found their hopes dashed in the wake of the Civil War, however. Having expended enormous energy to emancipate slaves, many of them hoped that women would receive the vote when it was given to freed slaves with passage of the Fourteenth and Fifteenth amendments. But male legislators, many women, and the Republican party were not willing to accept this major policy change.[35]

The women's movement focused on suffrage in the Gilded Age but divided into two factions. The American Women's Suffrage Association circulated petitions that beseeched each of the state legislatures to change their constitutions so as to grant women the vote, whereas the National Women's Suffrage Association sought a range of reforms for women, including passage of a federal constitutional amendment to enact universal suffrage. Both groups were frustrated, despite some modest gains. Most states and the Congress resisted universal suffrage, because of the sexism of the era as well as the determined lobbying of the liquor industry, which was certain that women would support prohibition. The two factions of the women's movement united in 1890 into the National American Women's Suffrage Association but had scant success in obtaining suffrage reforms during the remainder of the century, though some states liberalized property laws and women continued to increase their enrollments in secondary and college education.[36]

SOCIAL POLICY AND INDUSTRIALIZATION

The speed of the American transition from an agricultural to an industrial society was unprecedented in world history; it is only rivaled by the pace of Japanese and Russian industrialization in the mid-20th century. No more than 20% of Americans lived in cities in 1860, and the nation ranked fourth in the world in the value of its manufactured products; in 1920, however, more than 50% of Americans lived in cities, and the nation ranked first in industrial output. Indeed, the total population of urban areas grew from five million in 1860 to 25 million in 1900.

Industrialization Before the Civil War

Industrialization began prior to the Civil War, when most nonagricultural workers were still employed in such skilled crafts as carpentry, blacksmithing and shoemaking. Textile, food-processing, and mining industries, as well as factory-based mass production of shoes, developed in New England in the 1830s and 1840s. Some textile plants located in rural areas, where they employed middle-class women who boarded on the premises; others located in urban areas, where they employed entire families. Even before the Civil War, factory owners used large numbers of children and women to minimize their labor costs, particularly in textile factories. Railroads were rapidly constructed in the North; indeed, by 1840, the United States had laid twice as much track as all of Europe.

In the absence of regulations, workers were subjected to brutal working conditions; they commonly worked for more than 12 hours per day (some worked as many as 15 hours) at abysmally low rates of pay and in unsanitary, dark, and dangerous conditions. Skilled workers who had made entire products in shops or homes before industrialization were often reduced to unskilled tenders of machines.

Industrialization was accompanied by a turbulent economic environment, marked by frequent recessions and cut-throat competition between domestic and foreign enterprises. England tried to sabotage the development of industry in America by imposing tariffs on American imports, by prohibiting the export of technology to America, and by dumping commodities on American markets at artificially low prices. American industrialists, in turn, were vulnerable to bankruptcy, because they accumulated enormous debts to build factories and acquire machinery.[37]

Already considerable in the colonial period, economic hardship in Eastern cities became even more serious as cities grew in size and recessions threw many into unemployment. To make matters worse, factory workers in the growing cities of New England had no fall-back strategies. Distressed farmers could try to maintain a subsistence living through simple bartering or by producing their own food, but urban dwellers often did not own land. Moreover, farmers could survive hard times by selling a portion of their lands or working for other farmers; city dwellers had no such opportunity. Finally, farm families could pool their resources in times of need, but that was not an option for many city dwellers, who were separated from their families. Industrialization spawned other problems, too. Unskilled factory work was repetitive and exhausting; and, because early equipment was often dangerous, work-related injuries were common.[38]

Industrialization During the Gilded Age

For a number of reasons, a truly dramatic acceleration of industrialization occurred during the Gilded Age, which extended from the Civil War to the end of the 19th century. Further expansion of the railroads opened up new markets and supplied agricultural produce and raw materials to the growing urban areas. Funds to build factories and purchase machinery were obtained from foreign sources, as well as a rapidly expanding American banking system.

Massive immigration provided a cheap and plentiful labor supply. From 1860 to 1890, nearly ten million northern European immigrants came to American cities (including three million Germans, two million English, Scottish, and Welsh, and 1.5 million Irish), to join the four million who had immigrated in the 1840s and 1850s. A subsequent wave of immigrants from southern and eastern Europe dwarfed prior immigration; nearly 18 million people arrived between 1890 and 1920. Hungry for cheap labor, industrialists actively resisted any effort to stem this immigration. (We discuss immigrants more fully in Chapter 6.)

Americans obtained a competitive advantage over Europeans because their new plants were able to incorporate rapidly developing technology. Moreover, the American business environment—high tariffs, minimal safety regulations, and low taxes—was very favorable to entrepreneurs. Finally, between 1885 and 1900, the Supreme Court restricted the right of government to regulate corporations, by ruling, for example, that manufacturing did not fall under the jurisdiction of the federal government because it was not "commerce" and that government could only gingerly regulate corporations because their rights were protected by the due process clause of the Fourteenth Amendment, which had originally been enacted to safeguard the rights of freed slaves. The Sherman antitrust legislation, which was enacted in 1890 to restrict corporate monopolies, was applied by the courts to union monopolies! Even the power of the federal government to collect income taxes was declared unconstitutional in a Supreme Court ruling in 1895. It is small wonder, then, that industrialization proceeded rapidly.[39]

Along with industrialization came rapid population growth. Cities expanded at phenomenal rates. Frontier towns, such as Cleveland, Detroit, Pittsburgh, and Chicago, became major industrial centers, and with this growth came increasing social and economic problems. In some cities, packs of wild dogs roamed the streets and maimed or killed children. Typhoid, cholera, and malaria epidemics were common and sometimes decimated the populations of entire cities. Dangerous work conditions led to scores of injuries and deaths. Immigrants were particularly subject to wretched housing and industrial exploitation. The prewar pattern of periodic and devastating recessions continued unabated after the war. Major recessions caused unemployment rates that often exceeded 25% in major cities; indeed, 10% of the population of New

York City was receiving welfare after the recession of 1873. Recessions sometimes lasted for many years; the devastating recession of 1873 (known as the long recession) lasted until 1878. Many people fell behind with their rent and were evicted. Unable to find work in the industrial order and lacking the security of family farms, large numbers of Americans became vagabonds and roamed the countryside. Indeed, 10–20% of Americans in the late 19th century lived in families where someone had "tramped." As they fell on hard times, citizens frequently came into contact with orphanages, workhouses, and police departments.[40]

Perhaps more than in any other period, American society was characterized by extreme economic inequality. Two classes predominated, the laboring and entrepreneurial classes. Because most people were poor, the middle class was small—no more than 16% of wage earners. Factory owners characteristically hired labor on a daily basis at factory gates and retained workers for only brief periods; in many plants, there was a complete turnover of labor each year. Americans of all social classes moved frequently, but transiency was particularly marked among the working class, whose members had to remain mobile to find jobs in an uncertain economy.[41]

In contemporary cities, relatively affluent suburbs encircle low-income urban areas. In the Gilded Age, by contrast, American cities were not segregated by social class. Because industry was located in the centers of cities, most people lived nearby to get access to work. The large ethnic enclaves—Irish, Italian, Jewish, and others—were overwhelmingly poor, but contained an array of small businesses, churches, and voluntary associations.

Prior to the Civil War, industrialization had been marked by the development of small industries. In the latter part of the century, however, massive corporations were formed and systematically drove small competitors out of business. Not content to concentrate on making one product, many tycoons bought related companies. Andrew Carnegie coupled his steel empire with railroad and mining interests, and John D. Rockefeller extended his oil empire to include railroads and refineries. Massive cartels monopolized the production of certain products, charged exorbitant prices, and conspired to bankrupt competitors.

The Failure of Regulation

Reformers obtained some policy victories during the Gilded Age, including the establishment of limits on the working hours of federal employees, local housing regulations, some local regulations on the working conditions of women and children, establishment of the Interstate Commerce Commission, and passage of the Sherman antitrust legislation. However, these policies did not begin to match the magnitude of social needs. Many jurisdictions did not enact regulations on industry, housing, public health, or employers' labor practices. Unemployment insurance, workmen's compensation, or pensions for the elderly were hardly discussed. The Interstate Commerce Commission was not able to regulate railroads, because it was not given formal powers or sufficient resources to accomplish its task.[42] The ineffectiveness of the Sherman Antitrust Act, enacted in 1890, was illustrated by the acceleration of the development of cartels after its passage.

Intolerance of poor persons increased after the disastrous depression of 1873. As the frontier closed and cities swelled with poor immigrants, many Americans feared that this growing class of landless persons could disrupt existing institutions and supported the repression of unions and strikes, as well as the suppression of "foreign radicals." At the same time, there was a surge in punitive policies toward Native Americans and freed slaves, whom many Americans believed to be unreceptive to educational and moral-uplift projects.[43]

The nation seemed to be returning to the mercantile policies of the colonial period. Land subsidies to railroads, high tariffs to discourage imports, subsidies to shipping industries and telegraph lines, and public funding of improvements to rivers and harbors were motivated by a desire to build America's economy. Colonial mercantilism had been a top-down policy, in which top officials and royalty engineered tariffs and subsidies to help the national economy and unemployed citizens. The bottom-up mercantilism of the Gilded Age was prompted by political pressures from corporations, which made flagrant use of bribes and lobbying to advance their economic interests.

Although no nation had developed advanced policies to assist industrial workers, to upgrade cities, and to help persons who experienced unemployment, European societies were beginning to fashion social policies to mitigate the social and economic hardships that accompanied industrialization. The English Parliament, for example, enacted factory regulations in 1833, 1844, 1847, 1853, 1867, 1874, and 1878, as well as many public health measures. Germany enacted old-age pensions and unemployment insurance in the 1880s. The United States, which had pioneered suffrage, land distribution, and public education, lagged behind other nations in enacting social reforms.[44]

Most historians—and the first two editions of this book—have emphasized that the federal government adopted virtually no ameliorative policies during the Gilded Age, when the reluctance of the American response to social needs was particularly evident. Sociologist Theda Skocpol has recently argued that the federal government authorized generous social spending for veterans' pensions after the Civil War. She notes that "this was not merely a military program" and that the government continued to make substantial outlays on pensions—one-fourth (or more) of its expenditures—until well into the 20th century. Eventually, she contends, the pensions became virtually an old-age pensions program; by 1910, 28% of all men aged 65 and over received federal benefits averaging $189 per year.[45]

Skocpol overreaches, however, when she argues that these pensions constituted major involvement in social policy by the federal government. While the pensions may have absorbed one-fourth or more of the federal budget, the federal budget itself was so meager that the nation devoted only 5.5% of its GNP to public spending (at all levels of government) in 1920, as compared to 25.5% for France and 19.1% for Great Britain.[46] (While some Civil War veterans had died by 1920, their numbers were

FIGURE 5.1   Spindle boys in a Georgia cotton mill

SOURCE: © Lewis Hines/Bettmann

INSERT 5.3   CRITICAL ANALYSIS: THE CONSERVATIVES' CONTRADICTION

We have noted how, with the victory of Jefferson in 1800, a limited vision of American government triumphed over Hamilton's perspective that government should actively intervene in the economic order to promote trade and economic growth. By the Gilded Age, industrialists publicly favored limited government. Yet they often used the power of government to advance their own economic interests—by supporting some policies (like tariff and tax policies) and opposing others (like regulations to require safe working conditions, to support union organizing, or to help unemployed workers). This contrast between word and deed has been called the conservatives' contradiction.

Discuss the causes of this contradiction. In light of industrialists' success in getting assistance from government, was the government truly limited in the Gilded Age?

Discuss examples of conservatives' use of government to advance their economic and political interests in the United States today.

augmented by large numbers of veterans of World War I.) One-fourth of such a small federal budget is not very much spending. Nor did the pensions breach the constitutional delegation of social programs to local governments, because the benefits were linked to a national war, which clearly belonged within the purview of the federal government. It was not until the New Deal of the 1930s that the federal government took a major role in social policy—and increased its social spending sufficiently to signal a sharp departure from its limited role in the previous 150 years.

Corporations and financiers took advantage of a power and policy vacuum after the Civil War. When the nation began to industrialize rapidly, agricultural interests were placed on the defensive and were fragmented. Unions would have been a logical countervailing force to business, but they were extraordinarily weak and focused on crafts and skilled trades rather than on unskilled workers in factories. Unions were organized by geographic locality and sought a basic wage for all skilled workers in that area. Their modest organizing successes in various cities in the 1830s were shattered by the recession of 1833, which allowed employers to violate agreements, to fire union members, and to hire nonunion members. There were a number of strikes and riots by factory workers in specific locations, but few unions larger than specific work sites developed. American courts, which began a pattern of rulings that severely limited the ability of

unions to organize, often declared unions to represent unlawful conspiracies or to violate the rights of workers by coercing them to enlist. Many American economists believed as well that the "unnatural" wage increases obtained by unions decreased economic growth, by absorbing funds from the pool of investment capital.[47]

Economists' theories hardly deterred workers from striking: Between 1881 and 1905, 7 million workers participated in 37,000 strikes. Some Americans began to fear that the nation was headed toward class war. After the Civil War, unions of unskilled workers were ruthlessly suppressed. Armed guards beat up strikers or intimidated union organizers. Owners of some Colorado mines forcibly placed strike leaders on a train to Arizona and told them not to come back. Industrialists found powerful allies in government and courts. Local politicians frequently used police and local militia to break strikes, and they were soon joined by federal officials, who used the national guard and federal troops. In 1877, President Hayes mobilized federal troops to break a national strike against the railroads in which nearly 100 people died as rioters torched railroad facilities. Other sensational strikes punctuated the 1880s and 1890s. In the 1886 Haymarket Square riot in Chicago, for example, policemen and strikers were killed. In the Pullman Strike of 1894, federal troops quelled a strike against the railroads, but only after 700 freight cars were burned and 13 people died.

Recessions and immigration frustrated the work of union organizers by breaking their momentum. Waves of immigrants provided industrialists with an inexhaustible source of cheap labor, which they used to break strikes and to depress wages. The weakness of unions in the late 19th century is illustrated by the strange saga of the Knights of Labor, a national organization that organized district assemblies of skilled and unskilled workers from many trades. The Knights engaged in secret rituals, often opposed unions and strikes on the grounds that brotherhood would solve industrial problems, and supported the development of self-employment and cooperative schemes. Although the Knights often supported progressive social legislation, their ideology precluded the development of effective pressure on industrialists.[48]

Corporate interests became major contributors to the Democratic and Republican parties at local and national levels and used campaign contributions to obtain antiunion legislation, defeat adverse regulations, obtain tax concessions, and get government contracts. The weakness of governmental institutions and the lack of competing groups, such as unions and agriculture, allowed corporate and banking interests to dominate the political field and to secure favorable policies.

Social reform was also impeded by changes in popular culture. Prior to the Civil War, many Americans had believed that the primary purpose in life was to lead a virtuous existence, which might lead to social mobility; most persons, it was widely believed, were destined to remain in relatively humble positions. Americans continued to emphasize moral virtues after the Civil War, but they placed far more emphasis on social mobility. Although pauperism had always been reviled, many Americans came to believe after the Civil War that poverty was itself an indication of personal failing. Increasingly, affluent persons were honored as models of success, who inspired Americans of humbler origins to redouble their efforts. The Calvinist ambivalence about wealth, which was both revered as a sign from God of His pleasure and feared as a corrupter of moral virtue, was increasingly transformed into unambiguous worship of wealth.[49]

This shift in culture was reflected in the stature of Herbert Spencer, an English writer who popularized and applied to society the theories of the English naturalist Charles Darwin. Darwin had fashioned a theory of the evolution of animal and plant forms to explain how different species emerged. He maintained that genetic mutations can provide some individuals within a species with a competitive edge, which allows them to survive— and breed—more effectively than other members of the species. As these new characteristics are perpetuated from generation to generation through natural selection, adaptive mutations thus lead to modification of the species. Spencer theorized that genes also influence how persons fare in society. He argued that persons who excel in business or other endeavors, much like animals or plants that survive in nature, possess superior genetic characteristics. His logic led him to conservative political conclusions: If affluent classes possess superior genes, he asked, should not society allow their numbers to increase, while adopting policies to bring reductions in the numbers of low-income persons? By propping up ne'er-do-wells, in Spencer's view, governments and social agencies were artificially and wrongly interfering with natural selection within the social order.[50]

Spencer's use of Darwinian theory represented a sloppy and misguided application of biological theories to society. Poverty and other social ills are caused by innumerable factors, including environmental and societal conditions, as is illustrated by the plight of people of color in the United States in the 19th century. No evidence has been found by contemporary scientists to suggest that groups— whether social classes or ethnic groups—possess genetic characteristics that predispose them to inferior educational and economic performance. (In 1994, reviving some very old ideas, Richard Herrnstein and Charles Murray argued in their book *The Bell Curve* that genetic characteristics caused "lower intelligence" among African Americans. However, the book's poor methodology and flawed data drew extensive criticism from social scientists.[51])

The influence of Spencer in the Gilded Age should not be exaggerated, however. Many Americans did not read him, and others ignored those portions of his teachings that urged the elimination of social programs. But his deification of affluent persons struck a responsive chord with many Americans during a period of phenomenal economic growth. Where Americans had once romanticized yeomen farmers, they now glorified affluent industrialists and businessmen within urban settings. Industrialists could not have wished for a more receptive environment!

 ## THE ABSENCE OF A WELFARE STATE

The three central experiences of this era—the frontier, the Civil War, and industrialization—posed different social welfare challenges. Each benefited many persons, yet each created social casualties—in particular, displaced Native Americans and Spanish-speaking persons, destitute farmers, and exploited laborers (the frontier); freed slaves and poor white refugees (the Civil War); and workers who were unemployed, underpaid, or disabled (industrialization).

Americans during the Gilded Age glamorized the successes, paid relatively little attention to the casualties, and chose not to construct policies to alleviate suffering. The nation virtually pursued a policy of genocide toward Native Americans and Spanish-speaking persons. Asian and Latino laborers were deprived of their fundamental rights and subjected to virulent racism in local communities. Freed slaves were left to wander in a racist society and were given scant assistance as they made the difficult transition from slavery to freedom. Industrialists had a free hand to exploit workers—including women and children—in dangerous working environments.

American interpretations of the frontier, the Civil War, and industrialization are striking in their similarity. Americans idealized the frontier as a place where Christian religion and values were defended against savages; they viewed industrialization as an American success story, in which self-made men rose to prominence by dint of hard work; and they perceived the Civil War as the triumphs of morality over the greed of slaveholders and of nationalism over the renegade Southern secessionists. By idealizing positive outcomes of these experiences, Americans more easily rationalized or denied the suffering that accompanied them.

Many Americans interpreted the negative outcomes of these three experiences in a manner that blamed their victims rather than American social institutions and values. In this interpretation, Native Americans caused their own demise by not farming land or by unleashing "unprovoked" attacks on white settlers. Their problems, settlers reasoned, surely arose because of their savage nature rather than because the settlers took their land. Asians and Latinos were perceived as the bearers of alien religious and cultural traditions that imperiled the culture of the white settlers; white laborers were apt to accuse them of stealing scarce jobs. Most Americans believed that the slaves, once freed, were given the same "fair shake" that had been extended to white immigrants; their lack of economic success was commonly attributed to personal shortcomings rather than to the racism of their society or the intrinsic difficulties in making a transition from slavery. Likewise, it was widely believed that any person in industrial society could achieve social mobility by working hard; consequently, union demands for fair pay were often viewed as the work of foreign agitators who wanted to introduce alien socialist institutions.

Moral treatment was an intervention based on the assumption that the moral character of individuals was the most potent factor in shaping their destinies, but this assumption was untenable when applied to landless, uneducated, and impoverished former slaves, who were released into a Southern society that detested them; to Native Americans, whose land was taken by false treaties or violence; and to the urban poor, who were at the mercy of exploitative employers and an unstable economy.

Few Americans in this era could even envision a major and ongoing social policy role for the federal government. The federal civil rights legislation, the

Freedmen's Bureau, and the stationing of troops in the South represented remarkable departures from the limited role of the federal government prior to the war, but these were ultimately regarded as temporary measures. Lacking a tradition of federal intervention, Americans were disinclined to regulate the emerging industrial order or to develop federal policies to distribute free lands to impoverished persons. While the federal government did enact pensions for Civil War veterans, as we have seen, these expenditures were very limited and did not set a precedent for an expanded federal role in social welfare.

Each of the three central experiences of this era also unleashed powerful political forces that prevented Americans from grappling with social problems. In the decades following the Civil War, the powerful and affluent agricultural interests who had instituted slavery regained their power in the South, established a strong Southern constituency for the Democratic party, and successfully bargained in the Congress for withdrawal of Northern troops and lifting of federal pressure to honor the civil and voting rights of freed slaves. (They were aided by Northern entrepreneurs who bought, sold, and profited from Southern cotton and tobacco and favored the use of the former slaves as cheap labor.) American land policy at the frontier empowered speculators, white settlers, and railroads, who pressured public authorities to repress Native Americans or to place them on reservations. A new and powerful class of entrepreneurs created by industrialization resisted unions and regulatory policies of the government.

By the end of the 19th century, Americans had developed a conservative consensus that embraced moralistic and punitive stances toward persons in poverty, embodied a restrictive concept of social obligation, portrayed social problems as temporary rather than endemic to the social fabric, and favored limited government. Especially striking, however, was the inability of most Americans to support compensatory strategies to help populations that needed special assistance. Most Americans believed that government risked favoritism if it singled out specific groups for assistance. No group in American history possessed such desperate needs as the freed slaves, whose economic problems stemmed so clearly from the horrors of slavery. The disinclination of Americans to use compensatory strategies in cases of obvious need during the 19th century represents a legacy of lost opportunity that has influenced social welfare policy to this day.

Indeed, the major policy roles of the federal government in the Gilded Age involved concessions to corporations. It repressed strikes on key occasions, issued rulings that chilled union organizing, gave huge land grants to railroads, raised tariffs to protect manufacturing (often at the expense of consumers), and failed to enact regulations—such as safe-working standards—that curbed the greed of corporations.

NOTES

1. Jack Sosin, *The Revolutionary Frontier, 1763–1783* (New York: Holt, Rinehart & Winston, 1967); Malcolm Rohrbough, *The Land Office Business: The Settlement and Administration of American Public Lands, 1789–1837* (New York: Oxford University Press, 1968), pp. 200–220.

2. Rohrbough, *The Land Office Business,* pp. 200–220.

3. Ibid., pp. 190–199.

4. Reginald Horseman, *Race and Manifest Destiny* (Cambridge, Mass.: Harvard University Press, 1981), pp. 116–138.

5. Stephen Jay Gould, *The Mismeasure of Man* (New York: Norton, 1981), p. 74.

6. Horseman, *Race and Manifest Destiny,* pp. 154–155, 220.

7. Angie Debo, *History of the Indians of the United States* (Norman, Okla.: University of Oklahoma Press, 1970), pp. 90ff.

8. Ibid., pp. 102ff; Robert Berkhofer, *The White Man's Burden: Images of the American Indian from Columbus to the Present* (New York: Knopf, 1978), pp. 157–165.

9. Carey McWilliams, *North from Mexico: The Spanish-Speaking People of the United States* (New York: Greenwood Press, 1968), pp. 98–105, 169–183; Richard Slotkin, *The Fatal Environment:*

The Myth of the Frontier in the Age of Industrialization, 1800–1890 (New York: Atheneum, 1985), pp. 161–207; and Rodolpho Acuna, *Occupied America: The Chicano's Struggle Toward Liberation* (San Francisco: Canfield Press, 1972), pp. 105–106.

10. Debo, *History of the Indians,* pp. 133ff.

11. Berkhofer, *White Man's Burden,* pp. 166–175; Debo, *History of the Indians,* pp. 276ff.

12. Ronald Takaki, *Strangers from a Different Shore* (Boston: Little, Brown, 1989), pp. 1–11, 79–131, 179–229.

13. James Davis, *Frontier America, 1800–1840: A Comparative Demographic Analysis of the Frontier Process* (Glendale, Calif.: Arthur H. Clark Co., 1977), pp. 15–17; Slotkin, *The Fatal Environment,* pp. 47, 281.

14. Kenneth Stampp, *The Imperiled Union: Essays on the Background of the Civil War* (New York: Oxford University Press, 1980), pp. 191–245.

15. James McPherson, *Ordeal by Fire: The Civil War and Reconstruction* (New York: Knopf, 1982), pp. 42, 72.

16. Stampp, *The Imperiled Union,* p. 192.

17. Lawrence J. Friedman, *Gregarious Saints: Self and Community in American Abolitionism, 1830–1870* (Cambridge: Cambridge University Press, 1982), pp. 168–169; James McPherson, *The Struggle for Equality* (Princeton, N.J.: Princeton University Press, 1964), pp. 147–148.

18. Friedman, *Gregarious Saints,* pp. 169–178; McPherson, *The Struggle,* pp. 143–147.

19. Charles Sellers, *The Market Revolution: Jacksonian America, 1815–1846* (New York: Oxford University Press, 1991), pp. 399–400.

20. McPherson, *Ordeal by Fire,* pp. 278–279; John Hope Franklin, *From Slavery to Freedom* (New York: Knopf, 1974), pp. 275–280.

21. McPherson, *Ordeal by Fire,* pp. 394–396; McPherson, *The Struggle,* pp. 189–191.

22. McPherson, *Ordeal by Fire,* pp. 509–511.

23. Ibid., pp. 396–398, 506–509, 579–580; McPherson, *The Struggle,* pp. 407–416.

24. McPherson, *Ordeal by Fire,* pp. 391–392, 476; McPherson, *The Struggle,* pp. 308–314.

25. Mark Neely, *The Last Best Hope of Earth* (Cambridge, Mass.: Harvard University Press, 1993), pp. 178–181.

26. McPherson, *Ordeal by Fire,* pp. 497–503, 513–533.

27. Ibid., pp. 543–546, 566–567, 576–577.

28. C. Vann Woodward, *Reunion and Reaction: The Compromise of 1877 and the End of Reconstruction* (Boston: Little, Brown, 1951), pp. 12–13.

29. John Franklin, "Public Welfare in the South During the Reconstruction Era," *Social Service Review,* 44 (December 1970), 379–392; Michael Perman, *The Road to Redemption: Southern Politics, 1869–1879* (Chapel Hill, N.C.: University of North Carolina Press, 1984), pp. 22–25.

30. Perman, *The Road to Redemption,* pp. 50–56, 149–178; Friedman, *Gregarious Saints,* pp. 264–280.

31. McPherson, *The Struggle,* pp. 256–259, 386–397, 407–412.

32. Franklin, *From Slavery,* pp. 324–338.

33. C. Vann Woodward, *The Strange Career of Jim Crow* (New York: Oxford University Press, 1957).

34. J. Owens Smith, *The Politics of Racial Inequality: A Systematic Comparative Macro-Analysis from the Colonial Period to 1970* (New York: Greenwood Press, 1987), pp. 105–126.

35. Eleanor Flexner, *Century of Struggle: The Women's Rights Movement in the United States* (Cambridge, Mass.: Harvard University Press, 1975), pp. 44–45, 71–77, 145–154.

36. Nancy Woloch, *Women and the American Experience* (New York: Knopf, 1984), p. 195.

37. David Brody, *Workers in Industrial America: Essays on the Twentieth-Century Struggle* (New York: Oxford University Press, 1980), pp. 3–9; Eric Foner, *History of the Labor Movement in the United States,* Vol. 1 (New York: International Publishers, 1955), pp. 51–53.

38. Richard Bushman, "Family Security in the Transition from Farm to City, 1750–1850," *Journal of Family History,* 6 (Fall 1980), 238–256.

39. Thomas Cochran, *The Age of Enterprise: A Social History of Industrial America* (New York: Harper & Row, 1961), pp. 129–153; Edward White, *The American Judicial Tradition: Profiles of Leading American Judges* (New York: Oxford University Press, 1976), pp. 86, 100–105; and Robert Steamer, *The Supreme Court in Crisis: A History of Conflict*

(Amherst, Mass.: University of Massachusetts Press, 1971), pp. 143–149.

40. Paul Boyer, *Urban Masses and the Moral Order in America, 1820–1920* (Cambridge, Mass.: Harvard University Press, 1978), pp. 123–131; Foner, *History of the Labor Movement,* Vol. 1, pp. 439–474; Herbert Gutman, "The Failure of the Movement by the Unemployed for Public Works in 1873," *Political Science Quarterly,* 80 (June 1975), 254–277; and Thomas Sugrue, "The Structures of Urban Poverty: The Reorganization of Space and Work in Three Periods of American History." In Michael Katz, ed., *The "Underclass" Debate: Views from History* (Princeton, N.J.: Princeton University Press), pp. 91–92.

41. Michael Katz, Michael Doucet, and Mark Stern, *The Social Organization of Early Industrial Capitalism* (Cambridge, Mass.: Harvard University Press, 1982), pp. 14–63, 102–130.

42. Stephan Skowronek, *Building a New American State: The Expansion of National Administrative Capacities, 1877–1920* (Cambridge: Cambridge University Press, 1982), pp. 150–160.

43. Gutman, "The Failure"; Slotkin, *The Fatal Environment,* pp. 477–498.

44. Derek Fraser, *The Evolution of the British Welfare State: A History of Social Policy Since the Industrial Revolution* (New York: Barnes & Noble, 1973), pp. 1–22; Deltev Zollner, "Germany." In Peter Kohler and Hans Zacher, eds., *The Evolution of Social Insurance, 1881–1981* (New York: St. Martins Press, 1981), pp. 4–33.

45. Theda Skocpol, *Social Policy in the United States: Future Possibilities in Historical Perspective* (Princeton, N.J.: Princeton University Press, 1995), pp. 37–71.

46. Carolyn Webber and Aaron Wildavsky, *A History of Taxation and Expenditure in the Western World* (New York: Simon and Schuster, 1986), p. 451.

47. Foner, *History of the Labor Movement,* Vol. 1, pp. 77–81, 101–113; Sidney Fine, *Laissez-Faire and the General Welfare State: A Study of Conflict in America, 1865–1901* (Ann Arbor, Mich.: University of Michigan Press, 1956), pp. 52–64.

48. Leon Fink, *Workingmen's Democracy: The Knights of Labor and American Politics* (Urbana, Ill.: University of Illinois Press, 1983), pp. 3–17; Foner, *History of the Labor Movement,* Vol. 2, pp. 47–92.

49. Carl Kaestle, *Pillars of the Republic: Common Schools and American Society, 1780–1860* (New York: Hill and Wang, 1983), pp. 36–39, 92.

50. Richard Hofstadter, *Social Darwinism in American Thought* (Boston: Beacon Press, 1955), pp. 41–50.

51. Richard Herrnstein and Charles Murray, *The Bell Curve: Intelligence and Class Structure in American Life* (New York: Free Press, 1994). For a critique of Murray's work, see the essay review by Leon Kamin, "Behind the Curve," *Scientific American* (February 1995), pp. 99–103.

6

C H A P T E R

Social Reform
in the Progressive Era

Selected Orienting Events

1882	Chinese Exclusion Act passed by Congress
1886	Formation of the American Federation of Labor (AFL) with Samuel Gompers as president
1889	Jane Addams establishes Hull House
1890s	Populist movement in rural areas
1890	Establishment of the National American Women's Suffrage Association
1893–1896	Depression of 1893 causes severe unemployment
1896	The Supreme Court legitimizes separate facilities for African Americans in its *Plessy* v. *Ferguson* decision
1899	Legislation establishing juvenile courts enacted in Illinois and Colorado
1901–1908	Presidency of Theodore Roosevelt
1904	National Committee on Child Labor organized
1905	Formation of Industrial Workers of the World (IWW)
1909	Initiation of the Pittsburgh Survey by Paul Kellogg; White House Conference on Care of Dependent Children
1909–1912	Presidency of William Howard Taft
1911	Fire at the Triangle Shirtwaist Company in New York City
1911–1920	Most states enact mothers' pension legislation, and many states enact workmen's compensation
1912	Unsuccessful Bull Moose campaign by Theodore Roosevelt and the Progressive party; Children's Bureau established
1913–1920	Presidency of Woodrow Wilson
1914–1918	World War I (entry of United States in 1917)
1916	Margaret Sanger opens first birth control clinic in New York City; passage of child-labor legislation by Congress
1918	Supreme Court overrules federal child-labor legislation
1920	Nineteenth Amendment to the Constitution grants suffrage to women
1921	Enactment of Sheppard-Towner legislation
1924	Enactment of Immigration Act of 1924

Quiescence was shattered in the 1890s, when a rural reform movement known as populism mobilized farmers of the Midwest and South to protest low agricultural prices, high interest rates, excessive charges by granaries and railroads, and profiteering by food processors. As the populists lashed out against bankers, Wall Street, and corporations, they obtained a variety of regulatory measures in local and state jurisdictions and developed cooperative storage facilities. Their reform momentum died as quickly as it had started, however, when farm prices improved, limits were placed on rates of railroads, and cooperatives were developed. Moreover, since populism was a rural movement, its impact on urban reform was negligible.

Urban reform had to await the turn of the century, when a reform movement known as progressivism developed. It was not a focused reform movement but embraced a variety of antimonopoly, city beautification, civil service, governmental, and social reforms. Progressives advocated prohibition, laws to outlaw prostitution, and efforts to limit immigration, along with policies to limit child labor, correct unsafe working conditions, and obtain unemployment insurance.

The number of reform projects that were included within the progressive movement makes it difficult to establish a profile of the typical progressive reformer. Many were middle-class Americans bewildered by the emergence of massive corporations, big-city bosses, and large urban immigrant populations; however, many affluent Americans, political machines, and trade unions also supported various progressive reforms. Progressivism was not dominated by members of the Democratic or Republican party. Despite its amorphous nature, progressivism was the first sustained reform movement in the United States that addressed a variety of urban issues.

REALITIES IN INDUSTRIAL SOCIETY

Immigrants bore the brunt of industrialization in Northern and Midwestern cities. Around 21 million of the total U.S. population of 92 million in 1914 were immigrants who had arrived since 1880. Major American cities consisted of separate ethnic settlements, each with its own churches, political machines, and newspapers. In the 12 largest cities, 40% of the population consisted of immigrants, and another 20% consisted of second-generation descendants; altogether, 60% of the U.S. industrial labor force was foreign born.[1]

Whereas immigrants prior to 1885 had largely come from northern and western Europe, so-called new immigrants from 1885 to 1924 predominantly came from southern and eastern Europe, particularly Italy, eastern Europe, and Russia. Most Italian immigrants were rural peasants who had been forced to leave villages by an agricultural depression, rising taxes and rents, and competition from factories that mass-produced products that the peasants formerly made in their homes and shops. Husbands or unmarried men often emigrated in hopes of returning to Italy with resources gained in the United States, but ultimately they often decided to pay the transportation costs of relatives, families, and brides. (In 1908, however, after a bad recession, as many Italians returned to Italy as entered the United States.) Russian Jews, by contrast, were mostly artisans and small merchants whose earnings had been eroded by competition with industrial products and who suffered appalling persecution. Entire Jewish families emigrated, usually with little desire to return. Both Italians and Jews were wooed by steamship companies, whose salesmen promised prosperity for the price of a ticket. But word of mouth was the primary recruiter, as preceding immigrants revealed that American life—though harsh in the industrial cities—was better than conditions in their homelands. As they streamed in torrents along roads to seaports, they were often robbed by bandits, only to then endure the epidemics of the steamship passage.[2]

Many immigrants were shocked to find themselves in dark and crowded tenements in Eastern and Midwestern cities, which differed from the outdoor living of their native villages. A typical apartment contained two or three rooms with no bathroom or inside toilet; people bathed in a large tub in the kitchen. They moved frequently in response to job markets, to find less exploitative landlords, or to escape eviction.

Traditionally, historians have viewed industrialization as ruining the homogeneous villages of agrarian society and replacing them with urban ethnic enclaves that were unpleasant places to live. To be certain, different ethnic groups *did* establish their own enclaves; for example, Polish, Jewish, and Italian areas were remarkably separate from one another. Moreover, these enclaves possessed many social problems. In the absence of public health regulations and modern refrigeration, food poisoning was commonplace. Medications sold on street corners and in pharmacies were touted as cure-alls for many conditions but often contained toxic substances or had no medicinal value. Residents lived in fear of devastating fires. The hastily constructed wooden tenements, many of them home to hundreds of families, were potential incinerators in the absence of housing codes. In some cases, entire sections of cities burned, as in Chicago in 1871 and in San Francisco after the 1906 earthquake. The fire at the Triangle Shirtwaist Company in New York City in 1911 killed 146 girls and women, many of whom were impaled on iron fences after they leaped from a ten-story building with no fire escapes. This catastrophe mobilized pressure for fire and occupational safety regulations. High levels of crime existed in American cities. Street gangs from different ethnic enclaves preyed on one another.

Despite these problems, however, we should not overlook immigrants' ability to craft a range of institutions to help them cope with adversity. The immigrants brought with them their customs, which differed markedly from American practices (see Figure 6.1). Children and adolescents were subject to strict discipline and generally remained with their families until they married. Daughters' marriages were often arranged by the family. Although fathers had ultimate authority, mothers collected the paychecks of all working members, purchased household goods, and parceled out sums to each family member. The immigrants shopped in crowded outdoor markets or from ever-present peddlers who sold produce on the streets. They

FIGURE 6.1 The ethnic European urban community in America: German-Americans participating in a Steuben Day festival

SOURCE: © Rogers/Monkmeyer

paid substantial sums to health-insurance, life-insurance, and funeral-benefit companies. Often with the aid of the Catholic Church, synagogues, or fundraising efforts in their communities, they constructed a range of self-help and benevolent organizations that helped them during adversity. Each of the immigrant groups organized itself, as well, within the political process; they often linked themselves to political machines that provided members of their groups with jobs, protection, and community amenities. Fearing hospitals, which they associated with death, they generally relied on midwives drawn from their own communities, as well as purveyors of folk medicine. The institutions of these urban ethnic enclaves, as well as the jobs and protections they received from political machines, allowed them to cope with a hostile environment in the absence of the governmental social policies that we take for granted today.[3]

Nor were these urban enclaves temporary.

INSERT 6.1 CRITICAL ANALYSIS: NONGOVERNMENTAL INSTRUMENTS

The term *social policy* usually connotes governmental policies, such as legislation and governmental budgets, but immigrants constructed and used an array of *nonpolicy* instruments to protect and advance their interests, such as political machines, self-help organizations, and charitable agencies. Moreover, people often fend off economic hardship by *personal strategies*—for example, by owning assets like homes, purchasing insurance policies, and hiring relatives in family businesses.

Compare and contrast nonpolicy strategies used by persons of low income, such as immigrants in the early 20th century, with strategies used by more affluent people. Even with immigrants' ingenuity in using nonpolicy strategies, was there a level playing field? What kinds of policy enactments, in eras *after* the progressive period, helped people of low income supplement their nonpolicy instruments?

When ethnic groups moved to obtain better housing, they moved en masse to new locations. Though historians once thought that ethnic traditions eroded quickly as immigrants assimilated, it now appears that many ethnic enclaves persisted for generations and their members retained considerable portions of their culture.[4]

Social workers and schools tended to encourage immigrants to adopt American child-rearing practices, medical practices, diet, and clothing and viewed with distaste the immigrants' outdoor markets, which they believed to be unsanitary. When the children of immigrants quickly adopted American customs, conflict erupted within immigrant families, which often pressured children to accept arranged marriages, not to Americanize their names, to date only with chaperones present, and to speak their own dialect.

Unfortunately, social workers did not recognize the immigrants' values and customs as salutary alternatives to the American emphasis on individualism. An ethic of mutual assistance was deeply rooted in the immigrants' culture; they were extraordinarily generous to one another, exchanged job information, formed many ethnic associations, exchanged resources during hard times, and supported political leaders who pledged to help them with jobs and food. Social workers tended to believe that immigrant parents were excessively authoritarian, but each family constituted a small welfare state, in which children's earnings were joined with other family assets and family members cooperated during hard times. The American disdain of the immigrants' diet, which emphasized potatoes or pasta, was equally misdirected, for this diet allowed them to survive with minimal resources.[5]

While their ethnic enclaves helped them cope with adversity, the immigrants encountered an industrial system that oppressed them. By 1900, many jurisdictions placed curbs on the hours of labor, but poor enforcement meant that six-day weeks and 12-hour workdays were commonplace. To override these statutes, moreover, employers sought to persuade workers to sign "voluntary agreements" to work long hours. Immigrants received abysmal wages. Though $15 per week was needed for survival by families in Pittsburgh in 1909, two-thirds of immigrants earned less than $12.50, and half earned less than $10. Barely half the workers in American industry could survive on one paycheck.[6]

Many workers were even more concerned about the dangerous working conditions than about low pay. Industrialization required the use of labor-saving machinery, but these machines lacked safety devices. Roughly 35,000 Americans were killed and 536,000 injured *each* year during the progressive era. In other words, the number of Americans injured in workplace accidents each year was about the same as the total of those killed or injured during the entire Vietnam conflict of the 1960s. Specific industries were particularly hazardous; 328 railroad workers were killed each month in this era, and 46 deaths and 528 injuries occurred in just one steel plant in South Chicago in 1906. American rates of industrial accidents were far greater than rates that existed in European nations, where factory regulations had been enacted and enforced. American workers were not likely to collect funds from their employers when they sued them after industrial accidents, because corporate attorneys were frequently able to delay litigation or to use a variety of legal tactics to place the blame for accidents on the worker. Workers collected in only 15% of disability lawsuits where employers were proven to be negligent.[7]

Employers were unsympathetic to union organizing. Many believed that their work force, much like their equipment and plant, was their personal property, and they feared that wage increases could bankrupt them in the wild and unpredictable economic climate of this period. Employers used a range of tactics to quell unions, such as lockouts, violence, spies, and private police forces. Local governments and courts frequently helped employers by issuing injunctions against strikes; denying permits for union demonstrations or picketing; threatening to deport aliens; and using police to intimidate or repress workers. Trade unions grew from 447,000 persons in 1897 to more than two million persons in 1904, but they were usually relatively weak, because they focused on skilled crafts rather than the unskilled workers who dominated the steel, garment, meat packing, and other basic industries. Nor was it easy for immigrants to organize unions *across* ethnic groups, because they spoke different languages and often possessed considerable prejudice against other nationalities.[8]

Periodic recessions were devastating to workers. In many jurisdictions, 30% of the labor force was unemployed in the depression of 1893, which lasted until 1897 and was a grim forerunner of the Great Depression of the 1930s. Unemployment was not buffered by insurance, Food Stamps, and other programs that contemporary Americans take for granted. Unemployed persons, who often had no savings, were frequently evicted from their homes and had to obtain meager benefits from breadlines or poorhouses. Social conditions can be summarized with the word *insecurity,* particularly for persons in the lower third of the economic lad-

der. Few policies or programs existed to protect persons from disease, poverty, discrimination, disability, crime, fires, and poor living conditions. It often seemed to citizens of humble means that social predators endangered them at every juncture, whether employers who overworked them, businesses who sold them dangerous foods or medicines, or slum landlords who exacted exorbitant rents.

Families were splintered by these adverse economic conditions. When destitute women with young children approached public authorities, they were sometimes told that they could receive assistance only if their children were placed in foster homes or with adoptive agencies, because officials assumed that their own households were unwholesome—or they voluntarily relinquished them because they could not support them. Many children were pressured by their parents to take jobs at an early age. Finally, families were often divided when their individual members went to different cities to seek work.[9]

THE GENESIS OF REFORM

Social Darwinism, the political power of corporations, and the national preoccupation with upward mobility made it seem unlikely, in 1900, that Americans would develop a major reform movement to address social problems. Political institutions seemed impervious to reform. Most state legislators met for a few months in alternate years and devoted themselves to housekeeping matters. Government was dominated at all levels by the use of patronage to obtain nomination to political office, to secure electoral victories, and to obtain governmental employment. In many cities, political machines used ethnic loyalty and the lure of jobs in municipal services to secure the support of ward and precinct workers, who worked to ensure that incumbents were reelected. In local, congressional, and presidential elections, the Democratic and Republican parties delivered nominations to persons who were connected to machines or who could bring corporate donations to the party. In an

INSERT 6.2   CRITICAL ANALYSIS:
CONFRONTING THE (NEARLY) BLANK POLICY SLATE

When analyzing the challenges confronted by reformers at the turn of the 20th century, we should remember that they lived in a society that possessed few of the policies that we take for granted today. Recall the discussion in Chapter 5 about the social problems that accompany industrialization and urbanization, such as unemployment, unsafe working conditions, poor housing, poverty, and victimization of workers. If we conceptualize ameliorative policies to address these problems as a puzzle, we realize that *all* of the pieces in Figure 6.2 were missing in 1900.

Imagine yourself as a reformer in a society that lacked most of these policies, as well as government bureaucracies capable of administering them *or* sufficient taxes to fund them. (Since a federal income tax did not yet exist, the primary governmental revenues derived from local property taxes, which were absorbed by schools and local services such as police departments.) Where would you start? How would you obtain popular support in a nation whose leaders extolled limited government and that lacked strong, grass-roots pressure for social reforms from such groups as organized labor?

Whichever reforms they chose to seek, progressive reformers knew that they would confront determined opposition. Conservatives would argue that many reforms were unconstitutional or too costly—or that they would expand government excessively. Corporate leaders would oppose many of these reforms on the grounds that they would diminish their profits or force tax increases. Even charity workers and private charities would often oppose some reforms—for example, welfare programs—on the grounds that government ought to leave charity in their hands. Often desperate for the funds that their children earned, some immigrants themselves could be expected to oppose curtailment of child labor. Undeterred by these realities, progressive reformers pressed forward. We shall ask in this chapter which pieces in Figure 6.2 they obtained—and which ones they did not obtain. Why did they win certain kinds of reforms, but not others?

era dominated by parties and lobbyists, presidents and governors were relatively weak figures who tended not to initiate legislation but to acquiesce in decisions fashioned in smoke-filled rooms.[10]

It seemed that government could not implement social programs or enforce regulations, even if they could be developed. In the absence of a modern civil service, patronage rather than competitive exams was used to fill most positions. Many bureaucrats could be bribed or intimidated by party officials. Perhaps the most damaging weakness of government, however, was its paltry size; Americans were unwilling to levy sufficient taxes to fund government institutions at any level.

Patterns of party support frustrated efforts to develop social reform. Voting patterns were dictated by complicated sectional and ethnic traditions, so that neither Democrats nor Republicans focused on the needs of the working class. Demo-crats were the dominant party in the South; Republicans had considerable strength in New England; and the two parties divided the votes in the Midwest and West. Various ethnic groups supported one of the two major parties on the basis of local tradition rather than for their positions on social issues.

Catalytic Events

The depression of 1893, which lingered through 1896, had a decisive effect on the nation. It triggered widespread discontent with the Democrats and President Grover Cleveland, who had the misfortune to be in office. Believing that his inactivity and economic policies had caused and sustained the depression, many voters changed their allegiance to the Republican party. (With the exception

FIGURE 6.2 The social reform puzzle

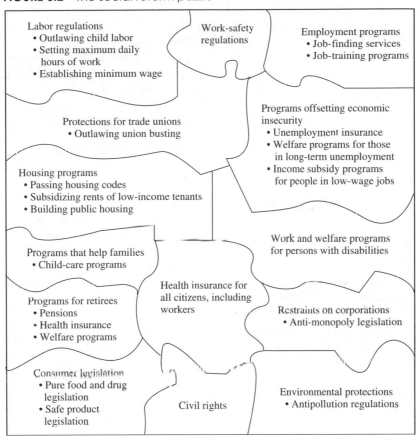

of Woodrow Wilson, who held the presidency from 1913 to 1920, Republicans dominated national politics until the Great Depression of 1929, when the political balance swung back to the Democrats.)[11]

The depression of 1893 also brought widespread disenchantment with corporate tycoons; these heroes of virtue, hard work, and success had not been able to usher in unlimited prosperity, as the script of the Gilded Age had dictated. Their willingness to fire workers, to shut down plants, and to use violent means of suppressing labor strikes during the depression tarnished their reputations. Many Americans read in the newspapers about industrialists' blatant efforts to garner special treatment for themselves and their corporations by bribing public officials or by threatening to relocate to other jurisdictions that promised more favorable tax concessions. Outlandish efforts to bribe politicians and to finance their campaigns were publicized. The flamboyant lifestyles of corporate executives—once considered a just reward for hard work—came to be resented when more than a quarter of adult males were unemployed in many areas.[12]

Some Americans began to wonder whether the fantastic growth of industry was an unlimited blessing. Industrialization had seemed at first to be a kind of new economic frontier that, like the Western frontier, could lead to unlimited opportunities for millions of Americans. But small entrepreneurs were increasingly driven from business by the ruthless tactics of corporate entrepreneurs, who managed to aggregate vast economic empires. Many Americans grew alarmed at the size and power of corporations, which prompted doubts that they could be effectively regulated. Lurid stories about the victimization of hapless workers, women and children among them, tarnished industrialists' reputation. Reports of adulterated food, unsafe medicines, and other defective products convinced many Americans that corporate executives had to be restrained by enactment of regulations. Social reform thrives when culprits are identified; their perceived infamies inflame the passions of the public and inspire efforts to regulate them. As tycoons were forced from their pedestals, they were subjected increasingly to proposals to limit their power over labor, to curtail the size of their companies, and to limit their ability to bribe politicians.

Intellectual Ferment and Public Opinion

The nation's major policy swings have been associated with shifts in emphasis between environmental and personal explanations of social problems. During conservative periods—such as the Gilded Age, the 1920s, the 1950s, and the 1980s—the focus is on personal and moral problems. In reform periods—such as the progressive era, the 1930s, and the 1960s—attention switches to environmental factors. Historians do not know why these tidal swings in public opinion occur.

By the turn of the 20th century, many Americans believed that environmental factors, such as overcrowding, tenements, and poor working conditions, thwarted the healthy development of city dwellers. Many progressives also feared that political machines, large corporations, and widespread corruption threatened democratic institutions. An environmental focus was critical to the development of a reform movement. When the public's attention was drawn to various environmental conditions that were believed to cause social ills, support for social reform to modify those conditions increased.

In the Gilded Age, reform was deterred by the conventional wisdom that the American Constitution was sacrosanct and should be interpreted liter-

ally and that the meaning of life derived from work, competition, and upward mobility.[13] By the late 19th century, however, many Americans questioned these verities. They countered the Social Darwinists' argument that life should be devoted to competition, for example, with the assertion that cooperation and creativity were higher values. Ministers known as social gospellers argued that the gospel required people to help the downtrodden. Social workers like Jane Addams and philosophers like John Dewey believed that people were intrinsically cooperative and became competitive only when they were exposed to environmental cues and models—including an American culture that emphasized winning at all costs. Addams extolled a "cooperative ideal" when she contended that government should try to instill a spirit of cooperation in its citizens, whether through example (by developing social programs, for instance) or through education. She argued that regulations and social programs represented expressions of altruism rather than unwarranted interference in the private affairs of industrialists and citizens.[14]

Addams and other reformers wondered how the competitive and materialistic values of Americans could be transformed. Unlike European radicals and socialists, who romanticized the working class and believed that its victory over bourgeois interests would transform society, Addams idealized different groups at different points in her career. She variously hoped that immigrants would infuse American society with their simple peasant and altruistic virtues; that the creativity and playful virtues of youth would be emulated by others; and that women would transform American society by asserting values of nurturance that stemmed from their family roles. Although each group proved unequal to her high expectations, she seemed never to become disillusioned.[15]

Many reformers also contended that, if unregulated, economic activity created unacceptable levels of social distress. Whereas economic theorists in the 19th century had commonly argued that the natural balance of supply and demand was disrupted when government exacted taxes or regulated hours and working conditions, writers like Richard Ely asserted that, unless regulated, business practices concentrated power in the hands of elites, who consigned workers to poverty and diverted their own wealth into nonproductive ventures such as speculation and corporate takeovers.[16]

A phalanx of theorists questioned provisions of the Constitution and the American legal system. Some argued that the Constitution constructed by the founding fathers adequately addressed the needs of an agricultural republic but was inadequate for an industrial society, which required government to assume an active role in economic and social affairs. Many progressives felt that the Supreme Court did not have the right to overrule progressive social legislation and proposed legislation to circumscribe its powers.[17]

Progressives also began to question whether America was a model society that should be emulated by the rest of the world. The nation *had* led the way in opening opportunities to citizens by enacting universal suffrage, land ownership, and education, but it had lagged in providing security to its citizens. On extensive trips to Europe, social workers Jane Addams and Grace Abbott, as well as other reformers, discovered various social programs and regulations that offered supports for workers and families.[18]

Some reformers obtained extraordinary popularity in the progressive era; in public opinion polls, for example, Jane Addams was voted the most exemplary American. Politicians of both parties who espoused various reforms were elected in large numbers to local, state, and national legislatures. As progressives opened up the political process by allowing voters to place issues (so-called initiatives) on the ballot, many reform measures were enacted even when legislators showed scant interest in them. The sheer number of progressive measures enacted in cities and states attests to the popularity of reform during this period.

Some historians have used concepts from social psychology to explain why middle-class Americans became more interested in reform in certain periods. Richard Hofstadter, for example, argued that middle-class Americans supported reform because they feared that corporations and political machines threatened their economic and social

roles. It seems unlikely, however, that a single motivation explains this swing in public opinion. Different persons and groups probably supported reform for different reasons. Many Americans supported reforms because of personal exposure to social ills: They read about the corruption of officials whom they had elected, trembled when epidemics struck their cities, read about or saw corporate executives' flaunting of power, or ate food or consumed drugs that made them unwell. Religion should not be ignored as a motivating force for reform in the progressive era. Many middle- and upper-class Americans felt guilty about the sorry condition of the bottom third of their society and the victimization of women and children by employers. Some realized, despite their prejudices, that the economic institutions of the nation from which they derived personal benefit were fueled by immigrants' labor.[19]

Furthermore, a pragmatism propelled many Americans toward reform, as they became convinced that conservative policies had not been effective. While conservatives in the progressive era continued to voice the laissez-faire homilies of the Gilded Age, they were on the defensive, because reformers successfully argued that their policies had led to a disastrous depression, the victimization of women and children, and the rise of monopolies. The fruits of capitalism had failed to reach some of the desperately poor immigrants who crowded American cities.[20]

Though portrayed by conservatives as outside agitators or socialists, reformers were able to enlist popular support by employing a symbolism that seemed respectable and American. They spoke of saving the American family, saving children, opening up politics to the people, increasing economic opportunity, and preventing poverty and crime. Many Americans believed that the family was in a state of serious decline, because children and women had to work, women were separated from their children when they applied for assistance, and children were placed in prisons because of the lack of juvenile facilities. Americans also feared that their political institutions were increasingly dominated by political machines or corrupt politicians, and favored proposals to save democracy itself, including the initiative and the civil service. Trust-busting was defended on the grounds that it would enhance economic opportunity for ordinary citizens. Once perceived as addressing these non-controversial goals, reform obtained widespread support.[21]

Many Americans in the progressive era also believed that they were rediscovering their own land. The rhetoric of the Gilded Age had suggested that the nation was free of problems and on a path of unlimited prosperity, democracy, and territorial expansion. By the turn of the century, however, reformers and journalists engaged in a frenzied search for factual evidence of social problems, such as the number of children and women exposed to dangerous working conditions, the number of children placed in adult prisons, the toxicity of many drugs, high rates of infant mortality among specific groups, and instances of political corruption. The appetite for facts and figures was insatiable; the social worker and reformer Paul Kellogg, for example, initiated an exhaustive six-volume survey of social conditions in Pittsburgh that described occupational hazards, housing, health, and other facets of residents' lives.[22]

As social facts were discovered, they were disseminated to the public through popular and professional journals and newspapers. Reforming journalists, popularly known as *muckrakers,* dramatized their findings by highlighting the evil nature of the wrongdoers and the innocence (and vast number) of the victims. Professionals and academics presented findings in more neutral terms. In either case, the general public was fascinated by the endless evidence of wrongdoing and suffering, which bolstered support for reform.

The Specter of Social Unrest

Progressive leaders were largely unconcerned with the possibility of social unrest by the millions of immigrant workers who provided cheap labor for American industry. With notable exceptions, most workers were relatively tranquil in this period, despite their appalling working and living conditions. Immigrants who did not speak English, who

lacked citizenship, who often hoped to return to Europe, and who feared unemployment were not likely to engage in militant protest. Most women were not amenable to strikes because they hoped to work only for a brief period before marrying.

Still, the emergence of fringe—but vocal and radical—organizations, such as the Socialist party and the Industrial Workers of the World, represented a new phenomenon in the nation. Their leaders espoused ideas that departed from the conventional political beliefs of the nation; many advocated political organization of the working class, supported national strikes, favored the nationalization of some industries, and called for a national minimum wage. As we shall see later in this chapter, fringe parties had scant success in obtaining political offices, except at the mayoral level; nonetheless, they constituted a political threat to many Americans, particularly because the unskilled labor force that they sought to organize was so huge. In this climate, many progressives presented themselves as moderates whose sensible and pragmatic reforms would blunt protest and maintain tranquility.

As many scholars have recently analyzed, a dark side of progressivism existed. While often siding with underdogs, many progressives were prejudiced against immigrants, whom they regarded as uncivilized, ignorant, and immoral. Charity workers often wanted to imbue immigrants with middle-class virtues. Progressives who enacted a modest welfare program for women known as mothers' pensions wanted to withhold it from immigrant women until they had been investigated to determine whether they deserved assistance and would use it wisely. Furthermore, many progressives were deeply prejudiced against African Americans, as we shall discuss in more detail later.

REGULATORY REFORMS IN THE PROGRESSIVE ERA

The number of regulations enacted during the progressive era is suggested by Box 6.1, which lists the major progressive reforms that regulated the

BOX 6.1   Selected Regulations Enacted in the Progressive Era

Regulations of Industrialists
- Curtailment of the size of trusts (federal)
- Limitation of working hours of women and children (local)
- Regulation of working conditions in plants (local)

Regulations of the Food and Drug Industry
- Restrictions placed on the content and labeling of food and drugs (federal and local)

Regulations of Developers and Owners of Rental Properties
- Housing codes (local) and development of zoning to govern construction

Regulations of Politicians
- Passage of the initiative, referendum, and recall (local)
- Restrictions on lobbying and campaign contributions (local)
- Limitation of patronage through passage of civil service legislation (local and federal)
- Curtailment of the power of machines and bosses through the establishment of nonpartisan elections and commissions (local)

Protections for Immigrants
- Controls on persons who hire immigrants (federal and local)

Protections for Women
- Curbs on interstate transportation of nonconsenting women to prevent kidnapping for prostitution (federal) and laws to restrict prostitution (local)

Development of Fire Codes
- Controls on construction of industrial facilities as well as housing (local)

Regulations of Taverns and Distilleries
- Enactment of prohibition (local)

Regulations of Immigration
- Many proposals advanced to restrict immigration (federal)

Regulations of Banks
- Laws regulating reserve requirements of banks (federal)

Regulations Governing Professional Activities
- Enactment of licensing laws for medical, dental, legal, and other professional activities (local)

Public Health Regulations
- Laws regulating disposal of sewage and garbage as well as food processing in restaurants (local)

Working Hours of Women and Children
- Laws regulating hours and working conditions of women and children (local and federal)

Working Hours of Federal Employees
- Federal legislation limiting the hours of work of federal employees

political process, banking and economic institutions, conditions of employment, food and drugs, employment of immigrants, and housing. Although most were enacted in local jurisdictions, they also gave state and federal governments new policy roles.

The regulatory emphasis of progressives is understandable in the context of the few social controls on corporations and political and social institutions. In the absence of public regulations, corporations could make products, establish working practices, and subject workers to hazardous conditions. In the absence of public scrutiny, politicians could accept bribes, hire relatives, and tamper with elections. Homer Folks, a reformer in New York State, found that state institutions were rarely audited, that laundry and food concessions were awarded to politicians' friends, that no system of external monitoring existed, and that it was impossible to distinguish staff from residents in some institutions because they were similarly dressed. He conducted a tireless campaign to establish audit, licensing, and monitoring programs for public bureaucracies; to place staff positions under the civil service; to oust political appointees; to establish standards of sanitation; and to enforce existing laws that required children and insane persons to be removed from almshouses. Similar projects were undertaken by many other reformers in other states.[23]

Many of the regulations were obtained only after exhausting political battles. Thus, advocates of child-labor laws, who formed reform organizations in each state as well as at the national level, fought those who argued that these laws violated parental rights, that immigrants needed the earnings of their children to survive, and that child labor prevented the overcrowding of schools. Reformers who sought federal labor laws, such as a minimum wage and maximum hours of work, were told that the Constitution did not give the federal government jurisdiction in social matters.

The regulatory reforms of the era were supplemented by efforts to rationalize the social services system and to develop a social work profession. The reformers viewed with horror the provision of services by amateurs and political appointees. The National Conference of Charities and Corrections sponsored conventions of administrators and staff of agencies to exchange information and provide training. The New York Charity Organization Society established an annual summer course for social workers in 1898, which was followed in 1903 by the formation of the Chicago School of Civics and Philanthropy and in 1904 by the New York School of Philanthropy and the Boston School for Social Workers. By 1919, the leaders of 15 schools of social work had formed the Association of Training Schools for Professional Social Work. These early social workers usually identified with private agencies; they tended to view public institutions as last-resort programs for people in extreme poverty, people with mental disorders, and criminals. However, they increasingly departed from the moralistic ethos of 19th-century social service staff (who had used such value-laden labels as deserving and undeserving) by providing services based on the analysis of familial, personal, and neighborhood

factors that contributed to their clients' problems. Instead of dictating to clients and offering personal models of morality, many social workers sought to develop give-and-take exchanges with clients and local interventions. Social work pioneers hoped to professionalize social programs by credentialing their staff in training programs.[24]

Progressive-era reformers such as Addams, who advocated coupling personal service with public-sector reforms, came into conflict with social workers who believed private agencies should dominate in the provision of outdoor relief and opposed the development of public programs. But this conflict had diminished by 1909, when Addams was selected as president of the National Conference of Charities and Corrections.[25]

THE LIMITED SOCIAL PROGRAMS OF THE PROGRESSIVE ERA

Although many new regulations were passed into law, the few social programs that were enacted underscored the limited nature of social reform in the progressive era, since none of them required the expenditure of large sums of money or the distribution of resources or services to poor persons. The main programs of the day included workmen's compensation, mothers' pensions, juvenile courts, the Children's Bureau, and protections for female workers in various states.

Policy Reforms for Women and Children

The mothers' pension movement swept the nation between 1911 and 1919, when most states developed such programs. Whereas today most single mothers have been deserted, have divorced, or have had children out of wedlock, in the progressive period most single mothers were widows. When they sought governmental assistance for single mothers, progressive reformers focused on the needs of women who had been widowed, in the belief that such women would be viewed more sympathetically than would women who had been divorced or deserted. Without governmental assistance, they contended, single mothers—whether widowed, divorced, or deserted—would have to work such long hours that they could not properly care for their children, and many of them would have to continue to divide their families by sending some of their children to orphanages.

Mothers' pensions can be viewed as a first breach in the American orthodoxy that the government should not provide outdoor relief to people in need. Indeed, many progressives hoped that it would be followed by other programs, such as unemployment insurance and old-age pensions. But mothers' pensions were hardly the far-reaching reform that sociologist Theda Skocpol suggests when she contends that Americans constructed a "maternalist welfare state" in the progressive era. As Linda Gordon notes, these pensions were granted to relatively few women—only 46,000 women nationally by 1919. Residency and citizenship requirements excluded many immigrants. The programs operated with such low appropriations that long waiting lists often existed. Many applicants were screened out as unsuitable due to health problems or poor housing. Even in Los Angeles, with a reputedly generous program, only 24% of single mothers received public or private assistance. Pensions were so miserly, moreover, that large numbers of women who received them *had* to work. While legislation rarely indicated that women with out-of-wedlock children or women who had left their husbands could not receive

mothers' pensions, local administrators could and sometimes did exclude them from the program on the grounds that they were morally undeserving. Many states allowed women to receive assistance even when their husbands were still present, but it is likely that such assistance was given reluctantly, lest it reduce the husband's incentive to work.[26]

Progressives succeeded in obtaining special courts, known as juvenile courts, in many jurisdictions. Prior to this reform, children were tried in adult courts, detained in jails for extended periods, and remanded to adult prisons, even though houses of refuge and legal precedents that exempted minor children from penalties established for adult offenders already existed in the 19th century. In many jurisdictions, children who were less than 14 years of age were exempted from capital punishment and from other penalties, but these exceptions could be waived in certain circumstances. Judge Ben Lindsey in Denver and many social reformers in Chicago and elsewhere believed that mixing children with adult criminals was harmful to children and that confinement did not address familial, school, and other causes of delinquency. Since probation hardly existed as an option, even children who had committed minor offenses were institutionalized.[27]

When children were tried in juvenile courts, judges and staff could explore their family situations, examine a range of options including probation, and, in principle, refer children to special juvenile institutions when they needed to be committed. In practice, however, judges still lacked innovative

INSERT 6.3   ETHICAL ANALYSIS OF KEY ISSUES AND POLICIES: THE STIGMATIZING OF SINGLE MOTHERS

As our discussion of mothers' pensions suggests, single mothers in the early part of the 20th century were viewed as morally suspect by many people, even by many advocates of mothers' pensions.

1. Speculate why single mothers were widely distrusted in American society in the early part of this century. What policies did progressives institute that reflected this suspicion?
2. What policies might progressives have considered that would have had greater ethical merit than mothers' pensions?
3. What similarities exist with contemporary portrayals of mothers on Aid to Families with Dependent Children (AFDC)?

community programs to which they could refer juvenile offenders. Furthermore, funding was insufficient to hire the staff needed, the courts lacked bilingual staff able to converse with immigrant children and parents in their native tongues, and most judges lacked training in social matters.

The idea of establishing a national Children's Bureau originated in 1904 in the National Committee on Child Labor, was reaffirmed in a White House Conference on Care of Dependent Children in 1909, and was finally enacted in 1912; it received the meager budget of $25,640, as compared to the $1.4 million that funded the federal Board of Animal Husbandry. Conservatives hobbled the agency still further by limiting its authority to data gathering and advisory functions that precluded it from providing resources directly to children or to local units of government. Its dedicated social work staff issued many seminal reports in the succeeding years, but the bureau did not provide a frontal attack on the poverty, malnutrition, or poor health of the nation's children; furthermore, the bureau tended to avoid controversial issues, such as national child-labor laws. Its greatest triumph was the enactment in 1921 of the Sheppard-Towner legislation, which provided federal matching funds for states to provide clinics for pregnant women and young children. However, the American Medical Association viewed the program as a competitor to private doctors, and succeeded in precluding programs funded by the legislation from providing medical services; thus, the programs were limited to educational and social services. Even this small program was terminated in 1929 on the grounds that it violated states' rights and represented socialized medicine.[28]

Reformers believed that they had made a lasting breakthrough in 1916 when they finally obtained passage of national legislation to restrict the use of child labor. Specifically, the legislation prohibited interstate commerce of the products of firms that employed children who were less than 14 years of age and mines that employed children less than 16 years of age. However, reformers' hopes were dashed when the Supreme Court nullified the legislation in 1918, on the grounds that the law fell outside the province of interstate commerce, which had been widely regarded as the only way that child-labor laws could be constitutionally legitimized. Although the ruling did not frontally challenge the right of the federal government to regulate child labor, and the staff of the Children's Bureau was able to obtain measures that prevented federal contractors from using child labor during World War I, the ruling had a chilling effect on social reform at the national level.[29] Moreover, in 1922 the Court declared unconstitutional a second anti–child-labor law, enacted in 1919 and based on the national power of taxation.

Progressives did obtain minimum wage legislation for women in 15 states and the District of Columbia by 1923 and legislation that established maximum hours of daily labor in 41 states by 1921. For reasons we shall discuss later, these measures applied only to women; it was not until 1938 that federal legislation that covered all workers was enacted.

Private Philanthropy

When discussing progressives' reforms, we should remember that they did not wish to supplant private philanthropy with publicly funded programs. Used to the sectarian and privately run institutions that evolved in the 19th century, they strongly supported the continuation of these institutions, as well as the construction of hundreds of sectarian hospitals across the nation as physicians developed surgical and diagnostic techniques that shifted medical practice from their offices and patient homes to institutional settings. Indeed, some social workers opposed certain publicly funded programs, such as mothers' pensions, on the grounds that they would wrongly supplant private charity.

Nor did strict boundaries exist between public and private sectors. Mothers' pensions were sometimes administered by private agencies. Judges sometimes committed neglected children to sectarian orphanages. Settlement houses often received contracts from public authorities.

Middle-class progressive reformers who had not personally experienced social problems made determined efforts to live among immigrants by establishing settlement houses in Eastern and Midwestern cities. Hull House, the settlement house that Jane Addams established in 1889, was modeled after Toynbee Hall in London, which had been founded by Arnold Toynbee, an English social reformer. Addams' Hull House was a remarkable institution. She carefully documented living conditions and the ethnicity of area residents, often as a prelude to seeking corrective legislation from local and state governments. She recruited large numbers of volunteers, who provided an array of services to immigrants. Hull House became a mecca for social reformers in the nation and the world, and held numerous seminars on social problems. Addams sought to organize immigrants against the political machine, on the grounds that it was corrupt and did not seek ameliorative reforms. More than 400 settlement houses had been established by 1910, many in white immigrant neighborhoods but some in African American neighborhoods in the North and the South. The settlement houses provided many services and programs, including arts, vocational training, crafts, cultural events, teaching English, preparing immigrants for citizenship, helping unionize workers, registering citizens to vote, and health services. Following Addams's example, the staff of some settlement houses developed surveys of housing and other social conditions in their neighborhoods, as a prelude to seeking regulations.

We should not idealize the settlements, however. While Addams made social action an important part of Hull House's program, other settlements were relatively inactive. Many settlement leaders were condescending to immigrants, whom they regarded as ignorant of hygiene, proper diet, and morality. Some sought to convert immigrants to Protestantism. Imbued with the racism of the period, some leaders moved their settlements out of the neighborhood when African Americans moved in, refused to serve them, charged them fees to keep them from services, or opened separate and segregated facilities for them. (Even Hull House had no African Americans on its board as late as the 1930s.) In an era when government funds were rarely used to provide contracts or grants to nonpublic agencies, the settlements' boards often consisted of affluent people with conservative ideology; this further constrained their social reform work.[30]

Even enlightened settlement staff worked under difficult circumstances. They had to raise funds to support their work, often from conservative people and institutions. The settlements existed in turbulent communities, where successive waves of immigrants moved in and out in complex patterns. The immigrants themselves tended to view the affluent white volunteers and staff as authority figures, and political officials were inclined to view them as competitors for the immigrants' allegiance.

These criticisms of settlements ought not to obscure some of their achievements. Unlike the settlement staff, most affluent white Americans avoided the immigrant enclaves of major cities. Those settlement workers who did engage in social reforms provided a style of work that contrasted with that of other private agencies, which often focused on a narrow casework approach, opposed even to such modest policies as mother's pensions. (We note subsequently that the social reform ideology of some contemporary social workers derives from these distant, settlement-house origins.)

Other Policy Reforms

Employers used a variety of legal defenses to place part or all of the responsibility for work-related injuries on employees. They argued that employees knew about dangers before they took employment; that employees were careless in their work; or that negligence of a fellow employee, rather than negligence of the employer, had caused work-related injuries. Litigation was so time-consuming that workers often died before awards were made to them. Its cost forced many workers into indebtedness and eventually into poor-relief programs. Despite their legal successes, employers also found the costs of litigation to be prohibitive; ever-mounting awards to disabled workers and the costs of liability insurance increased their costs of doing business.

Workmen's compensation laws, which had been adopted by virtually all states by 1920, provided a partial remedy that was acceptable to many employers and to some unions. The laws established a state fund that received its revenues from a payroll tax levied on employers. Workers who were injured were entitled to obtain an award, the amount of which was determined on the basis of the specific type of injuries. Under the legislation, workers usually forfeited their right to sue employers.

Workers soon discovered that workmen's compensation was not a panacea. The payment schedules for specific injuries were appallingly low—indeed, far lower than jury awards that had preceded the enactment of workmen's compensation. Nevertheless, the legislation took the edge off discontent, and consequently pressure to make the workplace safer was eased. Unions were divided in their attitudes to workmen's compensation; some believed this legislation was an improvement, but others believed it helped employers more than workers. Moreover, workmen's compensation covered only bodily injuries; in Great Britain, by contrast, industrial diseases were also covered.[31]

Finally, the progressive era saw the introduction of an initial set of aftercare services for people who had been institutionalized in mental asylums. As late as 1905, virtually no aftercare services existed in the United States; released mental patients had to fend for themselves with no assistance from anyone. Beginning in New York State and expanding to other states, social workers were employed by mental institutions to follow their wards on release and to give them services. Moreover, the work of Clifford Beers, himself a former mental patient who had written about his ordeal in public institutions, led to the establishment of nongovernmental societies for mental hygiene in various states, as well as the National Committee for Mental Hygiene, which pressured public authorities to improve mental hospitals and to develop programs to prevent mental illness.

The Limited Nature of Progressives' Social Reforms

When viewed from the perspective of the 19th century, progressives achieved extraordinary reforms in a brief period of time; they passed a variety of regulations, reforms for women and children, and workmen's compensation. These reforms required sustained effort for a period spanning 20 years.

When viewed from a contemporary perspective, however, the progressives' reforms underscore the reluctance of the American welfare state. Most importantly, progressives' reforms did not require large government expenditures; they did not involve major benefit or service programs. As we have discussed, both mothers' pensions and Sheppard-Towner were minuscule programs. As we noted in Chapter 5, government spending in the United States in 1920 was only 5.5% of the GNP, as compared to 19.1% in Great Britain and 25.5% in France, and a considerable portion of these American expenditures went to veterans' payments—not only to the surviving veterans of the Civil War and the Spanish-American War but to recent veterans of World War I.[32]

Besides the political and cultural barriers to reform, which we shall discuss shortly, another serious obstacle was that state, local, and federal governments lacked revenues to fund major social programs, even had the progressives desired them. We have noted that local property taxes were the primary source of governmental revenues in this period—and they were used primarily for schools and public services. The Congress had enacted a federal income tax in 1894, only to have the Supreme Court declare it unconstitutional. In 1913, to bypass the Court, progressives secured the 16th Amendment to the Constitution, which empowered the Congress "to lay and collect taxes on incomes," but the rates were established at such low levels that most citizens paid no income taxes at all.

CULTURAL AND POLICY REALITIES THAT LIMITED REFORM

Despite their skill in uncovering the devious actions of corporate tycoons and exploiters of powerless populations, progressives were often naive in their approach to social reform. They assumed that regulations would bring dramatic changes when, in fact, they often had negligible effect. The naivete of progressives took two forms. First, their *legalistic bias* made them assume that laws would lead to dramatic changes in the behavior of wrongdoers, though they soon learned that persons and institutions subject to regulations were resourceful in evading them—whether by coopting or bribing government officials or by escaping detection because regulatory agencies lacked funds and staff to adequately monitor compliance.

Furthermore, their *procedural bias* led them to believe that changes in the procedures of government would make government dramatically more responsive to the needs of the people; thus, they fought for the passage of such laws as the initiative, the referendum, and the recall, which, respectively, allowed citizens to place legislation on the ballot; to hold popular votes on measures that had already been enacted by legislators; and to vote from office public officials who were believed to be corrupt or misdirected. These measures assumed that an aroused citizenry would vote for progressive legislation; as reformers soon learned, the same techniques could also be used to recall liberal legislators or to place conservative measures on the ballot. (It is an irony of history that conservative initiatives to cut government social spending, such as California's Proposition 13 in 1978, were one legacy of progressive procedural reforms.)

Few persons in the progressive era would have argued that regulations to control the actions of industrialists, politicians, and landlords were unnecessary. However, a law enforcement approach, which fostered the use of regulatory strategies, precluded the enactment of major programs to deliver resources and services *directly* to these powerless groups. Some progressives sought unemployment insurance, health insurance, and other programs, but many emphasized regulations.

Progressive reformers also diminished their effectiveness by relying on local governments—whether cities, counties, or state legislatures—to take the lead in addressing the mounting social ills of the nation. Child-labor, workmen's compensation, mothers' pension, and many other reforms were enacted locally; tens of thousands of regulations and proposals were advanced at local levels of government. Local reforms were needed, of course, but national programs offered certain advantages. A strategy of policy localism required expenditure of vast amounts of energy in reinvent-

ing the wheel in each of the states and local jurisdictions. Moreover, resistance to reforms in specific localities was often heightened by opponents' argument that a specific local reform—such as prohibition of child labor—might make industry move to other localities where this restriction did not exist.

Since most Americans and some reformers believed that social welfare issues belonged to local governments under the Constitution and by the precedent of the poor laws, efforts to secure national reforms occurred belatedly during the progressive era and were limited to modest reforms like the Children's Bureau. Other national initiatives included the 1916 child-labor legislation and the 1910 Mann Act, which prohibited the transportation of women across state lines for immoral purposes. Efforts at the national level were further hampered by the Supreme Court, which continued to limit the power of the federal government—for example, in rulings that restricted the federal government to those functions specifically enumerated in the Constitution.[33]

Progressives' effectiveness was also diluted by the range of their interests. At least six overlapping reform agendas existed.

1. Some progressives, who emphasized procedural reforms in government, sought policies to reduce corruption, to give more power to experts in governments, and to foster greater participation by citizens in government.
2. Some progressives sought regulation of the economic system, to restrict the size of corporations or to develop federal controls over banking and currency.
3. Members of such professions as medicine, nursing, law, teaching, and social work sought to develop licensing laws and accredited educational programs, in order to upgrade the knowledge and skills of professionals.
4. Some progressives sought legislation to restore morality to American life by curbing immigration, restricting gambling, ending prostitution, or limiting alcohol consumption.
5. Some reformers focused on regulations to limit the ability of corporations, owners of rental

housing, and others to victimize workers or the public.

6. Some progressives pursued programs to redistribute resources to impoverished workers, destitute women, and other groups.

Most progressives embraced more than one of these agendas.[34]

The range of the reform agendas limited progressives' impact in several ways. First, by devoting their energies to many causes and issues, reformers decreased the likelihood that they could significantly affect any one of them. Furthermore, not all of the six agendas received equal attention: Reforms that assisted powerless and impoverished groups tended to attract less support than did other reforms. In particular, trust-busting, good-government reforms (such as the initiative, referendum, and recall), prohibition, and the limitation of immigration absorbed the attention of many reform leaders and the general public.[35]

These emphases reflected the middle-class perspectives of many reformers. Middle-class citizens did not monopolize progressivism; various of the six progressive agendas were supported by trade unions, political bosses, and immigrant groups. Nonetheless, they shaped the direction and content of many reforms. Relatively affluent persons often had scant personal knowledge of the problems that immigrants and factory workers encountered in their daily lives. Trust-busting, city beautification, civil service, professional licensing, and other such reforms did not directly address the appalling social conditions of poor persons. The prominence of moral reforms during the progressive era also suggests the imprint of middle-class reformers, many of whom sought temperance, termination of gambling, elimination of prostitution, and anti-crime measures. Some progressive reformers were biased against immigrant groups and sought legislation to limit immigration. Despite valiant attempts, reformers like Jane Addams were unable to prevent Congress from passing anti-immigration legislation, which would have become public law had it not been vetoed by Presidents Taft and Wilson. We have already noted the punitive administration of mothers' pensions to immigrant widows,

who had to convince investigators that they were deserving before the pension would be granted.

This middle-class imprint on reform can usefully be contrasted with England and other European nations, where strong political parties dominated by factory workers and radicals were beginning to emerge. While the Labor party was still in its infancy by 1910, its presence led to competition between the Conservative and the Liberal parties for workers' votes—a competition that partly led Lloyd George, the leader of the Liberal party, to support a range of social legislation. (By 1924, Ramsay MacDonald became the first Prime Minister from the Labor party.) Even those progressives who most favored social reforms were often uncomfortable with class conflict and had little sympathy for groups that advocated sweeping reforms.[36]

POLITICAL REALITIES THAT LIMITED REFORM

Even had they focused on helping immigrants and workers, the reformers would have had minimal policy successes. The Supreme Court, as well as local and state courts, impeded social reforms by making a succession of adverse rulings; for example, a state law that sought to limit hours of bakers to ten hours per day was ruled unconstitutional.

Neither the Republican party nor the Democratic party focused on the needs of workers, persons with low incomes, or oppressed groups such as African Americans, because voters in the progressive era tended to vote not on the basis of social class but according to local and family traditions that stemmed from ethnicity and sectionalism. (To the extent that workers and persons of low income voted at all, they split their votes between the two major parties, though African Americans usually voted for the Republican party because of its historic role in ending slavery.) Because party leaders lacked an incentive to concentrate on assistance to those in need, social reformers often found it difficult to get their attention.[37]

Reformers also had difficulty obtaining assistance from the groups that most needed social reforms—immigrants, workers, and African Americans. Political cooperation among immigrant groups was impeded by language barriers, ethnic rivalries, and residential segregation. Immigrants often distrusted middle-class reformers, who proposed civil service and other reforms that seemed irrelevant to their practical needs, and resented reforms to curb corruption in politics—including the political machines that represented the primary vehicle for distribution of jobs and food to immigrants.[38]

Unions, which largely represented skilled crafts, were uncertain allies for social reformers. Samuel Gompers, the leader of the American Federation of Labor (AFL), attributed the demise of the Knights of Labor in the 1880s to its diversion to extraneous political and social issues, and resolved, in consequence, to concentrate exclusively on union members' wages and fringe benefits and on organizing skilled or semiskilled white, native, and male workers. His tactical defensiveness was increased, moreover, by repeated court injunctions that declared specific strikes to be illegal. Gompers's tactical decisions helped the AFL make gains in the early years of this century but at the price of indifference to social reforms and to organizing workers who were unskilled, female, immigrants, or people of color. Furthermore, the trade union movement remained weak. Employers mounted a decisive counterattack by means of court suits, bloody repression, spies, scabs, and red-baiting. The fledgling movement was fraught with internal dissension and outmoded organizing techniques. In the 19th century, factories had been dominated by skilled craftsmen, who possessed considerable autonomy and worked within highly defined trades. But in the 20th century factories were dominated by machinery, which relegated workers to tedious and unskilled work under the scrutiny of central management. Instead of organizing the workers of entire factories, unionists still tried to rally those groups of skilled workers within factories who performed specific tasks; that tactic left many workers unorganized and led to turf rivalry between competing craft unions within specific factories. Gompers's decision to avoid political partisanship also limited labor's ability to develop political power and to obtain support for minimum-wage and collective-bargaining legislation. Labor's noninvolvement in politics was illustrated in 1908, when the AFL raised only $8,000 for electoral campaigns![39]

Even had they tried, trade unionists would have found it difficult to organize and politically mobilize unskilled and semiskilled workers, who formed a massive constituency. Immigrants, who composed 60% of the industrial workforce in 1913, had extraordinary economic and social needs and were not likely to protest low wages, particularly when they knew that they could be easily replaced by other immigrants. African American workers, who constituted more than 10% of workers in Northern iron and steel plants, felt beholden to foremen who had hired them in an era of intense racial discrimination and were reluctant to make trouble. Female workers, who dominated the garment industry, often hoped to work only for a brief period before they married. The nation possessed, then, an enormous pool of relatively passive laborers, who were susceptible to victimization and feared retribution from local courts and police forces if they supported strikes.[40]

Gompers did not provide much assistance to social reformers. The AFL often opposed health insurance to workers on the grounds that it would undermine union efforts to obtain fringe benefits from employers. Many union leaders opposed the development of workmen's compensation laws on the grounds that workers could obtain larger awards from court litigation. A powerful radical movement might have pressured politicians to redistribute resources to the working class, but its power was limited. The Socialist party, which was established in 1901, managed to elect 56 socialist mayors, but its power resided mostly in local jurisdictions, and its elected officials were often indistinguishable from other progressive reformers. The Industrial Workers of the World (IWW) was organized in 1905 and had 100,000 members by 1916, but it had little power in large industries; it represented only extremely poor workers in mining, lumbering, and agricultural sectors. (Most of its members lived in Western states.) As the Socialist candidate in the presidential election of 1912, Eugene Debs, a fiery labor leader, succeeded in obtaining nearly one million of the almost 15 million votes cast, but he was not a serious threat to the major political parties.[41]

Social reformers were themselves impeded by their lack of interest in partisan politics during much of the progressive era. Many of them were contemptuous of existing parties, which they believed were corrupt and not interested in promoting reforms. Since many believed that their strength derived from the morality of their positions buttressed by public exposure of wrongdoing and social ills in the mass media, they envisioned social reform as a nonpartisan activity to pressure leaders of both parties to support reforms. Nonpartisanship allowed the progressives to maintain their political purity, but it prevented them from developing a partisan reform constituency. Their efforts to obtain support from politicians in both political parties meant that they controlled neither of them. Relatively conservative persons remained in control of the caucuses and conventions of the two major parties and often dictated their policies— under the influence of corporate interests, who remained the major source of campaign contributions for many political candidates.[42]

In many cases, reformers' energies were depleted by the task of continually raising funds to maintain staff for their nonpartisan organizations. Thousands of reform groups and settlements were formed in local, state, and national settings; these organizations often vied with one another for philanthropic contributions, and their leaders sometimes found that they had to tame their activities in order to retain the support of affluent donors.[43]

WOMEN AND CHILDREN: SEIZING THE OPPORTUNITY

If these various cultural and political obstacles impeded the enactment of benefit and services programs, how *did* progressives enact considerable legislation that benefited women and chil-

dren? Curiously, the Supreme Court, while overruling laws that limited hours of work and minimum wages for men, *allowed* similar legislation for women, as in *Muller* v. *Oregon* (1908), which upheld an Oregon statute. Were not women, after all, particularly vulnerable and weak and did not the nation depend upon their health to produce progeny?

Given a legal loophole that did not extend to men, women were not timid in seizing the opportunity. Women's organizations were remarkably numerous and well organized in the progressive era. Unlike European nations, which hardly allowed women to obtain higher education, nearly one-third of college students were women in 1900; that figure rose to one-half by 1920. Not allowed to enter the professions or many occupations—and otherwise limited to nursing and secondary school teaching—many of these well-educated women invested themselves in social reform activity; in many cases, they even decided to forego marriage. Starting from local literary clubs, the General Federation of Women's Clubs became a massive national organization, with local chapters that had over one million members in 1911. The U.S. Women's Trade Union League sought to organize trade unions among female workers. The National Consumers League, headed by Florence Kelley, sought child-labor laws and protectionist legislation for women. A network of more than 400 settlement houses organized grass-roots pressure for various reforms. While focusing on prohibition, the Women's Christian Temperance Union also supported a range of social legislation that would help women and children. The female leaders of these organizations, frequently in contact with one another, maintained pressure on politicians through petitions, lobbying, and publicity. They formed alliances with male-dominated interest groups in state capitols on frequent occasions. They were remarkably adept, moreover, in using moral arguments with male legislators, by contending that reforms for women and children were needed to protect them from victimization by employers.[44]

Even the tactical ingenuity of these dedicated women, however, proved insufficient to obtain unemployment insurance, old-age pensions, or major federal legislation. Indeed, the focus on women's and children's legislation merely underscores the reluctance of Americans in addressing a range of social needs that exist in any industrialized and urbanized society.

SOCIAL REFORMERS AND THE BULL MOOSE CAMPAIGN OF 1912

During the first decade of the 20th century, both the Republican and Democratic parties were often dominated on specific issues by conservative politicians, who insisted that federal authorities ought not to assume social welfare roles; who believed that social activists were "demagogues," "socialists," and "sentimental idealists"; and who sought to focus party platforms on international, tariff, currency, national defense, and related issues. Various conservatives supported specific pieces of social legislation—many of them, for example, favored the establishment of the Children's Bureau—but they often opposed specific reforms. Each party contained an insurgent wing that favored social legislation and other reforms, but its members were often outmaneuvered by conservatives in party nominating conventions and in legislative arenas. Corporate officials continued to assume a dominant role in American politics and often tried to persuade candidates from both parties to oppose such reforms as lower tariffs; it was not until 1914 that Woodrow Wilson was able to slash tariffs and thus reduce prices of many commodities for workers and immigrants.[45]

Social reformers such as Jane Addams and Paul Kellogg experienced many policy successes in municipal and state arenas during the first decade of the 20th century as they secured passage of mothers' pension, workmen's compensation, and juvenile court legislation. They grew more confident as they became national celebrities. Many were frequently requested to give speeches; some authored popular books; and Jane Addams was called an American reform goddess!

But frustration also made many of the reformers want larger policy victories. The prodigious effort to enact legislation in many states and municipalities took its toll; why not, some asked, obtain sweeping national legislation to regulate the working conditions of women and children, establish upper limits on the hours of work, establish a progressive tax system, establish a minimum wage, and extend the vote to women? A few avant-garde reformers even favored passage of national health insurance, unemployment insurance, and old-age pensions.[46]

Many social reformers dreamed that a fundamental political realignment might occur, so that voters could choose between a relatively liberal party (with a constituency of intellectuals, workers, immigrants, and social reformers) and a relatively conservative party (with a constituency of businesspeople and affluent persons). It seemed that reformers' dream of realignment might come to pass in the election of 1912. Theodore Roosevelt, who became president in 1901 on the assassination of William McKinley, had gingerly broached various reforms in his first term, but had refrained from supporting many controversial reforms so as not to alienate the conservative wing of the Republican party, which he needed if he was to obtain the party's nomination in 1904. He became bolder during his second term, however; on the eve of leaving office, he left a lengthy reform agenda to Vice President William Taft, which he hoped Taft would support if elected in 1908.

Roosevelt's hopes in Taft were misplaced. Taft became a captive of the conservative wing of the Republican party during his term in office from 1909 to 1912. A large, phlegmatic man, Taft believed that major social reforms were not needed. As Taft became more conservative, the charismatic and energetic Roosevelt became more liberal. Dashing to and from his wild-game safaris in Africa, he added support of national child-labor legislation, a progressive income tax, and workmen's compensation to his reform agenda. He proposed the creation of an industrial commission to conduct national economic planning, which would be charged with fostering economic growth and regulating trusts so that their power and job-creation potentials could be realized. Feminists

persuaded him to support a constitutional amendment to give women the vote.

Taft feared that Roosevelt, backed by social
reformers, would try to regain control of the Republican party by seeking its presidential nomination in
1912. Many reformers had maintained a nonpartisan
stance prior to 1912 and had supported neither of the
two major parties, but a number of them, including
Jane Addams and Paul Kellogg, openly advocated
supporting Roosevelt for the nomination.

The stage was set for a confrontation at the
Republican convention in Chicago in summer
1912. However, the hopes of social reformers were
dashed when Taft and entrenched party leaders
secured the nomination for Taft in a series of power
moves. They were further disheartened when the
Democratic party nominated Woodrow Wilson, the
governor of New Jersey and former college president, who favored states' rights and focused on
trust-busting and lowering tariffs. Instead of realignment, *both* parties seemed to be following a
conservative course.

Many social reformers believed that realignment might still occur if a new political party were
established with Roosevelt as its leader. With light-
ning speed, reformers called a convention of the
Progressive party in Chicago and persuaded a
reluctant Roosevelt to accept its presidential nomination. The new party and its nominee were hardly
rabid social reformers—only 25% of its platform,
as well as of his acceptance speech, was devoted to
social reforms—but they were far more reformist
than alternative parties and candidates. Their platform included support for social insurances, workmen's compensation, a minimum wage, women's
suffrage, and a child-labor law. Jane Addams
became the first woman to address a major political
convention when she seconded the nomination of
Roosevelt. Party members entered the campaign in
an atmosphere of religious and moral fervor, but
many practical problems bedeviled them. They had
to secure a place on the ballot in the various states,
obtain campaign funds, and develop a massive
constituency in a nation that was wedded to the
Democratic and Republican parties. Roosevelt
doubted that he could prevail in the election of
1912, but he and others hoped they could educate

the public sufficiently that workers and liberals
would support the Progressive party and it would
replace the Republican party.[47]

Wilson, who had supported some progressive
reforms as governor of New Jersey, tried from the
outset to portray Taft as an extremist on the right
and Roosevelt as an extremist on the left. He persuaded Samuel Gompers and many other union
leaders to support him, by promising them that he
would seek legislation to improve the legal status
of organized labor. When portrayed as a left-
winger by both Wilson and Taft, Roosevelt coun-
terattacked vigorously by arguing that Taft and
Wilson had outmoded and conservative ideas. He
succeeded in differentiating his positions from
those of Wilson by questioning Wilson's assertions
that a minimum wage would depress prices, by
arguing that a welfare state was needed in an industrial society, and by insisting that states' rights had
to be superseded by national planning. He drew
enormous and enthusiastic crowds in his campaign
appearances. When the results were tallied, Roosevelt made a respectable showing but lost the
election, because ethnic and regional loyalties, as
well as the allegiance of many immigrants to political bosses, led many Democratic voters to support
Wilson. Wilson won, not because he was overwhelmingly popular—he received less than 50% of
the popular vote—but because the Republican vote
was split between Taft and Roosevelt.[48]

Many persons who had voted for Roosevelt still
believed that political realignment was possible if
the Progressive party could be kept intact and if it
waged successful campaigns in the congressional
elections of 1914 and the presidential election of
1916. The reformers hoped that Roosevelt would
win in 1916, that the Republican party would die,
and that conservatives would gravitate to the Democratic party. To ensure that the Progressive party
maintained its reforming mission, social reformers
succeeded in creating a national department of the
party, directed by Jane Addams, that focused on
social research and the development of social policies. Promisingly, 20 members of Congress
declared their allegiance to the party, as did a number of local officeholders.

Practical realities doomed the reformers'

dreams of political realignment, however. Political experts decided that party funds should be devoted to hiring political experts and financing campaigns, and so, to the dismay of reformers, the social service department of the party was terminated. The party was unable to raise the funds necessary to get on the ballot in some jurisdictions. Most damaging to the Progressive party, however, was Woodrow Wilson's unexpected support for social legislation during his presidency. Although he had argued in the campaign of 1912 that federal authorities should not enact a minimum wage or place restrictions on child labor and had lambasted the idea of a welfare state as paternalistic, he realized in the aftermath of his victory that he could significantly add to the political base of the Democratic party if he adopted some of the reforms proposed by the Progressive party. He even cautiously wooed social reformers like Jane Addams. He enacted child-labor legislation, banking legislation, tariff reductions, and eventually women's suffrage.[49]

The fate of the Progressive party was virtually sealed by its poor showing in the congressional elections of 1914. Except in a few scattered locations, the party was defunct well before the presidential election of 1916. Roosevelt tried to secure the Republican nomination in 1916 but was again rebuffed by party conservatives, who nominated Charles Hughes. Wilson again ran successfully on the Democratic ticket, with the assistance of many progressive reformers.

The failure of the Progressive party during and after 1912 demonstrated that social reform could not proceed beyond the limited policy successes of the progressive era unless reformers could obtain a power base, by capturing a major party that had significant support from liberals, the working class, and people of color. The demise of the Progressive party also illustrated the precarious position of social reform in America, despite growing social problems in the cities. It would take a catastrophic depression in the late 1920s to galvanize workers, the poor, and people of color behind social reforms—and it would be a distant cousin of Theodore Roosevelt, Franklin Delano Roosevelt, who would finally accomplish the political realignment that the progressives had sought.

 ## OUTGROUPS IN THE PROGRESSIVE ERA

It would be a mistake to view progressivism as a reform movement fought for, by, and in behalf of the immigrants who constituted such major portions of the nation's urban population. Americans of this era harbored very contradictory opinions about this huge population; though they freely used—and depended on—immigrants as cheap labor to fuel industrial growth, they resented, and sometimes even feared, this population for reasons of eugenics (would they dilute the Anglo-Saxon race?), social unrest (could America have a revolution if "agitators" awoke these immigrants, and did the big-city political machines constitute a threat to democracy?), public health (did the immigrants pass diseases, such as tuberculosis, to others?), and culture (did Catholicism, Judaism, and ethnic culture threaten Protestant and American culture?). Nor were the progressives, aside from many settlement workers and certain other reformers, free from racism; indeed, no significant civil rights legislation was enacted or seriously considered in this period, and some decided setbacks occurred. Although women were often in the vanguard of social reform in the progressive era and made some economic and other gains (for example, regulation of their working conditions and hours), they remained shackled by traditional notions of their role in society.

People of Color

The civil rights gains of freed slaves were nullified following the Civil War: Southern whites regained their political power when Northerners withdrew military and legislative pressure on the South and when the Supreme Court rendered federal civil rights laws useless. Republicans hoped to regain their Southern constituency, but Democrats had become the dominant party of the South by 1900 and staunchly resisted federal efforts to protect or help African Americans. Most African Americans lived in rural areas as tenant farmers; low wages and indebtedness to plantation owners enmeshed them in grinding poverty. Increasing numbers moved to Southern cities where, aside from a small elite group of affluent African Americans, they were unemployed or worked as domestic servants or in other low-paying and unskilled jobs; rich or poor, they all lived within a segregated society. Americans had developed, in effect, a social system that approached apartheid and was maintained by Jim Crow laws, police, courts, and white racism.[50]

The situation was more favorable for African Americans in the North, but only modestly so. Poverty and lack of jobs in the South led to a steady and growing migration of African Americans to Northern cities, where their presence was still relatively small in 1915. The enticement of jobs in burgeoning industries like meatpacking and steel drew African Americans to the North, where their wages, though low, were nonetheless considerably higher than what they could earn in the South. Neighborhoods occupied by African Americans were even more blighted than those occupied by other immigrant groups, were more likely to be the headquarters of organized crime and drug interests, and had virtually no health or other services. African Americans experienced extraordinary discrimination in job markets; they were excluded from skilled trades and unions, were often used as scabs to break unions, and were subject to race riots and mob violence when they competed with whites for jobs. Most African Americans in the North, like their urban counterparts in the South, worked in unskilled jobs.[51]

African Americans in both the North and the South evolved ingenious strategies for coping with their adversity and for seeking social reforms. African American women assumed even more assertive roles than white women in promoting self-help and charitable projects. They developed mutual benefit societies that provided insurance for sickness and funerals. They participated in church groups such as the Women's Convention of the Black Baptist Church, which had 1.5 million members in 1907. They formed Women's Clubs to promote charities, such as the National Association of Colored Women. They formed their own settlement houses. And they established 200 hospitals and nurse-training schools. Unlike white women, African American women placed particular emphasis on education; they regarded schools—from kindergarten to college—as a kind of antipoverty program. In the South, educational needs were extreme. Because local jurisdictions underfunded public schools for African Americans, private support had to be found; even as late as 1940, only 1% of African Americans, male and female, had four or more years of college; and many Southern colleges for African Americans were only the equivalent of secondary schools.[52]

In the broader African American community, a conflict between Booker T. Washington and W. E. B. Du Bois reflected the dilemma of oppressed people. Washington, the son of a slave woman and her white master, preached accommodation; he wanted African Americans to conquer racism by honesty, hard work, and the help of kindly patrons. But Du Bois wanted African Americans to develop political power, so that they could obtain civil rights laws and get access to the same educational advantages as whites. Du Bois and other African American leaders formed the National Association for the Advancement of Colored People (NAACP) in 1909 and succeeded in getting 6,000 members by 1914, mostly from the African American middle class.

Asian immigrants on the West coast also suffered discrimination and poverty. As we noted in Chapter 5, hundreds of Chinese immigrants came to California in the late 19th century to work on the railroads and in the mines and were followed by Japanese immigrants over the next two decades. Many Americans believed Asians to be sinister and untrustworthy people, and worried that they brought diseases to America; editorialists wrote hatefully of the "yellow peril." To survive, many Japanese Americans capitalized on their ability to farm hillside land, and both Chinese and Japanese immigrants developed specialized niches in urban America; they ran laundries and small businesses. However, both groups frequently encountered prejudice and adverse policies.

California enacted Alien Land Laws in 1913

and 1920 to prohibit land purchases and ownership by Japanese residents. Even in this period, long before World War II, many people feared that the Japanese would overrun the West Coast and even attack the United States. Many Americans urged extension of the provisions of the Chinese Exclusion Act of 1882 to the Japanese but had to content themselves with measures such as the Gentleman's Agreement of 1907, in which Japan agreed to stop the migration of laborers to the United States. (For diplomatic reasons, Roosevelt did not want to antagonize the Japanese government by legally prohibiting Japanese immigration.)[53]

In both Hawaii and California, the Japanese immigrants fashioned an ingenious survival strategy. Taking advantage of a shortage of craftspeople and artisans and also of entrepreneurs, the Japanese quickly filled these economic positions. In Hawaii, their access to supplies from Japan and the difficulty of obtaining supplies from the United States, because of the distances involved, allowed them to develop a monopoly of retail grocery and dry-goods stores. In California, bringing skills in hillside and irrigated farming from Japan, they leased or owned substantial acreage and were able to monopolize the burgeoning fresh-vegetable crop. As in Hawaii, Japanese Americans were adept at becoming entrepreneurs; by 1919, they owned 45% of the hotels and 25% of the grocery stores in Seattle. Both Chinese and Japanese Americans achieved these stunning successes by pooling funds in their own communities to allow one another to invest and thus sidestepping the restrictive lending policies of commercial banks. Far weaker on the West coast, unions did not systematically prevent Asian Americans from entering the trades, unlike unions in the East and Midwest that denied entry to African Americans.[54]

In the Southwest lived large numbers of Latinos, whose land was taken from them in the middle and late 19th century. Their numbers were swelled by Mexican immigrants, who were able to move freely across a relatively unrestricted border until 1924, when the U.S. Border Patrol was created. It is impossible to know precisely how many Latinos came across the 2,000-mile border, but some scholars estimate roughly 195,000 migrated between 1900 and 1920; their numbers grew dramatically in the wake of the economic dislocation accompanying the Mexican revolution of 1910. By 1930, the U.S. population included more than 2 million people who had been born in Mexico.

These immigrants, as well as the indigenous Latino population, became the labor force for the irrigated cotton, vegetable, and fruit enterprises of the Southwest. Along with ranching and meat processing, these enterprises expanded enormously after the Reclamation Act of 1902 provided large federal funding for irrigation projects. Latinos worked not only in the fields but in numerous canning and food-processing plants. They lived in barracks in remote rural areas and were subject to the punitive labor policies of large landowners, who paid low wages and brutally suppressed protest. Like many rural African Americans in the South, they were denied education and excluded from economic opportunities that developed in urban America.

Nor were conditions much better for those Latinos who settled in growing urban areas of the Southwest, where employers used them as a reserve labor force to break strikes and depress wages. Those few business ventures that were owned by Latinos were located in Spanish-speaking communities and were mostly small stores.[55] As a strictly regional population in the Southwest (only 15% lived outside the Southwest even as late as 1930), Latinos were isolated politically and subject to local and regional groups, such as growers, who wished to subjugate them. The Mexican government frequently protested the working conditions and suppression of the Latino population to the U.S. State Department, but to no avail.[56]

These Spanish-speaking persons in the Southwest differed markedly from European immigrants —and from African Americans. Like African Americans, they met the labor needs of white landowners, who could tap an inexhaustible supply of workers who migrated back and forth across the border. Indeed, in the wake of the Mexican Revolution, about 10% of the population of Mexico had emigrated to the United States; most were "unofficial immigrants," who evaded various fees, visas, and (after 1917) literacy tests. Also like African Americans, they could not easily enter the economic mainstream because they had limited access to schools, lived in areas where industrialization had hardly emerged, and lacked capital or the capital-raising techniques used by Asian immigrants.[57]

Unlike African Americans, however, these Spanish-speaking people had not been forcibly taken from their homeland or placed in bondage. Moving back and forth frequently between Mexico and the United States, they developed a "sojourner mentality"—a belief that they would soon return to Mexico. While this mentality impeded their development of economic roots, for example, by buying homes, it allowed them to retain their culture, with its emphasis on Catholicism, families, communities, and mutual assistance. Communities organized *mutualistas,* or mutual aid funds, to provide insurance, funeral, and limited welfare benefits. They observed Mexican holidays and traditions. This vibrant culture allowed Latinos to maintain their equilibrium even when they confronted oppressive conditions and grinding poverty.[58]

As a sojourner group that served the economic needs of white agricultural entrepreneurs, Spanish-speaking people of the Southwest would be linked in ensuing decades to immigration policy. Growers, who craved cheap labor, wanted no limits on immigration or else lax enforcement. They counted on ineffective border patrols and often sought exclusions for Latinos when restrictionist immigration policy was passed at the national level; for example, they had Western-hemisphere people exempted from restrictive quotas in the National Origins Act of 1924 (though Asian immigration was eliminated altogether). Growers also sought to define a special class of immigrants, known as *braceros,* who would be allowed to enter the nation only for specific harvests or brief periods; this program was first initiated in 1917, when almost 80,000 workers were admitted. With a relatively open border in the 1920s, many Mexican immigrants came to the United States. Considerable prejudice against Latinos in the broader population, however, led to strident efforts to restrict the flow of migration in the 1930s and subsequent decades, as illustrated by the 1994 passage of Cali-

fornia's Proposition 187—a measure that proposed to bolster border patrols *and* deny "illegal" Latinos educational, health, and other benefits.[59]

Many progressive reformers saw no contradiction between social reform and racism, as the actions of Theodore Roosevelt and Woodrow Wilson make plain. Roosevelt raised storms of protest when he invited Booker T. Washington, the African American leader, to the White House for lunch during his first term. Though Washington, unlike Marcus Garvey, was no militant and favored accommodation to existing policies, this luncheon led Roosevelt's foes to portray him as a radical on racial issues; even as late as 1912, the luncheon was cited as evidence that Roosevelt was a "nigger lover." Roosevelt was hardly a defender of civil rights, however. After the luncheon with Washington, he refrained from all public meetings with African Americans. He took no actions against Jim Crow legislation in the South; sided with white authorities in the infamous Brownsville incident in 1906 (in which African American soldiers were executed on undocumented charges that they had raped white women); and did not contest lily-white delegations to Republican conventions from Southern districts. Jane Addams vainly protested Roosevelt's acceptance of white Southern delegations to the convention of the ostensibly reformist Progressive party in 1912.

Like most white Americans in this era, Roosevelt upheld a racial ideology that extolled the virtues of the Anglo-American race to the detriment of other races, including African Americans, Asians, Latinos, and Native Americans. The racial doctrines that had fueled manifest destiny, which we discussed in Chapter 5, lived on in many white Americans, who believed that the superiority of Anglo-Americans was proven by scientific evidence (later discredited) such as alleged differences in skull size and intelligence. Roosevelt's ideological orientation and his desire to obtain white Southerners' support for the Republican party led him to neglect the problems of African Americans and other people of color.[60]

Woodrow Wilson was even less sympathetic than Roosevelt to the needs of African Americans. Raised in the South, he had adopted the racial orientations of affluent Southerners. Moreover, he was the presidential nominee of the Democratic party, which had relied on race baiting throughout the late 19th century to secure the support of Southern whites. Whereas Roosevelt had given African Americans some token posts in government, Wilson refused even to give the ambassadorship to Liberia to an African American, openly supported segregated restroom facilities in federal departments, and condoned lynching in the South. So detestable were his policies to African Americans that most of them continued to vote Republican, even though many social reformers switched their allegiance from the defunct Progressive party to Wilson in 1916.[61]

The courts reinforced prevailing attitudes. In *Plessy* v. *Ferguson* (1896), the Supreme Court condoned a state law that mandated separate facilities for African Americans, on the grounds that state legislation that implies a legal distinction between two races does not destroy legal equality between them. Moreover, the Court did not overturn prior rulings that federal civil rights legislation of the Reconstruction era applied only to the discriminatory acts of individuals rather than to the state and local governments.[62]

Jane Addams and a small band of social reformers were exceptions to the alliance of progressivism and racism. She supported the establishment of settlement houses in African American communities, sought to improve schools, and urged better protection of African Americans from lynching and race riots. She argued that African Americans possessed qualities of altruism and gentleness that made them superior in some respects to the dominant population. Her beliefs were not shared, however, by most policy makers in the North or South or by most Americans.[63]

Women and Politics

As we discussed in Chapter 5, the issue of women's suffrage became the central reform issue of the women's movement with the formation of the National American Women's Suffrage Associa-

tion in 1890. Between 1890 and 1905, women presented many petitions requesting state legislatures to modify their constitutions so as to grant women the vote, but they had scant success. Even many women regarded the issue as tangential to their economic and social needs. The male and female leaders of antisuffrage organizations contended that women would destroy the unity of households by voting for their own interests and would fall prey to demagogues because of their "hysterical" tendencies. Moreover, the liquor interests strongly opposed suffrage on the grounds that women would support temperance.

More progress was made after 1905, because feminist leaders had developed sophisticated organizing skills and because women's prominent roles in the reform era made the issue seem less radical. Indeed, 12 states had granted women the vote by 1916. Instead of emphasizing feminist arguments, suffragettes argued that voting women would support progressive reforms on education and family issues—an argument that was received favorably by males imbued with the 19th-century belief that women's superior moral qualities and temperament made them best suited to attend to family matters and children. Immigrant husbands increasingly supported suffrage for women, who were providing a major source of labor for the garment industry. Militant suffragists, who used disruptive organizing tactics, alienated some voters but dramatized the issue. A dramatic breakthrough occurred during World War I, when Woodrow Wilson finally agreed to support the issue, after such leaders as Carrie Chapman Catt threatened to target Democratic candidates for defeat and argued that suffrage was needed to maintain national unity during the war. The Nineteenth Amendment to the Constitution was finally enacted in 1920.[64]

Though suffrage got the most attention, other developments were of equal importance to women. There were major increases in female employment in industrial settings, as well as clerical, stenographic, and sales positions. (These occupations, as well as teaching, social work, and nursing, were gender-segregated and poorly paid, however.) Moreover, there was a sizable increase in the number of married women who worked; whereas only

14% of all women workers were married in 1900, more than 24% were married in 1910.

But economic gains ought not to be overstated. Protective labor laws were developed to "protect" women from exertion that could endanger their reproductive functions or expose them to excessive mixing with men, who might debase them morally and sexually. Abramovitz argues that these laws served to preserve "a sex-segregated labor market, the relative subordination of women to men, and the overall marginalization of women workers." Women were rarely unionized and represented a relatively docile labor force, although there were some dramatic strikes in the garment industry, such as the 1909 shirtwaist strike, in which tens of thousands of women in New York City and Philadelphia protested unsafe working conditions and low wages. Whereas 20% of men were organized according to a national survey of 15 occupations in 1905, only 3% of women belonged to unions. Mothers' pension laws, which might have been fashioned to provide major resources to single heads of households—or to help them get day care so that they could continue to work—were primarily developed with the needs of children in mind. As in prior eras, it was assumed that women with children ought not to work, and so the pensions were devised to provide just enough money so that they could stay at home. Little organized day care existed for working women in this period.[65]

Moreover, obstacles to women's sexual freedom persisted. The repertoire of birth control techniques had expanded to include condoms and diaphragms, but women learned of these techniques only by word of mouth and through vaguely worded advertisements, rather than at public family-planning clinics; even physicians often opposed their use on the grounds that they interfered with the natural reproductive functions of women or reduced the growth of the white population. Moreover, the obscenity laws of most states prohibited public discussion of these techniques or the distribution of birth control devices. As we noted in Chapter 4, the Comstock law, enacted in 1873, outlawed the distribution of birth control information through the federal mails.

Margaret Sanger founded a birth control movement, but its leaders were frequently jailed under obscenity laws. Realizing the futility of trying to change obscenity laws, Sanger focused increasingly on persuading physicians to prescribe birth control, since they could legally do so when medical needs existed. She also used the conservative argument that birth control would decrease the number of persons with mental disorders and developmental disabilities in the population and would slow the rate of increase of the low-income population. These kinds of arguments gained the support of the medical profession, which often prescribed birth control by the late 1920s. Most low-income persons lacked personal physicians, however, and did not have access to birth control because public birth control clinics were still outlawed in many jurisdictions.[66]

In this period, women were subjected to medical practices that contemporary Americans can scarcely fathom. Assuming that women's reproductive systems were the cause of many of their physical ailments, physicians performed large numbers of hysterectomies. (Even in the 1990s, rates of hysterectomy in the United States far exceed those of European nations, with little evidence that they yield medical benefit.) Indeed, some physicians assumed that women's *normal* state was to be sick. Menstruation, menopause, and childbirth were viewed as essentially medical conditions that required endless medications and surgeries. As "delicate" people, women had to be shielded, moreover, from those occupations that required physical (or even mental) exertion. Women were also commonly believed to be subject to bouts of hysteria—a condition that required bed rest in darkened rooms for weeks or even months at a time, on the theory that the absence of stimuli would allow them to recover.[67]

By 1930, little progress had been made in dispelling the cult of domesticity for married women, which had originated a century earlier. Women were endlessly exhorted to use materials from child psychology and home economics in perfecting the science of homemaking and to refrain from careers or other employment. Men objected if eminent women were nominated to serve on commissions or in administrative positions, even within the emerging social work profession. Moreover, women's access to many professions, which had increased in the progressive era, eroded in subsequent decades. Once childbirth was defined as a narrowly medical condition, for example, midwives were eventually supplanted by physicians in many jurisdictions, in contrast to European societies where this occupation remained intact.[68]

Immigrants and the Closing of the Doors

We have discussed the torrent of immigration to the United States from European nations in the period from 1880 to 1920. With the frontier closed, immigrants concentrated in major cities and became a low-paid labor force for the industrial system of the United States.

Deliberating in a nation already dominated by immigrants, the founding fathers finally decided to make no mention of immigration in the Constitution, and to allow Congress to shape the relevant policy. In the succeeding years, Americans adopted an extraordinarily liberal policy for white immigrants; they applied no annual limits, required no literacy test, and allowed people to naturalize within five years. No one anticipated, however, that immigrants would arrive in such numbers in the 19th century and the early part of the 20th century—or that many of them would not be Protestants. As Higham suggests, Americans have oscillated between periods of confidence, when they believed the nation could absorb immigrants without threat to their culture or economy, and periods of fear, when they believed the nation could be endangered by the immigrants' religions and culture; when they feared immigrants would take their jobs; and when they feared that immigrant anarchists or radicals would bring social unrest. We have already discussed nativism during the Irish immigration of the 19th century. However, confidence reigned supreme in the first decade of the 20th century, when many Americans

believed that the nation could socialize and convert immigrants to American culture. Moreover, immigrant groups, such as the German-American Alliance, Irish groups, and Jewish groups, developed considerable political power; they fought efforts to limit immigration by threatening not to vote for candidates who supported restrictive immigration policies.[69]

Even in this period of confidence, however, groups such as the Immigration Restriction League devised ways of limiting immigration—for example, by imposing literacy tests. The racist ideas associated with the doctrine of manifest destiny in the 19th century—for example, the fierce concern to prevent the "dilution" of Anglo-Saxon stock—began to resurface with the continuing influx of immigrants, who averaged 650,000 per year between 1907 and 1917. (Immigrants of other races, such as Asians, were perceived as a particular threat.)[70] Anti-Catholicism, always present, began to reemerge. The rise of the Industrial Workers of the World (IWW), a radical labor group, was linked by many people to "foreign agitators." A sharp economic downturn during and after 1913 led to a growing sense that immigrants threatened local jobs. And the immigrants of this era, like the Irish before the Civil War, were widely believed to bring with them diseases; a popular book of the era stated:

> The new immigration contained a large and increasing number of the weak, the broken, and the mentally crippled of all races drawn from the lowest stratum of the Mediterranean basin and the Balkans, together with hordes of the wretched, submerged populations of the Polish ghettoes. Our jails, insane asylums, and almshouses are filled with human flotsam and the whole tone of American life, social, moral, and political, has been lowered and vulgarized by them.[71]

Those seeking to restrict immigration found that their power increased steadily in the years preceding World War I. One victory was to enact a literacy test for immigrants who wished to become citizens in the Immigration Act of 1917. However, a curious combination of industrialists (who wanted immigrant labor) and friends of immigrants (such as the National Liberal Immigration League) held off restrictionist legislation; President Wilson vetoed legislation enacted by Congress in 1914. World War I and its aftermath vastly increased fear of foreigners; Americans were angered by various European powers and alarmed by the Russian Revolution. A "crusade for Americanization" developed during and after the war to make foreigners speak English and to identify and prosecute "bolsheviks" in a red scare that led to the imprisonment of many foreigners. After passage of a series of lesser measures, the Immigration Act of 1924 not only limited overall rates of immigration but also gave preference, within the diminished flow, to people from Northern Europe; it accomplished this by the ingenious device of limiting immigration to 2% of the population of the corresponding nationality in the United States in 1890, when relatively few Japanese, Italians, Eastern Europeans, or Russian Jews had arrived. Thus restricted, Italian immigration dropped from 42,000 to 4,000 persons per year and the Japanese immigration to 40 per year. Only Mexican immigrants escaped the restrictions, probably because their regional isolation in the Southwest made them less frightening to nativists and because agricultural, food-processing, and railroad interests in the region wanted to exploit them as cheap labor.[72]

FIGURE 6.3 Jane Addams: Pioneer social worker and social reformer

SOURCE: Corbis-Bettmann

THE RESILIENCE OF JANE ADDAMS AND HER ALLIES

Progressive reformers such as Jane Addams (see Figure 6.3) tried to develop social reforms in a society where individualism and competitiveness blinded its citizens to social problems. Unlike European reformers, who had trade union support, American reformers had to raise funds from the wealthy to establish organizations for social reform. There were few social welfare precedents, aside from local poorhouses and charities. Reformers had to obtain statistics about the incidence of various social problems, educate the public, fashion legislative testimony, engage in lobbying, network with reformers in other jurisdictions, and build coalitions. Despite their national popularity, they encountered extraordinary hostility from corporations, political machines, affluent citizens, conservatives, and even groups they sought to help, such as trade unions and immigrants. When Addams courageously attacked U.S. involvement in World War I, she was reviled as a traitor, even by many of her fellow reformers.

The persistence of the reformers was striking. Many began their work in the 1890s and continued to seek reforms until the United States entered World War I in 1917. During and after the war, when the nation turned toward conservatism, many collapsed from exhaustion, left the country, converted to conservatism, or turned to psychotherapy, which became a vogue in the 1920s. Some reformers bucked the conservative trend even during the 1920s, however. Addams continued to reside in Hull House, sought many new reforms, and correctly predicted that the United States would need to address the needs of the expanding African American population in Northern cities.

THE EMERGENCE OF SOCIAL WORK

An important question had to be answered in the progressive era: Who was to staff those social agencies that helped immigrants, poor people, children who could not remain with their natural families, and so many other troubled individuals? By 1920, a new profession, called social work, had developed schools in which people were trained to give these kinds of services. The development of social work was marked by considerable tension between different factions, each of which left an imprint on the profession; these complex origins foreshadowed much controversy about the direction of social work during the remainder of the 20th century.

In particular, there was a striking difference in approach between those who came from settlement houses and those intent on developing a methodology for helping people in one-on-one transactions. Recall from Chapter 4 that, even as early as the 1840s, various agencies in Eastern cities undertook to systematize relief giving to people in poverty by using volunteers to interview them, determine if they were truly needy, and supervise them while they received assistance, with an eye to making them independent as soon as possible. In some cases, agencies compared their records, so as to be certain that people were not receiving assistance from more than one source.

In the decades after the Civil War, these early attempts to make relief giving a disciplined process were enlarged in many jurisdictions. Local, nongovernmental agencies—called charity organization societies (COS)—developed in most cities to provide assistance to destitute people. Initially, these agencies did not actually give relief to individuals; instead, they sought to coordinate relief giving, with an eye to preventing people from seeking simultaneous assistance from two or more agencies. The agencies were administered by a paid male who recruited and supervised female volunteers—usually relatively affluent, white, English-speaking women; these women who came to be known as friendly visitors, were supposed to provide moral uplift to impoverished people. Some COS agencies eventually came to give out relief themselves, thereby joining the various sectarian agencies that had long provided aid to destitute persons. To coordinate and systematize their growing operations, private relief-giving agencies came to hire staff, usually women who remained in nonadministrative posts.

Relief giving by private agencies in the latter part of the 19th century was a grim undertaking. Friendly visitors and paid staff were taught to engage in a careful diagnostic and supervising process, as they screened, aided, and finally discharged poor people who needed assistance. Above all, they were to avoid giving indiscriminately or letting their emotions dictate their actions. Indeed, it was their duty to turn away, or refer to poorhouses, those people who were not bent on achieving independence and moral improvement; these qualities were monitored both at point of intake and throughout the helping process. The friendly visitors did detailed research on the motivations, history, and living arrangements of families as they decided whether and how to help destitute people. Moreover, they were to provide instruction to their wards, both through teaching (such as how to keep a clean house and prepare decent meals) and through personal example. As models of hard work, thrift, and morality, they could, it was hoped, inculcate those virtues in their clients. These friendly visitors probably exhibited contradictory tendencies in their work—both punitive attitudes and a desire to help. In screening "undeserving" from "deserving" poor people, they were certainly punitive. As white, English-speaking people, they most likely were perceived as condescending and harsh by their immigrant wards. They were often unaware that the poverty of the immigrants stemmed not from faults of character, such as laziness, but from the lack of available work or discrimination in hiring. Yet they could be advocates for their wards with local police, educational, and other agencies and provided hands-on assistance by actually visiting the homes and neighborhoods of their clients.

Some leaders of the charity societies formed quasi-public organizations at the state level to inspect state mental institutions, to collect data about pauperism and other social problems, and to combat patronage and corruption in public institutions. A national organization, the National Conference of Charities, was established in 1879 after members of various state boards of charities, who had been meeting annually in the American Social Science Association, decided that they needed their own organization; it convened annual conferences of leaders in this emerging field. (In 1884, it changed its name to the National Conference of Charities and Corrections.) Admission was also open to people engaged in private, nongovernmental charity in local agencies, who soon dominated the organization.[73]

The paid staff who supplanted volunteers in the last decades of the 19th century were the forerunners of the social work profession; they articulated a helping methodology called casework, which explained the techniques charity workers should use when helping individual clients.

We can now contrast the charity organization societies with people who administered and worked in settlement houses. These two factions were quite different, even though they both attended the annual meetings of the National Conference of Charities and Corrections. Settlement staff tended to be somewhat more reform oriented, more inclined to decrease the personal distance between paid staff and neighborhood residents, and less convinced that helping could be reduced to a science. These differences sparked frequent conflict between the two groups. For example, during the progressive era, many charity organization leaders opposed the development of mothers' pensions, which, they argued, represented an unwarranted intrusion into the work of nongovernmental agencies. By contrast, Jane Addams and many other social workers who were identified with social reform militantly supported mothers' pensions. (Even as late as 1932, some social workers

believed that private agencies could manage the economic destitution due to the Great Depression, which began in 1929.)[74]

How was a profession to be molded from these two disparate factions? Both charity workers and settlement staff realized that extended training was necessary if they were to develop a profession—and training had mostly taken the form of practical experience on the job, brief seminars, or courses in sociology, which had begun to be taught in universities in the 1890s.

Wenocur and Reisch contend that the charity organization movement seized the initiative, with the assistance of the Russell Sage Foundation.[75] Mary Richmond, who was a noteworthy theorist in the methodology of investigating and assisting individuals and had worked extensively with the Baltimore Charity Organization Society, had long espoused the development of a training school to be affiliated with a university. Her fledgling efforts, such as a six-week summer program of the New York Charity Organization Society in 1898, whetted appetites for more ambitious projects. The training period was extended to one year and then, with the establishment of the New York School of Philanthropy in 1910, to two years. (This program later became the Columbia University Graduate School of Social Work.) In quick succession, other schools were established in Boston and at institutions of higher education, including Bryn Mawr, Ohio State, Indiana University, and the University of Minnesota. Casework became the dominant curriculum focus of these various schools, although smatterings of other subject matter were included. In 1907, settlement leaders in Chicago founded the Chicago School of Civics and Philanthropy, which later became the School of Social Service Administration of the University of Chicago. However, its existence did not fundamentally challenge the dominance of those who saw the profession essentially as an extension of the charity societies' work. The emerging casework, as articulated by Richmond in her classic book *Social Diagnosis,* lacked the punitive qualities of much of the charity societies' work and was geared toward helping individuals with personal problems rather than toward determining whether they "deserved" monetary assistance, but it still focused on one-on-one trans-actions.[76] The founders of the Chicago School worried that the emphasis on casework, so entrenched in many of the early schools, would provide an excessively narrow focus for the new profession.

Wenocur and Reisch contend that the leaders in this early movement to develop a profession were constrained by economic realities. The budding profession depended, after all, on affluent philanthropists and university elites to provide resources and institutional support for the new training programs and agency services. From this vantage, the emphasis on personal casework was an ideal choice, for it was far less controversial than the social reform practiced by some settlements. Moreover, it seemed scientific in its emphasis on careful investigation and diagnosis, by comparison with the mix of social reform, recreational, and socialization services offered by settlements—and the leaders of the new profession could convincingly argue to universities, philanthropists, and the Russell Sage Foundation that this "core technology" required extended training in professional schools. (To obtain public support, professions needed to convince others that, without the training they provide, consumers would be endangered—an assertion the leaders of the new profession made unabashedly as they argued that good intentions and altruism, by themselves, were insufficient to provide assistance to destitute families, disrupted families, mental patients, and other people in need.) The emphasis of the new profession on training staff to work in nongovernmental agencies was also attuned to an era that had few governmental services, aside from poorhouses, mental institutions, and correctional facilities.[77]

If we place the emerging profession in the larger context of the progressive era, we can see that its leaders were captive to the intellectual currents and political assumptions of the period. Many of them were content to seek the regulation of child labor, women's working conditions, and other specific situations; they did not envision major social programs such as those in the New Deal. Many of them sought reforms of government, including the eradication of patronage and corruption from the administration of mental institutions and poor-

houses. Many brought into the profession a preoccupation with the investigation and diagnosis of dispossessed and impoverished individuals that derived from charity projects in the 1840s and later decades. Just as social reformers often stood at the periphery of progressivism, which was mostly preoccupied with the establishment of "good government," trust-busting, and moral issues like temperance, they often were at the periphery, also, of the emerging profession; indeed, Mary Richmond believed that the settlements' mixture of social reform, recreation, and socialization work was an unsuitable methodology for the new profession—and even inimical to its survival. Like the leaders of the charity societies, most leaders of the new profession assumed that nongovernmental agencies would provide the focus of its work; indeed, they looked with considerable cynicism at patronage-ridden public agencies such as mental institutions and poorhouses.

It was too soon to tell, in 1920, precisely how the new profession would develop. Given that both the charity society and settlement movements shared an emphasis on helping people in poverty, that aspect of social work was likely to continue. A social reform impulse deriving from the influence of settlement workers and certain charity society people, such as Homer Folks, was likely to remain. But a clever prognosticator might have guessed that tensions in the profession at its inception would also persist. Might not casework, soon to be married to the just-emerging tenets of Freud (and later the tenets of so many other psychological theorists), lead some practitioners to want to serve neurotic individuals from the middle and even upper classes *rather* than poor people? Might not the descendants of Jane Addams within the profession—those who wished to emphasize macro matters such as policy, administration, organizing, and social reform—be marginalized in a profession whose organizing principles reflected the person-to-person transactions of the charity societies? Would not endless disputes emerge about the precise educational content of the professional schools—and even whether a master's degree in a graduate facility was necessary or whether certain tasks could be performed by people with only a bachelor's degree? (We discuss in Chapter 7 and elsewhere how some of these tensions emerged over the next few decades.)

Lest we imply that social workers alone were subject to the limitations of their time, consider physicians and attorneys, who tightened the educational requirements of their disciplines in this era and made salutary advances but also made decisions that set back the course of social reform in the United States. Though the profession of medicine had existed for centuries, it did not possess a monopoly over health care in the mid-19th century; prior to the discovery of bacteria and an understanding of their role in illness, herbalists and other folk practitioners seemed as credible as physicians. The revolutionary scientific discoveries in Europe in the last four decades of the 19th century, which led to the development of inoculations, safer surgical techniques, and effective medications, checked scourges such as cholera, syphilis, and typhoid fever—and lent to physicians, who claimed credit for these new findings, a credibility that rival professions lacked. Seizing the moment, physicians organized a grass-roots campaign— conducted by chapters of the American Medical Association—to have state legislations pass licensing laws that would restrict surgical and pharmaceutical remedies to people who had obtained a medical degree. Like social workers, they linked their training facilities to universities and required a bachelor's degree for admission to them.

Who is to argue that this profession did not make salutary contributions to society as it waged war on ancient epidemics? But the medical profession also retarded social reform and, in some cases, restricted human rights. As we have already noted, the profession medicalized many of women's health conditions, such as childbirth, and subjected women to strange remedies such as months of bed rest and an epidemic of hysterectomies. Many physicians opposed the use of birth control on the grounds that women should not interfere with natural laws of reproduction. Moreover, physicians were not reluctant to profess knowledge of sexual matters; their pronouncement that homosexual behavior was medical pathology was not reversed until the 1980s.

Leaders of the American Medical Association (AMA) had entertained the notion of government health insurance (by the various states) in the early 20th century, as they observed successful projects by the English and Germans, but swung against the notion in the years before and after World War I. Indeed, they launched a campaign of virulent invective against the proponents of health insurance, which included many progressive reformers and social workers; health reformers were called "bolsheviks," "communists," and a threat to "the doctor-patient relationship." When they coupled this invective with a well-financed lobbying campaign in all states that were entertaining the idea of health insurance, they established the AMA as the primary lobbying group in the health field. The AMA's campaign helped convince large segments of the public that health insurance was un-American; it was so effective that it sabotaged the enactment of health insurance in the 1930s, the late 1940s, and the 1970s—and nearly blocked passage of lesser measures such as Medicare in the 1960s. The AMA also retarded the development of a strong public health system in the United States, by arguing on many occasions that even inoculations should be done only by private physicians.[78]

The AMA's reactionary tendencies were illustrated by its strident opposition to the Sheppard-Towner bill, a modest measure initiated by social workers in 1918 that sought to improve maternal and child health facilities and services in rural areas through federal grants to state health departments. Although the legislation was enacted in 1921, its proponents had to overcome charges that it represented "state medicine." Pathetically small, this program finally succumbed in 1929, largely because the medical profession "sought (successfully) to wrest control of infant and maternal health from female-run public clinics and place it, instead, in the hands of private, male physicians."[79]

The legal profession also threw roadblocks in the path of reform. Recall that progressives were interested in regulatory reforms, mostly in state and local jurisdictions. As we have already noted, the Supreme Court struck down legislation to limit hours of work for men and to prohibit child labor. Moreover, many Supreme Court justices continued to believe that the Constitution did not sanction the federal government's intrusion into social matters, *except* under very limited conditions that involved a specified power of the federal government, such as its jurisdiction over interstate commerce. (Recall from Chapter 3 that the Constitution reserved to the states all powers not specified in it—and, aside from vague clauses like the general welfare clause, the Constitution was silent on social policy matters.) Social reformers thus had to ponder how to frame social legislation so that it would conform to the narrow and specific wording of the Constitution. Amending the Constitution, although possible in principle, was difficult in practice. Congress passed a constitutional amendment in 1924 to authorize federal laws regulating the labor of youth under the age of 18, but the amendment failed to gain ratification by three-fourths of the states, and thus did not pass into law.

The intransigency of the courts, and particularly the Supreme Court, enraged progressive reformers like Theodore Roosevelt. Since the Constitution gives Congress the power to organize and establish rules for the Supreme Court, progressive reformers proposed taking the powers of constitutional review from the Supreme Court by legislation—or increasing the size of the Court to dilute the power of its sitting justices. These projects were not successful. In 1916, however, reformers did succeed in securing the appointment to the Court of Louis Brandeis—an attorney who advocated "sociological jurisprudence," which would factor the effects of laws on the well-being of citizens into constitutional rulings—over an avalanche of protests by many jurists and conservatives who alleged that he would disregard the intentions of the framers of the Constitution.

These legal disputes in the progressive era gave the Supreme Court a central role in the unfolding of social reform. Until about 1938, as we note in ensuing chapters, a succession of adverse rulings by the Supreme Court enormously delayed the federal government's assumption of responsibility for social policy. Even after the Court had acceded to the notion that the federal government could establish social programs and regulations, it remained a key player in shaping the content of those deci-

sions. (We note in later chapters how relatively liberal rulings of the 1950s and 1960s assumed enormous importance in speeding social reforms and how a succession of more conservative rulings in the 1980s and 1990s aligned the Court against social reformers.)[80]

 THE EVOLUTION OF THE RELUCTANT WELFARE STATE

Progressives dramatically expanded social obligation to include a host of regulations, as well as a limited set of social programs such as mothers' pensions and workmen's compensation. These accomplishments may not appear dramatic or far-reaching to contemporary citizens, but they constituted remarkable innovations in a society where social policy had previously been restricted to poorhouses, mental institutions, prisons, schools, and houses of refuge.

The progressives made a contribution to the development of the modern welfare state by championing the role of government in addressing social problems, although their emphasis was usually on regulation at state and local levels. Government, they believed, could serve as a force for the amelioration of social needs rather than as merely a passive umpire that preserved law and order. Further, many progressives believed that government need not merely provide funds and concessions to affluent persons and corporations but also ought to assist vulnerable populations such as women, children, immigrants, and factory workers. In a sense, then, progressives legitimized a vision of positive and compassionate government that had not hitherto been expressed as widely or as articulately in a nation preoccupied with laissez-faire doctrines and the deification of monied elites. The policies, that they enacted, in turn, served to educate the nation's citizens to the possibilities of governmental action, as workers, renters, and consumers benefited from improvements in working conditions, housing, and public health.

Nonetheless, the progressive movement must be

viewed as having made only modest social welfare innovations in a nation with extraordinary social needs. Regulations hardly constituted frontal assaults on poverty, low wages, or industrial accidents. Workmen's compensation and mothers' pensions were limited programs by any standards. When compared to European nations, the United States spent paltry sums on domestic programs—sums that were not markedly increased by the progressive reformers. Few Americans empathized with the social needs of African Americans, Latinos, and Asian Americans; indeed, many progressives were deeply suspicious of these groups—and were also prejudiced against immigrants.

Many reformers realized that low-income and working-class Americans would need to rally behind a reform-minded president if the nation were to develop more far-reaching reforms. But it was unclear how such a reform constituency could develop; the failed campaign of the Progressive party in 1912 illustrated how far there was still to go. As we discuss in Chapters 7 and 8, it took the catastrophe of the Great Depression to push the nation to develop major federal social programs and it took the leadership of a president who managed to achieve the political realignment that the progressives had fantasized might be possible.

NOTES

1. David Brody, *Workers in Industrial America: Essays on the Twentieth-Century Struggle* (New York: Oxford University Press, 1980), p. 15.

2. For comparisons of Russian and Italian immigrants, see Elizabeth Ewen, *Immigrant Women in the Land of Dollars: Life and Culture on the Lower East Side, 1890–1925* (New York: Monthly Review Press, 1985), pp. 30–57.

3. Ibid., pp. 112–113, 131; Timothy Walch, ed., *Immigrant America: European Ethnicity in the United States* (New York: Garland, 1993), pp. ix–xiv; and Edward Kantowicz, "The Changing Face of Ethnic Politics: From Political Machine to Community Organization." In Walch, ed., *Immigrant America,* pp. 179–197.

4. John Bodnar, *Steelton: Immigration and Industrialization, 1870–1940* (Pittsburgh: University of Pittsburgh Press, 1990), pp. 127–149; David Salvaterra, "Becoming American: Assimilation, Pluralism, and Ethnic Identity." In Walch, ed., *Immigrant America,* pp. 29–54.

5. Ewen, *Immigrant Women,* pp. 76–91.

6. Brody, *Workers,* p. 16.

7. James Weinstein, "It's Good for Business." In Arthur Mann, ed., *The Progressive Era: Major Issues of Interpretation* (Hinsdale, Ill.: Dryden Press, 1975), p. 112.

8. Brody, *Workers,* p. 24; Lizabeth Cohen, *Making a New Deal: Industrial Workers in Chicago, 1919–1939* (New York: Cambridge University Press, 1990), pp. 11–52.

9. Mark Leff, "Consensus for Reform: The Mothers' Pension Movement in the Progressive Era." In Frank Breul and Stephen Diner, eds., *Compassion and Responsibility: Readings in the History of Social Welfare Policy in the United States* (Chicago: University of Chicago Press, 1980), p. 245; Roy Lubove, *The Struggle for Social Security* (Cambridge, Mass.: Harvard University Press, 1968), pp. 98–99.

10. Stephan Skowronek, *Building a New American State: The Expansion of National Administrative Capacities, 1877–1920* (Cambridge: Cambridge University Press, 1982), pp. 39–42, 45–46, 165–176.

11. Arthur Link and Richard McCormick, *Progressivism* (Arlington Heights, Ill.: Harlan Davidson, 1983), pp. 18–20; David Thelen, "Not Classes but Issues." In Mann, ed., *The Progressive Era,* pp. 40–42.

12. Thelen, "Not Classes," pp. 42–45.

13. Sidney Fine, *Laissez-Faire and the General Welfare State: A Study of Conflict in America, 1865–1901* (Ann Arbor, Mich.: University of Michigan Press, 1956), pp. 126–168; Robert Steamer, *The Supreme Court in Crisis: A History of Conflict* (Amherst, Mass.: University of Massachusetts Press, 1971), pp. 149–171; and Edward White, *The American Judicial Tradition: Profiles of Leading American Judges* (New York: Oxford University Press, 1976), pp. 105–108.

14. Jane Addams, *Newer Ideals of Peace* (New York: Macmillan, 1907), p. 85.

15. She idealizes youth, immigrants, and women, respectively, in these books: *The Spirit of Youth and the City Streets* (New York: Macmillan, 1909); *Twenty Years at Hull House* (New York: Macmillan, 1961), pp. 169–185; *The Long Road of Women's Memory* (New York: Macmillan, 1917).

16. Fine, *Laissez-Faire,* pp. 198–251.

17. Charles Beard, *An Economic Interpretation of the Constitutional Convention* (New York: Free Press, 1965), pp. 152–188; Frederic Howe, *Confessions of a Reformer* (New York: Scribner's, 1925), p. 169; John Gable, *The Bull Moose Years: Theodore Roosevelt and the Progressive Party* (Port Woolington, N.Y.: Kennicat Press, 1978), pp. 11–13.

18. Lela Costin, *Two Sisters for Social Justice* (Urbana, Ill.: University of Illinois Press, 1983), pp. 31–38; Allen Davis, *American Heroine: The Life and Legend of Jane Addams* (New York: Oxford University Press, 1973), pp. 24–52.

19. Link and McCormick, *Progressivism,* pp. 15, 19–20; Thelen, "Not Classes," pp. 40–45; William Allen White, *The Autobiography of William Allen White* (New York: Macmillan, 1946), p. 484.

20. Fine, *Laissez-Faire,* p. 168; Thelen, "Not Classes," pp. 40–41.

21. Joseph Castrovinci, "Prelude to Welfare Capitalism: The Role of Business in the Enactment of Workmen's Compensation Legislation in Illinois, 1905–1912," *Social Service Review,* 50 (March 1976), 277; Lynn Gordon, "Women and the Anti-Child Labor Movement in Illinois, 1890–1920," *Social Service Review,* 51 (June 1977), 314, 319. For a discussion of the sheer power of the save-the-children ethos, see Michael Katz, *In the Shadow of the Poorhouse* (New York: Basic Books, 1986), pp. 113–115.

22. Richard Hofstadter, *Age of Reform: From Bryan to FDR* (New York: Knopf, 1955), pp. 185–195; Clarke Chambers, *Paul U. Kellogg and the Survey: Voices for Social Welfare and Social Justice* (Minneapolis, Minn.: University of Minnesota Press, 1971), pp. 33–40.

23. Walter Trattner, *Homer Folks: Pioneer in Social Welfare* (New York: Columbia University Press, 1968), pp. 76–84.

24. Roy Lubove, *The Professional Altruist* (Cambridge, Mass.: Harvard University Press, 1965), pp. 3–54.

25. Allen Davis, *Spearheads for Reform: The Social Settlements and the Progressive Movement, 1890–1914* (New York: Oxford University Press, 1967), p. 195.

26. Theda Skocpol, *Social Policy in the United States: Future Possibilities in Historical Perspective* (Princeton, N.J.: Princeton University Press, 1995), p. 76; Linda Gordon, *Pitied but Not Entitled* (New York: Free Press, 1994), p. 49.

27. Charles Larsen, *The Good Fight: The Life and Times of Ben Lindsey* (Chicago: Quadrangle Books, 1972), pp. 27–32.

28. Trattner, *Homer Folks,* p. 107; Costin, *Two Sisters,* pp. 100–118; and Josephine Goldmark, *The Impatient Crusader* (Urbana, Ill.: University of Illinois Press, 1953), pp. 100–104.

29. Costin, *Two Sisters,* p. 52.

30. Many monographs on settlements have recently been written, including *A White Man's Indian: Images of an Indian from Colún to Preston* (New York: 1978); Mina Carson, *Settlement Folk* (Chicago: University of Chicago Press, 1990); Ruth Crocker, *Social Work and Social Order* (Urbana, Ill.: University of Illinois Press, 1992); Howard Karger, *The Sentinels of Order* (Lanham, Md.: University Press of America, 1987); Elisabeth Lasch-Quinn, *Black Neighbors: Race and the Limits of Reform in the American Settlement House Movement, 1890–1945* (Chapel Hill, N.C.: University of North Carolina Press, 1993); Rivka Shpak Lissak, *Pluralism and Progressives* (Chicago: University of Chicago Press, 1989); Ralph Luker, *The Social Gospel in Black and White* (Chapel Hill: University of North Carolina Press, 1992); and Judith Ann Trolander, *Professionalism and Social Change* (New York: Columbia University Press, 1987). For an excellent overview of settlements, see Alfreda Iglehart and Rosina Becerra, *Social Services and the Ethnic Community* (Boston: Allyn and Bacon, 1995), pp. 107–148.

31. Lubove, *The Struggle,* p. 52–57; Skocpol, *Social Policy,* pp. 73–74; and Weinstein, "It's Good for Business," pp. 113–114.

32. Carolyn Webber and Aaron Wildavsky, *A History of Taxation and Expenditure in the Western World* (New York: Simon and Schuster, 1986), p. 451.

33. Steamer, *The Supreme Court,* pp. 149–171.

34. Link and McCormick, *Progressivism,* pp. 69–70, 72; Paolo Coletta, *The Presidency of William Howard Taft* (Lawrence, Kans.: University Press of Kansas, 1973), p. 139; Davis, *American Heroine,* p. 189;

Gable, *The Bull Moose Years,* pp. 90–91; and Link and McCormick, *Progressivism,* pp. 69–70.

35. John Buenker, *Urban Liberalism and Progressive Reform* (New York: Scribner's, 1973), p. 43; Michael Rogin and John Shover, "From Below." In Mann, ed., *The Progressive Era,* pp. 20–30; Davis, *American Heroine,* pp. 176–184, 189; Link and McCormick, *Progressivism,* pp. 69–70, 100–104; Paul Boyer, *Urban Masses and the Moral Order in America, 1820–1920* (Cambridge, Mass.: Harvard University Press, 1978), pp. 205–219; and Daniel Levine, *Jane Addams and the Liberal Tradition* (Madison, Wis.: State Historical Society of Wisconsin, 1971), pp. 144–159.

36. George Dangerfield, *The Strange Death of Liberal England* (New York: H. Smith and R. Haas, 1935), pp. 214–330; H. V. Emy, *Liberals, Radicals, and Social Politics, 1892–1914* (Cambridge: Cambridge University Press, 1973), pp. 235–280; and G. D. H. Cole and Raymond Postgate, *The British Common People* (New York: Barnes and Noble, 1961), pp. 481–496, 567–576.

37. Skowronek, *Building a New American State,* pp. 24–26.

38. Addams, *Twenty Years,* pp. 222–223; Hofstadter, *Age of Reform,* pp. 254–269; and Levine, *Jane Addams,* p. 75.

39. Brody, *Workers,* pp. 23-30, 82–88; Eric Foner, *History of the Labor Movement in the United States,* Vol. 2 (New York: International Publishers, 1955), pp. 184–188.

40. Brody, *Workers,* pp. 14–21.

41. Ibid., pp. 32–39.

42. Chambers, *Paul V. Kellogg,* p. 48; Davis, *American Heroine,* pp. 186, 193, 194; and Gable, *The Bull Moose Years,* pp. 6–7.

43. Davis, *American Heroine,* pp. 54–56, 125.

44. Gordon, *Pitied but Not Entitled,* pp. 67–87; and Skocpol, *Social Policy,* pp. 116–117.

45. Gable, *The Bull Moose Years,* pp. 6–7; Coletta, *The Presidency of William Howard Taft,* pp. 21–25.

46. Lee Kreader, "Isaac Max Rubinow: Pioneering Specialist in Social Insurance," *Social Service Review,* 50 (September 1976), 293–298.

47. Ibid., pp. 16–20; Gable, *The Bull Moose Years,* pp. 6, 112–113.

48. Gable, *The Bull Moose Years,* pp. 131–133.

49. Davis, *American Heroine,* p. 197.

50. John Dittmer, *Black Georgia in the Progressive Era, 1900–1920* (Urbana, Ill.: University of Illinois Press, 1977), pp. 8–22.

51. Florette Henri, *Black Migration: Movement North, 1900–1920* (Garden City, N.Y.: Doubleday, 1975), pp. 81–131.

52. Gordon, *Pitied but Not Entitled,* pp. 111–122.

53. Roger Daniels, *The Politics of Prejudice: The Anti-Japanese Movement in California and the Struggle for Japanese Exclusion* (Berkeley, Calif.: University of California Press, 1977), pp. 46–78; Jack Chen, *The Chinese of America: From the Beginnings to the Present* (San Francisco: Harper & Row, 1982), pp. 88–89, 99, 109–115.

54. J. Owens Smith, *The Politics of Racial Inequality: A Systematic Comparative Macro-Analysis from the Colonial Period to 1970* (New York: Greenwood Press, 1987), pp. 86–91.

55. Leobardo Estrada, F. Chris Garcia, Reynaldo Macias, and Lionel Maldonado, "Chicanos in the United States: A History of Exploitation and Resistance." In F. Chris Garcia, ed., *Latinos and the Political System* (Notre Dame, Ind.: University of Notre Dame Press, 1988), pp. 39, 41; Rodolfo Acuna, *Occupied America: The Chicano's Struggle Toward Liberation* (San Francisco: Canfield Press, 1972), pp. 130–135; Ronald Takaki, *A Different Mirror: A History of Multicultural America* (Boston: Little, Brown, 1994), p. 317; and Paul Boyer et al., *The Enduring Vision: A History of the American People* (Lexington, Mass.: D. C. Heath, 1995), p. 532.

56. Estrada et al., "Chicanos in the United States," p. 40.

57. Lawrence Fuchs, *The American Kaleidoscope: Race, Ethnicity, and the Civic Culture* (Hanover, N.H.: Wesleyan University Press, 1990), pp. 118–122; Takaki, *A Different Mirror,* p. 317.

58. Ibid.; Alfreda Iglehart and Rosina Becerra, *Social Services and the Ethnic Community* (Boston: Allyn and Bacon, 1995), pp. 51–57, 159; Ronald Takaki, *A Different Mirror,* pp. 336–339.

59. Fuchs, *The American Kaleidoscope,* pp. 120–122; Takaki, *A Different Mirror,* pp. 331–334.

60. Thomas Dyer, *Theodore Roosevelt and the Idea of Race* (Baton Rouge, La.: Louisiana State University Press, 1980), pp. 21–44, 105; Gable, *The Bull*

Moose Years, p. 74; Dittmer, *Black Georgia,* pp. 108–109.

61. Dittmer, *Black Georgia,* pp. 181, 186.

62. Steamer, *The Supreme Court,* pp. 125–126, 149–150.

63. Steven Diner, "Chicago Social Workers and Blacks in the Progressive Era," *Social Service Review,* 44 (December 1970), 231–236; Levine, *Jane Addams,* pp. 192–194.

64. Eleanor Flexner, *Century of Struggle: The Women's Rights Movement in the United States* (Cambridge, Mass.: Harvard University Press, 1975), pp. 319–337.

65. Mimi Abramovitz, *Regulating the Lives of Women: Social Welfare Policy from Colonial Times to the Present* (Boston: South End Press, 1988), p. 188, 190–193, 199, 248–255.

66. Nancy Woloch, *Women and the American Experience* (New York: Knopf, 1984), pp. 363–380.

67. Barbara Ehrenreich and Deirdre English, *For Her Own Good: 150 Years of the Experts' Advice to Women* (New York: Anchor Books, 1979), p. 110, 131–133.

68. Ibid., pp. 93–98.

69. Fuchs, *The American Kaleidoscope,* p. 16; John Higham, *Strangers in the Land: Patterns of American Nativism, 1860–1925* (New York: Atheneum, 1972), pp. 106–130, 158–193.

70. Higham, *Strangers in the Land,* p. 108.

71. Ibid., p. 159.

72. Ibid., p. 110; Estrada et al., "Chicanos in the United States," p. 44.

73. Walter Trattner, *From Poor Law to Welfare State,* 4th ed. (New York: Free Press, 1991), pp. 213–214.

74. Stanley Wenocur and Michael Reisch, *From Charity to Enterprise: The Development of American Social Work in a Market Economy* (Urbana, Ill.: University of Illinois Press, 1989), pp. 50–52.

75. Ibid., pp. 47–60.

76. Mary Richmond, *Social Diagnosis* (New York: Russell Sage Foundation, 1917).

77. Wenocur and Reisch, *From Charity to Enterprise,* pp. 77–78.

78. James Burrow, *Organized Medicine in the Progressive Era* (Baltimore: John Hopkins University Press, 1977), pp. 32–66; Ronald Numbers, *Almost Persuaded: American Physicians and Compulsory Health Insurance* (Baltimore: Johns Hopkins University Press, 1979), pp. 4–5.

79. Trattner, *From Poor Law to Welfare State,* pp. 198–200.

80. Gable, *The Bull Moose Years,* pp. 82, 93.

7

The Early Stages of the New Deal

Selected Orienting Events

1921–1923	Presidency of Warren Harding
1925–1928	Presidency of Calvin Coolidge
1929	Stock market crashes; Great Depression begins
1929–1932	Presidency of Herbert Hoover
1932	Reconstruction Finance Corporation established; Emergency Relief and Construction Act passed
1933–1945	Presidency of Franklin Roosevelt
1933	Civilian Conservation Corps (CCC), Agricultural Adjustment Agency (AAA), Public Works Administration (PWA), and Federal Emergency Relief Administration (FERA) established; Civilian Works Administration (CWA) established by executive order; Tennessee Valley Authority (TVA) created; Emergency Farm Mortgage Act and Farm Relief Act enacted
1934	Securities and Exchange Commission (SEC) created; CWA terminated by Roosevelt

During the Great Depression of the 1930s, Americans finally fashioned a series of social reforms that far surpassed the local and regulatory reforms of the progressive era and brought the federal government into a position of policy prominence. Governmental institutions, the presidency, politics, and the courts were also transformed in this fateful decade, which changed social welfare policy in the United States forever. Although ambitious by American standards, the reforms were relatively timid by international or today's standards.

Reforms in the Great Depression can best be understood by analyzing the unfolding of reform in four periods.

1. In the *era of denial* (1929 to March 1933), Americans seemed stunned by the economic catastrophe and took little corrective action.
2. During the *period of emergency reforms* (March 1933 to January 1935), Americans supported a bewildering number of reforms but tended to believe that prosperity would soon return and that many reforms could be relatively temporary.
3. In the *era of institutionalized reform* (January 1935 to January 1937), Americans decided to make a number of reforms permanent.
4. Finally, during an *era of policy stalemate* (January 1937 to December 1941), the momentum of New Deal reform was decisively broken.

THE 1920s

The progressive reform momentum was shattered when Americans focused on preparations for World War I, the war effort, and postwar diplomacy, including an ill-fated League of Nations, although this period did yield a few reforms, such as federal directives requiring recipients of war contracts not to use child labor.[1] In the 1920s, as in the 1950s and the 1980s, many Americans believed that private enterprise, left unfettered by government, would bring unlimited prosperity. The nation was presided over by three Republican presidents, Warren Harding, Calvin Coolidge, and Herbert

Hoover, who strenuously resisted efforts of a small cadre of social reformers.[2] Harding stated his philosophy succinctly when he said, "What we want in America is less government in business and more business in government."

A second American industrial revolution occurred during the 1920s. Steel, mining, and railroad industries had developed during the first revolution; the second focused on consumer products—such as cars, radios, and refrigerators—and on the electrification of homes and industries. Enormous consumer needs remained unmet in the United States: Only one in ten urban homes was electrified in 1920; only one in one hundred households possessed radios; and only one in three families had cars. Consumer appetites for new products were whetted by the rise of a large advertising industry.[3]

A trickle-down economic philosophy was dominant. Officials believed that economic assistance to affluent persons and industry stimulated investments that could bring jobs to poor and working-class Americans. The low tariffs of the prewar era were supplanted by protective tariffs for American industry; federal taxes had been increased to pay off the national debt in the wake of World War I, but new tax laws reduced them to one-quarter of their previous level; and many regulations that had been enacted in the progressive era were relaxed, not implemented, or struck down by the courts.[4] Policies that empowered industry and affluent persons were supplemented by vigorous suppression of organized labor. Companies sought to obtain the goodwill of employees by stock-sharing schemes, providing fringe benefits, and starting company unions that ostensibly gave workers a mechanism for negotiating higher benefits and wages. When unions tried to organize, their leaders were often intimidated or fired—and strikes led to unabashed use of scabs, local police, the national guard, and injunctions from courts that were usually favorable to management.[5]

Social reformers were on the defensive during the 1920s; some were stigmatized as radicals, communists, or traitors. African Americans continued to live under oppressive Jim Crow laws in the South, encountered race riots and residential segregation in the North, and found it difficult to find jobs in the industries that were now producing consumer goods in the second industrial revolution. Although African Americans were a significant presence in many Northern cities, most continued to work for white planters in the South.[6] Latinos and Asian Americans continued to experience rampant prejudice and adverse policies in the West and Southwest.[7] Women experienced new sexual freedoms in the era of the flapper, but found that their voting privileges did not lead to major policy reforms that would give them access to more remunerative work or to the professions.[8]

Americans were intrigued by social change and often tended to glamorize technology and science, but they were also fearful of new ideas; in the famous Scopes trial in 1925, for example, a school teacher was successfully prosecuted for teaching the theory of evolution in a Tennessee school. (The verdict was later overturned on a technicality.) Prohibition, enacted in the form of the Eighteenth Amendment to the Constitution in 1919, was supported by many Protestants, who insisted that local and federal officials strictly enforce the legislation.[9] Many Americans supported stringent reductions of immigration, whether on racial grounds or because they believed the nation could no longer absorb immigrants. The Immigration Act of 1924 was blatantly racist: Its goal was to maintain the "racial preponderance [of] the basic strain of our people." A limit of 150,000 people was placed on immigration each year, with quotas for each nationality in proportion to its size in the existing population. This policy was intended to reduce the proportion of immigrants from southern and eastern Europe. A complete prohibition was placed on Japanese immigration.[10]

In contrast to these conservative reforms, which sought to restore traditional American values, there was a new interest in exploring sexual liberation and the psyche. Sigmund Freud was not taken seriously in his native Europe, but his theories—though not immediately adopted by social work practitioners—swept America, much as those of Herbert Spencer had done in the Gilded Age.[11]

The profession of social work grew rapidly during the 1920s. By 1929, 25 graduate schools existed, several professional associations had developed, and three journals disseminated information. Casework emerged as the central skill during the decade; its practitioners outnumbered other kinds of social workers by a threefold margin. Mary Richmond's classic treatise during the progressive era had emphasized familial, neighborhood, and societal realities, but in the 1920s, some caseworkers became excited about the personality—so much so that they risked ignoring environmental realities as well as the need for social reforms. Caseworkers tended to be employed in not-for-profit agencies and were often relatively contemptuous of public agencies, which, they believed, should only aid paupers and persons with chronic and severe mental conditions.[12] There were still those who proposed more fundamental reforms, but they were decidedly on the fringes of American society.

Surface impressions of prosperity in the 1920s were misleading, because unemployment ranged from 5% to 13%, and agriculture was in a state of depression throughout the decade. Although the upper third of the populace conspicuously consumed consumer products, the lower third were often unemployed or lived near or below poverty in a society that had few governmental income-transfer programs.[13]

Controversy exists about the precise causes of the Great Depression in 1929.[14] Some theorists contend that the nation's economic expansion was halted because industry and affluent persons had insufficient capital at their disposal. However, the aforementioned trickle-down policies placed vast sums of money in the coffers of affluent persons and corporations. Other theorists argue convincingly that the Great Depression occurred because American consumers lacked sufficient resources to purchase consumer goods. Some economists implicate excessive speculation and protective tariffs. Whatever its precise causes, the Great Depression of 1929, like the depression of 1893, put an immediate and decisive halt to prosperity; suggested that trickle-down policies were not a panacea; and alerted Americans to the realities of poverty, unemployment, and economic injustice.

THE PERIOD OF DENIAL: 1929–1933

The immediate reality of massive unemployment, depressed stock prices, lost fortunes, bankrupt companies, and deflated prices was obvious to everyone in 1929, including Herbert Hoover, the incumbent president. Americans had experienced many economic downturns in their history, however; most persons assumed that economic growth would resume.

Herbert Hoover at first seemed ideally suited to solve the nation's problems. A civil engineer who had orchestrated a massive food relief program for starving Europeans after World War I, he prided himself on a problem-solving style in which political considerations were given little role. He believed, like most Americans, that modest tinkering with the economic system would bring the nation out of its economic doldrums. In accordance with trickle-down economics, he favored passage of the Reconstruction Finance Corporation (RFC), which processed $2 billion for loans to corporations and banks, as well as various projects to encourage economic activity by bankers and corporations. To appease critics, and because he did not believe in major governmental programs, however, Hoover implemented these policies in a restrictive manner; he insisted, for example, that corporations and banks prove that they were on the verge of bankruptcy before providing them with loans under the RFC.[15]

Hoover also believed that private agencies, principally the Red Cross and family service agencies, could address the needs of unemployed and poverty-stricken Americans without governmental assistance. He shared Franklin Pierce's ideology—enunciated in the Pierce veto of nearly a century earlier—that welfare issues belonged to local government and to private philanthropy. Some historians have emphasized progressive elements of Hoover's ideology, but the preponderance of evidence suggests that he was an inflexible conservative adhered to Social Darwinism and equated federal social programs with socialism.[16]

Hoover's measures did not address the mounting economic needs of local governments, which were moving toward bankruptcy as their welfare expenditures increased. Pressure from the Congress to help local governments finally led to passage of the Emergency Relief and Construction Act in 1932, which authorized federal loans to local governments that could prove they had become bankrupt. However, as the Depression worsened, some Americans began to wonder whether more drastic measures were needed. A small group of liberal politicians in the House and the Senate proposed measures that seemed radical to many Americans, such as federal funding of major public works projects; the development of federally funded employment offices; federal funding of unemployment and old-age insurance; the development of dams; and reforestation projects to create jobs and economic growth in rural areas.[17] Senators Robert Wagner of New York, Robert La Follette of Wisconsin, and Edward Costigan of Colorado led this small cadre of reformers. They drew from some proposals fashioned in the 1920s by the American Association of Old Age Security, a reform group headed by Isaac Rubinow, who introduced to the United States concepts of social insurance that had been pioneered in Europe.[18] Even relatively conservative big-city bosses, such as Mayor James Curley of Boston, urged job creation and public works programs that went beyond the timid measures of Hoover.[19]

Hoover became more conservative, however, as the nation gradually moved toward more liberal ideas. An inflexible man who was isolated from, and insensitive to, political realities, he resorted to budget-balancing and various monetary solutions to complement his woefully inadequate programs. He bitterly attacked liberals, who, he believed, advocated socialistic measures that would compound the nation's economic problems.[20]

The nation's confidence in business—and in Hoover—began to waver by 1930. Hoover had won a sweeping victory in 1928, but the Republican party suffered such extensive losses in the congressional elections of 1930 that its majority was reduced to a narrow margin. Most Democrats were

INSERT 7.1   CRITICAL ANALYSIS: WHICH SOCIAL PROBLEMS ARE RECOGNIZED?

When Hoover failed to recognize the extent and duration of unemployment from 1929 onward, he illustrated a recurring tendency of policy makers to deny the existence of important problems.

1. Identify some major social problems in recent American history that policy makers failed to recognize or to take seriously.
2. Identify some other social problems that policy makers *did* take seriously (for example, by proposing major legislation or allocating major funding to address them).
3. What political, cultural, economic, or other factors seem to make policy makers deny some problems, while taking others seriously?
4. Can advocates for specific social problems speed up the clock? In other words, is there some way they can gain policy makers' attention more promptly?

as confused by the situation as Hoover, however, since they, too, tended to favor budget-cutting, tax reduction, and trickle-down economics to cope with the Depression. Though many social workers supported Roosevelt, Jane Addams and some other reformers voted for Hoover in the pivotal election of 1932.[21]

Franklin Delano Roosevelt (FDR) was not a liberal in the presidential campaign of 1932; he expressed more sympathy for the unemployed than did Hoover, and talked vaguely of reforestation schemes, but he advocated a balanced budget and conservative fiscal policies and even derided Hoover for spending too much federal money. However, Roosevelt and the Democrats won a sweeping victory in 1932 because, after three ineffectual Republican presidents, Americans wanted to give the Democrats a chance to address the nation's problems. Although few believed that Roosevelt favored policies strikingly different from those of Hoover, some who knew him believed that his policies would prove more liberal than his rhetoric. As assistant secretary of the navy in World War I, he had participated in the mobilization of national resources by the federal government. As governor of New York State between 1928 and 1932, he oversaw the operations of the state's Labor Department, which administered a variety of regulations pertaining to child labor and

work safety, and the Temporary Emergency Relief Administration (TERA), a modest program that provided state funds to local units of government for outdoor relief to the unemployed. He knew many social workers, including Frances Perkins, who headed the Labor Department, and Harry Hopkins, who had worked in private philanthropic agencies and directed the TERA. He was married, moreover, to a remarkable woman, Eleanor, who had been immersed in a range of social reforms during the 1920s.[22]

THE ERA OF EMERGENCY REFORMS: 1933–1935

When Franklin Roosevelt won his decisive victory in November 1932, it was unclear what he would do with his mandate. Policy drift was no longer possible, because the banking system was threatened with collapse due to insufficient funds to cover withdrawals of panic-stricken depositors. Local governments encountered staggering welfare burdens because 20–60% of Americans were unemployed in many cities and neighborhoods. Millions of Americans, many of them youths whose parents could no longer support them,

FIGURE 7.1 Men eating bread and soup in a bread line during the Great Depression

SOURCE: The Bettmann Archive

roamed the nation, obtained beans, coffee, and floor space from local police, and were told to move on the next day. Economic inequality, which had always been severe, became even more obvious at a time when unskilled and uneducated persons and people of color were massively unemployed. Many farmers, who were suffering catastrophic losses in a worldwide depression of prices of agricultural produce, lost their farms when they could not make mortgage or loan payments; many fled an extraordinary drought that had developed in Oklahoma and adjacent states.[23]

American business was in disarray. Prices of products decreased as demand plummeted and as exports were slashed owing to the depressed economies of European nations. Consumer demand decreased further when employers reduced their work forces. Businesses went bankrupt as they slashed their prices in a desperate effort to retain customers. The suicide rate of investors, bankers, and company executives rose sharply.[24]

Unions, which had made slow but certain progress in the late 1920s, went into virtual collapse; workers were too desperate for jobs to contest employers' wage-cutting policies.

Roosevelt faced several difficult choices.

1. He had to decide whether to focus on the victims of economic distress, such as unemployed and hungry persons, or to seek a range of reforms to improve the economic system.
2. When addressing the problems of destitute persons, he had to decide what combination of funds, goods, and jobs to provide them.
3. He had to decide whether to define the situation as an emergency or as a set of conditions that required permanent programs.
4. He had to decide whether to give the federal government major policy roles or to provide funds to state and local governments so that they could address social and economic problems within their boundaries.

A variety of forces pushed Roosevelt and his advisors toward limited, localistic, and temporary reforms, but other forces prompted him to consider ongoing federal programs. The actual reforms that were enacted in 1933 and 1934 can be understood only in the context of this set of contradictory forces.

Forces That Promoted Major Reforms

Roosevelt's sweeping personal victory in 1932 was the largest plurality a president had received since 1864 and provided him with a power base during the remainder of the decade. The progressives' dream of a relatively liberal political party, which failed in 1912, was partially realized when Roosevelt obtained the votes of an unprecedented proportion of working-class voters, who wanted government to take an active stance in addressing unemployment and poverty. (Republicans, by contrast, obtained most of their support from middle- and upper-class voters.) This substantial realignment of parties on the basis of social class, which continued throughout the 1930s, was crucial to the development of social reforms in the Roosevelt Administration and in succeeding decades.[25]

Roosevelt had extraordinary power because he had gained support not only from the working class but also from a sizable portion of the middle class, to whom Roosevelt appealed because he exuded confidence, because they no longer believed that Republicans could solve the economic problems of the nation, and because many of them had been directly affected by the depression.[26] As the progressive period had demonstrated, an era of major reform cannot develop until considerable reform sentiment emerges within the American middle class, so as to offset opposition from corporations, affluent persons, conservatives, and middle-class persons who oppose reforms.

The strongest pressure for reform derived, however, from the magnitude of human suffering that existed during the 1930s. Persons of all social classes were devastated by economic suffering and resorted to desperate and improvisational survival strategies. Some persons moved into tents in the countryside during the summer; three or more families shared apartments; groups of single women shared apartments and lived from the wages of a single worker; persons tried to grow produce in gardens; and teenagers roamed the countryside when their families could not support them. Lorena Hickok, a reporter who was commissioned by Eleanor Roosevelt to tour the country in a car, documented the suffering of members of all social classes in daily letters to the first lady.[27] White-collar Americans feared foreclosure or evictions, had to pawn family possessions, were ashamed that their neighbors might discover they were on relief, and shunned clothes made in the sewing rooms of relief programs. Malnutrition and starvation were widely reported; in some cases, thousands of children were placed in summer camps to give them adequate food. Medical care was lacking for members of all classes, since many physicians and hospitals refused service to persons with no money. Even on welfare, many individuals lacked funds to heat or light their homes or to purchase clothing. Foreclosures, evictions, layoffs, family disruption, and suicides were commonplace. When touring major American cities in 1932, Harry Hopkins observed that the hundreds of thousands of Americans who lined the streets to watch FDR's procession did not protest, yell, or applaud but stood in stunned silence.[28] This widespread suffering persisted throughout the decade, despite periodic upturns in the economy. Even when the economy improved slightly, vast numbers of persons could not find employment. When Congress impatiently imposed a rule in 1939 that no one could receive more than 18 months of work relief, investigators found that more than two-thirds of recipients had to return to work relief because they could not find jobs.[29]

Roosevelt's freedom of action was enhanced by the disarray of Republicans and conservatives following his overwhelming defeat of Hoover.[30] Business interests, which had traditionally pro-

INSERT 7.2   CRITICAL ANALYSIS: WHEN WOULD NATIONAL REFORMS HAVE EMERGED WITHOUT THE GREAT DEPRESSION?

Hypotheticals—that is, surmises about the course of history if certain historical incidents had *not* occurred—are sometimes useful, because they force us to analyze history and to place specific developments in a broader perspective. Speculate whether major social programs would have been enacted at the federal level had the Great Depression *not* occurred. If they would not have been enacted in the 1930s, would *other* pressures or forces have eventually forced Americans to evolve major national social programs? How would we view Franklin Roosevelt had he *not* presided over the nation during the Great Depression?

vided considerable support for conservative politicians, were discredited by the economic collapse, because their speculation and greed were widely perceived as one cause of the economic downturn. The catastrophe of the depression shook the nation to its foundations; confronted with such widespread and prolonged suffering, Americans looked for bold leadership and were willing to contemplate policies that would have been unthinkable several years earlier.

Roosevelt and his aides were often in disarray themselves, but they came into office with relatively well-developed ideas and many areas of consensus.[31] Above all, they wanted to use the resources and power of the federal government to intervene in economic and social affairs, in the belief that purposeful action could solve problems. They rejected both Adam Smith's laissez-faire economics and John Locke's restricted definition of government, which had provided the buttress for conservative philosophy in the United States through the Hoover administration. Roosevelt and his inner circle of advisors, the so-called brains trust, did not know the precise solutions, but they reasoned that interventions could be devised in trial-and-error fashion until something worked. Old verities had not worked to solve the economic malaise. Roosevelt had an open field, and he chose to seize the moment; the legislation and programs that he proposed transformed the nation and, in the process, created an American welfare state that endured even the conservative administration of Ronald Reagan 50 years later.

Forces That Limited Roosevelt's Initial Policy Initiatives

Roosevelt realized that conservatives were a potential threat to social reforms. The conservative National Economic League had fought even the limited reforms of the Hoover administration. Although many businessmen supported specific pieces of New Deal legislation, they tended to be suspicious of Roosevelt both for his rhetoric—he often singled out the wealthy, bankers, and speculators for criticism—and for his policies, such as tax measures that raised corporate and individual taxes. The U.S. Chamber of Commerce stoutly resisted reforms in local and national arenas.[32]

Roosevelt encountered formidable political opposition from both political parties throughout the decade. Coopted by corporate interests during the 1920s, the leadership of the Democratic party favored high tariffs, limited assistance to poor persons, and a small federal bureaucracy. Roosevelt's victory over Newton Baker in the Democratic convention in 1932 was a decisive blow to this traditional leadership, but it maintained a strong—and hostile—presence in the party and often opposed Roosevelt's initiatives.[33]

In the early 1930s, most churches were profoundly conservative; Boston clergy from most faiths, for example, opposed federal and state programs to help the poor.[34] Many leaders of the Catholic Church became staunch defenders of the New Deal, but its bishops nonetheless opposed regulation of child labor, which they believed interfered with the privacy of the family.[35] Even though more than half the American population lived in cities during the 1930s, local, state, and national legislatures were dominated by rural legislators, who were often insensitive to the needs of urban residents.[36]

Labor leaders tended not to be fierce advocates of social reforms during the New Deal, because they were preoccupied with securing the right to organize. At the start of the decade, fewer than three million American workers were organized (which was two million fewer than in 1920), and most were skilled workers in various AFL craft unions. In the early 1930s, considerable unrest developed among assembly-line workers and miners under the leadership of men such as John L. Lewis, who headed the United Mine Workers. But the AFL eyed these unskilled workers nervously, because they were unlikely candidates for skilled electrical, carpentry, and other unions. Prompted by worker unrest, and sensing that the New Deal provided workers with a less hostile environment than under prior administrations, Lewis impatiently prodded the AFL to allocate resources to unions of unskilled workers. In 1936, giving up on the AFL, he formed the Congress of Industrial Organizations (CIO), which finally provided a home for steel, auto, mining, and other unions. But the bloody strikes and the sheer effort of organizing these unions meant that Lewis and others devoted limited effort to securing broader social reforms for American workers. Indeed, in roughly one-half of the strikes during the New Deal, the goal was to obtain the right to form a union rather than to secure higher wages.[37]

Union leaders such as Lewis focused on traditional union issues partly because they were intent on building membership in a period when most unskilled workers were unorganized.[38] Union membership did increase, but not until relatively late in the 1930s, when employers decided that tolerating unions would decrease strikes and so preserve their profits from the upturn in the economy and from munitions contracts. (Massive increases in union membership also occurred during World War II, when the government supported collective bargaining to allay labor unrest.) By 1936, labor had become the major single contributor to the campaigns of Roosevelt, but labor was uncertain in its support for some New Deal legislation and was hampered by internal dissension.[39]

Indeed, the American Federation of Labor (AFL) maintained a relatively conservative posture throughout the decade. It sometimes argued that government work programs represented forced labor but then fought opportunistically to obtain jobs in government programs for its own members. It rarely initiated policy ideas and even feared the development of governmental policies that might facilitate the organizing of unskilled workers by rival unions in automobile, steel, and other plants.[40]

The specter of adverse rulings by the Supreme Court hung over the New Deal from the outset. The Court had declared federal child-labor legislation to be unconstitutional in 1918, on the grounds that the federal government's power to regulate interstate commerce was not applicable in that case. In the New Deal era, four of the justices, known as the four horsemen, consistently opposed federal social legislation on the grounds that it was not an enumerated power in the Constitution; when joined by two moderate justices, they were able to overrule social legislation. (Only three relatively liberal justices were on the Court.)[41]

The United States also lacked fiscal and governmental institutions to implement sweeping reforms. The federal income tax was initiated in 1913, but taxes had been drastically cut during the 1920s and only modestly increased by the Federal Revenue Act of 1932; most Americans paid no income tax at all, even after this legislation. The government financed social welfare programs by running deficits in its budget, but many Americans, including some of Roosevelt's advisors, believed that deficits exacerbated the economic problems of the nation.[42] A federal civil service system was in place, but federal bureaucracies were relatively small in 1932 and riddled with patronage and corruption. When Frances Perkins was appointed secretary of labor, for example, she found that many of its top officials were receiving payoffs in return for obtaining immigration papers and visas for political supporters; they were hoping she would stay away from her office so that they could continue to receive these payoffs.[43] Local governmental institutions were even more archaic. Many public welfare offices, for example, were staffed by cronies of local politicians; welfare funds often found their way into the pockets of politicians; and punitive policies, such as publicizing the names of recipients, were used in some jurisdictions.[44]

Legislatures at national and local levels and even the presidency itself were unpromising vehicles for social reform. Many state legislatures met only every two years and busied themselves primarily with pork barrel and patronage matters. The Congress was saddled with a seniority system that rewarded older, Southern, and conservative legislators, who chaired key committees. Committees generally lacked staffs to help them analyze legislation and develop positions. Patronage was frequently entangled with policy; when legislators or presidents broached policy recommendations, it was often assumed that their major motivation was to secure patronage for loyal supporters.[45] The institution of the presidency was unequipped to develop policy. The presidency had become a symbolic post during the 1920s, when presidents satisfied themselves with budget-balancing and patronage functions. Roosevelt dramatically changed the presidency from a symbolic institution to a policy-initiating institution in his first year, when he presented a full legislative package to the Congress.[46]

Another factor that slowed the pace of reform was the absence of a well-developed radical movement in the United States. Strong union, socialist, and radical movements had obtained national unemployment programs in England during the 1920s. Though these movements demonstrated less strength and militance in the 1930s, some politicians in England feared that class conflict could lead to revolution and were reluctant to rescind the extremely liberal unemployment and welfare benefits that had been enacted.[47] Dramatic strikes should not obscure the fact, however, that American workers were stunned by the Depression and,

in the main, were politically quiet from 1929 to 1934. Only a small fraction of workers participated in the sitdown strikes of 1937. When a challenge from the left did develop in 1934 and 1935 (which we shall discuss later), it was poorly organized and focused only on the personal agendas of charismatic leaders.[48]

Local organizations of unemployed persons sprang up spontaneously in many localities, but their national impact was limited because they were not nationally coordinated and their emphasis was on obtaining higher benefits from existing work and relief programs.[49] Local agricultural protest movements flourished but also focused on improving the benefits of existing programs, as well as on policies to stem the tide of foreclosures. Interest groups—which assumed far greater prominence in the United States than in European societies, where class-oriented organizations were dominant—did not understand the full range of programs that constituted the New Deal legislative strategy.[50] Each group, such as labor, agriculture, and business, emphasized policies to help its members. In this welter of specific groups, a philosophy that defined and embraced public obligation for the nation's citizens seemed strangely absent.[51] No alliances formed between groups that represented urban workers and distressed persons in rural areas; indeed, many farmers turned against the New Deal in the late 1930s because they resented its emphasis on urban reforms.[52]

Reform momentum was also impeded by dissension among Roosevelt's advisors, some of whom favored conservative policies. The inner circle of advisors included budget-conscious persons, such as Henry Morgenthau (secretary of the treasury) and Lewis Douglas (director of the Bureau of the Budget), who sought to reduce social spending and often contended with Harry Hopkins, who favored increasing social spending, even when it required massive deficits. Some advisors, such as Frances Perkins, sought federal policies that ceded major policy roles to the states, in contrast to advisors like Harry Hopkins, who tended to favor federal policy roles. Louis Brandeis, the attorney general, believed that a trust-busting strategy should be used, whereas Senator Robert Wagner believed trust-busting hurt economic growth. Roosevelt often received contradictory advice and was himself confused about various issues, such as the merits of deficit spending.[53]

Roosevelt was not a radical. His defenders argued that conservative political pressures compelled him to include compromises in his legislation, but his critics contended that he was often too cautious even when he had firm control of the Congress. He did not favor the ongoing assumption of major welfare programs by the federal government; he liked social insurance programs that were funded by payroll deductions rather than from general revenues; and he often acceded to advisors who advocated cuts in social programs in order to decrease federal deficits.[54]

Finally, Southern Democrats chaired the major committees of Congress and constituted a substantial block of votes in the Democratic party. Throughout the decade, Roosevelt realized that his social reforms could be enacted only if he kept the support of these conservative legislators, who could form a majority of the chamber if they chose to vote with Republicans.

Emergency Relief

Roosevelt created a variety of programs that propelled the federal government for the first time into the social welfare arena. These programs provided relief, jobs, and food to Americans who needed them.

Many states and localities were verging on bankruptcy in 1932 because of mounting welfare costs and diminished revenues. Roosevelt's solution was the Federal Emergency Relief Administration (FERA); this emergency program provided funds to states for persons who needed financial assistance. It was virtually a carbon copy, though on a larger scale, of the Temporary Emergency Relief Administration (TERA) that Roosevelt had developed in New York.[55]

The legislation did not give a carte blanche to state and local governments. Hopkins was a man of strong convictions, who realized that poor law traditions in states and localities were often punitive, particularly to persons capable of working—the very group that now comprised the bulk of the population that needed welfare. He was also incensed by the orientations of many private agencies, which insisted on intensive casework screening of applicants as a condition of relief. Hopkins did not hold the widespread belief that the poor should receive in-kind relief or food vouchers to prevent them from spending welfare funds on alcohol, tobacco, and other luxuries. If wealthy persons can drink martinis, he asked, why not allow poor persons to drink beer? Hopkins also realized that firm federal administration of relief giving would be needed if corruption and patronage were to be avoided. He did not want intensive casework to be used with recipients, but he wanted trained social workers to be hired in supervisory positions, so as to enhance the professionalism of welfare services and provide services to those who needed them.[56]

The subsequent legislation, which evolved in the course of consultations between Hopkins, Perkins, Senator Robert Wagner, and Roosevelt, contained provisions to minimize these various dangers. It required each state to designate a state commission that was separate from the existing welfare apparatus, both to underscore the temporary nature of the federal assistance and to establish new agencies that would not be punitive. The state commissions were required to establish offices in the various counties and to establish uniform eligibility processes to be used throughout the state. Federal officials had veto power over high-level appointments, to guard against patronage appointments, and required the use of social workers in key supervisory positions. The legislation gave federal authorities the right to federalize FERA programs in states where irregularities such as corruption or excessive patronage were discovered. It authorized $500 million in federal aid to destitute persons, of which half was given to states in a one-to-three match; the other $250 million was used as

ERIN
751-0289

755-90Mark

Call Mark Colleta ask
if I could borrow a sleeping
bag.
Write a letter to
Glenda, ask for permanency.

619-
2384

fax # 755-2822

755-4058

751-3196
Drew

grants to states that could prove they lacked funds. FERA was technically supposed to provide welfare payments only for unemployed persons, but many states also gave funds to the working poor, many of whom were unable to survive on their low wages. Its major thrust was to help states and localities with the costs of sustaining unemployed persons, but the FERA also funded and ran camps for transients, helped college students with loans, funded cooperatives among farmers, and purchased more than four million acres of land for resale to tenant farmers.[57]

The FERA was a startling departure from prior American welfare traditions. It represented the first major federal welfare program in the nation's history. Though innovative, it also had conservative features. It was not intended to be ongoing legislation; Roosevelt was convinced that public welfare rightly belonged to states and local jurisdictions. He hoped, as well, that the depression would run its course. The legislation did not require local units of government to give recipients a minimum level of benefits; such a requirement would have been widely interpreted as undue interference with local prerogatives. Many recipients were returned to local, and often punitive, welfare agencies when the FERA was terminated in 1935. Although federal authorities expected local government to use FERA funds to supplement their existing welfare expenditures, many cut their local funding, so that welfare recipients scarcely benefited from the infusion of new federal money.[58] Even with the federal funding, welfare programs were marked by uncertainty. Foodless holidays were declared when funds ran out. Because many citizens resisted the enactment of state bond issues to raise local matching funds, federal funding was sometimes terminated for brief periods. Many local areas continued to emphasize in-kind rather than cash assistance, despite Hopkins's conviction that in-kind assistance was demeaning.[59]

Nonetheless, it is to the credit of FERA administrators that they put this massive program in place with remarkable speed and efficiency. The country was divided into five regions, whose federal administrators worked closely with directors of state emergency relief organizations to ensure that federal guidelines were followed. They were often greeted with hostility by local and state officials, who resented federal intrusion and sought to maintain patronage systems and punitive practices. The regional and federal administrators were not afraid to persevere to correct local abuses; indeed, they federalized FERA operations in six states because of irregularities.[60]

Critics pointed out that the FERA did not provide work to unemployed persons and even discouraged work in those cases where recipients were afraid to leave FERA rolls in order to take jobs. Many recipients feared that they would not be recertified for welfare if their companies went bankrupt or slashed wages below the level of the FERA grants, which were barely sufficient for subsistence. Some observers even suspected that, by allowing states to provide FERA funds to people who were working but still poor, the program was encouraging employers to reduce wages. Accepting those criticisms of the program, Hopkins himself argued in the summer of 1933 that the FERA dole was holding back large numbers of persons who were able and willing to work.[61]

An obvious solution to these problems was to create a public works program. Aubrey Williams, an assistant to Hopkins, proposed the use of FERA funds to create public works; this program would be administered through county offices of the FERA in the various states, and its work projects would be developed by local FERA staff in consultation with local governmental officials. Roosevelt, who also disliked the use of doles for the able-bodied poor, quickly concurred with Williams's scheme by creating, through executive order, the Civilian Works Administration (CWA) as part of the FERA. Another job-creation program, the Public Works Administration (PWA), favored technically complex projects, such as airports, dams, flood-control projects, and military installations. These projects required so much technical planning that few had been initiated by the fall of 1933.[62]

CWA funds came from the FERA budget, as

well as surplus funds commandeered from the PWA program. Between November 1933 and January 1934, the federal government initiated 190,000 work projects that employed 16 million Americans—a remarkable feat by any standard, even though the CWA still did not reach many unemployed persons. The program was funded by a federal-local matching formula, in which the federal government paid most of the direct costs.

Most work projects were proposed by local officials, who submitted tens of thousands of ideas, not only because they wanted to help the unemployed but also because an enormous backlog of road repair and other public needs existed in bankrupted local jurisdictions. The projects were approved by local officials and state FERA officials, except for those that were initiated by federal staff and approved in the Washington headquarters of the FERA. Road-related construction projects accounted for 8% of CWA funds; other local improvement projects under the program included recataloging books in public libraries, constructing retaining walls, digging drainage ditches, and cleaning local parks.[63]

Many practical eligibility and reimbursement details had to be quickly solved to allow these projects to be implemented. Hopkins angered unemployed persons who were not on FERA rolls when he decided to require that 50% of the enrollees come from FERA relief rolls, but he remained adamant because he felt welfare recipients should receive priority. (He also feared that unions, which saw the program as a chance to obtain employment for unemployed union workers, would dominate the recruitment process and insist that virtually all jobs go to their members, to the detriment of FERA recipients.) State employment offices certified that CWA workers were unemployed and had tried to find jobs in the private sector. Reimbursement levels were established in Washington; workers in jobs that were classified as unskilled received far less pay than did skilled workers, and adjustments were made to reflect regional wage and cost-of-living levels. Hopkins succeeded in allocating most of the job slots to unskilled persons, so that the program would not be monopolized by skilled work-

ers. CWA wage levels were hardly munificent; indeed, workers with relatively large families often had to supplement their CWA paychecks with FERA assistance in order to survive.

Roosevelt also had to contend both with Republican fears that the CWA would be used for patronage purposes by his administration and with Democratic officials who wanted to reward party members with jobs. He decided not to appease the Democrats who desired patronage; instead of placing supervisorial positions under the civil service, as they wished, he insisted that the federal FERA staff carefully screen the thousands of applicants for project supervisor positions and delete persons who lacked requisite skills, even when they were nominees of Democrats. Given the size of the operation (it involved 190,000 separate projects) and the speed of its implementation, it is remarkable that only 240 charges of serious irregularity were ever proved.[64]

The CWA was a bold initiative that gave new social welfare roles to the federal government. It was a massive program, even by today's standards, but was nonetheless an emergency measure that gave minimal benefits to destitute persons and reimbursed unskilled labor at significantly lower levels than skilled labor.

Even before he was elected, Roosevelt had promised to enact a scheme that would address unemployment among the nation's youth by devising conservation projects in national and state parks. No reform measure was more popular during the New Deal than the Civilian Conservation Corps (CCC), which was enacted in 1933 and provided assistance to 2.5 million young men. Its popularity stemmed from its assistance to youth; from its conservation projects, which were often located in the districts of conservative legislators who might normally have opposed the program; and from its reduction of welfare rolls.

Eligibility was restricted at first to males between the ages of 18 and 25 who were currently on welfare rolls but by 1937, in response to widespread protest against this restrictive eligibility policy, officials allowed any unemployed youth to apply. To spread CCC benefits to as many youths as possible, Roosevelt tried to limit enrollees to one year's residence but then allowed youths to extend their stay for another year because of their difficulty in finding jobs in the private economy. Recruits were paid as little as $1 a day and required to send half their wages to their parents. The army and the Department of Interior were given joint roles in administering the CCC; the former administered the camps, under a strict regimen supervised by sergeants, and the latter planned and oversaw the work projects in the national and state forests to which the youths were sent each day in small work groups.

It would be hard to exaggerate the meaning of the CCC to unemployed youths. Because the unemployment rate among youths was often double the rate for adults, many young persons would have been consigned to welfare for years had the CCC not existed. Transported great distances from Midwestern and Eastern cities to parks in the West, the participants underwent an extraordinary and broadening experience. The program was implemented with remarkable speed; 300,000 youths were placed in camps by the summer of 1933, and 500,000 by 1934.

Nevertheless, the program was not perfect. Critics feared that the CCC was militarizing America's youth, by placing them in regimented settings under the control of the army. Others noted that the CCC did not prepare the youths for jobs after they had left the CCC; it did not provide technical skills, emphasize remedial education, or offer employment counseling. The program was not large enough to meet the needs of the vast numbers of youth who needed jobs during the Great Depression. African American youths were placed in segregated camps, and the program did not address the needs of young women.[65]

Many internal improvements were needed in the nation—whether to address such natural disasters as floods and droughts or to build airports, roads, bridges, and military installations. Work on these projects, Roosevelt contended, served both the public interest and the needs of unemployed Americans. Accordingly, he developed the Public Works Administration (PWA) in 1933. Because large-

scale projects can easily become enmeshed in corruption and patronage, Roosevelt appointed as its director Harold Ickes, a stern perfectionist who insisted on the highest technical standards. His administrative style and philosophy contrasted with those of Harry Hopkins. Ickes believed that the hurriedly arranged projects of the CWA did not provide lasting economic benefit to the nation. Hopkins often persuaded Roosevelt that unemployed workers needed immediate work and that unskilled workers did not benefit from complex projects, which required skilled labor. Ickes was furious when Hopkins was able, repeatedly, to raid PWA funds for the CWA and its successor, the Works Progress Administration (WPA).[66]

Ickes subjected each project to an identical—and lengthy—review process that made extensive use of engineers and other experts, in order to convince legislators that projects were funded on their merits. He took care to assemble a skilled work force, project managers, and contractors who could build a project to precise specifications. Because he distrusted corporations, which he regarded as placing profits ahead of the public interest, he contracted projects to the private sector only with reluctance and monitored them carefully.

The PWA represented the first massive peacetime involvement by the federal government in complex public projects. By 1937, the PWA had constructed astonishing numbers of bridges, airports, dams, and school buildings. The program was bedeviled by many problems, however. Roosevelt often reduced PWA funding on the grounds that less complex projects were needed immediately to put millions of Americans to work. The PWA often became embroiled in politics and troublesome lawsuits, as political and community rivals developed alternative projects or even alternative versions of the same project. Because the PWA required local units of government to contribute a large share of the cost of specific projects, a good many projects had to be canceled when local funds were not forthcoming. Finally, many Americans questioned whether the federal government was competing with private business and thus exceeding its proper role.[67]

Prior to 1933, only 23 states had developed employment offices to help unemployed workers find jobs. But with the passage of the Wagner-Peyser Act in 1933, federal funds were made available to the states for that purpose, and each state created a network of state employment offices. As well as helping unemployed workers find jobs, these offices were used extensively to recruit and screen persons for work in the CWA, CCC, and PWA.[68]

The federal government instituted a range of food programs in the Great Depression, even though Hopkins and others preferred cash assistance to in-kind assistance. These included a food stamp program for federal workers who could show evidence of need and a massive surplus commodities program that distributed agricultural produce to the nation's poor.[69]

Reform of the Economic System

The FERA, CWA, CCC, and PWA rescued persons for brief periods from economic misery, but they did not directly address the collapse of the economic system itself, which had created the economic misery in the first place. Since the trickle-down theories of Herbert Hoover had not worked, Roosevelt proposed a combination of fiscal, monetary, regulatory, and market-support strategies. Indeed, Rosen argues that Roosevelt valued these economic policies more than his welfare and jobs programs.[70]

Hoover had feared federal deficits, but Roosevelt drastically increased social spending even though it led to unprecedented peacetime deficits. Federal taxes had been raised somewhat by 1933, but federal revenues were still wholly insufficient to cover the mounting costs of New Deal programs. The federal deficits were nonetheless modest by wartime standards or by those of the Reagan and Bush administrations of the 1980s and 1990s. Indeed, Roosevelt did not understand that even more drastic increases in social spending could have been a potent economic weapon against the Depression.[71] Since many conservatives, as well as

some of Roosevelt's advisors, viewed these modest deficits with horror, Roosevelt was under constant pressure to slash social spending. (The theories of the English economist John Maynard Keynes, which provided a rationale for incurring large deficits during recessions and depressions, were not widely publicized or accepted in the United States until 1936.)[72]

During the 1920s, many banks had insufficient reserves to provide a margin of safety if large numbers of depositors decided to withdraw their funds or to cover bad loans and investments. The Federal Deposit Insurance Corporation, established in 1933, provided federal insurance to cover deposits when banks became insolvent. Restrictions were also placed on stock market transactions when the Securities and Exchange Commission (SEC) was established in 1934 to forestall undue speculation by investors and stockbrokers. These banking measures established confidence in economic institutions and prevented speculative abuses that had precipitated the stock market crash of 1929. Today, Americans take many of these policies for granted, but they represented an unprecedented expansion of the role of the federal government in economic affairs.[73]

Roosevelt's most difficult problem was to devise strategies for arresting the vicious circle of bankruptcies, price slashing, curtailment of production, and decreased spending power that contributed to the depression. When confronted with unsold merchandise, businesses often slashed prices to increase their sales, but decreased prices led to lower profit margins, which, in turn, required reduction in work forces or in wages. As unemployment thus increased, consumers possessed fewer resources to purchase goods and services.

Roosevelt addressed this vicious circle with passage of the National Industrial Recovery Act of 1933, which established the National Recovery Administration (NRA). Business leaders in various economic sectors, such as the steel, coal, and mining industries, were convened to agree on prices that they would charge for products in their sectors, so as to arrest the destructive slashing of prices and the erosion of profit margins. To curtail slashing of wages, they were also required to establish common wage levels for specific kinds of workers, though with regional variations to account for differences in the cost of living. Production quotas were devised for each company, so as to decrease the dumping of products on slack markets.[74]

Critics feared that businesses would use this participatory process to make excessive profits, by establishing self-serving policies—whether excessively low wages, high prices, or low levels of production to drive up prices. Some persons claimed the NRA was unconstitutional because it allowed businesses to use monopolistic practices, such as price and wage fixing, that were forbidden by the Sherman Antitrust Act.

Roosevelt tried to develop safeguards to forestall these abuses while still obtaining the benefits of regulation of prices, wages, and production. Business leaders had to agree to establish prices that were fair, to refrain from using child labor, to allow workers to join unions, to honor specified minimum working conditions, to exclude women from dangerous occupations, and to include union representatives in industry-wide negotiations. Roosevelt tried, in effect, to use the NRA not only to establish a process to stabilize prices and wages but also to advance indirectly the cause of social reform by abolishing child labor and legitimizing unions.[75]

Its goals were ambitious, and the NRA was hampered by many problems. Liberals who argued that the NRA put foxes in charge of the henhouse found their fears realized when some NRA negotiations led to price increases and production cutbacks that decreased employment while adding to the burdens of consumers. Employers who honored the minimum-wage requirements of the NRA often worked their employees to exhaustion in order to recoup wage increases, whereas others resorted to a policy of labor turnover to reduce their labor costs and decrease labor unrest. Many employers ignored provisions of the NRA by 1934, when they became convinced that it was unconstitutional.[76] Businesses also found ways of harming labor. Since the provisions that allowed workers to organize unions were exceedingly vague, many employers formed company unions to thwart the establishment of independent unions and then told

the NRA that their workers were already organized. General Hugh Johnson, the director of the NRA, took an aggressive stance in opposing efforts to form longshoremen's unions in California and even urged the use of federal troops to repress some legitimate unions on the grounds that their organizers were communists. Southern firms often succeeded in keeping extremely low wage levels for jobs held by African Americans, by contending that regional wages were lower than in the North.[77]

The NRA was terminated in 1935, when the Supreme Court declared that its delegation of power to nongovernmental entities was unconstitutional. However, its demise had been widely predicted, because it had not been effective. An elaborate bureaucracy was required to arrange and oversee negotiations in thousands of industries; price and labor codes were established in virtually every industry—including, for example, firms that made fishhooks. Because federal administrators could not effectively monitor so many codes, companies' compliance was far from perfect. Finally, the National Labor Board, which was established to monitor the provisions protecting workers who sought unions, had too few staff and too little power to help most workers.

Depressed prices were also a problem in rural areas, where millions of farmers were verging on bankruptcy. To address this agricultural depression, Roosevelt established the Agricultural Adjustment Agency (AAA). It convened producers of the same crop to negotiate the amounts of acreage they would grow, and then reimbursed farmers for *not* planting some of their land. Planners hoped that, by curtailing production, farmers would get a higher price for their crops and would thus remain solvent, and there would be fewer evictions of tenant farmers and sharecroppers, who constituted the poorest and most vulnerable groups within agriculture. Funds to finance the AAA were obtained by levying a tax on food processors.[78]

As with the NRA, however, large producers often used the AAA to advance their own financial interests: They established production policies that were favorable to themselves but harmful to small farmers and took their poorest land out of production, to avoid having to reduce their overall output.

Many producers pocketed their growing profits and evicted tenant farmers and sharecroppers.

The AAA developed safeguards to forestall abuse of tenant farmers by landowners but, because it lacked the staff to monitor landowners, evictions continued. The AAA required landowners to pass on to tenants a specified percentage of the monies they obtained from the government for withdrawing acreage from production, but many landowners gave sharecroppers a smaller percentage or nothing at all. In 1934, the Southern Tenant Farmers Association was formed to try to stop evictions, but grass-roots advocacy was difficult because the tenant farmers and sharecroppers, many of them African Americans, were dispersed and impoverished.[79]

Roosevelt tried to provide assistance to millions of farmers and homeowners threatened with foreclosure. Farm mortgages were directly purchased and refinanced by the government when the Emergency Farm Mortgage Act and the Farm Relief Act were enacted in 1933. As to homeowners, the Roosevelt administration decided to take an indirect role; rather than helping homeowners directly, the National Housing Act of 1934 established the Federal Home Administration (FHA) to insure mortgages and home improvement loans, so that banks could refinance them at lower rates of interest.[80]

Why not, some persons asked, use the power of the federal government to orchestrate the economic development of entire regions? With federal assistance, vast river systems in the United States, including the Mississippi and Missouri rivers, could be made to yield power if dams, generators, and transmission lines were constructed. The most prominent legislative advocate of regional development schemes was George Norris, a progressive Republican senator from Nebraska, who had made river development his major interest and who worked closely with Roosevelt to secure its passage.

The first project, the Tennessee Valley Authority (TVA), was initiated in 1933 and governed by a commission that was established to oversee development of a network of dams and generating plants. The TVA sold electricity to power cooperatives and local towns, manufactured and sold fertil-

izer, reforested vast amounts of land, and built flood-control projects. It was partially responsible for the economic rebirth of a vast region and, thanks to the proceeds from the sale of power and fertilizer, the cost to the government was minimal. Private power companies, which often charged excessive fees for their power, protested vigorously that the federal government was competing unfairly with them. Their many legal and political strategies to sabotage the TVA included attempts to place allies on the commission that established TVA policy. Defenders of the TVA were able to institutionalize the experiment, however, even if they were unable to extend their bold design to the Missouri and other large river systems.[81]

EMERGENCY OR PERMANENT PROGRAMS?

Federal social programs evolved as much from necessity as from philosophy. As the nation's citizens and its local and state governments teetered on the brink of bankruptcy, Americans *had* to take ameliorative action. However, socialism, which extolled major governmental roles and the redistribution of resources from the rich to the poor, had no strong roots in the United States. Would Americans, then, institutionalize their social reforms of 1933 and 1934 or dismantle them at the first opportunity?

Events of early 1934 were not encouraging to social reformers. Roosevelt, under severe pressure to cut spending in order to reduce deficits, terminated the CWA in 1934, despite protests from reformers.[82] Slowing the momentum of social programs also had a political rationale. Although Roosevelt had won a sweeping victory in 1932, as well as control of both houses of Congress, he feared that widespread grumbling about welfare cheaters and loafers in the FERA, CWA, and PWA would fuel a conservative resurgence in congressional elections in November 1934. Business and conservative interests, which had been on the defensive and in disarray in 1933 and early 1934, had also

INSERT 7.3   ETHICAL ANALYSIS OF KEY ISSUES AND POLICIES: FEDERAL LEADERSHIP VERSUS DEFERRING TO THE STATES

The central innovation of the New Deal was its development of the federal government's social policy roles. States and localities were the prime movers in social policy before the New Deal, as our discussion in Chapters 3–6 suggests.

1. Using the New Deal as an example, analyze FDR's decision to make assertive use of federal power from an ethical perspective. What ethical criticisms would he have encountered had he *not* developed national programs in the Great Depression? Consider the fiscal resources of the federal government (for example, its tax and borrowing powers) when compared to state governments. Consider, as well, some other reasons why states often cannot or will not develop social policies, such as state officials' fears that corporations will relocate if state taxes are raised to pay for social programs.

2. Speculate whether social justice goals are advanced more effectively where the federal government assumes policy roles than where the federal government cedes social policy to the states. Consider whether advocacy groups for outgroups find it easier to obtain federal, rather than state, assistance.

begun to develop a political counteroffensive. Moreover, Roosevelt had his own doubts about the advisability of a strong federal role in public welfare, since he had always favored giving local governments the responsibility for welfare problems. He had developed the FERA because states were verging on bankruptcy in 1932, but he did not want to institutionalize it, and he did not want the federal government to assume a permanent job-creation role. He continued to hope that easing of the economic depression would permit a reduction in size of the federal programs, though advisors like Hopkins feared that the government would have to continue to fund public works indefinitely.[83]

Americans tend to believe that social problems are abnormal or unusual phenomena that can be solved by the development of specific policies. This optimistic and problem-solving orientation is illustrated by the prolific efforts of 19th-century reformers to end pauperism, mental illness, crime, and alcoholism, as well as by the regulations that some progressives believed would eliminate exploitation by corporations, politicians, landlords, and drug companies. Likewise, some New Deal reformers hoped that a frantic round of reforms would restore prosperity and eliminate poverty and unemployment. Alas, none of these reformers— and none who have succeeded them—has been able to make American society into the problem-

free utopia that Jefferson had imagined at the inception of the republic. Perhaps it is sensible to create and sustain many social programs that help citizens who are in need, while we continue to try (as best we can) to develop solutions.

THE EVOLUTION OF THE RELUCTANT WELFARE STATE

The years 1933 and 1934 could easily be selected as the most decisive years in the emergence of the modern American welfare state. The nature of social obligation was broadened to include farmers, the unemployed, teenagers, homeowners, inhabitants of large river basins, and transient persons. Government officials initiated projects not only to help destitute individuals but also to develop public works; they undertook a host of fiscal and monetary interventions and efforts to stabilize wages and prices. Furthermore, when the federal government became the prime funder and organizer of these various undertakings, the tradition of reliance on local welfare programs was decisively shattered, even if federal authorities asked the states to collaborate in funding and implementing the new programs.

Many Americans began to change their notions about some of the five moral issues we discussed in Chapter 1 as they viewed the new policy developments of Roosevelt's first two years in office. Policies and ideas that had hitherto been taboo or restricted to a few avant-garde reformers were now both acceptable and operational. Federal authorities could develop national programs with speed and efficiency—and those programs were widely perceived to mean the difference between life and death for millions of Americans. Once the new policies were in place, there was no turning back to the restrictive welfare traditions of the 19th century; Americans had seen that the new policies, though imperfect, were preferable to the traditional approaches, which now seemed mean-minded and anachronistic.

NOTES

1. Lela Costin, *Two Sisters for Social Justice* (Urbana, Ill.: University of Illinois Press, 1984), pp. 11–116.

2. William Leuchtenberg, *Perils of Prosperity, 1914–1932* (Chicago: University of Chicago Press, 1958). Some reformers remained active, as discussed by Clarke Chambers, *Seedtime of Reform: American Social Service and Social Action, 1918–1933* (Minneapolis, Minn.: University of Minnesota Press, 1963).

3. Leuchtenberg, *Perils,* pp. 179, 186.

4. Ibid., p. 98.

5. David Brody, *Workers in Industrial America: Essays on the Twentieth-Century Struggle* (New York: Oxford University Press, 1980), pp. 48–78.

6. John Kirby, *Black Americans in the Roosevelt Era: Liberalism and Race* (Knoxville, Tenn.: University of Tennessee Press, 1980), p. 3; Raymond Wolters, *Negroes and the Great Depression: The Problem of Economic Recovery* (Westport, Conn.: Greenwood Press, 1970), p. 7.

7. Cary McWilliams, *North from Mexico: The Spanish-Speaking People of the United States* (New York: Greenwood Press, 1968), pp. 215–226.

8. Nancy Woloch, *Women and the American Experience* (New York: Knopf, 1984), pp. 382–388.

9. Leuchtenberg, *Perils,* pp. 204–224.

10. Maldwyn Jones, *American Immigration* (Chicago: University of Chicago Press, 1960), pp. 270–281.

11. Leuchtenberg, *Perils,* pp. 163–188; Roy Lubove, *The Professional Altruist* (Cambridge, Mass.: Harvard University Press, 1965), pp. 85–89.

12. Lubove, *The Professional Altruist,* pp. 124–156; John Ehrenreich, *The Altruistic Imagination: A History of Social Work and Social Policy in the United States* (Ithaca, N.Y.: Cornell University Press, 1985), pp. 43–77.

13. John Galbraith, *The Great Crash, 1929* (Boston: Houghton Mifflin, 1957), pp. 180–183.

14. Robert McElvaine, *The Great Depression: America, 1929–1941* (New York: New York Times Book Co., 1984), pp. 25–50.

15. William Bremer, *Depression Winters: New York Social Workers and the New Deal* (Philadelphia: Temple University Press, 1984), pp. 88–100; Charles Trout, *Boston, the Great Depression, and the New Deal* (New York: Oxford University Press, 1977), pp. 90–92.

16. Eliot Rosen, *Hoover, Roosevelt, and the Brains Trust: From Depression to New Deal* (New York: Columbia University Press, 1977), pp. 39–65.

17. Chambers, *Seedtime of Reform,* pp. 185–207; Joseph Huthmacher, *Senator Robert F. Wagner and the Rise of Urban Liberalism* (New York: Atheneum, 1968), pp. 71–102.

18. Chambers, *Seedtime of Reform,* pp. 217–218; Lee Kraeder, "Isaac Max Rubinow: Pioneering Specialist in Social Insurance," *Social Service Review,* 50 (September 1976), 293–298.

19. Trout, *Boston,* pp. 62–63, 97–100.

20. McElvaine, *The Great Depression,* pp. 69–71.

21. Allen Davis, *The Life and Legend of Jane Addams* (New York: Oxford University Press, 1973), pp. 287–288.

22. Bremer, *Depression Winters,* pp. 101–113.

23. William Leuchtenberg, *Franklin Roosevelt and the New Deal: 1932–1940* (New York: Harper & Row, 1963), pp. 1–3, 18–31; Trout, *Boston,* pp. 71–93.

24. Trout, *Boston,* pp. 56–72.

25. Eric Schattschneider, *The Semisovereign People* (New York: Holt, Rinehart & Winston, 1960), pp. 86–89.

26. McElvaine, *The Great Depression,* pp. 6–7.

27. Richard Lowitt and Maurine Beasley, eds., *One Third of a Nation* (Urbana, Ill.: University of Illinois Press, 1981).

28. Leuchtenberg, *Franklin Roosevelt,* p. 1.

29. Arthur MacMahon, John Millett, and Gladys Ogden, *The Administration of Federal Work Relief* (Chicago: Public Administration Service, 1941), pp. 183–184, 334–341.

30. James Patterson, *Congressional Conservatism and the New Deal* (Lexington, Ky.: University of Kentucky Press, 1967), pp. 4–7.

31. Rosen, *Hoover,* pp. 303–328.

32. Patterson, *Congressional Conservatism,* pp. 13–31.

33. Rosen, *Hoover,* pp. 308–314.

34. Trout, *Boston,* p. xi.

35. George Flynn, *American Catholics and the Roosevelt Presidency, 1932–1936* (Lexington, Ky.: University of Kentucky Press, 1968).

36. Ronald A. Mulder, *The Insurgent Progressives in the United States Senate and the New Deal* (New York: Garland, 1979), pp. 12–13; Patterson, *Congressional Conservatism,* pp. 154–155, 160–161.

37. Brody, *Workers,* pp. 82–105.

38. Ibid., pp. 166–172.

39. Ibid., pp. 107–116.

40. Lowitt and Beasley, *One Third of a Nation,* p. 213; Trout, *Boston,* pp. 208–209.

41. Edward White, *The American Judicial Tradition: Profiles of Leading American Judges* (New York: Oxford University Press, 1976), pp. 178–199.

42. Henry Adams, *Harry Hopkins* (New York: Putnam, 1977), pp. 60–62; Bremer, *Depression Winters,* pp. 135–136.

43. George Martin, *Madam Secretary: Frances Perkins* (Boston: Houghton Mifflin, 1976), pp. 245–247; Lillian Mohr, *Frances Perkins* (Croton-on-Hudson, N.Y.: North River Press, 1979), pp. 131–133.

44. John Salmond, *A Southern Rebel: The Life and Times of Aubrey Willis Williams, 1890–1965* (Chapel Hill, N.C.: University of North Carolina Press, 1983), pp. 45–56.

45. Patterson, *Congressional Conservatism,* pp. 32–76.

46. Leuchtenberg, *Franklin Roosevelt,* pp. 326–328.

47. G. D. H. Cole and Raymond Postgate, *The British Common People, 1746–1946* (New York: Knopf, 1939), pp. 587–614.

48. Brody, *Workers,* pp. 120–129.

49. Lowitt and Beasley, *One Third of a Nation,* pp. 5–6, 12–13, 31–32.

50. Ibid., pp. 70–71, 78–82, 94–95.

51. Leuchtenberg, *Franklin Roosevelt,* pp. 87–89.

52. Margaret Weir and Theda Skocpol, "State Structures and the Possibility of 'Keynesian' Responses to the Great Depression in Sweden, Britain, and the United States." In Peter Evans, Dietrich Rueschemeyer, and Theda Skocpol, eds., *Bringing the State Back In* (Cambridge: Cambridge University Press, 1985), p. 145.

53. Leuchtenberg, *Franklin Roosevelt,* pp. 145–149, 256; Martin, *Madam Secretary,* pp. 258–260; and Salmond, *A Southern Rebel,* pp. 68–70.

54. Bremer, *Depression Winters,* pp. 134–141, 155–157, 165, 167–170; Martin, *Madam Secretary,* pp. 258–259; and McElvaine, *The Great Depression,* pp. 250–263.

55. Bremer, *Depression Winters,* p. 129.

56. Adams, *Harry Hopkins,* pp. 52–53, 71–72.

57. Josephine Brown, *Public Relief, 1929–1939* (New York: Holt, 1940), pp. 146–159, 171–190, 218–298.

58. Trout, *Boston,* pp. 148–149.

59. Lowitt and Beasley, *One Third of a Nation,* p. 46.

60. Salmond, *A Southern Rebel,* pp. 45–56.

61. Harry Hopkins, *Spending To Save* (New York: Harper & Row, 1936), pp. 108–110.

62. Salmond, *A Southern Rebel,* pp. 55–56.

63. Ibid., pp. 57–63.

64. Ibid., p. 59.

65. John Salmond, *The Civilian Conservation Corps, 1933–1942* (Durham, N.C.: Duke University Press, 1967).

66. Adams, *Harry Hopkins,* pp. 57–58, 82–88.

67. Richard Lowitt, *George W. Norris: The Triumph of a Progressive, 1933–1944* (Urbana, Ill.: University of Illinois Press, 1981), pp. 95–109.

68. Martin, *Madam Secretary,* pp. 296–298; Mohr, *Frances Perkins,* p. 141.

69. Gilbert Steiner, *State of Welfare* (Washington, D.C.: Brookings Institution, 1971), pp. 198–199.

70. Rosen, *Hoover,* p. 59.

71. Susan Lee and Peter Passell, *A New Economic View of American History* (New York: Norton, 1979), pp. 383–387.

72. Dean May, *From New Deal to New Economics: The American Liberal Response to the Recession of 1937* (New York: Garland, 1981), pp. 160–161.

73. Leuchtenberg, *Franklin Roosevelt,* pp. 38–39, 42–46.

74. Wolters, *Negroes,* pp. 83–90.

75. Ibid., pp. 83–90.

76. Lowitt and Beasley, *One Third of a Nation,* pp. 341–346, 356.

77. Mohr, *Frances Perkins,* pp. 163–170; Wolters, *Negroes,* pp. 169–192.

78. Wolters, *Negroes,* pp. 3–38.

79. Ibid., pp. 21–77.

80. Leuchtenberg, *Franklin Roosevelt,* p. 52.

81. Lowitt, *George W. Norris,* pp. 16–25, 110–125.

82. Bremer, *Depression Winters,* pp. 134–136.

83. Adams, *Harry Hopkins,* p. 61; Leuchtenberg, *Franklin Roosevelt,* pp. 91–94.

8

Institutionalizing the New Deal

Selected Orienting Events

1934	Committee on Economic Security established by Roosevelt
1935	FERA terminated; Social Security Act passed, with its constituent programs of Aid to Dependent Children (ADC), Old-Age Assistance (OAA), Aid to the Blind (AB), unemployment insurance, Social Security, child welfare, and public health programs; Supreme Court declares the NRA to be unconstitutional; Senator Huey Long assassinated; Works Progress Administration (WPA) established
1936	Father Coughlin and Francis Townsend support the Union party; Congress of Industrial Organizations (CIO) founded; passage of Wagner Act, establishing the National Labor Relations Board; Supreme Court declares the AAA to be unconstitutional; Roosevelt wins landslide victory for his second term
1937	Deep recession ends nation's economic recovery; Wagner-Steagall Housing Act passed
1938	Fair Labor Standards Act enacted
1939	Federal Security Agency established
Early 1940s	CCC, WPA, and the National Youth Administration (NYA) are terminated
1940	Roosevelt elected to third term
1941	America enters World War II; Executive Order 8802 prohibits discrimination in war industry
1942	Some 120,000 persons of Japanese ancestry evacuated to relocation centers
1945	Roosevelt dies and is succeeded by Harry Truman

TOWARD ONGOING PROGRAMS

New reforms that supplemented or replaced earlier programs were introduced in the period from November 1934 to November 1936, which has been called the second New Deal. This term unduly emphasizes discontinuity in New Deal reforms, however. Roosevelt, Perkins, Hopkins, and others had supported from the outset many of the policies enacted in this period, including old-age pensions, unemployment insurance, and higher taxes on wealthy persons. Accordingly, it is more accurate to portray New Deal policies in 1935 and 1936 as a logical sequel to reforms in the preceding two years. The important distinction is that the early reforms were improvisational and focused on rescuing bankrupt local governments and righting the economy, whereas the reforms in the second period represented Roosevelt's more considered efforts to decide which ongoing welfare functions the federal government should assume and what its relationship toward organized labor should be.[1]

Liberal Forces

When Roosevelt won a smashing victory in the congressional elections of November 1934, Harry Hopkins and other social reformers believed they could finally prevail over both Republicans and budget-balancers within the Democratic party. Hopkins said to fellow reformers:

> Boys, this is our hour. We've got to get everything we want—a works program, social security, wages and hours [regulation], everything—now or never. Put your minds to work in developing a complete ticket to provide security for all the folks of this country up and down and across the board.[2]

Hopkins proposed the End Poverty in America (EPIA) plan, which included an ongoing federal jobs program, a massive low-cost housing program, a set of insurance programs, establishment of large manufacturing centers, and new rural programs to help poor farmers acquire land and equipment.[3]

Liberals generally supported the New Deal programs; more radical groups and individuals, while endorsing the goals of Roosevelt's reforms, wanted him to go much further. Huey Long, the charismatic and demagogic senator from Louisiana, pressured Roosevelt to place heavy taxes on incomes and estates of millionaires, to greatly expand federal works programs, and to pay a higher wage to workers in public works projects. He believed that the NRA and the AAA did little more than protect the interests of large industrialists and landowners. He criticized the low wages paid by the CWA and attacked the budget-cutting inclinations of Roosevelt. As a militant defender of small farmers and small businessmen, he believed that their economic opportunities remained limited, he resented affluent elites, and he tended to dislike the large New Deal bureaucracies.[4]

Father Charles Coughlin, a Jesuit priest from Detroit, attracted a massive audience to his national radio show when he proposed a variety of federal regulations of the banking system and monetary reforms. His initial support for Roosevelt turned to opposition when FDR failed to support his economic measures.[5] (Coughlin later turned sharply to the right and became virulently anti-Semitic.) Other reformers concentrated on single issues. Francis Townsend, a dentist in Long Beach, California, proposed and popularized a scheme to pay a monthly pension of $200 per month to all American citizens over the age of 60 on the condition that they pledge to spend it within 30 days and agree to give up all other income. It was to be financed from a federal sales tax. He hoped the scheme would simultaneously relieve grinding poverty among the elderly and revive the economy by requiring them to spend their monthly pensions before the end of each month. He obtained 20 million signatures on a petition by 1936.[6]

Representative Ernest Lundeen of Minnesota proposed a scheme of unemployment insurance in 1934 to pay compensation from the general revenues of the nation to all persons who were unemployed through no fault of their own. (Unemployed workers were to receive benefits equal to prevailing wages, and persons with part-time work were to have their wages supplemented to bring them up to the prevailing standard.) The scheme was to be administered by worker and farmer organizations.[7]

A bipartisan cadre of liberals often voted together on public housing legislation, legislation protecting the rights of unions, legislation to oppose lynching (of African Americans), and fair labor standards. Indeed, Senator Robert F. Wagner, a leading figure in this liberal bloc, initiated reform measures without FDR's approval, as a means of pressuring the administration to be more daring.[8]

Roosevelt experienced mounting pressure from reformers and social workers. An influential contingent of social workers from New York State had assumed a particularly important role in supporting reforms during the early years of the New Deal when they offered suggestions and assumed key positions within the administration. (Hopkins and Perkins were merely the most visible members of this community.)[9] Many of them had become disenchanted with the New Deal by 1934, however; they resented the termination of the CWA, the opportunistic exploitation of the NRA by many businessmen, and the low levels of relief provided by the FERA and the CWA. Their anger mounted during 1935, when they believed Roosevelt hoped to disband federal assistance to many unemployed persons and destitute families. A radical contingent of the profession, led by Mary Van Kleeck, urged social workers to become radical critics of the New Deal rather than be coopted by Roosevelt.[10]

Pressure for reform also came from the burgeoning unions that represented unskilled workers. These workers and their organizers had been radicalized by the inhuman labor practices of the corporations, high rates of unemployment among unskilled workers, and the bloody suppression of strikes in automobile and steel plants and in coal mines. Such union leaders as Walter Reuther in the auto industry and John L. Lewis in mining developed growing constituencies and power. Although they had supported the establishment of the NRA because of its protections for unions, they wondered why the Roosevelt administration seemed content with the vague and poorly enforced provisions of the NRA to protect collective bargaining.[11]

In 1934, the Southern Tenant Farmers Associa-

tion (STFA) was formed to protect millions of agricultural laborers who found their lot even worse after passage of the AAA. A few African American sharecroppers were helped by the FERA and the Resettlement Administration to obtain their own land; most, however, remained enmeshed in poverty and heavily indebted to landowners, who charged them excessive prices for seed, fertilizer, and food. To make matters worse, as landowners curbed production to reap payments from the AAA, they evicted their tenant farmers. The STFA asked the administration to stop this wave of evictions and to help landless persons obtain their own farms.[12]

Although workers, liberals, and African Americans were often critical of Roosevelt, they nonetheless regarded him as preferable to the Republican leaders, who became even more conservative and opposed to reform after the 1934 election. This support from the left emboldened Roosevelt to initiate and support reforms, not only because he wanted to keep their support but also because he wanted to prevent the emergence of a more radical rival. A poll in 1935 suggested that Huey Long would receive six million votes if he were to run for president in 1936.[13] Father Coughlin and Townsend supported the Union Party, which frontally attacked Roosevelt as too conservative and sought to defeat both the Democrats and Republicans in the elections of 1936. Rivalry among figures and groups on the left, the assassination of Huey Long in 1935, and Roosevelt's sheer popularity and tactical brilliance doomed the political aspirations of many of these leaders, but they pushed Roosevelt to consider policies that he might otherwise have neglected.[14]

A determined group of social reformers, including Isaac Rubinow, pressured Roosevelt and his aides to enact old-age pensions, unemployment insurance, and national health insurance. Some of them had sought such legislation even in the progressive era—and had continued their work during the 1920s by advocating so-called social insurances in various states. While they differed over program details, these reformers were convinced that economic security would never be realized in the United States if these reforms were not enacted.

Conservative Pressures on Roosevelt

Though conservatives never loved Roosevelt, they sometimes tolerated him because of the nation's economic straits. A conservative coalition consisting of Republicans, Southern Democrats, and some political moderates had developed considerable cohesion within the Congress by 1935, however, and rallied opposition to FDR's policies. Southern Democrats, who held many committee chairs in the House and Senate and had traditionally possessed a good deal of power in the Democratic party, felt that their party had been taken over by liberal Northerners and by urban reformers such as Senator Wagner. Their anger mounted when they were not consulted by Roosevelt on many policy issues. Business interests, which had often supported Democratic candidates, increasingly gave their allegiance and money to Republicans when confronted with legislation to markedly increase the taxes of affluent persons and corporations. With Roosevelt's electoral successes, Republicans' opposition to the New Deal became increasingly militant; they realized that they might remain the minority party for decades if they could not arrest Roosevelt's political momentum.[15]

Roosevelt's political problems were compounded by the increasing opposition of a group of 13 Republican senators, called the insurgent progressives, who were ideological descendants of the progressive era. They had provided vital support to New Deal programs during Roosevelt's first term and had championed agricultural reforms, the TVA, antimonopoly policies, and higher taxes on the wealthy, but they disliked large federal bureaucracies, feared Roosevelt had too much power, wished to preserve strong policy roles for states, and feared the use of social programs for political patronage. They increasingly resented the deployment of a major portion of New Deal resources to urban areas and workers. Their distrust of Roosevelt and his policies reached paranoid proportions by 1936, when they were convinced that he sought to establish a dynasty beholden to urban interests. Their anger mounted in 1937, when Roosevelt attacked the Supreme Court and did not publicly rebuke the disruptive tactics of automobile

workers. Furthermore, they had come to detest the size of the federal government. Their distrust of Roosevelt was expressed in negative votes on many pieces of legislation and in increasing cooperation with Southern Democrats and more conservative Republicans.[16]

Many middle-class Americans became less enamored with Roosevelt's policies by late 1935. Convinced that individuals were personally responsible for their unemployment, they resented federal work and relief programs, which they believed sapped the initiative of recipients. They increasingly questioned Roosevelt's economic policies as the nation remained mired in depression. Considerable animus developed toward Harry Hopkins, who was perceived to be a welfare czar and was widely believed to reward Democrats with jobs in the federal bureaucracy. Many Americans resented the burgeoning of the federal bureaucracies, which had become highly visible during the implementation of hundreds of New Deal programs. They also disliked the brains trust, academicians, and theorists, whose ideas had not solved the nation's economic malaise.[17]

The Supreme Court gave legal sanction to the conservatives when it declared the NRA and AAA unconstitutional, in 1935 and 1936, respectively; indeed, between January 1935 and June 1936, the Court issued 12 rulings against the New Deal that rested on an assortment of constitutional objections. Roosevelt wondered whether virtually all major New Deal programs might be rescinded by the Court.[18]

 ## LEGISLATION IN THE SECOND HALF OF THE NEW DEAL

These conservative pressures led Roosevelt to abandon certain reforms, to support some of them belatedly, and to dilute or compromise others. At the same time, the liberal pressures pushed FDR to sustain his reform momentum. This bewildering combination of liberal and conservative pressure contributed to confusing patterns of deletions, continuations, and enlargements of New Deal programs, as well as to compromises in new legislation. Some of the initial programs were discontinued—because Roosevelt had misgivings about them (the CWA and the FERA) or because they were declared unconstitutional (the AAA and NRA); others, such as the CCC and PWA, survived. Major new programs were created in the second half of the New Deal, including the Social Security Act, the National Labor Relations Board (NLRB), the Works Progress Administration (WPA), and the National Youth Administration (NYA), but their form and size often reflected compromises with conservatives. Still other pieces of legislation were proposed but not enacted, such as antilynching, tax, and public housing legislation.

The Social Security Act

The Social Security Act, which is the foundation of the American welfare state, contained many programs to address a variety of social problems. Roosevelt wanted to decide, once and for all, which relief functions would be maintained by federal and local governments. He also wanted to prevent destitution by developing social insurances to address the economic needs of persons who were unemployed and elderly. Finally, he wanted to develop some permanent and ongoing programs to constitute his legacy to the nation. Roosevelt had many policy interests, but he wanted a single piece of legislation to encapsulate them, because he realized that some relatively controversial measures, such as unemployment insurance, would not pass unless they were part of a larger piece of legislation that also contained more popular programs, such as old-age pensions and welfare assistance for older persons. He reasoned as well that the Supreme Court would find it more difficult to attack specific programs if they were part of multifaceted legislation.

To plan this legislation, Roosevelt appointed a Committee on Economic Security in June 1934. The committee, chaired by Frances Perkins, included the secretary of the treasury, the attorney general, the secretary of agriculture, and the administrator of the FERA. A large advisory committee and a technical committee were also formed. The committee accomplished its complex task with remarkable speed and was able, after marathon sessions during the Christmas holidays, to issue its final report on January 15, 1935. The legislation passed overwhelmingly in the Congress and was signed into law by Roosevelt in August 1935. The Social Security Act contained two social insurance programs, three relief programs, and other smaller programs.[19]

Social insurances, principally unemployment insurance and old-age pensions (Social Security), were attractive to Roosevelt for several reasons. They were self-funding programs; their benefits were financed from payroll taxes levied on employers and employees. Roosevelt favored the payroll tax so that future generations would not have to fund these programs from general revenues. He also believed that these insurance programs would reduce the size of welfare rolls, as the benefits paid to older persons and unemployed workers in these programs lifted them above the threshold of poverty. Moreover, he knew that insurances were politically acceptable to many Americans because they represented earned benefits rather than welfare payments.[20] Roosevelt initially showed little interest in Social Security, because he was preoccupied with the needs of unemployed workers, but he vigorously declared his support of it when critical stories appeared in the press in 1934.[21]

Despite the political popularity of these programs, Roosevelt believed he needed to make concessions to conservatives to ensure their passage. Over the protests of some liberals, he supported a regressive system of payroll taxes that levied stiffer taxes on low-income wage earners than on more affluent persons, and he refused to contribute general revenues to Social Security. (Liberals believed the use of general revenues would have been more equitable and would have allowed major increases in the size of benefits.) Some liberals also opposed his decision—supported by Southern agricultural interests—not to cover farm and domestic workers.[22]

Although Roosevelt made concessions to conservatives, he also made policy choices that

FIGURE 8.1   Franklin Delano Roosevelt signing the Social Security Act

SOURCE: UPI/Bettmann

defied them. Some persons believed that participation in Social Security should be voluntary, but FDR insisted on mandatory participation. Frances Perkins, a believer in states' rights, initially favored allowing each state to keep its own Social Security fund, but FDR rejected this policy on the grounds that movement of workers between states would make it unworkable.[23]

Originally conceived as a measure to provide pensions to retired workers, Social Security was broadened in 1939 to include family members of the worker. Arthur Altmeyer, chair of the Social Security Board, explained that "this system, formerly a plan to provide old-age annuities for individual wage earners, has become a broad system of family insurance, which protects not only the wage earner but his wife and children, and if they are dependent on him, his aged parents."[24] Social Security was amended to include benefits to the wives, widows, and children of retirees—a salutary step even if it was grounded on a patriarchal notion

of the family, in which men were regarded as breadwinners and it was assumed that women would not work.[25]

Senator Wagner and other liberals had introduced various versions of a federal unemployment insurance program since 1933, but much controversy existed about how best to proceed. Should funds collected by a payroll tax on employers be kept in a central pool in Washington or in each of the states? Should central funds exist, or should separate accounts be maintained for each industry? Should the federal government assume the lead in administering the funds, devise the level and duration of unemployment benefits, and levy taxes? Should employers' participation in the scheme be mandatory or voluntary?

The unemployment insurance program embodied in the Social Security Act represented an ingenious compromise between these policy alternatives. A payroll tax was levied on employers by states; though participation was technically voluntary, participating employers were given generous federal tax credits to offset most of their payroll taxes. States collected the payroll taxes, but they gave the revenues to the federal government, which maintained a central fund for each state that was then used to pay unemployment benefits to workers. The federal government paid the states' costs of administering their programs. Although this plan sounds complicated, it was a rather simple scheme to allow the federal government to bear most of the costs of unemployment insurance, while lending the appearance that participation by employers was voluntary.[26] Each state enacted its own unemployment insurance law, which determined benefit levels and duration. Many liberal critics contended that the legislation penalized states with high levels of unemployment, whose funds would be more severely burdened than states with low levels of unemployment. Others feared that conservative states might choose to pay low benefits to unemployed persons. Why, some liberal critics asked, should workers have to be unemployed for four weeks before obtaining benefits? Many liberals favored federal contributions to the program to enable it to pay higher benefits and for longer periods. They feared that workers would be forced onto welfare rolls because they could not survive on the meager assistance, which was limited to around 14 weeks in many states. Liberals were also unhappy that Roosevelt capitulated to special interests when he excluded domestics, cannery workers, and farm laborers from coverage. They were nonetheless delighted that FDR supported the concept of unemployment insurance and that he withstood pressure for each state to have its separate unemployment program.[27]

Most liberals supported the Federal Emergency Relief Administration because it gave relief to a broad range of needy Americans—including families, single persons, older persons, and nonworking and working poor persons—and they were furious when it became apparent that Roosevelt had decided to scuttle the FERA and replace it with federal relief programs to only three groups of persons in need—elderly persons (Old-Age Assistance, or OAA); children in families with one caretaker (Aid to Dependent Children, or ADC); and blind persons (Aid to the Blind, or AB).[28] All other

destitute persons, including single nonelderly persons and families with two parents, were returned to local or general assistance welfare programs, which were entirely funded by state and local resources. Many of these poor relief agencies were punitive in orientation and racist in their practices.

These three programs followed a similar format. States received matching or formula funds from the federal government. Under OAA, for example, the federal government paid one-half of local grants for each eligible person, as long as local grants did not exceed $30 per month. (The federal government paid only one-third of ADC grants.) Federal authorities insisted that a state agency be designated to implement the programs, that uniform standards of eligibility be established within each state to preclude specific counties from developing relatively punitive policies, and that fair hearings be established so that aggrieved recipients could appeal eligibility decisions.[29]

Liberal critics were pleased that Roosevelt had developed some permanent programs, but they were displeased that many persons were shunted to local welfare programs. They contended that the legislation mistakenly gave states the power to establish eligibility standards and levels of benefits. Would not Southern and relatively conservative states, they asked, make their programs so restrictive that they would deny assistance to vast numbers of poor persons and people of color? Since federal authorities were given no power over the states' personnel decisions and were not required to use social workers in supervisory positions, critics wondered if patronage would dominate local agencies.[30] Some liberals were also unhappy that the ADC program restricted assistance to families with a single parent or that the welfare grants to these families included funds only for the children and not for the parent. The policy limiting the grants to children was not amended until 1950, when the name of the program was changed to Aid to Families with Dependent Children (AFDC). Even this restrictive program was more liberal than a version advocated by some social workers, who wanted relief to be given only to those children who were found, on casework investigation, to reside in "suitable homes," on the grounds that many destitute mothers pro-

INSERT 8.1 ETHICAL ANALYSIS OF KEY ISSUES AND POLICIES: ROOSEVELT'S DILEMMA: WHAT TO DO ABOUT SOUTHERN DEMOCRATS?

Southern Democrats presented Roosevelt with an ethical dilemma. They were a large part of his Democratic party and controlled virtually every Congressional committee. When they voted with Republicans *against* New Deal legislation, they could defeat social reform measures.

Roosevelt's dilemma was this: When should he oppose the policy preferences of Southern Democrats and when should he defer to them? Should he have risked passage of the Social Security Act by demanding more liberal provisions in it, such as national minimum standards for welfare grants? Or was he correct in acceding to many of their demands? Discuss the ethical merits of *both* approaches and then decide, on balance, whether he made the ethically meritorious choice.

Roosevelt also confronted a related ethical dilemma. Northern liberals, like Senator Robert Wagner, wanted federal legislation to make the lynching of African Americans (a common occurrence in the South) a federal crime. Believing the Southern Democrats would oppose his New Deal if he supported antilynching legislation, Roosevelt maintained a discreet silence on the legislation until late in the decade; even then, his support was tepid. Did he err, ethically, when he made this choice?

vided improper care.[31] As liberals had predicted, eligibility standards and grant levels were far more restrictive in Southern and rural states than in industrial states, and Southerners kept benefits low, partly to force African American women and their children to labor for miserable wages in cotton and tobacco fields, and partly because Southern states lacked the tax revenues to fund more munificent programs.[32]

Limited as they were, OAA, ADC, and AB were the first permanent and major federal relief programs. Many persons believed in 1935 that they would be extremely small programs; Social Security benefits, it was thought, would allow elderly persons to escape the OAA program; ADC did not attract much attention since most people thought it would be a federal-state version of mothers' pension programs; and AB applied only to a relatively small population of persons with a specific disability.[33] Had they guessed the future size of OAA and ADC rolls or realized that Aid to the Blind would be expanded in the 1950s and subsequent decades to include persons with mental and physical disabilities, many conservatives—and possibly Roosevelt himself—might have thought twice about establishing these federal programs.

Reformers were able to obtain provisions in the Social Security Act that provided grants to locali-

ties for child welfare and maternal health programs (Title V) and public health programs (Title VI). The amounts of money involved were small; $1.5 million was authorized for the child welfare funds, but the money was allowed to be used only for the administrative costs of state agencies. These small grant programs nonetheless represented grudging acceptance of the notion that local governments needed federal assistance in providing a range of social welfare services. Not until the 1960s were federal programs enacted to fund a range of mental-health, health, and other services.

The Social Security Act created programs that would have been unthinkable five years earlier. (See Table 8.1 for a summary of its major provisions.) It committed the federal government to permanent funding of an assortment of programs. However, many concessions were made to Southern Democrats and other conservatives in the specific programs, and many programs were missing from the legislation altogether. Roosevelt had contemplated including national health programs in the act, but he changed his mind because he feared that opposition from the American Medical Association and conservatives could imperil its passage. A public works program was not placed within the Social Security Act because of the controversy it would have generated.[34]

TABLE 8.1 Summary of the major provisions of the Social Security Act

Title I: Grants to States for Old-Age Assistance

Nature of grants	Secretary of treasury pays to each state 50% of the sums expended in a year for assistance to people over age 65 who are not inmates of public institutions, but not including that portion of payments that exceeds $30 per month—and 5% of the federal payments are used to administer the programs by the states.
Requirements that states must meet	Each state must: • have a state plan for old-age assistance that is in effect in all political subdivisions of the state and that is mandatory on them • pay for the nonfederal share of the costs of assistance • designate a single state agency to administer the plan (or supervise the plan if local jurisdictions administer part of it) • establish an opportunity for a fair hearing before the state agency for anyone who is denied assistance • provide for method of selecting personnel and administering the grants that are found by the Social Security Board to be necessary for the efficient operation of the plan • provide to the Social Security Board any information and data that it requests • pay to the United States one-half of the net amount collected by any state (or its subdivisions) from the estate of any recipient of old-age assistance
Requirements that the Social Security Board cannot impose on the states	An age requirement of more than 65 years Any residence requirement that excludes any resident of a state who has resided therein five years during the nine years immediately preceding application and who has resided therein continuously for one year immediately preceding the application

Title II: Federal Old-Age Benefits

Establishing the trust fund	An account is created in the U.S. Treasury, known as the Old-Age Reserve Account, to which funds are appropriated for each fiscal year in an amount sufficient to provide for the payments under this title to retired persons.
Definition of eligibility	People who are at least 65 years of age who have received after December 31, 1936, and before reaching age 65 a total amount of wages not less than $2,000. Ineligible categories of work include: • agricultural labor • domestic service • casual labor not in the course of the employer's trade or business • service performed as an officer or member of the crew of a vessel documented under the laws of the United States or of any foreign country • service performed in the employment of the United States government • service performed in the employment of state governments or political subdivisions thereof • service performed in the employment of not-for-profit agencies
Amounts of benefits	If total wages after December 31, 1936, and before the age of 65 are not more than $3,000, the old-age benefit shall be at a monthly rate of one-half of 1% of such total wages. If these total wages are more than $3,000, the monthly rate will be one-half of 1% of the first $3,000 plus one-twelfth of 1% of total wages that exceed $3,000 and do not exceed $45,000. But in no case shall the monthly rate exceed $85. If someone dies before reaching 65, there shall be paid to his estate an amount equal to 3.5% of the total wages determined by the Board to have been paid to him with respect to employment after December 31, 1936.

(continued)

(continued)

Title III: Grants to States for Unemployment Compensation Administration

The federal government authorized to be appropriated funds to help states administer their unemployment compensation laws (Title IX discusses the actual unemployment program) provided that the state provides fair and efficient methods of implementing the program, including fair hearings. (If a state agency denies benefits unfairly, the Board can stop making further payments to that state.)

The Social Security Board, on collecting funds in the unemployment fund of each state, will give it to the secretary of the treasury, who will place it in the Unemployment Trust Fund.

Each state agency administering the program pays its benefits from funds from the Unemployment Trust Fund that are forwarded to it by federal authorities.

Title IV: Grants to States for Aid to Dependent Children

Nature of grants

States make payments of needy dependent children with the federal government paying to each state an amount equal to one-third of the total of the sums expended in a given quarter, but not counting the amount of grants that exceed $18 per month with respect to one dependent child (in a family) and $12 per month with respect to each additional dependent child.

Eligibility

The term *dependent child* means a child under age 16 deprived of parental support by reason of death, continued absence from the home, or physical or mental incapacity of a parent—and the child must be living with his father, mother, grandfather, grandmother, brother, sister, stepfather, stepmother, stepbrother, stepsister, uncle, or aunt in a place of residence maintained by one or more of such relatives as his or their own home.

Requirements that states must meet

The requirements are similar to those for Title I, but states cannot deny aid to any child who has resided in the state for one year immediately preceding the application or who was born within the state within one year of the application if the child's mother has resided in the state for one year immediately preceding the birth.

Title V: Grants to States for Maternal and Child Welfare

There are five parts to Title V:

Part 1

Provides funds to be paid to the states to enable them to extend and improve services for promoting the health of mothers and children, especially in rural areas and in areas suffering from severe economic distress. (States must have plans for the services funded by the part approved by the chief of the Children's Bureau. (The state plan must include state contributions to the services and administration or supervision of the spending by the state's health agency.)

Part 2

Provides federal funds to help each state extend and improve services for locating children with disabilities and providing them with medical, surgical, corrective, and other services and care, particularly in rural areas and areas with severe economic distress. State plans must be approved by the chief of the Children's Bureau.

Part 3

Provides funds for the purpose of enabling the Children's Bureau to cooperate with state public-welfare agencies to establish, extend, and strengthen public welfare services, called child welfare services, for the protection and care of homeless, dependent, and neglected children, and children in danger of becoming delinquent.

(continued)

(continued)

Title V: Grants to States for Maternal and Child Welfare	
Part 4	Provides funds to the states to allow them to extend and strengthen their programs of vocational rehabilitation of people with physical disabilities—and to allow them to continue to carry out legislation enacted in 1920 to provide vocational rehabilitation to persons disabled in industry or otherwise to help them return to employment.
Part 5	Provides funds for the maintenance of the Children's Bureau.

Title X: Grants to States for Aid to the Blind	
Nature of the grant	The federal government pays one-half of the funds expended by a state for aid to blind persons but not counting expenditures exceeding $30 a month—and 5% of the federal funds are to be used to administer the program. Inmates of public institutions cannot receive assistance under this title.
Requirements that states must meet	The requirements are similar to those for Title I.

Labor and Public Works Legislation

The National Labor Board that was established under the NRA had mediated conflicts between thousands of employers and employees. Senator Wagner proposed legislation that more clearly defined specific procedures to be followed when employees wanted to initiate a union and proposed establishment of an independent board to enforce the rights of union organizers. He fervently believed that such legislation would not only eliminate conflict but bring economic recovery, by increasing consumer purchasing power through the wage increases that would follow the growth of unions.[35] He proposed that employees should be allowed to circulate petitions to their fellow workers if they wanted an election to choose a collective bargaining agent and that secret elections, to be monitored by a National Labor Relations Board (NLRB), should be required if more than 50% of employees requested it. Employers would have to officially recognize any collective bargaining agent that received support from a majority of employees in the secret ballot, could not fire or intimidate organizers, and could not claim that a company union sufficed when workers wanted to hold elections.

When Senator Wagner introduced his legislation in 1934, Roosevelt withheld his support, because he wanted union organizing to proceed gradually, so as to avoid political backlash from business and the general public. He also wanted to place the NLRB within the Department of Labor rather than establishing it as an independent agency, so that Frances Perkins could administer it. When the NRA was declared unconstitutional in May 1935, however, Roosevelt supported Wagner's legislation, which had already been enacted in the Senate.[36] Despite strong opposition from business, the Wagner Act was enacted in 1936. It was partly responsible for an upsurge of union membership, which increased from 3.3 million workers in 1935 to 14 million workers in 1945, but its role should not be exaggerated. Many employers ignored it; many companies finally capitulated to unions because they feared strikes would decrease their profits; and then during World War II the government vigorously enforced collective bargaining to avert work stoppages.[37]

Soon after he terminated the CWA in early 1934, Roosevelt decided to develop a new work program to consolidate existing federal jobs programs into one piece of legislation. The legislation, entitled the Emergency Relief Appropriation Act, was enacted in 1935. He required most of its funds to go directly to wages rather than to administrative overhead and to be spent quickly rather than held back for long-term projects. He mandated socially useful projects to be allocated to areas in relation to the number of workers who were on welfare rolls.[38]

The intense rivalry that had existed between Ickes and Hopkins in 1933 continued following passage of the legislation. Both men wanted to head this new consolidated agency and sought Roosevelt's support. Roosevelt favored Hopkins, but he had to move gingerly so as not to alienate Ickes, congressional conservatives who disliked Hopkins, or congressmen who wanted to exercise patronage in the massive new jobs agency. (Congress insisted that appointments of all persons earning more than $5,000 be subject to the consent of the Senate.)

Roosevelt developed regulations that allowed the work programs to avoid undue patronage and placed them under Hopkins' control. He made himself the nominal head of the agency in order to curtail efforts by senators to place political friends in key jobs. He placed Ickes in charge of a large decision-making committee that had the official power to decide which work projects to fund, but he placed Hopkins in charge of a division that was empowered to recommend small work projects and to veto other project applications. As mayors, governors, and other local officials initiated thousands of modest street, library, and public improvement projects, Hopkins forwarded them to the decision-making committees, which *had* to fund them to meet Roosevelt's guideline that work funds be spent immediately. Hopkins used his veto power to defeat many of Ickes's large and complex projects, on the grounds that they competed with the private sector or that insufficient skilled labor existed to implement them. When the frustrated Ickes obtained a ruling that all projects of more than $25,000 should be given to the PWA rather than to Hopkins's division, Hopkins merely divided the larger projects into bundles of smaller ones.[39]

The programs of Hopkins's division, named the Works Progress Administration (WPA), dominated Roosevelt's public works strategy. Between 1935 and 1940, $14 billion were allocated to it, and 7.8 million persons received work relief. The WPA completed a remarkable array of projects and assumed a major role in disaster relief work, including floods, droughts, and hurricanes. Mil-

lions of Americans took on some semblance of dignity as they worked on these projects. The WPA inherited the local, state, and federal staff of the FERA, which was phased out following passage of the Social Security Act. Ultimate approval of projects came from Washington, but district or state branches of the WPA initiated and approved projects in consultation with local and state officials. Various administrative arrangements were established; some projects were completely supervised by local officials, and others by WPA staff. Local units of government were usually required to contribute some 20% of a project's budget through provision of in-kind costs.[40]

The WPA was criticized from both the left and the right. Conservatives believed that it provided make-work jobs, that it enticed some people to become dependent on public jobs rather than seeking employment in the private sector, and that it competed with the private sector. Hopkins's tireless advocacy of the program and his troubleshooting to deal with periodic crises in the field proved enough, however, to offset conservative criticism. Organized labor demanded that the WPA pay prevailing wages, but Roosevelt preferred a so-called security wage that was pitched between relief benefits and prevailing wages. Critics questioned Roosevelt's decision to restrict the WPA to persons who were already on welfare rolls, since this policy penalized many destitute persons who had avoided welfare. (Roosevelt consented to a compromise policy in which roughly 85% of WPA enrollees came from welfare rolls.) Other critics objected to the discrepancy between the wages of unskilled and skilled workers; the former received half the wages of the latter. To distribute WPA jobs broadly, only one member of a family was allowed to participate; this policy often meant that women and adolescents could not receive work relief, because administrators gave jobs to male heads of household. The WPA did not provide training to its workers or match workers to jobs so that they could increase their employment prospects while holding WPA jobs. It did not enjoy good working relationships with public welfare and employment offices, which lacked the staff to make sufficient referrals to it.[41] The WPA was never funded at levels to help more than two-thirds of eligible persons, and Roosevelt declined to institutionalize it by placing it within the Social Security Act, because some of his advisors did not want temporary programs placed within the act.[42] Both Congress and the president seemed to fear that a declaration of a permanent works program implied an admission to voters that they had failed to correct the nation's economic problems, and so the program struggled along with an uncertain future.[43]

At the insistence of Eleanor Roosevelt, who was a determined advocate for youth, the National Youth Administration (NYA) was established within the WPA, with Aubrey Williams as its director. A broad range of programs was established, including college aid for impoverished students, aid for high school students, public jobs in recreation centers and municipal services, and camps for rural youth to provide them with trade skills. In 1936 and 1937, 600,000 youths, many of them in extreme poverty, were aided by the NYA, even though NYA wages were only one-third of prevailing wages.[44]

THE ERA OF STALEMATE: 1937–1941

Roosevelt won a resounding victory in 1936, with the support of the liberal coalition of intellectuals, workers, Jews, and people of color. As much as 80% of the working class voted for him, as compared to only 42% of affluent persons. He also retained the support of the conservative South, which had traditionally voted Democratic. After Roosevelt's smashing presidential victory in November 1936, everyone was asking where the New Deal would go next. Hopkins, Senator Wagner, and others believed that Roosevelt had received a mandate to continue New Deal reforms—to obtain public housing programs, federal regulation of child labor and working conditions, an expansion of the WPA, and antilynching legislation.[45] Other advisors believed that the victory represented only a personal mandate and urged him merely to consolidate his gains in a quiet second term. Although he

often sought liberal reforms, Roosevelt's reform momentum halted in this era of stalemate.

Roosevelt's policies during this period manifested the same curious mixture of liberalism and conservatism that had marked other phases of the New Deal. He wanted to sustain his reform momentum, because he had become increasingly irritated by business, banking, and industrial elites and their continuing attacks on New Deal programs and the proposed tax increases. He used class-oriented language in the election of 1936, when he railed at the selfish and conservative attitudes of business elites. He was furious at Southern Democrats, who had increasingly allied themselves with Republicans to attack New Deal programs. Furthermore, he feared that his legislation would be dismantled by the Supreme Court, which had declared the NRA and the AAA to be unconstitutional in 1935 and 1936, respectively. When the economic resurgence of 1935 and 1936 ended with a recession in 1937 that increased national unemployment rates to 17%, he realized that deficit spending would be needed to stimulate economic growth.[46]

However, Roosevelt was cautious about expanding New Deal reforms, and he even made drastic cuts in some programs. Advised that the economic resurgence of 1935 and 1936 could be maintained only if federal deficits were reduced, he slashed funding for many New Deal programs, over the objections of liberals.[47] As he watched Hitler militarize Germany in the middle and late 1930s and became convinced that America had to respond, he sought increasingly to appease conservatives, whose support would be needed for rearmament.

With the realignment of political parties by social class in the 1930s, many middle-class persons joined working-class voters to give Roosevelt smashing victories in 1932, 1934, and 1936. However, as the decade wore on, some middle-class voters began to hedge their reform interests, because the nation's economic ills continued and the unprecedented expansion of government bureaucracy led them to wonder if Roosevelt was leading America toward socialism. However, anger at the New Deal often focused not on Roosevelt, who retained his personal popularity throughout the decade, but on some of his advisors and programs. Hopkins was widely believed to want unlimited personal power. Perkins was perceived as soft on militant labor unions and as a charity-minded social worker who blindly supported new programs. Many persons resented the intellectuals who formed Roosevelt's brains trust.[48] Some middle-class Americans also became alarmed by labor organizations, such as the Congress of Industrial Organizations (CIO), which they feared would gain inordinate power. The sitdown strikes of 1937, in which workers occupied automobile plants, were profoundly disturbing to many middle-class citizens, who believed that such disruptive techniques exceeded the bounds of fair play.[49] Thus, in the late 1930s and early 1940s, middle-class voters gradually shifted their support to the Republican party; indeed, when reelected in 1944, Roosevelt won only 53% of the votes cast.

These growing doubts about New Deal reforms among the middle class were supplemented by widespread opposition to Roosevelt's attempts to pack the Supreme Court and to purge the Democratic party in 1937. Many liberals had been furious at the Court for its adverse rulings and had developed various legislative proposals for neutralizing it—for example, a proposal requiring a two-thirds vote of the justices to declare legislation unconstitutional. (Congress has the constitutional power to determine the size and voting procedures of the Court.) Had Roosevelt not acted, Congress might have enacted legislation to limit the Court, because 150 such measures were introduced in Congress in 1937.[50]

Roosevelt remained silent on the issue until 1937, when he introduced a legislative proposal to allow the president to appoint a new justice every time a justice failed to retire within six months of his 70th birthday. Perkins advised him not to introduce this proposal because the Court not only appeared to be wavering in its attacks on New Deal programs but was widely regarded as sacrosanct.[51] When Roosevelt persisted, he ran into a storm of political protest; he was charged with upsetting the constitutional balance of powers, seeking unlimited personal power, and trying to establish a fascist dictatorship.[52]

Moreover, Roosevelt was unable to purge the Democratic party of dissident Southern Democrats, whose conservative opposition was magnified by their fears that Roosevelt would support civil rights measures. Enraged by these defections, he targeted several Southern politicians for political attack, by traveling to their districts to campaign for their rivals. However, he suffered a humiliating defeat when each of the politicians was reelected.[53]

Roosevelt's political effectiveness in the early and middle 1930s depended in part on his image of political invincibility. He had obtained so many

INSERT 8.2   CRITICAL ANALYSIS: WHY NOT DEVELOP A TRULY LIBERAL PARTY?

Roosevelt often dreamed of realigning American politics even more markedly than he had done in 1932, when he brought large numbers of low- and moderate-income people, including many immigrants and ethnic voters, into the Democratic party. But this Democratic party still contained its Southern contingent, which tended to be conservative on many issues and downright reactionary on civil rights issues. Many European nations possess labor parties that predominantly draw upon the support of workers—a fact that makes them more likely to support relatively liberal, or radical, policies.

Analyze why such realignment is more difficult in the United States than in Europe. Consider the orientations of American workers when compared to European workers; for example, do they identify with their social class or with the middle class? Consider historic reasons why the South became solidly Democratic, by reviewing political developments just before, during, and after the Civil War, such as Southern opposition to the Republican party headed by Abraham Lincoln. Consider the weakness of the American trade union movement.

Were a truly liberal party to exist, would it be successful in getting and keeping power in the United States with a winner-take-all system of elections?

legislative and electoral victories that many opponents believed it would be fruitless to oppose his
policies and feared that he might deny them patronage or personal support in their campaigns. His
Supreme Court and political defeats in 1936 and
1937 tarnished his image of invincibility, however,
and emboldened members of the conservative
coalition, as well as some moderate Democrats, to
question his policies.[54]

Roosevelt was accused of fascist tactics when
he attacked the Court and tried to purge his party,
but he was one of a relatively small number of
Americans who became alarmed by Hitler's rise to
power in the early 1930s. He first tried to work
indirectly to alert Europeans to the impending danger and to offer them economic assistance, because
he knew that many Americans, including many liberals, favored isolationism. As his espousal of rearmament became more obvious, isolationists in
both parties attacked his domestic policies, which
also languished as he devoted more time to foreign
policy. Roosevelt's preoccupation with foreign
affairs was illustrated when he appointed Hopkins
to be secretary of commerce in 1938 to develop
rapport with top American industrialists, whose
support and technical knowledge was needed during rearmament.

During World War II, social reform came under
strong attack. Many Americans demanded cutbacks in nonessential government programs,
because the war effort produced federal deficits
that dwarfed those of the 1930s. Indeed, the war
provided a splendid opportunity for the conservative coalition, whose members were determined to
rescind New Deal programs. As one historian
noted, "Republicans viewed the war as a struggle
for supremacy at home and abroad. . . . At home,
the enemy was reform. . . . The war provided an
opportunity to dismantle the New Deal [with]
reestablishment of the traditional American system
of unfettered private enterprise at the end of the
war."[55] Roosevelt hoped to maintain his New Deal
programs for the duration of the war, so that a new
round of reform activity could occur when it had
ended. However, he was unable to stop conservatives from terminating the CCC, NYA, PWA, and
WPA, partly because he had to mute his defense of
these programs in order to retain conservatives'

support for his international policies. It is difficult
to fault his decision to give precedence to international affairs in light of the barbarism of Nazi Germany, but liberals watched nervously as prized
programs were eliminated.

POLICIES DURING THE ERA OF STALEMATE

Roosevelt was able to obtain some major policy
reforms after 1936, despite the loss of his reform
momentum. The funding of the WPA, CCC, and
NYA, particularly after the recession of 1937, was
increased. Perhaps his signal accomplishment,
however, was passage of the Fair Labor Standards
Act of 1938. Fair working conditions and minimum
wages had been established for each industry under
the NRA, but many industries returned to sweat-
shop conditions when the Supreme Court declared
the NRA to be unconstitutional. With assistance
from Perkins, Roosevelt supported legislation that
established minimum wages and maximum hours,
but he had to make concessions to conservatives to
secure its passage. Farm labor was excluded from
the legislation, to appease Southern and Western
agricultural interests. Wage-and-hour standards
were phased in gradually so that the minimum wage
rose from 25 cents per hour to 40 cents per hour in
seven years. The maximum length of a work week
diminished from 44 to 40 hours per week in three
years.[56] Even this legislation aroused considerable
controversy. Southern Democrats feared it would
elevate the wages of poor African Americans, even
when agricultural laborers were excluded from it.
The AFL opposed it because they feared the minimum wage might establish a ceiling on wages and
would decrease the motivation of workers to join
unions. Some critics were unhappy that the Department of Labor would administer the legislation,
because they believed Perkins favored unions.[57]

In 1937, Roosevelt was able to obtain passage
of the Wagner-Steagall Housing Act, which established the United States Housing Authority to provide low-interest loans to local authorities to build
public housing.[58] The Roosevelt administration

INSERT 8.3   CRITICAL ANALYSIS: LIMITS OF NEW DEAL REFORMS

When viewed from the perspective of its era, the New Deal seems truly revolutionary in its policy enactments. It gave major social policy roles to the federal government for the first time in American history.

When viewed from the perspective of contemporary society, New Deal reforms seem quite limited in their focus. Identify kinds of reforms that were *not* enacted in the New Deal—ones we take for granted in contemporary society. Speculate why these reforms were not enacted in the 1930s.

expended considerable energy in implementing the many programs of the Social Security Act. Federal regulations and policies to govern OAA, ADC, AB, and unemployment insurance programs were issued. States were monitored to be certain that uniform standards of eligibility were used, that names of recipients were not published, and that political criteria were not used in eligibility decisions. Federal officials pressured states to develop their ADC and OAA programs rapidly; nonetheless, some states had barely started their programs by 1940. Federal authorities occasionally threatened to cut off federal funds to states that were remiss in administering their programs.[59]

Roosevelt realized by 1937 that he also needed to simplify the organization of federal programs; social welfare programs were scattered in the Departments of Interior, Treasury, Labor, and Agriculture, as well as in independent commissions and elsewhere. No department focused on social welfare issues, and no cabinet-level secretary coordinated the planning and implementation of social programs. He appointed a committee to examine this issue; the committee recommended the establishment of a Department of Public Works and a Department of Welfare, whose directors would sit in his cabinet. The plan was defeated in the Congress in 1938, because legislators feared that it had been masterminded by Hopkins to enhance his personal power, to increase Roosevelt's political patronage, and to increase the power of the federal government. The plan was also attacked by advocates of existing programs, such as the CCC, who feared that these programs would lose power if they were transferred to the new agency.[60] Roosevelt reluctantly retreated to a more modest proposal to create a subcabinet agency known as the

Federal Security Agency (FSA) and a Federal Works Agency under the Reorganization Act of 1939. The FSA contained the CCC, the NYA, the Public Health Service, the U.S. Employment Service, and the Social Security Board, whereas the WPA and the PWA were placed in the Federal Works Agency. This legislation was enacted, but not until 1953 was the Department of Health, Education, and Welfare finally created to house the nation's social programs.

Despite these various policy gains, Roosevelt suffered many policy losses during the waning years of the New Deal. A program to provide a large revolving federal fund to finance public works was defeated. Knowing they would be rebuffed, Roosevelt declined to support health legislation and a redistributive tax act. As the nation rearmed, Congress periodically raised the national debt limit but, as the price of their compliance, conservatives demanded and often obtained major cuts in social spending. Roosevelt failed in his bids in 1937 and 1939 to have the CCC made a permanent program, because conservatives did not want to establish the principle that ongoing federal programs were needed for the nation's youth. An ambitious proposal to develop programs like the TVA in seven other river basins was defeated.[61]

OUTGROUPS IN THE NEW DEAL

In the New Deal, attention focused on the problems of unemployment and relief, since millions of Americans were economically devastated by the Great Depression. But the nation's outgroups, including women, bore a disproportionate share of the economic suffering and sometimes wondered whether the New Deal spoke to their broader needs as well as their economic deprivation. In some cases, the economic plight of whites heightened animosities between the dominant population and outgroups, both during the Depression and during World War II.

African Americans

As the New Deal began, discrimination against African Americans continued unabated in both the North and the South. Because Jim Crow laws remained in force throughout the South, African Americans were disenfranchised, forced to live in segregated neighborhoods, required to sit at the rear of buses, and placed in segregated schools. Bad as these violations of civil rights were, they were overshadowed by the many instances of violence against African Americans. The Ku Klux Klan, long a presence in the South, had a resurgence in the 1920s and struck terror in the hearts of African Americans with a sustained campaign of lynchings and beatings.

Hard times increased racism, because many whites feared that African Americans would take employment from them. Faced with layoff decisions, many employers fired African Americans and retained white employees, sometimes in response to agitation by white citizens. As had been common before the 1930s, African American workers were denied membership in many unions and were used as scabs by employers to break strikes. Southern whites were furious, too, that African Americans received far higher wages under the WPA than they had received in the fields—and feared that the New Deal programs would disrupt the political and economic structure of the South by dramatically improving the economic condition of African Americans.[62]

African Americans desperately needed federal civil rights legislation that would rescind Jim Crow laws and outlaw discrimination by unions and employers, as well as job and service programs to provide resources and employment. But Roosevelt, during most of the New Deal, refused even to sup-

port legislation that would make lynching a federal crime; he finally gave it no more than verbal support late in the 1930s. Nor did he support legislation to eliminate the poll tax, which was widely used in the South to disenfranchise African Americans, or legislation to counter segregation in housing markets, despite urging by African Americans and Senator Wagner.[63]

Why didn't Roosevelt throw his support behind civil rights legislation? He knew that Southern Democrats would become determined opponents of his domestic legislation if he supported civil rights legislation, particularly if they voted with Republicans in the so-called conservative coalition. (As we have seen, Roosevelt's forebodings came true in 1937 and succeeding years, when the conservative coalition militantly attacked many New Deal initiatives.)[64] Indeed, even before 1937, Roosevelt had to make key concessions in unemployment, Social Security, public welfare, NRA, and fair labor and standards legislation to obtain the support of Southerners.[65]

Roosevelt and his aides also felt that African Americans were discriminated against because they were poor *rather than* because they were African American, and thus New Deal programs like the WPA, which gave jobs to African Americans, would end discrimination more effectively than would civil rights legislation. This perspective was tragically naive. Racism exists as a force that is independent of social class; in contemporary society, for example, affluent and well-educated African Americans still experience discrimination in job and housing markets. In the New Deal era, as we have already noted, some whites became even more hostile to African Americans, whom they viewed as competitors for jobs and even WPA positions. And the disposition of some whites to lynch African Americans was hardly linked to their precise economic status, as the epidemic of lynchings throughout the 1930s illustrated.

If many New Dealers were disinclined to support federal civil rights legislation, they were also reluctant to develop programs that specifically provided African American populations with resources and jobs. The creation of special programs for African Americans or even a policy of requiring quotas for African Americans in specific New

Deal programs were opposed because they were perceived to represent reverse discrimination.[66] Without such special treatment, however, it was doubtful that African Americans could overcome the economic and social chasm that existed between themselves and the white population.

African Americans nonetheless obtained notable policy concessions. Since it was obvious that many local officials and project-review committees would exclude African Americans from eligibility in the FERA and CWA programs in 1933, Hopkins, Williams, Perkins, and Ickes appointed African American advisors to monitor implementation of programs and to work in tandem with investigators to detect flagrant cases of discrimination.[67] Considerable success was obtained in enrolling African Americans, who constituted 10% of CCC enrollees and more than 15% of WPA workers.[68] The PWA and NYA were particularly innovative: The PWA established a quota system that required its private contractors to reach specific goals in their hiring practices; and the NYA was the only major New Deal agency that established special programs restricted to African American enrollees.[69] The inclusion of millions of African Americans in New Deal programs represented a major policy feat in a nation that had often denied African Americans access to local relief programs.

Discrimination nonetheless existed within New Deal programs. Except for a few camps in New England, the CCC was segregated. Roosevelt feared racial conflict within integrated camps as well as political opposition from Southerners. (Ugly incidents occurred in a number of camps before they were segregated.) African American enrollees were not transported to CCC camps in other states because of opposition by whites and fear for their safety.[70] Housing built by the PWA was often segregated.[71] Many New Deal programs —in particular, programs to help farmers refinance their mortgages or obtain loans—were of no assistance to African Americans, most of whom were tenant farmers. The NRA often allowed Southern industrialists to establish wage codes that froze the existing inequitable wages for African American workers.[72] Moreover, as we have seen, payments made to landowners under the AAA for withdrawing acreage from production were often not passed on to African American tenant farmers and sharecroppers, despite legislation that required such transfers.

Curiously, African Americans gained a major victory during World War II, when reformers asked why African Americans should sacrifice their lives in the war if units of the army were segregated, if African American workers in war industries had to live in segregated housing, and if African Americans encountered discrimination in wartime industries. Many whites, including some liberals, exhorted African Americans not to raise these issues during the war, in order not to divide the nation, but A. Phillip Randolph, the fiery African American director of the Brotherhood of Sleeping Car Porters and Maids, was so incensed by the prevalence of job discrimination against African Americans, even in war industries desperate for labor, that he advocated a massive march on Washington to force Roosevelt to sign federal legislation that would ensure the fair employment of African Americans in the defense industry. So as not to disrupt the war effort, Roosevelt finally relented in 1941, by signing Executive Order 8802 to prohibit discrimination in employment in the defense industry on the basis of race, creed, or national origin—on the condition that plans for the march be abandoned. (Executive Order 8802 also established the Committee on Fair Employment Practices to monitor the private sector, though the committee was given such scant funding that it could not assertively investigate many complaints of discrimination.)

Since Randolph was unable to persuade Roosevelt to sign an order to desegregate the armed forces, the war was fought with segregated battalions, until President Truman finally desegregated the armed forces at the war's end.[73] Hundreds of thousands of African Americans who returned from the military at the end of the war encountered extraordinary prejudice in both the North and the South. Moreover, the African Americans who had migrated to cities during the war constituted a growing underclass with limited economic prospects.

Thus, the civil rights accomplishments of the New Deal were very limited. A huge chasm existed between white and African American populations in this era, as suggested by public opinion polls. Poll data in 1939, for example, indicated that 69% of whites thought African Americans were less intelligent and that most whites endorsed segregated restaurants, neighborhoods, and schools (respectively, 99%, 97%, and 98% of Southerners and 62%, 82%, and 58% of Northerners).[74]

An African American social worker ominously predicted in the 1930s that provision of welfare benefits to African Americans without civil rights and jobs legislation risked perpetuating their inferior economic and social status. Three decades later, Jesse Jackson, a former aide to Martin Luther King, Jr., repeated that warning when he noted the existence of a massive population of African Americans who encountered bleak job prospects, poor educational programs, and minimal job-training programs and whose survival hinged on the receipt of welfare benefits.[75]

Women

The achievement of suffrage did not lead to policy gains for women, who found themselves unable to vote as a bloc or to agree on policy issues. Some women, including Eleanor Roosevelt, favored passage of protective legislation that shielded women from dangerous or physically taxing occupations; other women, who believed that protective legislation would merely close certain jobs to women, supported an equal rights amendment to the Constitution to grant women legal equality.[76]

Eleanor Roosevelt became a determined advocate for women during the early years of the New Deal. Because the CCC camps were statutorily limited to males, she persuaded her husband to establish 45 camps for 8,500 women under the FERA. Working closely with Molly Dewson, director of the women's division of the Democratic party, she secured the appointment of many women to high-level posts in the FERA, the WPA, and other agencies.[77] Almost no women obtained work relief in the CWA, but 15% of WPA recruits were women. The Wagner Act helped spur organizing of women; between 1930 and 1940, for example, the International Ladies Garment Workers Union tripled its membership, to 800,000 persons.

Although many women—about 20%—lost their jobs during the Great Depression, others found their employment to be more secure than men's; they tended not to work in heavy industry but rather in gender-segregated occupations that were relatively unaffected by the economic downturn. With the expansion of government programs, vast numbers of clerks and secretaries were hired, and the percentage of women in the federal work force rose from 14% in 1929 to 19% in 1939—or twice the rate of increase of male employment.[78]

Women also made major strides in obtaining sexual freedom. The flapper of the 1920s partially escaped Victorian moral codes. A majority of middle-class married women used birth control during the 1930s; their physicians provided them with the information they needed. However, many poor women, who could not afford doctors, lacked access to birth control information as a result, because birth control clinics were still illegal in many areas under the obscenity laws that had hampered Margaret Sanger two decades earlier.[79]

The economic and social gains of women in the New Deal should not obscure the continuing discrimination against them. It was widely assumed that married women should relinquish their positions to allow the employment of unemployed men; indeed, some women lost federal jobs after federal legislation in 1932 (which was not rescinded until 1937) stipulated that husbands and wives could not both hold federal positions. Many administrators in the CWA and the WPA assumed that husbands should receive priority in work relief programs. NRA labor codes tended to establish lower wages for women than for men in identical positions. Widows were not entitled to receive Social Security benefits of their deceased husbands until 1939; even under the new policy, the woman was not entitled to the benefits unless she was living with her husband at the time of his death.[80] Social Security was also expanded in 1939 to give modest benefits to the wives of retired workers—so long, that is, as she had been his wife for at least five years and was living with him at the time of the application. (Divorced women and remarried women had to forfeit these benefits.) Because Social Security benefits were tied to wage levels, female retirees, who usually came from low-wage occupations, received lower benefits than did males. Women who worked as domestics or in agriculture were not included in Social Security at all.[81] Unemployment insurance also discriminated against women. Because applicants were required to have a recent and extended employment record, women who left the labor force to have a child—or for other family reasons—could not easily reestablish eligibility after they resumed work. Many women were also denied benefits because they refused a "suitable job" that was a distance away or that required they work hours that were incompatible with their family responsibilities.[82] Nor were benefits paid for pregnancy or maternal (or paternal) leave—an omission that remains in place in the 1990s. Until 1950, the ADC program did not provide benefits to the heads of households, but only to the children, and federal authorities provided a smaller share of the funding of ADC than of OAA. Because it provided grants only to children in families headed by a single mother, ADC offered no assistance to the children of married women, many of whom were in considerable need. Trade unions generally excluded women from leadership positions and often negotiated contracts that gave women lower pay than men. The AFL leadership even demanded that women who were married leave their jobs so as to make available more employment for males.[83]

The cult of domesticity, which had dominated American family life for a century, remained intact; many married women who worked encountered hostility from their husbands and peers, even when they limited their horizons to gender-segregated and low-paying jobs. Moreover, psychologists, psychoanalysts, and physicians, such as Dr. Gesell and Dr. Spock, defined the role of the mother (*not* the father) as an all-encompassing one that was dictated by the needs of their children. Love between mother and child was the magic and necessary ingredient to be provided in "a perfectly nourishing environment" with mothers avoiding

"outside commitments so as not to 'miss' a fascinating stage of development" so that mother and child "could enjoy each other, fulfilling one another's needs perfectly, instinctively, as if Nature in her infinite wisdom has created them [to be] two happily matched consumers consuming each other."[84] Thus defined as supermom, women were truly confined to their homes through much of their married lives.

Latinos

Spanish-speaking persons constituted the majority of field workers in the irrigated farms of the Southwest by 1930. Despite some successes, violent suppression of agricultural unions, as well as red-baiting, led to the demise of pioneering unions. Since farm workers were not covered under the Wagner Act of 1936, they did not have collective bargaining rights that were enforced by the federal government; thus, employers could fire anyone they suspected of trying to organize the workers. In remote farming areas, the workers lacked access to lawyers or advocates. Even the few unions that had developed ended with the onset of World War II, when many organizers and workers were drafted or migrated to cities. As we have already noted, farm workers did not receive Social Security benefits or unemployment insurance.

When thousands of unemployed Latinos sought welfare in the 1930s, local welfare officials demanded massive "repatriation" (forced evacuation) to Mexico. Around 400,000 Latinos were forced to leave the country between 1929 and 1934. Many of them, with $14.70 in their pockets from the U.S. government, were placed on trains to Mexico City; the impact on families and communities was devastating.

When faced with the need to produce huge quantities of food during World War II, the federal government initiated the bracero program through a bilateral agreement with Mexico in 1942. The Mexican government, which wanted to alleviate domestic unemployment, allowed a specified number of Mexicans to enter the United States to meet labor shortages on farms; in return, the U.S. government pledged to ensure a minimum wage and to guarantee their just treatment. Extended annually until 1964, the program brought a total of five million Mexican laborers to the United States. In addition, many undocumented workers continued to flow into the United States during this period. But not bound by *any* agreements with the Mexican government regarding undocumented workers, employers that hired them—mainly agribusiness and mining companies—were able to treat them virtually as they wished.

Despite efforts by the Mexican government to secure their rights, braceros were subjected to countless abuses—in particular, poor wages, lack of housing, and lack of health care—and unions were no more successful during and after World War II than in the 1930s.

During World War II, sizable Latino populations had settled in urban areas; they worked in munitions factories, ship building, and other industries. Like African American workers of the period, they lived in segregated communities, in neighborhoods that had been abandoned by white populations fleeing to areas with better amenities. These urban Latinos encountered considerable racial animosity. In Los Angeles, for example, white sailors on shore leave frequently attacked Latino youth who wore zoot suits—flamboyant outfits featuring long jackets with padded shoulders. Resentment at these attacks led to the so-called zoot-suit riots. The Los Angeles police, well known for their brutality against Latinos, regularly conducted mass roundups and incarcerations.[85]

Asian Americans

The migration of Asians to the United States was effectively curbed with the Immigration Act of 1924, which limited annual immigration from specific countries to a percentage of the population of the corresponding group in the United States in 1890, when few Asians had migrated. (Chinese migration was banned altogether by the Chinese Exclusion Act of 1882.) Though not allowed to own land in many areas by state legislation, Asian residents had shown extraordinary ability to con-tinue farming—by leasing land or by finding cooperative Americans who put their own names on the deed but allowed the Asians to work the land. Moreover, Chinese American and Japanese American communities channeled their energies into developing a thriving network of small businesses. The Nisei (second-generation Japanese Americans, the children of the Issei, or first generation), who were U.S. citizens by virtue of birth, placed extraordinary emphasis on education, which was seen as a way of overcoming the barriers imposed by discrimination. Truly caught between American and Japanese culture, the Nisei nonetheless sought, with their parents' blessing, to master English, to go to college, and to use their educational achievement to obtain jobs that had been denied their parents.[86]

But a strong undercurrent of racism existed toward this outgroup. This racism could be shockingly intense, as Takaki points out. He cites the example of a young Japanese man from Hawaii who went to get his hair cut: On hearing that he was Japanese, the barber drove the young man out of his shop "as if he were driving away a cat or a dog."[87] People even spat on Japanese persons whom they encountered on the street. First-generation Asian Americans were denied citizenship on the grounds that they were non-Caucasian aliens—and then denied access to relief programs during the Great Depression on the grounds that they were not citizens! Nor were the Nisei able to escape discrimination, even with their college degrees. As the depression hit, most Nisei were unable to find jobs for which they had been trained; virtually no jobs were open to them in engineering, manufacturing, business, or even high school teaching. Trapped in family businesses, almost no Nisei worked for white employers even as late as 1940.[88] Chinese Americans worked largely in restaurants and laundries; a pattern of systematic discrimination prevented them from working in other occupations.

Recall that many Americans on the West coast had feared an invasion from Japan even at the start of the century and had demanded the immediate cessation of all immigration from Japan. The attack on Pearl Harbor in 1941 brought an immediate fear that Japanese Americans would conspire with Japanese agents to facilitate an invasion by the

Japanese. As other Asian Americans tried frantically to show that they were not of Japanese ancestry, Japanese Americans found themselves isolated and subjected to hatred and violence. They waited fearfully to see what would happen.

Roosevelt had received confidential reports before and soon after Pearl Harbor that the Japanese Americans did not constitute a threat to national security. The press, however, printed a chorus of rumors that Japanese Americans were conspiring with Japanese agents and reported widespread calls for their immediate internment. Unlike General Delos Emmons in Hawaii, General John DeWitt of the Western Defense Command became a zealous persecutor of Japanese Americans and conducted many search-and-seizure operations to find hidden transmitters. White farmers, who resented the success of Japanese American farmers, demanded their evacuation, partly out of a desire to obtain their land.

Roosevelt was urged by his attorney general not to evacuate the Japanese Americans, and it was obvious that rounding them up without due process would be an infringement of their civil rights. Nevertheless, Roosevelt and other advisors were determined to proceed—and often used blatantly racist language in their private conversations.[89] Executive Order 9066, although it did not mention Japanese Americans, empowered the secretary of war to develop "military areas" where he could confine whoever he thought was a security risk. Rumors that Italian Americans and German Americans might be apprehended sparked widespread protests, but no protests emerged when about 120,000 Japanese Americans were rounded up and taken to internment camps located in remote rural areas, with no due process and no hearings. Because they were able to take only what they could carry, they were forced to sell their houses and belongings within a matter of days; in the circumstances, they were often forced to accept nominal amounts for their possessions.

The Japanese Americans were given numbers and were required to wear them on tags from the point of evacuation onward. They were housed in assembly centers, shipped to remote internment camps with no idea where they were going, and greeted by barbed wire and guard towers in the camps. Curiously, the American authorities, who had incarcerated them as security risks, soon sought to persuade draft-age youth to volunteer for the armed services, but only after they agreed to sign loyalty oaths; partly to protest the internment, many of them did not volunteer—and draft protests broke out in 1944 when the military tried to conscript them. Nonetheless, 33,000 Nisei served in World War II, many with distinction.

Evacuation orders had been rescinded before the end of the war, and some of those internees who agreed to sign loyalty oaths were allowed to settle in cities not on the West coast, such as Denver and Chicago. But the damage had been done to several generations of Japanese Americans. Those who were still alive finally received symbolic compensation in the 1990s.

This incident involved a unique situation, but is not trivial. It was (and is) widely perceived by Asian Americans as an illustration of the impact of racism on American social policy. Leaders who had implemented dozens of humane policies were nonetheless able to take extraordinary actions that were fueled by racism; indeed, those actions provoked scant protests even from liberals.

To critics, the episode was the tragic culmination of the New Deal's consistently poor record on civil rights, not just for Asian Americans but for other people of color and women as well. The American government did, however, finally rescind its ban on Chinese immigration in 1943—over sixty years after its original passage. In the end, the ban was lifted for utilitarian rather than moral reasons; the United States could not justify Chinese exclusion without endangering its alliance with the Chinese.[90]

SOCIAL WORKERS IN THE NEW DEAL

By the end of the 1920s, social work had consolidated its position, with the development of many schools, most of which were associated with universities. An explosion of demand for social work occurred as, freed from the old preoccupation with relief giving, the profession attended to a host of problems, including family disruption, medical problems, child pathology, school problems, and outpatient services to persons released from mental institutions. The old charity organization society agencies, some 200 nationwide, developed the American Association for Organizing Charity, where they officially changed their mission from relief giving to family casework. In the 1920s, nongovernmental social agencies developed so-called federated fund raising, in which many agencies banded together to seek donations from corporations and their employees in a united drive; this later became known as the United Way. In 1921, the new profession developed a mass-membership professional organization, the American Association of Social Workers, even if most of its early members lacked professional training. The future looked promising for this new profession; it had developed a core technology (social casework), a network of social agencies, sources of funding (the federations), and many schools.[91]

Social casework, though emphasizing diagnosis and "scientific work," still bore some resemblance to the older charity work because it emphasized the person-in-the-environment. Both in diagnosis and interventions, caseworkers were to examine environmental factors that shaped the problems of their clients and to help them cope with situational realities. But in the 1920s, the primacy of social casework was challenged by the emergence of psychiatric social work, which drew heavily on the ideas of Freud and his disciples, as illustrated by the works of Virginia Robinson and others, which were markedly different from older works by Mary Richmond.[92] Psychiatric social work did not dominate the profession in many schools and agencies, but it was a highly visible wing of social work and had a particularly strong hold on certain schools, such as Smith College and the University of Pennsylvania, and certain kinds of agencies, such as child guidance agencies and psychiatric hospitals. Some proponents of social casework feared that this new contender, which emphasized intrapsychic matters and family relationships, could sever social work from its person-in-the-environment emphasis as well as its work with relatively impoverished populations.

Social workers were not usually involved in social reform projects or in public agencies during the 1920s. Even many of the old settlements, though still existing, lost their reformist qualities, as well as their visible leadership within the profession. Social workers were not highly active in partisan politics, although they supported specific candidates whom they believed were interested in certain social issues.

Many social work leaders took an intense interest in the national presidential campaign of 1928, however. They couldn't agree on which candidate to support: Al Smith had been receptive to social workers during his tenure as governor of New York State; and Herbert Hoover had pursued humanitarian work after World War I in Europe and shown interest in unemployment issues during the 1920s.[93] Nevertheless, a sizable number of social workers continued to believe that social work should remain separate from partisan politics altogether.

Thus divided, the profession was as unready for the political upheaval of the Great Depression as many other citizens were. Many leaders maintained, as did Hoover, that private agencies would suffice to manage the economic destitution that occurred in 1929 and 1930. They were in for a rude shock, however, when they found that private agencies, like the Red Cross, lacked the funds to help the throngs of destitute people. Indeed, vast numbers of social agencies, one-third of them in New York City alone, went bankrupt because of the rising caseloads and the drop-off in private philanthropy. Increasing numbers of social workers realized by 1930 that strong governmental action was needed, even if many of them still did not see the Democratic party as the necessary instrument of reform. (As we have already seen, Jane Addams voted for Hoover, not Franklin Roosevelt, in 1932.)[94] By 1932, however, many social work leaders had come to dislike Hoover for his disinclination to take bold action to help unemployed people.

Curiously, the Great Depression and World War

II actually benefited the social work profession. Whereas most social workers had been employed in private agencies in the 1920s, thousands of jobs opened up in New Deal agencies in the 1930s. The number of people in social work positions increased from 40,000 in 1930 to 70,000 in 1940.[95] During the 1920s, a cohesive community of leaders in New York City became acquainted with Eleanor Roosevelt and Harry Hopkins and assumed leadership and consultative roles to Franklin Roosevelt during his governorship of New York State. Many of these social workers assumed influential positions in the New Deal, supported the FERA, the NRA, and the CWA, and sought to professionalize New Deal programs by insisting on prominent roles for social workers.[96] Indeed, Hopkins supported many training programs for social workers. When the Social Security Act mandated the creation of the Social Security Board, social workers received key appointments to it and also to its Bureau of Public Assistance, which supervised ADC and the other welfare programs.

Social casework proved to be adaptable to these new public agencies, which sought to screen, refer, and give brief assistance to the many destitute people who used the New Deal programs. At the same time, the psychiatric wing of the profession continued to ply its trade in various private agencies, which existed throughout the 1930s.

Many of the new social work positions were filled by untrained people. Paid relatively low salaries and acutely aware that the New Deal programs provided only meager benefits to desperately poor people, these staff members developed lively protest movements—to seek both better pay for themselves and greater benefits for their clients.[97] Mary Van Kleeck and the publication *Social Work Today* issued fiery denunciations of the New Deal, which many believed was captive to corporate interests. The so-called rank-and-file movement of nonprofessional public employees of New Deal programs developed unions of public employees, supported sweeping social reforms, and often joined with or helped to organize poor persons as well as their own clients. By 1937, however, their protests had dissipated, perhaps because many of them had become part of the establish-

ment and civil service protections had been extended to them.[98]

World War II brought more growth to the profession. Social workers were hired by the Red Cross and other agencies that helped soldiers. Private agencies worked with relocated workers, day care, and other social issues on the home front.[99]

At various points during the 1930s and 1940s, social workers wrestled with the question of how selectively the profession should define its boundaries. One faction wanted the profession to markedly increase its membership so as to include the legions of untrained people who worked in public programs—and, in the 1940s, to include people with only a bachelor's degree. They believed that the power of the profession would increase as it broadened its boundaries and that the quality and prestige of many social work positions could be increased by including their incumbents in the profession. Another faction wanted to restrict membership in the profession to individuals with a graduate degree, so as to keep the caliber of professional work at a high level and maintain the prestige of the profession. The two factions often clashed but, for the moment, the selective faction was victorious.[100]

As in the progressive era, the opinions of the social work profession reflected attitudes within the broader society. Most of the leadership was sympathetic to Roosevelt, even if they were sometimes embittered by, for example, his termination of the CWA and some of the conservative features of the Social Security Act. In the 1930s, virtually all social workers were converted to the need for government to fund and deliver a host of services; thus, the curious hold of nongovernmental agencies on social welfare was ended forever. Perhaps we can say that social work became a part of the broad coalition that Roosevelt had fashioned in the New Deal, to the extent that the profession was viewed as liberal in succeeding decades as well. When Richard Nixon and other conservatives cast about for enemies some decades later, they unhesitatingly seized on social workers; some social workers took that as a sign that the reformist traditions of the profession remained at least somewhat intact.

Yet some social workers supported relatively backward-looking policies during the New Deal—for example, restriction of ADC grants to those families whom caseworkers judged to provide "suitable homes"; that policy would have given social workers a strange veto over the intake process in public welfare.[101] And some social workers remained safely outside the turmoil of the New Deal, in child guidance and other agencies with a psychiatric focus.

On the left, a small faction sided with decidedly radical protest in the 1930s, including the Communist party, the rank-and-file movement, and the Socialist party. They often argued that social work had been coopted by Roosevelt to participate in inadequate social programs and that, by doing so, it was blunting significant social change that could occur only by aligning the profession with grass-roots dissent.

This discussion of social work in the 1920s and 1930s suggests that a lively controversy existed within the profession over a number of issues. For example, to what extent should the profession engage in social action rather than just counseling? Should the profession have relatively broad or narrow membership? And to what extent should the profession ally itself politically with liberal forces? We can see certain central tendencies in the developments of the 1920s and 1930s, such as the dominance of casework, the decision by most social workers to support relatively liberal social policies but not radical reforms, and the preference for a relatively restrictive membership policy. But these central tendencies ought not to obscure conflict within a profession that, in some respects, was a microcosm of the society that enveloped it.

THE EVOLUTION OF THE RELUCTANT WELFARE STATE

When viewed from the perspective of the progressive era, the New Deal represents a striking departure from traditional American policies on two counts. First, unlike progressive reformers, who focused on state and local reforms, Roosevelt created a *national* welfare state that superseded local programs. Second, he created social programs rather than focusing on a regulatory strategy, as was illustrated by the first major social programs in the United States that distributed jobs (the CWA, WPA, CCC, and PWA) and resources (the FERA and the Social Security Act) to destitute and elderly Americans. By going beyond the legalistic approach of progressives, Roosevelt drastically altered the scope of the American welfare state.

It is easy to criticize the New Deal from the vantage point of contemporary society; New Deal reforms did not include the range of civil rights, medical, housing, Food Stamp, and other programs that were developed in subsequent reform eras, and they often were diluted by compromises with conservatives. Roosevelt nonetheless accomplished his reforms in a society where virtually no national social programs had existed and in the face of profound social, legal, and political opposition. In venturing into new policy territory, he often stumbled and changed directions, but he developed precedent-shattering policies that helped millions of citizens survive an economic catastrophe. He opportunistically changed policies as political realities changed, but he was remarkably consistent in his basic policy goals. He was a firm believer in capitalism, but he sought regulatory, tax, and social welfare policies to mitigate economic uncertainty and the suffering that accompanied it. He opposed ideology, whether socialism or unfettered capitalism, and preferred instead to seek practical reform policies in the political context that he encountered. In 1932, Frances Perkins wrote on a piece of paper a series of six reforms that she favored; by 1940, only health insurance had not been enacted.[102]

Roosevelt's social welfare innovations were matched by political accomplishments that prevented conservatives from dismantling his social reforms after World War II. He created the modern Democratic party, which, for all its faults, embraced a relatively liberal constituency. Voting preferences in the nation were associated for the first time with social class and with political ideology; African Americans, workers, Jews, and intellectuals tended to support the Democratic party, whereas affluent Americans tended to vote Republican. The numerical size of this liberal constituency made it difficult for Republicans to rescind the New Deal—unless they could persuade large numbers of working- and middle-class voters that social reform was not in their best interest. This did not happen to any significant degree until the administration of Ronald Reagan in the 1980s.

Still, viewed from the vantage of today's society, New Deal reforms were timid. The social reform agenda of the 1960s and 1970s was largely fashioned to address social problems that were not included within New Deal reforms—federal medical programs, national civil rights legislation, federal assistance for persons with mental disorders, programs to help persons with disabilities, educational and nutritional programs for those with few resources, and job-training programs. The various New Deal programs often helped less affluent persons survive their immediate destitution, and Roosevelt did obtain some tax reforms, but the federal tax system was not so fundamentally reformed as to alter existing economic inequality. The realignment of the political parties was not accompanied by an economic or social revolution that redressed inequalities between classes or races.

As a consummate politician, Roosevelt was sometimes overcautious in supporting social reforms. He did not aggressively support union organizing; did not try to institutionalize a public works program; delegated many social welfare functions to states and localities when the Social Security Act was enacted; and often resorted to budget cutting even when it led to widespread suffering. Moreover, he did not seize the opportunity to mobilize a liberal party as aggressively as he might have; he was too enamored with coalition politics, except when he ineffectually tried to purge Southern Democrats. Roosevelt did not grasp the political uses of the labor movement until late in the decade.[103]

Particularly when prodded by conservatives, Roosevelt and Perkins gave states considerable discretion in setting eligibility and program standards in many of the New Deal programs, even when this policy allowed conservative and Southern states to impose punitive and racist standards.

Workers in America were more heavily burdened by the payroll taxes of the Social Security program than were affluent persons, and they received only short-term and relatively miserly unemployment benefits. Americans in poverty who did not fit the restrictive eligibility requirements of OAA, ADC, and AB were forced to receive welfare assistance from relatively punitive local programs.

Where do we place the blame for these various shortcomings in New Deal policy? To some extent, Roosevelt reflected the hesitations and biases of American society. Because the nation entered the decade with no tradition of federal leadership in social welfare, the first programs were greeted with suspicion and uncertain funding. So preoccupied were reformers with establishing the precedent of federal programs that they often could not seek their enlargement or had to make compromises to conservatives in both parties to establish them.[104] Many of Roosevelt's advisors, as well as a large contingent of liberals in the Congress, had their ideological roots in the progressive era, when emphasis was placed on local reforms, and were reluctant to develop a large federal bureaucracy or permanent federal programs.[105] There was widespread prejudice against programs that assisted urban dwellers and workers, though most Americans lived in cities. Work relief programs were controversial in a society that assumed industrious persons could find work or that believed government should not interfere with the private sector. Deficit spending was also unpopular.

Roosevelt was able to enact the policies of the New Deal only because the Great Depression brought unprecedented suffering and thereby created a political climate in which social reform could be tolerated. Roosevelt lacked strong and certain allies on the left whom he could rely on for consistent support. Charismatic but eccentric leaders such as Father Coughlin and Huey Long were as adept at demagoguery as they were at supporting reforms. The CIO proved a more certain ally, but the AFL was lukewarm about the Fair Employment Practices Act and opportunistically used programs like the WPA to secure jobs for its own members.

It is ironic, in retrospect, that President Ronald

Reagan attacked Roosevelt's New Deal in the 1980s as America's venture into socialism. It was hardly socialism; it was a tentative foundation for a welfare state that would provide minimal public benefits to some people in poverty and to older Americans. The nation's social and economic inequalities, as well as its racist and sexist policies, remained intact.

NOTES

1. Eliot Rosen, *Hoover, Roosevelt, and the Brains-Trust: From Depression to New Deal* (New York: Columbia University Press, 1977), pp. 115–119.

2. Henry Adams, *Harry Hopkins* (New York: Putnam, 1977), p. 71.

3. Ibid., pp. 71–72.

4. Alan Brinkley, *Voices of Protest: Huey Long, Father Coughlin, and the Great Depression* (New York: Random House, 1982), pp. 8–81.

5. Ibid., pp. 82–142.

6. Abraham Holtzman, *The Townsend Movement: A Political Study* (New York: Octagon Books, 1975).

7. Paul Douglas, *Social Security in the United States: An Analysis and Appraisal of the Federal Social Security Act* (New York: McGraw-Hill, 1939), pp. 74–83.

8. Ronald A. Mulder, *The Insurgent Progressives in the United States Senate and the New Deal, 1933–1939* (New York: Garland, 1979), p. 73.

9. William Bremer, *Depression Winters: New York Social Workers and the New Deal* (Philadelphia: Temple University Press, 1984), pp. 126–132.

10. Ibid., pp. 158–163; John Ehrenreich, *The Altruistic Imagination: A History of Social Work and Social Policy in the United States* (Ithaca, N.Y.: Cornell University Press, 1985), pp. 102–108.

11. Melvyn Dubofsky and Warren Van Tine, *John L. Lewis* (New York: New York Times Book Co., 1977), pp. 203–221.

12. Raymond Wolters, *Negroes and the Great Depression: The Problem of Economic Recovery* (Westport, Conn.: Greenwood, 1970), pp. 39–55.

13. Brinkley, *Voices of Protest,* pp. 207–208.

14. Ibid., p. 255.

15. James Patterson, *Congressional Conservatism and the New Deal* (Lexington, Ky.: University of Kentucky Press, 1967), pp. 50–76.

16. Mulder, *The Insurgent Progressives,* pp. 292–308.

17. Robert McElvaine, *The Great Depression: America, 1929–1941* (New York: New York Times Book Co., 1984), pp. 281–282; Richard Polenberg, *Reorganizing Roosevelt's Government: Controversy over Executive Reorganization, 1936–1939* (Cambridge, Mass.: Harvard University Press, 1966); and Charles Trout, *Boston, the Great Depression, and the New Deal* (New York: Oxford University Press, 1977), pp. 310–312.

18. Robert Steamer, *The Supreme Court in Crisis: A History of Conflict* (Amherst, Mass.: University of Massachusetts Press, 1971), p. 199.

19. George Martin, *Madam Secretary: Frances Perkins* (Boston: Houghton Mifflin, 1976), pp. 341–356; Lillian Mohr, *Frances Perkins* (Croton-on-Hudson, N.Y.: North River Press, 1979), pp. 203–206; and Edwin Witte, *The Development of the Social Security Act* (Madison, Wis.: University of Wisconsin Press, 1962), pp. 1–111.

20. Bremer, *Depression Winters,* p. 151; Martin, *Madam Secretary,* p. 345.

21. Mohr, *Frances Perkins,* p. 205.

22. Douglas, *Social Security,* pp. 62–68; Martin, *Madam Secretary,* p. 351.

23. Martin, *Madam Secretary,* p. 348.

24. Quoted in Mimi Abramovitz, *Regulating the Lives of Women* (Boston: South End Press, 1988), p. 253.

25. Ibid., p. 254.

26. Douglas, *Social Security,* pp. 28–54, 129–150.

27. Bremer, *Depression Winters,* pp. 150–155; Clarke Chambers, *Paul U. Kellogg and the Survey: Voices for Social Welfare and Social Justice* (Minneapolis, Minn.: University of Minnesota Press, 1971), pp. 156–157.

28. Josephine Brown, *Public Relief, 1929–1939* (New York: Holt, Rinehart & Winston, 1940), pp. 303–312; Bremer, *Depression Winters,* pp. 166–167.

29. Douglas, *Social Security,* pp. 151–157, 185–196, 203–205.

30. Brown, *Public Relief,* pp. 303–306, 308, 312.

31. Winifred Bell, *Aid to Dependent Children* (New York: Columbia University Press, 1965), pp. 29–30.

32. Frances Piven and Richard Cloward, *Regulating the Poor: The Functions of Public Welfare* (New York: Pantheon Books, 1971), pp. 123–145; Bell, *Aid to Dependent Children,* pp. 41–46, 76–110.

33. Gilbert Steiner, *Social Insecurity: The Politics of Welfare* (Chicago: Rand McNally, 1966), pp. 18–26.

34. Chambers, *Paul U. Kellogg,* p. 157; Douglas, *Social Security,* p. 68; and Martin, *Madam Secretary,* p. 347.

35. Joseph Huthmacher, *Senator Robert F. Wagner and the Rise of Urban Liberalism* (New York: Atheneum, 1968), pp. 190–191.

36. Martin, *Madam Secretary,* pp. 381–383.

37. David Brody, *Workers in Industrial America: Essays on the Twentieth-Century Struggle* (New York: Oxford University Press, 1980), pp. 110–112.

38. Adams, *Harry Hopkins,* pp. 72–73.

39. Ibid., pp. 73–88.

40. Arthur MacMahon, John Millett, and Gladys Ogden, *The Administration of Federal Work Relief* (Chicago: Public Administration Service, 1941), pp. 313–314.

41. Bremer, *Depression Winters,* pp. 137–141.

42. MacMahon, Millett, and Ogden, *The Administration,* pp. 26–27.

43. Ibid., p. 390.

44. John Salmond, *A Southern Rebel: The Life and Times of Aubrey Willis Williams, 1890–1965* (Chapel Hill, N.C.: University of North Carolina Press, 1983), pp. 121–140.

45. McElvaine, *The Great Depression,* p. 281.

46. Ibid., pp. 283, 299.

47. Ibid., pp. 299–300.

48. Martin, *Madam Secretary,* pp. 323–324, 399–419; Polenberg, *Reorganizing Roosevelt's Government,* pp. 55–78.

49. Martin, *Madam Secretary,* pp. 399–406.

50. Steamer, *The Supreme Court,* p. 209.

51. Martin, *Madam Secretary,* pp. 387–390.

52. Mulder, *The Insurgent Progressives,* pp. 165–213.

53. Ibid., pp. 272–274; Patterson, *Congressional Conservatism,* pp. 277–287.

54. Patterson, *Congressional Conservatism,* p. 127.

55. Richard Chapman, *Contours of Public Policy, 1939–1945* (New Haven, Conn.: Yale University Doctoral Dissertation, 1976), p. 262.

56. Martin, *Madam Secretary,* pp. 391–395.

57. Ibid.; Mulder, *The Insurgent Progressives,* pp. 224–227; Patterson, *Congressional Conservatism,* pp. 149–154.

58. Huthmacher, *Senator Robert F. Wagner,* pp. 224–228.

59. Charles McKinley and Robert Frase, *Launching Social Security: A Capture-and-Record Account* (Madison, Wis.: University of Wisconsin Press, 1970).

60. Barry Karl, *Executive Reorganization and Reform in the New Deal* (Cambridge, Mass.: Harvard University Press, 1963); Polenberg, *Reorganizing Roosevelt's Government.*

61. Chapman, *Contours,* pp. 1–80.

62. John Kirby, *Black Americans in the Roosevelt Era: Liberalism and Race* (Knoxville, Tenn.: University of Tennessee Press, 1980), pp. 97, 101–102, 141–142.

63. Ibid., pp. 34–35; Huthmacher, *Senator Robert F. Wagner,* pp. 171–173, 242.

64. Patterson, *Congressional Conservatism,* pp. 98–99.

65. Kirby, *Black Americans,* pp. 30–34, 57–62, 82–83.

66. Ibid., pp. 32, 61, 73–74; Salmond, *A Southern Rebel,* pp. 126–127.

67. Kirby, *Black Americans,* pp. 19–26, 37–47, 51–53, 58–59, 106–151.

68. Ibid., p. 142; John Salmond, *The Civilian Conservation Corps, 1933–1942* (Durham, N.C.: Duke University Press, 1967), p. 101; Wolters, *Negroes,* pp. 203–209.

69. Salmond, *A Southern Rebel,* pp. 126–127; Wolters, *Negroes,* pp. 196–206.

70. Salmond, *The Civilian Conservation Corps,* pp. 91–94.

71. Kirby, *Black Americans,* p. 34.

72. Wolters, *Negroes,* pp. 98–102.

73. John Hope Franklin, *From Slavery to Freedom* (New York: Knopf, 1974), pp. 559–563.

74. Gerald Jaynes and Robin Williams, eds., *A Common Destiny: Blacks and American Society* (Washington, D.C.: National Academy Press, 1989), pp. 59–60.

75. Kirby, *Black Americans,* pp. 142–145.

76. Nancy Woloch, *Women and the American Experience* (New York: Knopf, 1984), p. 424.

77. Susan Ware, "Women and the New Deal." In Harvard Sitcoff, ed., *Fifty Years Later: The New Deal Evaluated* (Philadelphia: Temple University Press, 1985), p. 120.

78. Ibid.

79. Woloch, *Women,* p. 443.

80. Abramovitz, *Regulating the Lives of Women,* p. 261.

81. Ibid., pp. 254–255, 292.

82. Ibid., p. 293.

83. Ware, "Women and the New Deal," pp. 121, 124; Abramovitz, *Regulating the Lives of Women,* p. 224.

84. Barbara Ehrenreich and Deirdre English, *For Her Own Good: 150 Years of Experts' Advice to Women* (New York: Doubleday, 1978), p. 221.

85. Leobardo Estrada, F. Chris Garcia, Reynaldo Macias, and Lionel Maldonado, "Chicanos in the United States: A History of Exploitation and Resistance." In F. Chris Garcia, ed., *Latinos and the Political System* (Notre Dame, Ind.: University of Notre Dame Press, 1988), pp. 50–51.

86. Ronald Takaki, *Strangers from a Different Shore* (Boston: Little, Brown, 1989), pp. 217ff.

87. Ibid., p. 179.

88. Ibid., p. 219.

89. Ibid., pp. 390–391.

90. Ibid., p. 378.

91. Stanley Wenocur and Michael Reisch, *From Charity to Enterprise: The Development of American Social Work in a Market Economy* (Urbana, Ill.: University of Illinois Press, 1989), pp. 115–135.

92. Virginia Robinson, *A Changing Psychology in Social Case Work* (Chapel Hill, N.C.: University of North Carolina Press, 1930).

93. Bremer, *Depression Winters,* pp. 16–24.

94. Ibid., pp. 34–37, 46–53.

95. Wenocur and Reisch, *From Charity to Enterprise,* p. 213.

96. Bremer, *Depression Winters,* pp. 126–132.

97. Wenocur and Reisch, *From Charity to Enterprise,* pp. 182–207.

98. Bremer, *Depression Winters,* pp. 159–165.

99. Leslie Leighninger, *Social Work: Search for Identity* (New York: Greenwood Press, 1987), pp. 103–124.

100. Ibid., pp. 125–150.

101. Bell, *Aid to Dependent Children,* pp. 29–30.

102. Ware, "Women and the New Deal," p. 119.

103. Brody, *Workers,* pp. 138–146.

104. Margaret Weir and Theda Skocpol, "State Structures and the Possibilities for 'Keynesian' Responses to the Great Depression in Sweden, Britain, and the United States." In Peter Evans, Dietrich Rueschemeyer, and Theda Skocpol, eds., *Bringing the State Back In* (Cambridge: Cambridge University Press, 1985), pp. 132–137.

105. Mulder, *The Insurgent Progressives,* pp. 1–34.

9

The Era of Federal Social Services: The New Frontier and the Great Society

Selected Orienting Events

1945–1952	Presidency of Harry Truman
1946	Full Employment Act
1950–1953	Korean War
1950s–1960s	Massive migration of African Americans from the South to the North
1953	Department of Health, Education, and Welfare established
1953–1960	Presidency of Dwight Eisenhower
1955	Bus boycott in Montgomery, Alabama, initiates civil rights movement
1960	John Kennedy wins presidential election
1961	Passage of Manpower Development and Training Act (MDTA)
1961–1963	Escalating racial violence and protest in the South
1962	Michael Harrington publishes *The Other America*
1963	President Kennedy delivers nation's first presidential address on civil rights; passage of Mental Retardation and Community Mental Health Centers Construction Act
1963	John Kennedy assassinated; succeeded by Lyndon Johnson
1964	Economic Opportunity Act, Food Stamps Act, and Civil Rights Act enacted
1964	Johnson wins a landslide victory over Goldwater in presidential election
1965	Medicare, Medicaid, Elementary and Secondary Education Act, Civil Rights Act, and Older Americans Act enacted
mid–late 1960s	Cesar Chavez organizes farm workers
1966	National Organization for Women formed
1967	Welfare amendments establish work incentives and work programs for AFDC recipients
1968	Martin Luther King assassinated
1968	Johnson decides not to seek Democratic nomination for another term
1969	Stonewall Inn riot initiates gay rights movement

Before he died, President Franklin Roosevelt hoped that a new reform era would begin after the end of World War II, but many conservatives were determined that this would not be the case. In fact, relatively few social reforms were enacted during the presidency of Harry Truman (1945–1952), and American policy was profoundly conservative during the two terms of Dwight Eisenhower (1953–1960). It was not until the presidency of John Kennedy (1961–1963) that the United States tentatively embarked on social reforms. The so-called Great Society during the administration of Lyndon Johnson (1963–1968) vastly increased the scope of the American welfare state, even if it was rudely interrupted by the Vietnam War.

WORLD WAR II, THE POSTWAR ERA, AND THE 1950s

Liberals watched with dismay as the New Deal was dismantled during World War II; many of the major social programs—including the WPA, the CCC, the PWA, and the NYA—were gone by 1943. Franklin Roosevelt failed to make much of an effort to save the programs, but they were probably doomed, in any case. The precipitous drop of unemployment during the war undercut the rationale for programs focused on providing jobs to the unemployed; the war gave conservatives more power (they could threaten not to cooperate with Roosevelt's foreign policy unless he axed social programs); and the huge wartime deficit made it difficult to justify spending that was not essential to the war effort.[1] All the programs within the Social Security Act survived the war, however.

During the war, liberals and conservatives sought to position themselves for the postwar period. Intent on not letting liberals seize the postwar agenda, the conservatives ended funding for the National Resources Planning Board (NRPB), which Roosevelt had established to conduct planning for the postwar period; staffed with liberals, it had recommended the creation of many social programs after the war, to avert an expected resump-

tion of the Great Depression.[2] Indeed, conservatives in Congress established several planning bodies of their own that, predictably, recommended no major increases in social spending after the war.

World War II required a total mobilization of the domestic economy and brought about huge, unprecedented deficits. This enormous effort distracted attention from the domestic social agenda. Instead of social reform, major domestic issues during the war involved the extent and nature of rationing, the extent wages and prices should be controlled (and at what levels), and the extent civilian goods should be produced in a wartime economy that focused on military production.

The Failure of Social Reform in the Truman Era

Despite the dissolution of the NRPB, some highly placed liberals within the administration sought to obtain reform in the immediate aftermath of the war. They tried to get Roosevelt's ear during the war and just before his death in March 1945 and then to enlist Truman's support before the defeat of Japan in August 1945. Following some of the earlier recommendations of the NRPB, these officials developed an intriguing and simple idea to achieve postwar social reform by indirection. Since a recession (or worse) was widely expected when military spending decreased after the war, why not commit the federal government to obtaining full employment and mandate spending on an array of social programs—such as health insurance, housing, and expanded Social Security—as the economic means to this goal? Social spending would thus be *required* to keep the economy in full employment. And why not establish in the White House a planning council of economists who would orchestrate this liberal scenario and also help the incumbent president to issue an annual economic report? After many meetings among themselves, with cooperation from some liberal congressmen and support from Truman, the legislation eventually was enacted as the Full Employment Act of 1946, which established a national full-employment goal and installed the Council of Economic Advisors in the White House.[3]

But the legislation hardly resulted in a renewal of social reforms. Conservatives were able to dilute its language so that the government was not *required* to increase social spending when unemployment became severe. (Moreover, the president was at liberty to ignore the recommendations of the Council of Economic Advisors.) In addition, to the surprise of many economists, there was no depression in the wake of World War II. For one thing, Americans had amassed enormous savings in the form of war bonds that they quickly used at war's end to buy the consumer goods denied them during the Great Depression and the war. Fueled by such spending, and by huge exports to nations whose economies had been devastated by the war, a postwar economic boom occurred, and conservatives sought to *reduce* government spending to avert inflation—hardly the scenario that the framers of the Full Employment Act had envisioned![4]

Other factors also prevented a postwar era of reform. Recall that a conservative coalition of Republicans and Southern Democrats had become relatively cohesive in 1937 and had fought many of Roosevelt's initiatives (or at least sought to dilute or modify them). When the Republicans won control of both houses of Congress in the national elections of 1946, they were able to develop an antispending crusade; wielding their ability to cut federal taxes, they forced Truman to refrain from increasing social spending, in order to avoid a serious deficit in the federal budget. (Like most Americans of this era, Truman was strongly against deficits. Thus, conservatives could constrain social spending simply by cutting taxes.)[5]

Nor were Americans enamored with social reform in this period, partly because they were preoccupied with enjoying the first extended period of relative affluence since the onset of the Great Depression in 1929. Imbued with savings from the war period and enticed by an array of appliances and cars, many Americans were oblivious to the needs of impoverished people in urban and rural areas—or to the needs of African Americans who still lived under the tyrannies of poverty and Jim Crow laws.

Social reform was also impeded by international developments. Idealists hoped that the end of World War II would usher in a period of international stability, orchestrated by the newly created United Nations. Indeed, in the immediate postwar period, military spending declined almost to prewar levels.

But international stability soon began to unravel, as the relationship between the United States and Russia became increasingly tense. Joseph Stalin, the Russian dictator, was convinced that Roosevelt had ceded Eastern Europe to him in the wake of the war, in return for the vast sacrifice of Russian soldiers and citizens on the eastern front. Thus emboldened and eager to build a buffer between his nation and the hated Germans, who had invaded Russia on several occasions, Stalin quickly asserted control over Poland, Czechoslovakia, East Germany, and other East European nations. Moreover, civil conflict in Greece and Turkey led Americans to fear that these nations could be taken over by the Russians. Believing that Stalin might even want to extend his empire to Western Europe, Truman developed the Marshall Plan, a program of U.S. economic assistance to Western Europe, in order to prevent the Russians from capitalizing on discontent and insurrections there. Although Truman refrained from increasing the military budget, the huge expenditures for the Marshall Plan ruled out any major increases in social spending, particularly when, as already noted, conservatives had cut the level of American taxes. Moreover, like Roosevelt in World War II, Truman gave only symbolic, verbal support to social reform between 1947 and 1949, because he needed the support of the conservative coalition for his foreign-policy objectives, such as the Marshall Plan.[6]

But the *real* diversion of resources and presidential effort to military spending and international affairs—indeed the Cold War itself—commenced in 1950. For several years, some top officials, including Dean Acheson and Paul Nitze of the State Department, had been advocating a dramatic increase in U.S. defense spending to counter a perceived Communist threat around the world. But they were worried that a budget-conscious Congress and president would refuse. Shortly after they sent Truman a secret report detailing the need for a larger military, North Korea attacked South Korea. Truman decided to use the invasion as a pretext for a massive, and ongoing, increase in American military spending.[7] American military spending rose from about $10 billion to $40 billion annually—and to considerably higher levels during the Korean and Vietnam Wars. In constant dollar terms, after correcting for inflation, the military budget remained at the same extraordinary level for the next 42 years; in 1991, military spending was roughly $300 billion.

Why, you may wonder, discuss the *military* budget in a book on social welfare policy? To some extent, any budget represents a competition between spending priorities. When Americans chose to spend close to 75% of their national budget in the 1950s on military spending, they could *not* spend these sums on alternative programs. Moreover, since high military spending was coupled with low federal tax rates (as compared to international standards), funds available for social spending were restricted even more. Military spending gradually declined as a percentage of the gross national product (GNP) over the next 40 years, because the American economy grew so rapidly, but even at that lower level it absorbed most of the federal budget. Indeed, even as late as 1975, military spending and military-related items (such as the Atomic Energy Commission, the National Aeronautics and Space Administration, and interest on the national debt, which largely derived from former wars) together constituted roughly three-quarters of the national budget.

Thus, when reading this and ensuing chapters, you should bear in mind that social spending was constrained by military (and military-related) spending. Moreover, the Cold War consumed a large portion of the energies of presidents and congressional leaders during its 40-odd years, probably to the detriment of attention to domestic matters.

Social reform in the Truman era was also retarded by the white population's racial animosities toward African Americans and by the African American community's lack of political organization. During World War II, the large influx of African Americans seeking work in the war industries angered white residents of Detroit and other urban centers; intermittent race riots broke out. Considerable racial tension remained in Northern cities after the war. Moreover, Southern legislators, with support from some Northern Republicans, secured the termination of the Fair Employment Practices Commission at the end of the war, resisted Truman's efforts to revive it, and blocked other civil rights legislation. Truman deserves credit for desegregating the armed services after the war was over, in the face of outright defiance by some generals.[8]

The dynamics of the Cold War put social reformers on the defensive in the postwar period and throughout the 1950s. Obsessed with the subversion of government and society by communists, cold-warriors demanded the dismissal of civil servants and the prosecution of ordinary citizens who were leftists or radicals—or who had once been members of the Communist party. Eradicating subversive people from government was a major campaign theme even in 1946, but it crescendoed into a veritable witch-hunt by the early 1950s, when federal officials developed lists of subversive civil servants, who were often terminated with no due process. The campaign met its ugly culmination in Senate investigating hearings in the early 1950s, at which Joseph McCarthy, who had already subjected many citizens to public interrogation, sought to obtain the dismissal of high-level officers of the army. When McCarthy was finally discredited and censured by the Senate, the witch-hunt subsided, but the whole process had led to widespread public suspicions of social reformers, who were often stigmatized as radicals.

Eisenhower and the Conservative 1950s

Elected as a World War II hero and as a candidate who promised to end the unpopular war in Korea, Eisenhower was a president who had had virtually no experience in nonmilitary domestic matters. He was no liberal, though he was frequently attacked by conservative Republicans for not cutting social

INSERT 9.1　ETHICAL ANALYSIS OF KEY ISSUES AND POLICIES: BALANCING NATIONAL-SECURITY AND DOMESTIC NEEDS

Any nation legitimately wants to protect itself from foreign intruders and to involve itself in foreign-policy issues that are germane to its interests. Yet nations also possess domestic problems that require the expenditure of resources, not to mention leadership from their elected officials.

Analyze the ethical merit of the decision during the 1950s to commit about 75% of the nation's budget to military and military-related expenditures. Would it have been ethically principled, even when confronting a dictator like Stalin, to limit military spending to a smaller percentage of the nation's budget? Would fewer missiles and fewer troops in Europe have sufficed to protect the nation's security needs?

Or should the nation have raised its taxes to allow *both* national-security and domestic programs?

While military spending is currently less than 10% of the nation's budget, it still consumes nearly $300 billion of the nation's resources. Is there ethical merit in the argument that, with the Cold War over, the nation should devote far less to its military budget in order to allow greater expenditures on domestic needs?

spending even further. Eisenhower wanted to keep taxes to a minimum, so that government did not interfere with the private economy. He had no interest in expanding social spending, aside from small programs here and there. He did make truly massive government commitments to infrastructure improvements, through the establishment of the interstate highway system and the St. Lawrence seaway, but he saw these measures in military terms: They would facilitate the transportation of troops and military hardware in the event of a world war. (He had marveled at the German's sophisticated transportation system during World War II.)[9]

Perhaps even more than Truman, Eisenhower was obsessed with Cold War diplomatic and military maneuvering. Flanked by the Dulles brothers (John Foster Dulles at the State Department and Allen Dulles at the Central Intelligence Agency), Eisenhower presided over numerous international crises abroad and innumerable debates within his administration about the size and composition of the American military forces. Fearing that the Russians wanted to bankrupt the United States by tricking it into excessive military spending, Eisenhower constantly sought to cut the defense budget. However, the costly technological advances of the

1950s—such as the development of missiles and advanced aircraft—and a continuing commitment to the defense of Europe left intact the large military budgets that Truman had initiated at the outset of the Korean War. Moreover, both Republican and Democratic members of Congress came to see military contracts as important sources of revenue for their districts—and political support for themselves—and would balk when Eisenhower broached cuts in military spending. It was ironic that Eisenhower, a former war hero, made an eloquent speech against the "military-industrial complex" as he left the presidency in 1960; he noted that every dollar spent on guns is a dollar not spent on humanitarian programs.[10]

The Democrats controlled the Congress during much of Eisenhower's tenure. In those circumstances, he made a deal with the Democratic leadership, including Lyndon Johnson. In return for support for most of his foreign-policy initiatives, Eisenhower agreed not to make an assault on those social programs that had survived the New Deal. Eisenhower realized that the American people, many of whom still vividly remembered the hardships of the Great Depression, wanted to keep those New Deal programs. Social Security was expanded in the 1950s to make it a family program that provided benefits to people with disabilities and to wives, widows, dependent children, and survivors of the men who had been its initial beneficiaries. When the Russians launched Sputnik into orbit, Eisenhower supported the National Defense Education Act, which provided federal funds for science and math training in the schools. But Eisenhower can hardly be called a reformist president, even if, unlike Ronald Reagan in the 1980s, he did not seek to undo social programs that had already been enacted.

Eisenhower's record on race relations was not progressive. Partly because of his numerous links with Southern governors and friends, he believed that the federal government should leave racial matters to the states. Accordingly, he did not assume leadership with respect to lynchings, Jim Crow laws, or the denial of suffrage to African Americans in the South. When the courts finally ordered the city of Little Rock, Arkansas, to allow African American children to attend its schools in 1957, he sent federal troops to enforce the order only when his hand was forced by escalating violence, including danger to the lives of the African American children.[11]

THE TURN TOWARD REFORM

Many persons wondered whether the policy quiescence of the 1950s would continue after the presidential election of 1960, which pitted Richard Nixon against John Kennedy, a relatively unknown Democrat who had served in the House (1947–1952) and had been elected to the Senate in 1952. Neither man projected a reform image; indeed, the campaign focused on the first televised presidential debates, in which the two men promised to pursue anticommunist policies. It was only when Kennedy was pitted against Hubert Humphrey, a liberal reformer, in a key primary in West Virginia that he made social reform a prominent part of his campaign; he promised to help elderly people with their medical bills, to develop programs to help Americans living in poverty in Appalachia and

inner cities, and "to get the country moving again." But his belated support of social reform and indifference to reform as a U.S. Senator did not endear him to liberals, including Eleanor Roosevelt, who gave her support to him only late in the campaign.[12]

A strange combination of affluence and poverty coexisted as the nation entered the 1960s. Several factors contributed to the postwar prosperity during the 1950s. With the economies of Japan and Europe devastated by World War II, the United States was uniquely positioned to become the major economic power in the world and to dominate world trade. Lacking economic competitors, American industry could both export at will and dominate domestic markets.[13] Economic growth was buoyed by rising wages, as well as funds that circulated in the economy from burgeoning Social Security and other social programs. It was also fueled by a partnership fashioned between government, the housing industry, and the automobile industry: The federal government provided cheap housing loans to veterans and other homeowners and underwrote a large share of the costs of a massive expansion of the nation's roads, which in turn, promoted a housing boom in the suburbs and the production of large numbers of automobiles. The federal government also contributed indirectly to economic growth through its tax policies, by allowing Americans to deduct interest payments on home mortgages and loans.[14]

Serious social problems existed, however. They were most obvious in the South and Southwest, where millions of African Americans, Latinos, and Native Americans experienced appalling poverty, as well as violation of their fundamental rights. Although they had traditionally resided in rural areas, increasing numbers settled in urban areas, where they encountered overt discrimination; they were prevented from voting, using public facilities and transportation, and living in white neighborhoods.

Even in the mid-1950s, there were signs that African Americans in the South would demand a new Reconstruction; leaders of African American churches, who had often been resigned to the oppression of their people, began to discuss strategies for attacking racist policies. The urbanization of African Americans in the South allowed them to organize more easily against rampant discrimination.[15]

The seeds of African American discontent in the North were sown in the 1940s and the 1950s by a massive migration from the South. African Americans fled the South for many reasons—to join friends who had already migrated to the North, to obtain jobs, or to escape oppression. Of the 4.5 million African Americans who migrated to the North and West between 1940 and 1970, 90% settled in the large cities of six states: California, New York, Pennsylvania, Ohio, Michigan, and Illinois.[16] They were segregated in densely populated urban ghettoes, denied housing in white areas, limited to unskilled jobs, denied membership in unions, placed within segregated and inferior school systems, disenfranchised, and subjected to police brutality.

Despite its prosperity, the nation was marked by extreme economic inequality in 1960: The average income of persons in the most affluent one-fifth of the population was roughly nine times the average income of those in the poorest one-fifth of the population.[17] Poverty existed in low-income urban areas and in rural areas such as Appalachia, where housing, infant mortality, health, and income standards were similar to those in many third-world nations. In 1960, Social Security, unemployment insurance, and AFDC provided a very inadequate safety net. AFDC was administered arbitrarily in many jurisdictions, with flagrant violations of the rights of persons who sought assistance.[18] Southern states paid scandalously low benefits. Because no subsidized nutrition program existed, many individuals—including those who received miserly AFDC payments—suffered malnutrition; indeed, surveys suggested that many children in Mississippi were malnourished even as late as 1967.[19] Since the federal government had developed no major medical programs, poor persons had to rely on underfunded county and municipal hospitals. There were virtually no neighborhood clinics for pregnant women or infants, for family planning, or for other special needs.

Since government health insurance programs did not exist, millions of elderly persons found that they could not afford medical bills when they lost the private medical insurance provided as a fringe benefit by many employers in the postwar era. Social Security pensions, which were received by millions of elderly persons, had helped ease their economic burdens, but about one-third of them lived below poverty levels even in 1967.[20]

Women first entered the labor force in large numbers during World War II, as replacements for male workers who had joined the military, but many of them were terminated when veterans returned. The millions of women remaining in the labor force—in clerical, check-out, sales, nursing, and teaching occupations—were usually consigned to low-paying jobs and rarely given assistance with their day-care needs.[21]

Blue-collar workers contended with hazardous working conditions in chemical, plastics, pesticide, and assembly-line plants that were not subject to adequate safety regulations. Despite major gains in unionizing workers, many blue-collar workers lacked private health insurance and were forced to rely on charity medicine in public hospitals when they became seriously ill. Workers were buffeted by three recessions in the 1950s.

Persons with mental illnesses, developmental disabilities, or physical disabilities encountered desperate problems. Since most jurisdictions lacked statutes that placed limits on the involuntary commitment of persons with mental disorders to institutions, many unjustified admissions were made. Persons with severe mental disorders had to be admitted to hospitals, since few community programs existed for them. Their rights were rarely safeguarded within institutions, where many remained for decades with little or no treatment. Along with a growing number of poorly monitored nursing homes, mental institutions also served as repositories for older persons, who had virtually no access to community-based services.[22] The plight of children with developmental disabilities and their families was equally desperate, because public schools often shunned this population, few community-based services existed, and parents often had no access to appropriate institutions for these children.[23] Persons with physical disabilities were provided with virtually no supportive assistance, other than disability assistance and inadequate health services in county and municipal hospitals.[24]

In the 1950s, homosexuality was widely perceived as a mental problem rather than a personal orientation. Since most states had statutes that defined their sexual practices as crimes, gay men and lesbians usually tried to disguise their sexual orientation, in order to escape criminal sanctions, insensitive services from mental-health professions, or discrimination by employers.[25] Some gay men and lesbians were involuntarily committed to mental institutions by relatives who believed them to be mentally ill because of their sexual orientation. Many were fired from the federal civil service, the State Department, and the armed forces in the 1950s. Quite apart from inadequate laws and social programs, widespread public discrimination existed against many outgroups in 1960, including people of color, people with disabilities, and gay men and lesbians.[26]

DOMESTIC POLICY DURING THE KENNEDY PRESIDENCY

The lethargy of the 1950s was broken by the election in 1960 of John Kennedy, the youngest president in American history. He remains a controversial figure. Some historians and biographers portray him as a socially minded leader whose legislation was defeated because he confronted a relatively conservative Congress and public. Had he not been assassinated in 1963, they argue, he would have been reelected in 1964, would have obtained a sweeping electoral victory, and would have secured the enactment of many social reforms.[27] His detractors present a less flattering portrait; they contend that he was relatively conservative, possessed a limited reform vision, adopted reform causes only under strong political pressure, and enmeshed the nation in the Vietnam conflict.[28] A true portrayal probably lies somewhere between these two poles.

Kennedy had a limited understanding of poverty and racism, because he was raised in a wealthy Boston family and attended private schools. He rarely assumed leadership roles on domestic issues while a congressman and senator in the postwar era, though he dutifully voted Democratic positions on many issues. His orientations toward social reform were reflected in his ambivalence about Franklin Roosevelt. His father, a wealthy businessman, had had a conflicted relationship with Roosevelt, which ended in his resignation from a high-level position in Roosevelt's administration.[29] Kennedy regarded New Deal reforms, which provided economic resources and jobs to the poor, as outmoded in an affluent era when, he believed, problems of poverty involved intergenerational pockets of poverty in inner cities and rural areas. Kennedy was a problem-solving pragmatist, whose advisors were adept at using economics and management tools to analyze complex problems. But social reform requires moral outrage—and it was the absence of a gut response to social problems that alienated many liberals from Kennedy in the late 1950s and led some of them to support his presidential bid only belatedly in 1960.[30]

Like many of his contemporaries, Kennedy accepted both cultural and structural explanations of poverty. The economic improvement of poor persons was impeded, he believed, by a culture of poverty that made them oriented toward the present, unable to defer gratification, and unwilling to perceive the utility of education. Structuralists believed that automation and technology consigned persons with few skills and little education to unemployment or dead-end jobs. In either case, remedies focused on changing poor individuals themselves, whether by providing them with different orientations or by giving them training or education.[31]

These approaches to poverty were based on questionable assumptions. Research suggests that, though structural unemployment exists, most low-income workers are able to find work but are subject to brief periods of unemployment because they work in seasonal occupations or for firms that are particularly subject to economic cycles. Perhaps more important than structural factors are overt and covert forms of discrimination that relegate people of color and women to low-paying unskilled and semiskilled occupations and subject them to adverse hiring and promotion decisions, particularly during recessions.[32]

The belief that poor people possess a distinctive and dysfunctional culture has also been questioned by many critics. Perspectives of poor persons often change when they receive work, which suggests that their presumed basic orientations are often adaptations to immediate situational realities. Certain attributes, such as present-orientedness, may be functional for populations that have little hope of saving money from low-paying jobs. Some critics have questioned the methodology of middle-class social scientists, whose conclusions about the different culture of poor people sometimes derived from biased research instruments. Others have noted that many of the characteristics attributed to the poor by social scientists in the 1960s were identical to 19th-century stereotypes of paupers—and also Irish Americans and other ethnic groups—as lazy and unmotivated. Both in the 19th century and in the 1960s, many Americans condescendingly believed that poor persons would be magically transformed if they were personally exposed to middle- or upper-class persons who could teach them to be industrious.[33]

The various explanations of poverty and unemployment that were commonly advanced in the early 1960s led to a preoccupation with policies to change people in poverty by providing them with services and training, to the neglect of policies to redistribute resources and jobs to them. Scant attention was given to public works, tax incentives to employers to hire certain kinds of workers, affirmative action, the development of a national welfare system, or redistributive tax reform.[34] Services, education, and job training may eventually help some persons escape poverty, but they do not help them with immediate economic needs or necessarily improve their economic condition relative to other citizens.

In Kennedy's defense, he encountered a difficult political situation in 1960. He did not receive a reform mandate from the voters when they narrowly chose him over Richard Nixon, and most Americans did not give priority, in public opinion polls of the early 1960s, to addressing issues of poverty or racial discrimination. Kennedy's political problems were magnified by divisions within the Democratic party: Southern conservatives, whose support he desperately needed to defeat Republican opposition, stoutly resisted domestic reforms, whereas a group of Northern liberals, including Senator Hubert Humphrey, insisted that Kennedy develop a range of social reforms, such as executive orders and legislation to protect the rights of African Americans in the South. Caught in this political cross-fire, Kennedy tried, with marginal success, to walk a political tightrope between the two factions. Many Southern conservatives believed he was a liberal reformer who might even vigorously seek a second Reconstruction, while Northern liberals thought him overconcerned with appeasing Southern Democrats.[35]

Kennedy's precarious political position was exacerbated by his political style. Unlike many politicians, who pride themselves on attention to legislative details, Kennedy was widely perceived by members of Congress to have been a relatively lazy legislator who missed key votes and was remiss in his legislative homework. Many powerful senior legislators also believed Kennedy had succeeded to the presidency before his rightful time and resented his disinclination to consult with them unless he absolutely needed their votes. Some politicians believed that he prematurely and fatalistically discounted his chances to win key votes. Witty, articulate, and adept at using television to advantage, Kennedy was an entertaining president who had limited ability to convince powerful politicians to support his legislation.[36]

Poverty and Civil Rights: Toward Reform

Kennedy grew up in a family tradition of Irish, big-city, machine politics. His grandfather, a prominent Boston politician, had developed his power base by assiduously helping citizens obtain jobs and resources. His father was quite conservative and anti-Semitic; nonetheless, he was active in Democratic politics and held the directorship of the Securities and Exchange Commission during the New Deal.

Kennedy did not actively seek a leadership position on domestic issues, but he usually voted liberal positions on social issues in Congress in the 1950s and consistently supported legislation that would help unions, which constituted a major portion of his political base. Because he had a sister with a developmental disability, he was somewhat conscious of disability issues. He possessed an activist philosophy that made him eager to tackle new problems, and he was supremely confident that any problem—even a complex problem like poverty—could be solved. He possessed an expansive conception of the presidency, which he believed should provide assertive leadership.[37]

Kennedy can best be described in the late 1950s as a potential liberal, because his background made him receptive to social reform but reluctant to give it precedence over foreign affairs. He was pushed leftward during the Democratic presidential primaries in 1960 when he ran against Hubert Humphrey, who successfully invoked the reform tradition of Franklin Roosevelt and, in the process, portrayed Kennedy as indifferent to social issues. When Kennedy also appealed to the Roosevelt tradition to win support of miners and other working-class voters in a pivotal West Virginia primary, he won a crucial victory and, with it, momentum that carried him eventually to the presidential nomination of his party. He realized, too, that he would have to actively pursue social reform if he wanted to keep the allegiance of the liberal wing of the Democratic party, a group that finally, if reluctantly, supported his bid for the party's nomination.[38]

Slow but decided shifts in public opinion facilitated Kennedy's movement toward social reform. Poverty and other social issues were rarely discussed in the 1950s in public or private arenas; indeed, a bibliography of academic writings on the subject of poverty in 1960 totaled two pages![39] The federal government had not even attempted to define poverty before the early 1960s; they finally created a standard that is still used. In 1962, when Michael Harrington published *The Other America,* a book that discussed problems of the "invisible poor" in rural and urban settings, he was surprised to discover that it became a bestseller.[40] Academics, too, discovered the poor, as reflected by a rapidly expanding literature on the subject in the early 1960s. As the progressive and New Deal eras had demonstrated, social reform is possible in America when sizable numbers of middle-class Americans empathize with disadvantaged persons.

It was the civil rights movement, however, that decisively pushed Kennedy and the nation toward social reform. It began quietly in the South in 1955, when a young African American minister, Martin Luther King, Jr., was chosen by its organizers to head a bus boycott in Montgomery, Alabama, to protest the policy that required African Americans to sit at the back of the bus. African Americans won a decisive victory when this policy was rescinded, but only after a lengthy period of tense confrontation that included sporadic acts of violence against African Americans. The bus boycott initiated a long sequence of protests that successively challenged segregation in interstate transportation, lunch counters, train stations, public swimming pools, public schools, and colleges. Involvement in these issues led, in turn, to protests against literacy tests and poll taxes that disqualified African Americans from voting in the South. Many Americans in the North began to realize that a tangled web of racist policies in the South trapped African Americans at virtually every step. The nation became further sensitized to Southern injustices as nonviolent protests of civil rights demonstrators were repeatedly countered by violence, unfair rulings by Southern courts, intimidation, and murder.[41]

A particular murder in the summer of 1955— the killing of Emmett Till, an African American child from Chicago who was visiting relatives in Mississippi—brought the civil rights struggle of the South to the attention of African Americans in the North, as well as the mass media.[42] Till had been warned by his mother to be meek when dealing with Southern whites; she said, "If you have to

FIGURE 9.1   Police using hoses against civil rights demonstrators

SOURCE: UPI/Bettmann

get on your knees and bow when a white person goes past, do it willingly."[43] But Till, who had not been reared in the South, bragged to several boys outside a grocery store that he had a white girlfriend up North. When one of them dared him to talk to the white female storekeeper, Till got some candy and told her, "Bye, Baby," as he was leaving. A girl who had heard about the incident predicted, "When that lady's husband come back, there is going to be trouble." Three days later, after midnight on a Saturday, the white woman's husband and his brother-in-law came to get that "boy who has done the talkin'."[44] They dragged Till from the country cabin, tortured him, murdered him, and dumped his body in a river. Later, they said they *had* to kill him, because he refused to repent or beg for mercy. When his mother saw the

mutilated body, she insisted on an open-casket funeral—and, indeed, a picture of the body, published in an African American magazine, so shocked Chicagoans that thousands attended the funeral. The subsequent trial of the accused white slayers was equally sensational: An African American man testified against them in open court—something that rarely happened in the South, because of its risks. When the all-white jury exonerated the defendants, mass rallies of African Americans occurred throughout the North. Although justice was never done in this case, Emmett Till became a martyr, and the civil rights struggle became a national movement. Ominously, however, white Southerners reacted with rage at the audacity of the African Americans who had testified against the men and at the Northern sympathy for Till. It was clear that the old South would not quickly relent.

The civil rights movement, like widespread unemployment in the Great Depression and child labor in the progressive era, provided an obvious and ongoing symbol that sensitized Americans to the needs of a particular group of people and forced political leaders to propose policy remedies. As in the 1930s, the vicious cycle of protest and repression would not disappear or yield to superficial remedies. Public opinion finally forced Kennedy to propose civil rights legislation in 1963.

The escalating protest and violence in the South in the early 1960s presented Kennedy and his brother Robert, the attorney general, with a dilemma. Kennedy needed the votes of Southern Democrats if the rest of his domestic and foreign policies were to be enacted, but he also needed the support of liberal Democrats, who were urging him to support federal civil rights legislation or, at the very least, to issue executive orders that prohibited job discrimination in federally funded projects.

Kennedy tried for several years to follow a middle course.[15] He gave African Americans and liberals a symbolic victory when he created a presidential task force headed by Vice President Lyndon Johnson, but it made little progress in addressing discrimination against African Americans in employment. Though Robert Kennedy used federal marshals and FBI agents to protect demonstrators in the South, he avoided the use of federal troops, even in the face of rapidly mounting violence, and insisted, moreover, that Southern jurisdictions were capable of protecting civil rights demonstrators, despite the obvious hostility of many Southern police chiefs. Kennedy refused to issue executive orders to outlaw discrimination or to develop federal civil rights legislation, because both he and his brother were convinced that the failure of Reconstruction was due to the imposition of civil rights policies on the South by the North.[46] They also naively hoped that civil rights legislation could be enacted by Southern states as more African Americans became enfranchised. Kennedy's middle course was successful in 1961 and much of 1962. Southerners believed that Robert Kennedy had not used federal marshals except as a

last resort, and most African Americans believed that the Kennedy brothers protected them from white extremists.

Some policy successes were obtained, even as violence escalated. Directives from the Interstate Commerce Commission to desegregate bus and train stations were met with compliance and the support of Southern police departments. But events soon made African Americans, liberals, and many Northerners realize that aggressive federal intervention was needed. Robert Kennedy had hoped that the civil rights protesters would focus on voting rights rather than on desegregation of public facilities and schools, because he thought registering African Americans to vote would be less likely to arouse a violent response and would eventually liberalize Southern politics.[47] When the Student Nonviolent Coordinating Committee (SNCC) brought thousands of white students to work alongside African Americans in registering voters in 1962 and 1963, however, activists were greeted with threats, intimidation, and physical violence. Many Southern authorities assumed a passive role, overlooked violence, or jailed activists. The mass media were filled with accounts of Southern atrocities, but Northern opinion was most aroused, African Americans ruefully noted, when white students or activists were murdered in voter registration drives.[48] Resistance by high-level Southern politicians to federal court orders to desegregate universities further angered Northerners.

As violence increased, liberals introduced a series of civil rights bills in the Congress and demanded support from Kennedy. Despite protests by some of his top advisors, Kennedy finally decided in 1963 to propose his own civil rights legislation, which prohibited job discrimination on the basis of race and gender as well as discrimination in voter registration.[49] To make the legislation acceptable to moderates in both parties, he diluted voting provisions. In June 1963, he gave a televised address to endorse the legislation, which was, sadly, the first presidential address in the nation's history devoted to civil rights issues. When Senator Everett Dirksen and other Republicans decided to join Northern Democrats, the legislation appeared destined for passage, but the ill-fated Kennedy could not claim credit for it because of his tragic death.

The Course of Reform: Failures and Successes

Kennedy promised in the 1960 campaign that he would support aid to education and medical insurance for older Americans, but both his medical and educational proposals became enmeshed in ideological controversy. Although European nations had developed national health-insurance schemes, many Americans believed that governmental financing of medical care would threaten the doctor-patient relationship and was, moreover, un-American. The American Medical Association led the opposition to *any* major federal programs, including public funding of inoculations, and was aided by disputes among legislators about financing and program details. Some legislators wanted to fund medical assistance to older Americans from Social Security payroll deductions, but others wanted to use a separate payroll tax or general revenues. Some legislators favored voluntary participation, and others wanted to make participation mandatory. Various legislative proposals went nowhere, though some progress had been made in congressional deliberations by the summer of 1963.[50]

As the nation's first Catholic president, Kennedy did not want to appear to favor parochial schools. When he excluded religious and private schools from funding under his education bill, however, he incited the wrath of the Catholic Church, which insisted that parochial schools receive funds as well. Kennedy's subsequent concessions to them emboldened Catholic leaders, as well as leaders of other denominations, to demand even more funds for their schools, to the chagrin of legislators who wanted to preserve strict separation of church and state. Passage seemed hopeless.[51]

Some economists believed that periodic recessions, pockets of unemployment, and low rates of economic growth were caused by inadequate pools of investment capital. Guided by economist Walter Heller, Kennedy proposed to increase depreciation allowances for businesses and to allow a tax credit for investments. These policies, which were enacted in 1962, were overshadowed by another proposal to drastically reduce the rates of taxes paid by businesses and wealthy persons. The bill encountered substantial opposition from conservatives, who feared that the tax cut could lead to government deficits. When Kennedy died, the legislation had passed the House, but it was not enacted until 1964. Judged in purely economic terms, Kennedy's tax measures probably spurred investment and economic growth but, from the vantage point of the poor and the working class, the policies contributed to economic inequality in the nation and drew attention from the need to reform the tax code so as to eliminate deductions and loopholes that benefited affluent taxpayers.[52] Moreover, as we later note, they reduced the funds available for social programs in the Johnson administration, when the Vietnam War absorbed increasing resources.

Believing that many unemployed persons could not find work because they lacked the necessary skills, Kennedy proposed and obtained passage of the Manpower Development and Training Act of 1962 (MDTA); 600,000 workers had completed technical training by 1968, but the program was plagued by problems.[53] The dropout rate was high; the skills taught were not always needed in local job markets; and relocation assistance was limited. Some critics contend that job-training programs allow one group of trained workers to displace nontrained workers if new jobs are not simultaneously created.[54] MDTA nonetheless represented the nation's first major job-training program. (The work relief programs of the New Deal had not focused on training.)

Kennedy sought and obtained major increases in the minimum wage, partly at the behest of unions, which hoped that this measure would deter companies from moving to the nonunionized and low-wage South.[55] Its supporters contended that it provided a wage floor for those workers—in particular, unskilled African American workers—who were severely underpaid compared to other workers, but some economists believe that it fostered unemployment, by stimulating employers to decrease the size of their labor forces.[56]

Kennedy established the Area Redevelopment Agency in 1961 to increase employment in depressed rural areas like Appalachia, by providing loans and subsidies to local businesses and by improving transportation systems.[57] Critics contend that the program created few jobs, because its subsidies were too low or were targeted to tourism and other businesses that employed relatively few persons. Marred by political favoritism and corruption, the program was terminated in 1965.[58]

The concerns of a number of mental-health experts about the absence of community-based care for persons who had been released from mental hospitals led Congress to establish a commission in 1955. The commission's report, *Action for Mental Health,* which was issued in 1961, recommended federal funding of community-based services. Kennedy secured the enactment of the Community Mental Health Centers Act of 1963, which provided federal funding for the construction of mental-health centers that offered a range of outpatient and preventive services. The act was quickly amended to provide funds for staff as well. Because appropriations for the legislation never met the expectations of its framers, it did not address all the community needs of mental patients, who often lived in substandard board-and-care and skid-row housing.[59] It nonetheless led to the establishment of a national network of centers that provided outpatient services to millions of people.

Many Americans were alarmed by the marked expansion of AFDC rolls in the early 1960s. In response, a services strategy was formulated in 1962. In this strategy, the federal government provided a 75% match to the states in order to encourage local welfare departments to provide social services to AFDC recipients. It was, at best, a naive proposal. The growth in AFDC rolls was the result of many factors, including migration of poor African Americans to urban areas in the North and the South, the absence of jobs for unskilled female workers, and the absence of day care. Furthermore, since rates of desertion by fathers are associated with social class, they are unlikely to decline unless jobs and resources are provided to low-income families. Continuing rise in AFDC rolls under the services strategy was inevitable, and it provided conservatives with the opportunity to propose punitive policies later in the decade.[60]

In rejecting the New Deal approach as outmoded, Kennedy missed an opportunity to develop a variety of tax, income, and nutritional programs to reduce poverty. Moreover, since he was convinced that the nation needed the capability to fight the Soviet Union, China, and one guerilla war at the same time, in order to counter communist insurgency, he launched the fastest peacetime buildup of the military in American history and introduced military advisors into South Vietnam.

INSERT 9.2   CRITICAL ANALYSIS: THE LIMITS OF SOCIAL SERVICES

Social workers are often asked to solve problems by working directly with the populations most affected by these problems, whether women on AFDC (as in the case of the services strategy of 1962), children who have been abused, homeless people, or mental patients. Yet the dilemmas of these clients are often profoundly shaped by economic factors, community factors, and family dynamics that the social worker cannot control. Most children who are reported as abused, for example, come from low-income families, where unemployment (or underemployment) is a stressor that causes or exacerbates the abuse.

Analyze options that exist for social workers in these circumstances:

• in their direct work with these clients
• in their social reform work

As always, this expansion of the military budget constrained social spending.[61]

Kennedy deserves praise, however, for shattering the conservative complacency that characterized the 1950s. He came to office with no mandate to enact major reforms and inherited a Congress in which Republicans and Southern Democrats possessed a majority. Although unable to secure passage of most of his major social legislation, he established a policy agenda for his successor: civil rights legislation, the War on Poverty, the Food Stamp program, Medicare, federal aid to public schools, and tax reforms. These Kennedy initiatives were enacted, though in modified form, by Lyndon Johnson after Kennedy was assassinated in November 1963.

KENNEDY AND JOHNSON: A STUDY IN CONTRAST

A novelist could not have fashioned a more unusual plot. The articulate and well-educated Kennedy, fearing lack of support from pivotal Southern delegates at the 1960 Democratic convention, chose Lyndon Johnson, a crude and politically astute Southerner, as his vice president, over the strenuous objections of Robert Kennedy. Political pundits saw it as a brilliant move to obtain the support of Southern Democrats. Who could have predicted that most of Kennedy's social legislation would eventually be enacted by Johnson, or that Johnson would carry the Vietnam policy that Kennedy had begun to its tragic conclusion?

Johnson excelled in political maneuvering. His grandfather and father had been involved in a strange mixture of populist and conservative Texas politics. His mother, an aristocratic figure unfulfilled in her marriage to an alcoholic Texan, urged him to rise above his humble origins. As early as college, when he was active in campus politics, Johnson displayed an uncanny ability to decipher the existing balance of political forces and to develop issues that could propel him into leader-

ship roles. After a brief stint as a teacher, he became an aide to a congressman, secured an appointment as regional director in Texas of a major New Deal program, and successfully ran for Congress.[62] On his second attempt, in 1948, Johnson was elected to the United States Senate, where he quickly became a protégé of Senator Richard Russell, a powerful legislator.

By helping Russell with laborious details and serving as his confidante, Johnson cleverly positioned himself to run for the position of Senate minority leader, to which he was elected in 1953; in January 1955, when Democrats won control of the Senate, he became majority leader. He became an expert in the intricacies of parliamentary procedures, honed his interpersonal and persuasive skills, and augmented his power by vesting in the majority leader the power to make committee assignments.[63] He had presidential ambitions but was not well known outside Texas and the Senate. Realizing that he could not advance beyond his position as majority leader, he accepted Kennedy's invitation to be vice president in 1960. He was deeply frustrated by 1963, however, because he was seldom consulted by Kennedy or his Ivy League staff. We can scarcely imagine how he felt when he learned, in a Dallas hospital, that Kennedy was dead and that he would soon be the nation's next president.

The Johnson administration achieved legislative successes that were matched only by Franklin Roosevelt; major federal resources were allocated for the first time for public schools, medical insurance for the elderly, subsidies for health care of the poor, legal aid for the poor, job training for impoverished teenagers, enforcement of civil rights for African Americans, nutritional programs, preschool programs, community development projects, health care for migrant labor, and medical services for pregnant women and for children. Whereas Franklin Roosevelt had succeeded in developing federal income and insurance programs for economic security, Johnson extended federal programs into areas that had fallen outside the province of federal policy. His legislative successes can be explained by a combination of facilitating factors.

When Kennedy died, many of his policy proposals were making their way through the legislative process. Thus, Kennedy provided Johnson with an instant agenda, which facilitated his legislative tasks.[64] Johnson was aided, moreover, by sustained pressure from civil rights groups. Violent reprisals against civil rights demonstrators, who continued to protest, inflamed public opinion in the North, which became more sympathetic not only to African Americans but to the plight of poor persons.

Nor should we ignore Johnson's genuine compassion for those in need. It is always difficult to determine motivation when examining the actions of politicians; this was particularly so with Johnson, who possessed much political ambition and was obsessed with personal failure. Did he pursue his policy agenda to obtain a high reputation, or did he genuinely seek to help people with problems? No doubt Johnson, like most politicians, had mixed motives, but one of his closest aides, Joseph Califano, argues persuasively that Johnson often had noble motives that derived from his populist origins.[65] In any event, Johnson was *driven* to seek social reforms, spent incalculable hours writing legislation, and repeatedly brought himself to the point of exhaustion in seeking its enactment.

Johnson used his political skills to advantage. He immediately wrapped himself in the mantle of Kennedy by promising to enact Kennedy's legislative measures and by keeping his top staff. By portraying himself as a humble successor to Kennedy, who would devote himself tirelessly to the fulfillment of the slain leader's unfulfilled aspirations, he endeared himself to the American people, as well as to legislators. He summoned to the White House virtually every legislator, lobbyist, interest-group leader, and citizen who could advance the progress of Kennedy's pending legislation. He obtained detailed information about their policy opinions, specific legislative objectives that they desired, and their willingness to compromise on key points. He assembled, in effect, a massive team to develop a legislative program in support of his domestic measures.[66]

Johnson was a welcome change to congressional leadership, because he discussed specific pieces of legislation with them before the legislation was introduced to Congress. He was adept, as well, at giving legislators credit for specific pieces of legislation during the legislative process and at signing ceremonies. He bridged the chasm between the White House and Congress, which had sabotaged Kennedy's legislation.

Johnson maintained political support from a broad spectrum of legislators and interest groups.[67] Many liberals, including Robert Kennedy, feared that, as a Southerner, Johnson would develop conservative policies, but Johnson dashed these fears when he declared his allegiance to Kennedy's entire legislative package, including civil rights. Indeed, his decisive commitment to civil rights, which he made almost immediately on succeeding to the presidency, was a remarkably bold move that signaled to Southerners, as it did to Northern liberals, that he would be a reform-minded president. Yet he was also adept at giving concessions to Southerners, as reflected by provisions in many pieces of legislation that gave Southern states a disproportionate amount of program funds by weighting their distribution to poorer states. (Southern states had the lowest per capita incomes in the United States.) He carefully cultivated support from both unions and business; he supported increases in the minimum wage, favored by unions, and he vigorously sought passage of Kennedy's tax cuts for businesses and individuals. His ability to appeal to both conservative and liberal audiences was illustrated by his support for both budget-cutting and social reform. He prided himself on fiscal conservatism; he sometimes proposed cuts in the federal budget that exceeded those desired by House Republicans, and he blocked efforts by liberals to drastically expand funding for the War on Poverty, the Food Stamps program, or the AFDC program. Yet he supported passage of a staggering number of social reforms and would brag, much like a fisherman who has had a good day, about the sheer number of programs that he had enacted.[68]

Johnson was a master of timing, negotiation, and compromise. Since he knew that momentum was crucial, he carefully introduced his legislation each year in a planned sequence, beginning with the easiest and ending with the most difficult. He made skillful compromises in legislation to defuse opposition, yet astutely avoided an image of softness by refusing to back down when he believed that vital principles were at stake or that compromises would make him appear overtimid. When he rewarded politicians with patronage and resources for their districts, it was not for votes on specific issues, which would have led them to expect rewards every time they supported measures, but rather for a pattern of support over an extended period. He had an uncanny ability to make slight changes in the wording of legislation so as to mollify objections of legislators or interest groups—but his compromises would be limited only to those changes that were necessary for passage.[69]

Johnson knew that his political honeymoon with the public would end and feared that his legislative successes would also come to a halt. However, he received extraordinary assistance from the Republicans when they nominated Barry Goldwater in 1964 to be their presidential candidate. The conservative Goldwater presented an easy target for Johnson when he violated the unspoken rule in American politics that legacies of the New Deal, such as Social Security and the Tennessee Valley Authority, would be placed above partisan politics. Since Goldwater both espoused foreign intervention against communist regimes and hinted that he might consider use of tactical nuclear weapons in such struggles, Johnson portrayed himself as a man of peace—a claim that still seemed plausible, because he had not yet committed thousands of troops to Vietnam.[70] Enough liberal and moderate Democrats were elected in the landslide victory of 1964 that Johnson's legislative program could not be scuttled by the conservative coalition of Republicans and Southern Democrats. He proceeded to use this mandate to enact Kennedy's pending legislation, as well as many proposals developed by his numerous task forces, under the rubric of the Great Society.

JOHNSON'S SOCIAL WELFARE LEGACY

Civil Rights Legislation

Johnson refused to compromise with Southerners in 1964 when they tried to dilute civil rights legislation drafted by the Kennedy administration. The Civil Rights Act of 1964 was a historic measure; it marked the first time since Reconstruction that the federal government assumed a major role in protecting the voting rights of African Americans in the South. The act required the desegregation of public facilities and prohibited discrimination in the hiring practices of firms and institutions that received federal contracts. The U.S. attorney general was also given the right to file suits to desegregate schools.

The immediate effects of this legislation were diminished because litigation was often required to bring compliance, but within six months it led to a civil rights revolution for African Americans in the South. Public accommodations and public transportation were desegregated by 1965. The attorney general initiated suits against local school districts that discriminated against African Americans and supported an ever-tightening series of guidelines that ultimately required them to use one set of facilities for all students. It was an extraordinary set of achievements by any standard. Southern whites found they were unable to persuade the Supreme Court to overrule federal civil rights powers, as had occurred during Reconstruction. The Department of Justice, often headed by officials who questioned various aspects of civil rights legislation, did not attack its central provisions.[71]

The Civil Rights Act of 1964 was flawed in several important respects, however. It outlawed the use of poll taxes and literacy tests, but the tedious case-by-case enforcement process allowed many jurisdictions to continue discriminatory practices. Johnson did not aggressively implement Title VII of the act, which outlawed discrimination in employment; for example, he failed to give the

Department of Labor a significant role in monitoring federal contracts for discrimination. Title VII established an Equal Employment Opportunity Commission (EEOC) to monitor discrimination in employment, but the commission did not receive the power to initiate suits until 1972. Furthermore, Johnson decided for political reasons not to aggressively attack de facto segregation of Northern schools.[72]

Johnson had not planned to introduce additional civil rights legislation in 1965, but he changed his mind when confronted with massive civil rights protests directed at continuing and widespread denial of suffrage to African Americans in the South. To allow faster legal action than had been possible in case-by-case litigation, the Civil Rights Act of 1965 gave the federal government the right to presume discrimination in any state or its subdivisions where less than 50% of people of color voted in federal elections and in areas that used literacy or other screening tests. In such areas, federal authorities were allowed to directly administer elections. These policies were remarkably successful in terminating the last vestiges of overt discrimination in voter registration.[73]

Earl Warren and the Supreme Court

The Supreme Court, under the leadership of Chief Justice Earl Warren between 1953 and 1969, provided its own impetus to the advancement of civil rights and civil liberties. Warren had been governor of California and an important Republican politician, who had, moreover, taken a number of conservative positions in California; indeed, as the state's attorney general, he had even assumed a key role in incarcerating Japanese Americans in World War II. Eisenhower, looking for a prominent Republican and owing a political debt to Warren, felt he would be an ideal conservative choice when he appointed him chief justice in 1953. But Eisenhower had misread his man; Warren believed, above all, in the doctrine of fairness. Guided by that doctrine, he presided over a Court that in 16 years made a series of liberal rulings that radically

transformed American jurisprudence. (Years later, Eisenhower believed the appointment of Warren was his biggest political error; he was not on speaking terms with Warren in the closing years of his presidency.)[74]

The precedent-shaking nature of the Warren Court began almost at the outset, with the historic *Brown* v. *Board of Education* ruling in 1954. Reverend Oliver Brown of Topeka, Kansas, had brought suit against his city's board of education, because his child had to take a bus to the other side of town when a school reserved for whites was much closer. Thurgood Marshall of the NAACP argued that segregation had such harmful psychological effects on people of color that the mere fact of segregation meant inferior education. He and other civil rights attorneys had been impressed by some experiments conducted by the African American social scientist Kenneth Clark. In tests with African American children in the North, Clark found that, when asked to identify a doll that most resembled themselves (by color), many African American children refused to answer or would cry and run out of the room. When the same test was given to African American children in the South, Clark found a different, but equally disturbing, result; the children would often point to the brown doll and say, matter-of-factly, "That's a nigger. I'm a nigger," thus accepting as given their subordinate status.[75] Although some of the civil rights lawyers did not want to use this "soft" evidence, Marshall and others prevailed; they felt that the Court would not hold segregated facilities to be a violation of the equal protection clause of the Fourteenth Amendment to the Constitution without it. By contrast, the attorney representing the board of education contended that no definitive proof had been shown that segregated students fare worse in life *because* of their segregation. Were the court to rule in Marshall's behalf, it would repudiate more than 50 years of tradition stemming from the *Plessy* v. *Ferguson* decision of 1896, which had upheld the separate-but-equal doctrine. What was at stake was the very structure of education in many Southern jurisdictions, which established so-called dual school systems, one for white students and the other for African American students—and possibly, further down the judicial road, the structure of Northern education, which had dual systems based not on law but on the combination of neighborhood schools and residential segregation. In the North, thanks to this system, vast numbers of children of color went to de facto segregated schools. Warren, who was appointed chief justice after the deliberations on the *Brown* case had been underway for many months, decided he wanted a unanimous ruling and finally got one that upheld the logic of the NAACP and gave due weight to the psychological testimony derived from Clark's work.[76]

Other rulings, some almost as controversial, followed in rapid succession—rulings that forced localities to reapportion voting districts to protect voting rights of minorities; to respect the rights of apprehended criminal suspects; to protect the rights of persons with radical beliefs; to give procedural protections to persons on death row; to enhance the power of the press; to strike down state laws that outlawed interracial sexual relations and marriage; to require the provision of public defenders to impoverished defendants; and to overturn laws that prohibited the sale of contraceptives. The cumulative effects of these and other rulings was enormous. Many conservatives, infuriated by these rulings, sought to develop a grass-roots campaign to impeach Warren and hoped that, one day, conservative presidents would make appointments that would turn the Court into a conservative institution. (As we note later, they succeeded in this objective during the 1980s.) We can say, then, that the Supreme Court was an important part of the social reforms of the 1960s under the leadership of Earl Warren. Though the Court is not a legislative body, its decisions had profound effects on the policies of local institutions that, in turn, affected the lives of people of color and people in poverty.

Medicare and Medicaid

An ingenious compromise fashioned by the administration and Wilbur Mills, powerful chairman of the House Ways and Means Committee, facilitated passage of Medicare and Medicaid programs in 1965 as Titles XVIII and XIX of the Social Security Act. Medicare received widespread attention, because of the political clout of elderly persons and the extensive discussion of their needs in preceding years. Kennedy's desire to obtain health insurance had been frustrated by controversy about details of the program, but Mills and Johnson developed a strategy that incorporated facets of the proposals by members of both parties.[77] The program was divided into two parts. Participation in Part A, which funded selected hospital services of elderly persons, was mandatory and financed by a payroll tax on workers and employers. Participation in Part B was voluntary. Part B financed physicians' services and was funded by a combination of monthly premiums on elderly persons and funds from the general revenues of the federal government.

Medicare was a godsend to many elderly persons, who lacked funds to pay for their medical bills without selling their personal possessions. Because the legislation made eligibility automatic on payment of payroll taxes and premiums, elderly persons were able to receive assistance without the stigma of a means test. They did not have to visit local welfare departments but obtained eligibility through Social Security offices. It is difficult to evaluate the effect of Medicare on the health and health practices of elderly persons on account of conflicting findings and methodological issues. For example, because most elderly persons participate in Medicare, it is difficult to assess whether they would have been more or less healthy without it. However, the program appears to have increased the utilization of physicians and hospitals by poor persons, who had often refrained from seeking medical care except in emergencies. Had the Medicare program not existed, it is likely that much greater numbers of elderly people would have become insolvent and forced on welfare rolls. Another factor is that, prior to Medicare, some medical care was donated to impoverished elderly persons by doctors and hospitals; with the passage of Medicare, such donations were reduced.[78]

Medicare can be criticized on several grounds. Since it subsidized acute health care services, it provided only a limited buffer against medical insolvency and did not help persons with chronic conditions. It reimbursed only a maximum of 60 days in the hospital, covered only 100 days of convalescent care, and did not reimburse out-of-hospital nursing home care. These restrictive policies meant that many elderly persons who exhausted their scanty Medicare benefits had to suffer the indignity of depleting their savings and assets in order to become eligible for Medicaid, which is a means-tested program.[79]

At the insistence of the American Medical Association, physicians were allowed to charge higher rates for Medicare than the maximum fees that authorities would reimburse, and so elderly persons had to contribute their own resources. Studies reveal that these costs, plus various other out-of-pocket costs for services covered and not covered by Medicare, meant that elderly persons in 1986 financed nearly the same percentage of their total medical costs as before its passage.[80] Elderly persons' out-of-pocket medical costs would have risen even more rapidly without the assistance of Medicare, however, because of the increasing use of expensive medical technologies and sharp increases in the real cost of medical services.

Medicare contributed to medical inflation by reimbursing providers at prevailing rates, so that they had no incentive to decrease their charges or to curtail unnecessary surgeries.[81] Because, in line with the disease model of medicine, it was confined to financing existing curative services, Medicare did not promote innovative alternatives to nursing home care, failed to foster preventive services for elderly persons, and did not provide outreach services to the frail elderly.[82] In short, Medicare funded conventional services for a population that needed innovative programs, and it covered only a small fraction of their medical needs.

We now turn to Medicaid. State, county, and municipal officials had funded medical services to poor persons for decades, but with considerable assistance from those physicians who donated their time. The costs of these programs had steadily increased, and many poor persons delayed treatment because they had no access to such services. The Medicaid program was enacted in 1965 to address the medical needs of welfare recipients, as well as so-called medically indigent persons, who, though not destitute, could not pay their medical bills.

Whereas Medicare vested financing, administration, and policy roles in the federal government, Medicaid was a matching grant program, like AFDC, in which federal authorities paid a substantial share of the medical services but ceded major administrative and policy roles to the states. States had to provide some basic services, such as outpatient and emergency care, had to enroll AFDC recipients, and were allowed to decide which, if any, additional services they wanted to provide and to devise eligibility criteria. As in the AFDC program, conservative and poor states covered fewer services and had more restrictive eligibility criteria than other states.[83]

Many legislators wrongly assumed that Medicaid would be a small program that would focus on the medical needs of AFDC recipients. Governors of New York and California, who had already been pressured to devise health insurance programs, believed that they could use the relatively generous federal match of the Medicaid program to develop free health services for their blue-collar citizens as well; indeed, at one point, 40% of the population in New York State was eligible for its Medicaid program. As congressional legislators observed the mounting federal costs of the Medicaid program and realized that a disproportionate share of federal funds went to a few liberal states, they enacted policies in 1967 that would restrict Medicaid coverage in all states by 1970 to persons who earned no more than 133% of a state's AFDC standard.[84]

It is difficult to gauge the precise effects of Medicaid on poor persons. Their use of outpatient services increased dramatically, and rural residents similarly increased their use of all medical services. Although Medicaid funding led many physicians and hospitals to discontinue free or low-cost services to poor persons, the total number of services available to the poor increased.[85] Nonetheless, Medicaid can be criticized in much the same way as Medicare. It encouraged inflation by infusing massive resources into the medical system, with few cost controls. It did not encourage the development of innovative outreach and preventive services to poor persons, who often distrusted medical authorities or postponed treatment until illnesses had become severe. Few poor persons entered the medical system used by middle-class Americans, since regular medical providers resented the restrictive levels of reimbursement that many states established. Many poor persons were served by Medicaid mills, where physicians reaped large profits from high-volume services. Two systems of care continued after the passage of Medicaid. Middle-class Americans used nonprofit or for-profit hospitals; low-income and medically indigent persons used public hospitals and inner-city clinics.[86]

Another program to aid elderly people, the Older Americans Act (OAA), passed Congress in 1965. Under Title III, it authorized the development of a national network of Area Agencies on Aging (AAAs) to coordinate services for elderly people.[87] Since its inception, OAA has subsidized many kinds of services, including nutritional programs, services for the homebound frail elderly, and training programs. Critics contend that AAAs, which were supposed to be vigorous advocates, have often been preoccupied with delivering services.[88]

Aid to Education

Kennedy's proposals to extend federal aid to public schools had foundered on constitutional and political issues associated with the relationship between church and state, but Johnson fashioned a clever compromise that eventually led to passage of the Elementary and Secondary Education Act of 1965 (ESEA).[89] It provided federal assistance to public schools with relatively high concentrations of low-income children, and it allowed private schools to share books and other materials that had been purchased by public schools.

Sharp differentials in educational spending at the local level between affluent and poor neighborhoods persisted even after ESEA was enacted. Its provision of funds with relatively few restrictions led many schools to use the funds to underwrite their regular expenses rather than to upgrade the instruction of low-income students; indeed, some

jurisdictions even reduced their level of educational spending after they received ESEA funds.[90] Gaps in educational achievement between middle- and upper-income students and low-income students continue to defy solution. Are the gaps due to poor facilities, poor instruction, or familial background? Do low-income children often discontinue school because they believe it will not lead to jobs? What combination of outreach, instructional, facility, and other changes are needed to help low-income students improve their educational performance?[91]

Johnson also developed a range of educational subsidies for low-income persons who sought junior college and college education.[92] Despite the shortcomings of ESEA and other legislation, striking educational gains were made by African Americans in the 1960s at both secondary and college levels.[93]

The War on Poverty, Welfare Reforms, and Food Stamps

When Kennedy realized in early 1963 that his domestic policy was stumbling, he commissioned top aides to develop an antipoverty program, but they had only begun assembling lists of job-training and youth-employment schemes when he died. The so-called War on Poverty was developed after his death and consisted of a collection of job-training, youth-employment, and medical services that various government departments had failed to enact during the Kennedy administration.[94] Specifically, the legislation included the Job Corps, to provide impoverished youth with job training in urban and rural residential centers; the Neighborhood Youth Corps, to provide teenagers with employment in local agencies; a legal aid program to provide free legal assistance to the poor; and medical clinics in low-income areas. The measure also included a community action program that established local community action agencies (CAAs) to coordinate local programs for the poor and to fund and operate various programs. (The popular Head Start program for preschool children was funded from community action funds.) To coordinate these programs, the legislation set up the Office of Economic Opportunity (OEO); Sargeant Shriver was its energetic director.

The community action program soon became the most controversial part of OEO. One group of officials believed the CAAs would concentrate on planning and coordinating functions in poverty areas. Another group, which included Richard Boone and David Hackett, believed that existing programs and agencies were unresponsive to poor persons and wanted the CAAs to be forceful advocates. To increase this likelihood, they placed in the legislation the requirement that the CAAs promote the "maximum feasible participation of the poor" in their governing boards.[95] Virtually no legislators noticed this phrase, but it was widely used by community activists in succeeding years to insist that poor persons be allowed to elect community representatives to the CAA boards.

Johnson and Shriver wanted OEO programs implemented as rapidly as possible, because they realized that demonstrable results were needed if the programs were to appeal to a wide spectrum of legislators. However, the speedy implementation of dozens of different programs, as well as the administratively complex CAAs, led to widespread charges of corruption, patronage, and inefficiency.[96] In the early planning of OEO, administration officials hoped to focus on demonstration programs in a limited number of cities, but Johnson insisted on broader coverage to enhance the visibility and impact of OEO. OEO was plagued, moreover, with incessant charges and countercharges as well as by local confusion about the objectives of the CAAs.

There have been many criticisms of OEO. It was not wise to suggest that a War on Poverty could be declared, waged, and won with a collection of small programs that were supplemented by an ill-defined advocacy program. It is impossible to wage even a limited action against poverty if no income or resources are given to the poor, but OEO provided only personal and community services. When Sargeant Shriver sought to include public works within OEO, he received a chilly reception from Johnson, who believed that services, training,

and coordination could somehow end poverty without income transfers or creation of new jobs.[97] Policy expectations were established that could not be fulfilled, and political opponents criticized the limited effectiveness of OEO in reducing poverty and demanded its curtailment or elimination.

Moreover, it is not politically feasible for governments to directly subsidize local protest organizations, even if the concept appears attractive at first glance. Governmental officials who are the targets of such protests will attack the advocacy program as unwarranted federal intrusion into local affairs; many of those officials will be powerful mayors, who constitute a significant part of the political constituency of the Democratic party. Republican members of Congress, who were desperately seeking issues to slow the momentum of the Johnson legislative avalanche, were delighted when local Democratic officials such as Mayor Richard Daley of Chicago attacked the CAAs.

OEO cannot be dismissed as a disaster, however. Many of its programs were highly innovative and, though transferred from OEO to other agencies in subsequent years, continue to exist. OEO initiated a large legal aid program that represented poor people against landlords, local merchants, and unresponsive government agencies.[98] Neighborhood health centers markedly improved the health of many low-income persons; nutritional and health programs for youth established.[99] OEO administrators' growing doubts about advocacy by CAAs led them to focus funding on such service programs as Head Start, a popular preschool program that combined recreational, educational, and health programs in summer as well as during the school year. The effectiveness of Head Start in raising the test scores of low-income children has been questioned, but some studies suggest that it has had long-term beneficial effects on the educational performance of its enrollees.[100]

Relatively muted in the 1950s, resentment against AFDC recipients mounted during the 1960s, when the program grew dramatically. One reason for this increase was that uprooted persons who fled rural areas and found bleak job prospects in urban areas were emboldened by civil rights protests to claim their right to AFDC. By the late

1960s, AFDC rolls were swelled further by women who realized that receipt of AFDC entitled them to receive Medicaid, Food Stamps, day care, and work-related incentive payments.

The mounting resentment against women on AFDC was fueled not only by the program's growth, but also by changing orientations toward work. Despite increases in the number of working women during the 1950s, many persons still believed that women should remain at home with their children. This sentiment decreased markedly during the 1960s, however, as more women of all social classes joined the labor force. With this change in attitude, conservatives began to demand that female welfare recipients obtain employment instead of welfare.[101]

In the face of conservative opposition to AFDC, the Johnson administration had a number of options. They could have capitulated to conservatives and accepted a variety of punitive strategies to force women off the AFDC rolls; they could have insisted that women on AFDC should not be compelled to work; or they could have devised programs to make it possible for women on AFDC to work. Most of the women wanted to work, but the latter option would have required careful planning, because adult AFDC recipients averaged only an eighth-grade education, often suffered discrimination in labor markets, required expensive day-care programs, sometimes possessed physical or mental problems, and often could not find employment. But the Johnson administration never chose a consistent strategy. Some conservatives wanted to force women on AFDC to work. Northern liberals, who had become supporters of welfare rights, opposed compulsory assignment to jobs for women with young children, insisted that jobs pay at least the minimum wage, and demanded that the level of AFDC grants be raised.[102] The administration did not believe it could oppose conservatives, since they had considerable strength in the Congress, and Johnson was unsympathetic to welfare recipients, whom he believed often sought benefits rather than employment.[103]

The administration's policy approach, which was reflected in the welfare amendments of 1967,

was a confusing mixture of incompatible policies; ultimately, it satisfied no one. Some punitive policies were adopted; in particular, all women who did not have children younger than 6 years of age were required to work, at prevailing rather than minimum wages. A federal freeze on funds for AFDC was enacted but, for technical and political reasons, never implemented. Liberals were delighted to obtain a series of exemptions in the law that allowed welfare women to escape the work requirement if they were ill or if work was "inimical" to the welfare of the family. Liberals also obtained a work-incentive provision that allowed women who obtained low-paying jobs to continue to augment their wages with welfare payments up to a certain cut-off point; thus, many low-wage working women were able to earn more than they would as nonworking welfare recipients. Although women who obtained relatively high-paying jobs lost their eligibility, this policy led, overall, to large increases in the welfare rolls. Some liberals also liked provisions that established the Work Incentive Program (WIN), which funded training programs and day care.

The 1967 amendments represented, then, a confused policy. Liberals were victorious, on balance, because exemptions meant that few women were forced to take jobs and the rolls increased rapidly in the wake of work-incentive provisions. Their victory came at a high price, however. Their insistence that women should not be forced to work blinded them to the reality that most women on AFDC wanted to work, though for decent wages. Instead of scheming to outmaneuver conservatives and dilute the work requirement, they could have tried more diligently to develop millions of public service jobs or subsidized jobs in private industry, backed up by good day-care programs. They would have encountered formidable opposition from conservatives, because the costs of day care, training, and job creation would have far exceeded the cost of merely providing AFDC grants or the cost of the WIN programs, which provided superficial training and inadequate day-care services. Still, had the administration developed an effective and humanistic work strategy that had actually reduced the size of AFDC rolls, they might have outflanked conservatives and taken the AFDC issue from them.

The Food Stamp program was enacted in 1964 in the wake of a series of pilot feeding programs during the Kennedy administration. Policy makers realized that distribution of surplus food to the poor was cumbersome and required recipients to travel to centralized storage sites. Instead, families were allowed to purchase Food Stamps—coupons—at a price considerably less than their retail value; a number of grocery stores across the country agreed to accept Food Stamps as payment. Families on welfare were automatically eligible, but many poor families not on welfare could also be certified by local welfare departments. Localities were given the option of participating in the program; the Department of Agriculture paid the entire cost. Successive amendments in 1968, 1971, 1973, and 1978 dramatically expanded funding for the program, established national eligibility standards, made the program mandatory in all states, and developed methods to allow recipients to receive coupons without having to make any cash payments. The Food Stamp program was a landmark achievement, because it gave millions of impoverished families the resources to purchase food in quantities not possible with meager welfare checks.

THE OVEREXTENDED PRESIDENT AND THE LOSS OF CREDIBILITY

Johnson's extraordinary legislative successes on the domestic front were unprecedented in American history when measured by their sheer numbers. His successes in 1964 carried into 1965, when he obtained passage of 84 of the 87 measures that he submitted to Congress, and into 1966, when 97 of 113 measures were enacted.[104] Nor did he obtain these successes by waving a magic wand; he invested enormous amounts of time in the legislative process.

But even in 1965, Johnson had decided to embark on a high-risk gamble. Kennedy had committed large numbers of military "advisors" to South Vietnam, where the Vietcong, a communist group, was waging guerrilla warfare against the corruption-ridden and conservative dictatorial government. In 1964 and early 1965, Johnson went through an extended period of discussion with his top aides to decide whether he should send large numbers of American troops to South Vietnam. The details of these talks fall beyond our purpose here, but the ultimate decision does not, because committing hundreds of thousands of troops to South Vietnam by the end of 1965 had profound consequences for Johnson's social policies.[105]

To understand the complex relations between Johnson's foreign policy and his domestic policy, we need to return to our discussion of the sheer size of American military spending *before* Johnson committed troops to Vietnam and a fateful decision in 1964 to drastically lower U.S. income taxes. Recall that Truman had committed the nation to extraordinary levels of ongoing military spending in 1950 and that, in consequence, most of the American federal budget went for military purposes. Kennedy increased military spending even further, because he believed that the United States needed the capability to fight two and one-half wars simultaneously—that is, a war against Russia (probably in Europe), a war against China, and a war in a third-world country such as Vietnam.[106]

As a true believer in the threat of communist insurrection around the world, Johnson accepted this large military commitment with alacrity. But Johnson *also* accepted another legacy from Kennedy and his economic advisors, who were convinced that American economic growth would suffer unless the nation pumped more money into the economy. To do so, they thought, the government had two options: either to raise the federal budget or to lower federal income taxes so as to stimulate consumer spending. Since conservatives were unlikely to allow an expansion of the budget, Kennedy's aides recommended large tax cuts, which Johnson obtained from the Congress in 1964 during the first year of his presidency.[107]

Johnson committed himself to ambitious

INSERT 9.3   CRITICAL ANALYSIS: LINKAGES BETWEEN TAXES AND SOCIAL POLICY

Few social policy theorists discuss taxes in their writings; they focus instead on policy enactments and social programs. But social programs are ultimately funded by tax revenues, whether from general taxes or from payroll taxes.

As a proportion of income, taxes in the United States are far lower than in European nations, where higher rates of taxation on personal incomes are supplemented by a value-added tax that far exceeds the size of local sales taxes in the United States.

In the context of U.S. history, what cultural and political factors promote Americans' distaste for taxes? What implications have low taxes had for social policy expenditures, particularly when the United States has also spent a far larger share of its domestic wealth on military programs?

domestic reforms, then, in an environment of economic scarcity occasioned by military spending and tax cuts—and this budgetary scarcity was further increased by his decision to send large numbers of troops to Vietnam in 1965. Another politician might have decided, in these circumstances, to reconsider the tax policies or the domestic policies or the decision to send troops to Vietnam, in order not to strain the budget excessively or not to anger the Congress, which might wonder how he could engage in multiple endeavors that so stressed the federal budget. However, Johnson was committed to *each* of these policies: He wanted to save the world from communism by decisively defeating the Vietcong; and he wanted to be the greatest reform president in American history.[108] Moreover, he knew that, if he asked the Congress to raise taxes in order to pay for the war and his social reforms, conservatives from both parties would demand, as their price, that he cut "nonessential" social spending, much as they had forced Franklin Roosevelt in World War II to terminate the WPA, CCC, and NYA.[109]

To extricate himself from this situation, Johnson engaged in activities that can only be called devious and manipulative. To minimize the strain on the federal budget and the size of the deficit, he sold huge amounts of American assets, including stockpiled metals such as aluminum and copper that the government had accumulated in case of war.[110] He made the true costs of Vietnam appear somewhat smaller by taking much of the personnel and equipment that had been devoted to defending

Europe and transferring them to Vietnam. He constructed his military budget on the premise that the war would be over by June 1966—hardly a realistic scenario. By this means, he was able to give the impression that spending on Vietnam would be relatively small.[111] Although he enacted vast numbers of social programs, he often devoted little money to each one, so as to diminish their fiscal impact. For example, the much-publicized War on Poverty never received more than $2 billion in any specific year.

These various tactics, in turn, angered political groups on whom Johnson depended. Conservatives of both parties, already angered by the numbers of social reforms that Johnson proposed, accused him of hiding the true costs of the war—a charge readily supported by antiwar factions, who resented the diversion of funds from social reforms. Social reformers wondered nervously if Johnson's Vietnam policy would curtail his domestic agenda; they also came to realize that, unlike previous wars, it was disproportionately fought by troops drawn from the African American and Latino communities.

THE BELEAGUERED PRESIDENT: 1967–1968

Precariously, Johnson managed to maintain his political balance through much of 1966. He refused to diminish his commitment to all-out war in Vietnam, despite discouraging reports from the battle-fields that the enemy was not likely to yield and that mounting numbers of Americans would lose their lives or be maimed. He refused to diminish his commitment to domestic reforms and obtained the passage of dozens of new social programs, though they were often meagerly funded. And he refused to push Congress to raise taxes, for fear of igniting pressure by conservatives to reduce social spending.

By early 1967, however, even the politically agile Johnson was running out of options. With changing circumstances, Johnson lost support across the political spectrum. Conservatives in Congress began to attack his credibility more assertively; they accused him of submitting decep-tive budgets and suggested he should cut social spending. Equally troubling were public opinion polls suggesting that the widespread sympathy of middle- and working-class Americans for the plight of low-income Americans and African Americans that had existed in 1964 and 1965 had waned by 1968.[112]

Once African Americans had obtained civil rights legislation that decreased discrimination in the South, they sought reforms to address poverty, housing discrimination, education, and other prob-lems in the North. Northern whites, who had often supported efforts to reduce discrimination in the South, were enraged when *they* became the targets of protest. Indeed, Martin Luther King, Jr., ob-served that he had never seen more hatred than he experienced in open housing marches in white Chicago suburbs in 1967.[113] The Northern whites who applauded when the Department of Justice attacked de jure segregation in the South did not realize that the de facto segregation in their school districts would soon become the focus of reform. Many of them opposed policies to desegregate Northern schools by the use of busing, viewed affirmative action with skepticism, and believed that the Warren Court had been too kind to criminal offenders. Scandals in the War on Poverty, which were seized on by Republicans and conservatives, also soured public support.

Many whites responded negatively, as well, to the increasingly militant tactics of African Ameri-cans (and also of women, Latinos, and Native Americans).[114] King, who remained an influential leader until his assassination in 1968, found it increasingly difficult to persuade a new breed of African American leaders that nonviolence repre-sented an inviolable principle rather than a tactic. Stokely Carmichael, who coined the term *black power* on a civil rights march in 1966, personified the trend among many African Americans toward separatism, the development of African American economic institutions, and violent protest.[115] This militance seemed to many white Americans to be reflected in the large number of urban riots and dis-turbances that occurred in Northern—and some Southern—cities between 1965 and 1968; 239 civil disturbances erupted, with 8,133 persons killed and 49,604 persons arrested.[116]

The uneasiness of white Americans was com-pounded by economic problems in the nation. When Johnson proclaimed the War on Poverty in 1964, it was widely assumed that economic growth would allow the condition of all social classes to improve simultaneously, but increasing rates of inflation and deficits led some Americans to con-clude that social spending was incompatible with economic growth. Inflation and other economic concerns had replaced social concerns in public opinion polls by 1968.

Johnson's popularity with liberals and social reformers also began to wane. Although many lib-erals had remained silent on Vietnam in 1966 and even early 1967, the silence was decisively broken in August 1967, when the *New York Times* called the war a "bottomless pit" and urged Johnson to curtail the American commitment to it.[117] More-over, some liberals even became disenchanted with Johnson's domestic policy, despite the torrent of reforms that were enacted. They noticed that many of the reforms were not well funded. Some were angered by periodic cuts in social spending that Johnson made to deflect conservatives' charges that he was fiscally irresponsible. And then there was the unfolding debacle in Vietnam, where John-son had engaged in a bombing campaign that was unprecedented in military history, against a small, largely agricultural nation, and had little to show for it except a weekly tally of returning body bags.

Johnson had escalated the Vietnam conflict from a few military advisors and spies in 1964 to more than 540,000 troops in 1968. The resulting military defeat had a staggering cost in lives and resources. By the conclusion of American involvement in 1973, more than 55,000 Americans had been killed and 304,000 Americans had been injured. The U.S. Senate estimates that 1.4 million South Vietnamese were killed and wounded, another 850,000 enemy soldiers were killed, and 10.3 million refugees were created. Americans expended more than $135 billion on the war.[118]

Johnson believed that a communist victory in South Vietnam would lead to others throughout Southeast Asia, and he assumed that the noncommunist regimes in South Vietnam possessed relatively broad support despite their corruption, intransigent resistance to land reform, and domination by conservative elites. Johnson reasoned that the U.S. Air Force, with napalm, helicopters, and B-52 bombers, could prevail over poorly supplied and sparsely clad Asians, that air strikes would demoralize the North Vietnamese, and that the enemy would accept his promises to provide them with billions of dollars on the cessation of hostilities. But Johnson underestimated the resolve of the North Vietnamese, who were deeply committed to a long-term conflict that they had already waged for decades.[119]

The war had both indirect and direct effects on social policy. By focusing attention on foreign affairs, it created an atmosphere that was not conducive to the continuation of social reform. The war also splintered the coalition that had supported civil rights and other reforms since many African Americans, liberals, young people, intellectuals, and clergy opposed it.[120] The increasingly militant demonstrations against the war antagonized some moderate whites who supported the war effort. The war also led to reductions in levels of funding for social programs.

Most of all, the war eroded Johnson's credibility. Many Americans remembered bitterly that Johnson had run in 1964 as a peace candidate against Goldwater. His deception in hiding the true costs of the war and his habit of overstating American military gains made many Americans distrust him.[121] Much as Franklin Roosevelt had squandered his landslide electoral victory of 1936 by attempting to pack the Supreme Court, Johnson lost his political momentum when he committed the nation to the war.[122]

Some liberals were also infuriated in 1968, when Johnson orchestrated a tax increase to pay for the war by promising conservatives that he would call for substantial cuts in social spending. He had long promised that the nation could have both "guns and butter," but he seemed now to acknowledge that Vietnam would lead to significant cuts in butter.

Caught in conflicting forces, Johnson tried to conciliate each side by making concessions. He consented to tax increases and cuts in social spending, as well as a continuing commitment to the war, in order to assuage conservatives. He continued to propose social reforms in order to keep the support of liberals—and generally chose to avoid coercive policies in the wake of the urban riots. Indeed, following the Detroit and Newark riots, he established, in 1967, the National Advisory Committee on Civil Disorders—often called the Kerner Commission after its chairperson, Otto Kerner—to investigate the causes of riots. As the political debate became increasingly polarized, however, his concessions to one side served to antagonize the other.

By the spring of 1968, Johnson's ratings in public opinion polls had sunk to such low levels that many pundits began to wonder if he could win reelection. His hand was forced by the New Hampshire primary, in which he was almost defeated by Eugene McCarthy, a relatively unknown senator running on an antiwar platform. Stung by this humiliation, Johnson withdrew from the presidential race, in the hope that he could orchestrate a peace settlement in Vietnam. In November, when Richard Nixon defeated Vice President Hubert Humphrey, the Democratic candidate, the Great Society came to an official close. But actually the Great Society had ended in the rice paddies of Vietnam, long before the election results were tallied.

Johnson left the presidency a tormented man. His international policies had led to uncertain outcomes and a loss of popularity. In his last year in office, he toyed with initiating some new and massive reforms—such as a child health program—but he realized that they faced certain defeat. Almost all Great Society reforms had been enacted in two years, 1964 and 1965—a period that seemed light years removed from the troubled final years of Johnson's presidency.

OUTGROUPS IN THE 1960s

Having already discussed policy reforms that affect African Americans throughout this chapter, we focus here on other outgroups.

The civil rights struggles of African Americans captured the attention of the nation from 1955—when Rosa Parks refused to move to the back of the bus and triggered the bus boycott in Montgomery—through most of the 1960s. It was an epic struggle, with drama, violence, defeats, and victories. This struggle especially captivated *other* outgroups who experienced discrimination, including women, Latinos, gay men and lesbians, Asian Americans, and Native Americans. Each of these groups, in turn, developed reformist leaders and engaged in various forms of protest. Indeed, the momentum of their mobilizing carried protest well into the 1970s, before reform ebbed somewhat in the 1980s.

Women

Things were never the same once Rosie the Riveter entered the work force. In World War II, millions of women went to work in production plants. They were supposed to return to their domestic roles when the war ended—and indeed 3.25 million women were forced, or persuaded, to leave industrial jobs after World War II. But the genie was out of the bottle. Women had tasted economic freedom, and a dramatic upturn in female employment occurred throughout the 1950s. By 1952, more

women were employed than at the height of World War II, and the trend continued during the next four decades.[123] But women were not made to feel good about their work; indeed, the mass media and many theorists implied or stated that working women risked harming their children or destroying their femininity.[124]

Following World War II, an effort to secure an Equal Rights Amendment (ERA) to the Constitution assumed center stage among female activists. A host of distinguished women—Margaret Sanger, Pearl S. Buck, and Katharine Hepburn among them—supported the amendment and formed a coalition of organizations under the Women's Joint Legislative Committee. Advocates hoped the ERA would sweep aside many state laws that still limited the rights of women to own and sell property, to make contracts, to control bequests, and to exercise parental authority. But other female leaders opposed the amendment on the grounds that women *needed* special protections, such as protective labor legislation, which might be erased by the amendment. Its fate was sealed, however, when it passed the Senate but failed to obtain the necessary two-thirds majority.[125] Other women sought legislation to guarantee women equal pay for equal work in private employment; many legislators opposed it on the grounds that higher female wages might entice many women to abdicate their parenting role.

But women who sought new challenges discovered innumerable barriers in the early 1960s. Relatively few women obtained access to work in the building trades or to training in male-dominated professions like law, medicine, and business; they were usually limited to gender-segregated jobs in clerical, sales, unskilled manufacturing, teaching, nursing, and social work. Women were widely perceived as fragile—they were not even allowed to run long distances in track—and so "protective laws" kept them from arduous work. Other cultural factors also hindered them: Women were required to be absent from the labor force for extended periods—often at least until their children had reached high school—and could not easily reenter it; if they did, they could not easily match the career gains of male workers who had been working continuously. Women had to contend, as well, with opposition from their husbands and lack of sympathy from their children, who often had expectations that women should do the bulk of household chores. Moreover, since the nation had virtually no governmentally subsidized child care in the early 1960s, working women had to pay for day care from their own—usually low—paychecks.

As the 1960s began, some female activists hoped that President Kennedy would be sympathetic. At first, he was unresponsive. Under pressure, however, he appointed Esther Peterson as director of the Women's Bureau in the Department of Labor. Peterson mobilized a campaign for enactment of equal pay legislation, which had foundered after World War II. Congress enacted an Equal Pay Act in 1963, but this legislation left out large groups of women, including domestics and farm workers, and did not speak to discrimination that blocked women from certain kinds of jobs and promotions.[126] (Because many women were confined to a gender-segregated workplace, the subject of equal pay was moot.) Moreover, Kennedy established a Commission on the Status of Women in 1961 to review existing policies regarding employment, social insurance, tax, labor, and social services. In its report, the commission recommended against an Equal Rights Amendment to the Constitution, on the grounds that women could bring suit under existing constitutional provisions such as the equal protection clause of the Fourteenth Amendment. The commission made many constructive suggestions; it advocated a reduction in gender-based pay and promotion discrimination in the civil service and recommended more high-level presidential appointees. (Kennedy had already issued an executive order in 1961 requiring private employers with federal contracts not to discriminate on the basis of race *or* gender.) It also recommended broadening women's access to education. However, the commission did not offer encouragement for women's entry into male-dominated fields; it did not attack the fundamental gender-role structure of American society or the prevailing

notion that women should have primary responsibility for child rearing; and it did not seek basic changes in Social Security, which discriminated against single women who were not dependents or widows.[127]

American women needed a theorist akin to Simone de Beauvoir, the French feminist who had so articulately analyzed the constraints placed on women in modern society. They found this theorist in Betty Friedan, whose classic book, *The Feminine Mystique,* was published in 1963.[128] Friedan dissected the malaise of the suburban woman who, "as she made the beds, shopped for groceries, matched slipcover material, ate peanut butter sandwiches with her children, chauffeured Cub Scouts and Brownies . . . was afraid to ask even of herself—'Is this all?'"[129] Friedan contended that society had developed a mystique of feminine fulfillment, in which the American woman achieved a kind of happiness as housewife and mother that no women had ever obtained in prior eras. If she lacked this happiness, Friedan contended, she was taught to blame herself—that is, to look inward for neurotic tendencies, "penis envy," or other personal failings. Isolated in her suburban "concentration camp," the married woman had no chance to explore options or seek new challenges.[130] Friedan's book ended with a ringing plea for "a new life plan for women"—a society in which, emancipated from past myths, women would "see through the delusions of the feminine mystique" to develop careers that would fully challenge them.[131]

Lyndon Johnson made a promising start when he appointed many more females to high-policy posts than had Kennedy, but Johnson was indifferent to the inclusion of a ban on gender-based discrimination in Title VII of the Civil Rights Act of 1964. A number of legislators opposed this provision on the grounds that it could threaten protective labor legislation for women, such as laws regulating the hours and conditions of women's work. Some powerful Southern legislators supported it for the wrong reasons: They hoped that the addition of the controversial provision would kill the entire Civil Rights Act, which they opposed. But

11 of the 12 female legislators in the House of Representatives spoke eloquently for the measure, by insisting that women deserved the same protections as the racial groups who were included in Title VII.[132] When the ban and the legislation were passed by the Senate, women had finally been included in major civil rights legislation, almost a century after their exclusion in the wake of the Civil War—but their inclusion did not stem from any militant support by the administration. Nor did the Equal Opportunities Commission, established to investigate discrimination in employment by Title VII, focus on gender-based discrimination; it was too preoccupied with racial discrimination. As Harrison notes, some of the EEOC commissioners and staff regarded the gender-discrimination provisions of the Civil Rights Act not as a legitimate protection, but as something conservatives had placed in the legislation in order to obtain its defeat.[133]

Some advances were made through legal rulings. For example, in 1965, the Supreme Court ruled in *Griswold* v. *Connecticut* that a law that made the use of contraceptives a crime was illegal. However, the ruling left intact the ban on abortions in many states and did not speak to the absence of family-planning clinics in many jurisdictions. Other court rulings abolished certain residency requirements, midnight raids, and man-in-the-house rules that various states had devised to cut AFDC rolls.

Although these early policy successes represented important gains, they were token measures or inadequately implemented. Recognizing that women needed to develop political clout, Betty Friedan and other women formed the National Organization for Women (NOW) in 1966 to seek federal action on women's employment issues, such as tighter bans on sex discrimination by federal contractors, the full deductibility of day-care expenses, and more enforcement powers for the EEOC. Most significant, NOW from the outset questioned the long-standing assumption that females should primarily be the child rearers and their husbands the breadwinners.[134]

NOW assertively sought to pressure Johnson to include women within the scope of his September 1965 executive order that required affirmative action programs to ensure equal opportunity for all races. By October 1967, they had succeeded; this paved the way for affirmative action programs by local and state governments, federal contractors, and the federal government—and established the precedent that the term *sex* would appear whenever the phrase "race, creed, color, or national origin" appeared.[135] NOW also initiated another bid for an Equal Rights Amendment and secured widespread support for the measure from many candidates.

A development that was as important as these political developments was that women had begun to form consciousness-raising groups, where issues like sexual abuse, harassment on the job, rape, women's health, abortion, and job discrimination became topics of conversation rather than taboo subjects. These issues would become important policy issues over the next several decades, though the government response was uneven and often inadequate.

By the end of the Johnson administration, then, women had made important gains but, in retrospect, they were only token advances. Though women had made huge gains in obtaining higher education, had received one-third of all the master's degrees granted in the United States by 1968, and represented 58% of the labor force, the economic position of white women relative to white men declined during the decades after World War II. Full-time female workers earned, on average, only 58.2% of the income of men in 1969, down from 63.3% in 1956.[136]

Critics of the feminist movement in the 1960s note that it often did not speak to the needs of African American or low-income women. African American women, who often had had to work, were less worried about the feminine mystique and more worried about the lack of economic opportunity and decent wages for themselves and for African American men. Another criticism was that, by their single-minded advocacy of women's right to a career, feminists made women who chose to emphasize child rearing feel guilty, much as working women in earlier periods felt guilty that they didn't prioritize child rearing.

Gay Men and Lesbians

The extent of prejudice against gay men and lesbians in the early 1950s is best revealed by a quote from Senator Kenneth Wherry (R., Neb.), who asserted that he wished to "harry every last pervert from the federal government services" on the grounds that "homosexuals in government are a moral and security issue . . . the lack of emotional stability which is found in most sex perverts, and the weakness of their moral fiber, makes them susceptible to the blandishments of foreign espionage agents."[137] This virulent prejudice must be placed in the context of long-standing harassment, incarceration, and discrimination against gay men and lesbians. Underlying this systematic homophobia was a combination of religious ideas, which equated homosexuality with sin; psychiatric and medical thought, which saw it as mental or physical pathology; and criminology, which was inclined to perceive homosexual behavior as criminal. (Sodomy and other homosexual acts were widely punishable as crimes.) In this social climate, many gay men and lesbians came to think of themselves as diseased.

World War II brought more attention to homosexuality, not only because the army made strenuous efforts to screen gay men and lesbians from service but also because so many escaped its net. For the first time, gay men and lesbians discovered that many others shared their sexual orientations—and same-gender associations were surprisingly common and open in barracks, dance halls, and combat zones.[138]

Soldiers formed gay communities in New York, San Francisco, Los Angeles, and other major cities following the war, and institutions such as gay and lesbian bars become widespread. Sexual behavior became more openly discussed in the conservative 1950s, as reflected by the widely read Kinsey report, which addressed taboo topics like masturbation. And Kinsey found that nearly 50% of males admitted erotic responses to their own sex, even if only 4% admitted that they were exclusively homosexual.[139]

But gay men and lesbians in the 1950s led a life constricted by societal laws and prejudices. Witchhunts against communists in government often included gay men and lesbians. Eisenhower, in an executive order aimed at dismissing loyalty risks from government, explicitly listed "sexual perversion" and proceeded to remove presumed homosexuals from government at the rate of 40 per month in the first 16 months after the order; job seekers who were judged to be homosexual by the interviewer were denied employment.[140] Moreover, 2,000 persons per year were removed from the military in the early 1950s—a number that rose by another 50% by the early 1960s. State and local governments screened their 12.5 million employees with similar zeal and also cited homosexuality as grounds for dismissal.[141]

Gay men and lesbians were also subject to arrests by local police and vice squads, who raided gay bars, restrooms, lesbian bars, and even personal residences. D'Emilio estimates that there were more than 1,000 arrests per year in the District of Columbia in the early 1950s.[142] Gay bashing by local gangs and petty criminals was also common.

The gay and lesbian community began to develop organizations and leadership in the 1950s, but these organizations lacked a mass membership and had little success in changing social policies. A major problem among gay men and lesbians was that they were reluctant to publicly reveal their sexual orientation, for fear of reprisal from law authorities or recrimination from landlords or employers. Moreover, many gay men and lesbians had internalized homophobia.[143]

The emergence of a less oppressive social climate in the 1960s promoted the development of activism among gay men and lesbians. A succession of court rulings had gradually limited the ability of local and federal governments to censor or prohibit "obscene literature," and so publications by gay and lesbian writers and groups could circulate more freely. As with so many other policies, the Warren Court led the way; finally, in 1967, it ruled that "a book cannot be proscribed unless it is found to be *utterly* without redeeming social value" even though the book is "patently offensive." In the more permissive climate of the 1960s, mass-based magazines like *Playboy* were circulated—an unthinkable development in the 1950s. Howard Becker and other sociologists wrote on deviance from a relativistic perspective. Avoiding moral judgments about homosexual behavior, they urged an end to criminal penalties and to exclusion from the armed forces. Lawyers began to develop suits against antisodomy statutes on the grounds that they violated personal liberty, and some local chapters of the American Civil Liberties Union (ACLU) became interested in pursuing discriminatory actions such as exclusion of gay men and lesbians from the civil service. Court decisions in a few states had legitimized the right of gay men and lesbians to assemble in local bars, and the possibility of further progress was suggested by movements in Europe that sought to decriminalize sex acts among consenting adults.[144] Some courageous clergy declared that the sexual orientations of gay men and lesbians were not immoral. And some city governments, such as the Civil Service Commission of New York City, began to relax the restrictions against the hiring of gay men and lesbians. Even mental-health and health professionals began to reexamine traditional perspectives, and a committee established by the National Institute of Mental Health in 1967, though it refrained from declaring their orientation to be normal, urged tolerance of gay men and lesbians.[145]

By the late 1960s, just as the black power philosophy emerged in the civil rights movement, the accommodationist and gradualist perspectives of other outgroups had begun to be supplanted by more radical perspectives. Thus, in 1969, a pivotal development in New York City ignited the gay liberation movement. Some police officers and detectives raided the Stonewall Inn, a gay bar in Greenwich Village. When the officers arrested the bartender, the Stonewall's bouncer, and three drag queens, a riot broke out; it spread into the Village and continued through the next night. In the wake of the Stonewall riots, the gay and lesbian movements attracted a mass membership and developed a political agenda—to modify government policies at every level and to change the diagnostic categories of the American Psychiatric Association. Moreover, they made "coming out" a key organizing strategy: They hoped to persuade millions of gay men and lesbians to publicly announce their sexual orientations, despite possible reprisals.[146] Organizers' spirits were buoyed by early successes, such as the decision of the American Psychiatric Association in 1973 that gay men and lesbians would no longer be regarded as mentally ill. But their work had barely begun. Generations of prejudice hung heavy over a nation that was only starting to rethink traditional stereotypes.

Latinos, Native Americans, and Asian Americans

Latinos   At the beginning of the 1960s, Latinos, like African Americans, still lived in their traditional rural areas—for example, on the farms and ranches of the Southwest and the farms of the upper Midwest—but had also formed rapidly growing communities in some urban areas—in particular, in the Southwest and in Midwestern cities like Chicago and Kansas City. In the 1950s, moreover, there was a huge influx of Puerto Ricans to East-coast cities, particularly New York City, where between 850,000 and 1.2 million Puerto Ricans resided by 1970.[147] They often came to the United States for economic reasons, because they had been displaced by the expansion of large American sugar and coffee corporations and because factories and service industries in New York wanted and solicited cheap labor. As with prior immigrant groups, many Puerto Ricans hoped to return to their homeland after they had improved their economic condition—but, in the end, most remained. Moreover, a substantial population of Cubans settled in the United States, particularly in South Florida, in the wake of the Cuban Revolution of 1959, which brought Fidel Castro to power.

The so-called Chicano movement signaled the beginning of militant organizing projects that centered on Mexican Americans and undocumented workers. That movement was led by a series of charismatic leaders, including Reies Lopex Tijerina, who sought to restore lost Spanish and Mexican land grants in New Mexico, and Corky Gonzales, who organized grass-roots groups in Denver. It was Cesar Chavez, however, who captured national attention when he developed the United Farm Workers Organizing Committee to empower Mexican agricultural laborers. Recall that the Wagner Act of 1936, which established federal protection for persons who sought to organize unions, did not apply to farm workers. As a result, organizers could be summarily fired or intimidated if employers thought they were making trouble. In 1966, after building a cadre of leaders, Chavez organized a march on Sacramento, the capital of California, to dramatize the plight of farm workers. This march was followed by a flurry of organizing activities—most memorably, by well-publicized national boycotts of crops like grapes and lettuce to pressure agribusiness to recognize farm workers' right to organize. Simultaneously, Chavez pressured politicians in California to enact legislation that would provide agricultural laborers with the kinds of protections that the Wagner Act afforded other workers. The Latino community was active on many fronts: voter registration drives; pressure on the EEOC to assertively investigate job discrimination against Latinos; the development of the Mexican American Legal Defense and Education Fund (a Latino counterpart to the NAACP); pressure that led to an extension of the provisions of the Voting Rights Act of 1965 to Latinos; and the development of various coordinating councils to link the work of many advocacy groups.[148]

Puerto Ricans, because of their strong personal ties to their homeland, had more difficulty in organizing protests against poor working conditions and wages, as well as atrocious living conditions; their patterns of migration back and forth to Puerto Rico undermined the cohesion of their communities in East-coast cities.[149] Moreover, unlike the farm workers, who had a relatively identifiable enemy in agribusiness, and African Americans, who could attack Jim Crow laws, most Puerto Ricans were enmeshed in the constellation of factors that perpetuate urban poverty.

Native Americans Native Americans had been placed on reservations during the 19th century following their eviction from their ancestral lands. These reservations were frequently assigned to one tribe; the government agreed to supply certain commodities or services (such as a school) in return for the tribe's agreement to cede its ancestral lands. The early reservation experience was difficult for Native Americans; because the reservations were too small to allow them to hunt and be self-sufficient, they had to rely on financial assistance from government agents and missionary groups. As we discussed in Chapter 5, the federal government decided in 1887, soon after establishing the reservations, to break up tribes; the Dawes Act individualized Native Americans' landholdings, made some of them American citizens, and provided them with a government school system, so as to socialize them to American ways. The chief instruments of this Americanizing strategy were the agents of the Bureau of Indian Affairs.[150] Congress conferred citizenship on all remaining Native Americans in 1924.

But the Americanization strategy did not work, because the Native Americans held on to their indigenous culture. However, many Native Americans lost their land to speculators and crooks, or else chose to lease it to others to farm; still living on or near reservations, they became dependent on government rations. The Indian agent and his staff were empowered by the Snyder Act in 1921 to help Native Americans with a range of education, welfare, health, agricultural, and other functions and to provide technical assistance to Native American policy makers and judges.

By the 1920s and 1930s, government policy had again reversed itself, to emphasize preservation of reservations and culture. Indeed, the Indian Reorganization Act of 1934 promoted the establishment of tribal organizations, economies, and government, as well as the purchase of additional lands for the reservations. This desire to help Native Americans become self-sufficient stemmed partly from their economic desperation in the Great Depression. In the 1940s and 1950s, the pendulum swung again, as legislators and officials sought to diminish federal responsibilities by adopting an assimilationist strategy. Termination acts in the 1950s and early 1960s ended federal responsibility for various tribes, who had to turn to state governments for economic and other assistance.

In the 1960s and 1970s, the pendulum swung back again: The War on Poverty placed considerable emphasis on supporting the culture of Native Americans, as well as their indigenous communities and tribal functions. Some of the reservations that had been terminated in the 1950s were restored to federal authority. Many Great Society programs channeled funds to the reservations for housing assistance, education, and economic development. The Bureau of Indian Affairs, which had often sought to force American customs on Native Americans, became an advocate for Native Americans "in the same manner as the Department of Agriculture is pro-farmer and the Department of Labor, pro-labor."[151] Both Presidents Johnson and Nixon strongly opposed the termination policy, sought to develop Native American participation in their governance, and favored continuation of federal technical and economic assistance to tribes. Indeed, the Indian Self-Determination and Education Assistance Act, as well as other legislation in the 1970s, sought to give tribes the authority to decide whether to assume responsibility for administering federal programs of the Interior Department or the Department of Health, Education, and Welfare.

Nor were Native Americans quiescent politically during the turbulence of the 1960s. Indigenous groups demanded compensation for lands that were taken from Native Americans illegally, sought protections for minerals and timber on reservations, and challenged stereotypical portrayals of Native Americans in films. Like African Americans and Latinos, they dramatized their demands by direct action—for example, the occupation of Alcatraz, an abandoned federal prison on an island in San Francisco Bay.

As with other people of color, a significant number of Native Americans moved to urban areas, where they often resided in deteriorated communities and in poverty. Caught between two cultures, and not inclined to assimilate to the extent that many other groups did, Native Americans often had difficulty establishing their personal and collective identities. When the colonists arrived in the 17th century, there were roughly ten million Native Americans, but by 1970 their numbers had dwindled to some 827,000, though many of them had been absorbed into the general population.[152]

Asian Americans   Asian Americans in Hawaii and California made important gains in achieving their civil rights in the wake of World War II and in the 1950s. Disenfranchised before World War II, Asian plantation laborers were registered in a massive drive by the International Longshoremen's and Warehousemen's Union during the war and secured an act by the Hawaii legislature that was akin to the Wagner Act. Sugar workers were able to unionize in a multiracial union that included Filipino, Japanese, and Portuguese laborers. Californian Japanese Americans were able to obtain from the Supreme Court a ruling that the California laws that prohibited a noncitizen alien from conveying his or her land to a citizen child were unconstitutional. The California Supreme Court ruled in 1948 that laws that prohibited people of different races from having sexual contact (antimiscegenation laws) were unconstitutional. In 1946, California voters decisively defeated an initiative that was placed on the ballot to reaffirm the alien land laws.

In 1956, Japanese Americans placed on the ballot an initiative to overturn the alien land laws altogether and won. In 1952, the federal government finally terminated provisions of the 1790 naturalization law that refused citizenship to nonwhite individuals, partly because of lobbying by Japanese Americans.[153]

But immigration limitations on Asians continued, despite token concessions to various nationalities following World War II. The blatantly racist immigration policies of the United States, which gave larger annual quotas to European nations than to Asian nations, were finally reversed in the Immigration Act of 1965. This act abolished the national-origin quotas and allowed annual admissions of 170,000 immigrants from the Eastern Hemisphere and 120,000 from the Western Hemisphere, not including immediate family members. As Takaki notes, "the new law represented a sharp ideological departure from the traditional view of America as a homogeneous white society."[154] Indeed, a second wave of Asian immigrants during the next 30 years brought a massive increase in the Asian population; significant Japanese, Chinese, and Filipino populations were supplemented by Vietnamese, Korean, Asian Indian, Laotian, and Cambodian groups, as we discuss in Chapter 11.

People of Color in the Urban Ghettoes

By the end of the 1960s, people of color in the United States had predominantly been segregated within urban ghettoes, but this pattern was to become even more marked over the next two decades. As Latinos and African Americans entered American cities, they tended to reside in segregated communities—often communities that had been abandoned by other ethnic groups as they fled to suburban areas. New York City provides an example; by 1970, whites composed 63.3% of its population, whereas African Americans and Latinos, respectively, composed 19.2% and 15.2% of its population. By 1990, the white population had declined to 41.3%, whereas the African American and Latino populations had, respectively, risen to

27.7% and 23.7%.[155] (The statistics for other major American cities were similar.)

Of course, Irish, Italian, Jewish, and other ethnic enclaves had traditionally existed in American cities, but their plight was enviable compared to that of people of color. Their upward mobility— that is, their ability to become wealthy, so that they could eventually afford more expensive housing in better communities and the suburbs—was enhanced by the fact that they immigrated just as the United States was industrializing, so that they secured a position from the outset in the growing American economy—albeit a position that was poorly paid at first. By the time large numbers of Latinos and African Americans reached the cities, in the 1950s, they found it difficult to penetrate an economic structure dominated by the whites who had preceded them. Moreover, white immigrants did not find themselves segregated by race in low-income communities that were encircled by vast middle-class suburbs, where most jobs were located. Denied education in rural areas before they left for the cities, African Americans and Latinos were probably less prepared to use education as the vehicle of upward mobility than were the Jews, Asian Americans, and white-ethnic populations of prior eras. Moreover, inner-city schools often lacked staff who could relate to African American and Latino youth, and the classrooms were usually overcrowded.

Moreover, the segregation of these communities into urban ghettoes was coupled with selective outmigration of those individuals who *were* upwardly mobile. As a result, those who remained behind not only lived in poverty but also often lacked the role models, indigenous businesses, vibrant churches, and community cohesiveness that white-ethnic groups had enjoyed.

 ## SOCIAL WORK IN THE 1960s

Social work emerged from the Great Depression with a determination to upgrade the profession, by making a bachelor's degree mandatory for admission to graduate programs and by making all graduate programs last for two years. Casework remained the dominant methodology of the profession; macro practice occupied a decidedly secondary niche. Moreover, social workers in many states wanted to establish state-enforced standards and tests to register or certify social workers; that is, they wanted to establish lists of certified social workers, who could then receive priority over non-trained workers in filling government and agency positions. The profession was trying, in effect, to distinguish its members from the legions of untrained staff who worked in government and nongovernment agencies.[156] Some people wondered if the profession risked being too elitist by requiring extended graduate training, but advocates of the master's degree insisted that it was required to improve standards and to obtain competence in casework.

The National Council on Social Work Education was established in 1946 to launch a study of social work education that would clarify relationships between undergraduate and graduate education; it was renamed the Council on Social Work Education (CSWE) in 1952. The study concluded that graduate education was needed for professional practice and that undergraduate education provided only a preprofessional base. Though diminished in status, undergraduate education nevertheless continued; in 1951, 400 schools taught undergraduate courses in social work.[157] In 1955, seven separate social work associations were merged to form the National Association of Social Workers (NASW), with roughly 18,000 members; new members were required to have completed two years of graduate study.

An important question remained: To what extent would this profession be committed to social action and social justice, in the tradition of Jane Addams and the rank-and-file movement of the 1930s? Would casework, with its emphasis on individual counseling, draw into social work only those students with a narrow focus on individual remedies? And would it socialize students to view social action as extraneous to professional work? Developments in the 1950s did not augur well for those who wanted a social action perspective to be prominent in the profession. The macro side of the profession, such as community organization and administration, remained ill defined. Social policy offerings in schools of social work were uneven and often emphasized historical materials, without giving students the tools to engage in advocacy for the poor or other populations. A prominent set of educators infused casework with so much psychiatric content that it became irrelevant to those working-class and poor persons unable or unwilling to participate in extended intrapsychic explorations. Still, a movement to have a generalist curriculum began to give social work students a breadth of content, rather than a narrowly defined casework training.

The profession was influenced by the turbulence of the 1960s. Even in the late 1950s, an exhaustive study of social work education recommended that community organization and administration join casework and group work as fully recognized interventions in social work, even if policy was still relegated to largely theoretical, philosophical, and historical roles. The advocacy of the War on Poverty infused life into community organizing and other macro aspects of social work; many scores of students joined these branches in the growing numbers of schools that offered relevant study.[158] The NASW engaged in extensive lobbying and advocacy in the 1960s, in contrast to its lower profile in the 1950s.[159] Social work, which remained the dominant profession in many nongovernmental social agencies, also retained its foothold in public agencies in the 1960s; its members were much involved in mental-health, child welfare, and public welfare agencies. Thus enriching its mission and buoyed by the expansion of the welfare state, social work seemed positioned to provide much of the staff for a range of agencies and functions, while retaining a reformist mission.

But the profession was hardly free from controversy. Some people believed it to be too conservative. Protests by students in various schools of social work in the 1960s and by activists at national conferences called for social workers to be more assertive in challenging existing programs and policies.[160] Questions remained about the continuing—though somewhat diminished—dominance of casework in social work. A decision by the NASW in 1969 to give regular membership to holders of bachelor's degrees from those undergraduate programs that met CSWE criteria was controversial within the profession; its advocates insisted that it would give NASW more political clout by vastly enlarging its membership, but its detractors insisted that it would lower standards and decrease the prestige—and thus the power—of the social work profession by diluting its membership.[161]

THE EVOLUTION OF THE RELUCTANT WELFARE STATE

Johnson possessed genuine sympathy for persons in need, yet he was no more disposed than Kennedy to expand income maintenance, public works, unemployment, or Social Security programs.[162] Fortuitous circumstances and his formidable legislative skills enabled him to enact a flood of social legislation. But critics contend that this highly ambitious man, who wanted to enact more programs than Franklin Roosevelt, became seduced by his legislative successes and equated quantity with quality.[163] So obsessed was he with enacting measures that he gave insufficient attention to their implementation. Moreover, because of Johnson's budgetary frugality, which stemmed from his dislike of big spenders and from his diversion of national resources to the Vietnam conflict, many of his programs received woefully inadequate funding.[164]

The Great Society represented a curious paradox; though it was a period of unprecedented social reform, the Great Society era was not marked by significant increases in social spending, when expressed as a percentage of total federal spending; this was partly because Johnson did not commit major funds to many of his initiatives and programs like Medicare had not become fully established.[165] The economic circumstances of poor persons and people of color improved considerably, but these improvements probably stemmed primarily from the economic growth of the period. Johnson nonetheless vastly broadened the policy roles of the federal government—to include federal funding of medical, nutritional, preschool, educational, legal, civil rights, and gerontologic programs. Roosevelt had established the foundations of the American welfare state; Johnson dramatically expanded its scope in a remarkably brief period.

Social reforms occurred at a dizzying pace in the 1960s but for reasons quite different from those in the New Deal era. In the 1960s, unlike the 1930s, reforms did not stem from the overall economic plight of the population; it was a period of economic growth in the United States. A combination of factors stimulated reform. One factor was that few new social programs had been established since the onset of World War II, owing to the conservative hold on Congress in the Truman administration, the conservatism of Eisenhower, the inability of Kennedy to obtain passage of his domestic measures, and the diversion of funds and presidential attention to the crises of the Cold War. We might say there was a pent-up demand for reform.

Furthermore, we can speculate that Kennedy reinstilled a sense of idealism in certain segments of the population, even if few reforms had been enacted by the time of his death. American public opinion was profoundly influenced, moreover, by the civil rights movement, which daily brought to the public gaze an unending series of atrocities in the South, as civil rights activists dramatically challenged a range of discriminatory laws and practices.

Nor can we underestimate the efforts of Lyndon Johnson, who seized the moment to turn Kennedy's assassination into a series of legislative victories even in 1964. Moreover, Johnson's landslide victory in 1964 gave the Democrats such commanding majorities in both chambers of Congress that Johnson could use his formidable skills to fashion a torrent of legislative successes. The civil rights movement, the women's movement, people with disabilities, gay men and lesbians, and other activist groups kept pressure on legislators to maintain the pace of reform. And the riots in the cities were a constant and grim reminder that America had a large population of citizens whose economic and social plight had not been frontally addressed by civil rights legislation.

As might be expected in a nation that had created a sizable welfare state so late in its history, substantial opposition to the rate of growth of federal social programs began to appear by 1966. There was a resurgence of racial animosity, dislike of big government, antipathy to the poor, and dislike of radicals and social reformers, which had been somewhat muted from 1964 to 1966. The Vietnam War probably accelerated and intensified polarization between factions who favored and opposed social reforms, because they also tended to take divergent positions on the war.

The Great Society was, then, a significant reform movement but, like the New Deal, it occurred in a nation that was reluctant to embrace an emerging welfare state. As the nation headed toward the 1970s, reformers wondered if the set of programs would endure or would be swept away in a new conservative era. As with the provisions of the Social Security Act, time would show the surprising resilience of many Great Society programs. By the same token, the size and nature of the American welfare state would prove highly controversial in the coming decades.

NOTES

1. Joseph Lash, *Eleanor and Franklin* (New York: W. W. Norton, 1971), pp. 597ff.

2. Richard Chapman, "Contours of Public Policy, 1939–1945." Unpublished dissertation (New Haven, Conn.: Yale University, 1976), pp. 300ff.

3. Stephen Bailey, *Congress Makes a Law* (New York: Columbia University Press, 1950), pp. 220–234.

4. Mary Hinchey, "The Frustration of the New Deal Revival: 1944–1946." Unpublished dissertation (Columbia, Mo.: University of Missouri, 1965).

5. James Savage, *Balanced Budgets and American Politics* (Ithaca, N.Y.: Cornell University Press, 1988), pp. 161–175.

6. See, for example, Barton Bernstein, "The Ambiguous Legacy: The Truman Administration and Civil Rights." In Barton Bernstein, ed., *Politics and Policies of the Truman Administration* (Chicago: Quadrangle Books, 1970), pp. 269–314.

7. Paul Nitze, *From Hiroshima to Glasnost: At the Center of Decision* (New York: Grove Weidenfeld, 1989).

8. Bernstein, "The Ambiguous Legacy," pp. 269–314.

9. Richard Davies, *Age of Asphalt: The Automobile, the Freeway, and the Condition of Metropolitan America* (Philadelphia: J. B. Lippincott, 1975).

10. Herbert Parmet, *Eisenhower and the American Crusades* (New York: Macmillan, 1972), pp. 570–572.

11. Stephen Ambrose, *Eisenhower, the President,* Vol. II (New York: Simon & Schuster, 1984), pp. 411–435.

12. William Leuchtenberg, *In the Shadow of FDR: From Harry Truman to Ronald Reagan* (Ithaca, N.Y.: Cornell University Press, 1983), pp. 78–84; Allen Matusow, *The Unraveling of America: A History of Liberalism in the 1960's* (New York: Harper & Row, 1984), pp. 15–17.

13. Charles Hulton, "The Legacy of Reaganomics." In John Palmer and Isabel Sawhill, eds., *The Legacy of Reaganomics* (Washington, D.C.: Urban Institute, 1984), p. 7.

14. Geoffrey Hodgson, *America in Our Time* (Garden City, N.Y.: Doubleday, 1976), p. 51.

15. Ibid., pp. 54–64, 184–189.

16. Ibid., pp. 58–60.

17. Paul Taubman, *Income Distribution and Redistribution* (Reading, Mass.: Addison-Wesley, 1978), p. 15.

18. Winifred Bell, *Aid to Dependent Children* (New York: Columbia University Press, 1965), pp. 93–110; Frances Piven and Richard Cloward, *Regulating the Poor: The Functions of Public Welfare* (New York: Pantheon, 1971), pp. 123–177.

19. Gilbert Steiner, *State of Welfare* (Washington, D.C.: Brookings Institution, 1971), pp. 226–227.

20. Peter Gottschalk and Sheldon Danziger, "Macroeconomic Conditions, Income Transfers, and the Trend in Poverty." In D. Lee Bawden, ed., *The Social Contract Revisited: Aims and Outcomes of President Reagan's Social Welfare Policy* (Washington, D.C.: Urban Institute, 1984), p. 191.

21. William Chafe, *The American Woman: Her Changing Social, Economic, and Political Roles* (New York: Oxford University Press, 1972), pp. 174–195.

22. Bernard Bloom, *Community Mental Health* (Pacific Grove, Calif.: Brooks/Cole, 1977), pp. 11–20.

23. Peter Tyor and Leland Bell, *Caring for the Retarded in America: A History* (Westport, Conn.: Greenwood Press, 1984), pp. 123–145.

24. The number of persons with disabilities is discussed by Frank Bowe, *Rehabilitating America: Toward Independence for Disabled and Elderly People* (New York: Harper & Row, 1980), pp. 24–54.

25. Jonathan Katz, *Gay American History: Lesbians and Gay Men in the U.S.A.* (New York: Harper Colophon Books, 1976), pp. 432, 596.

26. Hodgson, *America in Our Time,* p. 45.

27. Theodore Sorenson, *Kennedy* (New York: Harper & Row, 1965); Arthur Schlesinger, Jr., *A Thousand Days: John F. Kennedy in the White House* (Boston: Houghton Mifflin, 1965); and William Manchester, *Portrait of a President* (Boston: Little, Brown, 1962).

28. Henry Fairlie, *The Kennedy Promise* (Garden City, N.Y.: Doubleday, 1973); Victor Lasky, *J.F.K., the Man and the Myth* (New York: Macmillan, 1963); and Richard Walton, *Cold War and Counterrevolution: The Foreign Policy of John F. Kennedy* (New York: Viking Press, 1972).

29. Leuchtenberg, *In the Shadow of FDR,* pp. 76–84.

30. Ibid., p. 77; Matusow, *The Unraveling of America,* p. 14.

31. Henry Aaron, *Politics and the Professors* (Washington, D.C.: Brookings Institution, 1981), pp. 17–25; James Patterson, *America's Struggle Against Poverty* (Cambridge, Mass.: Harvard University Press, 1981), pp. 115–125.

32. Aaron, *Politics and the Professors,* pp. 35–49, 220–225.

33. William Ryan, *Blaming the Victim* (New York: Pantheon, 1971), pp. 112–135.

34. Vincent Burke, *Nixon's Good Deed: Welfare Reform* (New York: Columbia University Press, 1974), p. 36; Hodgson, *America in Our Time,* pp. 82–98.

35. Tom Wicker, *JFK and LBJ: The Influence of Personality upon Politics* (New York: Morrow, 1968), pp. 85–87.

36. Ibid., pp. 90–92.

37. Ibid., pp. 25–28; Hodgson, *America in Our Time,* pp. 99–110.

38. Leuchtenberg, *In the Shadow of FDR,* pp. 85–88.

39. Aaron, *Politics and the Professors,* p. 17.

40. Michael Harrington, *The Other America: Poverty in the United States* (New York: Macmillan, 1962).

41. Matusow, *The Unraveling of America,* pp. 60–96.

42. Juan Williams, *Eyes on the Prize: America's Civil Rights Years, 1954–1965* (New York: Viking, 1987), pp. 39–61.

43. Ibid., p. 41.

44. Ibid., pp. 39–61.

45. Matusow, *The Unraveling of America,* pp. 62–63.

46. Carl Brauer, *John F. Kennedy and the Second Reconstruction* (New York: Columbia University Press, 1977), pp. 16–17, 204.

47. Ibid., pp. 112–113.

48. Matusow, *The Unraveling of America,* p. 348.

49. Ibid., pp. 90–91; Brauer, *John F. Kennedy,* pp. 265–268.

50. Theodore Marmor, *The Politics of Medicare* (Chicago: Aldine Books, 1975), pp. 39–53.

51. Wicker, *JFK and LBJ,* pp. 132–146.

52. Hodgson, *America in Our Time,* pp. 247–248.

53. Matusow, *The Unraveling of America,* pp. 104–105; James Sundquist, *Politics and Policy: The Eisenhower, Kennedy and Johnson Years* (Washington, D.C.: Brookings Institution, 1968), pp. 85–91.

54. Matusow, *The Unraveling of America,* p. 105.

55. Ibid., p. 100.

56. James Singer, "A Subminimum Wage—Jobs for Youths or a Break for Their Employers?" *National Journal* (January 24, 1981), 146–148.

57. Sundquist, *Politics and Policy,* pp. 97–105.

58. Matusow, *The Unraveling of America,* pp. 100–102.

59. Bloom, *Community Mental Health,* pp. 19–25.

60. Steiner, *State of Welfare,* pp. 35–40.

61. David Halberstam, *The Best and the Brightest* (New York: Random House, 1972), pp. 154–301.

62. Robert Caro, *The Years of Lyndon Johnson* (New York: Knopf, 1982); Doris Kearns, *Lyndon Johnson and the American Dream* (New York: Harper & Row, 1976), pp. 19–96.

63. Kearns, *Lyndon Johnson,* pp. 103–106.

64. Ibid., p. 179; Wicker, *JFK and LBJ,* pp. 161–163.

65. Joseph Califano, *The Triumph and Tragedy of Lyndon Johnson: The White House Years* (New York: Simon & Schuster, 1991), pp. 106–121.

66. Wicker, *JFK and LBJ,* pp. 163–169; Kearns, *Lyndon Johnson,* pp. 170–176.

67. Kearns, *Lyndon Johnson,* pp. 190, 224–227; Wicker, *JFK and LBJ,* pp. 209–211.

68. Vaughn Bornet, *The Presidency of Lyndon B. Johnson* (Lawrence, Kans.: University of Kansas, 1983), pp. 134, 225, 333, 343; Patterson, *America's Struggle,* p. 141; and Wicker, *JFK and LBJ,* pp. 177–178.

69. Kearns, *Lyndon Johnson,* pp. 190, 224–227.

70. Wicker, *JFK and LBJ,* pp. 212–235.

71. Sundquist, *Politics and Policy,* pp. 259–271.

72. Matusow, *The Unraveling of America,* pp. 203–213.

73. Ibid., pp. 180–187.

74. Ambrose, *Eisenhower, the President,* Vol. II, p. 425.

75. Williams, *Eyes on the Prize,* pp. 23, 32.

76. Ibid., p. 23.

77. Paul Starr, *The Social Transformation of American Medicine* (New York: Basic Books, 1984), pp. 369–370.

78. Ibid., pp. 97–103, 373; Frank Thompson, *Health Policy and the Bureaucracy: Politics and Implementation* (Cambridge, Mass.: M.I.T. Press, 1981), pp. 180–185.

79. Nancy Eustis, Jay Greenberg, and Sharon Patten, *Long-Term Care for Older Persons: A Policy Perspective* (Pacific Grove, Calif.: Brooks/Cole, 1984), pp. 135–137.

80. Ibid., pp. 133–135.

81. Starr, *The Social Transformation,* pp. 375–378.

82. Many legislative proposals to develop innovative outreach and community projects have been considered. See Eustis, Greenberg, and Patten, *Long-Term Care,* pp. 189–192.

83. Rosemary Stevens, *Welfare Medicine in America: The Case of Medicaid* (New York: Free Press, 1974), pp. 51–71.

84. Ibid., p. 131.

85. Karen Davis and Cathy Schoen, *Health and the War on Poverty: A Ten-Year Appraisal* (Washington, D.C.: Brookings Institution, 1978), pp. 62–67; Thompson, *Health Policy,* pp. 148–153.

86. Davis and Schoen, *Health and the War on Poverty,* pp. 67–91; Dorothy Kupcha, "Medicaid: In or Out of the Mainstream?" *California Journal,* 10 (May 1979), 181–183.

87. Donald Gelfand and Jody Olsen, *The Aging Network: Programs and Services* (New York: Springer, 1980), pp. 9–16.

88. William Lammers, *Public Policy and the Aging* (Washington, D.C.: Congressional Quarterly Press, 1983), pp. 180–183.

89. Sundquist, *Politics and Policy,* pp. 210–215.

90. Matusow, *The Unraveling of America,* pp. 223–226.

91. Aaron, *Politics and the Professors,* pp. 70–92.

92. Bornet, *The Presidency of Lyndon Johnson,* pp. 223–224.

93. Ibid., pp. 224–227.

94. Sundquist, *Politics and Policy,* pp. 134–150.

95. Daniel Moynihan, *Maximum Feasible Misunderstanding: Community Action in the War on Poverty* (New York: Free Press, 1969), pp. 79–100.

96. Matusow, *The Unraveling of America,* pp. 243–265.

97. Burke, *Nixon's Good Deed,* pp. 18, 23–24.

98. Matusow, *The Unraveling of America,* pp. 266–267.

99. Davis and Schoen, *Health and the War on Poverty,* pp. 133–134, 177–189.

100. Matusow, *The Unraveling of America,* p. 266.

101. Bruce Jansson, *The History and Politics of Selected Children's Programs and Related Legislation in the Context of Four Models of Political Behavior.* Doctoral dissertation (Chicago: University of Chicago, 1975), pp. 145–146, 160–161.

102. Steiner, *State of Welfare,* pp. 40–50.

103. Burke, *Nixon's Good Deed,* pp. 22–24, 35–41.

104. Califano, *The Triumph and Tragedy of Lyndon Johnson,* p. 149.

105. William Gibbons, *The U.S. Government and the Vietnam War: Executive and Legislative Roles and Relationships,* Part III (Princeton, N.J.: Princeton University Press, 1990).

106. Michael Boll, *National Security Planning: Roosevelt Through Reagan* (Lexington, Ky.: University of Kentucky Press, 1988).

107. See oral histories by Walter Heller at the Lyndon Johnson Presidential Library.

108. Califano, *The Triumph and Tragedy of Lyndon Johnson,* pp. 106–121.

109. Ibid., pp. 94–97.

110. Ibid., pp. 97–98.

111. Ibid., p. 111.

112. Matusow, *The Unraveling of America,* pp. 204–206.

113. Ibid., p. 205.

114. Ibid., pp. 422–426; Hodgson, *America in Our Time,* pp. 368–383.

115. Matusow, *The Unraveling of America,* pp. 345–360.

116. William Leuchtenberg, *The Perils of Prosperity,* (Chicago: University of Chicago Press, 1958), p. 173.

117. Califano, *The Triumph and Tragedy of Lyndon Johnson,* p. 248.

118. Gloria Emerson, *Winners and Losers* (New York: Random House, 1976), p. 357; Guenter Lewy, *America in Vietnam* (New York: Oxford University Press, 1978), p. 445; and Alan Millette, ed., *A Short History of the Vietnam Conflict* (Bloomington, Ind.: University of Indiana, 1978), p. 131.

119. Kearns, *Lyndon Johnson,* pp. 251–275; Wicker, *JFK and LBJ,* pp. 252–253.

120. Matusow, *The Unraveling of America,* pp. 376–394.

121. Kearns, *Lyndon Johnson,* pp. 302–304.

122. Leuchtenberg, *In the Shadow of FDR,* pp. 147–150.

123. Susan Faludi, *Backlash: The Undeclared War Against American Women* (New York: Crown Publishers, 1991), p. 56.

124. Ibid., p. 57.

125. Cynthia Harrison, *On Account of Sex: The Politics of Women's Issues, 1945–1968* (Berkeley: University of California Press, 1988), pp. 3–23.

126. Ibid., pp. 89–105.

127. Ibid., pp. 139–156.

128. Betty Friedan, *The Feminine Mystique* (New York: W.W. Norton, 1963).

129. Ibid., p. 15.

130. Ibid., p. 282.

131. Ibid., pp. 338–378.

132. Harrison, *On Account of Sex,* pp. 176–180.

133. Ibid., pp. 187–191.

134. Ibid., p. 200.

135. Ibid., pp. 201–202.

136. Ibid., p. 171.

137. Jonathan Katz, *Gay American History,* p. 99.

138. John D'Emilio, *Sexual Politics, Sexual Communities: The Making of a Homosexual Minority in the United States, 1940–1970* (Chicago: University of Chicago Press, 1983).

139. Ibid., p. 35.

140. Ibid., p. 44.

141. Ibid., p. 46.

142. Ibid., p. 49.

143. Ibid., pp. 124–125.

144. Ibid., pp. 129–148.

145. Ibid., p. 217.

146. Ibid., p. 235.

147. James Jennings, "The Puerto Rican Community: Its Political Background." In F. Chris Garcia, ed., *Latinos and the Political System* (Notre Dame, Ind.: University of Notre Dame Press, 1988), p. 65.

148. Juan Gomez Quinones, *Chicano Politics* (Albuquerque, N.M.: University of New Mexico Press, 1990), pp. 101–153.

149. Jennings, "The Puerto Rican Community," p. 75.

150. Theodore Taylor, *The Bureau of Indian Affairs* (Boulder, Colo.: Westview Press, 1984), pp. 18–19.

151. Ibid., p. 25.

152. Ibid., p. 27.

153. Ronald Takaki, *Strangers from a Different Shore* (Boston: Little, Brown, 1989), pp. 406–420.

154. Ibid., p. 419.

155. Angelo Falcon, "Black and Latino Politics in New York City: Race and Ethnicity in a Changing Urban Context." In Garcia, ed., *Latinos and the Political System,* pp. 172–173.

156. Stanley Wenocur and Michael Reisch, *From Charity to Enterprise: The Development of American Social Work in a Market Economy* (Urbana, Ill.: University of Illinois Press, 1989), pp. 211–213.

157. Ibid., pp. 252–255.

158. Jack Rothman, "Macro Social Work in a Tightening Economy," *Social Work,* 24 (May 1980), 274–282.

159. Leslie Leighninger, *Social Work: Search for Identity* (New York: Greenwood Press, 1987), p. 217.

160. Ibid., p. 217.

161. Ibid., pp. 214–215.

162. Burke, *Nixon's Good Deed,* pp. 20, 22–24, 36–39.

163. Lawrence O'Brien, *No Final Victories: A Life in Politics from John F. Kennedy to Watergate* (Garden City, N.Y.: Doubleday, 1974), pp. 196–197.

164. Kearns, *Lyndon Johnson,* pp. 282–284.

165. Jack Meyer, "Budget Cuts in the Reagan Administration: A Question of Fairness." In D. Lee Bawden, ed., *The Social Contract Revisited: Aims and Outcomes of President Reagan's Social Welfare Policy* (Washington, D.C.: Urban Institute, 1984), p. 36.

10

C H A P T E R

The Paradoxical Era: 1968–1980

Selected Orienting Events

1968	Richard Nixon wins narrow presidential victory over Hubert Humphrey
1969	Nixon proposes Family Assistance Plan
1970	Family Planning and Population Research Act enacted; Occupational Safety and Health Act (OSHA) enacted
1971	National eligibility standards established for Food Stamp program
1972	Local Fiscal Assistance Act establishes general revenue sharing; Social Security benefits indexed to rise with inflation; Supplementary Security Income (SSI) program established
1972	Nixon wins landslide victory over George McGovern
1973	Comprehensive Employment and Training Act (CETA) enacted; Food Stamp program federalized and made mandatory; Rehabilitation Act passed
1973	Supreme Court issues *Roe* v. *Wade* decision, which legalizes abortion
1974	Juvenile Justice and Delinquency Prevention Act enacted; Title XX (social services) added to Social Security Act
1974	Nixon resigns presidency under threat of impeachment due to the Watergate scandal and is succeeded by Gerald Ford
1975	Education for All Handicapped Children Act passed; earned-income tax credit (EITC) enacted for poor wage earners
1976	Jimmy Carter elected president
1977	Carter introduces welfare reform plan, which is later defeated
1978	Report of President's Commission on Mental Health issued
1979	Carter introduces unsuccessful national health-insurance plan; Office of Education separated from the Department of Health, Education, and Welfare (HEW), which becomes the Department of Health and Human Services (DHHS)
1980	Adoption Assistance and Child Welfare Act enacted; Mental Health Systems Act passed

Presidents Richard Nixon (1969–1974), Gerald Ford (1974–1976), and Jimmy Carter (1977–1980) were relatively conservative presidents who had little outward interest in major social reforms. Yet social spending rose dramatically during this ostensibly conservative period. Indeed, few people realize that the first term of Nixon's presidency (1969–1972) ranks as a major period of social reform. Sar Levitan, a noted policy commentator, argued that "the greatest extensions of the modern welfare system were enacted under the conservative Presidency of Richard Nixon with bipartisan congressional support, dwarfing in size and scope the initiatives of Lyndon Johnson's Great Society."[1] Although Levitan seems to forget that many of Nixon's reforms consisted of simply expanding programs he inherited from the Great Society, such as the Food Stamps program, he correctly notes that many social reforms and considerable increases in social spending occurred in the Nixon years; Tom Wicker, a biographer of Nixon, concurs.[2] Nevertheless, Nixon was extremely conservative in much of his rhetoric and turned sharply to the right in 1972. With its conflicting tendencies, this was a transitional era between the reformist period of the Great Society and the conservative presidency of Ronald Reagan in the 1980s.

RICHARD NIXON: POLITICAL OPPORTUNIST

Richard Nixon achieved early successes in House and Senate races in the late 1940s and early 1950s by alleging that his opponents had left-wing tendencies and by spearheading congressional investigations of Alger Hiss, a State Department official who was accused and ultimately convicted of spying for Russia. These tactics earned him the disdain of liberals, but they brought sufficient public support that Dwight Eisenhower chose Nixon as his running mate in his presidential campaigns of 1952 and 1956. Nixon obtained the Republican nomination for the presidency in 1960, but narrowly lost to John Kennedy. After losing a bid for a California Senate seat in 1962, he retired from politics, only

to resurface as the Republican presidential candidate in 1968 against Hubert Humphrey, whom he subsequently defeated by a thin margin.

Liberal critics of Nixon had long accused him of willingness to use red-baiting and other dubious tactics to secure power, but his opportunism also led him to support liberal domestic policies when he believed they would enhance his political career. These calculations sometimes led him to support moderate positions during the 1950s, when Republicans understood that frontal attacks on New Deal programs, such as Social Security, were unpopular.[3]

Nixon correctly perceived that a power vacuum existed in the Republican party in the wake of the Democratic landslide victory over Goldwater in 1964. By assuming the role of mediator and statesman within the leaderless and demoralized party and by aggressively campaigning for Republicans of all persuasions in succeeding years, he successfully positioned himself for the presidential bid in 1968.[4] Nixon obtained the nomination for the presidency in 1968 because he convinced each segment of the Republican party, including liberal, moderate, and conservative wings, that he represented them.[5]

His election campaign in 1968 did not suggest that he would soon initiate or support a series of domestic reforms. Sensing that the Democratic contender, Hubert Humphrey, was vulnerable among working- and middle-class voters because he was identified with the Vietnam conflict and with black power and other reform groups, Nixon avoided major social issues, promised peace with honor, and pledged he would be tough on the issue of crime. He appealed to Southerners by promising to terminate federal efforts to desegregate schools and by giving Senator Strom Thurmond, a conservative Southerner, a prominent role in selecting the law-and-order theme of his campaign. He chose Spiro Agnew as his vice president in an obvious effort to appeal to white backlash sentiment and repeatedly attacked alleged social reform excesses of the Great Society.[6]

Nixon's conservative rhetoric in the campaign of 1968 was not a good predictor of his subsequent policy choices, particularly in the first three years of his presidency. His motivation for supporting various social reforms defies easy analysis, because he was an enigmatic man, to whom Churchill's characterization of Russia ("a riddle wrapped in a mystery inside an enigma") might aptly apply. Wicker contends that Nixon was not devoid of sympathy for the poor, because of his own experience of poverty during his childhood; however, Wicker also notes that Nixon's choices were dictated by political concerns, such as his desire to broaden the base of the Republican party.[7] Indeed, other writers place considerable stock in the Disraeli thesis—that is, that Nixon's reading of English history inspired him to be an American conservative who, much like Disraeli, the English conservative prime minister of the 19th century, would support certain reforms in order to pull new working-class constituents into his political party.[8] Likewise, many theorists believe that he was persuaded by the arguments of Kevin Phillips, who maintained that the Republican party could construct a new majority by attracting large numbers of working-class voters, Catholics, members of white ethnic groups, and residents of the Sunbelt.[9] Yet other commentators suggest that much of his behavior derived from a perverse pleasure in upstaging or surprising the Democrats.[10] Another intriguing theory is that Nixon supported social reform mainly to retain the support of liberals in both political parties for his foreign policies, including his Vietnam policy.[11] If this was indeed the case, it represented an interesting reversal from Franklin Roosevelt and Lyndon Johnson, both of whom had to *cut* social spending to placate conservative congressional foes. Nixon also knew that Democrats, who controlled both houses of Congress, would push him to support many liberal measures. Doubtless, Nixon was often driven by some combination of these motivations, but the bottom line was that he supported or agreed to an array of social reforms.

Nevertheless, Nixon's reform strategy rested on profound ambivalence, both ideological and political. Nixon was not instinctively a liberal, even if he was willing to espouse liberal causes for political reasons. He despised many liberal Republican sen-

ators, such as Charles Percy of Illinois. Many of his advisors, as well as broad sections of his party, were conservative and unlikely to support liberal policies. An inner circle of ambivalence thus existed in the White House in Nixon's first term and led to contradictory policies. By 1972, this ambivalence turned to outright opposition to many social policies and to a determination to cut social spending, even by impounding funds that Congress had already appropriated for specific programs.[12]

NIXON'S STRATEGY: FLOATING COALITIONS AND OUTBIDDING

Nixon both initiated social legislation and responded positively to congressional initiatives. When Nixon supported social reforms, he used a floating coalition and political outbidding. The *floating coalition strategy* depended on fashioning a coalition that included the support of some liberal Republicans, some moderate Republicans who were loyal to the president, and some Democratic liberals and moderates who placed their ideology before their party—that is, a bipartisan coalition of moderates and liberals to oppose conservatives; the precise composition of the coalition varied from issue to issue.[13] In the *political outbidding strategy,* he endorsed social reforms that were initiated by Democrats but offered expansive amendments to them—or accepted them with little change—so that he could obtain partial credit for their passage.[14] It was a strange spectacle to many political observers; no Republican president since Theodore Roosevelt had sought to enact so many domestic reforms, much less to try to beat the Democrats at their own game.

Floating coalitions and outbidding represented bold strategies that could be successful only in a particular political environment. To employ this strategy, Nixon first had to want to expand the political base of the Republican party and had to believe, as well, that blue-collar and white ethnic voters desired social reforms. Second, he had to

INSERT 10.1   CRITICAL ANALYSIS: SERVICES VERSUS HARD BENEFITS

Nixon framed social policy as a choice between social services and hard benefits. Was he correct?

1. Analyze the functions of *both* service and benefit programs in the welfare state.
2. What would society look like if either kind of program were largely eliminated?
3. Choosing any major social problem, discuss how those upon whom it has the greatest impact often need both social services and hard benefits.

believe that he could persuade members of his own party that the social reforms he developed were different from the Democratic reforms that they had opposed since the New Deal. Where Lyndon Johnson had sought programs that emphasized social and medical services, community participation of the poor, and expanded roles for the federal government, Nixon sought reforms that provided jobs and income, expanded the policy roles of local governments, and used private market mechanisms rather than direct government provision.[15] He believed that, by portraying his programs as "hard benefits" that were superior to the social services offered by Democrats, he could gain the support of many Republicans and also of blue-collar voters, local officials, and the business community. To underscore the distinctiveness of Republican reforms, Nixon unleashed scathing attacks on the innovations of the Great Society, which he depicted as undisciplined and ineffective programs that enriched bureaucrats and social workers.[16]

Third, Nixon had to believe that increased domestic spending would not jeopardize the nation's economic growth by causing deficits or by drawing capital from investments. He believed that, following the Vietnam conflict, there would be economic surpluses sufficient to fund new programs, and he favored the use of increased social spending to bring about economic recovery during and after a sharp recession in 1970.[17] Finally, he needed to have a significant number of liberal advisors to provide him with reform ideas and to fend off conservative advisors who were beholden to the conservative wing of the Republican party; nevertheless, in keeping with his policy ambivalence in his first term, he also appointed many

conservative advisors.[18] He named the relatively liberal Robert Finch as his secretary of the Department of Health, Education, and Welfare and, when Finch suffered a nervous breakdown, replaced him with Elliot Richardson. He appointed Daniel Moynihan, a moderate Democrat who was critical of the Great Society but favored income, job, and other reforms, as the director of his Urban Affairs Council.

 FROM STRATEGY TO POLICY

Reforms enacted during Nixon's first term (1969–1972) included the Supplementary Security Income (SSI) program; major revisions in the Food Stamp program; indexing of the Social Security program; revenue sharing; the consolidation of social services in Title XX to the Social Security Act; addition of a family planning program to the Public Health Act; assorted health legislation; development of affirmative action policies; establishment of the Occupational Safety and Health Administration (OSHA); and policies that led to the desegregation of virtually all Southern schools. These policy enactments, which would have represented a remarkable achievement even for a Democratic president, were supplemented by two major proposals that were not enacted: a proposal to reform welfare programs (the Family Assistance Program, or FAP) and a proposal for national health insurance. In Nixon's second term (1973–1974), the Comprehensive Employment and Training Act (CETA), the Community Development

Block Grant Program, the Rehabilitation Act of 1973, and the Child Abuse Prevention Act of 1973 were enacted.

Welfare Policy

Virtually no one was satisfied with the AFDC program. Liberals believed it limited assistance to families with single parents in many states and disliked its low eligibility levels and often paltry grants; conservatives believed it encouraged substantial numbers of women not to work and included too many working mothers who had retained their eligibility owing to the work-incentive provisions of 1967.[19] Faced with this cross-fire from liberals and conservatives, Nixon had several options. He could have sought incremental and liberalizing reforms to increase the levels of benefits in low-benefit states, as suggested by a task force headed by Richard Nathan; or he could have favored incremental and conservative reforms, such as those suggested by economist Arthur Burns, to strengthen the work requirement and to create public service jobs.

At the urging of Daniel Moynihan, however, Nixon decided to seek a comprehensive reform of the nation's welfare system, partly because his advisors feared that the Democrats would preempt the issue by announcing their own reform measure from a commission that had been appointed by Johnson.[20] Moynihan convinced Nixon that his plan offered a lasting policy solution to a vexing problem, because it focused on provision of income, work incentives, and public service jobs. At a critical juncture, Moynihan told Nixon that the new program would permit the termination of scores of social workers, whom Nixon detested and associated with Democratic reforms, and would extend benefits to many blue-collar and white ethnic voters, since intact families and working (but poor) persons were both eligible.[21]

Democrats and Republicans alike were astonished when President Nixon announced in August 1969 that he wanted to revamp the nation's welfare programs by establishing a Family Assistance Plan (FAP) to replace the AFDC and AFDC-U programs with a program that would provide federal assistance to all families who fell beneath a federally prescribed minimum income. (Enacted in 1961, AFDC-U had given states the option to offer AFDC assistance to families with unemployed fathers, but fewer than half of them had exercised this option.) FAP provided for all intact families a nationwide guaranteed income that was higher than prevailing welfare standards in many Southern states. It had even more generous work incentives than the 1967 provisions, proposed the creation of large numbers of public service jobs for welfare recipients, and contained a large day-care program. In one policy stroke, then, FAP proposed to repeal the AFDC program and replace it with a national program. It did not constitute truly massive redistribution of resources to the poor, however; it would have provided only $4.5 billion in additional federal outlays.[22] FAP soon became enmeshed in the same cross fire between liberals and conservatives that had plagued the AFDC program. Fearing its defeat by a combination of Republican and Democratic conservatives, Nixon stressed that FAP contained a strong work incentive and work requirement. The legislation breezed through the House, because of the diligent help of Wilbur Mills, chair of the Ways and Means Committee, but it encountered opposition from conservative Republicans and Democrats in the Senate Finance Committee, who succeeded in demonstrating that thousands of FAP recipients would lose eligibility for Medicaid, public housing, and Food Stamps as their welfare benefits and earnings catapulted them above the eligibility ceiling of these programs. Loss of these benefits would, they argued, severely jeopardize recipients' incentives to work.[23] Many liberal senators also attacked FAP because trade unions, which supported the minimum wage, objected to provisions that required federal authorities to pay only the prevailing wages in local jurisdictions. The National Welfare Rights Organization (NWRO), the grass-roots protest movement of welfare recipients, contended that the national minimum benefit should be significantly increased and also objected to work requirements in the legislation. Most members of NWRO, who resided in Northern cities within high-benefit states, would have obtained little direct benefit from FAP, which emphasized improvement of benefits in low-benefit states in the South. NWRO leaders sought amendments to increase benefit levels, weaken the work requirement, expand day-care provisions, and raise wage levels in public service jobs.[24]

Despite this sniping from both conservatives and liberals, FAP came surprisingly close to passage, thanks to numerous amendments that the administration introduced to appease both factions; however, it finally lost a decisive vote in the Senate in 1970. Reintroduced with minor changes in 1971, it was caught in an even more furious exchange between liberals and conservatives and was finally defeated in 1972.[25] FAP's demise was hastened by lack of constituency support; some key legislators noted that they did not receive a single supportive letter in 1971.

An important policy reform was nonetheless achieved. An obscure provision attached to the welfare reform measure in 1971 proposed to replace the adult welfare programs of Old-Age Assistance, Aid to the Blind, and Aid to the Disabled with the Supplementary Security Income (SSI) program.[26] While FAP was defeated, its SSI provision was enacted in 1972. SSI proposed to federalize these adult programs, just as FAP had proposed to federalize AFDC, but older persons and those with disabilities were not associated with the long tradition of controversy that had beset AFDC beneficiaries, who were variously accused of malingering, seeking welfare funds to have more kids, and leading immoral lives.

The federal government assumed responsibility for most of the welfare costs for these adult recipients under SSI. Since SSI was administered by the Social Security Administration and its local offices, elderly citizens no longer received their financial support from public welfare offices and so were spared the stigma visited upon welfare recipients. The legislation rescued older persons from the often punitive federal-state Old-Age Assistance program, assisted hundreds of thousands of deinstitutionalized persons with mental disorders, and provided funds for many persons with physical disabilities, including Vietnam vets. Over the years, the SSI rolls expanded considerably—from 3.1 million persons in 1970 to 4.1 million persons in 1980.[27]

SSI nonetheless had serious flaws. Elderly persons and those with disabilities were allowed to keep their homes and could not have their estates attached, but they were not entitled to use Food Stamps. Grants were hardly munificent. Additionally, elderly persons who lived in states that did not supplement the federal minimum benefits received lower benefits than their peers in more generous states. The early federal guidelines that defined mental and physical disability were vague; Presidents Carter and Reagan instituted guidelines and procedures that discontinued grants to tens of thousands of persons with serious disabilities.[28]

Democrats had initiated and received political credit for the Food Stamp program when it was enacted in 1964. They continued their leadership in this area when George McGovern, the liberal Democratic senator, held hearings during the late 1960s on issues of nutrition and hunger in the United States.[29] He contended that the Food Stamp program addressed the nutritional needs of only a small fraction of hungry Americans. Furthermore, conservatives had shown that the eligibility criteria for Food Stamps did not mesh with the FAP criteria. Nixon believed that he could both solve the technical problems of Food Stamps and regain the initiative from the Democrats by federalizing Food Stamps, establishing national eligibility standards, making participation in the program mandatory for all states, and developing a revised benefit schedule that would provide additional benefits to families with no earned income, as well as larger families. By securing these bold changes, Nixon transformed Food Stamps from a welfare program to a program used by large numbers of the working poor.[30] These liberal reforms were enacted in 1970 and 1973 and dramatically increased the size of the program—from 10.4 million enrollees in 1970 to 19.4 million enrollees in 1980.[31] A broad constituency of protest groups, liberals, agricultural interests, and conservative politicians from rural areas supported these reforms.

Social Security

Congress had periodically revised Social Security benefits upward to compensate for their erosion by inflation; this ritual was used by both Democrats and Republicans to garner support from elderly constituents. But members of both parties saw a need to index benefits—that is, to adjust benefits automatically and annually so as to compensate for the erosion in their value due to inflation. Nixon proposed a small benefit increase in Social Security and indexing in 1972. However, Wilbur Mills, a Democratic Congressman with presidential aspirations, realized that championing the needs of elderly voters would benefit Democrats in the 1972 elections and consequently proposed not only indexing but also a 20% increase in benefits![32] Such generous increases would normally have required major increases in payroll taxes. However, Mills refrained from proposing such tax increases, in part to avoid the ensuing political outcry but also because actuaries for the Social Security Administration, whose new economic models were based on overoptimistic assumptions, predicted that the trust fund would remain solvent even with massive increases in benefits. Nixon decided to support Mills's proposals, so as to obtain partial credit for them and to compensate for the defeat of FAP, which had deprived his administration of credit for a major social reform.[33]

Everyone realized that indexing would increase benefits, but virtually no one predicted that the onset of double-digit inflation in the 1970s would lead to extraordinary increases in Social Security benefits—or that the technical formulas used to compute benefit increases would allow these increases even to exceed rates of inflation.[34] The old system of incremental and periodic benefit increases had been replaced by an automatic system that led to rapid increases in benefits without associated increases in payroll taxes. Furthermore, an increase in the ratio of benefit receivers to employed workers also depleted the fund. Benefit outlays of the Social Security program increased from $68.2 billion in 1970 to $135 billion in 1980.[35]

As with FAP and SSI, competitive bidding between the two parties and Nixon's desire to expand the base of the Republican party led a conservative president to support massive increases in social spending. Nixon's failure to increase payroll taxes, when coupled with a steady decline in the proportion of wage earners to retirees, ensured the emergence of a funding crisis for Social Security, which had to be addressed by subsequent presidents. However, it's largely as a result of the Social Security increases that the percentage of elderly persons below the poverty line decreased from 29.5% to 15% between 1967 and 1979—and to less than 5% when the value of in-kind benefits, such as medical care, was included.

Revenue Sharing and Social Services

In response to Republican concerns that the New Deal and the Great Society had concentrated excessive power in the federal bureaucracy, Nixon developed the idea of revenue sharing: He proposed to give federal funds directly to local units of government, with few strings attached, so that local officials could decide how they wished to use them. Nixon also had more sinister motivations for this policy. He had become increasingly paranoid about the federal bureaucracy in his first three years of office and was convinced that federal bureaucrats, in liaison with sympathetic legislators and supportive (liberal) interest groups, had wrested power from him. By giving funds directly to the local and state units of government, he hoped to bypass the federal bureaucracy and even, to some extent, the Congress, which no longer would be able to develop specific programs. (Congress would merely allocate funds that local governments could use, more or less, as they pleased.)[36]

The Local Fiscal Assistance Act of 1972 gave funds to local governments to use for their operating expenses. To supplement this general revenue sharing, Nixon also proposed special revenue sharing, in the form of six block grants to local governments to provide resources in broad areas such as housing and job training. This special revenue sharing would, Nixon argued, eventually replace many of the existing federal programs, which he portrayed as encumbered by excessive federal rules, guidelines, and regulations.[37] Why not, he asked, simultaneously terminate some existing programs and give local governments relatively unrestricted funds to spend on broad program areas? He had little success in obtaining special revenue sharing, however, because many members of Congress did not want to relinquish their control of federal programs and feared that some states would deny support to relatively powerless groups who benefited from existing federal programs. Nixon obtained passage of only two special revenue-sharing programs, the Comprehensive Employment and Training Act of 1973 (CETA) and the Community Development Block Grant portion of the Housing and Community Development Act of 1974 (CDBG).

General and special revenue sharing were suited to Nixon's political strategy, for they represented a brand of social reform that was different from traditional Democratic programs. Some of Lyndon Johnson's advisors, notably economist Walter Heller, had themselves urged passage of revenue sharing, but Johnson had demurred in favor of traditional categorical programs.[38] The policy field was thus open to Nixon, and he seized the opportunity to enact his version of reform. By so doing, Nixon hoped to gain the support of state and local officials, who liked revenue sharing because it augmented their funds. Between 1973 and 1980, the federal government paid roughly $6 billion a year in general revenue sharing to local governments, which substantially eased their fiscal problems during the 1970s.[39] Critics noted, however, that local authorities often did not use these resources to help disadvantaged citizens. In one city, CDBG funds were used to build a municipal golf course!

Job-training programs had proliferated in a disorderly fashion during the 1960s. Nixon proposed to consolidate them in the Comprehensive Employment and Training Act (CETA). The administrative mechanism devised for CETA vested considerable power in state and local organizations, known as prime sponsors, which issued contracts with public agencies and industry to provide jobs

INSERT 10.2   ETHICAL ANALYSIS OF KEY ISSUES AND POLICIES: SHOULD WE BLOCK-GRANT ALL FEDERAL PROGRAMS?

The concept of returning federal funds to the states has deep roots in American history. For example, President Andrew Jackson proposed such transfers when he ran a budget surplus. More recently, the liberal economist Walter Heller was a prime advocate of revenue sharing in the 1960s.

The federal government *could* transfer all of its tax revenues, save those used for military and international programs, to the states and localities. Were this to happen, what would be the consequences? Would certain vulnerable populations, like impoverished single mothers, be adequately helped by state and local governments once they lost the entitlement status that they enjoy under the AFDC program? What about the medical needs of older people who use Medicaid—or poor people who currently use the Food Stamp program?

Yet some transfers of funds are probably beneficial, because local and state governments do not possess the borrowing power, or the large income-tax revenues, of the federal government. What kinds of programs could states and localities implement with little or no guidance from federal authorities—and which ones should federal authorities retain?

and job training. Under Title VI, CETA subsidized hundreds of thousands of public service jobs in both public and nonprofit agencies. These jobs were not means-tested; applicants had merely to demonstrate that they were unemployed. Incredibly, a Republican president had proposed and obtained enactment of a proposal that recalled the public works programs of the 1930s.[40]

As we discussed in Chapter 9, Congress gave states 75% matching funds in 1962 to provide social services to existing or potential recipients of AFDC. Some states seemed unaware of the legislation or used the money only for traditional services, such as home visits to AFDC recipients, but discerning policy analysts in various states, including California, Oregon, Pennsylvania, and Washington, realized that they could use these funds to develop a range of programs. Furthermore, when a federal administrator who prized expansiveness replaced a cost-conscious one, the use of the funds increased dramatically; some state officials were allowed to use the funds for drug, mental-health, public education, and even highway construction programs.[41] In 1972, the Nixon administration sought to place a ceiling on this runaway program. To protect the program and to counter HEW regulations that limited its services to persons currently receiving or applying for welfare, the Congress created Title XX of the Social Security Act, which allocated funds to states according to a prescribed formula for use—with broad latitude by each state—in programs to enhance individuals' ability to be self-supporting, family care or self-care, community-based care, and institutional care. The legislation was enacted in 1974.[42] States usually chose relatively traditional services, such as day care, that were provided by established agencies. To impose discipline on the program, a ceiling of $2.5 billion was established for annual expenditures—a figure that remained relatively constant in succeeding years. Title XX represented the first time that the federal government had officially committed itself to funding a variety of social services to persons who were usually near or under the poverty line. It also illustrated the reformist nature of Nixon's first term. Nixon, who despised services and social workers, did not veto legisla-

tion that covered services for existing and potential welfare recipients in a block grant.

Civil Rights

Nixon's strange mixture of conservative rhetoric and liberal deeds was nowhere more conspicuous than in civil rights. Nixon had won five Southern states in the presidential election of 1968 and hoped to increase his Southern gains in 1972, but he feared that George Wallace would again try to sweep the South by supporting racist policies. Thus, Nixon did not support desegregation of Southern schools in 1969 and 1970. He fired a liberal attorney in the Justice Department who favored cutting federal funds from segregated districts, and he supported a proposed constitutional amendment to prohibit busing. Nixon often used rhetoric that relied on code words—for example, "the silent majority of law-abiding citizens"—to appeal to racial animosities in the broader population.

Yet some commentators believe that Nixon's policies on racial issues constitute a strength of his administration.[43] When federal courts insisted that intentional segregation had to be terminated, Nixon finally relented and empowered George Shultz, his secretary of labor, to organize a series of Southern committees that succeeded in securing voluntary desegregation. When the number of African American students in segregated Southern schools was reduced from 68% in 1968 to 8% in 1972, the cycle of reform in the South that had begun with the Civil Rights Acts of 1964 and 1965 was completed.[44] Nixon's successes in the South were not matched by similar efforts in the North, however; he chose not to use busing to combat de facto segregation.

Between 1971 and 1974, Congress and the administration enacted a variety of laws and administrative measures that prohibited gender-based discrimination in training programs and employment. HEW instituted legal action to force colleges to end discrimination against women, just as the Supreme Court struck down various local laws that discriminated against women. The Justice Department brought suit against such corporations as American Telephone and Telegraph (AT&T) and won large awards for women who had been denied promotions. Women made extraordinary gains in obtaining training and membership in the professions and business.[45] Nixon approved the Equal Employment Opportunity Act of 1972, which gave the Equal Employment Opportunity Commission the power to use court rulings to enforce its orders. His administration included women in affirmative action orders that were sent to federal contractors.[46]

Moreover, the Nixon administration developed the so-called Philadelphia plan, which required building contractors that obtained federal contracts to institute affirmative action—a policy stoutly opposed by trade unions. This plan was subsequently extended to all federal contractors, as well as to state and local employees such as local police and fire departments. (These policies led to extraordinary increases in the employment of people of color and women by public agencies.)[47]

The Rehabilitation Act of 1973 was a historic measure to accord persons with disabilities protections from discrimination; section 504 states that "no otherwise qualified handicapped individual . . . shall . . . be excluded from participating in, be denied the benefits of, or be subjected to discrimination under any program of activity receiving federal assistance." This legislation, as well as associated lawsuits, led to massive efforts to make buildings, public transportation, and jobs accessible to persons with disabilities.[48] Funds were appropriated to assist the mainstreaming of students with disabilities in public schools under the Education for All Handicapped Act of 1975.[49]

Health Policy and Other Legislation

Various health and family measures were enacted during Nixon's administration. Medicare was revised in 1973 to extend coverage to nonelderly persons with kidney disease. The Health Maintenance Act of 1973 provided seed money to promote the establishment of medical organizations funded by annual payments from enrollees rather than traditional fee-for-service payments.[50] The Family

Planning and Population Research Act of 1970 had helped four million low-income women, including 1.3 million teenagers, obtain family-planning services by 1980.[51] The Juvenile Justice and Delinquency Act of 1974 provided resources to local juvenile diversion projects to help runaways and truants, who had previously been stigmatized by court and juvenile detention services.[52] The Child Abuse Prevention Act of 1974 provided research funds to be disseminated to universities and pilot projects to develop effective interventions.[53]

The Occupational Safety and Health Act of 1970 was landmark legislation that propelled the federal government into oversight of the safety standards in American industry, in an era when toxic chemicals and new technology demanded new protections. The Department of Labor was charged with devising standards and establishing local agencies to implement inspection.[54]

Finally, legislation enacted in 1975 established an earned-income tax credit: Workers who earned less than $4,000 were given a tax credit (a payment) equivalent to 10% of their earnings. Though modest, it was the first legislation to use the tax system as a vehicle for giving resources to the poor.

NIXON'S SHIFT FROM REFORM TO CONSERVATISM

Social reform flourished in the first three years of Nixon's first term: Spending for poverty programs had increased by $27 billion in the Kennedy and Johnson administrations (in 1986 dollars), but it increased by $54 billion in the Nixon and Ford administrations.[55] When confronted with a deep recession, trade deficits, and inflation, Nixon even imposed wage and price controls in 1971.[56] But during this liberal period, Nixon's rhetoric remained staunchly conservative, even as he supported reform measures; he regularly lambasted programs of the Great Society, "big spenders," and liberalism and remained silent on the subjects of civil rights and race relations. He repeatedly attacked service programs staffed by social workers, child development specialists, psychologists, psychiatrists, and community activists. He believed that these programs were ineffective, coddled the poor, and represented a misguided Democratic approach to social reform. He sought major reductions in federal funding of neighborhood health centers, community action programs, and community mental health centers.[57] Head Start was saved from massive cuts only because of its extraordinary political popularity.

Nixon's antipathy to service programs was illustrated by his veto of child development legislation in 1971. The Head Start program had stimulated interest in expanding funding for preschool, day-care, regional planning, and advocacy services for children, and some experts were convinced that many families were endangered by high rates of dissolution and women's increasing rates of employment. In that context, legislation was initiated in House and Senate committees to provide a variety of free or low-cost services to American families.

It was uncertain whether Nixon would support this legislation. When his HEW secretary, Elliot Richardson, insisted in 1971 that the legislation be amended to make it more acceptable to the administration, some observers took this as a promising sign. But Nixon vetoed it, with conservative language that reflected the right wing of the Republican party. He charged that the legislation would destroy the institution of the family, which should be retained "in its rightful position as the keystone of our civilization [and] would commit the vast moral authority to [institutional] child rearing as against the family-centered approach." It was a devastating blow to reformers, who were unable to obtain similar legislation in succeeding years.[58]

A changing political climate shaped Nixon's decision by summer 1972—and even more obviously by fall 1973—to disavow new social legislation. It had been reasonable to assume in 1968, after the Great Society, that blue-collar and white ethnic Americans could be wooed by social initiatives like FAP, SSI, national health insurance, and the indexing of Social Security. Partly because of the conservative rhetoric of Nixon and Agnew, however,

many white ethnic, blue-collar, and middle-class persons had become preoccupied with issues of crime, inflation, and government spending by 1972 and had become resentful of African Americans, who were, they believed, receiving unwarranted or disproportionate benefits from federal programs. The term *white backlash* has been used to characterize the resentments of these citizens.[59]

White Americans had also become alarmed by the tactics and language used by the various reform groups that had emerged in the late 1960s.[60] The new militance of these groups stemmed in considerable measure from disillusionment with the Great Society. African Americans realized that the civil rights gains of the 1960s, which had largely addressed legal and overt discrimination in the South, had not slowed the segregation of African Americans into urban ghettoes or the expansion of an African American underclass, whose members had limited education and high unemployment and often depended on AFDC, Food Stamps, and other social programs. Leaders of outgroups—African Americans, women, Latinos, Native Americans, gay men and lesbians, and people with disabilities —spoke of the feelings of inferiority that stemmed from living in a society that overtly or covertly discriminated against them. African Americans urged one another to develop pride in their race and heritage; women advocated feminist education to develop solidarity; Native Americans and Latinos organized protests against government officials, schools, and universities; leaders of the gay and lesbian communities urged their members to declare their sexual orientations publicly and pressured politicians and employers to end discriminatory practices; and people with disabilities demanded access to jobs, buildings, and public transportation. Efforts to mobilize these populations alienated many Americans, who resented the separatism and the challenge to dominant policies that the new rhetoric implied.

Nixon and Agnew realized that they could exploit this situation for their political benefit.[61] Why not, they reasoned, condemn the rhetoric and tactics of these groups in order to turn working- and middle-class persons against activists and reformers? Why not try to identify the Democratic

INSERT 10.3 CRITICAL ANALYSIS: WHAT CREATED ARCHIE BUNKER?

People in the working class or in the lower middle class ought, in theory, to support social programs. Possessing relatively meager resources and experiencing job insecurity, they or their family members sometimes use social programs such as Medicaid and Food Stamps, just as their parents use Medicare. Yet white backlash developed most acutely in this group, such as Catholic voters in the North and white blue-collar voters in the South. Its most celebrated representative is the fictional character Archie Bunker from the TV show "All in the Family."

Analyze why this group, whose ancestors had often been part of the Roosevelt coalition in the New Deal, became disenchanted with the American welfare state, voted for such Presidential candidates as George Wallace in the 1960s, Richard Nixon in the 1970s, and Ronald Reagan in the 1980s, and granted Newt Gingrich a Republican landslide in the 1994 Congressional elections.

What, if anything, might reformers have done differently to retain the good will of this group?

party with these groups—and themselves with "the silent majority of law-abiding citizens"? Their resolve was strengthened when public opinion polls indicated that crime and inflation were the issues of most concern to many Americans, who believed that civil rights, social spending, and social reform efforts had proceeded too rapidly. These sentiments were linked to the growing economic distress of *stagflation,* the combination of high unemployment and inflation.[62] Economic stagnation made some blue-collar Americans fear that African Americans, women, and others might take jobs from them, and inflation reduced the real income of many families and made credit hard to obtain as interest rates soared. Furthermore, many Americans believed that the only way to decrease the rate of inflation was to cut social spending.[63]

Nixon was also quick to capitalize on developments within the Democratic party. Following the 1968 election, Democrats made a concerted effort to increase participation by African Americans, women, and others in party councils, at the expense of the power of incumbent politicians and powerful brokers, such as Mayor Richard Daley of Chicago. These reforms, however, boosted the political fortunes of Richard Nixon, who was able to argue that the Democratic party had been taken over by special interests. When the party reforms allowed a particularly liberal senator—George McGovern— to obtain the Democratic nomination for the presidency in 1972, Nixon portrayed him as an extremist who was beholden to these interests.[64]

Nixon's conservative policies were also promoted, of course, by Republican conservatives, who believed that they represented the mainstream of the party. At first, Nixon's conservative advisors, such as the economist Arthur Burns and Martin Anderson, had been outflanked by liberal advisors, such as Robert Finch, Daniel Moynihan, and Elliot Richardson, but there was a definite thinning in the ranks of liberal advisors as Nixon's first term progressed. Indeed, by 1972, the conservative John Ehrlichman emerged as his leading advisor on domestic matters.[65]

Soon after his reelection in 1972, Nixon began a personal war against liberals that was motivated by his political decision to move toward the right, to fight inflation with budget cuts, and to discipline federal civil servants, who, he had come to believe, colluded with special interests and liberal congressional aides to resist the implementation of conservative policies. Nixon manipulated the civil service system to place into office conservative persons of dubious merit, impounded funds that had already been appropriated by Congress for social programs, proposed major decreases in the funds of most major programs, and demanded a major reduction of the federal work force. Because many members of Congress and the federal bureaucracy were embittered by these tactics, an atmosphere of suspicion and polarization developed in the Capitol.[66]

Nixon's effectiveness in waging this war against liberalism was stymied, however, by the aftermath of a break-in at the Democratic campaign headquarters in the Watergate Hotel in 1972. Investigations by the Justice Department and by Congress, which focused at first on the burglars, soon implicated presidential aides, cabinet officials, and Nixon himself. The Congress was on the verge of impeachment proceedings when Nixon resigned from office in August 1974. He was succeeded by Vice President Gerald Ford.

THE BRIEF REIGN OF GERALD FORD

Ford was a political conservative who had spent years in the Congress criticizing programs of the Great Society. He was, moreover, an unimaginative man, who was unable to initiate legislation even when urged by his advisors. As did Nixon, he became even more conservative as his term progressed. Nelson Rockefeller, his vice president, pressured Ford to endorse urban development reforms, to expand health care, and to support other policy reforms, but his power, as well as that of other liberal Republicans, was soon eclipsed in internal power struggles within the administration.[67] Ford's major policy became the presidential veto, which he used with remarkable frequency to stymie legislation and spending increases proposed by the Congress.

Because of Democratic majorities in both houses, Congress was able to override a number of vetoes and to increase funding for school lunches, education, and health-care programs. Ford finally realized that increases in social spending were needed to counter the deep recession of 1975, though Congress had to override his veto to establish a public works program to help the unemployed. His term can best be characterized as a continuing stalemate between conservatives and liberals over the size of social spending.[68]

Little social legislation was enacted during Ford's tenure. The Education for All Handicapped Children Act, passed in 1975, provided federal subsidies to schools so that children with physical and mental disabilities could be mainstreamed into regular classes. Although it allowed many children with disabilities to escape special institutions, inadequate funding in succeeding years much diminished its effect.[69]

JIMMY CARTER: OUTSIDER IN THE WHITE HOUSE

A journalist who had covered five prior presidential campaigns wrote that he had never experienced more pervasive suspicion of government among the electorate than in 1976.[70] Jimmy Carter, an astute Southern politician who had recently finished his term as governor of Georgia, decided in 1972 to mount a campaign to secure the Democratic nomination for the presidency in 1976. He was relatively unknown outside the South and had virtually no links to trade unions, powerful incumbent politicians, or other groups that usually helped Democratic aspirants, but his relative obscurity became an asset in the post-Watergate political climate of 1976. When he lambasted the federal bureaucracy, red tape, and undue centralization of authority in the nation, he did not seem hypocritical, because he had not participated in their development.[71]

Carter's outsider status enabled him to develop a strategy to appeal to a cross section of political opinion. His attacks on the political establishment appealed to some populist liberals. To obtain support from conservatives, he emphasized moral values, his religious convictions as a born-again Baptist, his Southern background, his dislike of big-spending liberals, and his support of major increases in defense spending. Moderates liked his cultivation of big business, his internationalism, and his emphasis on making the federal government less corrupt and more efficient. Most moderates and conservatives liked his antigovernment rhetoric. Carter told all groups that he was an efficient problem solver who would not succumb to politics-as-usual when making decisions.[72]

Carter obtained the Democratic nomination by developing grass-roots organizations in primary states before other Democratic candidates did so. He also ran a clever race against Gerald Ford, who was tainted by his prior association with the discredited Nixon—and, in particular, by his decision to pardon Nixon and so exempt him from prosecution for Watergate. Ford's membership in the Washington establishment and the recession of 1975 were also liabilities. Carter won the election by a slim margin when he carried the South and key Midwestern states.

Even the most astute president would have found it difficult to govern in 1976, however. Congressional legislators insisted on full participation in the legislative process after Watergate and were eager to demonstrate their resentment of Carter's repeated criticisms of Congress. Many legislators had also developed specific programs that they wanted to enact, after a string of vetoes by Nixon and Ford.[73] Carter encountered a bleak economic situation, as well. He inherited a massive deficit from Ford, high rates of inflation, and increasing levels of social spending. Inflation became a national crisis when Middle Eastern countries decided to stop shipments of oil to the United States, in reprisal for American assistance to Israel. When gasoline prices rose from 37 cents per gallon in 1970 to $1.60 in 1977, double-digit inflation became a reality.

Carter was ill equipped to contend with these harsh political and economic realities. As an aloof problem solver, he did not enjoy the give-and-take of the political process. He liked to tackle problems in the isolation of the White House.[74] His condescending attitude toward legislators infuriated them, as did his disinclination to consult them. Carter surrounded himself, moreover, with untested advisors from Georgia who did not communicate with legislators. Several years after the election, Tip O'Neill, the Democratic majority leader in the House, had not even met Hamilton Jordan, Carter's chief advisor. Carter failed to develop alliances with groups and legislators who would normally have assisted a Democratic president. Union leaders distrusted him because he opposed increases in the minimum wage; Catholics and Jews were antagonized by his flaunting of his Protestant fundamentalism; big-city mayors believed that he did not understand urban problems;

and social reformers believed him to be indifferent to the needs of the poor.[75] Carter was unable, moreover, to intelligently schedule his domestic measures. Disdaining partial or incremental approaches in favor of comprehensive solutions, Carter overwhelmed Congress with his rapid-fire delivery of comprehensive energy, welfare, government reorganization, and health measures.[76]

Carter's Domestic Legislation

Unlike Roosevelt, Truman, and Johnson, Carter was not much interested in domestic legislation. His priorities were reorganization of the federal bureaucracy, the Middle East, renegotiation of the Panama Canal Treaty, and energy policy. He did not like proposals that required major funding of social programs, because he favored reductions in federal spending.[77] Critics contend, as well, that he was ill disposed to welfare recipients, alcoholics, and drug addicts, whom he believed to make fraudulent use of government programs.[78] He enacted relatively little social legislation, because of his political style and intrinsic conservatism, as well as the difficult political and economic environment that he encountered.

Carter supported national health insurance in his campaign of 1976 but, once elected, he took no action on this measure until Senator Edward Kennedy, brother of the late president, accused him of reneging on his campaign promise. Fearing that this issue could be used against him if Kennedy opposed him for the presidential nomination in 1980, Carter belatedly introduced his own version of health insurance in 1979. Carter's proposal combined an insurance plan for employees, to be financed by payroll deductions, and a government-funded scheme for nonworkers.[79] Kennedy's scheme favored government controls, government financing, and government regulation of health care. Neither Carter's nor Kennedy's scheme was politically feasible in the climate of 1979, however, when double-digit inflation and large deficits made politicians unwilling to increase government spending.

In 1977, Carter introduced a comprehensive scheme for welfare reform, which, like Nixon's a few years earlier, became caught in a cross fire between liberals and conservatives. Carter's scheme was imaginative and more ambitious than FAP. He proposed to consolidate AFDC, food stamps, and SSI so as to provide a national minimum income for families, individuals, and elderly persons. He envisioned a three-tiered benefit system, in which able-bodied but nonworking persons received the lowest benefits, persons who were exempted from work (persons with disabilities and women with preschool children) received middle-level benefits, and the working poor received the highest benefits (when added to their earned income). He also proposed the creation of 1.4 million public service jobs for recipients.[80]

Controversy was heated and wide ranging; Joseph Califano, secretary of the Department of Health and Human Services from 1977 to 1979, described welfare reform as the Middle East of domestic politics.[81] Conservatives wanted to exempt only women with children under the age of 6 from the work requirement, whereas many liberals wanted to exempt women with children under the age of 14. Conservatives insisted that persons holding public service jobs receive prevailing wages, whereas liberals wanted them to be paid the federal minimum wage. Some defenders of Food Stamps and SSI objected to their merger into the larger welfare reform program. Legislators quibbled about the relative size of the minimum benefits for nonworking recipients and the monies to be spent on work incentives for the employed poor. Many conservatives feared that the extension of governmental benefits to working persons would pauperize them.[82]

Not surprisingly, then, welfare reform was defeated in the Senate in 1978. Califano concluded in 1981 that comprehensive reform of the American welfare system was probably not politically feasible; attention should focus instead on incremental improvements, as well as experiments to test controversial policies.[83] This pessimistic appraisal could be extended to national health insurance, which seemed as politically elusive as welfare reform.

Despite the existence of CETA, millions of Americans had suffered the trauma of unemployment during the 1970s, at least briefly; its toll on their physical and mental health was considerable. People of color and teenagers bore a particularly heavy burden; more than 30% of them were unemployed in many areas. In 1974, Senator Hubert Humphrey and Congressman Augustus Hawkins introduced legislation to improve the situation by requiring the creation of federal public service jobs whenever the national unemployment rate exceeded 3%.[84] The legislation was strongly opposed by the Ford administration, on the grounds that it was not feasible to create this many jobs, that federal jobs would draw persons away from the private sector, that the cost of the measure was prohibitive, and that public sector jobs would make many persons dependent on government.[85] Humphrey and Hawkins reintroduced their legislation in 1976, after Carter had been elected, in hopes that strong support by the administration would facilitate its passage. Though he gave his support, Carter did not aggressively fight efforts by conservatives to amend the legislation. When finally enacted in 1978, the Full Employment and Balanced Growth Act was so diluted as to be meaningless.[86]

Carter's conservatism curbed his support for various measures to help children. His legislation to provide comprehensive services to families headed by teenagers was enacted but was hardly funded, because the administration did not decisively promote it.[87] He did not support expanded federal funding of child care, since it would have required major new federal expenditures.[88] Carter vacillated on legislation to extend federal subsidies to local centers that helped battered women; strong opposition from conservatives, who insisted that social workers exaggerated the extent of the problem, defeated the legislation in 1980.[89]

Carter was nonetheless able to obtain passage of legislation that sought to rescue children from long-term stays in the foster care system, which provided inadequate care and shuffled children from one short-term placement to another. Although AFDC paid the costs of court-ordered foster care placements, the federal government had traditionally left the funding and planning of adoption and foster care services to local public and private agencies. Hundreds of thousands of children were served by this system; unless they were adopted or returned to their parental homes, children had no escape from it. Those most likely to remain in foster care were children of color, older children, and children with serious physical and mental disabilities. To encourage local child welfare agencies to pursue adoptions for these children, the Adoption Assistance and Child Welfare Act of 1980 provided federal subsidies to families that adopted children and required states to maintain status reports on all children in foster care, so that they could be expeditiously placed into adoption or returned to their parental homes within specified time limits. In addition, the legislation expanded federal assistance to states for foster care.[90]

Carter was also able to enlarge Medicaid programs to screen and treat low-income children and to help pregnant women.[91] The federal government had required local authorities to screen low-income children under the 1965 Medicaid legislation, but compliance had been inadequate, and screened children were often not helped with treatment even when serious problems were found.

In the area of civil rights, Carter seemed more intent on consolidating existing laws than adding new protections, because he wanted to retain the support of Southerners, who had been indispensable to his victory in 1976. He was sufficiently indifferent to issues of affirmative action that he supported a white plaintiff, Allan Bakke, who sued a public medical school of the University of California on the grounds that its admission policies gave preference to people of color with lesser qualifications. After Joseph Califano, the HEW secretary, persuaded the administration to oppose Bakke, the Justice Department provided testimony that eventually influenced the Supreme Court to uphold the principle of affirmative action while disallowing the use of numerical quotas.[92]

The rights of persons with disabilities were enhanced during the Carter administration, though only after extensive pressure from certain interest groups. The Architectural and Transportation Compliance Board, established in 1973, issued regulations in 1980 that required extensive modifications in federal buildings.[93]

Rosalyn Carter, the wife of the president, made mental health her major domestic issue and assumed an important role in establishing a Presidential Commission on Mental Health. In 1978, this commission issued a four-volume report that analyzed many program, policy, and financing issues in the mental-health system. The report cited the lack of insurance coverage for outpatient services; inadequate community services for persons with chronic and severe mental problems in community settings; and the lack of services for elderly and adolescent populations.[94] Its findings did not lead to major reforms, however, for the resulting legislation, the Mental Health Systems Act of 1980, did not provide centers with sufficient funds to implement the new services that it mandated.

A financing crisis in the Social Security program prompted an important policy debate in the administration. Califano believed that Social Security should provide a safety net for those elderly persons who were poor, but proposed taxing the benefits of more affluent elderly persons, so that proceeds from the tax could be used to bail out the trust fund. However, some of the founders of the Social Security program, such as Wilbur Cohen, believed that benefits should continue to bear a strong relationship to the amount of payroll taxes that persons had paid into the system—that affluent persons, having paid higher taxes, should receive higher benefits than other persons. Cohen feared that Califano's proposal would encourage the transformation of Social Security into a welfare rather than a universal program.[95] Califano lost this battle, but his recommendation was approved during Ronald Reagan's first term, when it became obvious that even the major increases in the payroll taxes that Carter had engineered were insufficient to preserve the solvency of the trust fund.[96]

The SSI program grew at a fantastic pace during the mid-1970s, because thousands of persons with mental and physical disabilities were using it. Carter resolved to slow its rate of increase by restricting benefits to the level of wages that recipients had received before their disability and by allowing them to retain their Medicaid benefits. He also pressured administrative judges, who were hired by the government to decide whether persons were entitled to SSI, to make fewer favorable decisions. Although there had been abuse of the program, the new policy had its own dangers, for it deprived some persons with severe disabilities of the benefits they needed.[97]

The Department of Health, Education, and Welfare grew rapidly during the 1960s and 1970s, but staff morale plummeted following successive cuts in personnel and heavier workloads. The staff needed leadership from a president who would empathize with their problems, reduce pointless regulations, and troubleshoot logistical and other problems.[98] Carter was often as paranoid as Nixon about federal bureaucrats. Nonetheless, he placed Medicare and Medicaid under a single office known as the Health Care and Finance Administration, eliminated many unnecessary regulations, and established a department for tracking and assessing programs and policies and imposing budgetary controls. Finally, in a controversial move that was partly inspired by Carter's desire to repay the National Education Association for its assistance in the 1976 election, the Office of Education was separated from HEW, which was renamed the Department of Health and Human Services (DHHS).[99]

By 1978, Carter had decided to effect massive cuts in social programs as part of his desperate effort to diminish double-digit inflation and to accommodate substantial increases in military spending. The budget cuts in the last two years of Carter's administration can be seen as the beginning of a long conservative assault on social spending, which extended through the presidency of Ronald Reagan.[100]

To the chagrin of feminists, Carter was militantly against abortion and supported a constitutional amendment to overrule the Supreme Court's 1973 *Roe* v. *Wade* decision, which had declared unconstitutional state laws that prohibited abortions during the first trimester. When a constitutional amendment proved to be politically impractical, Carter supported legislation to prohibit use of federal Medicaid funds for abortions.[101] The legislation, eventually enacted, allowed the use of Medicaid funds for abortions only in very narrowly defined circumstances; in practice, low-income women could only obtain abortions with Medicaid funds if their lives were endangered by childbirth or else within 72 hours of a rape or incest.[102] As a result of this legislation, the number of federally financed abortions declined from 275,000 in 1976 to 1,250 in 1978, and most abortions for low-income women had to be financed by local government and charitable institutions. Unlike more affluent women, some poor women were driven to illegal (and frequently dangerous) low-cost abortions or delivered unwanted children because of the difficulty of obtaining abortions from local institutions.[103]

Carter's Fall

Only two years after his election, Carter had the worst popularity rating of any president in recent American history at a comparable point in his term. It sank even further by 1979, in the wake of soaring oil prices, continuing stagflation, a Congress that wanted to assert its independence, and widespread public disenchantment with government.[104]

Carter was nonetheless able to obtain the Democratic nomination for the presidency in 1980, despite a vigorous challenge by Senator Edward Kennedy. But Carter faced another outsider, who used many of the same anti-establishment tactics that he himself had used in 1976. This time, however, Carter was the insider; the outsider was Ronald Reagan, his Republican opponent. Carter was dealt a final misfortune when he failed to free a group of hostages captured by a band of terrorists who overran the American embassy in Iran. Reagan defeated Carter easily in the 1980 election and began a new era of conservative policies that attacked the liberal reforms of the preceding 50 years.

THE HIDDEN SOCIAL SPENDING REVOLUTION OF THE 1970s

The policy changes that were made in the 1970s constitute a hidden social spending revolution in American social policy. Nondefense spending went from 8.1% of the gross national product in 1961 to

TABLE 10.1   Increases in outlays for specific programs (in billions of constant dollars) during the 1970s

| | 1970 | | 1980 | |
	Federal	Total	Federal	Total
Food Stamps	2.0	2.0	10.0	10.0
SSI	—	4.1	7.0	8.6
Unemployment insurance	7.7	7.7	18.5	18.5
Medicaid	5.8	10.9	15.3	25.4
Medicare	15.2	15.2	38.3	38.3
AFDC	5.1	9.2	8.8	13.9
CETA and MDTA	2.4	2.4	3.6	3.6
Social Security*	68.2	68.2	134.8	134.8
Housing assistance	2.8	2.8	4.9	4.9
Total	109.2	122.5	241.4	258.0

* Expenditures include federal costs as well as spending from funds generated by payroll taxes.

11.3% in 1971 and 15.6% in 1981. About two-thirds of this domestic budget consisted of social insurance and means-tested social programs. Total federal social spending rose from $67 billion in 1960 to $158 billion in 1970 (in 1980 dollars) and to $314 billion in 1980.[105] Many social programs grew tremendously in their total cost during the 1970s, as Table 10.1 illustrates.[106]

For the first time in American history, a relatively sophisticated safety net of social programs existed for persons who lacked resources, whether because they were old, unemployed, ill, or poor. Many persons used only a single program. A man who became unemployed during the recession of 1976 might use only unemployment benefits, because he considered use of Food Stamps or Medicaid programs to be unnecessary or stigmatizing or because his net income made him ineligible for them. Other families used only the Food Stamps program, and still others only received Medicaid. The range of different cash-transfer, in-kind, and services programs allowed families to select specific programs that improved their quality of life at a specific point in time.[107]

Other consumers used combinations of programs. A single woman with several preschool or school-age children might receive AFDC, Food Stamps, and health services reimbursed by Medicaid, and live in publicly subsidized housing. An elderly family might use Medicare, SSI, and Social Security benefits. A young adult who had received a kidney transplant could receive SSI as well as medical services from Medicare. An unemployed person could receive unemployment insurance, job training from CETA, Food Stamps, and Medicaid. The availability of combinations of programs was crucial to many individuals and families—especially to large families, whose members needed a range of services and resources.[108]

Many persons used such programs as unemployment insurance, Food Stamps, and Medicaid for brief periods of unemployment, illness, or poverty; others needed assistance for longer periods. Of all the recipients of the nation's welfare programs, about 50% used them for less than three years; about 33% used them for three to seven years; and about 12% used them for eight or more years.[109] Impoverished women with children were likely to use AFDC, Food Stamps, and Medicaid. Unemployed men tended to use unemployment insurance and Food Stamps. Elderly people used SSI, Social Security, Medicare, and Medicaid. Persons with disabilities used SSI and Social Security disability benefits. (The Social Security program had become far more than a pension program for elderly people by the 1970s, because its benefits often subsidized surviving family members when a parent died and helped pay for the education of surviving children.)[110] The programs were not used only by low-income persons; indeed, roughly three of every four dollars of social welfare benefits (whether cash, in-kind benefits, or services) were delivered in programs that were not means-tested, such as Medicare, Social Security, and unemployment insurance.[111] Government loan programs for college students were greatly expanded in the 1970s and were used extensively by middle- and even upper-income families. Countless people found their quality of life improved by receipt of cash, in-kind benefits, or services from one or more of the social programs.

Evidence also suggests that extraordinary progress was made during the 1970s in reducing the incidence of poverty, as measured by the percentage of the population that fell under official poverty lines. By this measure, the poverty rate declined from 14.2% of the population in 1967 to 11.1% in 1979. When in-kind transfers, such as Food Stamps and Medicaid, are also included, the poverty rate declined to 6.4% in 1979—an extraordinary accomplishment. However, 15% of African Americans, 12% of Latinos, and 18% of female-headed households remained in poverty.[112]

The reduction in poverty during the 1970s was even more impressive than the gains made during the 1960s, which were facilitated by the Vietnam War and the economic activity that accompanied it. Expenditures for the military declined from 8% of the GNP in 1966 to 5.5% of the GNP in 1981.[113] Indeed, in contrast to the boom of the 1960s, the economy was plagued by stagflation in the 1970s. The striking successes in reducing poverty in the 1970s can be attributed in considerable measure to expansion of cash and in-kind social programs. The average value of payments, benefits, and services to families and individuals was $1,252 in 1970 (in 1980 dollars), but it reached $1,896 in 1980.[114] Thus, progress in reducing poverty was made only because social programs were more comprehensive than during any other period in American history.

Of course, increases in spending on entitlements did not address the job-related income of Americans. Because the United States had dominated world markets through the 1960s, few people realized that vast numbers of unionized, industrial jobs were disappearing, whether through migration of American firms abroad in search of cheaper labor or from competition with European nations and Japan. In the 1970s, little attention was given to job-training programs, improvements in public education, and relocation of jobs to inner city areas.

The progress in improving the material status of Americans was accompanied by a revolution in human rights. Regulations and litigation by the Equal Employment Opportunity Commission (EEOC) were supplemented by many court rulings that bolstered the rights of people of color and women in job markets and in college admissions. The rights of persons with physical and mental disabilities were advanced by important court decisions, by legislation, and by government regulations. These measures significantly decreased the extent to which people with disabilities were warehoused in custodial institutions and increased their access to public facilities. Advocates for gay men and lesbians defeated local government attempts to deny them teaching positions.

WHY WAS THE SPENDING REVOLUTION HIDDEN?

In the 1980s, secure in the knowledge that one of their own—Ronald Reagan—was in the White House, conservatives attacked social spending and the welfare state. They focused their attacks on the New Deal and Great Society reforms, but they ought also to have attacked Richard Nixon and his presidential successors during the 1970s, who permitted startling increases in social spending that rivaled earlier periods of reform. Many factors combined to hide the extent of the 1970s reforms. Nixon's political rhetoric was often conservative, in contrast to Roosevelt's denunciation of "monied interests" and Johnson's expressions of sympathy for those in poverty. Each of the three presidents in the 1970s began their administrations with relatively liberal emphases but ended their terms as determined conservatives, which made them appear to focus on reductions rather than increases in social spending. Nixon was far more conservative in his second term than in his first, Ford more conservative in 1976 than in 1975, and Carter more conservative after 1978 than in his first two years.[115] Each president was forced to abandon reform measures by their Southern constituencies, high inflation and deficits, and public indifference to reform.

Moreover, the nature of the 1970s reforms tended to render them invisible. Whereas Democrats had typically sought new programs, some of Nixon's reforms—such as the indexing of Social Security, federalizing of Food Stamps, and SSI— were simply procedural and administrative changes in existing programs. Nixon's reforms often had a conservative appearance because they deemphasized the role of the federal government; both CETA and revenue sharing allocated funds to localities. Such appearances are deceiving, however, because CETA and revenue sharing were substantial additions to the American welfare state, as Ronald Reagan realized a few years later when he succeeded in virtually eliminating them. Nixon's reforms were also unobtrusive because they lacked a dramatic name like the New Deal.

Finally, where the New Deal and Great Society reforms resulted from the successful mobilizing of a liberal coalition of unions, intellectuals, Jews, blue-collar voters, racial groups, and other interest groups against conservatives, passage of reforms in the 1970s often resulted from a more complex and less dramatic political process, in which members of both parties sought partial credit for reforms.

OUTGROUPS IN THE 1970s

Changes in Tactics and Organization

Groups representing women, people of color, and gay men and lesbians made important changes in tactics and organization in the 1970s. The middle and late 1960s saw the emergence of relatively radical leadership, who focused on nonviolent marches and demonstrations, building group pride, and recruiting mass membership. Among African Americans, the nonviolent precepts of Martin Luther King, Jr., were losing ground to the black power philosophy of Malcolm X and Stokely Carmichael.

In the mid-1970s, as this first wave of outgroup activists burned out, experienced intimidation by the FBI and other federal officials, or became discouraged by intragroup dissension between radicals and those more inclined to accept incremental changes, they were replaced by a second wave.[116] It had also become clear by the mid-1970s that each of the outgroups faced dauntingly complicated problems in obtaining legislative and legal advances for their groups—problems that could not easily be addressed by direct action. They needed to work on a number of fronts simultaneously, to obtain expert legal advice, to surmount honest differences within their groups about how best to proceed, and to develop staying power as complex legal initiatives were processed and litigated. Indeed, within each movement, specialized groups that worked on specific issues supplemented the older general-purpose groups such as the National Association for the Advancement of Colored People and the National Organization for Women.

The women's movement illustrates this transformation of outgroup organizing in the 1970s. Women found that they had to work on multiple fronts—to redress job discrimination; reform state laws on rape; develop funding for battered women's shelters; seek resources for child care; obtain legislation allowing maternal (and paternal) leaves for pregnant women and for parents of newly born children; secure equal pay for comparable work; increase child-support payments from divorced or absent fathers; increase training and assistance to "displaced homemakers"; work for enactment of an Equal Rights Amendment; develop lawsuits to force promotions and hiring of women in the face of discrimination; contest court rulings that threatened affirmative action; and seek

FIGURE 10.1 The women's liberation movement

SOURCE: © Ron Bennett/UPI/Bettmann

legislation to ban sexual harassment in the workplace. Specialized organizations formed to deal with each of these issues; they developed loose connections with each other and with the National Organization for Women.[117]

The women's movement also illustrates how different groups had to try to overcome dissent *within* their movement. African American women and other women of color sometimes contended that the leadership of the established groups was insensitive to their needs; thus, some African American women thought that more attention should be devoted to the needs of poor women and that radical feminists' attacks on the institution of

marriage did not reflect the interest of the African American community in supporting African American males within their marriages.[118] Old controversies resurfaced, such as those between women who favored protectionist legislation and women who favored strict equality for women and men. Whereas protectionists wanted legislation that gave *women* maternal leaves, custody rights, alimony, and child support, other women wanted legislation that gave men and women complete equality under the law—that is, that gave men and women equal rights to child support, alimony, support payments, and leaves.[119] Heterosexual women and lesbians disagreed about how much emphasis the women's movement should place on fighting discrimination encountered by lesbians.

The Mobilization of New Sets of Outgroups

We discussed African Americans, Asian Americans, Latinos, Native Americans, and women in Chapter 9, but the members of other outgroups also developed leadership and organizations in the late 1960s. Many policies that affected older persons were developed in the 1960s and early 1970s, including Medicare, the Older Americans Act, Supplementary Security Income (SSI), and indexing of Social Security benefits.[120] A "gray lobby" was energized by rapid growth in the membership of the American Association of Retired Persons (AARP), the National Council of Senior Citizens (NCSC), the Gray Panthers, and many other groups.[121] Indeed, by the 1980s, AARP used its vast resources to mobilize support for those legislators who were sympathetic to programs that benefited older persons.

In the 1960s, automobile accidents and the Vietnam War led to substantial increases in the numbers of Americans with disabilities. Towards the end of the decade, a robust movement to assert the rights of people with disabilities developed. Various groups had long represented veterans with disabilities, persons with vision and hearing impairment, those with developmental disabilities, and people with specific diseases such as cerebral palsy. However, none of these groups focused on the civil rights of persons with disabilities, and each was dominated by providers of specific services. While long-standing programs such as the federal vocational rehabilitation program already provided services to persons with physical disabilities, the emerging interest in extending their rights was first reflected in the 1968 Architectural Barriers Act, which promoted the modification of federal facilities. Various local groups with an interest in civil rights, such as the Center for Independent Living in Berkeley, California, developed in the 1960s and early 1970s. Persons with disabilities came to be concerned about discrimination in the workplace and about the many physical impediments—such as the absence of ramps and elevators—that made their access to transportation and facilities problematic. However, there was little networking among individuals with different disabilities until 1972, when President Nixon vetoed the Rehabilitation Act. In response, an array of persons demonstrated in support of the legislation at the annual conference of the President's Committee on Employment of the Handicapped. The disability movement took off after the enactment of the Rehabilitation Act of 1973, whose section 504 prohibited discrimination against persons with disabilities. The American Coalition of Citizens with Disabilities (ACCD) sought to pressure the Nixon, Ford, and Carter administrations to put resources, legal advocacy, and commitment behind the civil rights provisions of the act.[122]

Americans had lagged behind Europeans in developing child care and children's allowances, but little pressure was placed on federal politicians prior to the mid-1960s, except by small professional organizations such as the Child Welfare League of America. A White House Conference on Children was held about every ten years, but it tended to be a symbolic event. The establishment of the Head Start program in 1964 provided a dramatic breakthrough for children, even if it was poorly funded. President Nixon's veto of child development legislation in 1971 provided the impetus for the founding of the Children's Defense Fund in 1973 by Marian Wright Edelman—the most assertive advocate for children in Washington, D.C., during the next two decades. Over the years, various coalitions of professional groups banded together to seek passage of measures like the Adoption Assistance and Child Welfare Act of 1980. Child advocacy groups developed in local and state jurisdictions, as well. Unlike groups with mass memberships, such as AARP, advocates for children had to depend on the goodwill and interest of other groups, such as the National Organization for Women, which often gave relatively little attention to the needs of children.[123]

The 1970s as a Revolution in Rights

Although civil rights are commonly associated with the pivotal Civil Rights Acts of 1964 and 1965, the rights revolution reached its zenith in the mid-1970s. Working with advocacy groups or within the Justice Department itself, attorneys who had received their training in the civil rights movement of the 1960s developed a vast quantity of litigation for the various outgroups. As one example, in *O'Connor* v. *Donaldson,* the Supreme Court ruled that individuals who are placed in mental institutions have a right to treatment and cannot simply be warehoused, as was so often done. Other rulings extended protections to immigrants in detention camps, to gay men and lesbians, to persons with disabilities, to the indigent, to persons with developmental disabilities, to persons in jail, and to prisoners on death row. The federal courts required the Justice Department to enforce their orders outlawing segregated school systems in the South. The courts also required Northern schools to end de facto segregation, often by means of busing. Women won class-action lawsuits against corporations such as AT&T, which were required to make back payments of huge sums of money to women who had been unfairly denied promotions or who had encountered wage discrimination. The Supreme Court's *Roe* v. *Wade* ruling disallowed state laws that prohibited abortion during the first trimester. The building trades, which had historically excluded people of color and women from apprenticeship programs and jobs, were the subject of Court judgments that forced them to train minorities and women. Litigation promoted by the Age Discrimination Act of 1967 and the Rehabilitation Act of 1973 required some employers to hire or retain elderly persons and persons with disabilities.[124] Advocates found a generally receptive response from the Supreme Court even after Earl Warren's retirement as chief justice in 1969 and his replacement by Warren Burger, who remained chief justice until 1986.

This explosion of litigation and rulings was supplemented by the growth of government regulatory bodies, such as the Equal Employment Opportunities Commission, whose budget rose from $3.25 million in 1966 to $111.4 million in 1979. Court rulings and regulatory pressure had a marked impact on the decisions of colleges, corporations, and public agencies such as fire and police departments. For example, the percentage of African American police officers in Atlanta increased from 10% to 29.9% between 1968 and 1975.[125]

The Beginnings of Backlash

Each of the outgroups obtained policy successes in the 1970s and 1980s, but each also encountered a significant backlash from conservatives and movements that opposed social change. In the case of women, Phyllis Schlafly became an outspoken critic of the Equal Rights Amendment (ERA), as well as several other policy measures that feminists sought. Schlafly wanted to preserve traditional sex roles and was convinced that the ERA would force women to take jobs in order to provide half the family's income, end laws that gave mothers custody of children, and deprive them of the right to obtain alimony.[126] During the 1970s and 1980s, many conservatives shared her opposition to policies that feminists sought.

Republican legislators, hopeful of gaining votes from low- and moderate-income whites who believed they were losing jobs to people of color, mounted a vigorous attack on affirmative action, as well as busing. Leaders of the building trades often chose to disregard federal regulations until forced to act by litigation or federal regulators.

Persons with disabilities, encountered resistance from many colleges and some employers, who made little effort to make buildings accessible and jobs available to them. At one point, frustrated by this resistance, they orchestrated a sit-down strike in the office of the HEW secretary, to force the drafting of regulations to implement the Rehabilitation Act of 1973.[127]

Gay men and lesbians encountered a backlash orchestrated by the New Right. Gay rights ordinances were repealed in 1977 and 1978 in Dade County, Florida, Saint Paul, Minnesota, Wichita,

Kansas, and Eugene, Oregon. In the late 1970s, a California legislator mounted a campaign for a ballot initiative to prohibit gay men and lesbians from teaching in public schools. Harvey Milk, a gay member of the board of supervisors in San Francisco, was assassinated in 1978, along with the city's mayor, who supported gay and lesbian issues.[128]

THE EVOLUTION OF THE RELUCTANT WELFARE STATE

We have emphasized the hidden nature of social reforms in the 1970s, but we can also discern in this paradoxical era the harbingers of a more conservative time. Though Nixon often supported, and even initiated, social reforms, his rhetoric in public utterances, as well as during private conferences with advisors, reflected racism and anti-Semitism. While he supported the Family Assistance Plan, he also led highly publicized efforts to attack welfare fraud. He sometimes supported policies for women and other groups, but he also endorsed FBI infiltration of dissident groups. His brooding presence symbolizes the contradictions of the 1970s; he balanced conservative rhetoric and support of social initiatives in his first term, only to swing decisively toward conservative policies in his second term. As we have noted, Presidents Ford and Carter were basically conservative in their domestic policies, even though they supported certain reforms. Full-fledged conservative movements against the supposed excesses of reform emerged in the form of a backlash against feminism, affirmative action, social spending, and taxes, so that advocates for women, gay men and lesbians, and people of color felt increasingly on the defensive.

With the end of the Vietnam War, major and ongoing reductions in military spending were expected. Sharp reductions *did* occur and were used to fund increases in social spending during the decade. By the mid-1970s, however, some Americans became convinced that the Soviet Union, which had dramatically increased the number and power of its missiles, threatened to overtake the American lead in military weapons. Angered by several arms control treaties, which they believed made undue concessions to the Russians, these Americans led a crusade to dramatically increase military spending—a plea that fell on the receptive ears of Ronald Reagan, who made increases in military spending a major pledge in his campaign of 1980.[129]

Historians sometimes err by characterizing historical eras as liberal *or* conservative. The decade of the 1970s was a peculiar mixture of both these tendencies. Major policy reforms took place but in the context of a nation with an emerging conservative movement, which came to view even Richard Nixon as too liberal. Conservatives confidently awaited the 1980 presidential election, and they were not disappointed by the results.

NOTES

1. Sar Levitan and Clifford Johnson, *Beyond the Safety Net: Reviving the Promise of Opportunity in America* (Cambridge, Mass.: Ballinger, 1984), p. 2.

2. Tom Wicker, *One of Us: Richard Nixon and the American Dream* (New York: Random House, 1991), pp. 484–541.

3. James Reichley, *Conservatives in an Age of Change: The Nixon and Ford Administrations* (Washington, D.C.: Brookings Institution, 1981), pp. 48–52.

4. Jules Witcover, *The Resurrection of Richard Nixon* (New York: Putnam, 1970), pp. 104–225.

5. Ibid., pp. 57–58.

6. Ibid., pp. 361–379.

7. Tom Wicker, *One of Us,* pp. 410–413.

8. Elliot Richardson, "The Paradox." In Kenneth Thompson, ed., *The Nixon Presidency* (New York: University Press of America, 1987), pp. 53ff.

9. Rowland Evans and Robert Novak, *Nixon in the White House* (New York: Random House, 1971), pp. 42–43, 108, 117–118, 211–214; William Leuchtenberg, *In the Shadow of FDR: From Harry Truman to Ronald Reagan* (Ithaca, N.Y.: Cornell University

Press, 1983), pp. 168–169; and Reichley, *Conservatives in an Age of Change,* pp. 58–70.

10. Hugh Graham, *The Civil Rights Era: Origins and Development of National Policy, 1960–1972* (New York: Oxford University Press, 1990), p. 322.

11. Leonard Garment, "Richard Nixon." In Thompson, ed., *The Nixon Presidency,* pp. 99ff.

12. Richard Nathan, *The Plot that Failed: Nixon and the Administrative Presidency* (New York: John Wiley & Sons, 1975), pp. 37–56.

13. Reichley, *Conservatives in an Age of Change,* pp. 79–87.

14. Bruce Jansson, *The History and Politics of Selected Children's Programs and Related Legislation in the Context of Four Models of Political Behavior.* Doctoral dissertation (Chicago: University of Chicago, 1975), pp. 54–55.

15. Reichley, *Conservatives in an Age of Change,* pp. 56, 72, 154–156.

16. Sar Levitan and Robert Taggart, *The Promise of Greatness* (Cambridge, Mass.: Harvard University Press, 1976), pp. 24–28.

17. Reichley, *Conservatives in an Age of Change,* pp. 219–224.

18. Ibid., pp. 59–64, 68–72; Evans and Novak, *Nixon,* pp. 37–74.

19. Daniel Moynihan, *The Politics of a Guaranteed Income* (New York: Random House, 1973), pp. 352–396.

20. Ibid., pp. 192–226; Reichley, *Conservatives in an Age of Change,* pp. 138–142.

21. Vincent Burke, *Nixon's Good Deed: Welfare Reform* (New York: Columbia University Press, 1974), p. 67.

22. W. Joseph Heffernan, *Introduction to Social Welfare Policy* (Itasca, Ill.: Peacock, 1979), pp. 241–250.

23. Moynihan, *The Politics of a Guaranteed Income,* pp. 458–483.

24. Ibid., pp. 439–452.

25. Burke, *Nixon's Good Deed,* pp. 177–187.

26. Ibid., pp. 198–204.

27. Timothy Smeeding, "Is the Safety Net Still Intact?" In D. Lee Bawden, ed., *The Social Contract Revisited: Aims and Outcomes of President Reagan's Social Welfare Policy* (Washington, D.C.: Urban Institute, 1984), pp. 75, 78.

28. Linda Demkovitch, "Administration About-Face on Disability Could Be a Blessing in Disguise," *National Journal,* 16 (April 28, 1984), 823–825; Donald Chambers, "Policy Weaknesses and Political Opportunities," *Social Service Review,* 1 (March 1985), 1–17.

29. Nicholas Kotz, *Let Them Eat Promises* (Garden City, N.Y.: Doubleday, 1971), pp. 206–213.

30. Levitan and Taggart, *The Promise of Greatness,* p. 67; Moynihan, *The Politics of a Guaranteed Income,* pp. 493–494.

31. Smeeding, "Is the Safety Net Still Intact?" p. 78.

32. Martha Derthick, *Policymaking for Social Security* (Washington, D.C.: Brookings Institution, 1979), pp. 345–368.

33. Ibid., pp. 358–362.

34. Craig Roberts, *The Supply-Side Revolution: An Insider's Account of Policy-Making in Washington* (Cambridge, Mass.: Harvard University Press, 1984), pp. 260–261.

35. Peter Gottschalk and Sheldon Danziger, "Macroeconomic Conditions, Income Transfers, and the Trend in Poverty." In Bawden, ed., *The Social Contract Revisited,* p. 191.

36. Nathan, *The Plot that Failed,* pp. 37–56.

37. Robert Magill, *Social Policy in American Society* (New York: Human Sciences Press, 1984), pp. 127–128; Reichley, *Conservatives in an Age of Change,* pp. 156–159.

38. Reichley, *Conservatives in an Age of Change,* p. 155.

39. George Hale and Marian Palley, *The Politics of Federal Grants* (Washington, D.C.: Congressional Quarterly Press, 1981), pp. 111–113.

40. Walter Williams, *Government by Agency: Lessons from the Social Program Grants-in-Aid Experience* (New York: Academic Press, 1980), pp. 42–43.

41. Martha Derthick, *Uncontrollable Spending for Social Services Grants* (Washington, D.C.: Brookings Institution, 1975), pp. 29–34.

42. Congressional Quarterly Service, Inc., *Congressional Quarterly Almanac,* Vol. XXIX (Washington, D.C., 1973), p. 575.

43. Wicker, *One of Us,* pp. 484–507, 522–523; Graham, *The Civil Rights Era,* pp. 475–476.

44. Reichley, *Conservatives in an Age of Change,* pp. 188–189.

45. Levitan and Taggart, *The Promise of Greatness,* pp. 150–155; Nancy Woloch, *Women and the American Experience* (New York: Knopf, 1984), pp. 524–526.

46. Graham, *The Civil Rights Era,* pp. 393–449.

47. Ibid., pp. 322–345.

48. Frank Bowe, *Rehabilitating America: Toward Independence for Disabled and Elderly People* (New York: Harper & Row, 1980), pp. 59–91.

49. Joseph Califano, *Governing America* (New York: Simon & Schuster, 1981), pp. 314–315.

50. Paul Starr, *The Social Transformation of American Medicine* (New York: Basic Books, 1984), pp. 396–401, 402–403.

51. Gilbert Steiner, *The Futility of Family Policy* (Washington, D.C.: Brookings Institution, 1981), pp. 49–50.

52. Lela Costin, *Child Welfare: Policies and Practice* (New York: McGraw-Hill, 1979), p. 49.

53. Bruce Jansson, *Theory and Practice of Social Welfare Policy* (Belmont, Calif.: Wadsworth, 1984), p. 335.

54. Frank Thompson, *Health Policy and the Bureaucracy: Politics and Implementation* (Cambridge, Mass.: M.I.T. Press, 1981), pp. 217–251.

55. David Stockman, *The Triumph of Politics* (New York: Harper & Row, 1986), p. 410.

56. Reichley, *Conservatives in an Age of Change,* pp. 219–221.

57. For example, funding pressures on neighborhood health centers are discussed by Isabel Marcus, *Dollars for Reform* (Lexington, Mass.: D. C. Heath, 1981), pp. 89–115.

58. Jansson, *The History and Politics,* pp. 233–309; Gilbert Steiner, *The Children's Cause* (Washington, D.C.: Brookings Institution, 1976), pp. 90–117.

59. Geoffrey Hodgson, *America in Our Time* (Garden City, N.Y.: Doubleday, 1976), pp. 412–428; Kevin Phillips, *The Emerging Republican Majority* (New Rochelle, N.Y.: Arlington House, 1969), pp. 168–175, 182–184, 321–330.

60. Hodgson, *America in Our Time,* pp. 401–411.

61. Reichley, *Conservatives in an Age of Change,* pp. 54–55; Tom Wicker, "Introduction." In John Osborne, *The Nixon Watch* (New York: Liveright, 1970), pp. viii–x.

62. Hodgson, *America in Our Time,* pp. 425–428, 455.

63. Reichley, *Conservatives in an Age of Change,* pp. 208–209.

64. Hodgson, *America in Our Time,* p. 366.

65. Reichley, *Conservatives in an Age of Change,* pp. 232–233, 239–242.

66. Ibid., pp. 234–237, 242–247.

67. Ibid., pp. 307–311.

68. Ibid., pp. 322–325.

69. Bowe, *Rehabilitating America,* pp. 102–107, 130; Peter Tyor and Leland Bell, *Caring for the Retarded in America: A History* (Westport, Conn.: Greenwood, 1984), p. 150.

70. Haynes Johnson, *In the Absence of Power* (New York: Viking Press, 1980), p. 114.

71. Robert Shogan, *Promises to Keep: Carter's First Hundred Days* (New York: Thomas Crowell, 1977), pp. 22–28.

72. Ibid., pp. 28–48.

73. Johnson, *In the Absence of Power,* pp. 38–48.

74. Ibid., p. 295.

75. Ibid., pp. 101, 154–168.

76. Ibid., pp. 163-164; Shogan, *Promises to Keep,* p. 199.

77. Califano, *Governing America,* p. 334; Johnson, *In the Absence of Power,* p. 217.

78. Shogan, *Promises to Keep,* p. 189.

79. Califano, *Governing America,* pp. 96–117.

80. Heffernan, *Introduction to Social Welfare Policy,* pp. 259–266.

81. Califano, *Governing America,* p. 321.

82. Ibid., pp. 320–366.

83. Ibid., pp. 364–367.

84. Reichley, *Conservatives in an Age of Change,* pp. 397–399.

85. Ibid.

86. Congressional Quarterly Service, Inc., *Congressional Quarterly Almanac,* Vol. XXXIV (Washington, D.C., 1978), pp. 272–279.

87. Steiner, *The Futility of Family Policy,* pp. 85–88.

88. Ibid., pp. 93–94.

89. Ibid., pp. 163–173.

90. Ibid., pp. 144–155.

91. Karen Davis and Cathy Schoen, *Health and the War on Poverty: A Ten-Year Appraisal* (Washington, D.C.: Brookings Institution, 1978), p. 86.

92. Califano, *Governing America*, pp. 231–243.

93. Ibid., pp. 258–262, 314–315; Timothy Clark, "Here's One Midnight Regulation That Slipped Through Reagan's Net," *National Journal*, 13 (February 7, 1981), 221–224.

94. U.S. President's Commission on Mental Health, *Report to the President* (Washington, D.C.: Government Printing Office, 1978).

95. Jansson, *Theory and Practice of Social Welfare Policy*, pp. 444–446.

96. Califano, *Governing America*, pp. 388–396.

97. Ibid., pp. 384–386.

98. Johnson, *In the Absence of Power*, pp. 49–81.

99. Ibid., p. 293.

100. Meyer, "Budget Cuts in the Reagan Administration." In Bawden, ed., *The Social Contract Revisited*, p. 36.

101. Califano, *Governing America*, p. 67; Johnson, *In the Absence of Power*, pp. 299–300.

102. Califano, *Governing America*, pp. 82–86.

103. Ibid.

104. Johnson, *In the Absence of Power*, pp. 277–317.

105. Meyer, "Budget Cuts in the Reagan Administration," p. 35; Gregory Mills and John Palmer, "The Federal Budget in Flux." In Gregory Mills and John Palmer, eds., *Federal Budget Policy in the 1980s* (Washington, D.C.: Urban Institute, 1984), p. 14; Stockman, *The Triumph of Politics*, p. 411.

106. Table 10.1 from Smeeding, "Is the Safety Net Still Intact?" p. 75.

107. Levitan and Taggart, *The Promise of Greatness*, pp. 70-74.

108. Ibid., pp. 72–73.

109. Blanche Bernstein, "Welfare Dependency." In Bawden, ed., *The Social Contract Revisited*, pp. 129–130.

110. Derthick, *Policymaking for Social Security*, pp. 254–270.

111. Meyer, "Budget Cuts in the Reagan Administration," p. 38.

112. Gottschalk and Danziger, "Macroeconomic Conditions," p. 191.

113. Mills and Palmer, "The Federal Budget in Flux," p. 14.

114. Gottschalk and Danziger, "Macroeconomic Conditions," pp. 188–189.

115. Evans and Novak, *Nixon*, pp. 227–228; Reichley, *Conservatives in an Age of Change*, p. 314; Califano, *Governing America*, pp. 402–448.

116. Flora Davis, *Moving the Mountain: The Women's Movement in America Since 1960* (New York: Simon & Schuster, 1991), pp. 137–138.

117. Ibid., pp. 137–154.

118. Ibid., pp. 362–367.

119. Ibid., pp. 305–307.

120. C. L. Estes, *The Aging Enterprise* (San Francisco: Jossey-Bass, 1979).

121. H. J. Pratt, *The Gray Lobby* (Chicago: University of Chicago Press, 1976).

122. Richard Scotch, *From Good Will to Civil Rights* (Philadelphia: Temple University Press, 1984), pp. 34–59, 82–120.

123. Susan Tolchin and Martin Tolchin, *Clout: Women's Power and Politics* (New York: Coward, McCann, and Geoghegan, 1974), p. 230.

124. Thomas Edsall, *Chain Reaction: The Impact of Race, Rights, and Taxes on American Politics* (New York: W. W. Norton, 1991), pp. 107–115.

125. Edsall, *Chain Reaction*, p. 117.

126. Donald Mathews and Jane Sherron De Hart, *Sex, Gender, and the Politics of ERA* (New York: Oxford University Press, 1990), pp. 154–165.

127. Scotch, *From Good Will*, pp. 111–120.

128. John D'Emilio, "Gay Politics and Community in San Francisco Since World War II." In Martin Duberman, Martha Vicinus, and George Chauncey, *Hidden From History: Reclaiming the Gay and Lesbian Past* (New York: Meridian Books, 1990), pp. 468–473.

129. Michael Boll, *National Security Planning: Roosevelt Through Reagan* (Lexington, Ky.: University of Kentucky Press, 1988), pp. 188–197.

11 CHAPTER

The Conservative Counterrevolution in the Era of Reagan and Bush

Selected Orienting Events

1978	Tax revolt initiated by the passage of Proposition 13 in California
1980	Ronald Reagan wins landslide victory over Jimmy Carter
1981	Omnibus Budget Reconciliation Act (OBRA) makes deep cuts in social programs and establishes seven block grants; Economic Recovery Tax Act of 1981 (ERTA) sharply reduces personal and corporate taxes; Presidential Task Force on Regulatory Relief established; Executive Order mandates review of regulations by the Office of Management and Budget
1981–1983	Nation's deepest recession since the 1930s
1982	Job Training Partnership Act (JTPA) enacted; Tax Equity and Fiscal Responsibility Act (TEFRA) raises corporate taxes and cuts social programs
1983	Diagnostic-related groups (DRGs) introduced by DHHS to finance Medicare's hospital fees; Social Security amendments increase retirement age, reduce some benefits, and subject pensions of some retirees to taxes
1984	Reagan wins landslide victory over Walter Mondale
1985	Balanced Budget and Emergency Deficit Control Act (Gramm-Rudman-Hollings Act) enacted
1986	Tax reform reduces highest tax rate and eliminates many deductions
1987	Enactment of Stewart B. McKinney Homeless Assistance Act
1988	Enactment of Family Support Act
1988	Election of George Bush
1990	Enactment of Americans with Disabilities Act and the Child Care and Development Block Grant program
1991	Enactment of Civil Rights Act
1992	Los Angeles riots

THE ASCENDANCY OF CONSERVATISM

Conservatism was the political mainstream of the nation in the Gilded Age, the 1920s, and the 1950s, when localism, limited federal social welfare roles, and unfettered capitalism prevailed, but it gave way to liberal policies during the Great Depression and in the early 1960s.[1] The minority status of conservatives was illustrated by the landslide defeat in 1964 of Barry Goldwater by Lyndon Johnson, who accused Goldwater of attacking Social Security, TVA, and other legacies of the New Deal. When the Goldwater defeat was swiftly followed by Johnson's legislative successes in 1965 and 1966, it seemed as if conservatism had run its course in national politics.

Between 1966 and 1980, however, a number of developments led to a remarkable resurgence of conservatism, which culminated in the election of Ronald Reagan. The standard of living of the American working and middle classes had improved markedly during the 1950s and 1960s, despite occasional recessions and sharp inflation in the early 1950s. Most people believed that government officials, armed with Keynesian economic theory, could continue this rosy scenario by adjusting government spending downward (to reduce inflation) or upward (to reduce unemployment). The American economy was widely perceived to be an expanding pie that would benefit all segments of the population.[2]

The simultaneous appearance of inflation and unemployment in the 1970s rudely upset this economic utopia. Many middle-class Americans found their earnings sharply eroded by inflation, which not only increased the cost of living but also pushed them into higher federal tax brackets.[3] Many local taxes were also rising, to cover the higher costs of local and municipal services and to pay the local costs of federally mandated programs.

In California, Howard Jarvis campaigned successfully in 1978 for Proposition 13, which drastically reduced local property taxes. This victory was followed by grass-roots tax revolts in many other states. Liberal legislators watched these local tax revolts with trepidation, for they realized that they could eventually stimulate protests against the federal tax system and the social programs it funded.[4] Social reform in the 1970s was also undermined by concern about federal deficits, which, according to conservatives, could only be reduced by sharp cuts in social spending.[5]

Conservatives' hopes were buoyed by the declining strength of the Democratic party. Richard Nixon carried five Southern states in 1968, a Republican achievement that had not been matched since Reconstruction. The liberal flank of the Democratic party began to weaken, as blue-collar workers became increasingly uneasy about social reform and preoccupied with their own economic problems. White backlash led to widespread opposition to affirmative action and social programs, which were widely perceived to disproportionately benefit women, African Americans, and other people of color. Many Jewish voters opposed the use of quotas, because this policy had often been used to exclude them from admission to colleges and the professions.[6]

Feminists and African American activists were increasingly viewed with suspicion in a nation that resisted affirmative action. Conservatives spoke of "big-spending liberals" as an anachronism in a society that experienced large deficits.[7] Trade unions, which had provided electoral and campaign support for the Democrats, were weakened as the economy shifted from manufacturing to service industries, as new jobs were increasingly located in the nonunionized South, and as many industries moved to foreign nations to reduce their labor costs. The ill-fated presidencies of Lyndon Johnson and Jimmy Carter, as well as the assassinations of John and Robert Kennedy, also weakened the Democratic party.

Americans had lived through a long period of social reform, from 1960 through the 1970s. In prior eras, they had only tolerated social reforms for a limited time, and so it was not surprising that the pendulum swung toward conservativism. Conservatives found the public to be more receptive to their arguments that social programs had not solved poverty and other social problems and that social spending was incompatible with economic growth.

The exodus of persons and jobs to the Sunbelt throughout the 1950s, 1960s, and 1970s, in which nearly 40 million Americans left the Northeast and the Midwest, depleted traditional Democratic bastions and greatly increased the electoral strength of conservatives. When placed in this new environment—and removed from trade unions, big-city mayors, and incumbent liberal politicians—these voters, who tended to be relatively conservative and middle class, often became even more conservative. Throughout the country, moreover, there was a continuing shift of population to the suburbs. Suburban voters were far more conservative than urban voters, because they had little stake in social programs for urban residents.[8]

The traditional strength of the Democratic party was also undermined by the maturing of the large war-baby generation, born from 1946 to the late 1950s. These Americans had not lived through the Great Depression and, if they lived in the suburbs, had little or no contact with people of color. They were often preoccupied with material wealth and with personal survival in labor markets crowded with young job seekers from their generation.[9]

Together, these various demographic and social trends placed the Democratic party in jeopardy, particularly as Republicans developed marketing and campaign tactics to reach Sunbelt, suburban, service-oriented, and youthful citizens. There was no sudden erosion in the strength of the Democratic party, particularly in local elections, but its power in senatorial and presidential elections had diminished significantly by the early 1980s.

The Republican party skillfully used these various developments in the 1970s to wrest from the Democratic party two specific groups of voters: Northern white Catholic voters; and working-class and lower-middle-class Southern white voters. Knowing that many of these voters believed that the Great Society had disproportionately assisted people of color and that their rising taxes were caused by this expansion of the welfare state, Republican strategists sought, often successfully, to associate the Democrats with welfare programs, urban riots, high taxes, busing, and affirmative action—and to identify their own party with law-abiding citizens. Using advanced marketing techniques, they addressed literature to these two groups of voters and succeeded in persuading many of them to vote for Republican candidates in presidential races. When added to their traditional suburban and relatively affluent constituency, these new voters gave the Republicans a decided advantage, particularly in the presidential elections of 1968, 1972, 1980, 1984, and 1988.[10]

The Legitimation of Conservatism

Liberal reformers had dominated political dialogue from the New Deal through the presidency of Lyndon Johnson.[11] During the 1950s and early 1960s, a cadre of conservative thinkers, such as sociologist Robert Nisbet, had promulgated theories about the merits of limiting the federal government's policy roles and about the need to establish the family, neighborhoods, and local government as buffers between citizens and central government. Other theorists, such as Richard Weaver, had established libertarian positions, which emphasized policies that maximized freedom by abolishing most government regulations and minimizing taxes. But conservative theorists of the 1950s were relatively isolated from the political process and even distrustful of the general public, who, they believed, were easily manipulated by liberals and the mass media.[12]

The defeat of Goldwater in 1964 made conservatives realize that they needed to participate in the political process if they were to gain power and that they had to use aggressive advertising and outreach to convince the American public to elect conservative legislators.[13] As we have seen, Nixon and his allies used the term *silent majority* in 1968 to describe their belief that most Americans favored localism, elimination of government regulations, and reductions in social spending.

In a departure from the abstract conservative philosophy of the 1950s, a number of theorists began to analyze public policy and to offer recommendations that stemmed from their conservative ideology. Milton Friedman, the conservative economist from the University of Chicago who published *Capitalism and Freedom* in 1962, discussed a series of policies to radically reduce the regulatory power of government; he denounced public housing programs, licensing of professionals, traditional welfare programs, and a host of other liberal policies.[14] In 1964, Martin Anderson advanced a critique of existing urban-renewal programs in *The Federal Bulldozer,* where he argued that private housing markets more effectively met consumer needs than government urban renewal and housing programs.[15] By the end of the 1960s, conservatives had established think tanks, including the American Enterprise Institute and the Heritage Foundation, to compete with such liberal organizations as the Brookings Institution and the Urban Institute. William Buckley initiated a national television show, "Firing Line," which he used as a forum to present conservative views, and developed *The National Review,* a conservative journal that supplemented viewpoints in *The Public Interest, Commentary,* and other conservative publications.

The chastening effect of the Goldwater defeat also made conservatives more willing to participate in political campaigns. Some analysts, such as Kevin Phillips, developed theories about how conservatives could wrest political power from the Democrats by appealing to blue-collar, white ethnic, and Sunbelt voters. Although Presidents Nixon and Ford preferred to have businesspeople and attorneys in their administrations, conservative economists such as Alan Greenspan and William Simon received top positions. The respectability of conservative points of view was further enhanced by criticisms of the Democratic party and Great Society reforms by prominent intellectuals, such as Nathan Glazer and Daniel Moynihan, who pointedly attacked social programs, community action programs, affirmative action, and liberalism.[16]

The constituency of conservatism expanded considerably in the late 1970s, when it obtained a large grass-roots following within fundamentalist religious groups, particularly the Southern Baptist Church. White parents who had sent their children to segregated private schools in order to escape integrated public schools, as well as curriculum they believed to represent secular humanism, were outraged that the Internal Revenue Service (IRS) did not grant tax exemptions to those schools, and turned to the Republicans, who promised to help rescind the IRS ruling.[17] The New Religious-Political Right (NRPR) was formed as an umbrella group that contained many independent congregations, individual members, and groups like the Moral Majority. By 1980, it contained 90 constituent organizations—from the national Pro-Life Political Action Committee to the Interfaith Committee Against Blasphemy.[18] Jerry Falwell, an outspoken Baptist preacher, quickly became the leader of the Moral Majority, a grass-roots pressure group that favored the abolition of abortion, censorship of literature to limit pornography, and policies to allow prayer in schools; the Moral Majority lent its support to many political conservatives who advocated sharp reductions in social spending. The various member groups of the NRPR engaged in educational programs, funded by tax-deductible contributions, in which millions of items of literature were distributed through the mails, at churches, and by personal contacts. Some groups also engaged in extensive political activities, including lobbying and contributions to political campaigns.[19]

Ronald Reagan as Catalyst

By the late 1970s, the political climate was ripe for the emergence of a conservative movement and it found a catalyst in Ronald Reagan, a former movie actor turned politician. Reagan came from a family in Illinois that had suffered some poverty and turmoil because Reagan's father was an alcoholic; it seems likely that Reagan's dislike of welfare recipients and poor people stemmed in part from the trauma his family encountered as it sought to remain independent despite his father's erratic behavior.[20]

In the 1930s, Reagan was a devoted follower of Franklin Roosevelt. However, during his postwar acting career, he became convinced that government regulations had unfairly forced a movie company with which he was associated to divest its holdings in a chain of theaters. He increasingly resented the high taxes that he had to pay as his income from movies increased. His distrust of communists, which was to assume paranoid proportions in succeeding decades, increased as he observed the power of radicals in his union, the Screen Actors Guild. During the late 1940s, he devoted himself to his movie career; he chose roles that mirrored his personal philosophy—for example, the Notre Dame football coach Knute Rockne, a self-made man who preached the virtues of hard work and morality. Reagan remained a Democrat until 1962, but he had gradually moved to the right during the 1950s, when he developed a national reputation as a public speaker for conservative audiences.[21]

Reagan idealized self-made men who achieved upward mobility through the traditional virtues of hard work, persistence, and risk taking. He realized that some Americans encountered hard times, but he was convinced that private philanthropy and the assistance of family and friends were usually sufficient remedies. Since he discounted the importance of racism and discrimination, he believed that, if they tried, African Americans, Latinos, and Native Americans could emulate the successes of white citizens.[22] The economy worked best, he believed, when government assumed virtually no role in its regulation and did not tax citizens beyond the minimal amount needed to fund defense spending and keep a police force. He regarded the 19th century as America's golden era, when individualism, localism, risk taking, and free enterprise dominated the nation. His political hero was Calvin Coolidge, who articulated a conservative philosophy and

made deep and successive cuts in federal taxes during the 1920s.[23] Although Reagan admired Franklin Roosevelt's political skills and decisive leadership, he held Roosevelt responsible for the introduction of alien and destructive policies, including the development of the federal bureaucracy, federal regulations, handouts or doles to millions of Americans, and heavy federal taxes. Roosevelt had systematically destroyed the vision of the founding fathers, Reagan thought, and developed massive welfare and public works programs to gain a political constituency for the Democratic party. Reagan was critical of liberal rulings of the Supreme Court in the 1950s and 1960s under Chief Justice Earl Warren; he believed that liberal justices had erred in limiting the powers of the police excessively. Reagan did not support federal civil rights legislation in the 1960s, because he believed that states could protect the civil rights of their citizens.[24]

His political philosophy can be criticized on many counts. The nostalgic view of American history that eulogized generations of self-made men overlooked the systematic oppression of people of color and women. Since his "frontier philosophy" accorded women primarily domestic functions, he did not appoint many women to policy positions during his terms as governor of California and as president.[25] He did not fully realize that many persons who led salutary lives often encountered hard times. Roosevelt's New Deal, far from consisting of a radical departure, provided a minimal set of subsistence supports for such persons. Reagan's emphasis on self-sufficiency precluded him from understanding the plight of millions of working but poor Americans who cannot support their families. He did not favor social welfare programs to aid

INSERT 11.1   CRITICAL ANALYSIS: REAGAN'S ROMANTIC VIEW OF THE 19TH CENTURY

Drawing on materials from Chapters 4 and 5 of this book, critique Reagan's romantic view of the 19th century and, especially, his belief that the nation benefited from the federal government's lack of involvement in social policy.

In light of our knowledge of social problems in the 19th century, why would Reagan believe that it was the golden age of American history?

poor persons because he regarded economic inequality as an incentive for the poor to improve their economic conditions.[26]

Other troubling characteristics of Reagan appeared even when he was governor, only to resurface during his presidency. Lou Cannon, a reporter who followed him over decades and interviewed him more than 40 times, believes that Reagan's childhood experiences with an alcoholic father led him to live largely in a fantasy world of movies, Western heroes, and war heroes that made him inattentive to details and unable to grasp the consequences of some of his decisions—for example, his irresponsible fiscal policies, which led to huge deficits.[27] He was too obsessed with the three themes of lowering taxes, increasing America's defenses, and cutting social spending to be interested in other issues.[28]

Reagan's Emergence as a National Hero

Those who shared Reagan's ideology were widely viewed as extremist in the 1960s, even by many Republicans, but Reagan began to shed the label of extremism by winning election in 1966, and again in 1970, as governor of California, a state where liberals, trade unions, and people of color are a considerable political force. Although his policies were decidedly conservative, Reagan often displayed political pragmatism. While criticizing intellectuals, he substantially increased the budget of the state university, as well as state assistance to public schools; while criticizing social spending, he permitted significant increases in the state's budget; while criticizing taxes, he increased the state's taxes by $1 billion; and while criticizing sexual permissiveness and abortion, he supported policies that allowed large state funding of abortions. Even as governor, however, these pragmatic accommodations were accompanied by harsh and uncompromising attitudes toward people in poverty; for example, he slashed the budgets of selected public welfare, mental-health, and child welfare programs. His open opposition to the federal Civil Rights Acts of 1964 and 1965 was matched by his indifference to civil rights as governor. Reagan also initiated a punitive workfare program that forced some recipients into low-paying and menial jobs. He appointed conservative "law and order" justices and continued the rhetoric that extolled conservative values.[29] Moreover, he exhibited a penchant for fiscal irresponsibility as governor by making such large tax cuts that he later had to increase taxes to reduce the budget deficit.[30]

Conservatives persuaded Reagan to run against Gerald Ford for the Republican nomination for the presidency in 1976, but his poor showing in the primaries suggested that he was still regarded as a political maverick. Unhappy with the politically moderate Ford, conservatives tried to persuade Reagan to start a new conservative party both during and after the 1976 race, but he refused, because he realized that it would ruin his chances to enter the mainstream of the Republican party.[31] He decided to pursue the presidency in 1980 in the aftermath of his defeat for the nomination in 1976 but, like Nixon before him, he realized that Republicans' traditional negative policies would not suffice to attract a broad range of voters.

Supply-Side Economics: A Positive Way To Be Negative

It was during this period of drift that Reagan and his aides chanced on a theory known as supply-side economics, which became a major theme of his candidacy.[32] Keynesian economics, which had dominated economic thinking in the United States since the late 1930s, emphasized the use of government spending and changes in interest rates to offset recessions and inflation. In recessions, spending was increased and interest rates were decreased; to combat inflation, these policies were reversed. Even Republican Presidents Eisenhower, Nixon, and Ford had used its tenets to guide their economic policies. But Keynesian economics was increasingly under attack by the mid-1970s, because it seemed inadequate to solve stagflation. Milton Friedman added new doubts when he suggested that monetary policy—increases or decreases in the supply of money—could powerfully influence the economy. When the government increased the money supply too rapidly, he argued, the nation experienced rapid growth with ensuing inflation, whereas severe reductions in the supply of money often caused recessions.

In this welter of economic theories, economist Arthur Laffer, whose ideas were popularized by journalist Jude Wanniski, argued that Keynesian economists had neglected the importance of the supply of capital to economic growth, because of their preoccupation with consumer demand, interest rates, and government spending. Laffer reasoned that economic growth requires steady increases in investment, but investment can occur only if sufficient amounts of capital are accumulated by wealthy persons and corporations and invested in job-creating businesses. However, affluent persons are unlikely to invest their excess money in such businesses, Laffer argued, if their money is subject to high marginal rates of taxation that reduce their profits from investments; in such circumstances, he contended, affluent persons buy expensive cars, antiques, and other luxuries rather than placing their funds in income-producing investments. No amount of consumer demand, Laffer concluded, can cause economic growth if a shortage of investment capital exists.[33] Some Republican politicians, including Congressman Jack Kemp, accepted the logic of supply-side economics and vigorously promoted tax reduction.

Quite apart from its technical merits, supply-side theory appealed to Reagan and his advisors on political grounds, because it purported to offer a solution to stagflation by simultaneously addressing problems of inflation and unemployment.[34] Increases in pools of investment capital would, they argued, increase employment by creating jobs, while inflation would decrease as entrepreneurs invested in technology and new machinery that made workers more productive. Supply-side economics also provided a justification for major reductions in taxes, which are usually popular with conservatives and with many voters. But would not tax cuts exacerbate the nation's mounting deficits, which had approached $50 billion by the mid-1970s? Not so, countered the supply-siders, because increases in investments prompted by the lower tax rates would stimulate economic activity and hence produce an overall gain in government revenues, even with reductions in tax rates.[35]

Supply-side economics also provided a convenient way to appeal not only to the traditional Republican constituency but to blue-collar voters. Supply-side theorists were most interested in tax reductions for affluent persons, but it was relatively easy to also introduce some reductions for blue-collar and middle-class persons, by proposing reductions in the appropriate federal tax brackets.[36] In short, Reagan hoped to achieve Nixon's dream of enlarging the base of the Republican party, not by the development of social programs but by economic policy.[37]

Ronald Reagan was not alone in his advocacy of supply-side economics. By 1978, the concepts had obtained sufficient appeal that tax-cut proposals nearly passed both houses of Congress with bipartisan support.[38] However, in 1980, Reagan was the only presidential contender in either party who strongly supported the theory; indeed, in the Republican primaries, George Bush attacked Reagan's policies as "voodoo economics."[39] Supply-side economics, then, provided a positive way to be negative. Reagan could demand tax cuts (a negative policy) in order to promote economic growth, reductions in both unemployment and inflation, reductions of the federal deficit, and increases in the income of Americans of all social classes (positive policies).

Since supply-side economists were convinced that economic growth would follow tax cuts, they did not believe that major cuts in government spending were required to curtail deficits. Reagan coupled supply-side economics, however, with his traditional demands that social spending be radically reduced and that many government regulations be rescinded. Reagan's demands for reductions in the role of the federal government might have been dismissed earlier in the decade as Republican negativism, but they struck a sympathetic chord in the political climate of the late 1970s, when Americans were distrustful of federal bureaucrats and Congress.[40] Moreover, many white Americans were convinced their taxes rose during the 1970s because of increases in spending for social programs that they believed were used primarily by people of color.

The Campaign of 1980: Two Styles

Reagan won the nomination of the Republican party in 1980, but Carter, the Democratic incumbent, enjoyed a substantial lead in polls in early September, scored heavily when he attacked Reagan as trigger-happy, and used his presidential access to the media to advantage.[41] The political climate of 1980 was very different from that of 1964, however, and Reagan was far more politically adept than Goldwater. His political success stemmed from his ability to adapt his political message to the mood of voters in 1980, with considerable aid from media and political consultants. Carter's response to the nation's economic ills was to cut social spending, but Reagan coupled this response with his supply-side vision of sweeping tax cuts. Carter projected an image of policy vacillation, but Reagan consistently presented his conservative philosophy and advocacy of rearmament. Reagan's rugged image appealed to those male voters who regarded Carter as soft. (Carter was more appealing to female voters, but not enough to offset Reagan's lead with male voters.) Carter's campaign promises to specific interest groups, such as the National Education Association, made him seem beholden to them, but Reagan claimed to be speaking for the entire nation. Carter emphasized the difficulties in righting the economy, but Reagan exuded an optimism reminiscent of Roosevelt's in 1932.

Reagan was aided by public opinion that strongly favored conservatism. After the trauma of Vietnam, Watergate, stagflation, and the Iran hostage crisis, many Americans wanted a respite with a president who could make the world seem simple, who could unite the nation behind patriotism and national pride, and who seemed to stand for moral values. Reagan appealed to many white Americans' distress at the pace of reform in the preceding two decades and their opposition to affirmative action, quotas, and busing. He made extraordinary promises that appealed to those Americans who sought easy answers to stagflation; he even predicted that he could cut taxes, increase defense spending, *and* balance the budget![42] He played on the racial and social fears of white voters by stressing opposition to busing, affirmative action, quotas, and welfare; indeed, he loved to recount the story of a "welfare queen" who had enriched herself through welfare fraud.[43] In the 1980 presidential election, Reagan won a landslide victory; he obtained a large majority of the male vote, carried the entire Southern and Western regions of the nation, and wrested large numbers of blue-collar votes from the Democratic party.[44]

 # THE REAGAN POLICY BLITZKRIEG

In the conservative equivalent of Roosevelt's first 100 days in office, Reagan during his first eight months secured major budget cuts, tax cuts, the elimination of many regulations, reductions in the federal government's policy roles, and massive increases in military spending. A number of conditions allowed Reagan to move quickly and successfully on his conservative agenda. First of all, the Democrats were thoroughly demoralized by the size of Reagan's victory in 1980. They feared that it might presage a permanent shift of blue-collar and white ethnic populations to the Republican party.[45] Thus intimidated by Reagan, the Democrats were also in disarray as they planned their political strategy. Some wanted their party to militantly oppose Reagan's policies and to reassert liberal principles; others feared that opposition would allow Reagan to accuse them of resisting the will of the people; still other Democrats hoped to obtain partial credit for conservative policies by offering budget and tax alternatives to Reagan's positions.[46] Democrats also encountered serious practical and leadership problems. Having obtained numerical superiority in the Senate in 1980, Republicans possessed a crucial bastion in the Congress as long as they remained united. In the House, the Democratic party maintained only a slim majority of 38 seats, which could be overcome if there were defections to the Republicans from conservative Southern Democrats, whose constituencies often favored Reagan's policies. The Democrats lacked effective leadership to develop their policy strategy, because Tip O'Neill, the majority leader in the House, was widely perceived to lack skills in initiating policies and had awarded crucial committee and party positions to conservative Democrats following an internal party struggle in 1980.[47]

Reagan and his aides plotted a brilliant strategy to capitalize on the Democrats' weakness and the desperate economic situation. Their tactics included militance, centralization, surprise, preparedness, cooptation of conservative Southern Democrats, and preemption of federal revenues through tax cuts and increases in military spending. Let's see how these tactics played out in practice.

The term *militance* is usually applied to the strategy of radicals, but it usefully describes the risk-taking orientation of Reagan and his top advisors, who wanted drastic reductions in social programs and regulations.[48] Reagan knew that he could not instantly eradicate most of the welfare state, because of political support for many social programs, but he hoped to reduce government spending from 23% to 19% of the GNP by 1984 and to hold government spending increases to 7% per year, which was far below the 16% increases in the last years of the Carter administration. Cuts in social spending were particularly needed because of projected massive increases in military spending, which Reagan wanted to increase by 160% over the defense budget during the next six years—rising from $142 billion in 1980 to $368 billion by 1986. Reagan's inner circle of advisors quickly decided that they could be successful only if they created a climate in which virtually every program and governmental unit were asked to sacrifice for the common good and opposition to cuts in particular programs was viewed as sabotaging efforts to reduce deficits and restore economic growth.[49] They intimidated recalcitrant members of Congress with the prospect of opposition from Reagan in upcoming elections, particularly in those districts in the South and West where Reagan had run more strongly than incumbents. They even hoped

to persuade some Southern Democrats to become Republicans in return for choice committee assignments and other political concessions.[50]

Although Reagan was committed to budget cuts, he was equally interested in tax cuts, both to instill economic growth and to reduce federal revenues that might otherwise be used to fund social programs.[51] In a sense, then, Reagan was using the tax cuts to force budget cuts. He calculated that, because tax cuts were politically popular, members of Congress would be pressured to enact them—and that the resulting decreases in revenues would *force* spending cuts unless the Congress wanted to take the blame for budget deficits.[52] Indeed, as David Stockman, the budget director, revealed to Senator Daniel Moynihan in 1985, Reagan had acknowledged in 1981 that he *wanted* a huge deficit in order to force Congress to cut costly social spending.[53]

Many Democrats were acutely aware of Reagan's strategy, but encountered a political predicament. In the conservative political atmosphere of 1980, it would have been difficult to oppose *both* tax and budget cuts. Accordingly, many liberal Democrats decided to support budget cuts and oppose tax cuts. They regarded tax cuts as particularly pernicious, since they diminished revenues that were needed to fund social programs.[54] Democrats reasoned, then, that consenting to large budget cuts would make it clear that they were not obstructionists, and so they would then be free to oppose the tax cuts. Their strategy backfired, however, because they did not realize that the tax cuts were so popular with their colleagues and with the electorate that the Congress would enact them despite massive budget cuts.

Military spending, while it had increased in absolute terms during most of the 1970s, had decreased from 49% of the federal budget in 1960 to 21% in 1980. President Carter had initiated increases in military spending. However, Reagan sought increases that were unprecedented during peacetime. Indeed, his advisors wanted to expend $1.46 trillion on defense in the next five years—a sum so large that even the hawkish David Stockman believed it would make a massive federal deficit inevitable.[55] These incredible increases in

INSERT 11.2   ETHICAL ANALYSIS OF KEY ISSUES AND POLICIES: WHEN TO RETREAT AND WHEN TO RESIST?

Most of the budget cuts of 1981 focused on programs for poor people; so-called middle-class entitlements like Medicare and Social Security were untouched. Northern Democrats, who represent the liberal wing of the party, faced a dilemma. Many Southern Democrats were defecting to the Republican budget and tax policies. The Reagan presidency seemed to be invincible; Democrats feared that they might be routed in upcoming elections if they obstructed his policies. Yet those policies contradicted deeply held liberal values and violated the principle of social justice.

Should liberal Democrats have made a last stand in 1981 against the budget cuts? Should they have opposed *both* budget cuts and tax cuts, on the grounds that the latter *forced* the budget cuts by depleting the government's revenue? Is a principled stand sometimes effective in politics?

defense spending, like the proposed tax cuts, were highly popular with an American public convinced that the United States needed to deal with the Soviet Union from a position of strength. Realizing that Reagan would obtain major increases in defense spending, members of Congress recognized that cuts in social programs would be needed to restrain budget deficits. The issue of guns versus butter surfaced once again; this time, many Americans believed that guns needed to take precedence. Like the tax cuts, the increase in defense spending was a threat to social spending because it diminished resources that could be invested in social programs.

Reagan soon realized, however, that his budget cuts would be endangered if he attacked social programs with powerful constituencies, such as Social Security, Medicare, Head Start, SSI, disability payments for veterans, summer jobs programs, and school lunch programs. In addition to declaring these programs immune from cuts, Reagan cleverly argued that he was not cutting aggregate social spending in absolute terms but was merely cutting the rate of increase in social spending. He also announced that he would preserve a safety net of basic programs for Americans who were poor or ill, so that none of them would lose welfare protections.[56] These arguments, he hoped, would make him appear compassionate, even as he proposed massive cuts in many social programs.

Reagan's decision to focus on means-tested programs rather than so-called entitlement programs like Medicare and Social Security had profound—and disastrous—consequences for many Americans. Entitlements constituted 41% of the nation's spending in 1980; indeed, Social Security alone constituted almost 33% of the nation's domestic budget. To achieve his target of $50 billion in cuts, therefore, Reagan had to slash programs that specifically gave services and resources to poor persons.[57] Certainly, his argument that he was only slowing the rate of increase of aggregate social spending was technically correct; nevertheless, many specific programs that assisted poor persons were eliminated or severely slashed. For example, Reagan proposed decreasing the federal share of AFDC, even though the real value of AFDC benefits had eroded during the late 1970s. He called for massive cuts in Food Stamps and Medicaid, as well as in nutritional, mental-health, and public health programs.[58]

Anticipating efforts by lobbyists and defenders of specific programs to mobilize opposition to his cuts, Reagan called on David Stockman and Edwin Meese to develop and implement a centralized strategy to push them through.[59] The youthful Stockman, formerly a conservative member of the House, had gained detailed knowledge of government programs and finance when he fashioned Republican alternatives to Carter's budgets in the late 1970s. Impressed by Stockman's knowledge, Reagan appointed him director of the Office of

Management and Budget (OMB), the agency that develops the president's budget. Meese, a conservative attorney who had been Reagan's attorney general in California, was given the authority to manage domestic policy decisions within the White House and to control the flow of paper to Reagan. He was joined by James Baker, a clever negotiator who orchestrated policy compromises with Congress, and Michael Deaver, an expert in public relations.

Reagan and his advisors realized that their objective of securing cuts in social programs could not be accomplished if they gave the opposition time to organize, if they allowed recently appointed cabinet officials to advocate increased funds for their departments, or if they gave opponents of specific cuts the opportunity to join forces with opponents of other cuts. Stockman, Meese, and Baker quickly held a series of briefings with recently appointed cabinet officials, where they announced plans for major cuts in their departments' programs and urged them to be team players. Richard Schweiker, the newly appointed secretary of the Department of Health and Human Services, conceded to most of the proposed cuts in social programs, not only because of the pressure that was placed on him but also because he had converted to conservatism after a relatively liberal voting record as a senator.[60]

Stockman also met with many members of Congress to inform them of proposed cuts and seek their ideas for further cuts. He compiled in a large black book the growing list of proposed cuts, which quickly totaled $50 billion, a staggering and unprecedented sum. No one was allowed access to this book, which was stored in a safe in his office, but the repeated leaks of proposed cuts kept the opposition off guard and strengthened the impression that everyone would have to sacrifice. Reagan's team created a siege atmosphere, in which it seemed unpatriotic to oppose cuts in specific programs.[61]

The Democrats threatened to defeat Reagan's policies in the House, where they held a majority, but Reagan remedied this situation by cultivating the support of conservative Southern Democrats who favored his tax, military, and budget-cutting policies. These renegade Southern Democrats, who were called boll weevils, repeatedly gave Reagan a majority of votes in the House. To gain their support, Reagan's team consulted with them and gave some of them, such as Phil Gramm of Texas, important roles as sponsors and designers of legislation. The boll weevils' threat of defection put House Democrats under even more pressure to capitulate to Reagan's policies, in the knowledge that they could be outvoted by the Reagan coalition of Republicans and boll weevils.[62]

The Triumph of Conservatism

Reagan's strategy led to three major victories for conservatives in 1981: Budget cuts were achieved through passage of the Omnibus Budget Reconciliation Act (OBRA) in July; tax cuts were enacted in August; and increases in defense spending were made final in the fall.

It is difficult under ordinary conditions for a president to control the budgetary process, because numerous congressional committees can override his budgetary suggestions. Without describing the complex budgetary maneuvering in detail, suffice it to say that David Stockman became the orchestrator of administration policy: To obtain enactment of OBRA, tax cuts, and increases in defense spending, he literally camped out in the Congress, arranged coalitions of Republicans and boll weevils, outmaneuvered liberal Democrats, and made extensive use of Reagan's popularity and the mass media.

OBRA made deep cuts in social programs and eliminated 57 social programs, by folding them into seven block grants: social services; community services; alcohol, drug-abuse, and mental-health services; maternal and child health services; community development services; primary health services; and preventive health services.[63] By creating block grants and allocating limited funds to each of them, Reagan was able to cut social spending for those programs within the block grants.

Reagan achieved another victory in August,

when the largest tax cut since the end of World War II was enacted. It made substantial reductions in the taxes of individuals and even larger cuts in the taxes of many corporations. This legislation markedly increased economic inequality by granting larger tax cuts to affluent persons than to middle- and working-class Americans, at the same time as social programs for the poor were being decimated. In the end, the tax cuts gained the support not only of boll weevils and Republicans but also of many Democrats who had initially planned to contest them but who feared retaliation from voters.[64]

Reagan also succeeded in obtaining the huge increases in defense spending that he had so fervently sought. By so doing, Reagan had obtained the counterrevolution that he had espoused since the early 1950s—tax cuts, social spending reductions, and defense increases.

When characterizing Reagan's policy successes in 1981, it is important to reiterate that, though he cut the funding of many programs that help low-income persons, he chose not to cut big-ticket social programs with large middle-class constituencies, such as Medicare and Social Security. In subsequent years, he again chose to exclude these programs from his cuts. Indeed, one commentator calls Reagan the guns *and* butter president, because aggregate social spending continued to rise along with defense spending.[65] He chose to make this strategic concession partly because his aides had calculated that Congress, including many Democrats, would not accede to his increased military spending if he also sought to cut these middle-class programs.

OBRA, Tax Reductions, and Deregulation

A host of conservative policies were included within the complex tangle of the OBRA legislation, which recommended budget cuts that totaled $40 billion for 1982 and an additional $50 billion by 1984. First, the legislation terminated some programs—for example, CETA, the public service program for unemployed workers. Second, deep cuts were made in many means-tested programs. The extent of the cuts in these programs for low-income persons was deeply disturbing to many liberals—and Reagan relentlessly sought to cut these programs further in succeeding years. All told, Reagan managed during his administration to cut AFDC by 17.4%; 400,000 persons were removed from the rolls. One million persons lost eligibility for Food Stamps; the program was cut by 14.3%. The social services block grant, which provided an array of services to poor people, was cut by 23.5%.[66] In the Department of Housing and Urban Development, funding for low- and moderate-income housing was reduced from $33.5 billion in 1981 to $14 billion in 1987—a cut of 57%.[67]

Third, OBRA enacted indirect methods of cutting expenditures. Believing that social programs should only assist truly needy persons, Reagan hoped to reduce the number of able-bodied persons who received welfare and other benefits.[68] To do so, he reduced eligibility for Food Stamps, state AFDC programs, and unemployment insurance. He also eliminated work-incentive payments in the AFDC program, so that many working women could no longer receive welfare benefits, even if they were beneath official poverty lines. AFDC rolls were cut dramatically by this policy, but it was ironic that an administration that wanted to encourage, even require, work for welfare recipients had provided a disincentive to work by forcing many women working in low-wage jobs to return to welfare rolls.[69]

The Economic Recovery Tax Act that passed the Congress in August 1981 provided for 20% cuts in the income taxes of most Americans, spread over three years, and a major reduction in corporate taxes.[70] But these cuts were highly inequitable. Between 1981 and 1985, for example, the combined tax rates for the lowest one-fifth of the population went from 8.4% to 10.6% (or $137 in additional taxes per payer), whereas the tax rate of persons in the top one-fifth declined from 27.3% to 24% (or tax reductions of $2,531 per payer). What made these tax increases even more onerous on poor persons was that their *pretax* income declined during the decade, because low-paid service jobs steadily replaced unionized industrial jobs.[71] The tax legislation also violated the principle of progressive taxation that liberals had traditionally championed: It gave larger tax breaks to rich people than to poor people. Further, the tax credits given in 1973 to low-income persons who earned less than $5,600 were not indexed; their value had been seriously eroded by the inflation of the 1970s.[72]

In 1981, Reagan issued an executive order that gave OMB the duty of reviewing government regulations and deleting those that were not demonstrated to be cost effective, and a cabinet-level Task Force on Regulatory Relief, chaired by Vice President George Bush, was established. Between 1980 and 1984, the number of federal regulations was reduced from 90,000 to 76,000. To the consternation of some liberals, the administration drastically reduced regulations in the EEOC, OSHA, and many social programs; key civil rights and other provisions were deleted.[73] Reagan severely curtailed the effectiveness of OSHA, the EEOC, and the Department of Labor's Office of Contract Compliance Programs. He cut their staffs; delegated many monitoring functions to states; sought to enforce affirmative action only when proof of discrimination by employers had been first obtained; and limited affirmative action monitoring to very large corporations. Reagan appointed officials who did not favor affirmative action to oversee its enforcement; for example, he chose Clarence Thomas to head the EEOC, and he appointed Clarence Pendleton to direct the Civil Rights Commission, where he used his power to fight the principle of affirmative action.[74]

Reagan's Loss of Momentum

It seemed in September 1981 that the Reagan counterrevolution would continue unabated for years to come, but he did not achieve striking policy successes during the remainder of his first term. There were a number of reasons for this loss of momentum. First, the administration split into two factions.[75] One group, headed by David Stockman and James Baker, feared that the federal deficit would continue to grow uncontrollably unless taxes were increased, further cuts were made in social spending, and reductions were made in defense spending. Another group, which included supply-side economists, adamantly opposed tax increases, which they feared would jeopardize economic growth. They believed that the economic growth generated by the 1981 tax cuts would produce additional tax revenues to ease the federal deficit. Some of them were so confident in this prediction that they did not believe further deep cuts in social programs were needed.

Stockman had embraced tax reduction policies uneasily during the early and middle 1980s because he feared massive increases in the federal deficit. However, he advocated delaying or reducing tax cuts in the summer of 1981.[76] In interviews during the summer and fall of 1981, which were published in December 1981, he admitted that top officials in the administration had tinkered with economic models so as to make it appear that federal deficits would not be exacerbated by the tax cuts, and he alleged that some officials in the administration had used supply-side theory as a convenient rationale for giving huge tax concessions to affluent persons and corporations.[77] Supply-siders were also furious with Stockman and Baker for not protesting the tight-money policy of the Federal Reserve Board. This policy had been devised by its chairman to drive down the extraordinary inflation that plagued the nation, but supply-siders feared that it would create a recession and thereby discredit their approach. Some even believed that Stockman would welcome a recession so as to discredit them.[78]

Both sides in this titanic struggle within the administration were convinced of the rightness of their cause and attributed evil intentions to their opponents. To the delight of supply-siders, Reagan resisted pleas by Stockman and Baker to increase taxes. However, in the spring of 1982, when he finally assented to a large tax increase known as the Tax Equity and Fiscal Responsibility Act (TEFRA), which took away some of the massive tax concessions given to corporations in 1981, some supply-side officials left the administration.[79] Rumors circulated of dissension among Meese, Deaver, and Baker. Meanwhile, observers began to wonder whether anyone was in charge at the White House, because Reagan appeared to lack understanding of policy issues.[80]

Another factor that slowed Reagan's momentum was a deep recession, which began in 1981 and extended into 1983. Unemployment rose to double-digit figures; its impact was greatest on people of color, teenagers, and women. The recession contributed to growing doubts about the administration's economic policies; it also increased the federal deficit, since government tax revenues decreased as economic activity slackened.[81] By the end of fiscal year 1984, the cumulative deficits in the Reagan administration had surpassed the cumulative deficits of *all* preceding American presidents; indeed, some commentators feared that the United States would be reduced to the status of nations such as Mexico and Brazil, which found their economic growth impeded by the size of interest payments on their national debts.

With the recession came growing awareness of the plight of poor persons, who were hard hit by unemployment and the cuts in means-tested social programs. National media ran extended stories about increases in poverty rates across the nation, the growing inequality between rich and poor Americans, and pockets of unemployment in cities like Youngstown and Cleveland, Ohio, where steel and other basic industries had closed plants in response to foreign competition.[82] Congress was unhappy about the lack of equity in administration policies. Reagan had declared virtually all the entitlement programs off limits for cuts, but he proposed further cuts of means-tested programs for the poor. His tax policies had led to windfall gains for many corporations and affluent persons. The charge that Reagan lacked compassion appeared to be gathering strength in 1982 and 1983, because of the cumulative effects of his budget-cutting and tax policies, as well as his fiscal and monetary policy, which had contributed to the recession.[83]

Many members of Congress also believed they had been manipulated by the White House and by Stockman during budget and tax deliberations in 1981. Should the OMB director, they asked, personally orchestrate budget objectives and goals of the Congress? Some in Congress felt betrayed by the White House; although Stockman had implied in 1981 that the OBRA cuts would suffice, he proposed further deep cuts in late 1981 and in succeeding years. Was it fair for Reagan, some asked, to force the Congress to make cuts in social programs by reducing government revenues—both by slashing taxes and by dramatically increasing military spending? Moreover, Reagan's frequent use of television and radio to apply public pressure on Congress made members increasingly resentful.[84]

Whereas many Democrats had capitulated to Reagan's blitzkrieg in 1981, they were more willing to resist Reagan's cuts during the remainder of his first term—especially now that, thanks to the recession, their constituents were more concerned about unemployment than about inflation. In addition, Reagan's ability to outvote Democrats with a coalition of boll weevils and Republicans was curtailed when the Democrats gained a number of House seats in congressional elections of 1982. Indeed, some liberal Republicans, known as gypsy moths, sided with Democrats against many spending cuts. Though still in disarray, the Democrats held their ground against further cuts, in the hope that they could defeat Reagan in 1984.

Social Security, Job Training, and Medicare

Reagan's policy successes during the remainder of his first term were modest, though he was able to obtain additional cuts in social programs, to make major changes in the Social Security program and Medicare, and to create his own job-training legislation.

Stockman had hoped from the outset to include Social Security and Medicare in the budget cuts, because they constituted a large portion of domestic spending. When he became further concerned about deficits, Stockman pushed the president to rescind the minimum Social Security benefit that was given to persons—such as elderly nuns—who had not paid into the trust fund during their working years. Stockman also sought to institute a penalty for those who sought early retirement benefits. A storm of political protest greeted these proposals when the president made them public. Democrats accused him of reneging on his pledge to exempt the Social Security program from budget cuts, and many Republicans dissociated themselves from policies that they believed could be politically disastrous. The proposals were defeated by a vote of 96 to 0 by the Senate in 1981.[85]

Reagan and most legislators realized, however, that changes had to be made in Social Security, because benefit outlays continued to exceed revenues from payroll deductions despite the sharp increases in payroll taxes introduced by President Carter. To deflect controversy from himself, Reagan appointed a blue-ribbon task force, which recommended that the option to take Social Security benefits at age 62 be rescinded and that benefits be delayed until persons reached age 68. The commission also concluded that retired persons whose earnings exceeded $20,000, whether from work or investments, should pay taxes on a substantial portion of their Social Security benefits, with ensuing revenues to be returned to the trust fund. To decrease the size of reductions in general benefits, many politicians supported the taxation of affluent persons' benefits, a policy that partially offset the regressive nature of Social Security payroll taxes.[86] Some of these recommendations received bipartisan support and were enacted in 1983, including the taxing of some benefits received by affluent persons and the phasing upward of the retirement age to age 67 by the year 2027.

Reagan also encountered a funding emergency in Part A of the Medicare program, whose outlays for hospital bills had increased faster than payroll tax revenues. Federal Medicare expenditures had increased from $15.2 billion in 1970 to $38.3 billion in 1980 because of the aging of the population, the increasing use of technology, and the failure of government authorities to prevent doctors and hospitals from charging excessive fees and providing unnecessary treatments.[87] Reagan's advisers developed an indirect method of restraining Medicare costs. To place pressure on hospitals to discharge patients as soon as possible and to prevent them from charging excessive fees, Congress established national levels of payment for 467 specific diagnoses or diagnostic-related groups (DRGs).

Thus, federal authorities paid hospitals an established fee for all patients who were admitted for appendectomies, no matter how long they remained in the hospital or whether they developed complications. The policy led to some decrease in health expenditures by 1986, but critics argued that this reimbursement approach created additional problems. Would not many hospitals try to discharge patients prematurely—or serve only those patients who were not likely to develop complications? Would not affluent persons purchase insurance to finance supplemental services so that, once again, public policy would create a two-tiered system of health care? The formula also appeared to favor the growing network of for-profit hospitals that primarily served those middle- and upper-class clientele who are least likely to experience medical complications.[88]

Federal authorities also wanted to contain the increasing costs of Medicaid, whose combined federal and state funding had increased from $10.9 billion in 1970 to $25.4 billion in 1980. They cut the federal share of Medicaid funding in the OBRA legislation and offered states incentives to reduce the growth rates of Medicaid. Finally, they encouraged states to offer Medicaid contracts only to those hospitals and clinics that offered low bids; as a result, Medicaid patients found that they could use even fewer providers than were previously available.[89]

The health-care system was characterized in 1986 by increasing competition and turmoil. There had been some easing of the rate of price increases for medical care by the middle of the decade, but basic flaws in the American medical system, such as its excessive use of technology and absence of preventive care, had still not been addressed.[90] Critics lamented continuing inequities in medical care. Roughly 30 million Americans had no health insurance and were ineligible for the means-tested Medicaid program and the age-tested Medicare programs. Millions of Medicaid patients could obtain treatment only in inner-city clinics, partly because most physicians would not serve Medicaid patients for reasons of financial self-interest: They received considerably larger fees from other insurers.[91]

Federal authorities had not developed adequate policies to help elderly patients with chronic health-care problems. Medicare was intended to help elderly persons with acute conditions. Those with chronic conditions soon exhausted it (and their private insurance) and had to deplete their assets to obtain eligibility for the means-tested Medicaid program, which covered ongoing costs of convalescent homes, nursing homes, and home health care. Medicaid authorities had, in turn, developed confusing and poorly monitored federal and state policies to regulate nursing home care and to fund community-based care of frail and elderly persons. Medicare and Medicaid authorities, as well as private insurance companies, had commissioned a series of experiments in the 1980s to test various community-based methods of helping frail elderly persons, but no comprehensive national policy had been developed by the late 1980s.[92] Perhaps the most serious health problem of the 1980s was the emergence of acquired immunodeficiency syndrome (AIDS), which we discuss in more detail later.[93]

Reagan was determined to terminate the CETA program, because he believed its subsidy of tens of thousands of public service jobs in public and not-for-profit agencies interfered with private job markets. After slashing its funds, Reagan finally abolished it in favor of his own program, the Job Training Partnership Act (JTPA), enacted in 1982. The federal government gave funds with relatively few restrictions to states, which, in turn, funded local private industry councils (PICs). PICs, made up of business, agency, and government officials, awarded contracts to job-placement agencies and to local industries, which received a fee for each person that they placed with private business. Critics contended, however, that the training and reimbursement policies of JTPA made it irrelevant to the needs of many low-income persons, because placement agencies often were reimbursed only for successful placements. Moreover, the failure of JTPA to provide training and day-care subsidies to placement agencies, businesses, or trainees made it impossible for many women and low-income persons to use the program.[94]

In 1981, Reagan had folded 57 categorical programs into seven block grants. In 1982, he proposed to reduce the federal role in social welfare much further by offering to undertake complete federal financing and administration of Medicaid if the states carried full costs and responsibility for AFDC, Food Stamps, and 43 other programs. To attract the support of governors, he offered to cede to states a limited proportion of federal gasoline and cigarette excise taxes. The proposed swap was defeated, however, for several reasons. Although Reagan claimed that he did not want to short-change the states, astute analysts computed that the scheme would lead them to suffer large net losses in revenue. As in the case of the OBRA block grants, Reagan could not resist the impulse to couple defederalization with budget cuts. Officials in industrialized states in the Midwest and New England, which had particularly high expenses for welfare, believed that defederalization would mainly benefit Sunbelt states, where oil and gas production, as well as high rates of economic growth, already provided sufficient resources to address social needs.[95] Many state officials were disinclined to support the scheme because they were still angry at the budgetary turmoil provoked by Reagan's earlier cuts. Reductions in federal funding for social programs had meant that local authorities had to assume additional expenses at the very time when popular tax revolts had led to sharp reductions in local taxes. Few federal legislators desired to carry defederalization further, because they derived political support from federal programs.

Indeed, it can be argued that the Reagan years reduced both federal and state budgets to chaos. The huge deficits at the federal level meant that congressional officials devoted more time to the budget process than to other, more pressing domestic issues. Moreover, the deficits placed extraordinary pressure on programs for low-income persons, as we have noted. The budgets of many states rose sharply in the 1980s, as they sought to address problems of family dissolution, homelessness, AIDS, and drug and crack babies; they also faced costs due to immigration from abroad, increased costs of prisons, remarkable increases in Medicaid and AFDC costs, and a doubling of their education spending—all during a decade when federal aid went from $110 billion in 1978, in inflation-adjusted dollars, to $88 billion in 1982 and only back up to $96 billion by 1990. Indeed, when AFDC and portions of the Medicaid program are not considered, federal aid to the states fell by one-third during the 1980s.[96] These escalating social costs, coupled with federal cuts, produced serious budget deficits in many local jurisdictions.

Moral Reforms

The Moral Majority had hoped that Reagan would take strong action to stop abortions, to attack pornography, to allow prayer in the public schools, and to provide tax concessions for tuition payments to private schools, but their confidence in him was premature. Reagan knew that these issues, like temperance in the 19th century and in the 1920s, were divisive. The demand for tax concessions for the tuition costs of private schools was widely viewed as public underwriting of educational segregation. Many women opposed a constitutional amendment to override the 1973 Supreme Court ruling that legalized abortion. Many persons in both parties opposed federal legislation or a constitutional amendment to allow school prayer in schools, and civil libertarians stoutly resisted federal laws to outlaw pornography. Reagan feared that personal identification with these divisive issues would jeopardize his other budget-cutting, tax, and deregulatory legislation.[97] Accordingly, he voiced support for moral reforms but did not invest time or resources in them.

Meese became Reagan's emissary to leaders of the Moral Majority and tried to placate them. Disappointed by Reagan's inaction, the Moral Majority nevertheless had notable victories. The Congress continued to disallow use of Medicaid funds for abortion and to cut funds for family planning, which the Moral Majority believed fostered promiscuity. The Justice Department advocated the

Moral Majority's position in court cases regarding pornography, school prayer, and other matters, though it received few favorable rulings. A Presidential Commission on Pornography requested national censorship of magazines like *Playboy* in 1986. The Supreme Court upheld a Georgia statute that declared acts of sodomy between consenting adults to be illegal.

The Moral Majority and its allies also developed expertise in targeting liberal legislators in election campaigns. Vast media, advertising, mailing, and door-to-door campaigns sought to portray liberal candidates as murderers (of fetuses), supporters of pornography, and atheists. By engaging in character assassination of liberal candidates, the Moral Majority and its allies allowed conservative candidates to take the high road and yet still reap the electoral benefits. These tactics contributed to the defeat of a number of liberal legislators in close races.[98]

But the nation was hardly embracing the tenets of the Moral Majority. Courts often ruled against them in school prayer, pornography, and abortion cases. Their tactics in political campaigns sometimes caused a sympathy vote for liberal candidates. Many observers wondered whether a secular and urban society would truly accept the ideas of individuals who, like temperance crusaders in earlier periods, sought to impose their moral standards on others.[99]

STALEMATE AND SCANDAL

The Election of 1984

Reagan relished the opportunity to face Walter Mondale, the Democratic candidate in 1984, who not only had served as vice president to the unpopular Jimmy Carter but was identified with unions and liberalism. After some vacillation, Reagan's resolve to run again was strengthened by improvement in the nation's economy following the recession of 1983.[100]

The election in 1984 was a rerun of the 1980 campaign. Many major Democratic candidates ran in the presidential primaries. Mondale obtained early endorsements from trade unions, as well as from professional groups, but Senator Gary Hart made Mondale appear politically vulnerable by winning decisive victories in key primaries. These two candidates represented a deep split in the Democratic party. Some Democrats, including civil rights groups, many trade unions, intellectuals, and some mayors, continued to embrace federal social welfare programs and civil rights. Mondale felt most at home with this group, but even here he had to contend with the African American civil rights activist Jesse Jackson, whose determined campaign mobilized unprecedented numbers of African American voters. Other Democrats, such as Hart, were neoliberals, who disdained major increases in social spending but favored federal incentives to promote American industry's ability to compete with the Japanese.[101] Hart's support came mainly from young professionals, who had little knowledge of social reform movements in either the Great Depression or the Great Society.[102]

Mondale finally won the Democratic nomination, but he did not overcome Reagan's lead in the polls. In a major victory for feminists, Mondale chose Geraldine Ferraro as the vice-presidential candidate, but her family finances became a major campaign issue that slowed Mondale's momentum. Mondale tried to make the mounting budget deficit a campaign issue—he actually proposed major increases in federal taxes—but the issue was too abstract for most voters, who did not believe the deficits slowed economic growth and did not like his remedy of increased taxes. As front-runner, Reagan avoided substantive issues during most of the campaign and focused instead on his leadership and personal skills, as well as his success in restoring economic growth. As in 1980, he targeted white voters and used code words like affirmative action and quotas to mobilize them against the Democrats. By holding his own during his second televised debate with Mondale, he deflected the charge that he was too old to be president. He won another landslide victory, though the Democrats maintained their numbers in Congress.

Reagan's Second Term

Unlike his victory in 1980, when tax and budget reduction were his central themes, his reelection in 1984 did not constitute a mandate for specific policies. The American people, who stood to the left of Reagan in public opinion polls, liked him as a person, believed him to be a decisive leader, and favored his buildup of the military, but did not elect him to continue his assault on the welfare state.

The politics of his second term can best be described as a stalemate. As in his first term, Reagan used the specter of the federal deficit to increase pressure on the Congress to reduce social spending. Once again, he proposed massive increases in defense spending—in particular, for the Strategic Defense Initiative (SDI), a space-based, laser-guided antimissile system for which appropriate technology had not yet been developed. At an estimated cost of $1 trillion, spread over a decade, this program quickly became a priority of defense spending. However, Congressional legislators balked at his proposals to cut domestic spending, and even made modest increases in some programs. Entitlements remained out of bounds for cuts, though Reagan tried to cut them indirectly, by proposing major increases in consumer fees for services subsidized by Medicare.

In this stalemated atmosphere, an unlikely coalition in Congress enacted legislation to address the unprecedented federal deficits, which had continued to increase. The Balanced Budget and Emergency Deficit Control Act, commonly known as the Gramm-Rudman-Hollings Act, was enacted by Congress in 1985. Furious that Reagan proposed neither tax increases nor cuts in military spending to alleviate the deficit, members of Congress assented to a measure that required across-the-board cuts in domestic and military programs if the budget did not meet targeted spending reductions in coming years, with a view to eventually balancing the budget. But this measure could hardly be expected to eliminate the deficit, inasmuch as it implied that the basic problem was *spending,* rather than the combination of inadequate *revenues* (from taxes) and large military budgets. It was this combination of tax cuts and increases in military spending that had led to the budget deficits in 1981, but few politicians wanted to propose tax increases, even though U.S. tax rates had plummeted far lower than those in any Western industrialized nation. A few legislators proposed sharp decreases in military spending, but most politicians were hesitant to cut the defense budget when it funded projects in their districts. Many commentators doubted that Congress would actually bring the budget into balance even with the enactment of Gramm-Rudman-Hollings.

Tax reform became a central issue in Reagan's second term and eclipsed deficit reduction in congressional deliberations. Finally enacted in 1986 after complicated political maneuvering, the resulting legislation simplified federal taxes by decreasing the number of tax brackets and loopholes, vastly increased corporate taxes, and took roughly six million low-wage earners from the tax rolls. But it also repudiated the liberal belief that the federal tax system should be progressive, by reducing the top tax bracket of affluent Americans to a modest 33%, which was not much higher than the rate paid by middle- and working-class Americans. Moreover, the tax reform did not generate considerably more revenues than the old tax system, and consequently the federal deficit was not reduced; federal revenues were still insufficient to fund social programs.[103]

Social reformers could nonetheless count several modest victories during Reagan's second term. The denial of SSI payments to persons with disabilities, which had often been arbitrary and unwarranted during Reagan's first term, was challenged by several court rulings, and benefits were restored in thousands of cases. The Department of Health and Human Services was forced to concede that many persons with mental disabilities such as schizophrenia could not work and required ongoing assistance from the federal government.[104] The Family Support Act of 1988 provided funds to the states for training projects and child care, in order to help AFDC recipients enter the labor force, though many critics doubted if the program was sufficiently generous to make much difference. Perhaps most important, Congress managed to fend off Reagan's continuing demands for further cuts in many social programs, even if funding for programs that helped poor people had not recovered from cuts earlier in the decade.

PASSING THE TORCH: FROM REAGAN TO BUSH

It was, some commentators have argued, the last campaign of the Cold War when George Bush, who had been Reagan's vice president, battled Michael Dukakis for the presidency in 1988.[105] Both candidates believed that the party that could attract blue-collar and white voters to its side would win the election. It was the quintessential public-relations campaign; both candidates were guided by advertising and marketing experts.

The candidates tried to depict themselves as tough on crime, as patriotic, and as believers in a strong defense. Bush sought to depict Dukakis as soft on crime; a television advertisement argued that, while governor of Massachussetts, Dukakis had inadvisedly released an African American prisoner called Willie Horton from jail. Bush accused Dukakis of being liberal; in the conservative 1980s, the opprobrium associated with liberalism was hardly less than the stigma of communism in the early 1950s! Dukakis, in turn, pledged that he would fight crime and drugs—and even rode, unconvincingly, in a tank to show that he would maintain a strong defense establishment. Social issues, such as poverty, homelessness, and AIDS, were hardly discussed during most of the campaign.

When it finally became clear that Bush was leading in the public opinion polls, Dukakis attempted to develop more traditional Democratic themes, such as social reform, but his newly found liberalism came too late to help him. Nor was the American public, which had been lulled to complacency by the Reagan administration, in a mood for fundamental changes in domestic or international arenas. George Bush was elected by an overwhelming majority, but the Democrats retained control of both chambers of Congress.

It was unclear when Bush took office how he would use his victory because, unlike Reagan in 1980, he had not developed a clear agenda. Once elected, he essentially continued the central themes of the Reagan administration—large military spending and resistance to tax increases. As former head of the Central Intelligence Agency and ambassador to China and to the United Nations, Bush was preoccupied with foreign policy for most of his term. He gave domestic issues extraordinarily scant attention, despite campaign pledges to be the education president, the environmental president, and the president who would wage a successful war on drugs. Even with the dissolution of the Soviet empire in the early 1990s, Bush was loath to markedly reduce funds for the American military establishment, which continued to absorb about $300 billion a year. Moreover, Bush was constrained by a campaign pledge not to raise new taxes. Although Bush was less fiercely opposed to social spending than his predecessor had been, and although he assented to increases in social spending far greater than had occurred in the Reagan years, he was largely passive on domestic matters and freely used his veto to stymie an array of measures proposed by Democrats.[106]

Caught in this fiscal bind, preoccupied with foreign affairs, and guided by a conservative ideology that was strongly enforced by John Sununu, his chief of staff until mid-1991, Bush offered few social initiatives that were backed up with funding. The Bush administration, which also had to contend with a Democratic Congress, was marked by the same curious combination of policies as the Reagan administration: on the one hand, deficits, massive defense budgets, and the absence of dramatic social reform initiatives; on the other, maintenance of almost all the existing programs of the American welfare state.

SOCIAL POLICIES OF THE BUSH ADMINISTRATION

Social Spending and the Politics of the Budget

The fate of social policy in the Bush era was considerably shaped during the annual budget process, when Congress and the executive branch determined what fraction of the budget to allocate to defense and social spending. The same had been true during much of the Reagan administration. Recall that Reagan's strategy to markedly reduce federal social spending by massively increasing the federal deficit—that is, by lowering taxes and increasing defense spending—had been only partially successful; though many programs for poor people found their funding decreased, overall social spending increased. Congressmen who favored retention of the American welfare state were, in effect, able to obtain their preferences in the heated budget negotiations of the period, while Reagan was able to retain his tax and military preferences.[107]

No less than Reagan, Bush was committed to the notion that the United States should maintain a worldwide military presence and large conventional and strategic forces. Like Reagan, he was committed to not raising taxes, as illustrated by his often-repeated pledge in 1988: "Read my lips, no new taxes." However, Bush was less able to counter increases in domestic spending than Reagan had been because the Democrats now controlled both houses of Congress and because Bush was less fervent in his opposition to federal programs. Thus, in the Bush era, the budget stalemate continued, with its huge deficits, but social spending rose at a much higher rate than in the Reagan administration.[108]

Social reformers were hardly satisfied with these gains in social spending, however, particularly in the wake of developments in Eastern Europe and the Soviet Union. Granted concessions by Soviet leader Mikhail Gorbachev and thus emboldened to assert their rights, Eastern European states achieved greater independence from the Soviet Union. Moreover, the Soviet Union rapidly disintegrated; it was dissolved by a historic decision of the leaders of its many republics in 1991.

Some social reformers perceived this thawing of the Cold War as a remarkable, unprecedented opportunity to recast the federal budget. Why not, they argued, declare a "peace dividend" to transfer as much as $150 billion annually from the military budget to the domestic-spending budget? Why not pull American troops from Europe and Asia, dramatically reduce American nuclear forces, and increasingly rely on multinational forces and the United Nations to keep the peace?[109]

The ensuing budgetary battle in 1990 rivaled the ferocity and duration of that in 1981, when Reagan had obtained tax cuts, spending reductions, and military increases at the inception of his presidency. Many legislators wanted to markedly decrease military spending and increase social spending, but the Bush administration was adamantly opposed to reductions in military spending. Legislators concerned about the budget deficit pushed to increase federal taxes, but Bush was under great pressure from conservatives to remain true to his 1988 pledge not to do so.

In a complex and extended set of negotiations, which culminated in the budget summit of 1990, Congress and the administration fashioned an uneasy compromise that gave something to everyone but avoided fundamental changes in the federal budget. Under pressure to reduce the deficit, Bush agreed to some new taxes. The ratio of military and domestic spending in the budget was preserved, but the overall budget was to be reduced incrementally in coming years, by placing caps on the aggregate social spending and military spending.[110] To

prevent social reformers from raiding the military budget, the agreement stipulated that reductions in defense spending could *not* be used to increase social spending. In effect, the agreement was a standoff, intended to delay reconsideration of budget priorities until 1993—conveniently after the next presidential elections. At that point, it was widely predicted, all hell would break loose, as the two parties battled to shape the new configuration of the federal budget. Would the military budget be severely cut? If so, would the savings be used for social programs or merely to reduce the vast deficit or even to fund new tax cuts?

Many social reformers were dismayed by the budget agreement of 1990. It made an immediate peace dividend impossible, because it explicitly disallowed the use of defense cuts to fund social programs. It required legislators to take funds from existing social programs whenever they proposed new social programs. Moreover, soon after the budget agreement, in early 1991, the war with Iraq quieted (for the moment) discussion of a peace dividend.

But it was clear that the budget settlement of 1990 was merely the first salvo in budget controversies that would extend through the 1990s and that would profoundly shape the course of the American welfare state. Nor were these budget debates likely to be amicable. Conservative Republicans, who had been bolstered and emboldened during the Reagan era, were so infuriated when Bush agreed to a modest tax increase in 1990 that they forced him to apologize for his decision in 1992 and to pledge never again to raise taxes. Having worshipped Reagan, they remained distrustful of Bush and pressured him to veto civil rights and other social reform measures and to resist efforts by liberals to raid the defense budget.[111] A strong coalition—between the Pentagon, the vast network of military contractors who existed in the districts of every federal politician, and politicians who retained a Cold War perspective—would likely resist major cuts in defense spending. And social reformers would find it difficult to enact new initiatives as long as the deficit remained and Americans continued to believe conservatives' claims that "you can't solve problems by throwing money at them" and "the federal government is the cause of the problem, not the solution."

Domestic Reforms

Few social reform initiatives were enacted from 1989 through 1992 because of budget deficits, the conservatism of Bush and his aides, and the president's preoccupation with international affairs. We will discuss some civil rights initiatives and childcare legislation when we consider the experiences of outgroups in the era of Reagan and Bush.

In the areas of education, antidrug programs, and welfare, Bush expressed lofty goals but committed few resources and little presidential attention.[112] Bush's policy on substance abuse, for example, called for new funds to interdict drugs from abroad but failed to emphasize treatment or prevention programs. His education policy emphasized procedural reforms, such as the development of national tests and proposals to test voucher systems, but provided little direct assistance to local schools, which often labored under severe shortages of resources.

Bush seemed oblivious of many other domestic issues. His plan for reform of the national health system, unveiled in 1992, proposed the use of tax deductions and credits to help low-income persons purchase private health insurance, but the suggested levels of these tax concessions were far beneath the likely health needs of low- and moderate-income Americans. He took little interest in the homeless population and took few steps to address the housing needs of millions of low-income Americans who often could not obtain decent housing or had to pay 50% or more of their modest income for it.[113] Nor did Bush attend to the problem of poverty, despite the increasing economic inequality that had developed in the United States during the 1980s.

Events in Los Angeles reminded Americans of

the hardships of inner-city life, despite the development of social programs following the urban riots of the 1960s. In the spring of 1991, an African American by the name of Rodney King was viciously beaten by Los Angeles policemen. Unlike many other instances of police brutality, the incident was recorded on videotape by a bystander. Most Americans—and virtually all African Americans—saw the tape on national television; it depicted 80 seconds of merciless beating of King by a group of policemen. After King brought charges against the police officers, an extended trial took place in spring 1992. At the end of the trial, the all-white jury found the officers not guilty. Most Americans were astonished, but African Americans in Los Angeles reacted with a fury that led to three days of burning and looting of business establishments. (Some Latinos also participated in the riots.)

Caught by surprise, the Bush administration initially blamed the riots on the Great Society social programs. When it became clear that this simplistic assertion was not widely accepted, the administration engaged in complex negotiations with the Congress to develop a program to provide various job-training, housing, recreation, and other programs for the inner cities—and for Los Angeles in particular—that would cost several billion dollars.

Critics of the emerging legislation suggested that it was grossly inadequate. Led by the mayors of many major cities, for example, about 150,000 people marched on Washington, D.C., on May 17, 1992, to demand massive increases in federal aid to the cities, as well as health, housing, and job-training programs for inner-city residents. They argued that spending for the military increased by $579 billion during the 1980s, while federal funds to cities and states were cut by $78 billion.

As Bush's first term neared its end, the Los Angeles riots raised important questions about the reaction of white, suburban Americans, who constituted a majority of the nation's voters. Physically and culturally distant from inner-city residents, would they be happy with law-and-order strategies and symbolic remedies, particularly in light of long-standing efforts by politicians—and especially the Republican party—to exploit white voters' antagonisms toward people of color? Or would they realize that, as the burning of some suburban shopping malls in the Los Angeles riots grimly suggested, their own well-being hinged on efforts to bring inner-city residents into the economic mainstream of American society? The early response of politicians of both parties was not encouraging, but some observers hoped that the events in Los Angeles, by dramatizing social distress in American cities, would invigorate a debate about national priorities in a period of reduced international tensions.

OUTGROUPS IN THE ERA OF REAGAN AND BUSH

Many outgroup members were dismayed when Ronald Reagan became president in 1980, because they knew that the implementation of conservative policies would jeopardize the gains that they had made in the preceding two decades. After all, the twin leaders of the conservative movement, Ronald Reagan and Barry Goldwater, had both strongly opposed the enactment of the Civil Rights Acts of 1964 and 1965, on the grounds that states should be charged with such matters. Conservatives tended to reject programs that sought to equalize conditions between groups in the population—for example, between people of color and the white majority—on the grounds that they represented reverse discrimination.

Outgroup members feared, as well, that Reagan (and then Bush) would pack the Supreme Court, as well as lower federal courts, with appointees who would overrule many of the decisions of the Warren and Burger Courts, which had supported civil rights, affirmative action, the legalization of abortion, and desegregation. Conservatives tended to take a strict constructionist approach to constitutional interpretation; that is, rulings had to conform

to the intentions of the framers of the Constitution. This doctrine was hardly promising for reformers, in that, as we noted in Chapter 3, the founders had legitimized slavery in the Constitution, and many contemporary social issues, such as abortion and affirmative action, had not emerged in colonial society. Moreover, enormous gains in employment opportunities for women and people of color had been obtained in the 1960s and 1970s through class action suits identifying patterns of discrimination. However, conservatives generally opposed the assertion of *group* rights and needs through class action suits; they were inclined to restrict legal recourse to instances when *individuals* could prove specific discriminatory actions had been taken against themselves by persons who *intended* to harm them.[114]

Members of the various outgroups realized, even before his election, that Reagan would seek to diminish the size and roles of regulatory agencies such as the Equal Employment Opportunity Commission. By weakening these agencies, the Reagan administration could prevent effective implementation of civil rights and related statutes.

Outgroup members were also acutely aware that the conservative movement in the 1970s had bitterly opposed policies to extend their rights, including the Equal Rights Amendment, affirmative action, school desegregation, and local ordinances protecting gay men and lesbians against job discrimination.[115]

Nor were outgroups and their advocates sanguine about the prospects for social programs to redress poverty, which provided assistance to many African Americans, Latinos, and Native Americans. Conservative politicians had sought throughout the 1970s to identify programs like AFDC, Food Stamps, public housing, and public employment with people of color in an effort to capitalize on, and enflame, white citizens' resentments; it was widely expected that the Reagan administration would scale back these programs.

As if these fears were not enough, many outgroup members expected Reagan's tax and economic policies to harm low-income Americans.

Supply-side economics, which was akin to the trickle-down economics of the 1920s, would give huge tax concessions to affluent persons, without necessarily lowering the taxes of poorer citizens. Strategies to induce economic growth in the economy would not likely include bottom-up approaches such as investing in the nation's infrastructure and schools or in training programs for its workers.

Predictions Come True

The Reagan and Bush years constitute the largest redistribution of resources and rights *upward* in the nation's history. Though the welfare state remained intact—and specific programs within it grew considerably—from 1980 through 1992, the actual economic situation of poor persons worsened, owing to a deterioration of wages, *and* reductions in social benefits and services, *and* increases in Social Security taxes. Those near the bottom of the economic ladder became poorer not only in absolute dollars (adjusted for inflation) but also when compared to the wealthiest Americans. Indeed, many persons fell out of the middle class in the 1980s; some observers wondered if the middle class would largely disappear, as in the Gilded Age. Moreover, the rights won during the 1960s and 1970s, such as protections against job-related discrimination and the right to abortion, were put at risk by the appointment of conservative justices to the Supreme Court and to lower courts.[116]

All the fears of outgroup members were realized during the Reagan period—particularly during his first term, when the Republicans controlled the Senate and often could muster a conservative majority in the House. Although Bush presented a more accommodating posture, his court appointments, as well as many of his policies, did not represent a fundamental departure from the politics of Reagan, despite conservatives' anger at Bush for consenting to tax increases and signing civil rights legislation.

Poverty and People of Color

By 1992, a good deal of evidence, assembled by an array of authors and studies, showed that the economic position of the lowest quintile—the lowest one-fifth—of citizens had eroded considerably during the tenure of Presidents Reagan and Bush.[117] The data implicated three factors.

1. With the loss of American industrial and unionized jobs during the 1970s and 1980s, increasing numbers of workers found an erosion in the real value of their paychecks. Moreover, many companies cut their fringe benefits, such as health benefits, during these two decades—though many enterprises that employed people in the lowest quintile had never provided health benefits or provided only residual benefits.

2. Poor individuals suffered economically as a result of the cuts in social benefits and services of the American welfare state. We have already discussed extensive cuts in AFDC, Food Stamps, and public housing programs. Poor persons also had to pay higher fees in Medicaid, Medicare, and other social programs.

3. Although some concessions were made in certain tax provisions—such as a tax credit extended by the federal government to some working but poor persons—the overall tax rates of poor and working persons increased, if payroll taxes for Social Security and Medicare are added to increases in the regular income tax.

The economic decline of the lowest quintile was matched by a decline of persons in the second-lowest quintile.[118] As the two lowest quintiles suffered these losses, many affluent Americans vastly increased their wealth; for example, the 400 richest Americans saw a tripling of their net worth in this period.[119] Viewed in this light, the Reagan and Bush years represented an economic counterrevolution. Some observers foresaw a transformation of the United States' economic structure to resemble that of some third-world nations, with vast disparities between rich and poor and a relatively small middle class—indeed, to resemble that in the Gilded Age, which we discussed in Chapter 5.

Economic data do not fully describe the constricted quality of life in the inner-city neighborhoods where low-income African Americans, Latinos, and Native Americans live. These segregated populations have extraordinary rates of poverty, drug usage, poor health, poor educational attainment, unemployment, homicides, and gang violence. Large numbers of low-income males are killed in violent encounters or are incarcerated. And the rates of single-headed families in these inner-city populations have markedly increased over the last 25 years.

In the 1970s and 1980s, conservatives dominated policy discussions of urban poverty, which were very limited in scope.[120] However, as Peterson notes, a range of theories to explain the social and economic problems of these segregated populations now exists. Some observers contend that the welfare state has been inadequately developed and does not sufficiently help inner-city residents with economic, health, social service, educational, and job-training remedies. Conservatives argue that inner-city residents are to blame for the conditions in which they live, and implicate cultural factors that prompt behaviors such as teenage pregnancy. Conservatives maintain that welfare and other programs provide "perverse incentives," which discourage poor people from seeking work and self-improvement. Others argue that the loss of well-paying unionized industrial jobs in the past 20 years has deprived relatively unskilled persons of employment or consigned them to service jobs that pay only the minimum wage.[121]

The Reagan and Bush administrations, as well as presidential candidates in 1980, 1984, and 1988, displayed scant interest in these inner-city problems. Although the Los Angeles riots of May 1992 suggested the need for sweeping social reforms to bring inner-city residents into the economic mainstream, the palliatives proposed by Congress and the Bush administration in the wake of the riots provided little prospect of decisive action. And

with huge federal deficits, as well as budget deficits in most states and major cities, funds to assist this population were not available—and would not be available, as long as the nation was disinclined either to raise its taxes or to dramatically cut its defense spending. Public opinion remained indifferent to inner-city residents, whose plight was largely invisible to the white suburban majority.

Immigrants

The enactment of the Immigration Law of 1965 and succeeding legislation—such as the 1975 Indochina Migration and Refugee Assistance Act and the 1980 Refugee Act—heralded a large influx of immigrants to the United States from Central America and Mexico and also from Asian nations such as Vietnam, China, Laos, Thailand, India, Cambodia, South Korea, and the Philippines. These new arrivals came to join relatives, to escape political persecution, or to seek better conditions. The Asian American population grew from one million in 1965 to five million in 1985; the number of Asians arriving in that 20-year period was almost four times as great as the Asian influx between 1849 and 1965.[122] Though immigrants settled disproportionately on the West coast, large enclaves existed throughout the nation.

The immigrant population was very diverse, and generalizations are fraught with danger. Some immigrants were highly educated professionals and persons with sophisticated technical skills. Others gravitated to businesses. Refugees from Vietnam, Central America, and the Caribbean, including boat people, came from a wide range of social backgrounds.

Even some entrants who possessed advanced skills found the adjustment problematic, not only because of language difficulties but also because of discrimination in employment and in society at large. About half of those Vietnamese refugees who reside in California were on public assistance in 1990.[123] Some refugees suffered from mental trauma due to harrowing experiences in refugee camps and war zones. As with immigrants in preceding eras, tensions often developed between first-generation immigrants and their children, who quickly learned English and the mores of the dominant culture.

Advocates for refugees from political persecution in countries like El Salvador fought a determined battle to stop their deportation, through the courts and through hearings of the Immigration Service; these refugees were offered sanctuary in churches and homes.

Gay Men and Lesbians

In the 1970s, gay men and lesbians had focused on winning civil rights, with some success. In the 1980s, however, they found themselves confronting the worst medical catastrophe of modern times, the AIDS epidemic. In spring 1982, researchers at the National Centers for Disease Control acknowledged the existence of an epidemic that had already killed 119 persons, but they did not know the cause of the disease and had not even assigned a name to it. However, they knew that it progressively destroyed the immune system and they had determined that it was concentrated in the gay male population. When the virus that caused the disease was finally identified in early 1984 (it was officially designated the human immunodeficiency virus, or HIV, in 1986), the horrific nature of the epidemic became clear. Transmitted by an exchange of fluids during sexual relations, the disease threatened to become a sort of biologic genocide visited on an unsuspecting population.

The gay community made unrelenting efforts to mobilize action against the epidemic. Edward Brandt, the assistant secretary for health, who asked in early 1984 for a modest outlay of $55 million on research to develop a blood test, a vaccine, and a cure, encountered indifference from the Reagan administration. The American Life Lobby, a conservative group, claimed that Brandt's plea to make AIDS a top priority of the Health Service was "an outrageous legitimization of a lifestyle repugnant to the vast majority of Americans."[124]

Researchers discovered by mid-1984 that the disease was also transmitted through blood transfusions, through intravenous drug use, by prostitutes, and by bisexuals to their spouses. The disease spread rapidly among African American and Latino addicts in the inner city who shared nonsterilized needles.

Americans are prone to cycles of interest in particular social problems. After a rash of news reports on the disease in 1983, coverage soon diminished, despite the mounting deaths. The Reagan administration requested only $51 million for 1985. At the same time, conservatives in Congress sought to require that health workers conducting blood tests for AIDS report positive results to public health departments. It was widely feared that this policy, which would compromise the confidentiality of the AIDS test, would lead to boycotts of the test, because persons with AIDS encountered virulent prejudice and discrimination in housing, in the workplace, and also from insurance companies. Though congressional pressure pushed funding to $96 million in 1985, the Reagan administration sought to *reduce* the funding to $85.5 million in the ensuing year, despite a prediction by government researchers that the epidemic could kill up to 50,000 persons (or the same number of fatalities as occurred during the Vietnam War) within a few years.[125] The gay community developed a massive education and self-help campaign, to provide assistance to people with AIDS and to promote safe sex, but they received scant assistance from the federal government. African American and Latino communities proved less able to develop self-help campaigns, partly because of prejudices against gay men in those cultures. Governmental authorities did not make it a priority to develop a determined preventive program in inner-city areas; this failure, which consigned thousands of persons to death, was a national disgrace.

With the revelation that movie star Rock Hudson had AIDS in mid-1985, and the publication of a report on the epidemic by Surgeon General C. Everett Koop in October 1986, government action increased markedly. However, increases in funding were still sufficiently modest that gay men, lesbians, and their allies repeatedly demonstrated in Washington; in 1987 a march attracted 600,000 people. Efforts to combat the disease continued to be hamstrung by prejudice: Many states failed to enact laws prohibiting discrimination against people with AIDS; there was widespread opposition to providing addicts with sterilized needles; many physicians decided not to treat persons who were HIV-positive; and conservatives continued to demand mandatory reporting of persons who tested HIV-positive. Nor did President Bush demonstrate active interest in the issue.

Moreover, the nation's disinclination to provide sex education and condoms to its youth had slowed effective preventive programs. Although the public schools of New York City decided in 1991 to distribute condoms to high school students, most other school districts were not as enlightened. Nor did Americans develop public service announcements, such as were widely used in European countries, to promote safe sex. Activists hoped that the announcement by basketball player Magic Johnson in late 1991 that he was HIV-positive might finally force a massive prevention program.

As the epidemic neared the end of its first decade in the United States, the death toll exceeded 138,000 persons and the disease was making rapid advances in heterosexual populations, particularly among intravenous drug users. About one million persons were HIV-positive in May 1992.

Though often preoccupied with AIDS, gay and lesbian activists also worked on many other fronts. They sought legislation in various states to outlaw job discrimination in the civil service, military, police and fire departments, and private markets; to outlaw housing discrimination; to allow same-gender couples to obtain access to Social Security, and job-related fringe benefits; to obtain the right to adopt children; to obtain custody and visitation rights; and to overturn antisodomy laws in 26 states.[126]

People with Disabilities

Buoyed by the Rehabilitation Act of 1973, a robust movement of persons with disabilities evolved and mobilized behind an "independent living centers" movement. Wishing to shed traditional images of helplessness, some advocates favored the term *physically challenged* to describe persons with disabilities. A national network of local organizations received federal funding to provide an array of outreach, educational, and advocacy services, with the intent of freeing persons from dependence on medical institutions. When possible, these organizations helped secure government payments for nonworking persons with disabilities, whether under the means-tested SSI program or under Social Security disability insurance (SSDI) for persons disabled on the job. With the use of technology and advocacy, they also succeeded in increasing the employment of persons with chronic physical, developmental, and mental problems. Many public facilities were made accessible by way of ramps, elevators, and other aids and vast progress was made in obtaining special programs to help persons with conditions like dyslexia in the educational system. Even with these improvements, many persons with chronic conditions remained mired in poverty or lacked access to the latest technology. Equally important, persons with chronic problems often needed personal assistants to help them with chores, transportation, and other matters, but government programs rarely provided these aides. Moreover, persons with chronic problems often encountered a dilemma: If they worked, their benefits would be taken from them, but the wages they could earn were so low that they needed their benefits to survive. Many persons with disabilities thus returned to their SSI or SSDI benefits rather than remaining in the work force.

Advocates obtained enactment of the Americans with Disabilities Act of 1990, which barred discrimination in the workplace, housing, and public accommodations. (It provided far more detailed language than the Rehabilitation Act of 1973.) Though this legislation represented progress, activists feared that the government would confine itself to policing the rights of persons with disabilities, rather than funding an array of services—such as personal aides—that they needed to become full-fledged members of society.[127]

Women

As Faludi notes, a curious paradox emerged in the 1980s: The women's liberation movement was widely blamed for depriving women of their femininity, their traditional rights to custody and alimony, and their special protections from hazardous work—in effect, for being too militant and thus jeopardizing traditional rights—yet women remained underpaid, denied access to many kinds of jobs, subject to a "glass ceiling," and greatly underrepresented in political offices.[128] Unlike other nations, moreover, the United States lacked a family leave program, and more than 99% of American employers did not provide child care. Family-planning services for the poor remained poorly funded, and the *Roe* v. *Wade* decision legalizing abortion seemed vulnerable to new court rulings. Attitudes toward women were cast into the public spotlight in 1981, when law professor Anita Hill alleged in Senate hearings that Supreme Court nominee Clarence Thomas had sexually harassed her while they both worked at the EEOC. The arrogance and insensitivity of the all-male group of senators conducting the hearings radicalized many women.[129]

Women encountered major political opposition in the 1980s from conservatives. Far from insisting that males should assume larger roles in parenting, some spokespersons for the New Right openly advocated turning the clock back to the 1950s with respect to women working, abortion rights, and women's rights. They fought the Equal Rights Amendment and even introduced the Family Protection Act in Congress in 1981, which sought to rescind federal laws that support equal education for boys and girls; prohibit what is called "inter-

mingling of the sexes" in sports or other school-related activities; require schools to endorse marriage and motherhood as the proper career for girls; cut off federal funding to any school that uses textbooks in which women are shown in nontraditional roles; and prevent women who seek abortion counseling or a divorce from obtaining federally funded legal aid.[130]

The decade was characterized by considerable backsliding—for example, fewer women were appointed to the judiciary and to top policy positions. The Supreme Court narrowed women's rights in the 1989 *Webster* v. *Reproductive Health Services* decision, which allowed Missouri to make major new restrictions on abortion; the 1991 *Rust* v. *Sullivan* decision, which upheld regulations of the Reagan administration that prohibited federally funded clinics from counseling pregnant women about abortion; and also various rulings attacking affirmative action and quotas. The labor force became even more gender segregated. In 1986, women earned, on average, 64% to every dollar earned by male workers—the same ratio that had existed 31 years earlier, in 1955. The EEOC no longer vigorously litigated cases against large corporations that excluded women from entire job categories—for example, from high-paying commission sales jobs.

The crusade by the New Right against abortions illustrates the temper of the 1980s. Anti-abortion groups burned or bombed 77 family planning clinics between 1977 and 1989. By 1987, 85% of counties in the nation did not provide abortion services; as a result, many women had to travel across county or state boundaries to find such services. Medicaid funding had not been available for abortions since the mid-1970s, and only 12 states continued to fund abortions; consequently, women had to obtain funding from a small number of private agencies or from private insurance or personal funds. Muzzled by regulations, health providers that received federal funds could not even discuss reproductive alternatives with women—and sex-education classes funded by the Adolescent Family Life Act withheld all information on abortion and birth control from students.[131]

The Democrats did not vigorously attack the Republicans' indifference to women's issues, even though many women felt alienated from the Republican party. Intimidated by the conservatives, they often reflected the antifemale bias of the decade; even Michael Dukakis, the Democratic contender in 1988, chose to be silent on women's issues.[132]

In 1990 women's groups and their allies were able to obtain legislation that channeled some funding for child care programs to the states. A coalition of labor, senior citizens', and women's groups lobbied for a family leave bill, which would allow men and women paid leave from work before and after the birth of a child. They were able to move it through the Senate in 1991 but ultimately failed to surmount opposition by conservatives, who argued that it represented an unfair obligation for corporations, even though the policy had already been enacted in many industrialized nations.[133]

Children

The well-being of children depends on the economic and social condition of their parents, as well as on the kinds of health, educational, and social-service programs that society provides them. In the 1980s, the score card was not impressive on either count. After declining in the 1960s and remaining stable in the 1970s, the rates of poverty among children and youth rose rapidly to around 25% in the early 1980s and then stabilized at those high levels for the rest of the decade. Whereas roughly 15% of white children were poor in 1989, about 44% of African American children and 36% of Latino children were poor. Falling earnings, low levels of AFDC and Food Stamps, and poor child support enforcement contributed to this high rate.

The poverty of growing numbers of children was linked, as well, to the growth in the percentage of families that had only a single head of household. The term *feminization of poverty* was coined to describe the extent of poverty in female-headed households. While only 23% of all poor families were headed by women in 1959, this figure had risen to 52% by 1989. About 51% of children in families headed by a woman were poor in 1989 compared to only 10% in two-parent families. Families headed by a woman tend to be poorer because they can draw on only a single source of wage income and because women tend to be segregated in lower-paying work.[134] According to Ozawa, increasing rates of teenage pregnancy and of divorce explain the growth in female-headed households.[135]

As well as poverty, American children faced an array of other problems, for which no adequate policies had been developed. Roughly 300,000 cocaine-addicted babies were born each year, and drug-treatment and prevention programs had failed to reach many teenagers who used drugs. Between 1965 and 1988, the arrest rate for violent crimes by 18-year-old males more than doubled; rates were particularly high in the lower economic strata. Homicides accounted for almost half of all deaths among young males. As Kozol documents in his book *Savage Inequalities,* the schools of poor children were overcrowded, lacked instructional aides, and often had less competent teachers than more affluent districts.[136]

There were many indications that the child welfare system could not cope with the sheer number of children who were reported to be neglected or abused by their care givers. In the wake of the Adoption Assistance and Child Welfare Act of 1980, which gave funds to the states to hire more child welfare staff and required them to develop a "permanency plan" for all children removed from their natural homes, the numbers of children in foster care was almost halved in five years. But the number zoomed upward by 29%, to about 360,000 children by 1991—and was predicted to exceed 500,000 children by the year 2000. Though staff were added in many jurisdictions, acute shortages developed because of a 147% increase in reports of abused and neglected children between 1979 and 1989, for an astonishing total of 2.4 million reported cases in 1989.[137]

Children's advocates nonetheless gained a number of incremental policy victories in the 1980s and seemed on the verge of some additional ones in 1992. By securing more funding for the Education for All Handicapped Children Act of 1975, millions of disabled children were mainstreamed into the regular public schools. The Medicaid program was amended to include a program that gave one million low-income children preventive checkups. Despite its inadequate funding and implementation, the Adoption Assistance and Child Welfare Act led to better foster care for many children, as well as higher rates of adoption and reunification with their natural families. In 1991, under pressure from children's advocates, Congress agreed in principle to expand the Head Start program to cover all children in coming years. In the 1980s, incremental increases had been obtained in the earned-income tax credit—a means-tested program that gave a tax rebate to qualifying families—and Congress agreed to raise the credit so that the benefit would rise another 70% by 1994. (A family earning less than $10,730 could claim a tax refund of almost $1,000 in 1990.)

With passage of the child care and development block grant in 1990, children's advocates finally obtained the first major, national child care program since World War II. It channeled funds through the states for child care services, administration, and staff training; though inadequately funded, it established a precedent that child care belonged within the purview of the federal government.

The AFDC program had been highly controversial since the mid-1960s, when many citizens became alarmed at its rate of growth. But the benefits of this program, which is supposed to help destitute heads of households and their children, had eroded during the 1970s and 1980s to the point where the grants of the median state were only 45% of the official poverty line in 1990, or only $367 a month for a family of three. Even when supplemented by Food Stamps and Medicaid, these resources were insufficient to meet the basic needs of many families. When the Family Support Act of 1988 was enacted, people hoped that its job-training and child care funds would allow many women on AFDC to enter the labor market, but the act fell far short of its potential, owing to inadequate funding at federal and state levels and the harsh realities of labor markets; relatively unskilled female workers often could obtain only minimum-wage jobs that rendered them even poorer than they had been on AFDC.

Thus, incremental gains in some aspects of children's welfare during the decade were offset by the rapid growth of social problems—such as cocaine-addicted babies and huge increases in reported cases of child abuse and neglect—that current programs could not adequately address. Children's advocates urged the United States to emulate programs in Europe and Canada, such as parental leave, expanded child care, and children's allowances.[138]

Aging Americans

Aging Americans appeared at first glance to have improved their condition in the 1970s and 1980s. Rates of poverty in this population had plummeted from 35% to 12.8% between 1959 and 1989. With the enactment of Medicare and the Older Americans Act in 1965 and the enactment of SSI and the indexing of Social Security in the early 1970s, older people obtained major new medical services, social services, and resources. Indeed, many commentators noted that a huge portion of the federal budget was devoted to older persons, including the 29.4% of the 1990 federal budget (or $341.4 billion) consumed by just two programs—Medicare and Social Security. Unlike poor Americans, elderly persons were largely spared the budget cuts of the 1980s, because Reagan (and then Bush) feared antagonizing this politically powerful group.[139]

But elderly persons had many serious problems of their own. Because consumer fees associated with Medicare were so high and so many services were not covered, elderly persons paid roughly 50% of their medical costs. Moreover, they paid upward of 50% of their costs for home health care and long-term care, because Medicare, with its focus on short-term, hospital-based care, offered scant coverage for those services. As a result, many older citizens experiencing catastrophic health conditions had to divest themselves of their savings, in order to obtain medical funds from the means-tested Medicaid program.[140] Moreover, many older persons and their families were heavily burdened—financially and otherwise—by Alzheimer's disease, which had become the fourth greatest killer of older persons by 1992. Day-treatment and other services for persons with Alzheimer's disease remained very limited.

As if these problems were not enough, older persons also had to contend with a strong movement in the 1980s that sought to cut social spending on their needs. Former Governor Richard Lamm of Colorado and others argued that many funds spent on older Americans should be diverted to children, since society would reap economic gains by making younger people more productive. Daniel Callahan, a prominent moral philosopher, advocated that the United States refuse heroic and expensive health remedies to all persons over the age of 80—for example, by disallowing stays in intensive care units—so as to permit these funds to be spent on younger people. Others argued that lobby groups representing older persons, such as the American Association of Retired Persons, possessed such power that older citizens were able

unfairly to obtain a disproportionate share of the public purse. In an era of deficits in federal and state budgets, many legislators feared making home health care and long-term care more available because of its likely costs.[141]

Homeless Americans

Many social problems of the 1980s and 1990s have an impact on individuals from several outgroups, as well as the general population. Consider homelessness. As the 1980s began, most Americans would likely have associated homelessness with relatively small areas of cities where alcoholic persons resided. (Such an area was often known as skid row.) A public opinion poll in 1991, however, found that 54% of Americans reported they saw homeless people in their communities or on their way to work—and the Urban Institute in 1987 estimated the homeless population of the United States at about 600,000 persons, including persons in shelters, using soup kitchens, and on the streets. Homeless people are a diverse group. When examining the characteristics of homeless people in cities of more than 100,000, the Urban Institute concluded that about one-fifth of them had a history of mental hospitalization; about 15% were children; about 81% were male; about one-third had been patients in a detoxification, alcohol treatment, or drug-treatment program; and about 29% of single men had served time in prison. These

INSERT 11.3   ETHICAL ANALYSIS OF KEY ISSUES AND POLICIES: PITTING GROUPS AGAINST ONE ANOTHER

It is true: Older Americans absorb a large share of the expenditures of the welfare state, partly on account of the high cost of their medical programs and long-term care programs. It is also true that children receive a small share of social spending in the United States.

Analyze the ethical merit of *cutting* expenditures on older people to divert funds to children. Some ethicists favor, for example, making a rule that no person over age 80 can receive extraordinary medical interventions. Others want older citizens to self-fund far larger portions of their health and other costs.

FIGURE 11.1   (*left*) A policy challenge: helping elderly Americans cope with adversity; (*right*) an American tragedy: childhood poverty in an affluent nation

SOURCE: (*left*) © Bernard Wolf/Monkmeyer; (*right*) © 1986 Andy Levin/Photo Researchers, Inc.

homeless people had an average monthly income of $135, or less than one-third of the federal poverty level, and half of them had not had a steady job in more than two years. Persons had been homeless for a median of ten months.[142]

The response of federal and state governments to this problem in the Reagan and Bush era was half-hearted, at best. Most vexing to advocates for the homeless was the presidents' disinclination to publicly discuss the issue; even Democratic candidates in 1984 and 1988 were unwilling to demand ameliorative policies. Congress enacted the Stewart B. McKinney Homeless Assistance Act of 1987, but it focused its resources on the construction costs for shelters and was burdened with bureaucratic delays in giving states funds. States and localities devoted considerable funds to the problem by the late 1980s and were particularly effective in meeting the emergency needs of those

homeless people who used their shelters. But most jurisdictions made little provision for outreach programs to homeless people who avoided organized services and shelters; transitional programs to help homeless people obtain housing and jobs; and programs to help prevent people from becoming homeless. Nor did most jurisdictions provide case management services to homeless persons, even in shelters. For want of leadership from federal or state authorities, voluntary agencies—including missions, churches, neighborhood coalitions, and social agencies—often took the lead in providing services.[143]

As Rossi notes, it is easy to ignore the simple fact that "the essential and defining symptom of homelessness is lack of access to conventional housing." The stocks of inexpensive housing were depleted in the 1980s by rising rents, conversion of many rental apartments to condominiums, and the continuing destruction of low-income housing (particularly buildings with apartments for single persons) for urban renewal.[144] As we have already noted, the Reagan administration virtually ended many programs of the Department of Housing and Urban Development. Furthermore, the policy of deinstitutionalizing the nation's mental hospitals from the early 1960s onward, when coupled with stricter rules for involuntary commitments, placed hundreds of thousands of mental patients on the streets, without adequate services. And increasing numbers of individuals and families could not afford housing because of the loss of industrialized, unionized employment in the United States in the 1980s.

The Erosion of Rights

A prime objective of Ronald Reagan and George Bush was to transform the federal judiciary into an instrument of conservative ideology. They succeeded to an extent unrivaled in modern times. With the appointment of Justice Clarence Thomas in late 1991, the number of liberals on the Supreme Court had been reduced to two justices (Harry Blackmun and John Paul Stevens). Under the leadership of William Rehnquist, who succeeded Warren Burger in 1986, the Court seemed poised to stress conservative goals in the 1990–1991 session, when it overturned a number of precedents and contemplated "shattering the Warren and Burger legacies . . . in the areas of abortion, separation of church and state, affirmative action, and free speech."[145] Moreover, by 1992, Reagan and Bush had appointed more than half of all the 828 federal appeals and court judges in the United States—judges who had usually been given "ideological litmus tests" to be certain that they would support conservative positions on controversial issues.[146]

It was too soon to tell precisely what directions the Supreme Court would take, but advocates for women and people of color feared a rollback in many policies that had been sanctioned by the Warren or Burger Court or by Congress. Advocates

realized that they would need to secure new legislation to offset adverse rulings by the Court; thus, gay activists, chagrined that the Supreme Court in 1986 upheld a Georgia statute that declared sodomy illegal, responded by pressuring state legislatures to overturn similar statutes. Advocates for people with disabilities secured the enactment of the Americans with Disabilities Act in 1990, after the Court had declined to cover people with disabilities under existing civil rights statutes.

Another landmark in this campaign of resistance was the Civil Rights Act of 1991, enacted after two years of negotiations between the Congress and the White House. This legislation was a response to a series of ten rulings by the Supreme Court that called into question the principle of affirmative action and limited individuals' ability to seek remedies to bias in the workplace. In its decision in 1989 in *Wards Cove Packing Co.* v. *Atonio,* for example, the Court held that the burden of proof rested with an employee who alleged that a company's practices had an adverse impact on people of color, women, or other groups; she or he had to prove that the practices did not serve a legitimate business purpose. The antidiscrimination provisions of the Civil Rights Act of 1991 applied to both governmental and private places of employment and reaffirmed the ability of employees to bring "disparate impact lawsuits" under Title VII of the Civil Rights Act of 1964—that is, lawsuits alleging that specific hiring or promotion decisions adversely affected women, people of color, or other groups. The legislation also allowed workers to seek monetary damages in cases of alleged intentional discrimination.[147]

Thus, the ideological divergence between Congress and the Supreme Court suggested that the House and Senate would be revisiting issues during the next decades that they *thought* they had resolved, until the Court declared the relevant statutes unconstitutional. In effect, the rulings of the Supreme Court were setting a major portion of Congress's legislative agenda, which was frustrating and time-consuming for liberal and moderate lawmakers. This standoff was reminiscent of the

New Deal era, when the intransigence of the conservative Court led Franklin Roosevelt to try to pack the Court with liberal justices. As a final example of the Court's uncompassionate rulings, note that in March 1992, by a 7 to 2 vote, the Court found that federal judges cannot force states to improve their care of abused and neglected children under the 1980 Adoption Assistance and Child Welfare Act, on the grounds that the legislation did not specifically mention that persons can sue in federal court. Outraged children's advocates faced the task of amending the legislation in Congress.[148]

THE SOCIAL WORK PROFESSION

The profession of social work proved remarkably resilient during the decades after the Great Society, despite the conservative attack on the kinds of social programs that employed social workers. Schools of social work at the graduate level held their own during this period, as did undergraduate programs. Membership of the National Association of Social Workers (NASW) exceeded 100,000 persons by the mid-1980s, and roughly nine-tenths of them had a master's in social work; more than 200,000 persons in the work force had either a bachelor's or master's in social work. About 40% of NASW members were employed in not-for-profit agencies, 45% in public agencies (mostly at state, county, or local levels), and the balance in for-profit agencies. Large numbers of social workers were employed in health, mental-health, and child-and-family sectors. Though most social workers held direct-service positions, many held administrative posts, and some worked in community-organizing and policy-making positions as well.

The profession had successes and failures in political battles to preserve its access to jobs. On the positive side, the profession succeeded in obtaining licensing in many states, which in turn, often led to the inclusion of social work in reimbursement by private insurance companies and Medicare. A number of public positions in agencies like child welfare, however, were declassified in the 1970s and 1980s in particular jurisdictions; that is, certain local authorities ceased to specify a social work degree as a qualification for particular kinds of jobs. But a number of public agencies actively recruited trained social workers by the early 1990s in fields such as protective services for abused children, and many positions in the large not-for-profit sector required a social work degree or even a social work license. The inexorable expansion of some social problems and the rise to prominence of others—including AIDS, substance abuse, homelessness, and Alzheimer's disease—created new openings for a field whose technologies could easily be adapted to an array of social needs.

Perhaps the most controversial issue concerned the role of private practice in the profession. Although most social workers were salaried, many had private practices on the side and aspired to full-time private practice, for its monetary rewards and the autonomy it offered. Critics feared that these private practitioners could draw the profession away from its role as service provider to persons with few financial means and as an advocate for relatively powerless groups.[149] Indeed, some private practitioners sought to avoid being called social workers; they preferred to be known, for example, as psychotherapists, though the term *clinical social worker* was also used.

It remained unclear precisely what effects the emergence of private practice would have on the profession. On the one hand, insofar as it represented a retreat from the precepts of social work, from agency practice, and from advocacy for groups with little power, private practice *was* a threat to the reformist mission of the profession. Private practice, however, did not appear to have fundamentally changed the field by the early 1990s; indeed, it seemed less of a threat to a broad-based mission for the field than psychiatric social work had been in the 1950s, when the profession seemed much more congruent with the conservatism of the era. Nor was it even clear that most persons who aspired to private practice rejected the mission of the profession; more than a few of them simply wished to avoid the stifling work requirements of some social agencies, particularly public ones, where workloads had often become excessive.[150]

Although we cannot use the positions of NASW as the only measure of sentiments within the profession, they suggest that social work had not veered to the right in the 1970s and 1980s. NASW in the 1980s, in its conferences, policy positions, and newsletter, frequently attacked the conservative positions of the Reagan and Bush administrations, assertively sought national health insurance and an array of social reforms, and actively participated in coalitions with advocacy groups such as the Children's Defense Fund. In 1975, it established a political action arm, the Political Action Committee for Candidate Election (PACE), that backed candidates who supported social reforms. Official policies that NASW's delegate assembly adopted over a period of 20 years suggest that the field took an array of progressive, even radical, positions on subjects as diverse as AIDS, economic policy, long-term care, and the rights of children.[151] (Of course, NASW's positions do not necessarily reflect the positions of rank and file social workers.)

Nor does the work of social work theorists suggest that the profession veered to the right in the 1980s. Most theorists maintained an ecological perspective that required social workers to examine human functioning in a broad context, including environmental and policy issues. There was an emphasis on *diversity*—that is, making social work services relevant to a range of oppressed populations, including African Americans, Latinos, Native Americans, women, gay men and lesbians, and the poor. Macro practitioners often remained on the fringes in many schools, but they maintained a determined existence and were strongly represented in national conferences of the Council on Social Work Education.[152]

By the same token, social work could hardly be called a radical presence in a society with enormous unmet needs. *All* professions are influenced by conservatizing forces, such as funding from government and business elites; referrals from other professionals; and recruits who are predomi-

nantly white and from the middle and upper classes. As Wenocur and Reisch established when discussing its origins, social work is no exception—and Rothman makes a similar point about the profession in the contemporary period.[153] But social work remained *relatively* more reformist than other professions such as law, medicine, and business, whose professional associations did not usually take controversial positions on current issues.[154] Social work should not be placed on a pedestal, but it should not be accused of forsaking its reformist heritage, either.

THE EVOLUTION OF THE RELUCTANT WELFARE STATE

The presidencies of Reagan and Bush constituted the first major era of conservatism since the 1950s. Their election required a shift in the votes of white Americans, particularly Northern white Catholics and Southern whites in lower and moderate income brackets. Skillfully using rhetoric that flamed racial animosities and social tensions, Reagan and Bush cultivated these white voters and secured their support in pivotal elections. They appealed, as well, to Americans who wanted political and social stability after such traumas of the 1960s and 1970s as Vietnam, Watergate, and stagflation.

Compared to many other nations, the United States developed a welfare state belatedly. Even after the spending increases of the 1960s and 1970s, U.S. governmental social spending, expressed as a percentage of the gross national product, fell short of that in other industrialized nations, and a host of serious social problems remained unresolved.

Just as programs established in the 1960s and 1970s began to address a variety of social needs, the Reagan administration decided to curb their funding. Reagan's conservative counterrevolution substantially reduced domestic spending, massively increased military spending, and drastically reduced the policy roles of the federal government.

Conservatives' successes were held in check, however, by the many legislators and citizens who did not share their goals and by the Democratic control of the House of Representatives throughout the Reagan and Bush years and of the Senate from 1986 onward.

Some historians are likely to criticize Reagan's policies as self-serving and inequitable. Far from cutting all social programs, the administration cut primarily those used by low-income Americans. Tax cuts in 1981 enriched affluent individuals and corporations far more than other Americans; the tax reform of 1986 drastically reduced the tax rates of affluent Americans. The defense industry reaped unprecedented peacetime profits, even without considering the trillion-dollar SDI initiative. Affirmative action policies were attacked by the president, the Justice Department, and the director of the Civil Rights Commission. By increasing deficit spending, Reagan was asking future generations to fund his defense and tax-reduction policies. Moreover, the administration hoped to foster conservative policies long after the 1980s by devising tax, deficit, and defense policies that would create a shortage of resources for social spending.

Crippled by international scandals in Iran and Nicaragua in late 1987, and reduced to lame-duck status, Reagan had lost political momentum by the midpoint of his second term. Democrats once again controlled both houses of Congress after the 1986 elections.

Although President George Bush was more responsive to some social problems than Reagan had been, and although his rhetoric was often more diplomatic, his policies were fundamentally the same. Partly because the Democrats had larger majorities in the House and Senate under Bush than under Reagan, Bush *had* to accept larger spending increases in many social programs.

By 1992, however, emerging political uncertainties suggested that conservative hegemony might one day end. Many Americans had descended from the middle class to lesser economic status, as unionized jobs were replaced (if at all) by lesser paying service jobs. The easing of the Cold War made it harder for conservatives to rally their constituency by invoking the threat of communism. Members of the various outgroups had reasons for wanting more liberal administrations, as they fought adverse court rulings and program cuts.

Still, many persons wondered whether, given budget deficits and a decade of conservative rhetoric, the nation could find the resources and the will to attack entrenched social problems as it moved toward the 21st century. Lack of medical insurance, homelessness, AIDS, growing economic inequality, poor schools, poverty in the racial ghettoes of inner cities, family violence, the feminization of poverty, gang warfare—all of these problems cried out for solutions and creative programs, but burdened human services systems were inadequate to the task.

NOTES

1. George Nash, *The Conservative Intellectual Movement in America Since 1945* (New York: Basic Books, 1976), pp. 253–295.

2. Geoffrey Hodgson, *America in Our Time* (Garden City, N.Y.: Doubleday, 1976), pp. 473–478.

3. Craig Roberts, *The Supply-Side Revolution: An Insider's Account of Policy-Making in Washington* (Cambridge, Mass.: Harvard University Press, 1984), p. 18.

4. Robert Kuttner, *Revolt of the Haves: Tax Rebellions and Hard Times* (New York: Simon & Schuster, 1980), pp. 349–350.

5. James Reichley, *Conservatives in an Age of Change: The Nixon and Ford Administrations* (Washington, D.C.: Brookings Institution, 1981), pp. 387–390.

6. Pete Hamill, "The Revolt of the White Lower-Middle Class." In Louise Howe, ed., *The White Majority: Between Poverty and Affluence* (New York: Random House, 1970), pp. 10–22.

7. T. R. Reid, "Kennedy." In David Broder et al., eds., *The Pursuit of the Presidency, 1980* (Washington, D.C.: Berkeley Books, 1980), pp. 68, 77; Martin Schram, "Carter." In Broder, et al., eds., *The Pursuit,* p. 116.

8. Kevin Phillips, *Post-Conservative America: People, Politics, and Ideology in a Time of Crisis* (New York: Vintage Books, 1983), pp. 53–63.

9. Susan Littwin, *The Postponed Generation: Why America's Grown-Up Kids Are Growing Up Later* (New York: Morrow, 1986), pp. 18–25, 191–213.

10. William Leuchtenberg, *In the Shadow of FDR: From Harry Truman to Ronald Reagan* (Ithaca, N.Y.: Cornell University Press, 1983), pp. 1–160.

11. Thomas Edsall, *Chain Reaction: The Impact of Race, Rights, and Taxes on American Politics* (New York: W. W. Norton, 1991), pp. ix–xiv, 1–7, 174.

12. Nash, *The Conservative Intellectual Movement,* pp. 36–56.

13. Ibid., pp. 291–295.

14. Milton Friedman, *Capitalism and Freedom* (Chicago: University of Chicago Press, 1962).

15. Martin Anderson, *The Federal Bulldozer: A Critical Analysis of Urban Renewal, 1949–1962* (Cambridge, Mass.: M.I.T. Press, 1964).

16. Peter Steinfels, *The Neoconservatives: The Men Who Are Changing America's Politics* (New York: Simon & Schuster, 1979), pp. 45–46, 108–160.

17. Edsall, *Chain Reaction,* p. 131.

18. Phillips, *Post-Conservative America,* pp. 180–192.

19. Samuel Hill and Dennis Owen, *The New Religious Political Right in America* (Nashville, Tenn.: Abingdon, 1982), pp. 51–76.

20. Robert Dallek, *Ronald Reagan: The Politics of Symbolism* (Cambridge, Mass.: Harvard University Press, 1984), pp. 13–18.

21. Lou Cannon, *Reagan* (New York: Putnam's, 1982), pp. 91–97.

22. Ibid., pp. 147–165.

23. Laurence Barrett, *Gambling with History: Reagan in the White House* (New York: Penguin Books, 1983), pp. 44–63; Rowland Evans and Robert Novak, *The Reagan Revolution* (New York: Dutton, 1981), pp. 91–95.

24. Dallek, *Ronald Reagan,* p. 34.

25. Barrett, *Gambling with History,* pp. 426–427.

26. See the views of a top aide, Martin Anderson, in *Welfare: The Political Economy of Welfare Reform in the United States* (Palo Alto, Calif.: Hoover Institution, 1978), pp. 87–132.

27. Lou Cannon, *President Reagan: The Role of A Lifetime* (New York: Simon & Schuster, 1991), pp. 206–231.

28. Haynes Johnson, *Sleepwalking Through History: America in the Reagan Years* (New York: W. W. Norton, 1991), pp. 65–76.

29. Cannon, *Reagan,* pp. 176–184.

30. Johnson, *Sleepwalking Through History,* p. 87.

31. Ibid., p. 197.

32. Evans and Novak, *The Reagan Revolution,* pp. 84–111.

33. Roberts, *The Supply-Side Revolution,* pp. 24–25.

34. Barrett, *Gambling with History,* p. 236.

35. Evans and Novak, *The Reagan Revolution,* pp. 95–96.

36. Roberts, *The Supply-Side Revolution,* pp. 12–13.

37. William Greider, "Republicans." In Broder et al., eds., *The Pursuit,* pp. 163, 168–169.

38. Roberts, *The Supply-Side Revolution,* pp. 69–88.

39. Cannon, *Reagan,* p. 325.

40. David Stockman, *The Triumph of Politics* (New York: Harper & Row, 1986), pp. 56–57.

41. Cannon, *Reagan,* pp. 273–278.

42. Johnson, *Sleepwalking Through History,* p. 131.

43. Edsall, *Chain Reaction,* p. 206.

44. "Death of the Pony." In Broder et al., eds., *The Pursuit,* p. 341.

45. Richard Cohen, "They're Still a Majority," *National Journal,* 13 (January 31, 1981), 189–191.

46. Ibid.

47. Barrett, *Gambling with History,* pp. 146–147.

48. Stockman, *The Triumph of Politics,* pp. 8–9, 11.

49. Timothy Clark, "Want to Know Where the Budget Ax Will Fall? Read Stockman's Big Black Book," *National Journal,* 13 (February 14, 1981), 274–281.

50. "Party Switchers," *National Journal,* 13 (June 20, 1981), 1095.

51. Robert Samuelson, "Reagan's Bet," *National Journal,* 13 (February 21, 1981), 301–307.

52. Evans and Novak, *The Reagan Revolution,* pp. 109–110.

53. Stephen Engelberg, "Moynihan Asserts Stockman Said Reagan Doubted Tax-Cut Theory," *The New York Times* (July 11, 1985), part A, 14.

54. Evans and Novak, *The Reagan Revolution,* pp. 109–110.

55. Stockman, *The Triumph of Politics,* pp. 269–298.

56. Ibid., p. 92; Barrett, *Gambling with History,* pp. 144–145.

57. Jack Meyer, "Budget Cuts in the Reagan Administration: A Question of Fairness." In D. Lee Bawden, ed., *The Social Contract Revisited* (Washington, D.C.: Urban Institute, 1984), pp. 33–68.

58. Clark, "Want to Know Where the Budget Ax Will Fall?" pp. 274–281.

59. Barrett, *Gambling with History,* pp. 94–106, 187–198.

60. Ibid., p. 71.

61. Clark, "Want to Know Where the Budget Ax Will Fall?" pp. 274–281.

62. Timothy Clark et al., "Congress Works a Minor Revolution—Making Cuts To Meet Its Budget Goals," *National Journal,* 13 (June 20, 1981), 1114–1115.

63. Richard Cohen, "For Spending Cuts, Only the Beginning," *National Journal,* 13 (August 8, 1981), 1414.

64. Barrett, *Gambling with History,* pp. 164–170.

65. Cannon, *President Reagan,* p. 279.

66. Edsall, *Chain Reaction,* p. 192.

67. Johnson, *Sleepwalking Through History,* p. 181.

68. Anderson, *Welfare,* pp. 43–58.

69. Blanche Bernstein, "Welfare Dependency." In Bawden, ed., *The Social Contract Revisited,* p. 138.

70. Robert Samuelson, "For the Economy, Unanswered Questions," *National Journal,* 13 (August 8, 1981), 1407.

71. Edsall, *Chain Reaction,* pp. 159–161.

72. W. Joseph Heffernan, *Introduction to Social Welfare Policy* (Itasca, Ill.: Peacock, 1979), pp. 179–180.

73. Murray Weidenbaum, "Regulatory Reform." In George Eads and Michael Fix, eds., *The Reagan Regulatory Strategy* (Washington, D.C.: Urban Institute, 1984), pp. 15–41.

74. Timothy Clark, "Affirmative Action May Fall Victim to Reagan's Regulatory Reform Drive," *National Journal,* 13 (August 11, 1981), 1248–1252.

75. Roberts, *The Supply-Side Revolution,* pp. 226–245; Stockman, *The Triumph of Politics,* pp. 320–323.

76. Roberts, *The Supply-Side Revolution,* pp. 165–179.

77. William Greider, "The Education of David Stockman," *Atlantic Monthly,* 248 (December 1981), 27–54.

78. Roberts, *The Supply-Side Revolution,* pp. 197–212.

79. Barrett, *Gambling with History,* p. 139.

80. Alexander Haig, *Caveat: Realism, Reagan, and Foreign Policy* (New York: Macmillan, 1984), pp. 303–316.

81. Charles Stone and Isabel Sawhill, *Economic Policy in the Reagan Years* (Washington, D.C.: Urban Institute, 1984), pp. 22–25.

82. "Reagan's Polarized America," *Newsweek* (April 5, 1982), 20–28.

83. Barrett, *Gambling with History,* pp. 401–402.

84. Ibid., pp. 348–349.

85. Stockman, *The Triumph of Politics,* pp. 192–193.

86. Timothy Clark, "Social Security Ball in Your Court, Greenspan Panel Tells Reagan, O'Neill," *National Journal,* 14 (November 20, 1982), 1889–1991.

87. Paul Starr, *The Social Transformation of American Medicine* (New York: Basic Books, 1984), pp. 383–388.

88. Linda Demkovitch, "Hospitals That Provide for the Poor Are Reeling from Uncompensated Costs," *National Journal,* 16 (November 24, 1984), 2245–2249.

89. Ibid.

90. Joseph Califano, *America's Health Care Revolution: Who Lives? Who Dies? Who Pays?* (New York: Random House, 1986), pp. 11–36, 58–68.

91. Dorothy Kupcha, "Medicaid: In or Out of the Mainstream?" *California Journal,* 10 (May 1979), 181–183.

92. Nancy Eustis, Jay Greenberg, and Sharon Patten, *Long-Term Care for Older Persons: A Policy Perspective* (Pacific Grove, Calif.: Brooks/Cole, 1984), pp. 1–7.

93. Marlene Cimons, "AIDS Shock Wave Due To Sweep U.S.," *Los Angeles Times* (December 7, 1986), 1, 35.

94. Richard Corrigan, "Private Sector on the Spot As It Prepares To Take Over Job Training," *National Journal,* 15 (April 30, 1983), 894–897.

95. Bruce Jansson, *Theory and Practice of Social Welfare Policy: Analysis, Processes, and Current Issues* (Belmont, Calif.: Wadsworth, 1984), pp. 133–134.

96. Neil Pierce, "The Myth of the Spendthrift States," *National Journal* (August 3, 1991), 1941.

97. Barrett, *Gambling with History,* p. 61.

98. Hill and Owen, *The New Religious Political Right,* pp. 72–76.

99. Peter Goldman and Tony Full, *The Quest for the Presidency, 1984* (New York: Bantam Books, 1985), pp. 35–36.

100. TRB, "Neoliberals, Paleoliberals," *New Republic* (April 9, 1984), 6, 41.

101. Goldman and Full, *The Quest for the Presidency,* pp. 48–58.

102. Ibid., pp. 368–374.

103. Jeffrey Birnbaum and Alan Murray, *Showdown at Gucchi Gulch* (New York: Vintage Books, 1988), pp. 284–291.

104. Donald Chambers, "Policy Weaknesses and Political Opportunities," *Social Service Review,* 59:1 (March 1985), 1–17.

105. Sidney Blumenthal, *Pledging Allegiance: The Last Campaign of the Cold War* (New York: Harper-Collins, 1990).

106. Burt Solomon, "Grading Bush," *National Journal* (July 8, 1991), 1331–1335.

107. Cannon, *President Reagan,* p. 279.

108. See, for example, the series of articles on the peace dividend in *The New York Times* in 1991, such as its editorial on May 9, 1990, part A, p. 30.

109. Barbara Sinclair, "Governing Unheroically (and Sometimes Unappetizingly): Bush and the 101st Congress." In Colin Campbell and Bert Rockman, eds., *The Bush Presidency: First Assessments* (Chatham, N.J.: Chatham House Publishers, 1991), pp. 174–181.

110. Ibid.

111. Bert Rockman, "Leadership Style of George Bush." In Campbell and Rockman, eds., *The Bush Presidency,* p. 1–35.

112. Paul Quirk, "Domestic Policy: Divided Government and Cooperative Presidential Leadership." In Campbell and Rockman, eds., *The Bush Presidency,* p. 69–91.

113. Solomon, "Grading Bush," p. 1335.

114. Edsall, *Chain Reaction,* p. 186.

115. Ibid., pp. 99–115.

116. Ibid., pp. 192–197, 215–255.

117. See, for example, U.S. House Ways and Means Committee, *The 1990 Green Book* (Washington, D.C.: Government Printing Office, June 5, 1990), pp. 1106–1107; Kevin Phillips, *Rich and Poor: Wealth and the American Electorate in the Reagan Aftermath* (New York: Random House, 1990), pp. 8–25, 74–91; and Edsall, *Chain Reaction,* pp. 160–161.

118. Phillips, *Rich and Poor,* pp. 8–25, 74–91.

119. Ibid., p. 166.

120. William Wilson, "Cycles of Deprivation and the Underclass Debate," *Social Service Review,* 59 (December 1985), 541–559.

121. Paul Peterson, "The Poverty Paradox." In Christopher Jencks and Paul Peterson, eds., *The Urban Underclass* (Washington, D.C.: Brookings Institution, 1990), pp. 9–16.

122. Ronald Takaki, *Strangers from a Different Shore* (Boston: Little, Brown, 1989), p. 420.

123. Sucheng Chen, *Asian Americans: An Interpretive History* (Boston: Twayne Publishers, 1991), p. 170.

124. Randy Shilts, *And the Band Played On* (New York. St. Martins Press, 1987), p. 456.

125. Ibid., p. 525.

126. *San Francisco Examiner* (June 5, 1989), 12.

127. Julie Kosterlitz, "Enablement," *National Journal* (August 31, 1991), 2093.

128. Susan Faludi, *Backlash: The Undeclared War Against American Women* (New York: Crown Publishers, 1991), pp. 59–72.

129. Ibid., pp. xiii–xxiii.

130. Ibid., p. 236.

131. Ibid., pp. 412–421.

132. Ibid., pp. 273–275.

133. Richard Cohen, "Family Leave Fight Perplexes Advocates," *National Journal* (November 23, 1991), 2878.

134. Children's Defense Fund, *State of America's Children* (Washington, D.C., 1991), pp. 24–25.

135. Martha Ozawa, "Introduction: An Overview." In Martha Ozawa, ed., *Women's Life Cycle and Economic Security* (New York: Greenwood Press, 1989), pp. 2–8.

136. Jonathan Kozol, *Savage Inequalities: Children in America's Schools* (New York: Crown Publishers, 1991).

137. Children's Defense Fund, *State of America's Children,* p. 122.

138. Sheila Kamerman and Alfred Kahn, "Social Policy and Children in the United States and Europe." In John Palmer, Timothy Smeeding, and Barbara Torrey, eds., *The Vulnerable* (Washington, D.C.: Urban Institute Press, 1988), pp. 351–380.

139. Robert Binstock, "The Politics and Economics of Aging and Diversity." In Scott Bass, Elizabeth Kutza, and Fernando Torres-Gil, eds., *Diversity in Aging: Challenges Facing Planners and Policy Makers in the 1990s* (Glenview, Ill.: Scott, Foresman, 1990), pp. 73–77.

140. Jack Meyer and Marilyn Moon, "Health Care Spending on Children and the Elderly." In Palmer, Smeeding, and Torrey, eds., *The Vulnerable,* p. 180.

141. Binstock, "The Politics and Economics of Aging," pp. 77–82.

142. Martha Burt and Barbara Cohen, *America's Homeless: Numbers, Characteristics, and Programs that Serve Them* (Washington, D.C.: Urban Institute Press, 1989), pp. 2–4, 27–31.

143. Ibid., pp. 141–161.

144. Peter Rossi, *Down and Out in America: The Origins of Homelessness* (Chicago: University of Chicago Press, 1989), pp. 181–184.

145. Joan Biskupic, *The Supreme Court Yearbook, 1990–1991* (Washington, D.C.: Congressional Quarterly, Inc., 1992), p. 10.

146. W. John Moore, "Righting the Courts," *National Journal* (January 25, 1992), 200.

147. W. John Moore, "In Whose Court?" *National Journal* (October 5, 1991), 2397.

148. Linda Greenhouse, "Justices Bar Using Civil Rights Suits to Enforce U.S. Child Welfare Law," *New York Times* (March 26, 1992), Sec. A, 15.

149. Harry Specht, "Social Work and the Popular Psychotherapies," *Social Service Review* 64 (September 1990), 345–357.

150. Amy Butler, "The Attractiveness of Private Practice," *Journal of Social Work Education* (Winter 1992), 47–60.

151. *Social Work Speaks: NASW Policy Statements,* 2nd ed. (Silver Spring, Md.: National Association of Social Workers, 1991).

152. Bruce Jansson, *Social Welfare Policy: From Theory to Practice* (Belmont, Calif.: Wadsworth, 1990), pp. 8–11.

153. Stanley Wenocur and Michael Reisch, *From Charity to Enterprise: The Development of American Social Work in a Market Economy* (Urbana, Ill.: University of Illinois Press, 1989), pp. 6–18; Gerald Rothman, *Philanthropists, Therapists, and Activists* (Cambridge, Mass.: Schenkman Publishing Co., 1985), pp. 155–161.

154. See the discussion of the American Medical Association throughout Paul Starr, *The Social Transformation of American Medicine* (New York: Basic Books, 1984).

12

C H A P T E R

Reluctance Illustrated: Policy Uncertainty During the Clinton Administration

Selected Orienting Events

1992	Bill Clinton defeats George Bush and Ross Perot
1993	Clinton announces an economic package that includes tax increases and spending cuts
1993	Clinton places Hillary Clinton in charge of a task force to develop a health-reform proposal
1993	Family and Medical Leave Act enacted
1993	Clinton signs the 1993 Omnibus Reconciliation Bill, which cuts the deficit, raises taxes, and increases the earned-income tax credit
1993	Clinton presents ambitious plan to reform health care
1993	North American Free Trade Agreement enacted
1993	Federal policy toward gay men and lesbians in the military is modified
1994	Congress enacts legislation that makes it a federal crime to intimidate abortion-clinic workers and clients by force or threat of force
1994	Crime Bill enacted
1994	Some Republican leaders issue Contract with America
1994	Republicans obtain control of both houses of Congress in landslide electoral victory
1995	Republican Newt Gingrich becomes Speaker of the House
1995	Congress enacts 1995 Omnibus Reconciliation Act, which seeks to eliminate the entitlement status of AFDC, Medicaid, and Food Stamps
1995	Clinton vetoes 1995 Omnibus Reconciliation Act, as well as specific appropriation bills
1996	Budget stalemate between Congress and President Clinton continues

In its first three years, the presidency of Bill Clinton was characterized by more conflict than any administration since the second term of Richard Nixon. In his 1992 campaign, Clinton ran on a relatively liberal agenda that featured increased spending on a range of social programs, as well as health and welfare reform. Clinton was able to enact some social reforms in his first two years in office and to avoid deep cuts in many social programs, but he was placed on the defensive in 1995, after Republicans under the leadership of Newt Gingrich swept the 1994 congressional elections and gained control of both houses of Congress. Republicans proceeded to advance a conservative agenda based on cutting taxes, slashing social spending, ending entitlements, and devolving many federal policy roles to the states. A titanic confrontation ensued between the Democratic administration and the Republican Congress. The central issues were the size and priorities of the national budget in 1995 and the nation's commitment to entitlements like AFDC and Medicaid.

Clinton's situation resembles that of another Democratic president, Harry Truman, who in 1947 and 1948 confronted a Republican congress determined to use its budget and taxing powers in order to impose its conservative agenda on the nation. We call the Truman, Nixon, and Clinton presidencies periods of policy uncertainty, in which liberal, moderate, and conservative ideologies were pitted against one another in dramatic fashion.

THE ASCENDANCE OF BILL CLINTON

Bill Clinton described his political career as a tale of rags to riches, a Lincoln-like ascent to power from humble origins in Hope, Arkansas through a succession of fortuitous events. As David Maraniss points out, however, the ascent was hardly accidental.[1] Developing a network of friends and patrons, winning elections, and gaining recognition by chairing national organizations, Clinton masterminded an ascent to power that realized presidential ambitions nurtured since (at least) high school. Unlike Lincoln, moreover, Clinton was raised in a middle-class family with easy access to a golf course and a swimming pool at a local country club. His primary adversity in childhood was not poverty, but an alcoholic and abusive stepfather.

Like Lyndon Johnson, Clinton was preoccupied with obtaining power; he sought it directly and he made connections for himself by participating in other people's campaigns. In his youth, he won class presidencies in high school and at Georgetown University. Using his contacts with Senator William Fulbright, he obtained a clerkship with the Senate Foreign Relations Committee while a college student and thus learned the inner workings of the Senate. By deft maneuvering, he obtained a Rhodes Scholarship, which allowed him to study at Oxford University for two years before obtaining a law degree at Yale. Even before he returned to Arkansas in 1973, at the age of 27, he had participated in four major campaigns at state and federal levels, culminating in the ill-fated presidential campaign of George McGovern in 1972. Throughout all of these experiences, Clinton developed thousands of contacts that he meticulously filed on index cards—contacts that he later cultivated and freely used to obtain funds, support, and advice for his own political races. Undeterred by a losing run for the House of Representatives from a rural part of Arkansas in 1974, he was elected attorney general in 1976 and governor in 1978; that victory made him the youngest governor in the United States in four decades. Aside from a single loss in 1980, he held the governorship for four terms; in 1991, during his fifth term, he decided to run for president. His political career was profoundly shaped by his wife, Hillary, who became his closest advisor in Arkansas and during his presidency.

The Search for the Real Bill Clinton

From the beginning of his career, Clinton has left many people uncertain where he really stood. He supported liberal policies on some occasions and moderate or conservative policies on others. He frequently retreated from liberal positions, to the dismay of liberal supporters, only to subsequently return to them.[2] His inconsistency stemmed from several sources. As a Southern politician, he *had* to present a moderate or conservative profile to succeed in a rural state that had supported such politicians as Orville Faubus, the governor who defied federal school-desegregation orders in the 1950s. Like many Southern politicians, including Jimmy Carter and ex-Senator Sam Nunn, Clinton feared that the Southern Democratic party might not survive Southern Republicans' attempts to win over white voters by means of antitax, antispending, and conservative rhetoric.[3] Yet Clinton had strong social reform and populist convictions. As a child, Clinton had been repulsed by the racist policies of Orville Faubus, as well as the segregationist policies of the South. John Kennedy was his personal hero. Partly because he opposed the Vietnam War but also because he possessed liberal views, Clinton campaigned for George McGovern in 1972. As populist or social reformer, Clinton sought reforms in the educational system of Arkansas, tried to lower utility rates, participated in a law suit against physicians who refused to serve Medicaid patients, and favored job training for welfare recipients. While he did not support civil rights legislation in Arkansas, he appointed many African Americans and women to governmental posts. He favored major tax increases in Arkansas to fund road construction and improvements in public education.[4]

Intensely ambitious and determined to win elections in his Southern state, Clinton was a chameleon even before he became president. He viewed himself as a social reformer, and felt most comfortable when championing social causes and attacking vested interests. Yet, when attacked by Southern opponents as a tax-and-spend Democrat, Clinton would backtrack if he believed his political base was jeopardized: He would repudiate former allies, such as organized labor or school teachers; seek tougher work requirements for welfare recipients; fail to seek civil rights legislation; or demand that the national Democratic party become more moderate. Clinton's political style contributed to fears that he lacked deep convictions. From 1980 onward, he relied heavily on Dick Morris, a political consultant who placed extraordinary reliance on political polls; under Morris's tutelage, Clinton shaped his rhetoric and positions almost daily to their latest findings. Morris preached that politicians should couple pragmatism with idealism, in a kind of permanent campaign.[5]

Observers began to wonder if Clinton possessed any core values. They worried that he was overly eager to be liked by everyone and unable to take strong, confrontive positions, even when confronted with arch conservatives. Some saw him as too academic, a policy wonk who mulled over endless options without reaching closure.

The Search for the New Democrat

Clinton's ill-defined views and Southern origins would have made his ascension to the presidency difficult in the 1960s, when Northern, liberal Democrats possessed considerable power in the national party. But by the early 1990s, these characteristics became assets rather than liabilities, for several reasons. With the extraordinary movement of people from the North to the Sunbelt from the 1950s through the 1980s, the electoral votes of the South and of California exceeded those of the Northern industrial states. The power of suburban voters had steadily increased since the 1960s, as well, to the point that a majority of voters in the 1992 presidential elections were suburbanites. Increasingly, Democratic leaders came to fear that, if they were to concede the South and Northern suburbs to Republicans, they might become a minority party for decades. Moreover, the ultra-liberal McGovern's one-sided defeat in 1972 led many Democrats to worry that the party was positioning itself so far to the left that it would no longer appeal to the white ethnic voters who had been a bastion of Democratic support since the 1930s. This threat had become more ominous by the 1980s, when substantial numbers of Republicans replaced Democrats in Congress. In an equally disturbing trend, some Democratic officeholders, such as Phil Gramm of Texas, had switched parties.

In the wake of McGovern's defeat, Democrats like Ben Wattenberg sought to move the party back to the center; they feared that it had been captured by special interest groups such as feminists, civil rights groups, and organized labor. These Democrats were particularly opposed to affirmative action, liberal welfare programs, and the eclipse of the states' policy roles.[6] Clinton signalled his decision to identify with the moderate wing of the party in 1980, by strongly supporting Jimmy Carter, a fellow Southern governor, against Teddy Kennedy's bid for the presidential nomination. In 1985, he helped cofound the Democratic Leadership Council (DLC), which sought to define a third way —that is, a political platform that fell between traditional liberal and conservative positions. Where traditional Democrats had favored redistribution of resources to the poor, civil rights legislation, affirmative action, and cuts in defense spending, the new Democrats emphasized a narrower range of economic reforms—job training, national standards in education, free trade, and infrastructure improvements. Where traditional Democrats favored new spending on social programs *and* retention of existing spending, the new Democrats favored balanced budgets. Where traditional Democrats were opposed to free trade, partly because trade unions feared it might hurt their domestic markets, new Democrats (with some exceptions) liked it; they believed that free trade would eventually expand markets for American goods by forcing efficiencies in American industry and lowering other nations' trade barriers. Where traditional Democrats wanted large cuts in the military in the wake of the Cold War, new Democrats favored only selective cuts. New Democrats were determined, as well, to challenge conservatives' charges that Democrats were soft on welfare and crime. Where traditional Democrats had often championed higher welfare benefits, new Democrats emphasized work requirements and limits on benefits. They often favored stiffer penalties for various crimes such as drug dealing, as well as extension of the death penalty to new crimes. Traditional and new Democrats tended to use different language; where the former discussed the obligations of citizens to help others, the latter emphasized the responsibilities of citizens—for example, to seek work, raise families, and help their communities. Perhaps most important, the new Democrats emphasized the economic needs of the middle class rather than low-income groups or racial outgroups, partly because they attributed the Republicans' upsurge in the 1980s to the alienation of white voters who perceived the Democrats as beholden to feminists, civil rights activists, and gays. Believing that this alienation was partly due to the erosion of living standards for many working-class and middle-class Americans, new Democrats often advocated education, job training, and tax cuts that would help this group; thus, they placed less emphasis on programs to help poor inner-city residents and other outgroups.[7]

Yet these new Democrats did not dominate the party in the early 1990s. Liberal Democrats maintained a strong presence in party councils, as did activists from an array of civil rights, feminist, and labor groups. Party chieftains in Congress, such as House Speaker Tom Foley and Senate Majority Leader George Mitchell, did not belong to the Democratic Leadership Council, even if they also feared the desertion of many white voters to the Republican cause.

Bill Clinton's ill-defined views positioned him perfectly to obtain the allegiance of the divided Democratic Party, if he could convince both factions that he favored their positions. He appealed to those Democrats who believed a Southern candidate was needed to avert further Republican inroads in the Sunbelt—and could point to his election as chair of the DLC in 1990 as proof that he could appeal to Democratic moderates and conservatives. Having campaigned for McGovern and sought various reform in Arkansas, he often spoke like a traditional Democrat. Himself a Baptist, he often spoke in African American churches and gave Vernon Jordan, a prominent African American attorney, important roles in his campaign and presidency. His wife, Hillary Rodham Clinton, who had chaired the board of directors of the Children's Defense Fund, broadened his appeal to liberals.

As an outsider who had never been elected to federal office, Clinton could also attract widespread support from independents and those citizens who were deeply cynical about the federal government and about the Congress. Many good reasons existed for cynicism. Americans had heard endless promises from politicians that budgets would be balanced since 1981, only to find mounting deficits. They had seen many news reports about government waste, in both defense and domestic agencies. They knew that many elections were bought by politicians who could obtain huge contributions from special interests and wealthy people. Finally, the bitter wrangling between Republican presidents and the Democratic Congress during the Reagan and Bush years, punctuated by presidential vetoes, had fueled widespread frustration at government gridlock.

THE PRESIDENTIAL CAMPAIGN OF 1992

Most Democrats regarded George Bush as unbeatable in fall 1991, in the wake of Operation Desert Storm, a highly popular war against Iraq. Facing candidates with little name recognition or uncertain reputations, like Paul Tsongas, John Kerry, and Jerry Brown, Clinton relied on his superior campaign skills, his adeptness at using the mass media, his vast network of contacts, and his ability to raise money and easily won the Democratic nomination in July 1992.

Clinton's road to the presidency was complicated by the third-party candidacy of Ross Perot, a maverick billionaire from Texas. Drawing on widespread cynicism about politicians and the government, Perot vowed to clean up Washington. Perot was vague about his likely policies, with one notable exception: He vowed to end the budget deficit soon after taking office, though he did not explain precisely how he would do so. By focusing on the budget deficit, Perot elevated that issue in the public's consciousness and stimulated other candidates to address it. Fearful that Perot would draw votes from them, both Bush and Clinton emphasized deficit reduction in their own campaigns; Clinton promised to halve the deficit within four years, from $237 billion to $118 billion.

Clinton fashioned a clever strategy in this complex environment. He maintained the allegiance of liberals by supporting the policy recommendations of Robert Reich, a professor Clinton knew from Oxford University and Yale Law School. Reich believed that the economy no longer revolved around nation states, but had become globalized, as corporations dispersed their operations in many nations, in search of cheap labor (for unskilled jobs) or educated, technologically sophisticated labor (for skilled jobs). In this globalized economy, Reich contended, the American work force was polarizing into two factions. Symbolic analysts, who had higher degrees and were adept at information-age technologies, had expanding options in an array of highly paid professional, technical, and corporate positions. By contrast, with the sharp decline in well-paid, unionized industrial jobs since the 1960s, tens of millions of Americans worked in low-paid, unskilled jobs. These low-paid workers in clerical, sales, and fast-food jobs faced a bleak economic future: Reich predicted that corporations would continue to place their manufacturing operations in low-wage nations, such as Mexico and Thailand and, in consequence, the wages and economic security of unskilled American workers would deteriorate even further. Concluding that the nation could retain and develop better-paying jobs only if it invested in its human capital and its infrastructure, such as roads and telecommunications, Reich recommended large expenditures in education, job training, and public improvements.[8] In addition to these social investment expenditures, which required outlays over many years, Clinton also advocated immediate spending—so-called stimulus spending—on an array of public projects to invigorate the stagnant economy.

Clinton also promised to reform the health-care system. He had long been concerned about the plight of Americans who lacked health coverage; as governor of Arkansas, he sought to develop public health, maternal health, and family-planning services in the state. In 1991, when Democrat Harrison Wofford ran a successful senatorial campaign in Pennsylvania on a health-reform platform, Clinton became convinced that public opinion favored an overhaul of the American health system. To strengthen his liberal credentials, he advocated unpaid parental leaves for childbirth and to help ailing relatives and he vowed to overturn the ban on gay men and lesbians in the military. He solicited support from environmentalists by selecting as his vice president Senator Albert Gore, Jr., who had supported many environmental causes. He cemented the support of liberal Democrats by promising to increase taxes on affluent Americans, who had, he argued, enriched themselves throughout the 1980s as a result of the Reagan administration's tax cuts.

Intent on capturing moderate and conservative votes and on securing the support of white ethnic voters, Clinton also used campaign language that the Democratic Leadership Council favored. Words like "responsibility," "community," and "opportunity" and glowing references to the middle class were scattered throughout his speeches. He promised to enact welfare reform that coupled strong work requirements with liberal subsidies for child care and job training. In a widely publicized statement, he criticized Sister Souljah, an African American rap singer, for militant language; that accusation brought a public confrontation with Jesse Jackson, the civil rights leader, who accused Clinton of currying the favor of white citizens. Clinton promised a significant tax cut for middle-class Americans, even though he had received confidential information that the federal deficit would be far higher than the Bush administration had publicly admitted. To neutralize Ross Perot, Clinton promised that he would support campaign reforms, consider some cuts in entitlements, and halve the nation's deficit during his term.

Most important, Clinton understood that presidential races often hinge on the state of the economy. To his astonishment, Bush failed to emphasize a strategy for reinvigorating the economy and thus alienated many of the working-class and middle-class voters who had defected to the Republican party from the Democratic party in the 1980s. Lacking a focus for his campaign in its early stages, Clinton's strategists successfully guided its later stages on the basis of a motto posted prominently in their campaign headquarters: "It's the economy, stupid."

Clinton won the election, but by the narrowest margin since 1968. He obtained only 43% of the popular vote, as compared to 38% for Bush and 19% for Perot. Clinton's support in California, industrial states of the Midwest, and New York State carried him to victory. Democrats controlled both houses of Congress. However, their margin in the Senate was insufficient to stop a Republican filibuster, and their majority in the House would be destroyed if only 30 conservative Democrats voted with the Republicans. Thus, in both the House and the Senate, Clinton would be vulnerable to a coalition of Southern (or border-state) Democrats and Republicans if they viewed his policies as excessively liberal.

CLINTON'S GRIM OPTIONS

Even before his inauguration, Clinton knew that his first challenge would be to fashion a budget and an economic policy. Perot's single-minded focus upon the budget deficit during the campaign had forced the issue to center stage. Were Clinton *not* to devise policies to reduce the deficit markedly, he would be accused of abandoning his campaign promise to halve it within four years—and would face a rebellious Congress, where many newly elected legislators were determined to diminish it.

Clinton's dilemma was that he had proposed contradictory policies during the campaign: He had promised to halve the nation's deficit, but he had also promised to fund social investments and an immediate economic stimulus. Moreover, he had promised a tax cut for middle-class citizens, and had downplayed the need for tax increases. To further complicate his deficit-reducing task, Clinton had rarely discussed spending cuts during the campaign; he had promised only to end subsidies to beekeepers and to consider modest premium increases for wealthy Medicare recipients.

With his advisors and cabinet named, Clinton came face to face with daunting economic realities that would further frustrate deficit reduction. While he had learned in August that the Bush administration would soon issue a higher estimate of the budget deficit, he had not focused on these figures.

Eventually, Bush estimated the deficit for 1997 at $305 billion, or $68 billion higher than he had predicted in the summer. (Many Democrats, including Clinton, feared it would rise to $360 billion or more.) With soaring Medicare and Medicaid costs, deficits would again begin to rise after 1997, even if a strong antideficit program were implemented in the interim.

These economic realities meant that Clinton had to seriously consider two options that were certain to attract political opposition: increasing taxes and cutting spending on existing programs.[9] Obstacles to tax increases had been introduced by Reagan, who had developed wide support for tax cuts, and by Bush, who had been vilified for breaking his promise to the 1988 Republican convention: "Read my lips. No new taxes." Nor were spending cuts palatable to the liberal wing of the Democratic party, which was anxious to enact a large agenda of social reforms after 12 years of Republican presidents.

Clinton also encountered another reality that would profoundly influence his economic strategy. During the campaign, he had emphasized spending increases as the primary means of stimulating the economy—a traditional Democratic method of restoring economic growth. Soon after he was elected, however, he met with Alan Greenspan, the Chair of the Federal Reserve Board. Greenspan contended that economic growth would hinge *not* on stimulus spending, but on interest rates charged to borrowers, such as home buyers, consumers, and corporations. Were interest rates to rise, these borrowers would have to pay more for their loans and would thus be discouraged from expenditures and investments. The best route to economic growth, Greenspan asserted, was to *cut* the large deficit: If the deficit were lower, he argued, interest rates would fall, because fewer investment funds would be diverted from the private sector to the purchase of government bonds. It became clear to Clinton, as well, that bond traders on Wall Street possessed extraordinary power over the economy, through their trading actions; they would sell and buy bonds at lower interest rates only if they believed that the government was pursuing antideficit policies—for example, by cutting social spending.

Greenspan implied, moreover, that he and the Federal Reserve Board would cut the so-called prime rate, which powerfully influences interest rates of banks, but only if the Clinton Administration developed a credible deficit-reduction plan. (At various points subsequently, Clinton felt that Greenspan and Wall Street bond traders controlled his policies; he feared that they might increase interest rates if he failed to emphasize deficit reduction over spending increases.)[10]

Before tackling his budget dilemma, Clinton devoted the month of December to selecting his cabinet and his economic team. His choices signified that he wanted an array of perspectives in his administration. On the conservative side, he chose advisors likely to emphasize deficit reduction—Senator Lloyd Bentsen as Secretary of the Treasury; Wall Street banker Robert Rubin to head his economic team; and deficit hawks Representative Leon Panetta and Alice Rivlin to run the Office of Management and Budget. He named the relatively liberal Laura D'Andrea Tyson to chair the Council of Economic Advisors. He also gave key posts to other liberal advisors—Robert Reich as Secretary of Labor; Donna Shalala as Secretary of Health and Human Services; and Henry Cisneros as Secretary of Housing and Urban Development. The liberal emphasis of his first two years was accentuated, moreover, by his decision to grant his wife, Hillary, a large role in overseeing domestic policy and by his frequent consultations with campaign strategists James Carville, Paul Begala, Stan Greenberg, and Mandy Grunwald, who insisted that Clinton follow through on his campaign promises to increase social investments.

FROM SOCIAL INVESTMENT TO DEFICIT REDUCTION

Even before his inauguration, Clinton was drawn in different directions by an array of powerful forces and people. Strong pressure for deficit reduction came from Bentsen and Rubin, who were convinced by Greenspan's logic. Members of

Congress from both parties—particularly those newly elected—believed they had been given a mandate by the people to push for deficit reduction. Clinton realized that he risked losing popular support if he did not take dramatic action against the deficit; he had promised to cut it in half within four years and it was rapidly expanding. He knew, as well, that the Republicans would make deficit reduction a central theme in their political strategy in 1993; they were eager to continue their attack on him as a tax-and-spend Democrat.

On the other hand, many people tried to convince Clinton not to abandon his campaign promises of social investments, health reform, and welfare reform. Liberal Democrats hadn't controlled the presidency for 12 years, and had seen many social programs severely cut during this period. They urged Clinton to pursue social investments and stimulus spending, as did many interest groups, such as the Children's Defense Fund and the American Association of Retired Persons. The strongest advocates for social investments within the Administration were campaign strategists like Carville, Begala, and Grunwald, sometimes joined by Reich, Tyson, and Hillary Clinton. Nor should we minimize Clinton's own social reform proclivities; he deeply believed that social investments were needed to help working Americans improve their economic options. In behind-the-scenes meetings during the first months of his administration, he frequently expressed reluctance to break his campaign promises.[11] With the Democrats in control of Congress, he had considerable political leverage to enact social reforms and to fund a liberal agenda.

Developing an Economic Package

Presidents who come into office for the first time inherit their predecessor's budget, even though they may modify it. Bush's budget emphasized cuts in social spending—including spending caps on many entitlement programs—and no new taxes and thus pressured Clinton to follow suit in his own economic plans.

Not content merely to adopt Bush's budget,

which did not reflect his interest in social investments, Clinton decided to develop his own economic package—a set of targets for spending, taxes, and deficit reduction that he wanted the Democratic Congress to incorporate in its Budget Resolution in the spring. (He planned to give the Congress his own detailed budget later in the spring, to show how he would meet the targets that he proposed.) In the course of many meetings with his top advisors, Clinton made several key decisions. He decided to backtrack from his campaign promise to halve the deficit by 1996; instead, he proposed to reduce it only to $205 billion in 1997. Even to reach this figure, he would need new tax revenues, particularly if he wanted immediate stimulus spending of $30 billion and social investments of $230 billion over five years. So he decided to include a broad-based energy tax based on the heat output (expressed in British thermal units, or BTUs); he also proposed to make permanent a 2.5-cents-per-gallon addition to the federal gas tax that had been scheduled to expire in 1995. He announced major tax increases for wealthy Americans; the new top rate would be 36% for couples earning more than $140,000 and individuals earning more than $115,000. Altogether, his tax increases totalled $328 billion over five years. He combined these tax increases with spending cuts of $375 billion over five years; among other things, he proposed to eliminate 100,000 positions from the federal government, to slow the rate of increase in fees paid to providers under Medicare, to extend a Medicare-premium increase that was due to expire, and to cut defense by $112 billion.

In effect, Clinton forged a compromise between his liberal and his conservative advisors that included both spending increases and deficit reduction. The president's package delighted many deficit hawks, including Greenspan, who viewed it as a major advance toward diminishing the deficit in his first term. Newspapers hailed the economic package and applauded Clinton's embrace of deficit reduction. Liberals liked its social investment and stimulus spending. Even at this early point, however, some liberal advisors within the administration were chagrined by the fact that deficit reduction, not social spending, was dominating discussion of the budget. They also knew that Clinton, already bowing to economic advisors like Bentsen, had cut his proposed social investments in behind-the-scenes discussions before he announced his economic package on February 17. In his speeches, moreover, he emphasized deficit reduction rather than social investments.[12]

A Brief Digression: The Budget Process

To understand the fate of Clinton's social investments—and the continuing conflict between Republicans, Democrats, and the president—we must first comprehend the budget process, which dominated the nation's politics in 1993, 1995, and much of 1996. An examination of this process will give us important insights into the reasons why many social programs, such as child care, child welfare, and mental-health services, are chronically underfunded.

The budget process begins when the president submits his proposed budget for the coming fiscal year, typically in February. He outlines how much money he wants to allocate to each program in the coming year, whether he wants new taxes, his estimate of the likely budget deficit, and his estimate of the likely effects of his budget on the budget deficit. Federal spending can be placed in two categories: entitlements and discretionary spending. Programs such as AFDC, Medicare, Medicaid, SSI, and Food Stamps are entitlements; the statutes that establish the programs lay out standards that recipients must meet, and the government automatically grants funds to pay the benefits of all recipients who meet those standards in a given year. Unlike entitlements, the funds for discretionary programs are determined annually by votes of the appropriations committees in each chamber. The Congress might decide in a given year, for example, to cut funding of a child nutrition program or to increase funding of a public health program.

In Clinton's budget proposal for the 1994 fiscal year (Figure 12.1), expenditures were divided among entitlements and mandatory spending (roughly 50% of the budget), discretionary spending (roughly 33% of the budget), and interest on

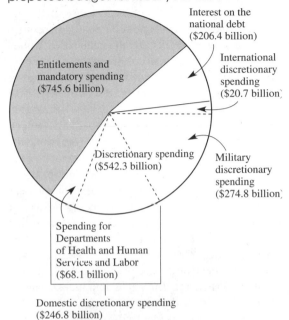

FIGURE 12.1   An overview of the President's proposed budget for fiscal year 1994

Interest on the national debt ($206.4 billion)

Entitlements and mandatory spending ($745.6 billion)

International discretionary spending ($20.7 billion)

Discretionary spending ($542.3 billion)

Military discretionary spending ($274.8 billion)

Spending for Departments of Health and Human Services and Labor ($68.1 billion)

Domestic discretionary spending ($246.8 billion)

SOURCE: President's budget. Office of Management and Budget, Appropriations Committee.

the national debt (roughly one-sixth of the budget). Inspection of Figure 12.1 reveals that the discretionary spending in Clinton's budget includes approximately equal components of domestic and military spending. Only $68.1 billion (or about 4% of the entire federal budget) is devoted to the combined discretionary programs of the Department of Health and Human Services and the Department of Labor, which constitute (aside from entitlements) the heart of the American welfare state.[13]

Four facets of this federal budget are of particular interest to social workers:

1. Funding of entitlements. Cuts in expenditures on entitlements severely impact social workers' clients, who often depend on Medicare, Medicaid, AFDC, SSI, and Food Stamps.
2. Domestic discretionary spending. This section of the budget, which accounts for only about 16% of the total, funds mental-health, child welfare, substance-abuse, public health, AIDS-treatment and AIDS-prevention, homelessness, child care, and many other social programs.

3. Tax policy. Tax cuts decrease the revenues needed to fund entitlements and domestic discretionary spending. Moreover, when taxes are cut excessively, budget deficits increase, and concern about budget deficits and the national debt often leads legislators to cut social programs.
4. Military spending. Military programs compete with domestic programs for discretionary funds.

Once the president has submitted his budget, Congress takes center stage. After reviewing the president's budget, a Budget Committee of each chamber puts together a Budget Resolution, a document that establishes spending goals for each entitlement program; develops spending goals for discretionary spending in 13 areas, including domestic and military programs; outlines tax-revenue targets for the coming fiscal year; and sets a target for the overall size of the budget deficit (or surplus). When the Budget Committees want to reduce the budget deficit, as was the case in 1993 and 1995, their Budget Resolutions mandate spending cuts or tax increases or some combination of both. (If a Budget Committee chooses to *reduce* taxes, as both Republicans in Congress and President Clinton proposed in 1995, its Budget Resolution must mandate even deeper spending cuts in order to reduce the budget deficit.)

Each chamber must vote on the Budget Resolution that its Budget Committee has fashioned. Once approved, these two documents are sent to a conference committee that includes members from each chamber. That committee negotiates a compromise Budget Resolution, which must then be ratified by both chambers. The resulting Congressional Budget Resolution instructs the committees of Congress to develop legislation and appropriations bills that conform to its directives. Rather than telling Congress specifically how to reach the spending, tax, and budget-reduction goals, the Budget Resolution merely instructs particular congressional committees to increase or decrease spending by stipulated amounts. It might want, say, $3 billion in cuts in Medicare over five years; Congressional committees then face the task of deciding how to achieve these savings by changing the Medicare statutes. The Budget Resolution in 1993

instructed the House Committee on Education and Labor, for example, to make changes in laws within its jurisdiction to allow increases in outlays of $118 million in the coming budget year and reductions in outlays in the succeeding three years totalling nearly $6 billion. To make laws conform to these directives, the House Committee on Education and Labor has to change eligibility and benefit levels of many programs in its jurisdiction, and the House Appropriations Committee, which recommends what funds will actually be spent in a given year, has to implement these funding guidelines in its spending recommendations. Similarly, the Budget Resolution instructs committees that deal with tax legislation to raise (or reduce) tax revenues by specific amounts.

To meet the targets of the Budget Resolution, then, a vast system of tasks must be implemented by the Congress. It is useful to conceptualize this system as consisting of two parallel tracks. One track deals with entitlements and tax legislation. In this track, the spending goals of the Budget Resolution are met by changing those statutes that govern specific programs and tax policy. The House Ways and Means Committee and the Senate Finance Committee assume pivotal roles here, because they process most tax legislation, as well as entitlements like Medicare, Medicaid, and AFDC. To obtain cuts in the Medicare program recommended by the Budget Resolution, the House Ways and Means Committee might consider such policies as raising premiums for elderly persons using Part B (physician services), cutting coverage of certain services (such as mental-health services), or lowering reimbursement fees for doctors and hospitals. The other track consists of legislative committees (such as the House Committee on Education and Labor) and appropriations committees (such as the House Appropriations Committee) that deal with domestic discretionary programs. As the House Ways and Means Committee is amending tax laws and entitlement statutes that govern such programs as Medicaid, other House committees are working to fashion spending (or appropriations) recommendations for programs such as Head Start that are funded by the discretionary budget.

Two kinds of recommendations emerge from the Congress. First, each chamber often bundles its entitlement and tax recommendations into a *reconciliation bill,* so called because its recommendations reconcile tax and entitlement policies with the spending and tax guidelines of the Budget Resolution. Each chamber must vote on its reconciliation bill; a conference committee then develops a compromise version that must be ratified by each chamber. Second, to specify discretionary spending, each chamber develops 13 separate *appropriations bills,* including one that focuses on programs administered by the Department of Health and Human Services and the Department of Labor. These bills conform to guidelines in the Budget Resolution. As with each chamber's reconciliation bill, conference committees fashion compromise appropriations measures that must be ratified by each chamber.

By late summer or fall, attention shifts back to the president, who has to decide whether to sign or veto the Congressional recommendations from both tracks. If he signs the reconciliation bills and the 13 appropriation bills, the budget is set for the coming year. If he vetoes any of these bills, the president and Congress must agree on a continuing resolution that temporarily funds federal programs. With the continuing resolution in place, Congress attempts to fashion modifications of the vetoed bills that the president is willing to sign. (If Congress and the president cannot even agree on a continuing resolution, some government programs may even come to a temporary halt, as occurred during the turbulent budget impasse of 1995 and 1996.)

The Demise of the Stimulus Package

Recall that, in his economic package, Clinton proposed two kinds of new spending: an immediate economic stimulus to get the economy moving; and social investments. House leaders introduced his $30 billion stimulus package in mid-February. (Only $16.3 billion was new spending; the rest consisted of business tax incentives and construction loans.) The stimulus spending was vulnerable on several counts. Because this spending was relatively small, it would not have a large economic effect even if enacted. Moreover, unlike the social investments, which were guided by Robert Reich's philosophy of making the nation competitive in a global economy, the stimulus package contained a lot of pork—that is, expenditures for various projects in the districts of important Democrats, such as road construction grants to particular cities. Conservatives were certain to attack it as inconsistent with deficit reduction.

Clinton moved to get immediate action on his stimulus package. The Republicans, urged forward by deficit hawks like Newt Gingrich and John Kasich, opposed it en masse and tried to portray the new president as a big spender. But the response of many House Democrats, particularly moderates and conservatives, was even more disconcerting. They wanted to cast their deficit-reduction vote *before* they cast their vote for stimulus spending, so that they could tell their constituents that they prioritized spending cuts. Consequently, they insisted that the vote on the stimulus package be delayed until the Budget Resolution, which emphasized deficit reduction, was also ready for a vote in the House.

After heavy lobbying by Clinton, the House did pass the stimulus package. But it was then subjected to devastating opposition from moderate and conservative Democrats in the Senate. Senators David Boren and John Breaux, who had been saying for weeks that Congress should make actual spending cuts before approving the stimulus package, wanted to spend only half of the stimulus package and to delay approval of the rest of it until Congress enacted those tax increases and spending cuts detailed in the House Budget Resolution. Strong-arm parliamentary tactics by Senator Robert Byrd, the Senate Majority Leader, angered Republican senators by making it impossible for them to amend the legislation. Realizing that they lacked the votes to stop it, Republicans decided to filibuster. When the Senate recessed and legislators returned to their districts to get constituents' feedback, Clinton received another bad piece of news; many voters told their representatives that *they* prioritized deficit reduction over stimulus spending.

When Clinton offered to cut the stimulus bill by one-fourth, to only $12.2 billion, Republicans insisted that *all* spending in the legislation be deleted, except for a $4 billion provision to fund extensions of unemployment insurance. Unable to stop the filibuster otherwise, the Democrats conceded on April 21 and, in gutted form, the stimulus package was finally passed.[14]

Early Warning Signs

If stimulus spending was gutted, what happened to the social investments in Clinton's economic package? They faced their first test when both chambers developed their Budget Resolutions. It seemed, at first glance, that Clinton won a decisive victory on March 19, when the House enacted Clinton's economic package in its Budget Resolution and thereby established the spending, tax, and deficit-reduction targets that Clinton had recommended. The Senate followed suit with a similar Budget Resolution on March 25. Budget Resolutions merely establish targets, however: Clinton now needed Congress to make appropriations that would allocate funds toward his social investments.

Early warning signs suggested that Clinton's social investments would not emerge unscathed during the appropriations process. House Democratic leaders encountered substantial pressure from conservative and moderate members to cut spending further; to mollify them, the House added $63 billion in deficit reduction in its Budget Resolution by making additional cuts in social spending, mostly from appropriated programs rather than entitlements. With John Kasich leading, Republicans tried to outbid the Democrats; they proposed $429 billion in deficit reduction over five years without *any* of Clinton's tax increases—a strategy that would have required huge cuts in social spending. Acting virtually in unison, the Democrats repelled this Republican effort.

Conservative dislike of the spending and tax provisions was even stronger in the Senate. To put conservative and moderate Democrats on the spot, Republicans forced them to vote against many amendments that sought to delete specific spending and tax increases in the president's package. They realized that the legislation's energy tax—the so-called BTU tax—was particularly vulnerable, both because key Democrats came from energy-producing states like Oklahoma and because it could be portrayed as hurting the middle class, the very group Clinton and the new Democrats wanted to help. Moreover, were this tax defeated, the whole plan could be thrown into turmoil because it would lack the revenues to fund the social investments.

Throughout the debates in the House and the Senate, conservatives demanded that spending cuts far *exceed* tax increases; they wanted spending cuts, rather than tax increases, to bear the burden of deficit reduction. (Clinton had wanted roughly even amounts of tax increases and spending cuts.) There was also considerable pressure to cut entitlements, which the president's economic plan left largely intact. An amendment to cap Medicare and Medicaid by Sam Nunn, a Southern Democrat, was narrowly defeated on the Senate floor.[15]

Because it processes tax and entitlement legislation, the Senate Finance Committee played a pivotal role in enacting the Senate's Budget Resolution—and this committee barely passed it, by an 11–9 vote. If even a single Democrat were to defect to the Republican side later in the summer, when the Congress enacted its reconciliation bill, the committee would be deadlocked.

Once the House and Senate versions were speedily reconciled in a Conference Committee, the Congress enacted its Budget Resolution on April 1. In its final form, the Budget Resolution retained many social investments, even if they would be diminished from $200 billion to $140 billion by 1998. But the Budget Resolution also contained a provision—not widely understood even by many liberals—that would have momentous implications for social investments. The Congress was instructed to hold discretionary spending to an overall limit about $12 billion less than that included in a 1990 budget-cutting agreement between President Bush and the Congress. Moreover, the Budget Resolution capped discretionary spending at $539 billion in 1994 and permitted an increase only to $548 billion by 1998. In the wake of huge cuts in discretionary programs for poor people in the Reagan and Bush years, this "hard freeze" meant that these programs would not even keep pace with inflation. Their prognosis was especially bleak, because the discretionary budget included defense spending: If cuts in defense spending did not continue, even greater pressure would be placed on domestic programs. (Many legislators already were balking at the initial cuts in defense spending that Clinton had proposed; even though the Cold War had ended, they argued that the cuts would imperil the nation's security.) This hard freeze also meant that Clinton's $140 billion in social investments would be imperiled in coming years. He could fund them *only* by cutting other discretionary domestic programs or by cutting defense spending. But such cuts in other domestic programs or defense would be strongly resisted by legislators; as a result, large increases in social investments were extremely unlikely. Nor would the outlook for social investments improve if Republicans were able to capture control of either chamber in the 1994 Congressional elections. Republicans might seek to cut taxes and thus force Congress to cut spending even further in order to reduce the deficit. Or they might seek major increases in defense spending, thereby forcing cuts in domestic spending.[16]

The Sacrifice of Social Investments

Enacting the Budget Resolution proved far easier than enacting specific tax, entitlement, and spending policies. The Budget Resolution merely set targets. Legislators now faced the task of approving specific tax and spending policies; this task, as they knew, required them to negotiate the conflicting objections of lobbyists and constituents to particular tax increases, cuts in entitlements, or cuts in spending. At the same time, in the deficit-cutting mood of 1993, legislators were aware that they would be heavily criticized for *not* cutting spending and entitlements. Deficit reduction was a priority for large numbers of newly elected legislators in both parties, including many moderate and conservative Democrats who were members of such groups as the Conservative Democratic Forum and

the House's Mainstream Forum, an organ of the DLC.[17]

The battle over the reconciliation bill, which contained Clinton's BTU tax and his cuts in Medicare, illustrated the extent that the Congress was in an antitax, antispending, and deficit-reduction mode. Clinton soon realized that he would have to work furiously to get the tax measures through the House. Many legislators wanted to delete, or drastically modify, the energy tax and wanted larger cuts in entitlements. He was able to obtain a close victory in the House on his energy tax—over the opposition of 43 Democrats and virtually all Republicans—only by agreeing that he would accede to large cuts in the energy tax and larger cuts in entitlements when the legislation came to the Senate.

The Achilles tendon of the entire package was its huge energy tax. Were the BTU tax not to be passed, the entire package might unravel, because the lost revenues would require huge new spending cuts or diminution of Clinton's social investments. The tax was bitterly opposed by an array of special interests, as well as by oil state senators under the leadership of Senator David Boren of Oklahoma. (Republicans continued to demand that *all* tax increases be deleted from the legislation and that the spending cuts be far larger.) At Boren's insistence, the BTU tax was deleted; another battle was then fought over the size of the gasoline tax. (A small gas tax was eventually approved.) When the dust had settled, Democrats partly offset these lost revenues by increasing Medicare and Social Security taxes, cutting tax breaks that Clinton favored for low-income persons, and scaling back tax breaks to encourage business to locate in so-called inner-city empowerment zones. Even with these changes, the legislation only passed by a 50–49 margin; Vice President Gore cast the tie-breaking vote.

At a raucous conference committee meeting to reconcile the House and Senate versions, members of the Congressional Black Caucus threatened to vote with Republicans if tax breaks for low-income persons or empowerment zones were dropped, and conservative and moderate Democrats threatened to oppose the legislation if certain energy taxes were restored. With more than 200 House and Senate members engaged in around-the-clock bargaining, a reconciliation bill was finally approved. The bill, which provided for $500 billion in new taxes over five years, included large tax increases on wealthy Americans and a gasoline tax, but the BTU tax that energy-state legislators disliked was removed. In the prevailing antitax climate, many legislators feared rejection by their constituents in forthcoming elections if they voted for these tax increases. Clinton won with a tight 218–216 vote in the House. (The crucial vote was cast by a grim-faced female Democrat from Pennsylvania, who knew she would probably lose her next election as a result; her forecast proved to be accurate.) The Senate approved the revised reconciliation bill only by a 51–50 vote; Gore's tie-breaking vote was needed again.

Once again, Clinton seemed to have prevailed. Over a five-year period, he achieved over $500 billion in deficit reduction by combining $250 billion in new taxes with $179 billion in spending cuts. When viewed in the context of his campaign promises for social investments, however, the reconciliation bill seemed less impressive. As we have seen, the reconciliation bill contained a hard freeze on discretionary spending that would force an additional $56 billion in cuts over five years. Even by August, it was clear that Clinton's social investments would be savaged by the Congress in the coming year. As Jonathan Rauch noted, "Clinton will get some of his investment agenda, but only about half over all, and more like 20 cents on the dollar for education. The total for new investment in [the coming year] looks to come out under $10 billion. In a $6 trillion economy, hardly anyone will notice."[18] As if these cuts in Clinton's domestic spending were not enough, the House leadership and the White House had to agree to *another* round of spending cuts in fall 1993, in appropriation bills that had already passed the Congress. (Cuts in appropriations that have already been enacted are called rescissions.) Debates over these additional cuts made clear that a bipartisan coalition of deficit hawks in the House would demand far more drastic deficit reduction in the future. Not content with Clinton's promise to reduce the fed-

eral work force by 252,000 people over the next five years or to rely on the hard freeze on discretionary spending through 1998, they wanted an additional $103 billion in cuts over five years, much of it from premium increases on Medicare recipients—and they wanted these cuts to be applied to deficit reduction rather than to be used to fund new programs. Many deficit hawks also wanted a balanced-budget amendment to the Constitution that would allow deficits in any particular year only if 60% of members of both chambers approved, except during wars. (They hoped this measure would take effect by 1999.) Additionally, they wanted a line-item veto to let the president cut appropriations already approved by Congress, subject to a vote by Congress on them. They reasoned that members of Congress would be more frugal if they realized that the president might veto wasteful spending and so force them to vote publicly to restore it.

The deficit hawks, led by Republicans like Newt Gingrich, were defeated in their efforts to seek large spending cuts, the balanced-budget amendment, or a line-item veto in fall 1993. However, they had publicized their intent to seek huge, additional spending cuts in the wake of the 1994 congressional elections if, as they correctly predicted, their numbers were swelled by voters who favored their cause. Indeed, they planned to attack Clinton as a tax-and-spend Democrat in those elections.[19]

THE SECOND YEAR: ANTICRIME LEGISLATION BUT NO HEALTH REFORM

The Fight for Health Reform

Long before the presidential campaign of 1992, Clinton realized that the American health-care system had many flaws. Unlike most other industrialized nations, the United States had developed a health-care system that revolved around employers and private insurance companies. Many employers paid, in part or in full, the monthly premiums on private health-insurance policies for employees and their families. This system often worked well for those who were covered by it, but others lacked coverage because they were unemployed, because their employers chose not to offer health insurance, or because chronic or catastrophic conditions had exhausted their benefits. Moreover, individuals beginning a new job might be denied coverage if the employer's health insurance company determined that they had a preexisting health condition. The enactment of Medicare and Medicaid had provided government-funded benefits to citizens over age 65 (Medicare) and to low-income persons who lacked private health insurance and met income-eligibility standards (Medicaid). Even with these programs, about 40 million Americans lacked private health insurance *or* access to Medicare and Medicaid in 1992.

In addition, the American health-care system was extraordinarily costly; it absorbed about 15% of the GNP in 1992, as compared to less than 10% in other industrialized nations. Costs were increasing at such an extraordinary rate that some experts guessed they would reach 20% of the GNP soon after the turn of the century. Americans had constructed a health-care system that provided physicians and hospitals with incentives to perform costly procedures and to provide expensive tests, in contrast to government-managed systems in Canada and most of Europe, where physicians' and hospitals' remuneration did not hinge on the volume of surgeries and procedures they provided. The use of private health-insurance companies, with considerable marketing and administrative overheads, added huge costs—estimated at about 20%—to the American medical system, as compared to Canada and Europe. Nor should we forget Americans' insatiable appetite for costly technology and drugs, which was further stimulated by the endless stream of innovations from huge biotechnology and pharmaceutical firms. Another factor increasing the nation's health-care costs was that tens of millions of poor and uninsured Americans, lacking access to primary-care and preventive services, sought services only after their medical condition had become serious.

Nor would it prove easy to surmount political barriers to basic reforms in the American health-care system. Many entrenched interests—including private health-insurance companies, physicians, hospitals, and pharmaceutical companies—would resist reforms that curtailed their profits, revenues, or autonomy. Americans who already had coverage might resist any reforms that they feared would raise their health-care costs or deplete their benefits. Moreover, those 40 million uncovered Americans—the people most needing health reforms—were not politically organized and often did not vote.

Aware of the complexity of the health system and the political barriers in his path, Clinton nonetheless chose to prioritize health reform, partly for moral reasons but also to enhance his political fortunes, in the way that educational reform had helped him in Arkansas. He decided in early 1993 to place Hillary Clinton in charge of health-care reform, with the assistance of Ira Magaziner, a liberal aide.

Even in spring and summer 1993, controversy erupted within the administration about the scope of health reform. Such advisors as Lloyd Bentsen and Robert Rubin cautioned Clinton not to seek comprehensive reform; they feared it might increase federal expenditures at a time when the administration was under political pressure to diminish the budget deficit. While restructuring the health-care system might eventually bring savings by reducing medical inflation, they warned that coverage of the 40 million uninsured Americans would require vast governmental outlays in the short term. Dismissing the warnings of Bill Clinton's economic advisors, Hillary Clinton and Magaziner chose universal coverage as the central goal. They were convinced that huge savings could be realized by using market forces to contain providers' fees and by using governmental power to force drug companies not to charge excessive prices. They realized, however, that health reform might mean large costs in the short run—even as much as $100 billion—to give uninsured Americans coverage. Indeed, they warned Clinton that health reform would require new taxes at the very time he was encountering increasing opposition to tax increases.[20]

Despite opposition from key advisors, Bill Clinton clearly agreed with Hillary Clinton and Magaziner that a major overhaul of American health care was required. He knew, however, that he could not get health legislation through the Congress in 1993, because he had to devote most of his energies to his economic package. He decided to establish a large task force, headed by Hillary Clinton and Magaziner, to define policy options. Partly as protection against special interests, such as physicians and hospitals, the task force met in secret. By early August, Clinton had made a pivotal choice: to establish universal coverage as the one principle for which he would risk losing the whole program; he was willing to negotiate other details of health reform.[21] He had decided by mid-August not to seek major new taxes to fund health care, but to rely instead on a tax hike on cigarettes, cuts in existing programs like Medicare and Medicaid, and savings from efficiencies resulting from government-enforced competition.[22]

Even before the task force began its work, Clinton had decided to rely on a market-driven system with private insurances, rather than a governmental single–payer system like Canada's and Britain's. In a single-payer system, the government pays the medical fees of citizens in a manner akin to the Medicare program; private insurance companies are unnecessary. As the single payer, the government has extraordinary power over the medical system, both through its purchasing decisions (it determines what procedures it will fund and at what cost) and its regulations (it can regulate providers and drug companies; it can even decide what fraction of physicians will be specialists or general practitioners). Clinton rejected the single-payer system for several reasons. He knew that entrenched medical interests, such as doctors, would strongly oppose it. He also knew that Republicans and conservatives would attack a single-payer system as "big government." Clinton also understood a simple economic fact: A single-payer system would require vast governmental resources at its outset; retention of the existing employer-funded benefits of the American system would demand far fewer tax revenues. When most citizens get their health benefits from employers,

government only has to fund benefits for those citizens who are not covered by employers, such as unemployed people or older citizens. Were the United States to make the government the prime funder of benefits, hundreds of billions of dollars would have to be found to replace the expenditures currently borne by employers.

Clinton released his plan in September, in a nationally televised address to a joint session of Congress. He hoped his proposals would appeal to both moderate and liberal factions. Its emphasis on market competition, employers' funding of benefits, and retention of private insurances made it consonant with the current health-care system. Its emphasis on universal coverage and requiring providers to give a basic package of benefits appealed to liberals.

In searching for a market-driven alternative to a single-payer system, Clinton drew on the work of many American economists, including Alain Enthoven. Enthoven had urged for many years that the government should enroll all Americans in health-maintenance organizations (HMOs). If the costs, quality, and scope of their plans were publicized, Enthoven reasoned, competition between HMOs would hold down health-care costs. Clinton's plan would establish regional health organizations (or alliances) that would provide competing plans—including both HMOs and plans initiated by insurance companies and providers—between which consumers could choose. The major provisions of Clinton's plan were as follows.

1. Most employers would be required to fund health care for their employees, with some government subsidies to small employers.
2. The federal government would fund the purchase of private health-insurance policies for unemployed people or part-time workers.
3. The government would establish the basic minimum coverage to be included in *all* health policies—including preventive services, drugs, and curative services.
4. Regional health-care alliances would be developed to publicize competing health-insurance policies, so that consumers could select the plan

that they wished—and change plans when they liked another plan.

5. Private insurance companies would not be allowed to discontinue coverage for preexisting conditions.
6. The government would develop controls over the prices charged by pharmaceutical companies for existing and new drugs.
7. The government would provide every American with a health-security card, to be used when seeking services from health-care plans.
8. Medicare and Medicaid would be retained, but their enrollees could join competing plans offered by regional health-care alliances.

Clinton outlined these general principles in September, and presented actual legislation on October 27. Already, however, battle lines had begun to be drawn. Many people criticized the sheer complexity of Clinton's plan; his proposed legislation totaled 1,342 pages. Even top advisors in the administration could not grasp many of its technical features. Questions arose about the plan's cost: Could it be funded only by efficiencies and a cigarette tax when it proposed to cover 40 million uninsured Americans and to add five new entitlements? (The Clintons insisted that the plan would cut the deficit by $91 billion by the year 2000, because they believed competition would markedly reduce costs.) Would insured Americans have to pay higher fees to help finance the plan? Would small employers be able to afford their employees' health costs, even with government subsidies? What about doctors, hospitals, insurance companies, and drug companies? They had been entirely left out of planning: Would they oppose the legislation? Would the regional alliances' preference for HMOs reduce freedom of choice?[23]

The foes of Clinton's plan wasted no time. Within days, rumors circulated that many insured Americans would pay higher fees. Polls showed that many Americans feared they would pay more for health insurance under the plan. Small businesses feared they would face huge new costs. Many middle-class Americans believed the plan would primarily help lower-income persons. Nor were providers and Republicans cautious about opposing the plan. Almost immediately, private health-insurance companies encouraged these fears by financing a television campaign that featured Harry and Louise, a fictional middle-class couple who discussed their concerns about the Clinton plan.

Neither liberals nor conservatives rallied to the plan. Many liberal Democrats favored a single-payer system akin to Canada's and supported a plan by Representative Jim McDermott. Conservatives proposed an array of plans that minimized government involvement in health care; some did not include requirements that all businesses cover their employees, or encouraged consumers to put aside savings for their own health-care expenses. In turn, moderates wanted a scaled-back version of Clinton's plan; some urged that universal coverage be delayed until after the turn of the century.

These political problems were accentuated by the logistical problems of enacting health care in the Congress, where it fell under the jurisdiction of several committees—three in the House and two in the Senate. Adrift in this maze of committees, the Clinton plan lost momentum; different committees came to differing conclusions. As providers continued to run advertisements attacking the legislation, the reservations of many middle-class citizens remained. Sensing an election-year issue, Republicans branded the Clinton proposal as unworkable or as excessively costly.[24]

It was painfully clear by August that no plan would command a majority of legislators in either chamber. It is easy to blame Clinton's plan for the failure of health reform, but it is not clear that *any* plan would have gained support from the Congress in 1994. In the extraordinarily complex U.S. health-care system, too many groups—not least the private insurance companies—have a vested interest in the status quo. The American health care system polarizes Americans into insured people (who mostly get their insurance through their employers) and uninsured Americans (who tend to be relatively poor); insured people are fearful that their coverage will suffer, or their fees will rise, if uninsured Americans are brought into their system.

The defeat of his health-care plan was a crushing blow to Clinton. He had gambled that it could be enacted just prior to the Congressional elections of 1994; instead, its defeat made him look ineffectual and renewed the public's distaste for government gridlock. By portraying his plan as a bureaucratic, big-government scheme, Republicans persuaded many voters that Clinton was a traditional liberal and thus eroded Democrats' support in moderate and conservative districts.

Anticrime Legislation

The largest measure to be enacted in Clinton's first term was not health care or other social reforms, but an anticrime measure. Realizing that many Americans listed crime as the nation's most serious problem, Clinton was determined not to let Republicans monopolize the issue. He outlined the basic elements of a Democratic anticrime plan in August 1993: funds for 100,000 new police officers; new federal death penalties; and fewer appeals for death-row inmates. By November 1993, Senate Democrats had obtained the Senate's approval for a huge, $22.3-billion bill that also included funds for prison construction, a ban on some semiautomatic weapons, and programs to prevent violence against women. In April 1994, the House approved a similar measure; the House version also included significant funds for social services to prevent crime, such as recreation programs. Responding to charges that death sentences were disproportionately levied on African American inmates, the House bill also included a controversial measure to allow defendants to challenge their death sentences as racially discriminatory, on the basis of sentencing statistics. After deleting this measure, a conference committee approved a $30.2-billion bill, an unprecedented involvement by the federal government in local law enforcement.

During deliberations on the conference report in the Senate, conservatives sought to portray the legislation as a monument to freewheeling Democratic spending; they were particularly offended by its generous funding of social services. In turn, Democrats charged that Republicans' opposition to the legislation was an effort to appease the powerful National Rifle Association, which opposed the ban on 19 assault-type weapons. When finally signed by the president in mid-September, the legislation provided $8.8 billion to hire 100,000 new officers; $7.9 billion to help states build new prisons and boot camps; and $6.9 billion for social programs, including $1.6 billion to fund the Violence Against Women Act, which provided federal penalties and programs to reduce domestic violence.

It is ironic that Clinton's major achievement in his first term proved not to be health care or social investments, but a huge anticrime bill that largely funded expansion of police forces and new prisons. In its size, this bill rivalled his new spending for social investments of 1993. Its expenditures for social programs barely survived an onslaught from conservatives, who viewed them as social reform through the back door—and conservatives vowed to rescind these social programs if they controlled Congress after the impending 1994 elections.[25]

BUILDING A REVOLUTION WITHIN THE COUNTERREVOLUTION

Ronald Reagan had fashioned a counterrevolution against Democratic liberalism in the 1980s, but many conservatives were deeply dissatisfied by the mid-1980s. While Reagan had cut many discretionary programs, total spending continued to escalate rapidly, largely driven by increased expenditures for Social Security, Medicare, and Medicaid. Even if Reagan had shifted many federal programs into block grants, many others remained intact. It was Reagan's tax and defense policies that created the huge budget deficit, but conservatives came to view it as a product of big-spending liberalism and special interests. Had social spending been radically cut, they reasoned, the deficit would not have been created or sustained. As the deficit soared during the 1980s and early 1990s, their frustration with government spending rose. Convinced in 1987 that Robert Bork, President Reagan's nominee for the Supreme Court, had been defeated by a coalition of feminist and civil rights groups, conservatives were determined not to let liberals shape future appointments. Many conservatives were still angry that President Bush accepted major tax increases as part of a deficit-reduction package in 1990; they had long wanted social spending cuts, not tax increases, to bear the onus for deficit reduction. (Since the New Deal, many conservatives had believed that the welfare state would only be curtailed if the tax revenues that funded it were slashed.) The election of Bill Clinton in 1992 infuriated conservatives further; they regarded him as a political threat, because he disguised his liberalism with conservative terms such as responsibility and values. They feared that, left unchecked, Clinton might win back Democrats who had voted for Republicans in the Reagan era.[26]

Increasingly discontented, some conservative Republicans believed that they could complete Reagan's work only by capturing control of the Congress, and especially the elusive House of Representatives, which had been controlled by Democrats since 1955. (Republicans would be well positioned to get spending cuts if they controlled the House, which initiates budget and tax legislation.) It fell to a politician by the unlikely name of Newt Gingrich to realize the conservatives' dreams. An army brat whose family lived on a succession of military bases, he had a great epiphany in 1958, when he visited Verdun, a battle site where 970,000 European troops had died in World War I. Determined to become a political leader who would prevent such cataclysms, he also decided that politics was like war, where brute power allows one side to prevail. Even by the mid-1970s, he wanted to become Speaker of the House, convinced that the Speaker was even more powerful than the president. After a brief stint as a college history teacher, Gingrich was finally elected to the House on his third attempt, in 1978. Initially a liberal Republican, Gingrich converted to conservatism after attending a campaign school run by Paul Weyrich, often called the father of the New Right. In a strategy meeting with Weyrich and others in 1980, Gingrich plotted how Republicans could take control of the House by 1992. He emphasized the importance of framing issues to allow conservatives to take the moral high ground from Democrats, by

contrasting the "conservative opportunity society" (portrayed as emphasizing lower taxes, protection of innocent people from crime, responsible fatherhood, and work) with the "liberal welfare state" (portrayed as emphasizing higher taxes, the rights of criminals, and welfare dependency). He placed extraordinary emphasis on *perceptions;* he argued that what actually happens is less crucial than how people perceive it. Conservatives could increase their power by manipulating and shaping popular perceptions to discredit liberals—a strategy that required frequent use of focus groups of voters to gauge what language and actions would allow conservatives to upstage liberals. He also emphasized tactics that featured surprise, manipulation, deception, and tactical ingenuity.[27]

Gingrich operated on two levels in the 1980s. He destabilized the House by waging a kind of guerilla warfare against its Democratic leadership; he performed this role with such relish that he was nicknamed Neutron. He also masterminded a national strategy for electing conservative Republicans when he became the chair of GOPAC, a private organization that funded Republican campaigns using resources from wealthy donors. Drawing on GOPAC funds, Gingrich targeted roughly 50 House districts; he carefully chose conservative constituencies, for which he could find candidates who met his conservative litmus test. He built a cadre of loyal supporters and trained them by means of tapes and seminars that provided tactical suggestions—for example, attacking Democrats as "traitors," "corrupt," and "sick." When elected, these conservatives acted cohesively in the Congress under his direction.

With a growing contingent in the House, Gingrich and his allies needed to get control of leadership positions in the Republican party, in order to supplant older Republicans like Bob Dole, the Senate Minority Leader, and Robert Michel, the House Minority Leader. These older leaders were unacceptable to Gingrich for several reasons. Having lived through World War II and its aftermath, they were not as critical of the welfare state as Gingrich; their generation had benefited from such government programs as the GI Bill, FHA housing, and Social Security. Used to serving in Congress as the minority party, they excelled at cutting deals with Democrats rather than adopting intransigent positions. Gingrich narrowly won the position of Minority Whip in 1989—and his close friend Dick Armey became chair of the House Republican Conference in late 1992. With Michel's retirement in late 1993, Gingrich became Minority Leader in early 1994.[28]

In addition to party leadership and GOPAC funds, conservatives supplemented their power with a "loosely knit group that included think tanks, foundations, columnists, direct-mail operations, talk-show hosts, and various self-appointed spokespeople."[29] Formed by Weyrich, the Heritage Foundation viewed itself as a public relations firm, providing conservative solutions to a range of issues. So-called profamily research groups, which stressed traditional family roles and antiwelfare positions, included the Family Research Council, the Eagle Forum (headed by Phyllis Schlafly), and Concerned Women for America. Republicans possessed remarkable access to the mass media. Weyrich's National Empowerment Television distributed conservative ideology to 11 million cable users; televangelists such as Pat Robertson coupled religious and political messages; and talk-show hosts like Rush Limbaugh reached tens of millions of Americans on radio and television. Conservative opinions were regularly disseminated by columnists such as Robert Novak and by the editorial page of the *Wall Street Journal*. Wealthy individuals, such as beer magnate Joseph Coors and Richard Scaife of the Mellon family, as well as large foundations like the Bradley and Olin foundations, contributed tens of millions of dollars to think tanks, publications, research, and political campaigns. The conservative message was also outlined in best-selling books by authors such as Charles Murray and William Bennett. Pat Robertson's Christian Coalition, the successor to the Moral Majority, continued to organize huge mailings to voters in pivotal districts.

Conservatives were more adept than liberals at reaching the broader public and using their economic resources to promote their ideas. While conservatives often depicted the media as liberal, the major news shows were usually neutral in their coverage; liberals had virtually no mass-audience outlets. Whereas the Brookings Institution and other relatively liberal think tanks operated in the same way as academic departments, conservative think tanks were intensely partisan; they disseminated research and opinions that conformed to conservative tenets. Whereas fundamentalist religious groups possessed large mailing lists and actively intervened in elections, relatively liberal religious groups lacked a massive grass-roots capability.[30]

THE HOUSE REPUBLICANS TAKE CHARGE

This conservative network was adept at shaping the public's perceptions of the Clinton administration in negative ways in 1993 and 1994. Armey's Republican Conference fashioned health-reform and welfare-reform proposals that emphasized market forces and work requirements, which Republicans contrasted with Clinton's proposals. The *Wall Street Journal* and Congressional Republicans publicized what they called the Whitewater scandal, which centered on allegations of financial improprieties by the Clintons in Arkansas. Talk-show hosts circulated sexual-misconduct allegations against Clinton. Not wanting Clinton to benefit in the 1994 elections, Republicans stymied his health-reform and welfare legislation in 1994. Even though Clinton had proposed a plan to reduce the federal deficit markedly in his first term, Republicans portrayed him as a big spender who did not care about the deficit. When Clinton raised taxes on affluent people, Republicans said that he waged "class warfare"; they neglected to mention that many of their policies would help affluent Americans. Nor were some Republicans hesitant to attack Hillary Clinton's policy roles as inappropriate for the first lady. Throughout 1994, the administration was aware that, historically, the party that sits in the White House has usually incurred some losses in off-year Congressional elections, but it clearly was not expecting the bombshell that hit Washington on November 8, 1994. The Republican gains in November were truly devastating for the Democrats. Not only did the Republicans gain majority status in both houses of Congress, thereby ending 40 years of Democratic control of at least one house, but they also gained a majority of the nation's governorships and control of 17 more state legislative chambers. (Not a single incumbent Republican governor or federal legislator was defeated.) A large majority of these Republican winners, especially in the House, were young and extremely conservative; they wanted to dismantle the remnants of the Great Society, which they felt had caused America's moral decline. (Gingrich now possessed a cadre of nearly 80 conservatives in the House, as well as many Republican moderates, who were dedicated to slashing government domestic spending.) Long a minority party in the South, Republicans emerged as its major party in national elections.[31]

Interpreting the election results as a repudiation of President Clinton and the Democratic party, Republicans vowed to enact a series of policies that were described in the Contract with America, a document created during the campaign by House Republican members and candidates.[32] The basic tenets of the Contract were articulated in February 1994: Individual liberty, economic opportunity, limited government, personal responsibility, and security at home and abroad. When they released the completed Contract on September 27, 1994, House Republican members and candidates promised that, if they controlled the House, they would enact its ten provisions in 100 days (Box 12.1).

With the Contract as its guiding framework, House Republicans took the offensive in spring 1995, when they dominated policy discourse in the United States. Clinton was relegated to a background role, as the House Republicans fulfilled their promise of enacting most items of the Contract within 100 days. (Some provisions were not enacted by the Senate, however.)

THE BUDGET CONFRONTATION OF 1995

In 1995, the major political event was a titanic budget confrontation between Democrats and Republicans and between the White House and the Congress. Republicans could only accomplish their goal of shrinking the federal government by shaping the federal budget through Budget Resolutions, a reconciliation bill, and 13 appropriation bills. Like Reagan in 1981, Gingrich wanted to use the budget process to implement his conservative agenda; he hoped to force huge spending cuts and the return of many federally funded programs to the states at the same time as he was enacting large tax cuts and significant increases in defense spending. More militant than Reagan, Gingrich wanted to terminate three entitlement programs (Food Stamps, Medicaid, and AFDC) by converting them to block grants to the states. This elimination of entitlements was a massive assault on the American welfare state; it attacked the fundamental concept that the federal government ought to avert starvation and dire suffering—an obligation first articulated by Franklin Roosevelt six decades earlier. Gingrich planned to use confrontive tactics; even in April 1995, he predicted that the government might have to shut down when the president and the Congress reached an impasse over the budget.

Gingrich needed a dramatic goal that would galvanize Americans and Republicans to support cuts in spending. Early in the debate, House members decided not merely to seek a constitutional amendment requiring a balanced budget but also to commit Congress to balancing the budget within seven years. Adopting a specific time frame forced Clinton and the Democrats onto the defensive; in 1993, after all, they had merely sought to *decrease* the annual deficits. When Senate Republicans supported the proposal to balance the budget in seven years, the stage was set for Budget Resolutions to accomplish this target.

In demanding that the budget be balanced by the year 2002, House Republicans took a calculated political gamble. They would have to cut more than $1.5 trillion from the budget, even without considering the large tax cuts and considerable increases in defense spending that they wanted. They could only reach their goal by focusing on entitlements, particularly Medicare, Medicaid, Food Stamps, and Social Security, which constituted the bulk of the domestic budget, as illustrated in Figure 12.1. (Analysts estimated that health costs would cause government spending *just* on entitlements to rise above the federal government's

BOX 12.1   Provisions of the Contract with America

1. Balancing the budget and tax limitation:
   * a constitutional amendment requiring that Congress submit a balanced budget each year;
   * a requirement that tax increases could be enacted only if a three-fifths majority of Congress voted for them—a policy that would usually put the burden of balancing the budget on spending cuts rather than tax increases;
   * a legislative line-item veto to restore fiscal responsibility.
2. Strengthening national defense:
   * legislation requiring that no US troops be placed under UN command;
   * restoration of funding for essential parts of national security.
3. Tax cuts to strengthen families and to benefit middle-class people:
   * a $500-per-child tax credit for families with annual incomes up to $200,000;
   * repeal of the marriage tax penalty, which causes many married couples to pay higher taxes than are levied on two single people;
   * creation of American Dream Savings Accounts to allow individuals to contribute up to $2000 a year to a tax-free account for retirement income, the purchase of a first home, education expenses, or medical costs.
4. Aid to senior citizens:
   * an increase in the Social Security earnings limit—which currently forces seniors out of the work force—from $11,160 to $30,000 over five years.
5. Welfare reform:
   * denial of welfare to minor mothers;
   * denial of higher payments to mothers who give birth to additional children while on welfare;
   * a strict two-years-and-out provision for recipients;
   * more stringent work requirements, to promote individual responsibility;
   * a cap on spending for AFDC, SSI, and public housing programs;
   * consolidation of nutrition programs such as Food Stamps, the Women's, Infants', and Children's (WIC) program, and the school lunch program into a block grant to states;
   * permission for states to opt out of the current AFDC program by converting their share of AFDC payments into fixed annual block grants.
6. Reform of unfunded mandates and incentives to business:
   * termination or reform of unfunded mandates, in which the federal government requires state and local governments to implement specific policies without providing the resources for them to do so;
   * a cut in the capital gains tax to stimulate investment.
7. Strengthening the family:
   * more stringent child-support enforcement;
   * larger tax incentives for adoption;
   * greater rights for parents in their children's education;
   * stronger child pornography laws;
   * tax credit for people who care for an elderly parent or grandparent.
8. Legal reforms to curb litigation:
   * loser-pays laws;
   * reasonable limits on punitive-damage awards;
   * reform of product-liability laws.
9. Anti-crime legislation:
   * stronger truth-in-sentencing laws;
   * effective death-penalty provisions;
   * elimination of social spending included in the 1994 Crime Bill and use of these resources to fund prison construction and additional police officers;
   * easier deportation of illegal aliens convicted of felonies.
10. Term limits:
    * Limits on the years that federal politicians can serve—for example, six 2-year terms for House members and two 6-year terms for senators.

INSERT 12.1   CRITICAL ANALYSIS: THE CAUSES OF BIRTHS TO UNWED WOMEN

Conservatives have often argued that "illegitimacy" stems from the "perverse incentives" provided by the welfare system. In this perspective, unwed women, often in their teens, decide to have children to secure welfare benefits.

Analyze this contention by asking the following questions.

1. Under what circumstances *are* our actions shaped or determined by externally imposed rewards or punishments. So as to be specific, identify cases where your actions are (or are not) shaped by rewards and punishments. (To get started, you might begin with relatively trivial actions—for example, whether the speed at which you drive is determined by the danger of receiving tickets. Then proceed to major life decisions of various kinds.)

2. In the case of unwed teenage women, to what extent are their pregnancies shaped or caused by:

   a. calculation of likely welfare benefits
   b. role models, such as a parent who was unwed at the time her children were born
   c. rape or forced sex
   d. lack of knowledge of birth control or lack of availability of birth control devices
   e. a desire for meaning or companionship in life
   f. cultural factors—for example, the belief among people of all social classes that unwed pregnancies are a legitimate lifestyle choice

3. To what extent do teenage women become pregnant because they believe that they lack economic, educational, or career options?

4. In light of the preceding discussion, would you expect coercive policies, such as denying or cutting benefits, to markedly decrease rates of births to unwed women?

---

total revenues in just over 25 years.) Republicans knew that these entitlements had strong support from the public, as well as from powerful interest groups—support so strong that even Reagan had demurred from seeking major cuts in them. They hoped that public support for deficit reduction would allow them to cut some entitlements and to terminate others by passing them to the states in block grants. Even in November, Gingrich had admitted that all entitlements except Social Security would be put on the table for trimming. Since discretionary spending had already been cut extensively during the Reagan and Bush years, as well as by Clinton's deficit-reduction plan of 1993, further cuts would not provide the bulk of the funds needed to bring a balanced budget.[33]

Once the House GOP announced its plans to balance the budget in seven years, the Congressional Democrats complained that the goal could be reached only by a mean-spirited slashing of America's social programs for the poor as well as for the middle class. The Democrats also charged the GOP with attempting to fund tax cuts for the rich by slashing social programs. They demanded that the House leadership reveal exactly how they would balance the budget in seven years. Aware that the public supported balancing the budget in general terms, the Democrats instead attempted to focus on the pain that would occur when *specific* cuts were made in programs widely used by Americans, such as Medicare.

Toward a Budget Resolution

The House Republicans originally intended to reveal their budget proposals in January 1995, but decided to wait until the president had presented his own budget in February. They were certain that he would not seek significant cuts in discretionary spending, because he had threatened to veto Republican attempts to cut his domestic service corps and the social spending included in the Crime Bill of 1994. They also knew that Clinton would not propose defense cuts; under Republican pressure on issues of military readiness, he had already promised the Department of Defense $25 billion in additional funds over six years. Thus, certain that the president would not make deep cuts in spending, the House Republicans waited for him to present his budget, so that they could reply that he was not serious about deficit reduction. If he *did* propose deep spending cuts, they could simply incorporate them into *their* spending cuts—and also make the president take the political heat for proposing them.

Clinton refused to walk into this budget trap. The president's budget neither dramatically reduced the deficit nor changed the level of spending for most government programs. Instead, the president offered something for everyone in his budget: a tax cut, in the form of a $500 per child tax credit; $25 billion in defense increases; and $81 billion in deficit reduction. Realizing that Republicans would have to cut entitlements in order to reach their balanced-budget goals, the administration wanted to force them to show their hand, and pay the political price. Clinton was also aware that any spending cuts that he proposed would make the Republicans' task easier. According to Joseph White, a budget expert at the Brookings Institution, "It would have been politically idiotic for the Administration to propose more spending cuts. The Republicans just would have turned around and used them to pay for their tax cuts."[34] Clinton's strategy paid off handsomely. When Republicans subsequently promised an array of cuts in social programs, Clinton attacked them. For example, he paid a number of visits to school cafeterias, where he declared that Republicans' cuts in subsidized school lunches would harm children.[35]

As was to be expected, the Republicans attacked the administration for its apparent lack of leadership and charged that it was not serious about reducing the deficit. Republican leaders also accused the president of failing to control the growth of entitlement spending and refusing to make any hard budget-cutting choices. House Republicans could stall no longer and finally presented their Budget Resolution for balancing the budget by the year 2002 on May 10. Over the seven years, it proposed a large tax cut of $353 billion and huge cuts in entitlement and discretionary spending that totaled nearly $1 trillion. More than half of these savings came from cuts in projected spending for Medicare and Medicaid. Medicare would be cut by $288 billion over seven years (reducing its growth rate from 10% a year to an average of 5.4% a year), and Medicaid would be cut by $187 billion, by converting it into a block grant (reducing its growth rate from 10% to 4% a year). The House Budget Resolution also targeted other entitlements—such as the earned-income tax credit for the working poor (EITC), welfare programs, federal pensions, veterans benefits, farm subsidies, and student loans—for a total saving of $219 billion over seven years. Discretionary spending, except that for defense, did not escape the budget knife: The House Budget Resolution called for $192 billion in savings over seven years from nonmilitary discretionary programs. The Republicans also wanted increased spending for the military.

The Senate presented its Budget Resolution in May. The major difference between the House and Senate plans was in the area of tax cuts. Whereas the House plan contained $340 billion in tax cuts, the Senate plan allowed tax cuts of up to $170 billion over seven years on condition that a deficit reduction plan was enacted and the Congressional Budget Office confirmed that the plan would balance the budget by 2002. Like the House version, the Senate Budget Resolution also made sharp cutbacks in projected spending for Medicare, Medicaid, and other entitlement programs, as well as discretionary programs.

When faced with these Republican budget-cutting plans, the administration complained that Republicans sought to balance the budget on the backs of the poor—that programs for the poor were cut but affluent people received large tax breaks. Congressional Democrats were even more critical of the plan; they highlighted the hardship that older Americans would face as a result of cuts in Medicare. Public opinion polls suggested that Democrats were gaining ground on Republicans and revealed widespread hesitation about the Republicans' plans to cut popular social programs.

Just as the Democrats' counteroffensive seemed to be working, Clinton dropped a bombshell on his party on June 13, by presenting his own plan to balance the budget in ten years—a mere three years longer than the Republicans' plan. The president's plan contained $105 billion in tax cuts for the middle class, as well as significant cuts in Medicare and Medicaid; it sought savings of $128 billion from the Medicare program and capped Medicaid's per-capita spending for savings of $54 billion. (Medicaid retained entitlement status, however.) Clinton's proposal also called for savings of $38 billion from poverty programs, such as AFDC, the EITC, and benefits for immigrants, but increased spending for nutritional programs such as WIC and Food Stamps. Clinton proposed cuts averaging 20% in domestic discretionary programs, for savings of $197 billion; he exempted programs that he favored, such as education, national service, health research, and crime control.[36] By developing his own deadline to balance the budget, Clinton hoped to prevent Republicans from monopolizing the balanced-budget theme. By selecting ten years rather than seven, he intended to emphasize the differences in priorities between his proposal and the Republicans'—including far lower cuts in Medicare, his decision not to rescind entitlement status for Medicaid and AFDC, and his opposition to huge tax cuts for affluent Americans.

The president's about-face infuriated Congressional Democrats, whom he did not consult in drawing up his plan. After they had invested extraordinary time in battling the Republicans' spending and tax cuts, they felt the president had left them high and dry. Democratic leaders, such as Senate Minority Leader Tom Daschle and House Minority Leader Richard Gephardt criticized even the scaled-back Medicare cuts that Clinton pro-

posed. Many Democrats believed that Clinton's switch betrayed his lack of core values, as well as his determination to fashion a political strategy for the 1996 presidential elections without concern for the priorities of Congressional Democrats.

Why did Clinton make this abrupt shift? With the guidance of his old pollster and advisor, Dick Morris, Clinton decided to take a decisively different strategy in the 1996 elections. He had been relatively liberal in his campaign of 1992, when he had promised social investments, and during his first two years, when he sought funding for these investments and pursued health reform. With advice from Morris, he became convinced that he could not win in 1996 if he did not distance himself from his liberal record and from liberal Democrats in Congress. Morris urged him to resort to triangulation, a strategy in which he would stand at the apex of a triangle above the other two corners— liberal Democrats and conservative Republicans. He should, Morris advised, alternately make concessions to, and flout, *both* groups in a complex, changing strategy that would present him to voters as a centrist who wanted to fashion compromises. Morris wanted Clinton to prevent Republicans from preempting such themes as balancing the budget or cutting taxes. Clinton should periodically give ground by acceding to some conservative demands, while nonetheless seeking centrist positions that would make conservatives seem extremist. Yet he should not be too strident in his opposition to conservatives, for fear of seeming too liberal—a perception that would frighten white centrist voters into the Republican camp or toward a third-party candidate. By shedding his liberal past, Clinton could run his campaign of 1996 as a centrist, with a focus on middle-class issues like education and the environment; social programs for the poor would be deemphasized.[37]

This strategy carried both political and ethical risks for Clinton, however. While Clinton could not win the 1996 election with liberal support alone, triangulation might alienate many liberal allies, much as they had become disenchanted with Lyndon Johnson in his second term and with Jimmy Carter when he ran in 1980. This zigzag

INSERT 12.2   ETHICAL ANALYSIS OF KEY ISSUES AND POLICIES: CLINTON'S DILEMMA

Clinton knew that he had received only 43% of the popular vote in 1992. He did not yet know if a popular third-party candidate—such as retired General Colin Powell, a much-admired African American with centrist views—might enter the race. Believing that he could not win with liberal support alone, he had to compete for moderate white voters in the North and the South.

Assume that marketing analyses provided by Morris suggested that these moderate voters wanted a balanced budget, but also wanted somewhat more compassionate policies than Republicans like Gingrich. Yet they remained suspicious of AFDC recipients, whom they believed largely to be cheaters. Assume, as well, that poll data showed that many were concerned with Medicare and Medicaid cuts.

Discuss alternative strategies that Clinton could take under these circumstances—and their ethical implications. Be certain to consider the liberals' nightmare: If moderate white voters rejected Clinton, he might be replaced by a Republican contender in 1996 *and* Republicans might still control both houses of Congress (with Gingrich still occupying the powerful Speaker's position).

Also consider whether Clinton had fully recognized the risks of his position, particularly in the light of polls that showed widespread support for the Democrats' opposition to the Republicans' harsh seven-year strategy.

strategy might confirm his reputation as someone who lacked core values, in the same way that Richard Nixon's opportunism had led people to distrust him. This strategy required Clinton to abandon poor people at the very time that their programs were under the most determined assault since 1981. Would he fight to retain entitlement status for AFDC, Food Stamps, and Medicaid in the face of the Republicans' Congressional onslaught? Would he accede to further, large cuts in domestic discretionary spending when it had already been savaged for a decade and a half? Would he accede to significant increases in defense spending, which he knew would further erode domestic spending?

Toward a Reconciliation Bill

The Republicans quickly dismissed Clinton's ten-year plan to balance the budget as inadequate. Once House and Senate negotiations had produced a Budget Resolution, Republicans worked over the summer to fashion a reconciliation bill and appropriations bills that would meet spending and bud-

get targets. Welfare provisions and health-care entitlements dominated policy discussion.[38]

Welfare Reform   Even before the House enacted its Budget Resolution in May, it had enacted a welfare reform measure on March 24 that conformed to the Contract with America. On September 15, the Senate enacted its version of welfare reform. Comparison of these measures proves the adage that *details* are critical in policy legislation. Let's first discuss the House version (in the left column of Table 12.1) and then note how the Senate version differed from it.[39]

The House version sought to change in drastic fashion the nature of the American welfare state. It sought to remove AFDC and Food Stamps from entitlement status by transforming them into block grants, while removing most federal regulations over them. It allowed states to contribute whatever sums they wished to their own welfare programs; states need not even increase their funding if the numbers of destitute persons rose. At the same time as they were giving states more authority over Food Stamps, child welfare programs, and child nutrition programs like school lunches, they imposed an array

TABLE 12.1 Comparison of the House and Senate versions of welfare reform

	House Bill	Senate Bill
Block grants	States would gain broad control over social service programs including cash welfare, child care, child protection programs such as foster care and adoption assistance, school meals, and nutritional aid to low-income pregnant women and their young children. In each case, states would receive federal money to help offset the costs of these programs in predetermined lump sums, or block grants. The bill would end the 60-year federal guarantee of cash aid to low-income mothers and children; instead, eligibility for the aid would largely be determined by states. States would also be able to transfer up to 30% of specific block grants to other programs. Finally, states could receive their Food Stamp funding in a block grant if they provided benefits through an electronic system.	States would receive block grants for cash welfare, child care, and job training. States could also opt to receive their Food Stamp funding in a block grant. As in the House bill, the federal guarantee of cash assistance to low-income mothers and children would end.
State funding	States could contribute whatever they wanted to their own welfare programs.	States would be required to spend at least 80% of what they spent in fiscal 1994 on cash welfare programs. They could use this money for specified social services, such as cash assistance and child care.
Work and time limits	Most recipients would be required to work within two years of receiving welfare benefits. Recipients would generally be ineligible to receive cash benefits for more than five years, though states could exempt up to 10% of their caseload from the time limit.	Most recipients would be required to work within two years of receiving welfare benefits. Recipients would generally be ineligible to receive cash benefits for more than five years, though states could exempt up to 15% of their caseload from the time limit.
Family cap	No federal funds could be used to provide welfare checks for children born within ten months of when a family received cash welfare benefits. Cases of rape or incest would be exempted. States could give vouchers redeemable for baby care expenses.	States would have the option to deny cash assistance for children born to families receiving welfare checks.
Teenage mothers	No federal funds could be used to provide welfare checks for children born out of wedlock to a mother under age 18, except in cases of rape or incest. The children would be eligible for cash benefits once the mother turned 18.	States would have the option to deny welfare checks for children born out of wedlock to a mother under age 18. The children would be eligible for cash benefits once the mother turned 18.

(continued)

(continued)

	House Bill	Senate Bill
SSI	Drug addiction and alcoholism would no longer be considered a disability under Supplemental Security Income (SSI), which provides cash to low-income elderly people as well as persons with vision impairment and other disabilities. It would be harder for children who have behavioral disorders to quality for SSI. Children not now receiving SSI could receive the cash benefits only if they required 24-hour care.	Drug addiction and alcoholism would no longer be considered a disability under SSI. It would be harder for children with behavioral disorders to quality for SSI.
Noncitizens	Most legal immigrants who are not citizens would be ineligible for five federal programs: SSI, cash welfare, social services block grant funds, Medicaid, and Food Stamps. The bill would dramatically increase the duration and circumstances under which an immigrant's sponsor would be financially responsible for that individual.	Immigrants who arrive after enactment would be ineligible for low-income social services for five years. Most noncitizens would be ineligible for SSI, and states could opt to deny them welfare checks and Food Stamps. The bill would increase the duration and circumstances under which an immigrant's sponsor would be financially responsible for that individual.
Overall savings	The bill would save about $62.1 billion over five years and $102 billion over seven years, according to the Congressional Budget Office (CBO). Most of the savings would come from Aid to Families with Dependent Children (AFDC), Food Stamps, and SSI.	The bill would save about $43 billion over five years and $70 billion over seven years, according to CBO. (Estimates do not reflect floor amendments.) Most of that would come from AFDC, Food Stamps, and SSI.

SOURCE: From "House, Senate Bills Compared," by J. L. Katz, *Congressional Quarterly,* September 1995, p. 2806. Reprinted by permission.

of restrictions on state-initiated programs for single mothers. Recipients would be required to work within two years of receiving welfare benefits and could not receive benefits for more than five years. Moreover, states could not use federal block-grant funds to provide welfare for children born within ten months of when a family first received welfare benefits or for children born out of wedlock to a mother under age 18. While retaining SSI as a federal program, the legislators decided to exclude alcoholism or drug addiction as qualifying conditions and chose to disqualify many children with behavioral disorders. Responding to a surge in anti-immigrant sentiment in the nation, the House declared that most legal immigrants who were not citizens could not receive benefits from a range of federal programs. The legislators hoped to save about $62.1 billion over five years.

In one bill, the legislators hoped to reduce drastically the power of the federal government, which would merely fund block grants; tens of millions of Americans would then be at the mercy of policies enacted by specific states. States would set their own eligibility requirements and benefit levels and would be able to transfer up to 30% of specific block grants to other programs. They could decide whether they wanted to supplement the block grants with their own funds. Whereas federal regulations had generally sought to protect the rights of AFDC recipients in the New Deal and subsequent eras, these new federal regulations *prohibited* relatively generous policies, even by those states who wished to pursue them.

Liberals were shocked by this legislation. As the history of AFDC amply suggested, many states had used the policy leeway given to them in the program to enact welfare benefits that were extra-ordinarily low. After the House passed this legislation, President Clinton immediately dismissed it as being "weak on work and tough on children" because it contained little or no funding for education, job training, and job placement, themes that he had outlined during his 1992 presidential campaign. He opposed the Republicans' plan to deny benefits to children whose mothers were under 18 or were already on welfare. Later in the week, a top administration aide warned that Clinton would veto the House welfare legislation unless it was changed by the Senate.

Many Congressional Democrats joined the President in criticizing the Republican measure. They emphasized that the measure would harm children—especially children whose teenage mothers were severed from rolls or children born to mothers who were already on the rolls. Above all, Democrats objected to ending AFDC as a federal entitlement that guaranteed federal funding for all single mothers meeting states' eligibility standards. (Under the Republicans' legislation, a specific state could decide not to fund benefits for some impoverished single mothers if the funds allocated for welfare in the state's budget had been exhausted.) Many Democrats feared that some states, faced with limited budgets, would prioritize other projects, such as highway maintenance. They also feared that states would embark on a race to reduce their benefits, so as to preempt an influx of welfare recipients from states with lower benefits. They accused the Republicans of stripping minimal financial support from millions of children, under the guise of granting states greater flexibility in utilizing federal funds. Democrats feared that, with block grants capped at current levels for five years, many states would be unable or unwilling to handle increases in the number of needy people. They also charged that the Republicans' welfare cuts were intended to finance cuts in the capital gains tax, which would help wealthy people. (Democrats failed to pass a provision that would have required any savings from welfare reform to be reserved for deficit reduction.)

Lacking a Democratic majority in the House, the administration hoped for extensive changes in the bill by the Senate, which tends to be more moderate. Indeed, the legislation immediately sparked controversy in the Senate. No Republican senator questioned the idea of ending the 60-year-old entitlement status of AFDC, but moderate Republicans in the Senate disagreed with the most controversial items in the House bill; they did not want to deny benefits to unwed teenage mothers and children born to welfare recipients. Conservative senators like Phil Gramm threatened to withhold their support from the welfare plan unless these items were included. Moderate Republicans also wanted to be sure that states would maintain their current level of welfare spending and that recipients who were required to work would have access to child care.[40]

Finally, on September 19, the Senate approved a welfare reform bill that was supported even by Democratic senators and the White House, who concluded that it was the best bill they could get. (See the right-hand column in Table 12.1.) While it retained the general direction of the House version, the Senate bill softened some of the more drastic provisions. It sought to protect destitute people by requiring states to spend at least 80% of their expenditures in 1993–1994; where the House bill had allowed states to exempt 10% of recipients from the five-year limit on benefits, the Senate bill raised that limit to 15%. It sought to give relatively liberal states more latitude, such as the option of not denying assistance to children born to families already receiving welfare benefits or to children born to mothers under age 18. Unlike the House version, which gave states a lump-sum payment for child welfare, the Senate version retained child welfare programs as separate programs with continuing federal oversight—and kept child nutrition programs under federal control.

As often occurs in policy debates, Democratic senators had to decide, on balance, whether changes in the details of legislation were sufficient to warrant its support. Many Democrats in the Senate reluctantly voted for the welfare reform plan because they feared that otherwise the House plan would prevail. (The bill passed overwhelmingly, by a 87–12 vote.) Minority leader Tom Daschle commented that the Senate's welfare plan was "the best bill that we are going to get under the circumstances." However,

Daschle and other Democratic leaders also cautioned that, if the welfare plan that emerged from the House-Senate conference committee was closer to the House plan, they would vote against it and urge Clinton to veto it. Clinton, in turn, implied he would veto welfare legislation if it was not similar to the Senate's version; he warned that, "if the Congress gives in to extremist pressure and walks away from this bipartisan American common ground, they will kill welfare reform."[41]

Many liberals disagreed with those senators who voted for the Senate version and were furious that Clinton had supported it. The National Association of Social Workers enlisted 1,000 social workers as sponsors of a full-page ad in the *New York Times* that demanded either congressional action to kill the bill or a presidential veto. Nor were they happy with the compromise version of welfare reform produced by House and Senate negotiators on November 13, because it retained many House provisions. It provided far less funds than the Senate version for jobs and child care and cut far more deeply into SSI cash benefits for disabled children, Food Stamp benefits, and social services for legal immigrants.

At this juncture, liberals knew that their only hope was a presidential veto. The president's press secretary said that Clinton was likely to veto the measure, whether it was part of the reconciliation bill or freestanding legislation. (Republicans *also* planned to introduce it as a freestanding welfare bill.)

Medicare and Medicaid   The Republicans' Budget Resolution called for savings of $270 billion from Medicare and $182 billion from Medicaid, but did not detail precisely how they would be made. Democrats demanded public hearings so that options could be openly discussed. In extended discussions behind closed doors, Republicans considered a range of options for cutting Medicare—for example, raising premiums for Part B (the monthly payment elderly people make to help defray physician costs); excluding certain services; raising deductibles (the amount patients pay *before* Medicare reimburses, such as $100 for surgeries); making wealthy elderly people pay higher premi-

ums or other charges; and lowering the reimbursable fees of providers. Many Republicans wanted to require older people to use health maintenance organizations (HMOs) rather than fee-for-service providers, on the grounds that they provide less expensive services. Still others wanted to encourage seniors to develop their own "medical savings accounts," so that they could even opt out of the Medicare program.

Realizing that the Republicans' proposals might excite political opposition, Gingrich orchestrated elaborate negotiations between providers so that he could sweeten the deal for each interest group. He granted the American Association of Retired Persons (AARP) their wish that the elderly pay only slightly higher premiums for Part B and that they not face additional deductibles for lab tests or home health care. Instead, affluent beneficiaries were charged more for Part B. Republicans decided not to *compel* seniors to use HMOs—a policy that private insurance companies opposed—but instead to encourage the use of HMOs by providing Medicare beneficiaries with a range of options: for example, joining an HMO; establishing a personal medical savings account coupled with a high-deductible insurance policy; or using a network of providers. The legislation granted the AMA many provisions for its doctors; they were allowed to charge more than 15% of Medicare-approved costs in certain circumstances, for example, and doctors and hospitals were allowed to form their own organizations to compete with HMOs. Republicans decided to cut levels of reimbursement to hospitals, doctors, and nursing homes and to establish uniform fees for home health services.

Democrats criticized the Medicare proposal—in particular, the small increases in premiums that seniors would pay for Part B. However, Medicare emerged relatively unscathed as compared to Medicaid, the health-care program for low-income individuals. Recognizing the limited political clout of poor people, Republicans decided to transform the federal-state entitlement program into a sharply reduced block grant, with a cap on the federal government's contribution. (Federal payments would be reduced from 50% of Medicaid costs to 40% under the new formula.) States would be given extraordinary latitude in designing their programs; the federal government would only require coverage of children and pregnant women falling beneath specific income guidelines.

As in the case of AFDC and nutritional programs, many critics wondered whether states would choose to fund medical care for poor people at reasonable levels, in an era of budgetary constraints. Even at current levels of Medicaid funding, beneficiaries had to endure extended waits for care of uncertain quality in antiquated facilities. What could they expect when federal reimbursement was diminished? In states where the numbers of poor persons increased, would coverage expand to meet the needs? As with welfare benefits, would some states diminish their health coverage to pre-vent immigration from states with lower coverage? Middle-class families failed to realize that nursing-home coverage for their elderly parents might be imperiled by Medicaid cuts. Many older people relied on means-tested Medicaid nursing-home benefits once they had exhausted their Medicare coverage and their personal savings.

Taxes   Clinton had achieved a remarkable policy victory in 1993 when he greatly increased the numbers of working-class Americans who received annual tax rebates (or credits). In a society where the disparity between the upper quintile and the lower three quintiles was rapidly increasing, this policy (the earned-income tax credit or EITC) seemed a sensible approach to reducing inequality.

INSERT 12.3   CRITICAL ANALYSIS: WHY KEEP ENTITLEMENTS?

In their quest to shrink the federal government, conservatives sought to end entitlement status for AFDC, Food Stamps, and Medicaid in 1995. Discuss the rationale for entitlements and the possible dangers of block grants by asking what forces or political factors might lead many states *not* to fund programs for poor people.

When discussing possible dangers, consider some economic realities in a federal system of government. Take your state as an example and assume that its legislators and governor are determined to be particularly generous to recipients of welfare, Food Stamps, and Medicaid once these programs have been block-granted. Also assume that such generosity requires a substantial increase in state taxes. Might the following adverse consequences ensue—and, if they did, would your state's voters and politicians soon decide to emulate less generous states after all?

1. Facing higher taxes, some corporate leaders threaten to relocate to lower-tax states. If they carry out their threat, the tax revenues needed to fund the state's programs will be depleted.
2. Low-income citizens from less generous states relocate to your state and, as a result, the cost of your state's welfare programs is increased.
3. Legislators in your state *fear* an exodus of corporations and an influx of poor individuals, even if they don't occur, and thus oppose generous programs. (Remember that *perceptions* often are more important in politics than actual events.)
4. A recession in your state is accompanied *both* by a decline in tax revenues *and* by a rise in welfare costs.
5. Local counties and cities are asked to bear some of the costs of your state's generous welfare, nutritional, and medical programs, but jurisdictions with large numbers of poor people, such as urban areas, are unable or unwilling to fund these programs.

Discuss whether entitlement status alleviates these problems. Also discuss whether advocates for poor people are better or less able to obtain relatively generous policies at the national or state levels of government.

Many Republicans viewed the EITC not as a tax benefit but as a welfare program; they believed it wrong to compel middle-income taxpayers to subsidize people who made somewhat less than themselves. The tax credits were cut by roughly one-fifth, by restricting eligibility, freezing the maximum credit, and eliminating the credit for taxpayers without children.

Republicans proposed huge tax cuts, totaling $245 billion. More than half of these cuts consisted of a $500 per-child tax credit for families with adjusted gross incomes of up to $110,000 per year. On its face, this tax credit also seemed sensible, because it reduced taxes on families. Some Democrats contended, however, that the cuts in the EITC for low-income families—as well as some cuts in AFDC and Medicaid—would not have been needed if Republicans had not proposed this tax credit or if they had limited it to less affluent families.

Nor were many Democrats happy with some other tax cuts in the reconciliation bill. Republicans wanted to expand individual retirement accounts (IRAs) so as to benefit relatively wealthy taxpayers. They favored cutting capital gains taxes by nearly one-third—a concession that would also favor wealthy families and corporations. They even proposed increasing the amount of estates not subject to inheritance taxes from $500,000 to $650,000, on the grounds that this provision had not kept up with inflation. Republicans notably failed to consider this factor in their deliberations on AFDC, whose real benefits had halved since 1970 because of inflation.

Discretionary Spending: Social Programs and Military Spending

As Republicans fashioned their reconciliation bill, with its tax and entitlement provisions, they forged ahead on 13 separate appropriations bills that had to meet their spending targets in the Budget Resolution—in particular, $10 billion in cuts below the 1994 levels for nondefense discretionary spending. As George Hager reported in July, "Republicans [in the appropriations committees] went straight at long-held Democratic priorities, slashing housing, environmental regulation, summer jobs and—in a seemingly personal twist of the knife—killing off two

of President Clinton's most cherished projects: the National Service initiative and the Goals 2000 education reform program."[42] In their early decisions, House Republicans made cuts even exceeding targets in the Budget Resolution. Democrats attacked some of the cuts; for example, they charged that Republicans waged a "midnight massacre" on children's programs such as Head Start and Healthy Start. Speaking through his Chief of Staff, Leon Panetta, Clinton vowed to veto the appropriations bill for the Department of Health and Human Services unless it was improved, but the House retained most of the cuts in the legislation that they enacted in early August. Some of the cuts were subsequently reduced, at least modestly, in the Senate.

At the same time that Congress was making huge cuts in social spending, it was adding to military spending. In early August, for example, the Senate added $6 billion to Clinton's $243-billion Pentagon budget. The Republicans approved funding for more jet fighters and warships than the administration had requested, on the grounds that they were needed to repel such countries as North Korea and Libya. In the fall, huge sums were added to procure heavy bombers.

CLINTON'S ZIGZAG COURSE

The Republicans and the Clinton administration engaged in a peculiar dance in November and December. To force the president to sign the reconciliation bill, Republicans refused to increase the national debt limit. Without such an agreement, the government could no longer borrow funds to pay its ongoing expenses, and many government agencies would be forced to shut down temporarily, until a continuing resolution was enacted. Aware that Clinton had already retreated on many previous occasions, Republicans assumed that, if they incorporated their draconian funding cuts and their tax cuts in the reconciliation bill, Clinton would meekly accept their policies and allow them to win the day. His startling proposal in June to erase the deficit in ten years seemed to have been a capitula-

FIGURE 12.2 Contending leaders meet the press during the budget negotiations.

SOURCE: © Wilfredo Lee/AP/Wide World

tion to the Republicans. Would he not, when pushed to the wall, agree to their seven-year timetable?

When the government did shut down, in November and again in late December, for a total of 43 days, people wondered where Clinton would draw his line in the sand. Would he demand that all entitlements be retained, even though he had already implied that he would agree to place AFDC in a block grant? Would he demand that Republicans' tax increases be rescinded, so that further cuts in discretionary spending could be avoided?

He chose neither of those paths. Instead, he continued his zig-zag course. In November, to secure Republican support for a continuing resolution to end the government shutdown, Clinton agreed to a seven-year deadline for balancing the budget. However, he also insisted that the agreement include a vaguely worded promise of adequate funding for the environment and medical programs. He remained noncommittal about other facets of the

reconciliation bill, such as its provisions on welfare and Food Stamps. However, he demonstrated that he would not accede to Republicans' demands on January 9th, 1996, when he vetoed a welfare reform bill that Congress had enacted outside of the rubric of the reconciliation bill.

Clinton became less inclined to compromise when polls showed that Newt Gingrich's popularity had plummeted in late 1995 and early 1996, while Clinton's had risen markedly. Although many Americans supported the idea of scaling back federal spending and authority, they often became apprehensive when faced with cuts in specific programs. Realizing that environmental, education, and health programs were particularly popular, Clinton adeptly focused on them in his budget negotiations with the Republicans in November and December; he contended that Republicans' policies would wreak havoc in these areas. Many voters, moreover, blamed Republicans for the partial government shutdown.[43] In addition,

Democrats continued to charge that Republicans' deep tax cuts would enrich affluent Americans and would be funded by cuts in social programs used by less affluent people. Clinton's resolve was further strengthened in early 1996, when a bitter primary battle between Republican presidential candidates revealed a split in the party between so-called fiscal conservatives (such as Steve Forbes, who emphasized balancing the budget and downsizing the federal government) and social conservatives (such as Pat Buchanan, who sought to end legalized abortion).[44]

Curiously, a staunch conservative, Pat Buchanan, stimulated renewed interest in the economic fate of American workers. Although he trailed far behind frontrunner Bob Dole in most of the primaries, he found that many white blue-collar voters resonated to his populist message. Buchanan called for government regulation of corporations to prevent them from moving production to low-wage nations and firing vast numbers of American workers. To protect American workers from foreign competition, he also wanted to rescind such treaties as the North American Free Trade Agreement, which was fashioned in 1993, with bipartisan support, to cut tariffs between Mexico, the United States, and Canada. Aware that the outcome of the 1996 election might hinge on the votes of fearful or displaced workers, leaders of both parties began to bid for those votes in March. Republicans like House Majority Leader Dick Armey evolved a nine-point agenda that included tax cuts for working families, cuts in the capital gains tax, and reductions in regulations to stimulate business, as well as tax concessions to corporations that would agree not to increase short-term profits by means of mass layoffs. In turn, Democrats like House Minority Leader Dick Gephardt sought tax cuts and considered tax incentives to discourage layoffs.[45]

The budgetary stalemate remained unresolved in March 1996. Accusing Congress of evading its responsibilities, Clinton avoided yet another partial government shutdown by signing a continuing resolution on March 15—the tenth in the current fiscal year. (Senate Democrats supported this $160 billion measure only after Republicans included additional environmental funds.) Five of 13 appropria-

tion bills had not yet been approved; Clinton pledged to veto any bills that cut health care, education, or environmental programs excessively. Meanwhile, Republicans used the continuing resolutions to effect severe cuts in social programs by only including partial funding for them; for example, they cut the Substance Abuse and Mental Health Services Administration by $400 million. Nor had the Republicans and the president reached agreement on measures in the reconciliation bill; each side was likely to seek a mandate for its position in the November 1996 elections. In late February, the Clinton administration indicated increased support for AFDC, Food Stamps, and child welfare when Donna Shalala criticized a compromise proposal put forth by the National Governors Association (NGA). Shalala rejected the AFDC block grant unless it included safeguards such as the requirement that states give support to children whose mothers exceeded the proposed five-year time limit on benefits. She also rejected the conversion of Food Stamps, foster care, and adoption programs to block grants. (Some liberals wanted Shalala—and Clinton—to go even further: to reject even the concept of a block grant for AFDC. They contended that eliminating the entitlement status of AFDC would violate a fundamental responsibility of the federal government for impoverished children.) Finally, she rejected the NGA's proposal that states should have complete control of Medicaid; she insisted on the need for federal regulation of nursing home care, the quality of services, and coverage of adolescents.[46]

On April 24, Congress and the White House finally agreed on a budget for the 1995–1996 fiscal year that covered discretionary spending. Republicans got $23 billion in cuts below the preceding year's level, though Clinton got $5 billion added for education, job training, and the environment. Left unresolved, and certain to be the subject of intense political conflict in an election year, were the fate of entitlements and the amount of tax cuts. Republicans planned to present Clinton with huge tax cuts and conservative policies on AFDC and Medicaid, hoping to force him to make politically damaging vetos that would help Bob Dole, his all-but-certain opponent in the 1996 elections. (In May

1996, Dole, the Republican Senate Majority Leader, resigned from his Senate seat to run against Bill Clinton in the 1996 presidential race.)

▊ OUTGROUPS

Affirmative Action

As we noted in Chapter 11, the worst urban uprising in American history occurred in Los Angeles in May 1992, in the wake of an all-white jury's decision to acquit three police officers accused of beating Rodney King, an African American. None of the political candidates for the presidency used the occasion to develop far-reaching proposals to help the largely African American and Latino residents of the nation's inner cities. While Clinton developed demonstration empowerment zones in some of the nation's major cities, this was a relatively small response to such large problems.

During Clinton's first term, policies to help persons of color came under increasing political attack. In California, Governor Pete Wilson, who was contemplating a run for the presidency, pledged to end affirmative action policies in the state. At his initiative, affirmative action was rescinded in the University of California system; he also supported a proposition on the California ballot in 1996 to end affirmative action throughout state government. Since their introduction, affirmative action policies had allowed many persons of color and women to obtain jobs, education, and government contracts, even if beneficiaries sometimes came from middle-class, rather than poor, families. However, the perception that white claimants were being denied positions and opportunities prompted some public resentment. Many civil rights advocates feared the erosion of job and college gains by persons of color if the government abandoned affirmative action altogether. Others feared that fundamental changes in the nation's economy—in particular, the growing importance of higher education and technical skills—would imperil the employment opportunities of African Americans and Latinos.

At the same time, influential books by conservative intellectuals disparaged government policies to provide special assistance to persons of color. As we saw in Chapter 5, *The Bell Curve,* by Richard Herrnstein and Charles Murray, asserted that African Americans are genetically predisposed to low intelligence.[47] While many social scientists critiqued the methodology and data used by Herrnstein and Murray, the book became a best-seller, and some readers came to believe that the authors had proved their assertion by using advanced social science statistics and methodology. In *The End of Racism,* Dinesh D'Souza alleged that "cultural dysfunctionality," not racism, is the main reason that African Americans lag behind the rest of the population economically.[48] Contending that affirmative action, as well as programs such as AFDC, institutionalized a culture of dependency among African Americans, D'Souza suggested that "race-neutral" policies, including the abandonment of affirmative action, would promote entrepreneurialism and the work ethic among African Americans. Though these two books implicated different causes, they came to the same conclusion: African Americans' economic status and educational performance derived from personal characteristics, whether their intelligence or their character, rather than from institutional racism or other social obstacles.

From a social policy perspective, both books provided simplistic analyses of complex phenomena. If African Americans are genetically or culturally inferior, why has a large African American middle (and upper) class developed in the three decades after the 1960s—that is, since the enactment of civil rights laws and opportunity-creating social programs, the mass migration of African Americans from rural to urban areas, and the use of affirmative action? Might not the low economic status of many African Americans be, in large part, a consequence of their segregation in rural Southern areas until relatively recently? Even if there has been a decline in the overt racism that was endemic until the early 1960s, do other, more subtle, forms of racism persist, as reflected in a pervasive bias by employers and gatekeepers of large institutions against African American candidates? And might these prejudices flourish if government pressure and protections were to be removed? Finally, if African Americans are characterized by permanent intellectual deficits, why do numerous pilot projects, as well as research on well-established job-training, Head Start, and educational programs, suggest that government intervention *can* improve the educational and economic standing of African Americans?

Perhaps most disturbing, *The Bell Curve* and *The End of Racism* lead us toward a policy fatalism. If impoverished African Americans possess characterological and intellectual deficits that are relatively intractable, government (or society) can play little role in helping them. However, to be fatalistic about African Americans, while believing that government policies can help other persons better their lot, is a kind of racism. If we are pessimistic about the efficacy of social policies in helping African Americans, should we not also be pessimistic about policies intended to help white citizens better their condition? Why should we pay for schools, nursery schools, and other amenities in white, suburban areas? These books are intent on blaming liberals for current social ills. Liberals might respond that conservatives' indifference to inequalities between the races has frustrated the implementation of more effective policies to help African Americans and other persons of color enter the economic mainstream. Even policies that are widely supported today, such as landmark civil rights laws and Medicare, were opposed by many conservatives.

Conservatives tend to argue that governmental initiatives are much less effective in addressing social problems than are community-based self-help strategies. An example of a self-help project was the Million Man March, called by African American leaders in the fall of 1995. Organizers of the march hoped to encourage the development of role models, community education, and social action to address such problems as crime, drug abuse, and teenage pregnancies. (African American women planned a similar march in 1996.) Whereas conservatives focused exclusively on such bottom-up approaches, liberals wondered whether they could be combined with government funding of innovative programs, as well as civil rights and affirmative action. Why not encourage partnerships between communities, not-for-profit agencies, and public agencies to address major problems?

Immigration

As we discussed in Chapter 6, anti-immigrant sentiment has often grown louder during periods of economic uncertainty. This pattern continued in the 1990s, when corporate downsizing and globalization brought economic insecurity and anxiety to many American homes. In 1994, California voters passed Proposition 187, which declared illegal aliens ineligible for medical, social, and educational services. Though its implementation was halted pending the outcome of court challenges and appeals, this law nonetheless triggered a national debate about immigration.

Are immigrants a burden on society? Immigrants certainly use health, welfare, and other government services on occasion, and some immigrants do commit crimes. However, as taxpayers, immigrants make a substantial financial contribution—a contribution that, according to some research, far exceeds society's expenditures on them. In general, they take the low-paying jobs that other citizens avoid, in hotels, restaurants, agriculture, garment factories, and hospitals, as well as in personal residences as domestics and home-health personnel. To deny immigrants the benefits of social programs and education would raise profound ethical concerns: Are Americans indifferent to the well-being of immigrants and their children? More pragmatically, such restrictions would also pose a threat to public health.

The nation needs to reexamine its immigration policies periodically, but it should not let its policies be dictated by xenophobia or prejudice.

Child Welfare

Knowing that Hillary Clinton was a former board member of the Children's Defense Fund, children's advocates hoped for major legislation to further their goals. Some marginal gains were made; for example, a nation-wide immunization program for children was initiated, and Congress approved $1 billion for demonstration programs in local jurisdictions to strengthen troubled families. However, major policy changes proposed by the Republican-controlled Congress—including the elimination of entitlement status for AFDC, the block-granting of Food Stamps, and revision of Medicaid policies to end the phased inclusion of children over age 12—threatened to cast even larger numbers of children into poverty.

The drawbacks of indiscriminate block-granting are well illustrated by child welfare. In 1996, 21 states were under court supervision for failing to properly care for children in child protective services and in foster care. Social workers, who have often been blamed for failing to detect child abuse or neglect, typically carried caseloads exceeding 50 cases, although the Child Welfare League of America, a respected private organization, recommended no more than 15. Many states, straining to meet the budgetary demands of education, Medicaid, and prisons, failed sufficiently to augment federal subsidies with their own resources. Yet Republicans insisted that the $4 billion in federal subsidies for child welfare be given as block grants to the states, which could administer them with few restrictions.[49]

The child welfare debacle also illustrates the cumulative effects of social policies. If cuts in AFDC grants were to be coupled with stringent requirements on AFDC recipients, many impoverished women, unable to find safe child care, would place their children in unsupervised care or neglect their basic needs. If the entitlement status of Medicaid were also eliminated and states failed to cover the adolescent children of working poor families, more children might not receive even basic medical care. If Food Stamps were also drastically cut, families would be unable to meet their nutritional needs. The outcome of those Republican policies would be extreme hardship for many Americans.

Women

Women's reproductive rights were under attack by conservatives in the Clinton era. Although Congress enacted a measure that made the use or threat of force against workers or clients of abortion clinics a federal crime, women found it difficult to exercise reproductive choice when confronted with pickets at clinics or when forced to travel fifty miles, on average, to find a clinic that would perform abortions.[50] The so-called morning-after pill, a simple means of abortion that was commonly used in Europe, was not widely available in the United States, partly because pharmaceutical companies feared boycotts of their other products by abortion foes. The medical profession itself retreated from abortion services: Most hospitals did not offer the procedure, and most medical students were not even taught how to perform it.[51] Conservative members of Congress, having succeeded in blocking the use of federal funds for abortions, attached riders to legislation to restrict abortion further. They hoped to make late-term abortions illegal, even when the mother's life was endangered. By attaching a rider to a defense authorization bill that President Clinton felt he had to sign, they secured the prohibition of abortions in military hospitals.

On the economic front, women had made substantial gains on some fronts in the 1990s. Large numbers of women continued to get admission to professional schools in law, business, and medicine. With the help of federally funded training programs, some women had entered nontraditional fields such as the trades. These gains were offset, however, by a continuing and extraordinary gap between the median wages of men and women. Moreover, many professional women continued to encounter the so-called glass ceiling. They were not promoted to higher positions even when their job performance excelled. Republicans' policies—in particular, their challenges to AFDC and the earned-income tax credit—threatened the economic standing of the many women who were single heads of families in low-wage jobs. Moreover, feminists feared that women's economic progress would lose its momentum if Republicans succeeded in terminating affirmative action and set-asides that reserved federal job-training slots and contracts for women.

Most European nations have funded absences from work for parents after the birth of a child or the death of a family member. In the United States, however, corporations and many conservatives have staunchly resisted such policies. Social

reformers gained a limited victory with the enactment of the Family and Medical Leave Act of 1993,
which required employers to give all but their top
employees up to 12 weeks of leave to take care of a
new baby or an ill family member. However, the
legislation excluded individuals who had not
worked for an employer for at least 12 months and
excluded businesses with fewer than 50 employees.
Although workers were guaranteed leaves, employers were not required to pay them during those periods. Thus, low-income workers were not easily able
to take advantage of this new policy.[52]

Gay Men and Lesbians

A policy controversy during Clinton's first months
in office illustrated the continuing discrimination
against gay men and lesbians. Clinton had made a
campaign promise to end the military's homopho-
bic policies, under which candidates known to be
gay men or lesbians were denied admission and
military personnel who came out as gay or lesbian
or were determined to have engaged in homosexual
acts were dismissed. (About 14,000 people had
been dismissed under these rules between 1983
and 1993; roughly 25% were women.) Most military leaders opposed any change in policy on the
grounds that gay and lesbian personnel undermined unit cohesion by alienating their heterosexual peers. However, a U.S. District Court judge had
ordered the Navy to reinstate Keith Meinhold, who
had been discharged after identifying himself as a
gay man on national television. Caught between
military leaders and conservatives, on the one
hand, and gay and lesbian activists, on the other,
Clinton fashioned an initial compromise in which
the existing policy would remain in place for six
months, pending consultation with military leaders, but all actions against gay men and lesbians
would be suspended, unless they had been charged
with homosexual conduct.

Unwilling to await the president's resolution,
Democratic Senator Sam Nunn held extended
hearings on the issue. Nunn advanced a "don't ask
and don't tell" approach, under which military
leaders would be prevented from questioning

recruits or personnel about their sexual orientation,
but could still dismiss personnel who identified
themselves as gay men or lesbians, engaged in
homosexual acts, or sought to marry a person of
the same gender. This compromise enraged many
gay men and lesbians, because sexual orientation
remained sufficient cause for dismissal, regardless
of the individual's job-related proficiency. When
the president accepted a "don't ask, don't tell"
approach, Senator Sam Nunn pushed for legislation that contained even more restrictive language
—for example, the declaration that those who
"demonstrate a propensity or intent to engage in
homosexual acts would create an unacceptable
risk" to military standards. Placed in a military
authorization bill, Clinton's compromise with
Nunn's tougher wording was finally codified into
law as part of a military authorization bill, in
November 1993.[53]

RELUCTANCE ILLUSTRATED

There was more conflict over social policy in 1995
than at any time since Harry Truman's confrontation
with the Republican Congress in 1947 and 1948.
While at one level the conflict centered on the federal budget and certain provisions of the Contract
with America, in a broader sense the domestic politics of 1995 represented a clash between conservative and liberal perspectives on the scope of the
American welfare state and on the widening gap
between wealthy and other Americans.

Some liberals had hoped that Clinton, as the
first president since the end of the Cold War, would
reorient the nation's priorities toward domestic
needs. Instead, the political debate became increasingly polarized, and liberals found themselves
forced on the defensive.

In the first two years of his presidency, Clinton
sought relatively liberal policies, including social
investments, health reform, and many smaller measures. A combination of forces frustrated his
attempts at reform. A resurgent Republican minority in both chambers was able to align with moderate and conservative Democrats who balked at the
president's proposals. Outside of Congress, large

numbers of Americans, cynical about government, did not want major social initiatives; they were more interested in an end to gridlock, campaign reforms, and a balanced budget. Nor had this electorate given Clinton a mandate; he was barely elected, with only 43% of the popular vote. Finally, Clinton and his advisers made many errors of their own during the first two years; in particular, the health-reform proposal that they developed was far too complex to win broad support.

The third year of the Clinton presidency might even be called the Newt Gingrich era, inasmuch as Republicans' victory in the 1994 elections left them in control of both chambers of Congress and left Gingrich to set the legislative agenda. Resorting to a zigzagging retreat by June, Clinton conceded most of the Republicans' budget demands as the year proceeded. This third year strongly resembled the politics of 1981, when Ronald Reagan had orchestrated huge cuts in domestic spending—except that the cuts in 1995 were orchestrated not by the president, but by a Congressional leader.

Some of the cuts in social spending were desirable. If Americans are unwilling to tax themselves sufficiently to fund a full domestic agenda akin to those of many European nations, affluent citizens probably need to pay a larger share of their Medicare and Social Security costs. However, some decisions—most notably the end to entitlement status for AFDC and Food Stamps—were certain to harm vulnerable populations.

The Clinton presidency illustrates how fragile the American welfare state is; social reforms are often challenged in later eras. In the two final chapters, we examine the forces that cause such reluctance and look to the prospects for social change in the future. If we are to seek humane policies in a nation that often deals harshly with vulnerable groups, we must understand the history of social policy. We will also need our own vision and values.

NOTES

1. David Maraniss, *First in His Class: A Biography of Bill Clinton* (New York: Simon and Schuster, 1995).

2. Ibid., pp. 72, 348, 366, 415.

3. Richard Cohen, "Democratic Leadership Council Sees Party Void and Is Ready to Fill It," *National Journal* (February 1, 1986), 267–270.

4. Maraniss, *First in His Class,* pp. 72, 239, 360, 453.

5. Ibid., pp. 407ff.

6. Ben Wattenberg, *Values Matter Most* (New York: Free Press, 1995).

7. Cohen, "Democratic Leadership Council."

8. Robert Reich, *The Work of Nations: Preparing Ourselves for Twenty-First Century Capitalism* (New York: Knopf, 1991).

9. *1993 Congressional Quarterly Almanac,* pp. 82–84.

10. Bob Woodward, *The Agenda: Inside the Clinton White House* (New York: Simon and Schuster, 1994), pp. 88ff.

11. Ibid., pp. 113–118, 135–138.

12. Ibid., pp. 43, 95, 108, 139–141.

13. Figure 12.1 uses budget data from the *1993 Congressional Quarterly Almanac,* p. 538.

14. Elizabeth Drew, *On the Edge: the Clinton Presidency* (New York: Simon and Schuster, 1994), pp. 119–123.

15. Graeme Browning, "The Old Shell Game?" *National Journal* (March 27, 1993), 746–748; *1993 Congressional Quarterly Almanac,* p. 105.

16. Jonathan Rauch, "Stage Two," *National Journal* (August 7, 1993), 1962–1966.

17. Viveca Novak, "After the Boll Weevils," *National Journal* (June 26, 1993), 1630–1664.

18. Rauch, "Stage Two," p. 1964.

19. Richard Cohen, "On the Edge," *National Journal* (December 4, 1993), 2888–2892.

20. Woodward, *The Agenda,* pp. 146, 164–168.

21. Drew, *On the Edge,* pp. 285ff.

22. Woodward, *The Agenda,* p. 315.

23. Drew, *On the Edge,* pp. 300–310.

24. For an extended discussion of health reform, see *1994 Congressional Quarterly Almanac,* pp. 319–357.

25. For discussion of the crime bill, see *1994 Congressional Quarterly Almanac,* pp. 273–293.

26. Jason DeParle, "Sheila Burke Is the Militant Feminist Commie Peacenik Who's Telling Bob Dole What to Think," *New York Times Magazine* (November 12, 1995), 32–38, 90, 100–105.

27. Howard Fineman, "The Warrior," *Newsweek* (January 9, 1995), 28–34; Connie Bruck, "The Politics of Perception," *New Yorker* (October 9, 1995), 50–76.

28. Bruck, "The Politics of Perception."

29. DeParle, "Sheila Burke."

30. Ibid.

31. Don Balz and Ronald Brownstein, *Storming the Gates: Protest Politics and the Republican Revival* (Boston: Little, Brown), pp. 240–245.

32. Ed Gillespie and Bob Schellhas, eds., *Contract with America* (New York: Random House, 1994).

33. Jeff Shear, "The Big Fix," *National Journal* (March 25, 1995), 734–735.

34. Jeff Shear, "Hey, What's Happened to the Budget?" *National Journal* (February 11, 1995), 357.

35. Burt Solomon, "As Republicans Sock, Sock, Sock, For Clinton Opportunities Knock," *National Journal* (March 18, 1995), 700–701.

36. George Hager, "Clinton Shifts Tactics, Projects Erasing Deficit in Ten Years," *Congressional Quarterly Weekly* (June 17, 1995), 1715–1720.

37. Jane Mayer, "Lonely Guy," *New Yorker* (October 30, 1995), 58–62.

38. George Hager and Alissa Rubin, "Last Minute Maneuvers Forge a Conference Agreement," *Congressional Quarterly Weekly* (June 24, 1995), 1814.

39. Jeffrey Katz, "House, Senate Bills Compared," *Congressional Quarterly Weekly* (September 16, 1995), 2806.

40. George Hager and David Cloud, "Clinton and Congress: Speeding Toward Collision over Budget," *Congressional Quarterly Weekly* (September 2, 1995), 2643.

41. George Hager, "GOP Ready To Take Debt Limit to the Brink and Beyond," *Congressional Quarterly Weekly* (September 23, 1995), 2908–2911.

42. George Hager, "Furor over First Spending Bills Promises a Stormy Summer," *Congressional Quarterly Weekly* (July 15, 1995), 2041.

43. George Hager, "A Battered GOP Calls Workers Back to the Job," *Congressional Quarterly Weekly* (January 6, 1996), 53–57.

44. Burt Solomon, "Christian Soldiers," *National Journal* (February 24, 1996), 410–415.

45. Jackie Koszczuk, "With Humor and Firm Hand, Armey Rules the House," *Congressional Quarterly Weekly* (March 2, 1996), 523–529.

46. Jeffrey Katz, "Shalala: Governors' Proposals Give States Too Much Power," *Congressional Quarterly Weekly* (March 2, 1996), 558–560.

47. Richard Herrnstein and Charles Murray, *The Bell Curve: Intelligence and Class Structure in American Life* (New York: Free Press, 1994). For a critique of Murray's work, see the essay review by Leon Kamin, "Behind the Curve," *Scientific American* (February 1995), 99–103.

48. Dinesh D'Souza, *The End of Racism* (New York: Free Press, 1995). For further explication of D'Souza's views, see the extended interview of D'Souza by Nicholas Lemann, "The End of Racism?" *American Heritage* (February/March 1996), 93–105.

49. For analysis of various states' child welfare programs, as well as the controversy about block-granting federal child welfare assistance, see Rochelle Stanfield, "Kids on the Block," *National Journal* (February 3, 1996), 247–251; Robert Pear, "Many States Fail To Meet Mandates on Child Welfare," *New York Times* (March 17, 1996), 1, 14.

50. Barbara Gottlieb, "Abortion, 1995," *New England Journal of Medicine* (February 23, 1995), 532–533.

51. Ibid., p. 533; Jan Hoffman, "The Morning After Pill," *New York Times Magazine* (January 10, 1993), 12–14, 30.

52. For provisions of the family leave law, see *1993 Congressional Quarterly Almanac,* p. 390.

53. For an extended discussion of the issue, see *1993 Congressional Quarterly Almanac,* pp. 454–462.

13

C H A P T E R

Why Has the American Welfare State Been Reluctant?

Now that we have brought our review of successive eras in U.S. social welfare history up to the present, let's change our focus and take a broader view of the American response to social needs. What characteristics of the American welfare state make it reluctant when compared to many European nations? What contextual and political factors, singly and in combination, explain this reluctance?

MANIFESTATIONS OF RELUCTANCE

As summarized in Box 13.1, we identify six manifestations of reluctance that distinguish the American welfare state from that of most European nations.[1]

1. Even when domestic expenditures of local, state, and federal authorities are aggregated, Americans devote a relatively small share of their GNP to domestic spending—roughly 23% when federal national-security and debt-servicing charges are not considered. (This figure includes local educational expenditures and a variety of state and federal programs.) By contrast, the Japanese spend 30%, the British and West Germans spend about 40%, and the Swedes spend about 50% of their GNP for comparable programs.[2]

2. Most nations provide a combination of universal programs, which deliver services or benefits to people regardless of their income, and means-tested programs, which can only be used by citizens who fall beneath specific levels of income. Whereas many European nations offer a range of universal programs, the United States emphasizes means-tested programs. Only elderly Americans benefit from anything resembling universal care, through the Medicare program—and even this program fails to cover long-term care and many specific services. Unlike most European nations, the United States does not provide a children's allowance to families—and restricts publicly funded child care to persons who meet specific income tests. In some European nations, housing programs, vacation subsidies, and even educational sabbaticals are not means-tested.[3]

3. Whereas European welfare programs are relatively stable, their American counterparts are subject to considerable volatility or uncertainty. New Deal public works programs, the National Youth Administration, many programs of the War on Poverty, and various housing programs have been terminated. Fluctuations in

BOX 13.1   Some Characteristics of the American Response to Social Needs

1. Low spending on social programs as a percentage of the GNP throughout the 20th century
2. Emphasis on means-tested programs rather than universal programs
3. Policy volatility: rapid changes in social policies within and between different eras
4. Significant out-of-pocket costs by consumers and citizens for an array of social needs
5. Particularly restrictive welfare programs, particularly for families with single (usually female) heads
6. Concentration of social problems and unmet needs in outgroups

program funding are endemic: Various New Deal programs underwent drastic cuts; the funding of many Great Society programs was cut in the late 1960s; and mental-health centers and a variety of means-tested programs for the poor suffered deep cuts in the administrations of Richard Nixon and Ronald Reagan. Liberal reformers have often found their legislative successes attacked in subsequent conservative periods, such as the 1920s, the 1950s, the 1980s, and the 1990s. While actual spending on many social programs has not diminished, the same is not true for others; for example, many programs that helped low-income people were slashed during the 1980s. Even when cuts were not made, *threats* to reduce domestic spending have often forced American reformers to devote considerable effort to maintaining existing funding. Flux has occurred in European nations, as well—for example, many had conservative regimes of their own during the 1980s—but the volatility of their programs has been less marked.[4]

The fragility of the American welfare state was dramatically illustrated in the wake of the 1994 Congressional elections, when the new Republican majority, under the leadership of House Speaker Newt Gingrich, proposed to end AFDC as an entitlement program, to terminate numerous federal programs, and to markedly reduce federal tax revenues. If European conservatives chafe at the size of their welfare states and often propose cuts in specific programs, they lack the assertiveness of the American counterparts, whose rhetoric, writings, and actions often attack the welfare state itself.

4. Many American consumers pay relatively large shares of their personal income for social,

medical, and educational services—a trend that has sharply increased in the 1980s and 1990s—and local and federal governments have increased fees and payment-shares for many public programs. Elderly persons, for example, pay a large share of medical costs under Medicare in the form of various fees associated with the program, and many must deplete their savings altogether when they develop chronic or catastrophic health-care problems. Mothers continue to fund a large share of day-care costs because of inadequate public funding or stringent eligibility conditions. We are not suggesting that consumers ought not to shoulder some share of the cost of the services they use, but Americans risk placing a sizable burden on many low-income, moderate-income, and middle-income citizens.

In a sense, Americans are gamblers against fate. Paying relatively low taxes when compared to Europeans, Americans must resort to personal savings, accumulation of assets, and fringe benefits (such as corporate pension funds) to self-fund major personal expenses. The many Americans who cannot save sufficient sums *and* who experience personal adversity—for example, a major health problem—must use means-tested programs such as SSI or Medicaid, but only after they have divested themselves of personal resources sufficiently to qualify. By contrast, Americans who *can* save money and who *do* qualify for liberal private pensions, and who are *not* beset by major social problems win the personal gamble; low U.S. taxes allow them to accumulate enormous personal resources.

5. In comparison with other European nations, the United States has subjected single heads of

households (usually women) and their families to extraordinarily harsh policies. It was not until the mid-1930s that a federal program was created to help them, and even this modest program had become engulfed in controversy by the early 1960s. In succeeding decades, it has been constantly attacked by conservatives; its modest benefits have been markedly eroded, and stringent restrictions on its beneficiaries have been proposed. As a corollary to this point, children in the United States are treated more harshly than are children in many European nations, partly because so many of them reside in families with single heads, and partly because the United States has not developed universal health care, universal child care, and childrens' allowances. Single heads of household in European nations endure hardships of their own, but they and their children have access to universal health care, free child care, efficient and cheap public transportation, well-funded vocational and training programs, and efficient job-search agencies.[5]

6. In this text, we have identified an array of outgroups, including racial, sociological, dependent, low-income, and socially stigmatized groups. Of course, all industrialized nations possess outgroups—that is, populations that suffer inequalities and discrimination. For various reasons, however, specific outgroups in the United States often confront even greater hardships than do their counterparts abroad. Take the case of low-income populations in the United States, as compared to the lowest quintile in many European nations. Contrast a walking tour of the great cities of Europe, such as Paris, Florence, Copenhagen, or Munich, with a walking tour of New York City, Los Angeles, Cleveland, or St. Louis. Cities on both continents include low-income areas, but the devastation found in American cities has not been seen in their European counterparts since the aftermath of World War II. Older Americans, while usually above the poverty line, encounter insecurities not known to the European elderly, such as fears of medical bankruptcy. Vast numbers of American children live with poor nutrition, poor health care, and physical danger from crime. We have already discussed the feminization of poverty in the United

States; European nations subsidize child care and offer more munificent payments to single mothers.[6]

No single reason exists for the deprivation of outgroups in the United States. One factor is the gaps and meager benefits of the American welfare state, as illustrated by the absence of a national health system, inadequate child care, and lack of a children's allowance. The American tax system does not redistribute income from the upper quintiles to the lower quintiles; Americans of all social classes pay roughly equal tax rates when all sources, including sales and property taxes, are included. We must look, as well, to historical factors, such as the prolonged exclusion of many African Americans, Latinos, and Native Americans from the industrial order and their subsequent attempts to play economic catch-up, with little assistance from white management and unions. Prejudice and racism, present in all nations, assumed a larger role in the United States than in Europe, partly because of the United States' larger populations of color, who experienced rampant discrimination. Nor can we ignore the effects of poverty and inequality upon outgroups themselves. Such social scientists as William Julius Wilson have argued compellingly that people who live under onerous conditions, such as inner-city populations, sometimes develop destructive behaviors that contribute to their plight, such as gangs, violence, and substance abuse, even if these behaviors may be attributed in part to the harsh social and economic environments in which they live.[7]

Even this cursory discussion suggests that a concentration of social problems in specific outgroups is linked to interlocking circumstances that do not affect their counterparts in Europe.

CONTEXTUAL CAUSES OF RELUCTANCE

A range of theorists have implicated various cultural, political, and institutional causes of reluctance of the American welfare state. Many of them identify a single primary cause. For example, Skocpol emphasizes political factors that shape

INSERT 13.1   CRITICAL ANALYSIS:
AMERICANS AND EUROPEANS APPROACHING RETIREMENT:
A COMPARISON

As Americans enter their 50s, they must engage in a series of financial maneuvers if they want to secure sufficient resources to protect themselves from economic bankruptcy in their retirement years. They can expect to encounter health problems as they grow older, and some significant fraction of them will experience chronic—long-term—health conditions that require them to obtain costly medical services for a protracted period. A significant number will have to enter a nursing home or receive long-term services in their homes—for example, from visiting nurses.

Many factors make such Americans nervous. With corporate downsizing, increasing numbers of employees in their 50s are losing their jobs, and may find that they deplete their personal resources even before they reach their 60s. As companies increasingly curtail or eliminate pensions, aging Americans face further drains on their personal resources. Some know that Medicare only funds *acute*—short-term—medical conditions, and that they themselves will be required to pay for medical care that extends beyond specific surgeries or other brief treatments. Some are anxious that even the Social Security and Medicare entitlements will not survive the uncertainties of the American political process: Might conservatives succeed in eliminating or further curtailing them? If they want to purchase medical security by entering retirement villages or homes, such as Leisure Village in Southern California, they need to have sufficient assets to pay the roughly $100,000 entrance fee *and* the roughly $1,500 monthly fees.

Contrast these aging Americans with their counterparts in Scandinavia, who know that they will enter their senior years with national health insurance that requires them to pay virtually nothing for short- *or* long-term care. Scandinavians know that government-funded retirement facilities charge minimal entrance fees and minimal monthly fees, even for relatively affluent people. Because their pensions are more munificent than American Social Security pensions, they have sufficient funds for recreation.

What are some implications of these two situations? Is the American gamble worth it, psychologically and financially? Do American policies create a class of citizens who enter their senior years with extraordinary life options and another class with very restricted options—as contrasted with a Scandinavian system where most citizens exceed a threshold of security?

policy choices—ideas of policy elites, organizational features of the U.S. state structure, and interest-group pressures; Hartz emphasizes cultural variables; Shalev emphasizes the power of working-class organizations such as trade unions; Edsall emphasizes the manipulation of race by political elites; and Berkowitz and McQuaid emphasize the role of corporate capitalists.[8]

It would be simpler, of course, if the reluctance of the American welfare state could be explained by a single cause. Preceding chapters in this text suggest, however, that many factors, singly and together, have contributed to the reluctance of the American welfare state. Were we to push for a single explanation, we would not only risk ignoring

the effects of other causes, but we would also fail to examine how the interactions of various factors shape the American welfare state.

When examining the reluctance of the American welfare state, we can return to Figure 2.1 (p. 13), where contextual factors and political processes are depicted as causing policy choices.

Cultural Factors

Americans have developed a multifaceted mythology to justify their failure to develop a relatively generous welfare state. It includes a set of interrelated beliefs: that social programs do more harm than good; that social problems can be easily solved; that problems can be avoided by creating equal opportunity; and that laissez-faire policies can suffice to solve social problems. We call these interrelated beliefs a mythology because they are unproven. Let's consider each in turn.

Doing Harm by Doing Good

Since the colonial period, Americans have been obsessed with the notion that charitable acts will bring adverse consequences. Benjamin Franklin contended that

> to relieve the misfortunes of our fellow creatures is concurring with the Deity; it is godlike; but, if we provide encouragement for laziness, and support for folly, may we not be fighting against the order of God and Nature, which perhaps has appointed want and misery . . . as necessary consequences of idleness and extravagance?[9]

Leaders of the charity organization societies and the Sunday School movement contended in the 19th century that generous relief to the poor would encourage laziness; this preoccupation led the charity societies to seek to provide every indigent person with a friendly visitor, who could screen out those persons who were corrupted by relief giving. Care was taken in the New Deal to set wage levels in public works programs so low that they would not tempt persons to rely on them. Welfare reform was defeated on successive occasions in the 1970s because many persons feared it would undermine the incentive to work. Conservatives and many liberals in the 1980s contended that overgenerous welfare programs had produced an African American underclass. Conservatives launched a far-reaching attack on welfare programs in the mid-1990s on the grounds that they promoted illegitimate births and rising AFDC rolls.

Concern about the deleterious effects of relief giving on poor persons has been complemented by fears that diversion of resources to charity would harm the nation's economy. Many economists opposed efforts by unions in the Gilded Age to seek higher wages on the grounds that such "artificial" increases would discourage entrepreneurs from making investments that were required to sustain economic growth. New Dealers often feared that large welfare expenditures would draw invest-

ment funds from the economy and thus diminish the number of jobs. Following World War II, opponents of efforts to raise the minimum wage contended that the policy would lead employers to reduce the size of the labor force. Conservatives argued in the 1980s and 1990s that diversion of a larger share of the nation's resources to social programs would decrease economic growth by depleting investment capital.

Fears that doing good might cause harm should not be dismissed as trivial; history is replete with altruistic projects that were unsuccessful. The temperance movement did not convert many Americans to abstinence. Crowded and custodial mental institutions and prisons may have harmed more persons than they helped. Dramatic increases in the minimum wage can bring layoffs for some low-wage employees. Welfare reforms that raised benefit levels far above existing wages for unskilled persons have tempted some to seek welfare as a substitute for work.

Analysis of history suggests, however, that Americans have often made premature judgments about the possible dangers of social reforms. Persons who leap to the judgment that altruism can be deleterious often fail to recognize that the status quo carries its own dangers. Low welfare benefits can bring economic desperation that leads to additional problems, such as stress, marital and family conflict, malnutrition, and despair. High unemployment brings a tragic toll of suicide, mental illness, and substance abuse. The dangers associated with punitive social programs or lack of economic opportunity are commonly overlooked in the zeal to identify the possible dangers of social programs.

Moreover, persons who highlight the dangers of altruism often neglect to note that social programs can be ineffective not because they are intrinsically defective but because their recipients live in a hostile world. A relatively generous welfare program may discourage some recipients from working, not because they are lazy but because they can find only positions that pay low wages. Raising the minimum wage would lead to some displacement of workers because many employers currently use teenage, undocumented, transient, and other low-paid workers to artificially boost their profits. If social programs were evaluated in their social context, then, more attention would be devoted to reforming injustices in society rather than assuming prematurely that the programs themselves are faulty.

Americans often contend not only that specific social programs lead to adverse consequences but that dramatic increases in social spending would decrease economic growth, by diverting funds from productive investments, and undermine the work ethic. If these arguments were correct, however, we would discern an inverse relationship between economic growth and the size of the welfare state, but many nations with a relatively large welfare state, such as Sweden and Germany, have higher rates of economic growth than does the United States.[10] European socialized health systems are associated with lower rates of mortality and morbidity than the private American system—and are considerably less expensive to operate. Arguments against an expansive welfare state sometimes reach comical proportions. Eisenhower surmised in 1956, for example, that the large Swedish welfare state caused many of its citizens to commit suicide by depriving them of the need to work hard, but historians discovered that the high suicide rate in Sweden had antedated the development of its welfare state—and that many other nations had higher rates.

Americans are fond of evaluating the effectiveness of social programs. If the evaluations indicate that they are not effective, the usual response is to call for the programs to be scaled back or terminated. These evaluations are often based on a single criterion. Thus, welfare programs are judged faulty if they induce more persons to seek welfare; the Head Start program is declared ineffective if it fails to raise the intelligence scores of its enrollees; and mental-health programs are declared unsuccessful when they do not reduce commitments to state hospitals. Since most social programs have multiple objectives, however, it is fallacious to evaluate them on only one criterion. Welfare programs provide sustenance to destitute persons, for example, and so the generosity of their benefits ought also to be considered. The Head Start program provides medical, nutritional, developmental, and parent-education services, and so its effective-

ness should be assessed in the context of all of these objectives. The mental-health system receives high marks for deinstitutionalizing mentally ill persons but low marks for consigning many of them to a lonely existence in board-and-care homes in skid-row areas.

Many assertions about the negative effects of social programs have not been proven or are challenged by research data. Take the alleged association between welfare and illegitimacy. A recent study in New Jersey suggests that increased welfare utilization did not increase rates of illegitimacy.[11]

Problems and Panaceas The American colonists had the dream that they could create a problem-free society. The Puritans sought to purge sinfulness from society by encouraging a regimen of work and morality. Thomas Jefferson, like many other colonial leaders, hoped Americans could create a republic of yeoman farmers and could avoid the problems of class conflict, poverty, and urbanization seen in European nations. This belief in the possibility of a utopian society engendered two social welfare fallacies.

First, it led many Americans to overlook harsh realities. Inequality and unemployment, as well as a relatively rigid class structure, were embedded in American society in the 19th century, both in the nation's cities and on the frontier; however, generations of Americans idealized the frontier as a place where anyone could prosper, saw the emerging industrial order as the source of new jobs, and believed that the nation provided unlimited opportunities to immigrants. Relatively high unemployment existed in the 1920s, yet the belief in unlimited prosperity led many of the nation's leaders to ignore danger signs that ultimately led to the Great Depression. Despite the growth of an underclass in the nation's cities and high rates of rural poverty, optimism returned in the 1950s, when many Americans believed that most families would soon possess suburban homes. Although inequality and poverty remained, conservative leaders of the 1980s, armed with supply-side economics, predicted that economic growth would eliminate poverty and increase tax revenues so substantially that the massive federal deficit would disappear, even with tax cuts and massive increases in military spending. Of course, just the opposite occurred, but the conservative rhetoric inhibited the development of social programs, by making Americans believe that persistent social problems did not exist.

Second, even when Americans acknowledged that serious social problems existed, they often believed that the problems could be easily solved. Jefferson believed that land ownership, education, and democratic institutions would eradicate poverty and other social ills; the moral-treatment reformers of the 19th century assumed that character-forming institutions could eradicate poverty, mental illness, delinquency, and crime; charity organization leaders placed faith in friendly visitors and case screening; progressives saw regulations as panaceas; New Deal reformers were convinced that Social Security would eliminate poverty among older Americans; framers of the welfare service amendments of 1962 hoped to markedly decrease welfare rolls by providing many families with the services of social workers; some reformers in the 1960s believed that the service and community programs in the War on Poverty would eradicate poverty, in the 1980s, supply-side economists were convinced that reductions in the nation's taxes would eliminate poverty; and in the 1990s, many conservatives believed that policies to place lifetime limits on AFDC usage would make welfare wither away.

This optimistic faith in simple solutions has impeded deeper analysis of the causes and persistence of social problems throughout the nation's history. Poverty is linked to structural causes, such as recessions, low wages in certain sectors of the economy, disabling mental and physical conditions, low levels of skills and education, and discrimination. Simple solutions did not eliminate or mitigate poverty in the 19th century, when breadlines formed during recessions or when immigrants found themselves at the mercy of employers who paid low wages. The government regulations of the progressive era did little to help destitute immigrant workers in the nation's cities. The Social Security program did not eradicate poverty among elderly persons, even though many of its framers were convinced that it would. Successive welfare reforms of the 1960s did not reduce the welfare rolls. The War on Poverty had minimal impact on the incidence of poverty in the United States. The Reagan administration's cuts in social spending and punitive welfare policies did not substantially reduce the size of welfare rolls.

Naive optimism that single programs can solve major social problems has fostered cynicism about the effectiveness of existing social programs. Time and time again, Americans have launched social programs with extravagant fanfare. When the programs failed to eliminate the problems, critics demanded their discontinuation, only to begin another cycle of hope and disillusionment. Americans have seldom realized that simple solutions rarely suffice to remedy complex problems or that the success of single programs is even less likely when they are poorly funded or implemented. The mental institutions of the mid-19th century became custodial institutions because they were poorly funded in subsequent decades. Regulations of housing and public health were often rendered ineffective in the progressive era because they were not monitored. The War on Poverty never received more than $2 billion in any given year.

Networks of mutually reinforcing programs are needed to address social problems. The problem of the feminization of poverty in the contemporary period could be reduced, for example, by a cluster of programs—a children's allowance, tax rebates and exemptions, enforcement of support payments from absentee fathers, and tax incentives to encourage employers to hire women who are single heads of households—but none of these remedies, by itself, would make a significant impact on the problem. It is also difficult for social programs to succeed without fundamental reforms designed to improve the economic and social status of disadvantaged persons. Individuals can benefit from services, job training, and improved education, but these positive benefits can be negated if they remain in blighted neighborhoods, suffer unemployment, or experience grinding poverty.

The Misleading Analogy of the Fair Footrace   Jefferson hoped that Americans could avoid the perils of a class-structured society by giving all citizens access to the land and to education. A combination of circumstances—the abundance

of frontier lands, the remarkable speed of industrialization, the prosperity of many Americans, economic growth, and success stories of immigrants who achieved wealth—encouraged the perpetuation of Jefferson's dream and the corollary notion that an expansive welfare state was not needed in a society that had created ample opportunities for its citizens to obtain wealth.

As our discussion in preceding chapters has indicated, many citizens had an unfair advantage. For example, contrast the descendants of an Irish immigrant family that came to this country in the 1850s and the descendants of African American slaves. The Irish immigrant family lived in appalling conditions in Philadelphia and encountered considerable prejudice, but many members of the first two generations worked in industrial plants and attended public school. By the third generation (roughly 1940), various descendants had purchased homes, obtained jobs from Irish ward bosses, and completed high school. In the fourth generation, many family members no longer lived in Irish communities but in the suburbs, and a number of them attended colleges and entered professions.

The African American family, once emancipated from slavery, lived in grinding poverty in the rural South of the postbellum years. Public education was not available to its members, who lived in shanty homes near the fields they tended as sharecroppers and field hands. For three generations, family members eked out a subsistence existence. Although some members sporadically attended segregated schools, successive generations perceived little utility in education, because rural African Americans could not enter occupations where literacy was needed. Family members learned to live in their segregated conditions and saw little hope of improving their economic status. When a family migrated north to Chicago in the 1950s, it lived in a vast segregated African American community, in a city that was dominated by white politicians, white trade unions, and businesses owned by white entrepreneurs. Unlike the descendants of the Irish immigrants, who by 1960 had wealth, education, and desirable positions in the economic order in the North, most members of the African American family were illiterate and unskilled and faced the task of catching up in a

society dominated by whites. They were subject to racial discrimination; they lacked the support of political machines; they found it hard to get industrial jobs; and the resources of African American churches in Northern cities had been overwhelmed by the enormous number of new arrivals from the South. Urban African Americans did not fare well in Northern schools, which were generally overcrowded and staffed by white teachers.

The analogy of a fair footrace ignores the fact that many citizens begin the race with a huge disadvantage. It is useful to improve education and services to disadvantaged populations, but their responses will be strongly conditioned by their social class and the experiences of their ancestors. Social policy that focuses on improving the education of disadvantaged citizens represents, at best, a long-term strategy; moreover, advantaged citizens are likely, in the meantime, to continue to improve their own educational status. Improvements in opportunity need to be coupled with programs that provide resources and jobs to disadvantaged groups in their present circumstances.

Beliefs About Markets and Government

American beliefs about markets and government have retarded the development of the welfare state. Many Americans have idealized private markets by suggesting that they worked best when left to themselves; this belief is perhaps best illustrated by economic theories in the Gilded Age, but has flourished more recently with the advocacy of conservative economists such as Milton Friedman. These theories—which were accepted in the United States more widely than in Europe—promoted opposition to factory regulations, taxes, redistribution of resources from affluent to less affluent persons, public works, and national economic planning. The welfare state itself has been viewed as interfering with private markets, because it diverts economic resources to nonmarket endeavors, such as income-maintenance programs.[12]

Ample evidence exists, however, that unregulated markets are not necessarily in the best public interest. Entrepreneurs have often victimized workers, consumers, and investors. Although many economic theorists have believed that implementation of their theories would end recessions, no one has yet succeeded. People of color and women have disproportionately borne the burden of economic suffering. Unregulated private markets do not bring an equitable distribution of wealth. If the problems created by capitalism are to be addressed, government regulations, social programs, taxes on affluent persons, and economic planning are needed. Many Americans have naively assumed, however, that social distress and inequality were caused by these interventions, rather than by capitalism itself. The idealization of capitalism in the United States stems in part from the fact that the economies of the colonies were capitalistic almost from the outset. Whereas the colonists assumed that capitalism was a natural way to organize economic affairs, many Europeans were suspicious of it, because they retained at least a vestige of feudal society's distrust of usury, speculation, fluctuating prices, and profits.

The capitalist mythology about free markets is often coupled with simplistic views of government that have emphasized its defects while ignoring its benefits. Many Americans in the colonial era believed that strong governments would subvert the freedoms of the people, absorb vast amounts of the nation's wealth, and contribute to the power of incumbents. These same fears were frequently expressed by opponents of New Deal and Great Society reforms and by conservatives in the 1980s and 1990s. But government programs, for all of their defects, arose to address intractable social problems that required a societal response. Red tape, inefficiency, and patronage have plagued government institutions, but these problems have been of lesser magnitude than those that would face the nation if the federal government remained as weak as in the Gilded Age. Many Americans have erroneously believed, moreover, that increases in social spending necessarily bring massive increases in the size of bureaucracies. When federal authorities provide matching funds and standards, while allowing local governments to implement programs, the growth of federal bureaucracies is limited.[13]

Beliefs About Equality   Prejudice against poor persons, which has fostered punitive strategies and benign neglect, has been supplemented by theories that extol the merits of economic inequality. Many European aristocrats and American leaders in the 18th century contended that the leadership of social elites would prevent the rise of demagogues, who, they feared, could capitalize on the ignorance, emotions, and licentiousness of the common people. When Benjamin Franklin wrote that "what the rich expend, the laboring poor receive in payment for their labour," he was arguing that affluence of an upper class is needed to support and sustain poor persons.[14] Many American politicians in the 20th century, including Calvin Coolidge and Ronald Reagan, argued that the nation had to increase economic inequality, so that an affluent class would have the resources to make investments that would ultimately benefit poor persons.

These prejudices and economic theories, which have deterred the development of generous social programs and other policies to decrease economic inequality, have been less influential in Europe, because they have been more effectively challenged by leaders of working-class organizations and political parties. European socialists and radicals countered that affluent persons were themselves social parasites, who used their resources to victimize the working class and to maintain extravagant lifestyles. American liberals, spared the need to articulate more progressive positions by the absence of a powerful radical movement, have often advocated policies surprisingly similar to those of conservatives. Thus, Franklin Roosevelt supported relatively meager unemployment benefits and regressive Social Security taxes; Kennedy and Johnson enacted tax cuts that markedly increased economic inequality; and many liberals have supported massive increases in military spending at the expense of social programs.

Americans have tended to consider equality of opportunity rather than equality of status or wealth. It is important, of course, to have equality in education so that citizens of different social classes and races have access to similar educational opportunities. But status and wealth are also important, because they reflect the degree of equality between members of different social classes. Partly because European nations have had powerful socialist or labor parties, they are more likely to consider equality of status and wealth—a propensity that leads them, in turn, to want to use the powers of government to redistribute resources from affluent to less affluent persons.

Economic Factors

Low Levels of Taxation Low levels of taxation contribute to the reluctant welfare state by depriving social programs of funding. Already meager by comparison with those of many European nations, federal tax revenues have been depleted from 1950 onward by large military expenditures. An overview of the evolution of American taxes suggests that U.S. history has been an extended Boston Tea Party; taxes have been perceived as alien even when imposed by the American government.

Americans first developed a federal income tax during the Civil War, but abruptly canceled it when the war was over. Although various reformers wanted an ongoing federal income tax, the Supreme Court declared an income tax law to be unconstitutional in 1894; this ruling set the stage for enactment of the Sixteenth Amendment to the Constitution in 1913. However, the federal income tax did not assume significant proportions until World War II, when it was finally levied on most citizens.

Without discussing the evolution of the income tax after World War II in detail, we confine ourselves to some important observations.

1. Americans have been sufficiently opposed to taxation that the revenue yields of combined federal, state, and local taxes have been far lower than the yields of most European nations, when computed as a percentage of gross national product.

2. The total yields have been frequently depleted by dramatic cuts in income and corporate taxes; important cuts were made by the Congress in 1948 over the veto of President Harry Truman, by Presidents Kennedy and Johnson in 1961 and 1964, by President Nixon in 1969, and by President Reagan in 1981.

3. Federal revenues have been further depleted by numerous loopholes in the tax code to benefit specific interests or groups in the population—for example, provisions that allow homeowners to deduct mortgage interest payments. Cuts have often been supported, as well, on the grounds that they will spur economic growth by providing more capital to entrepreneurs and to affluent persons, who, it is assumed, will use their additional funds to invest in jobs—a sometimes dubious assumption, as illustrated by the relatively few jobs created in the wake of President Reagan's massive tax cuts in 1981.

4. The relatively low levels of American taxes have placed significant downward pressure on budget allocations for social programs. Prior to the Reagan and Bush eras, most Americans opposed large budget deficits. Given their chronic reluctance to increase taxes, the budget could only be balanced by restraining expenditure. In this context, the nation's firm commitment to large military expenditures meant that social spending had to be kept in check. This tension between guns and butter was most dramatic during the Vietnam War, but existed throughout the Cold War.

5. Social spending rose during the Reagan and Bush eras, but its rate of increase was diminished by the huge budget deficits that President Reagan created by lowering taxes in 1981 while increasing military spending.

6. Even with the end of the Cold War, the size of the budget deficits, coupled with the traditional American disinclination to raise taxes, has continued to constrain the rate of increase in social spending in the United States.

7. Republicans' proposals to cut federal taxes dramatically in the 1995 Congress placed considerable downward pressure on social spending: To eradicate the national deficit in seven years and *increase* military spending, they would have to make huge cuts in domestic spending.

This summary of recent tax history suggests that welfare historians should place more emphasis on the revenue or tax side of the welfare state, because the reluctance of the American tax system has contributed to the reluctance of the American welfare state.

Military Spending From 1950 onward, scarce federal revenues have been depleted by military spending. Though Britain and France had significant armed forces, their military budgets, as a percentage of GNP, were much smaller than U.S. defense spending. Throughout the Cold War, West Germany and Japan spent far smaller amounts.

Since 1950, the U.S. military budget has absorbed roughly $300 billion per year in constant 1992 dollars, for a staggering total of some $12.6 trillion. President Reagan increased military spending at a rate that was unprecedented during peacetime. He hoped to add another trillion dollars to military spending with his Strategic Defense Initiative, but Congress balked when its costs became evident. Bill Clinton made some cuts in military spending, but they were undramatic. While the United States was expending these huge resources on defense, European nations and Japan were devoting their revenues instead to productive investments and social programs.

Conflicts between social and military spending had occurred earlier in American history. Jane Addams fought Theodore Roosevelt's rearmament plans in the years preceding World War I, and liberals vainly opposed efforts by conservatives to cut social spending during and after World War II. However, nothing compares with the Cold War, when the military drained the nation's resources for more than 40 years.

Liberals often did not contest the military budgets—because they believed the communist threat to be real, because they chose to demonstrate that they weren't soft on communism, or because they wanted defense jobs for constituents. Thousands of corporate officials, as well as the Pentagon's congressional liaison staff applied formidable pressure to the nation's appropriations and legislative committees, which often gave precedence to military expenditures.

The competition between guns and butter was perhaps most conspicuous during the Vietnam War and immediately afterward. In that standoff, conservatives obtained cuts in social spending as their price for accepting higher taxes to fund the war, but liberals secured some major cuts in the defense budget. This skirmish was inconclusive. Advocates of guns over butter more than made up their losses

later, however, in the huge military buildup of the Reagan administration.[15]

It's true that military spending *now* consumes a smaller portion of the federal budget than it did in the 1950s. This is primarily because the budget has grown vastly larger, while military spending has remained relatively constant, allowing for inflation. Military spending has continued to place downward pressure on domestic spending, however, because it still consumes a large share of the discretionary, or controllable, portion of the federal budget that funds most domestic programs.

We should note, of course, that military spending, though it reduced rates of spending on social programs, also had social welfare functions. Low-income youth and people of color often enlisted because the military provided them with secure employment and training. The Veterans Administration became a massive health system for millions of poor veterans and their families. The defense industry provided economic growth and employment in many sections of the nation, and its leaders vigorously lobbied for the expansion of military contracts. Such welfare functions of the military had negative consequences as well. People of color often found when they left the military that the skills they had acquired did not easily transfer to jobs in the civilian economy. Moreover, the economies of many towns, cities, and regions became so dependent on military spending that they were vulnerable to economic hardship when the Cold War eased in the 1990s.

Institutional Factors

Jurisdictional Confusion The American welfare state has been characterized by jurisdictional confusion, particularly from the New Deal onward. Unlike most welfare states in Europe, where national social programs that were funded by central governments developed decades or centuries ago, the American welfare state evolved from the bottom upwards—that is, from local governments (in the colonial period and the early 19th century) to state governments (from the mid-19th century to the New Deal) to the federal government (from the New Deal onwards). Local sponsorship of social programs, such as workhouses, mental institutions, and mothers' pensions, was fostered by the Constitution, which failed to enumerate social policy as a function of the federal government, as well as by the near absence of federal tax revenues until World War II. From the New Deal onward, conservatives have generally opposed the assumption of large social policy roles by the federal government; they have sometimes demanded that federal programs be rescinded or given back to state and local governments.

There has been jurisdictional confusion not only within the public sector, but also between public and nongovernmental entities. Until the inception of the New Deal, for example, a significant share of financial assistance to impoverished people was handled by not-for-profit agencies, such as family service agencies, just as most adoptions were managed by private agencies. Indeed, as we have seen, many immigrants, whether Jewish, Japanese, or Italian, brought with them rich traditions of mutual assistance. They developed civic associations, mutual-aid organizations, and social welfare activities within their churches and temples. They hired persons from their own groups in their businesses, created agencies that specialized in services to members of their groups, and developed political organizations to obtain government jobs and contracts for their own people. These immigrant traditions complemented an extensive pattern of private philanthropy that, since the colonial era, had fostered a proliferation of private agencies and volunteer activities.[16]

These nongovernmental associations and agencies have been widely regarded as substitutes for publicly funded programs. Many Americans also favored corporate and tax benefits to public programs. Corporations provided fringe benefits such as pensions and life insurance by the 1920s—and these fringe benefits were supplemented by health insurance in the late 1940s and succeeding decades. (As many people discovered in the 1980s and 1990s, however, such largesse can be rescinded when corporate generosity lapses.) Unlike most European nations, moreover, Americans have liberally used tax concessions and loopholes to enable individuals to provide for their own needs,

without government intercession. For example, Independent Retirement Accounts (IRAs) serve as a substitute for government-administered pensions; tax deductions for home mortgages help Americans to own homes; and tax deductions reduce the financial burden of certain medical expenses and child care.

Many Americans have also favored letting private entrepreneurs and corporations implement publicly funded services through the use of so-called voucher programs. Medicare and Medicaid programs made extensive use of private physicians, for-profit nursing homes, and private hospitals, but the advocates of vouchers want to extend this principle enormously; they even advocate that, in place of the public school system, citizens should be given publicly funded vouchers that they could use to purchase education for their children from for-profit schools.

These jurisdictional rivalries have contributed to the meager size of many public programs in several ways. Until the New Deal, social reformers who wanted to expand federal policy roles contended with a phalanx of people who wanted to vest most social policy functions with private philanthropy or with local or state governments. Confusion over jurisdictional roles has often led to buck-passing where major policy roles are undertaken by no one because people cannot agree who should take the lead. While some people want the states to take the lead in providing health insurance in the 1990s, for example, others want the federal government to develop national health insurance. Complex negotiations about the appropriate roles of state and federal governments have stymied several social reforms, including welfare reforms, national health insurance, and national child care policies.

Social Factors

Racism and Prejudice   European societies are more homogeneous than the United States, because they have not experienced waves of immigration. Moreover, most include few, if any, people of color when compared to the combined population of African Americans, Asian Americans, Latinos, and Native Americans.

Attitudes to ethnic and racial outgroups have certainly contributed to the relatively slow growth of the American welfare state. Because of the persistence of racism and prejudice, Americans have been inclined to believe that unemployment, crime, and other social ills were concentrated within ethnic and racial outgroups rather than distributed throughout the population. Consequently, they have felt little need to develop comprehensive welfare institutions. At various times, Irish Americans, Italian Americans, Russian Jews, African Americans, Asian Americans, and Latinos have each served as the scapegoat for the nation's social ills.

Negative stereotypes of African Americans, Latinos, and Native Americans have been invoked by opponents of civil rights legislation and welfare programs. Even many abolitionists believed African Americans to be intrinsically lazy. Progressive leaders such as Theodore Roosevelt and Woodrow Wilson were deeply prejudiced against people of color. While a few African Americans were appointed as high-level advisors to New Deal programs, and millions benefited from them, Roosevelt did not support antilynching and civil rights legislation. John Kennedy did not support civil rights legislation until the mounting pattern of violence in the South forced his hand. Republican and Democratic leaders conspicuously failed to seek far-reaching policies to help inner-city residents, who were disproportionately members of racial outgroups.

In addition to prejudice against people of color and women, prejudice against low-income persons —that is, classism—has often inhibited social reforms. In 19th century England, Malthus and many theorists contended that persons in the lower class were brutish creatures given to procreation, crime, and alcoholism. In the United States, likewise, Benjamin Franklin argued that "it seems to be a law of nature, that the poor should be to a certain degree improvident, that there may always be some to fulfill the most servile, the most sordid, and the most ignoble offices in the community."[17] In the Gilded Age, animosity toward unemployed

paupers, who were reviled as subhuman, was extended to all poor persons, who were sometimes believed to possess inferior genes. Americans have long been inclined to believe that the economic status of poor Americans may be attributed to their cultural predispositions. Over the years, the terms used have changed: Writers in the 1840s contended that poor persons were lazy and shiftless; social scientists in the 1960s described them as "unable to defer gratification" and "present-oriented."[18]

Prejudices against other groups have similarly impeded the development of the American welfare state. Sexism hindered the development of family-planning, day-care, and affirmative action programs; prejudice against mental patients slowed the growth of expenditures for a range of community services, such as halfway houses; homophobia delayed a social response to discrimination against gay men and lesbians and to the AIDS epidemic; and ageism delayed the development of humanitarian community-based alternatives to nursing homes, as well as the funding of policies for chronic medical conditions.

Politicians have used prejudice against outgroups to their own advantage. In election campaigns, conservatives invoke racism and sexism to inflame opposition to social programs among white male Americans, particularly in the lower and lower-middle classes. Hoping to draw these voters from the Democratic party, many Republican strategists over the past 30 years have sought to associate social programs and taxes with persons of color—even though most users of most social programs are predominantly white—and with Democratic social reformers. As part of this strategy, Republicans attacked affirmative action as an unfair policy that takes jobs from white males and gives them to persons of color and to women. This approach worked brilliantly; it produced such massive defections from the Democratic party that Republicans were able to win presidential elections in 1968, 1972, 1980, 1984, and 1988—and to win control of both houses of Congress in 1994.[19]

Looking back over American history, we see that Southern white politicians often sought to turn poor white Southerners against African Americans in the colonial period and during Reconstruction;

FIGURE 13.1   Recency of the American welfare state

that many white Americans distrusted immigrants in the progressive era; and that many Southern whites resented the use of social programs by African Americans in the New Deal. In the progressive era, competition between whites and African Americans in large cities like Chicago sparked a white backlash that culminated in race riots in 1919. George Wallace, the governor of Alabama, campaigned for the presidency in the late 1960s and early 1970s by inflaming whites against Great Society social programs and affirmative action. White Americans in the mid-19th century believed that poorhouses were exclusively used by immigrants, just as they believe today, in defiance of the facts, that recipients of AFDC, Food Stamps, and other programs are largely African Americans.

White Americans' resentments against the beneficiaries of social programs have few parallels in European nations. While some middle- and upper-class Europeans have criticized people who use social programs, these criticisms have lacked a *racial* dimension, because most Europeans are white. Moreover, because European social programs are relatively universal, the welfare state is regarded as belonging to the entire nation rather than to specific subgroups.

The Sequence of Events

The Late Development of the American Welfare State
When discussing the history of the American welfare state, a central fact is apparent: It emerged relatively recently, in the New Deal era (Figure 13.1). (As we argued in Chapter 5, Civil War pensions did not breach the American tradition of not vesting the federal government with social policy functions.) In many European nations, by contrast, an array of generous national

programs—such as health insurance, old-age pensions, housing programs, and unemployment benefits—were already well established by the 1930s. After World War II, moreover, most European governments presided over a vast expansion of social spending, such as the Beveridge plan in Great Britain, whereas in the United States social spending actually fell below New Deal levels. Most of the major programs of the U.S. welfare state were not enacted until the 1960s and 1970s.

This late development of the American welfare state contributed to its reluctance in several ways. Traditionally opposed to a significant social welfare role for the federal government, Americans would not support a generous welfare state until they learned that social programs could benefit a wide range of citizens. As we see, this learning process began relatively late in the nation's history.

The late development of the American welfare state also helps to explain the intensity of conservative opposition to it. From their perspective, the welfare state is an intruder on a society that emphasized localism and state policies, as well as private philanthropy. By contrast, European conservatives, used to monarchies, centralized government, and centralized social policies, viewed their emerging welfare states in the 20th century as a continuation of governmental activities that had long been present.

The Military State Precedes the Welfare State
We have already discussed how military spending diverted funds from social spending from 1950 onward, but the *timing* of the military state's inception is also important. When the American welfare state finally emerged in its contemporary form in the 1960s, it had to compete with a military state already established by the large Cold War increases in military spending of the 1950s. The

military state *already* absorbed nearly three-fourths of the federal budget in the 1960s, so that it had first claim on the bulk of federal resources. While conservatives depict the Great Society as an era of runaway social spending, funding for its programs was relatively limited, partly because of prior budgetary commitments to military programs. Even after the Great Society programs were established, military and social programs competed for the limited discretionary component of the federal budget, that is, the annual appropriations of Congress. In eras of financial stringency, this component is vulnerable to cutbacks, unlike the entitlements, whose benefits are automatically funded each year. In this way, military spending continued to place strong downward pressure on a range of social programs into the 1990s. Imagine if the welfare state had preceded the military state, and military programs had to fight for funds that had already been largely committed to social programs!

Legal Factors

As we have noted in previous chapters, the Constitution slowed the growth of social programs in the United States by not explicitly defining social policy roles for the federal government. Coupled with a political philosophy that extolled local and state governments while criticizing the federal government, this constitutional silence enabled generations of politicians to stifle a federal welfare state until the New Deal. Even after the New Deal, conservative politicians tended to regard the federal welfare state as an intruder with no legal standing and attempted to return policy roles to local and state governments.

■ POLITICAL PROCESSES

Whatever the contribution of contextual forces, the reluctance of the American welfare state has also depended on political processes, as expressed in the policy decisions of local, state, and federal legislators.

The Absence of a Powerful Radical Tradition

The working class has the most to gain from the development of pension, welfare, work inspection, factory regulation, and other social programs, because its members are most subject to economic uncertainty, poverty, and exploitation by employers. Welfare states are therefore likely to grow most rapidly in those nations where the working class is organized to demand the enactment of social programs and regulations and where radical ideology, such as socialism, promotes class struggle and the expansion of the welfare state. Indeed, radical ideology served two functions in European societies. First, it emphasized the need to develop programs and policies that would assist the working class. Second, it emphasized common or collective needs of the whole society—for example, public health measures and old-age pensions. Both functions enhanced the expansion of the welfare state.

While many conservatives in Europe supported the expansion of the welfare state, the primary impetus generally came from leftist parties. Socialist and labor parties were remarkably effective in national elections in the late 1940s, 1950s, and 1960s. These class-based parties had large constituencies, often held power, *and* possessed an ideology—in particular, socialism—supportive of large welfare states.

At first glance, the U.S. Democratic party would seem analogous to these European leftist parties: It represented a significant segment of less affluent people, held significant power in the decades after World War II, and subscribed to a relatively liberal ideology. This American party was different from its European counterparts in several ways, however. Not least, it included a major wing that was decidedly conservative—the Southern Democrats, whose threats to vote Republican often forced concessions from Democratic leaders in Congress. Moreover, Democratic ideology was not as leftist as that of many European parties, which openly endorsed socialist ideas. Whereas the political base of the European leftist parties was the trade union movement, which militantly favored the expansion of the welfare state, American unions, with important exceptions, focused on measures relating to their own legal, collective-bargaining powers.

The Democratic leaders also had to contend with the Republican leaders, who were more strongly opposed to social reforms than were their counterparts in Europe. Whereas Republican leaders liked to tar Democrats as tax-and-spend reformers, many European conservatives, used to centuries of large central governments, supported social reforms; for example, Benjamin Disraeli, the 19th century English conservative, believed that the affluent classes bore a responsibility to advance the welfare of the nation and of the lower classes.

Nor did the Democratic leaders pursue policies that enabled the nation to munificently fund social programs. They often supported large tax cuts; for example, the huge tax cut of 1964 depleted government revenues just as Lyndon Johnson was initiating the Great Society. And they supported large military expenditures during the Cold War, often without even pondering their implications for the domestic budget.

Americans have not lacked for social protest or radical movements. Utopian theorists favored the development of communal villages in the 19th century; legions of radical workers engaged in strikes and organizing in the 19th and 20th centuries; and radical organizations (such as the Industrial Workers of the World, the Socialist party, and the Communist party) were active in the progressive and New Deal eras. As compared to European societies, however, working-class protest and radical ideologies were weak.[20]

In the absence of a working-class movement, advocacy organizations for outgroups provided considerable impetus for reform. In eras when the federal government was relatively weak, outgroups found it hard to develop policy changes in conservative state and local legislatures, which were often dominated by agricultural and business interests. Political organizing was particularly hard when women and persons of color were denied suffrage

and civil rights. When outgroup mobilization accelerated in the 1960s and early 1970s, however, insurgent leaders were able to place considerable pressure on legislators and high-level officials. Nevertheless, social reform is less likely, as a rule, in response to pressure from specific outgroups than under pressure from an organized social class, which was common in European nations under the aegis of Labor, Socialist, and Communist parties. Moreover, it was difficult to build large coalitions of different outgroups, and so social reform in the United States was fragmented. Such coalitions must withstand tensions between their constituent groups—for example, competition for scarce jobs between African Americans and women in the decades after the 1960s, conflicts between African Americans and Latinos in the Southwest, and uneasiness between heterosexual women and lesbians in the feminist movement.

Encountering widespread discrimination, the various outgroups often focused their political efforts toward gaining *rights* for their members. Civil rights activists in the 1950s and early 1960s sought to erase Jim Crow laws; Latinos sought collective-bargaining powers for field workers; Asian Americans fought to eradicate laws that limited their rights to own land earlier in the century; and feminists sought to eradicate discrimination against themselves in education, employment, and medical settings. We do not mean to criticize the emphasis on civil rights, because each of the outgroups experienced profound prejudice and discriminatory policies, but this focus, however necessary, may have detracted from efforts to obtain national health insurance, day care, more munificent job-training programs, and other social programs.

The development of working-class power in the United States was complicated by the successive waves of immigration and by the internal migration to Northern cities. Immigrant groups spoke different languages and established their own communities and political organizations. Conflict sometimes erupted, as their members competed for jobs and local political offices.[21]

Another complicating factor is that many American workers did not identify strongly with their social class. In a nation that has strongly favored upward mobility, many Americans wanted to join the middle class, in contrast to European traditions of working-class solidarity. In the colonial period, indentured servants and immigrants aspired to own their own land or to start new businesses. In the 19th century, many working-class persons aspired to obtain gold, land, or wealth through hard work and luck. More recently, many blue-collar workers have aspired to and gained the trappings of suburban life, complete with two cars and home ownership. Seeking upward mobility, American workers have seldom pursued governmental programs to advance the interests of the working class.

In the absence of a powerful radical tradition in the United States, political compromises have been fashioned between moderate and conservative politicians. When Franklin Roosevelt and John Kennedy wrote their tax and social legislation, they were unconcerned about the views of radicals; rather, they were afraid that a coalition of Republicans and conservative Democrats would scuttle their domestic legislation. Had radicals also been part of the negotiating process, major legislation might have been more redistributive, made fewer concessions to the rights of states, and been broader in scope.

In the absence of class-based politics, interest groups have assumed far more importance in the United States than in Europe. Unfortunately for citizens seeking relief from social problems, the most powerful interest groups tend to represent corporations and conservatives, whose needs have been disproportionally represented in the negotiating process.[22]

Nonvoters

Voting rates in the United States have long been lower than in European nations. Significantly, nonvoters are predominantly from low-income groups —the very persons whose interests would be served by social programs. This group is so large that it could aptly be called the party of nonvoters. Social scientists differ in their explanations of the size of this group: Some emphasize procedural barriers to registration and voting, which have been slightly eased by recent policy enactments; others believe that low-income Americans are even more cynical about American politics than are middle-class citizens. Believing the deck is stacked against them and that private interests, corporations, and affluent Americans dominate politics, many decide that their votes count for nothing.[23]

The Power of American Conservatives

American conservatives have fought social reforms because such reforms required increases in taxation, enlarged the federal government, interfered with local prerogatives, equalized economic and social conditions, or ran counter to the economic interests of corporations. Conservative defense of the status quo had its golden era in the United States in the 19th century, but its proponents possessed extraordinary power even during the liberal reform periods of the progressive, New Deal, and Great Society eras, because they could meld the power of the Republican party with conservative Southern Democrats.

American conservatism provided a more devastating resistance to the development of social reforms than did European conservatism. European conservatives had helped construct the strong monarchies and central governments of European nations from the 16th through the 19th centuries because they wished to facilitate national economic planning; preserve their own prerogatives; place controls and regulations on industrialists and bankers, whom they sometimes regarded as rivals; or advance their paternalistic traditions in helping the downtrodden. Even when conservatives supported a central government to quell social uprisings, they enhanced its power and hence its ability to finance and administer social programs. By contrast, American conservatives obtained their ideology not from the traditions of the landed aristocracy but from theorists like John Locke. Whereas European aristocrats often used government to perpetuate their paternal status, American conservatives wanted to obliterate government, except as it specifically helped corporations, facilitated economic growth, and served national defense.

In Europe, there was often tension between the aristocracy and industrialists. American industrialists, however, had no serious competitors in local and national governments in the Gilded Age. Taxes, tariffs, and subsidies were devised to advance their interests. Their power was gradually diminished in the 20th century, as unions, reformers, and citizens demanded various regulations, but corporate lobbying efforts and campaign contributions have made them powerful political forces. Corporations have not always opposed the expansion of the welfare state, but organizations like the U.S. Chamber of Commerce and the National Association of Manufacturers have consistently fought proposals that would significantly increase government welfare expenditures or subvert their corporate interests.

Moral Crusades

Although the term *crusades* may seem melodramatic, it describes the fervor of many temperance, antidrug, anti-obscenity, antigay, anticrime, and anti-abortion projects (see Figure 13.2). Throughout American history, determined reformers have expended enormous effort in trying to eradicate immoral behavior, whether by prohibiting it or by engaging in public education. These crusades have diverted attention from other kinds of social reforms and have often exacerbated discrimination against persons whose personal lifestyle choices were publicly condemned.[24]

Preoccupation with public morality has often focused on poor persons and racial and ethnic groups. Moralists in different eras believed that poor persons' values prompted them to be lazy, to engage in crime, or to have limited horizons—proclivities that were presumed to cause their poverty. Moral reforms—the Sunday School movement, antipauperism projects, efforts of the charity organization societies, some settlement houses of the progressive movement, and some service programs of the Great Society—offered middle-class models of behavior, provided surveillance, and sought to discipline, to convert, or to teach frugality and morality to the poor. This portrayal of paupers as amoral, shiftless, criminal, and lazy has hindered

efforts to provide them with resources, jobs, education, housing, and tax concessions.

In the contemporary era, the efforts of the Christian Coalition and kindred groups have focused on lifestyle issues, such as restricting the rights of gay men and lesbians, limiting women's access to abortions, obtaining prayers in public schools, fighting programs to give sex education and condoms to youth, and opposing efforts to prevent the spread of AIDS through distribution of sterilized needles. Each of these projects, in turn, has required outgroups to develop protracted and difficult countercampaigns. In European societies, where such moral clashes are less common, reformers can pay more attention to advancing their agenda.

A Rigged System

Powerful interest groups and well-heeled contributors have exercised extraordinary influence over American elected officials, to the detriment of social reform. Despite recent efforts to limit their influence, wealthy people and corporations continue to shape policies by using numerous loopholes in campaign-funding legislation. Our discussion of the Gilded Age in Chapter 5 suggests that these contemporary phenomena have deep historical roots.

Within the legislative process, relatively conservative legislators possessed power far beyond their numbers during the crucial decades when the American federal welfare state was being constructed—from the 1930s until the mid-1970s. During these decades, the chairs of powerful Congressional committees were determined by seniority, a policy that gave legislators from the one-party South control of key committees. Many of the conservative features of New Deal and Great Society social programs stemmed from concessions that Democratic presidents were forced to make to appease these powerful legislators.

The relatively conservative nature of the South from the mid-1930s to the present has also given conservatives an advantage in the Congress. Ostensibly the liberal party, the Democratic Party has possessed a conservative Southern wing since the Civil War; the South initially voted Democratic in

FIGURE 13.2   "Right to lifers" seek to outlaw abortions in the 1980s

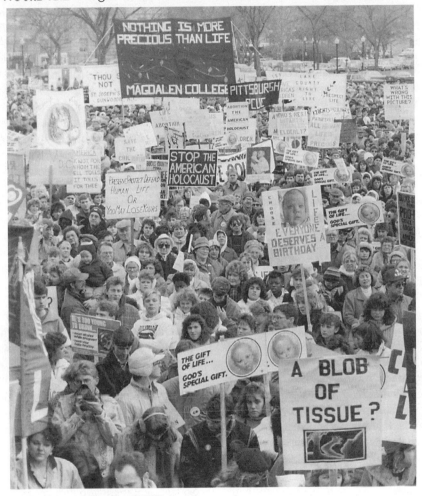

SOURCE: © Tim Clary/UPI/Bettmann

reprisal against Republicans' role in the Civil War and eventually by force of tradition. Had liberal Democrats *only* had to worry about Republicans, they would more easily have obtained social reforms, but they often contended with a marriage of ideological convenience between Southern Democrats and Republicans—a marriage that defeated many reforms and that forced the dilution of many others, even when Republicans were a minority party in Congress. Starting in the early 1970s and accelerating through the mid-1990s, Republicans bolstered their power, by winning increasing numbers of Southern votes and hence additional Congressional seats. While the South

was reliably conservative, liberals possessed no similar regional bastion. Even New England, perhaps the most liberal region, often supported conservative politicians in Congressional and presidential elections.

RELUCTANCE AS THE OUTCOME OF NUMEROUS FACTORS

Even a cursory examination of social policy history suggests that no single factor suffices to explain the reluctance of the American welfare state. Many theorists identify a piece of the puzzle and mistake it for the whole solution. Radical historians are correct in noting that the power of conservatives and corporations, unchecked by a forceful radical tradition, was often used to defeat or to dilute social reforms. In many cases, however, conservatives and corporations did not have to assume a dominant role, because the nation's culture, its powerful social welfare mythology, and the influence of racism and prejudice predisposed politicians not to develop social programs, to redistribute wealth, or to massively expand the welfare state. Conservatism has often been less than monolithic, as suggested by the division in the ranks of Republicans over Richard Nixon's social reforms. Some radical historians erroneously conclude that, because a radical left was often excluded from policy decisions, little conflict occurred in the United States over social welfare policy. In fact, American liberal reformers had to battle as hard as their radical counterparts in Europe to obtain even limited successes in a society that was relatively hostile to reform.[25]

Theorists who emphasize the impact of culture on the American response to social problems are correct in noting its deterrent effects on the development of the welfare state, but they often do not capture its complexity. We suggest that reformers in the United States have consistently been forced on the defensive by a multifaceted social welfare mythology, which enshrines the view that reform brings more harm than good. Combined with racism, prejudice, the idealization of limited government and unregulated markets, and patriotic sentiment, this mythology fueled powerful opposition to the development of social welfare policy. Important as this multifaceted culture was, however, it is not a sufficient explanation for the reluctant welfare state, because groups in Europe maintain similar beliefs. It was the absence of a powerful radical faction that gave these beliefs a peculiar importance in the United States, inasmuch as powerful opponents were not present to contest them.

The proponents of political or cultural explanations fail to devote enough attention to the effects of the American welfare state itself in deterring its own growth. The limited size of the American welfare state in the 19th and early 20th centuries was both a manifestation and a cause of American reluctance to fund a welfare state. A nation with a strong mythology against welfare had to be educated to the fallacies of that mythology by actually experiencing—in their families and communities—the beneficent effects of social programs. This educational process did not seriously begin until Americans benefited from social programs in the New Deal. Welfare states contribute to political pressures by encouraging the beneficiaries of their programs to demand expansion of existing programs, by stimulating reformers to emulate the successes of prior reformers, and by encouraging politicians to support the expansion of social programs as a means of obtaining votes. These educational and political effects of the American welfare state did not come into play until the nation developed its first set of federal programs in the New Deal, nearly 150 years after the birth of the republic.

When it finally emerged, the American welfare state was structured so as to deter widespread support. The eligibility of many means-tested programs was established at such low levels that white, blue-collar workers, who provided strong support for the expansion of European welfare states, found social programs irrelevant to their needs; indeed, they were inclined to believe that its programs were primarily used by people of color. Fewer universal programs existed in the United States. Funding and policy responsibilities were so dispersed that it was difficult for reformers to know where to apply pressure. Moreover, support for social reform was scattered among a large number of outgroups, whereas in Europe it was sustained by class-based, mass political parties such as the Labor, Socialist, and Communist parties.

To illustrate how different factors interact, let's discuss the Republicans' surprising successes from the early 1970s to the mid-1990s in attacking the scope of the American welfare state. We can begin with the relative conservativism of American workers, who have rarely sought far-reaching social reforms, even if labor organizations were relatively liberal in the decades following the New Deal. In the 1970s, 1980s, and 1990s, a second antireform factor was white backlash, itself a euphemism for racism; large numbers of white ethnic voters defected from the Democratic party to the Republican party. A third factor was the Republican tenet that doing good causes harm; accepting this premise, many ethnic voters came to believe that the generosity of American welfare programs had *caused* a precipitous rise in welfare rolls and the economic plight of African Americans. Finally, Congressional action in the 1980s and 1990s was profoundly constrained by powerful moral crusades of the Christian right, which gave Republicans additional grass-roots and campaign support. When discussing the recent attacks on the American welfare state, then, we need to link at least four factors: the absence of radical pressure from working-class Americans; racism; the belief that welfare programs do harm; and moral crusades.

SOME INTERPRETIVE CHALLENGES

It is not easy to decide which factors most shaped the reluctance of the American response to social problems in specific periods. Nor should we overstate the extent that Americans lagged behind Europeans.

Variations Between Eras and Issues

It is tempting to generalize about causes of reluctance across many eras and issues, but variations exist between them. Take the case of corporate power. When compared to the Gilded Age and the 1920s, the power of corporations to impede social enactments was somewhat weakened during the Great Depression, because of the hardships that citizens experienced and communicated to their legislators. A theory that emphasized the role of corporations in retarding social reform would have to admit that their power was not constant, but changed in different eras and with respect to different issues. Nor would corporate explanations be useful in periods of American history when the

nation was overwhelmingly agricultural—for example, the colonial era and the early part of the 19th century.

In similar fashion, racism has come to assume a particular vicious role in retarding the enactment of *federal* social policies only in the decades since the Great Society, even if its ugly presence in prior eras promoted punitive policies in local and state jurisdictions, such as Jim Crow Laws, the disenfranchisement of Latinos, the exclusion of Chinese immigrants, and the slaughter of Native Americans. (It also surfaced in the New Deal, when farm laborers were excluded from the protections of the Wagner Act and from Social Security.) As Edsall has cogently argued, it was only in the 1960s that conservatives fashioned their strategy of associating social programs with persons of color; this strategy conveniently overlooked the fact that most beneficiaries of social programs were white. Conservatives could not easily have inflamed white backlash in earlier decades, when the largest social programs were middle-class entitlements, principally Social Security and unemployment insurance —hardly good material for racial polarization, because they were extraordinarily popular with white Americans. Only with the creation of large means-tested programs in the 1960s, as well as the War on Poverty and eventually affirmative action, could conservatives contend that social programs were "for *those* people." At the federal level, then, racism has been a particularly powerful variable in promoting reluctance from the 1960s onward, although in the progressive era and the 1920s ethnic and racial prejudice was invoked to enact regressive immigration legislation.[26]

Nor is it easy to generalize across eras and issues about the role of cultural factors. Americans *do* generally accept the dominant welfare state mythology and want limited government. Yet Americans are also surprisingly supportive of many social policies and programs, even though they resist radical reforms. Once major social programs were enacted, many Americans resisted Republicans' efforts to dismantle them; in the 1980s and 1990s, for example, polls suggested that Americans wanted to retain substantial portions of the welfare state. In short, cultural orientations are not fixed in

INSERT 13.2   CRITICAL ANALYSIS:
DID THE ABSENCE OF FEUDAL INSTITUTIONS FOSTER RELUCTANCE?

It is interesting to speculate whether Americans' reluctance to spend funds on social programs stemmed, in part, from the absence of feudalism in the United States. Recall from Chapter 3 that immigrants to the colonies came from nations that had strong, but unraveling, feudal traditions, where mutual obligation and communal villages existed. Moreover, feudal society contained hierarchical classes or groups, from noblemen at the top to serfs at the bottom.

Discuss whether these ancient traditions and institutions—largely absent in the colonies—might have fostered support for social policies in far-removed contemporary periods in Europe. Consider whether concepts of mutual obligation in agricultural societies might have been resurrected in later industrial periods, when the urban working class replaced serfs. Might urban workers in European cities have possessed greater cohesion than American workers because their ancestors had been serfs in feudal times?

In discussing these possibilities, contrast European developments with the individualism implicit in land ownership and the frontier in the early years of the New World. Could this dispersed pattern of land ownership have fostered different values, which were transmitted to succeeding generations of Americans, even in distant industrial periods?

How certain can we be about our ultimate conclusions, whatever they might be?

concrete, but change through time as Americans observe and benefit from specific policies.

Gauging Missing Factors

In analyzing the American welfare state, we sometimes try to guess what missing factors accentuated reluctance. Take the absence of strong Labor, Socialist, and Communist parties in the United States, as compared to many European nations. On the basis of European history, we can surmise that such parties would have brought stronger pressure for social reform in the United States, but we do not know with certainty whether they would have dramatically transformed the politics of social policy, because we do not have the luxury of viewing their actual effects.

Barriers to Social Reform in Other Nations

Americans *have* lagged behind many industrialized nations in developing their welfare states, but we ought not to overstate the extent of the lag. While European nations possessed various smaller programs, the major burst of social reform occurred in the immediate aftermath of World War II. That was when Great Britain, for example, enacted the Beveridge plan, including national health insurance, national social services, and other economic reforms. Canada followed suit, as did many other European nations.

In short, despite pressure from relatively radical parties, many European nations were insensitive to the needs of their citizens until relatively recently. And their reforms were not immune from rollbacks, such as Margaret Thatcher's sweeping cuts in Britain's social programs in the 1980s or cuts made in Canadian social programs in the 1990s.

In discussing obstacles to social reforms in the United States, then, we should not imply that obstacles did not exist in other nations. Nor should we overstate the size of their welfare states prior to the end of World War II.

SOME REDEEMING FEATURES OF THE AMERICAN WELFARE STATE

We do not mean to imply that the American welfare state lacks redeeming qualities just because it is reluctant. The emphasis on individual rights in the U.S. Constitution has prompted outgroups to invest enormous energy in obtaining legal guarantees of their rights, with notable successes. People with disabilities provide an excellent example. Though Germany often provides better services to individuals with disabilities, it has not developed legislation that accords them protections against job discrimination.

American society has also made higher education widely available. Thanks to extraordinary funding of junior colleges and four-year colleges, about one-half of American youth seek schooling beyond high school, as against 10% in some European nations. (Budget cuts in the past few decades have put increasing pressure on American colleges, however.) Some critics of expansive postsecondary education contend that many American youth would be better served by vocational education and job training that outfitted them for specific positions in the job market. Those critics underestimate, however, the considerable benefits of postsecondary education, which has expanded the job opportunities for millions of American youth. In a world where unskilled positions are increasingly scarce, widespread participation in postsecondary education must be regarded as a remarkable American innovation.

Nor should we ignore the salutary benefits of nongovernmental organizations (NGOs). In nations such as Denmark, a tradition of not-for-profit organizations hardly exists. For most Danes, the publicly funded welfare state is the only source of assistance for their social needs. By contrast, Americans have emphasized the not-for-profit sector from the origins of the republic. An exponential increase in sectarian agencies in the 19th century and the early 20th century was followed by the development of nonsectarian agencies, including previously sectarian agencies that shed their religious origins. For example, many hospitals still possess the names given to them by their sectarian founders, such as Cedars Sinai Hospital, a Jewish hospital, but they have essentially become nonsectarian agencies that serve clients or patients regardless of their religion or ethnicity.

While we ought not to exaggerate their contributions, nongovernmental agencies have provided many benefits; they have, in effect, become part-

ners with the public welfare state. By administering public programs under contract or grants with government, they have provided a network of facilities that allow outreach into every American community. To Americans who feel stigmatized when they use public programs, they provide an acceptable alternative. Less restricted by public regulations and civil-service requirements, not-for-profit agencies have often pioneered innovative services. Millions of Americans have enriched their lives by volunteering in not-for-profit agencies—opportunities that would not exist if the nation relied exclusively on public services.

The viability of the not-for-profit sector has been threatened during the past two decades, however, by the reluctance of the American welfare state. As public funding of an array of programs has been reduced, not-for-profit agencies have increasingly lost their public contracts and grants. In turn, cuts in public programs have increased competition for the resources of philanthropical agencies and donors, so that hardpressed not-for-profits have found it difficult to offset cuts in public funds from other nongovernmental sources. The result, some critics argue, has been increasing reliance by not-for-profits on the fees and memberships of clients—a reliance that has made them increasingly inaccessible to low-income persons, who lack the resources to pay these charges.

The American welfare state also places greater reliance on for-profit agencies, both as freestanding entities that fund themselves from fees or memberships and as partners of public programs that receive government contracts and grants, as well as reimbursements from such public programs as Medicare. Policy analysts do not agree about the relative merits of for-profit agencies and the extent to which their role should expand. For-profit agencies dominate the nursing home industry; own a significant share of American hospitals and child-care centers; own a significant share of American psychiatric hospitals and substance-abuse programs; and have even entered such areas as prison administration. Deriding the inefficiencies of public programs such as schools, some people want the role of for-profit agencies to be vastly increased through the use of vouchers that allow citizens to select services from competing (and frequently for-profit) agencies.

It is beyond our scope to analyze the relative merits of for-profit agencies in detail. Some provide innovative, high-quality services; others try to increase their profits by making excessive cuts in their programs, as illustrated by poor-quality nursing homes. Some critics see them as profit-maximizing entities that actually *increase* the costs of services, by diverting resources to advertising and to owners' profits, and point out that they often locate their facilities only in areas where fee-paying clients exist, such as suburban communities. Many defenders of for-profits contend, however, that market competition forces them to provide services that are responsive to consumers' needs—and some argue that it is virtually impossible to distinguish the services of for-profits and not-for-profits, which themselves try to maximize their income from fees and from efficiencies.

Curiously, the reluctance of the American welfare state may increase the role of for-profits, which can raise capital from private sources—for example, from issuance of stock and from investors' funds—whereas not-for-profits must rely on increasingly scarce donors and public contracts to accumulate resources. In some cases, funding cuts in the public sector also increase the role of for-profits by enabling them to purchase failing not-for-profit hospitals and other agencies.

FROM DETERMINISM TO SOCIAL ACTION

That policies are shaped by contextual and political tendencies ought not to suggest, of course, that they are *determined* by them. In the last analysis, people—whether legislators, advocates, presidents, jurists, or government officials—make policies. Once aware of the influence of contextual and political factors on decision makers' policy choices individuals have to decide which policies are meritorious and which are not—and then try to change those policies that they dislike. As we discuss in

Chapter 14, analysis of the reluctant welfare state can prompt us to engage in social reform ourselves.

NOTES

1. The term *reluctant welfare state* was coined by Harold Wilensky and Charles Lebeaux, *Industrial Society and Social Welfare* (New York: Free Press, 1965), pp. xii–xxv.

2. David Stockman, *The Triumph of Politics* (New York: Harper & Row, 1986), p. 392.

3. Mary Walsh, "Germany's Reckoning," *Los Angeles Times* (February 25, 1996), D1.

4. Ibid.; Joel Blau, "Why the United States Is Not Sweden," *Journal of Progressive Human Services,* 4 (1993), 1–16.

5. Patricia Evans, "Targeting Single Mothers for Employment: Comparisons from the United States, Britain and Canada," *Social Service Review,* 55 (September 1992), 378–398.

6. Ibid.

7. William Julius Wilson, "Studying Inner City Dislocations: The Challenge of Public Policy Research," *American Sociological Review,* 56 (February 1991), 1–4.

8. Theda Skocpol, *Social Policy in the United States: Future Possibilities in Historical Perspective* (Princeton, N.J.: Princeton University Press, 1995), pp. 11–36, 78–86; Louis Hartz, *The Liberal Tradition in America* (New York: Harcourt, Brace, 1955); Michael Shalev, "The Social Democratic Model and Beyond: Two Generations of Comparative Research on the Welfare State," *Comparative Social Research,* 6 (1983), 315–351; Thomas Edsall, *Chain Reaction: The Impact of Race, Rights, and Taxes on American Politics* (New York: W. W. Norton, 1991); and Edward Berkowitz and Kim McQuaid, *Creating the Welfare State: The Political Economy of Twentieth-Century Reform* (New York: Praeger, 1980).

9. Quoted in June Axinn and Herman Levin, *Social Welfare: A History of the American Response to Need* (New York: Dodd Mead, 1975), p. 29.

10. Lester Thurow, *Zero-Sum Society* (New York: Basic Books, 1980), pp. 1–9, 155–190.

11. *New York Times* (October 22, 1995), xiii-NJ, 11.

12. For the classic statement of this position, see Milton Friedman, *Capitalism and Freedom* (Chicago: University of Chicago Press, 1962).

13. John Chubb, "Federalism and the Bias for Centralization." In John Chubb and Paul Peterson, eds., *The New Direction in American Politics* (Washington, D.C.: Brookings Institution, 1985), pp. 292–301.

14. Quoted in Axinn and Levin, *Social Welfare,* p. 30.

15. For a discussion of lobbying pressure by the Pentagon and corporations, see James Fallows, *National Defense* (New York: Random House, 1981).

16. For a summary of historical research on the development of mutual-aid and self-help projects, see Clarke Chambers, "Toward a Redefinition of Welfare History," *Journal of American History,* 73:2 (September 1986), 407–433.

17. Quoted in Axinn and Levin, *Social Welfare,* p. 30.

18. Orientations toward the poor in the 1960s and the 19th century are compared by Steven Schlossman, "The 'Culture of Poverty' in Ante-Bellum Social Thought," *Science and Society,* 38:1 (Spring 1974), 150–166.

19. Edsall, *Chain Reaction.*

20. Hartz, *The Liberal Tradition,* pp. 134–136, 266–270.

21. Lizabeth Cohen, *Making a New Deal: Industrial Workers in Chicago, 1919–1939* (New York: Cambridge University Press, 1990), pp. 53–98.

22. Geoffrey Hodgson, *America in Our Time* (Garden City, N.Y.: Doubleday, 1976), pp. 247, 484–490.

23. Frances Fox Piven and Richard Cloward, *Why Americans Don't Vote* (New York: Pantheon Books, 1988).

24. No one better captures the fervor of moral crusades than Paul Boyer, *Urban Masses and Moral Order in America, 1820–1920* (Cambridge, Mass.: Harvard University Press, 1978).

25. David Brody, *Workers in Industrial America: Essays on the Twentieth-Century Struggle* (New York: Oxford University Press, 1980), p. 127.

26. Edsall, *Chain Reaction.*

Policy Perspectives:
Past, Present, and Future

We discuss in this chapter whether the development of an American welfare state during and after the New Deal has made our society a better place, even considering the imperfections of specific policies. After arguing that the welfare state has, on balance, improved our condition, we suggest that a new generation of policy activists needs to build on the reform tradition in the United States.

THE CASE AGAINST THE WELFARE STATE

Conservatives often contend that the American welfare state has failed because social problems persist. At first glance, their assertions possess merit, because society today seems as bedeviled by social problems as at any time in the past. Growing inequality in the United States during the 1980s and 1990s is reminiscent of economic conditions in the Gilded Age, when wide discrepancies in wealth existed and the nation possessed only a small middle class. In the 1950s and 1960s, the United States enjoyed an economic advantage over foreign nations whose economies were devastated in World War II but, by the mid-1970s, many other nations had become fully competitive, and many Americans in such industries as steel and automobiles were thrown out of work. Moreover, many American corporations aggravated unemployment by relocating plants to low-wage nations. With the end of the Cold War in the late 1980s, many areas in the United States lost defense-related jobs. While economic growth continued throughout the decades after the 1960s, its benefits increasingly went to affluent people, as the wages and benefits of working-class Americans—and also some middle-class Americans—diminished.

By the mid-1990s, older Americans could look for assistance to an array of programs, but they still had to contend with worrying fiscal and social predicaments. As extended families gave way to nuclear families, in a long process extending from the colonial period onward, many older people had to fend for themselves when they retired. While the Medicare program in 1965 provided assistance for older peoples' health expenses, it did not fund chronic health conditions or long-term care. Where many older persons in the 19th century could only obtain care by entering poorhouses or mental institutions, their counterparts in the mid-1990s had to deplete their life savings to get access to the means-tested Medicaid program, which reimbursed nursing home care. As had been true prior to the 1960s, there were large inequalities in older persons' access to retirement communities, nursing homes, and medical care in the 1990s. Life was much easier for those with abundant savings, assets like homes, and pension plans.

In developments reminiscent of the Great Depression and also of the 19th century, hundreds of thousands of Americans lived on the streets in the 1980s and 1990s. Their numbers included single persons and families who could not afford housing, deinstitutionalized mental patients, and individuals with substance-abuse problems. Although many private agencies rose to the challenge, major federal funding of integrated services for homeless people had just emerged in 1995. Cuts in the funding of federal housing-subsidy programs and of community mental health centers exacerbated their problems.

Nor had women markedly improved their economic condition in American society. While many women entered the workforce during and after World War II and made strides in entering professions and occupations that had been closed to them in prior eras, discrepancies between male and female salaries and wages remained relatively constant in the decades after the 1960s.

Social policy clearly has not eradicated many kinds of problems. Moreover, some problems were arguably worse in the 1990s than in some earlier portions of American history. Most observers agreed that the word *crisis* accurately described the condition of the nation's families. The numbers of families with two parents had plummeted in the decades after the 1960s. While single-headed families can provide a salutory environment for children, they often confront daunting economic, health-care, and child care obstacles in a society that fails to provide adequate supportive programs. Millions of single parents were forced to take low-wage jobs, were unable to afford decent housing, and were mired in poverty.

Problems of family violence included wife abuse, child abuse, and elder abuse. We do not know whether these problems have increased in recent decades, because many victims failed to report their plight in prior eras and poor records were kept, some experts surmise that family violence has escalated in recent decades. Federal planners had hoped that federal subsidies to states would encourage adoptions, but they had little effect in decreasing the number of children and adolescents who rotated between foster care placements. Here, too, we do not know if the neglect and abuse of children has increased since many cases were (and are) unreported, and the practices of child welfare workers, such as their propensity to remove children from biological parents, has varied between jurisdictions and historical eras. But the problem of abuse and neglect had reached remarkable proportions by the late 1970s when 500,000 children were in foster care. By 1983, following the enactment of federal legislation, that figure fell to 251,000 children. Experts predicted, however, that the number of children would again exceed 500,000 children by the year 2000, partly because few people want to adopt teenagers, because nearly 300,000 infants are born to addicted parents, or because African American and Latino adoptive parents are difficult to recruit.

Teenagers often encountered hardships that were arguably even more formidable than preceding generations'. Like adolescents in the middle of the 19th century, they faced uncertain job prospects. High rates of substance abuse existed among them. Liberated from restrictions on sexuality, they were exposed to AIDS and other sexually transmitted diseases.

Less affluent African Americans in inner cities live in conditions in the 1990s that are even more brutish than those encountered by the generations of Irish, Italian, Eastern European, Russian, Jewish, and other immigrants who preceded them. While European immigrants encountered discrimination, it was not *racially* based. Nor were they encircled by relatively affluent suburbs, where jobs were increasingly located.

THE CASE FOR THE WELFARE STATE

While conservatives correctly argue that social problems persist despite the existence of the American welfare state, they fail to consider that many problems would be even worse if Americans had not developed social policies. Assume, for example, that Medicaid had not been enacted in the mid-1960s. Without Medicaid, the health care needs of low-income populations, already seriously underserved by public clinics, would have reached catastrophic proportions, because local and state governments lacked the resources to address them. Older citizens who had exhausted their Medicare benefits would have been unable to rely on the Medicaid program; thus, hundreds of thousands of them would have been forced into nursing homes even worse than those they encountered in the 1970s and succeeding decades. Persons with AIDS, often financially devastated by the expense of medical procedures, would have received no services unless physicians and hospitals had donated them.

Indeed, we can proceed through each of the major enactments of the 1960s and succeeding decades and render a similar prognosis. Assume, for example, that Medicaid, SSI, Food Stamps, *and* AFDC did not exist. Would not this erasure of social enactments lead to a homeless population many times the size of that existing in the 1980s and 1990s? Without these programs, what would have happened to economic inequality in the United States, which is already far greater than in European nations, Canada, and Japan?

Some conservatives would retort, "But would not the reductions in government spending allow further tax reductions and thus increase the funds available for investment and consumption? And would not greater investment and consumption fuel higher rates of economic growth, which would ultimately help low-income populations to find work?" The historical record provides little evidence that economic growth follows reductions in social spending. Affluent people use excess cash in many ways; they may make such nonproductive expenditures as luxury cars, second homes, and expensive vacations, or invest their funds abroad rather than in the United States. Moreover, expenditures on social programs themselves produce positive economic effects. Programs such as Medicare and Medicaid have funded hundreds of thousands of jobs and, by increasing the resources of

their beneficiaries, vastly increased consumption not only by the beneficiaries themselves but also by relatives who might otherwise have had to fund the beneficiaries' medical services.

We ought not to concede, moreover, that *all* problems have become more severe in recent decades. Considerable progress has been made, for example, in addressing poverty among elderly persons; challenges to the civil rights of outgroups; unemployment and lack of services for persons with disabilities; malnutrition; the health needs of certain groups in the population, such as persons with kidney failure; the preschool needs of low-income children; and psychological conditions such as depression. Many persons of color markedly improved their economic and social situation in the decades following the 1960s; there are now significant numbers of middle-class and upper-middle-class African Americans and Latinos, partly as a result of affirmative action and civil rights laws prohibiting job-related discrimination. Children in Head Start classes often show educational gains years after their enrollment.

Nor should we ignore the short-term humanitarian function of social programs. Even when they do not solve social problems, they provide resources and support to people who are experiencing unemployment, catastrophic health conditions, or mental trauma, for example. The much-maligned AFDC program has provided resources to millions of women in the wake of divorces or separations, when they and their children could not survive without them.

In many cases, problems that were seldom recognized in prior eras were publicized and addressed by new policies. Rape, child abuse, Alzheimer's disease, spousal abuse, reading and learning disorders, discrimination against gay men and lesbians, and the needs of people with disabilities have existed throughout American history, but have come to be widely recognized as important problems only recently. Victims of rape, for example, have often been subjected to punitive treatment, such as imputations of blame by judges and doctors. Children with developmental disabilities were routinely placed in institutions in the 1950s, in contrast to efforts to mainstream them in schools, communities, and employment in the 1990s. Children with reading difficulties were routinely discontinued from school in the 1950s, whereas they often receive special services in the 1990s. Persons with Alzheimer's disease in the 1950s were rarely diagnosed and seldom received day treatment and other services.

Government policies both emanated from heightened public awareness of these problems *and* contributed to the public's knowledge of them, as individuals saw the benefits of social programs to themselves, their relatives, or their friends. Moreover, the existence of social programs has often raised public expectations about the rights and needs of specific groups in the population. Whereas Americans in 1950 commonly assumed, for example, that paraplegics would be bed-ridden and institutionalized, many Americans in the 1990s were aware of these individuals' rights and capabilities, such as access to mechanized wheelchairs, independent living arrangements, occupational therapy, and employment.

We can reasonably argue that the nation would have suffered harm in the absence of reforms enacted in the progressive era, the New Deal, and the Great Society, expansions of civil rights and entitlements in the 1970s, or specific reforms of the 1980s and 1990s like the child care and development block grant of 1990. We can hardly imagine what the United States would be like were it to return to social policies that prevailed at the beginning of the 20th century. American life has been profoundly changed by policy initiatives of various types. Let's consider the various categories.

- *Regulations* of many kinds and at all levels of government have restrained corporations, landlords, businesses, realtors, and restaurant owners from exposing the public to hazards and have kept wages above certain minimum levels.
- *Needs-meeting policies* have provided basic health and economic benefits to citizens who might otherwise starve, lack health care, or suffer unacceptable poverty.
- *Opportunity-enhancing policies* have helped citizens obtain education and training to allow them to enter the economic mainstream; such policies

include vocational education, Head Start, and teacher aides in schools with large concentrations of low-income children, as well as affirmative action, which has resulted in greater integration of the work force and more equal participation by women.

- *Social services,* such as mental-health and child welfare services, have sought to help citizens redress individual and familial pathology.
- *Referral and linkage programs,* such as case-management services, have helped citizens get assistance from social programs that address their needs.
- *Equality-enhancing policies* have targeted resources and services to specific populations that lag behind the rest of the population; examples include Medicaid, AFDC, Food Stamps, and progressive taxation.
- *Rights-conferring policies,* such as civil rights legislation and policies granting grievance procedures, seek to protect citizens from discrimination.
- *Public-improvement policies* benefit all citizens; they fund parks, public transportation, roads, bridges, and so on.
- *Economic development policies,* such as tax incentives and loans to inner-city businesses, promote economic growth.
- *Asset-accumulation policies,* such as income-tax deductions for mortgage payments, have disproportionately helped affluent Americans but often help less-affluent people, as well.

When the welfare state is defined broadly so as to include these many kinds of people-helping policies, its scope becomes clear; it assists every member of the population at many points during their lives. Affluent people take *their* welfare state for granted; they seldom recognize its effects on their lives nor question the efficacy of those benefits that they receive. Unfortunately, the programs and tax benefits that persons of lesser means receive are often attacked and cut, as occurred during the Reagan years and in the wake of the Republicans' 1994 election victories.

Of course, citizens in the latter portion of the 19th century *did* survive without most of these kinds of policies. Unlike Marvin Olasky, who contends that the latter portion of the 19th century was an idyllic, nearly utopian, period, however, most historians agree that citizens in this period were bedeviled by inequality, economic insecurity, epidemics, unsafe working conditions, food poisoning, unsafe housing conditions, rampant discrimination against persons of color and women, and many other social problems.[1]

If conditions in the late 19th century were so brutish, why did Americans tolerate them? While many factors contributed, we must partly implicate public expectations. Most citizens *expected* life to be hazardous and insecure, much as they expected epidemics to kill their children. Unemployed people expected to be placed in workhouses or to join soup-and-bread lines during recessions. Relatives of older people with senile dementia expected to place them in mental institutions or even workhouses—or to care for them at extraordinary personal sacrifice in their own homes. During hard times—or at any time for many poor people—people expected not to eat well. Persons of color could not even imagine that their descendants might live in a society without lynchings and segregated public facilities.

Even those who wanted social reforms knew they lived in a society where change would be difficult. Corporations and banks dominated the politics of the Gilded Age; they freely used their funds and power to attack social reforms and sought to defeat regulations that would diminish their autonomy. Lacking a federal income tax and a substantial civil service, Americans did not know that large programs could be funded or implemented.

While specific policies have often failed or had mixed results, the combined effects of social policies that have been enacted in recent American history have transformed the lives of Americans in positive ways. They have made life somewhat less insecure and unpredictable for many people—and have sometimes dramatically improved their lives by giving them rights, opportunities, protections, and benefits. It is easy to dwell on the shortcomings of specific social programs, while forgetting that many reforms have indisputably made American society more humane. Many contemporary Americans cannot remember and can hardly comprehend the institution of slavery, imprisonment for indebtedness, capital punishment for relatively minor crimes, poorhouses, 14-hour work days, unsafe working conditions, child labor, routine denial of civil rights and welfare benefits to people of color, lynchings of African Americans, race riots, flagrant violation of the legal rights of radicals, incarceration of persons who publicly discussed birth control, the routine firing of gay men and lesbians, widespread malnutrition, and the denial of education to persons with disabilities. Even this partial list suggests that American reformers have had surprising successes, though they sometimes had to work for generations to accomplish them.

Has the welfare state benefited Americans? As we have seen, no simple answer can be made. Extraordinary progress has been made on certain fronts, but older problems fester and are supplemented by new problems.

1. Social problems that have become worse include the plight of those people who live within many inner-city areas. African Americans in many cities lead more hazardous and difficult lives now that upwardly mobile members of their communities have emigrated to more affluent areas, jobs have moved into suburban locations and abroad, and drug dealing and crime have escalated. However, we can legitimately argue that some of these social problems would have become even worse had ameliorating policies not emerged.

2. Some social problems may not have gotten worse; we have simply become more aware of them. Reading and learning disorders belong in this category: We do not know their incidence in prior eras because they were largely unrecognized, but they are now widely recognized as serious problems. We cannot blame the welfare state for making these problems worse.

3. Some social problems have clearly been redressed by social policies. As one clear example, some flagrant violations of the civil rights of persons of color and of women have been diminished by civil rights legislation as well as changing social values.

4. Some new problems have emerged. For example, the AIDS epidemic represents a serious

health crisis; this disease probably migrated to the United States in the 1970s from Africa. The existence of the welfare state had nothing to do with the emergence of this problem. People with AIDS would certainly have had an even harder time coping if programs such as Medicaid had not existed.

5. In some cases, social problems have not changed, but we *believe* they have gotten worse because our expectations have changed. Take the case of drunk drivers. Large numbers of Americans have been killed in car accidents involving intoxicated drivers since the 1920s, but Americans have come to take this problem seriously only in recent decades, partly because of the determined advocacy of Mothers Against Drunk Driving (MADD).

6. New factors have aggravated some older problems. For example, unemployment has been increasing as a result of American corporations' practice of shifting operations to new facilities in low-wage countries since the 1970s. Here, too, we cannot hold the welfare state responsible for these changes. While American social programs and regulations have increased corporations' operating costs somewhat, wages in third-world nations would still be far lower than American wages even if the American welfare state were cut in half.

7. In some cases, social programs have been poorly administered, have wasted funds, and have even had negative consequences for their clientele. Some school districts, for example, have used federal education subsidies to provide educational services that are not innovative or culturally sensitive —or to help them fund bloated bureaucracies. When public programs *are* poorly administered, ineffective, or wasteful, we should try to improve them. But such programs hardly support the case that the welfare state should be scrapped or reduced in size.

◼ MISSED OPPORTUNITIES

Conservatives often overlook another possibility: that some social problems fester not because of the welfare state but because Americans have failed to construct ameliorating policies—or have failed to

fund existing policies sufficiently. The Gilded Age illustrates how, in the absence of work regulations and unemployment insurance, millions of Americans suffered work-disabling conditions and poverty. Americans in the Gilded Age were subject to a far higher rate of work disabilities than were their English counterparts, who enjoyed stronger protections.[2] The progressives enacted many salutory reforms, but failed to develop health insurance, unemployment insurance, and old-age pensions. Preoccupied with keeping unemployed people from starving, New Dealers failed to enact health insurance and many other programs that had to await the Great Society.

The failure of Americans to develop and fund innovative vocational programs provides an excellent example of missed opportunities. Both the Germans and the Japanese have developed sophisticated programs that place many of their high-school students in apprentice programs with industry, where they learn on-the-job skills and obtain certification in technical fields even before graduating. By contrast, American vocational programs often place students in fast-food or other low-skill jobs, so that they are unable to enter industry upon graduation. The Germans carry their job-training programs even further: They offer unemployed adults extended stays in vocational-training centers as a prelude to matching them with jobs across the nation.

Moreover, as conservatives rarely note, some social programs are ineffective in redressing specific problems *not* because they are intrinsically flawed, but because they are funded at excessively low levels. Take the case of child welfare departments in the 1990s. Confronting huge caseloads and the demands of crisis management, their staff often lack the time to work creatively with families who need intensive services. As Fabricant and Burghardt persuasively argue, many inner-city bureaucracies have been mortally wounded by successive budget cuts of the 1980s and 1990s; their staff are demoralized and overworked.[3]

As we have seen, we cannot argue that the United States has become a better place during the past decades, or even in this century, but we can reasonably argue that social policies have redressed some problems, raised our expectations with regard to others, and rendered some problems less severe than they would otherwise have been. Eliminating social policies would reduce society to a condition unacceptable to virtually all citizens, even the many affluent people who currently devote extraordinary energy to attacking the welfare state.

ADMITTING ERRORS

Intent upon fighting to preserve existing programs, social reformers fail to admit that some social programs have been misdirected. Meant to provide low-income persons with housing, the large public housing buildings that were constructed in most major cities in the 1950s and 1960s, for example, harmed many tenants by placing them in unwholesome, often segregated environments with few supportive services. Many of these buildings are currently being destroyed by the public authorities that built them.

When admitting errors, of course, we should realize that some of the faults of social programs stem from the self-serving actions of vested interests. The health-care system provides an excellent example. Groups like the American Medical Association fought for decades to preserve the autonomy and the incomes of physicians and hospitals; they would accede only to those public programs that incorporated policies acceptable to them. Concerned only with curative services for existing illness, they fashioned a health-care system with virtually no preventive programs. The failure of Medicare and Medicaid to prevent illness is partly due to defective provisions introduced in response to self-serving lobbying by special interests.

THE LIMITATIONS OF PUBLIC POLICY

While they correctly note that many social programs have flaws, conservatives rely on the false premise that *any* social programs can magically make major social problems disappear. As we have noted, social problems such as family violence and substance abuse have multiple, complex causes. These problems exist in every nation, regardless of the ideology of their leaders or the nature of their social programs. When viewed from the vantage point of history, social problems display a remarkable persistence, even in the face of technological advances and policy enactments. This must be due, in part, to persistence of the factors that cause them: for example, social and economic inequalities (which breed alienation, desperation, stress); lack of economic opportunities for unskilled people (which breeds unemployment, substance abuse, and crime); genetic factors (which promote certain diseases, particularly when coupled with poor diet and substance abuse); viruses (which bring new ailments such as AIDS, even as old ones persist); biology (which is responsible for degenerative diseases and new diseases like AIDS); corporate greed (which causes unsafe working conditions, pollution, and low wages); discrimination (which works to exclude specific populations from opportunities and jobs); family pathology (which underlies family violence and the problem of runaway youth); and individual pathology (which is associated with mental illness, suicide, and substance abuse). These various factors interact with one another, often in complex fashion, to cause specific problems. Substance abuse, such as alcoholism, often stems from the combined interaction of biology, corporate advertising, family pathology, individual pathology, and lack of economic opportunities. Social programs can provide much-needed assistance and even promote certain changes in cultural attitudes, but, even if they are well-conceived and well-funded, they often cannot eradicate major social problems.

Many social problems come from capitalism itself. Left to its own devices, capitalism does not necessarily provide economic equality or a living wage. As Kevin Phillips has superbly documented, economic inequality increased markedly during the 1980s, in a trend that has continued during the 1990s; some people now predict the near demise of the middle class.[4]

Nor can social programs magically change the

behaviors of individuals, families, and communities. Considerable research documents that students' achievement in schools hinges in considerable measure upon their families. Children who are not encouraged, or are even discouraged, by their parents are less likely to make educational progress, no matter how skilled their teachers. Innovative schools that enlist the help of parents often cannot obtain it. Health providers cannot force people to stop smoking or using other harmful drugs, nor can they force people to consume healthy diets or to exercise.

Nor are social programs likely to succeed in an inegalitarian society that possesses a huge population with inadequate resources. Those who face bleak economic prospects in the 1990s include single (mostly female) heads of households and their children; former factory workers forced into unemployment or low-wage service jobs; impoverished inner-city populations of racial outgroups; persons working at or near the minimum wage; and older citizens who lack pensions or who confront chronic medical conditions.

We cannot say with precision how many people develop *additional* social problems because of the desperation and alienation provoked by their bleak economic conditions. Despite the remarkable persistence and resilience of people in these groups, considerable evidence suggests that their economic status contributes to their problems. Unemployment greatly increases such problems as substance abuse, family violence, and mental illness. The vast majority of children in foster care come from low-income families, partly because economic desperation contributes to neglect as well as family violence. While discrimination within the court system contributes, economic circumstances must also help explain why American prison cells are largely inhabited by low-income African American males, who also experience high rates of substance abuse and deaths from homicides.

Our discussion suggests that social policies cannot be expected to miraculously solve major social problems. When conservatives contend that the American welfare state has failed because it has not solved problems like poverty and homelessness, they are arguing from a false premise: In the

real world, social policies do not eradicate social problems.

WOULD CONSERVATIVES' POLICIES SOLVE MAJOR SOCIAL PROBLEMS?

Suppose we accept conservatives' contention that social policies have generally failed. Would *their* policy alternatives be dramatically more successful? Would lower levels of social spending solve major social problems such as homelessness and poverty? Let's analyze some likely effects of five policies often supported by conservatives: reducing social spending; delegating most policy functions to state and local governments; privatizing social services; relying more heavily on private philanthropy; instituting deterrent policies for welfare recipients; and rewarding personal responsibility.

Reducing Social Spending

Some social programs *do* waste resources on unnecessary administrative staff—and some consumers make fraudulent use of programs' benefits. But the preponderant share of programs' costs go to benefits (in the case of benefit programs like Food Stamps and AFDC) or to salaries (in the case of service programs like mental-health and child welfare programs). While some adjustments and economies can be made, large spending cuts in social programs are usually achievable only by making deep cuts in benefits or in staff. Fraud rarely consumes a large share of social programs' costs.

Demands for cuts in program costs, then, often rest on an unrealistic assumption that huge savings can be achieved without sacrificing quality of services or the amounts of benefits. In the absence of major waste or fraud, this quest for huge savings often leads to poorer services and more meager benefits.

Nor does indiscriminate cost cutting address the *real* problems in human services, such as turf boundaries. Take the case of child welfare programs. Many critics contend that, to help families that neglect or abuse their children, it is not enough to rely on occasional visits from a child welfare worker. Rather, child welfare staff need to engage schools, courts, child guidance agencies, case managers, substance-abuse agencies, and job-training agencies in a collaborative effort. Slashing the budgets of child welfare agencies hardly promotes such collaboration—and may even impede it, by forcing overworked social workers to focus on crisis management.

Cuts seem most feasible in medical programs, such as Medicare and Medicaid, whose costs have escalated extremely rapidly; the United States expends greater resources on medical care than other nations do. However, cost cutters encounter formidable obstacles even when seeking to scale back the budgets of these programs. Their high costs partly stem from inefficiencies in the medical system as a whole—such as high fees charged by doctors and hospitals, the emphasis on curative rather than preventive services, and extraordinary use of costly medical procedures even in the last months of life. Large cuts in Medicaid and Medicare would not address these broader causes of the rise in medical spending and would often subject elderly and poor patients to less effective services. If their fees were dramatically cut, physicians and hospitals would increasingly refuse to serve Medicaid and Medicare beneficiaries, who would thus be forced into public hospitals and clinics, which are already underfunded by counties and municipalities. Overall spending for medical care in the United States must be reduced, but that calls for reform of the American medical system, rather than large cuts in publicly funded programs. Policy makers seeking to cut medical costs must remember that roughly 40 million Americans lack health insurance *or* access to Medicare and Medicaid. How can public funding of medical services be cut when so many people are currently not covered by public or private programs?

Cuts in specific programs sometimes cause increases in the costs of *other* programs. Thus, confronted with cuts in their Medicaid and Medicare reimbursements, providers raise fees on their other patients. Likewise, if we cut prenatal programs or

programs that provide food to young children and their mothers, we may find that costs of medical programs increase correspondingly.

Delegating Policy Responsibilities to State and Local Government

Some policy functions can usefully be delegated to local and state governments, which already assume major responsibility for public education and the correctional system. They share responsibility for many social programs with federal authorities; under the block-grant program enacted by the Nixon and Reagan administrations, federal authorities provide money to states for programs and impose relatively few stipulations on their administration. In the 1990s, even in programs where federal authorities have traditionally exercised strong policy roles, such as AFDC and Medicaid, the federal government has increasingly issued waivers that grant permission to states to devise their own programs.

Conservatives often want to carry delegation of policy roles to far greater levels. They sometimes imply that it will save vast sums of money or that it will strikingly improve the quality of programs. While state and local governments can sometimes achieve economies by deleting federal regulations, they often discover that most program costs are absorbed by benefits and salaries. Delegation, in short, often brings scant savings *unless* state and local governments cut the size of programs inherited from the federal government. Indeed, facing budget difficulties of their own and lacking the large revenues of the federal income tax, state and local governments often do cut benefits or services when granted exclusive responsibility for funding social service programs. The dangers of delegation are particularly marked when federal authorities fail to impose minimum standards, such as requirements that states provide certain basic services in their Medicaid programs or give certain protections to AFDC clients.

We should remember that the federal government took on funding and oversight roles in the Great Depression and the Great Society because states and localities lacked the resources for social programs. Unlike the federal government, states and localities often want to keep taxes at low levels, in order to stop corporations from fleeing to locations with lower tax rates. Given their reluctance to increase taxes and the considerable costs of prisons and educational programs, states are unlikely to fund programs for relatively powerless populations like single mothers, unless federal requirements force them to do so.

Privatizing Social Services

Many conservatives want to place the administration of social services in the hands of for-profit corporations. Some for-profit corporations provide exemplary administration of social programs and even cut costs by management techniques drawn from private industry. Yet privatization carries dangers of its own. Unlike public and not-for-profit agencies, for-profit corporations divert funds as profits to owners and stockholders—profits that add costs to social programs. To maximize profits, corporations sometimes achieve efficiencies by cutting services to clients, hiring untrained staff, and providing no fringe benefits to staff. Alternatively, they may exclude people with serious problems from their services—whether by discriminating against them or by locating their services in relatively affluent areas.

Of course, some not-for-profit agencies provide inferior services—and many for-profit agencies and corporations *do* provide quality services. *Whenever* the government contracts with nongovernmental agencies, it needs to establish clear standards that are carefully monitored.

Seeking Nongovernmental Substitutes for Publicly Funded Programs

Conservatives often suggest that private philanthropy, volunteers, and communities can serve as substitutes for government-funded social programs. These nongovernmental entities already intertwine with governmental programs extensively—far more than in many European nations. Not-for-profit agencies usually receive more than half of their budgets from the government. Volunteers work for not-for-profit agencies, as well as some public ones. Private philanthropy augments public funding in many social agencies.

Useful as supplements to publicly funded services, these nongovernmental entities cannot easily become substitutes for them. Private philanthropy funds a network of not-for-profit agencies that provide valuable services to many Americans, but the extent of these services is a mere fraction of those provided by publicly subsidized programs. By the late 1980s, many not-for-profit agencies found themselves unable to sustain their budgets from existing donations and, moreover, faced cuts in their federal subsidies. In response, they turned toward fee-based programs and thus curtailed their services to impoverished clients, at the very time that the federal government was making cuts in programs serving the poor.[5] A large share of philanthropic dollars goes, moreover, to the so-called respectable charities—including universities, hospitals, private schools, and cultural activities—rather than to agencies that serve stigmatized populations, such as persons who are homeless or mentally ill.

Volunteers play a vital role in the human services system, but they cannot substitute for paid staff. Lacking training, many volunteers cannot help clients with complex problems. Some volunteers serve for relatively brief periods; they may burn out, as many agencies helping people with AIDS have discovered. Moreover, since the 1970s, the pool of available volunteers has shrunk, as more women have entered the work force.

When public authorities rely on volunteers excessively, they risk exploiting them. Consider the lack of public services for older Americans with chronic problems. Many women, unable to find adequate home health care for their parents and relatives, take on the care-giving role themselves, even though they already have jobs and heavy parenting responsibilities. Viewed from a feminist perspective, politicians who refuse to provide public funding for home health care are extorting unpaid labor from those women.

Skilled social workers often use informal networks to help specific clients or to enhance community support for a specific project, such as a halfway house. They cannot easily be substitutes for publicly funded services, however, because many individuals are not linked to informal networks, do not want community members to know about their problems, or are enmeshed in destructive networks.

Our discussion ought not suggest that volunteers, informal networks, and communities cannot assume important roles in the human services, but it is wrong to suppose that they can massively substitute for public programs.

Deterrent Policies

Deterrent policies—whether 19th-century workhouses or conservatives' efforts to place a three-year ceiling on AFDC benefits in 1995—sometimes diminish the costs of social programs, by frightening existing or potential users from seeking their benefits or by abbreviating their use. Penalties and investigations probably prevent fraudulent use of services by some people, much as audits by the Internal Revenue Service induce some people not to cheat on their taxes.

Deterrence often does not cut the costs of programs markedly, however, because it does not address the basic causes of social problems. Take the case of the AFDC program, which provides low benefits and imposes many requirements on beneficiaries. A woman who cannot find employment that pays enough to support herself and her children will seek AFDC, no matter what its regulations. If she does find a job, she may lose eligibility for Medicaid, subsidized child care, and Food Stamps. In those circumstances, placing a cap on their use of AFDC could risk depriving women of income.

In some cases, deterrent policies may even *raise* the costs of social programs, as Michael Kingsley recently argued. If the Internal Revenue Service simply distributed cash directly to people falling under poverty standards, public authorities would not need to fund the vast bureaucracy that currently investigates AFDC clients. (Kingsley also pointed out that middle-class recipients of social benefits, such as tax deductions for mortgage payments, are not subjected to frequent investigations or caps on their benefits.)[6]

Paradoxically, deterrence sometimes *increases* the incentive to cheat. Assume that you are a single mother with three children and that AFDC benefits are cut in half. Also assume that you can only find work that pays the minimum wage. Unable even to survive on these benefits, your economic incentive not to report certain income or to hide assets would increase as benefits were cut.

When seeking deterrent policies, conservatives risk overstating the extent to which people's decisions are influenced by rational considerations. For example, there are many reasons why teenagers become pregnant. Some young women are raped. Some become pregnant in the hope of cementing a relationship with a boyfriend. Some become pregnant for lack of information about birth control. Others want a child to make their lives more fulfilling. In light of these complex motivations, many social scientists doubt that deterrent policies, such as refusing or severely limiting public benefits to teenagers, *will* reduce out-of-wedlock birthrates— and they point to data from New Jersey where these birthrates *increased* when deterrent policies were imposed.[7]

Finally, deterrent policies sometimes violate ethical principles. If individuals have become dependent on public programs because well-paying work is not available to them, punitive policies punish them for events that they cannot control. If public benefits are denied to unwed teenagers who have children, those children will often experience malnutrition and other harmful outcomes.

Relying on Personal Responsibility

Conservatives often argue that the American welfare state has created a culture of dependency, within which people are accustomed to public subsidies when they encounter misfortune or to light sentences when they commit crimes. They want Americans to develop instead a culture of personal responsibility, which prizes personal efforts to be self-sufficient and to help others who experience social problems. If people are not self-sufficient or develop certain problems, conservatives often contend, they should shoulder the consequences, such as poverty or incarceration.[8]

No one would argue that citizens should not try to remain self-sufficient, but the ideology of personal responsibility often assumes that personal character is the primary reason people do, or do not, develop social problems. Even when they act responsibly, many people develop social problems. Many homeless people, for example, are unable to pay the rent because they became unemployed when their employer downsized or because they work in low-wage jobs. People with high-school educations occupy a precarious position in the service-oriented economy of the 1990s; while they can usually obtain work, they often receive wages that place them under poverty standards. Carried to an extreme, the ideology of personal responsibility blames victims of social circumstances for their plight, much as Americans in the 19th century assumed that poverty stemmed from poor character or laziness.

In some cases, public policies *should* reward responsible behaviors; for example, it is reasonable for nonsmokers to have lower health-insurance premiums. People who commit destructive acts—for example, those who drive while drunk—should suffer penalties, such as prison sentences or suspension of their licenses. When carried too far, however, the idea of personal responsibility can unduly penalize people for conditions that they cannot readily control. People with substance-abuse problems often have physiological and mental addictions, which they cannot easily overcome even if they confront extraordinary penalties. If addiction is a disease, is it fair to penalize addicts excessively?

 ## THE SOCIAL REFORM TRADITION IN AMERICAN HISTORY

Curiously, conservatives are more adept than liberals at identifying their historical roots; they boast of their affinity with many of the ideas of the founding fathers, for example. Indeed, some conservatives equate their ideology with patriotism itself, with the obvious implication that reformers possess alien ideas.

For all its faults and omissions, however, social reform in the United States is a rich and vibrant tradition and is just as integral to the nation's history as conservatism. Jane Addams exhorted Americans to define patriotism in the context of cooperative or sharing values rather than militaristic or competitive values and to find the meaning of their society from the altruism that was so evident in immigrant communities and among women. Reform ideas can sometimes be found in unlikely places. For example, Jefferson and many of the founding fathers were afraid that undue differences in wealth might cause social turmoil and demoralize persons in the lower economic strata. Dwight Eisenhower, who committed his life to a career in the military, warned of "the conjunction of an immense military establishment and a large arms industry" and urged Americans to "guard against the acquisition of unwarranted influence by the military-industrial complex."[9]

Reformers should not forget that conservative eras have been followed by liberal periods since the inception of the republic. It is worth remembering that abolitionists, progressives, New Dealers, and liberal reformers of the 1960s had their formative experiences not during reform periods but during the conservative eras that preceded them. Many reformers had despaired that their nation would again experience reform and had been accustomed to hearing rhetoric to the effect that conservative trends would dominate the nation for decades. Conservatives in the Gilded Age, the 1920s, and the 1950s had confidently predicted that the nation would experience unending prosperity and that its citizens would gratefully pay homage to corporate and conservative officials by choosing them to lead the nation. In each case, however, the nation had soon embarked on social reform, whether because citizens had tired of the narcissism and materialism of conservative eras; because of catastrophic events such as the Great Depression; because of popular anger against the exploitation of women, children, workers, or African Americans; or because of the failures of conservative policy

FIGURE 14.1   Young women demonstrating against child labor during the progressive era

SOURCE: American Heritage Library/Forbes, Inc.

prescriptions such as trickle-down economics, limited government, and unregulated markets.

In our analysis, we have emphasized the materialistic and individualistic characteristics of American culture, but these qualities coexist with altruism and other moral principles. Some social scientists contend that Americans have both private and public tendencies; whereas materialism and personal goals prevail during conservative periods, altruism and concern about societal needs prevail during liberal periods. This insight into American culture, which is confirmed historically by the rhythm of conservative and reform periods, suggests that reformers can successfully appeal to those aspects of American culture that emphasize assistance to innocent victims, assurance of equal rights, and provision of resources to needy citizens.[10]

Reformers should realize, too, that social reform is possible even during conservative periods. Fine and Chambers, respectively, note that reformers obtained some successes even during the Gilded Age and the 1920s.[11] Partly because many Americans remembered how New Deal programs saved them from the hardships of the Great Depression, President Eisenhower did not attack those social programs that had survived World War II, and he even made substantial additions to the Social Security Act. We have noted that, in the 1970s, conservative presidents consented to increases in social spending that equaled those of the 1960s. Although President Reagan made devastating cuts in means-tested programs, his major policy successes occurred during the first year of his presidency. Indeed, public opinion polls suggest that he did not markedly change American policy preferences on domestic matters during his presidency and that most Americans favored retention (or even expansion) of existing federal social programs.[12] Reagan felt compelled to agree that he would preserve safety-net programs from cuts. When he tried to frontally attack Social Security and Medicare, he suffered stinging defeats during both his first and second terms. Indeed, David Stockman, who favored sweeping cuts in social spending, noted remorsefully in 1986 that the Reagan revolution had failed.[13] Democratic candidates at local, state, and congressional levels bucked the national Republican trends not only in the 1980s but also in the 1920s and the 1950s. Both Eisenhower and Reagan had to contend with powerful Democratic contingents in both chambers of Congress—and in state and local governments—that resisted cuts in social spending.

We do not yet know whether the 1994 Congressional elections presage an extended Republican domination of national politics, as occurred in the late 19th century when Republicans defeated Grover Cleveland. As we have seen, however, social problems are persistent and conservatives' efforts to address them will most likely fail. In that case, we might expect a slow buildup of social discontent and an eventual resurgence of social reform.

Reformers should also note the rich traditions of resistance within the many groups that have experienced discrimination in the United States. The emphasis in the late 1960s and the 1970s on the rights of women, African Americans, gay men and lesbians, Latinos, and Native Americans had the salutary effect of making these groups more aware of historical reformers and of the possibility of political redress for grievances. A reform heritage has arisen to challenge conservative mythology; the formerly obscure names of distant and courageous persons have been brought to light, along with infamous events and persecutions. Discovery of older reform traditions has stimulated many Americans to become involved in social reform today.

During the nation's history, reformers have often benefited from the pragmatism of the American people, who tend to place problem solving above ideology. Conservatives can preach free-market and limited-government ideology, but Americans are unlikely to follow their dictates if they believe that assertive interventions are needed to redress pressing problems. Theodore Roosevelt, Franklin Roosevelt, John Kennedy, and Lyndon Johnson adeptly contrasted their activist, interventionist policies with the passivity of conservative politicians. Even some white, male, blue-collar voters who turned away from the Democratic party in the 1980s may come to realize that, in an era of economic globalization and extreme job insecurity, they can benefit from social policies such as vocational training. A poll conducted by the *New York Times* found that 63% of Americans who had been hard hit by layoffs believed the government "should step in to do something about layoffs and loss of jobs," as compared to only 42% of those still untouched by layoffs.[14]

As in preceding eras, a central challenge to reformers in the 1990s is to make expansion of the welfare state an issue of concern to many of the groups who are becoming increasingly influential in the nation's politics. Elderly voters, who have traditionally supported relatively conservative candidates, have medical and social welfare needs that are poorly addressed by existing policies. Workers in the service sector, including clerical and sales personnel, receive limited fringe benefits and are increasingly being supplanted by temporary workers. Women have day-care problems, often receive low wages, and face discriminatory hiring and promotion policies. Latino voters in Southwestern states contend with problems of poverty, poor education, and substance abuse. African Americans have high unemployment rates and would benefit from a variety of educational and social welfare benefits. Many young people realize that their economic prospects are bleaker than their parents'.

Reformers may despair at the difficulties of establishing coalitions of the disparate groups that have the most to gain from expansion of the welfare state, but coalitions of reform-oriented groups have occurred at numerous points in the nation's history. We noted in Chapter 6 that immigrant, middle-class, and working-class voters supported progressive politicians. Franklin Roosevelt fashioned a coalition of blue-collar workers, people of color, intellectuals, Jews, and ethnic voters that maintained considerable cohesion during the three decades following the New Deal. Although this liberal coalition frayed during the 1970s and 1980s, it could be restored if the separate hardships of different groups lead their members to believe that reform-oriented candidates are again needed. But reformers will need to be skillful in forging coalitions in a society riven by racism and economic rivalry. They need to construct proposals that address the needs of diverse groups and to develop broad-based support for social reforms.

By understanding American social welfare history, social reformers can gain a greater sense of their importance and can also take courage from the endurance of their predecessors. However, analysis of this history should also prompt expanded definitions of reform. More than the liberal reformers of past eras, today's reformers need to broaden their concerns to include tax policies, economic planning, and military spending, all of which have important consequences for social welfare policy. Traditionally, social welfare policy has focused on income maintenance or public welfare, child welfare, mental health, and housing. Although these policies are vitally important, they do not address the needs of all citizens. The failure to develop regional and national economic planning in recent decades has made it difficult to help displaced workers, to assist low-income inner-city populations in entering the economic mainstream, or to channel resources to depressed areas.

In coming decades, social reformers need to emphasize the positive roles of social programs in helping the nation cope with the globalized economy. Large segments of society will be left behind as the importance of technological skills increases. Changing careers many times in their lives, Americans will need continuing access to education; they will need medical programs that are not provided by particular employers; and they will need income supports during their transitions between jobs. In short, they will need an array of social programs to help them cope with economic and career uncertainties.

Moreover, reformers should advocate policies to reduce economic inequality. The wealth of the highest quintile is now ten times that of the lowest quintile. This extraordinary difference offends the principle of social justice and contributes to the economic suffering of persons in the lowest economic strata. Despite its importance, this issue has been missing from the agendas of most reformers in preceding eras.

Finally, social reformers should not be timid about making explicit reference to the values that justify their proposals. When Harry Hopkins told critics of his programs that relieving hunger was not debatable, he affirmed the principles of beneficence, social justice, and equality.

TOWARD POLICY PRACTICE

Social reformers in American history rarely achieved their successes without investing time and effort—and without developing specific policy-changing skills. No matter how meritorious they may be, policy proposals fail if their proponents do not gain the support of decision makers, whether in legislatures, organizations, or communities. Reformers like Dorothea Dix, Jane Addams, Margaret Sanger, and Harry Hopkins were actively involved in the political process for decades.

Some professionals take a dim view of politics; they regard those involved in politics as opportunistic, power-hungry, or wedded to special interests. It is difficult to imagine a world where politics does not exist, however, because political processes provide the means for addressing the many value-laden issues in policy making.

The political playing field often is not level, as social policy history repeatedly demonstrates. Advocates for corporations possess greater resources to hire lobbyists and engage in public relations campaigns than do advocates for stigmatized populations. The organized electorate readily throws its support behind some issues, such as tax cuts, while proposals to fund a guaranteed income or a children's allowance, for example, tend to attract less support. Far from curing or improving politics, social reformers who withdraw from the political process simply strengthen its inequities.

People who prize social justice, fairness, and beneficence need to develop organizational, community, and legislative skills in policy advocacy. Let's contrast some approaches to securing policy changes that are illustrated by historical events.

Participating in Social Movements Welfare recipients in the early 1960s were treated unfairly by many welfare offices across the nation. African Americans were often denied benefits in Southern states, in defiance of federal regulations that prohibited racial discrimination in the administration of AFDC. Even in Northern welfare offices, they often endured long waits, slow processing of claims, underpayments of benefits, and derogatory treatment by staff. Sparked by George Wiley, a national welfare rights movement was initiated in the early 1960s. With the help of community workers hired by settlement houses and other agencies, local chapters of welfare recipients were organized, not only to pressure local offices to be more responsive, but to initiate law suits to force compliance with federal regulations. Wiley headed the National Welfare Rights Organization, which sought to raise federal standards for benefits.

Establishing Advocacy Organizations Having participated in the civil rights movement, as well as antipoverty programs to help children in Mississippi, Marian Wright Edelman formed the Children's Defense Fund in 1973. Securing grants from foundations and private donors, she developed research and lobbying capabilities that she used to document a variety of problems encountered by the nation's children—in particular, inadequacies in the implementation of programs such as the Adoption Assistance and Child Welfare Act of 1980. She lobbied assertively for many pieces of legislation and played a key role in the enactment of the child care and development block grant of 1990, which provided the first major federal subsidies for child care in peacetime.

Seeking Social Reforms from Within the Government Wilbur Cohen's long career in the federal government, where he held various appointments in the executive branch, illustrates the tactics of officials who work inside bureaucracies. He favored what he called a salami approach to social reform; that is, he sought incremental slices that, when finally put together, represented major changes. Using this approach, he was able to gradually transform Social Security from merely an old-age pension to a family-assistance program, which provides benefits (and financial aid for college education) to surviving members of families who have lost a parent. He also helped to secure benefits from Social Security for persons with permanent disabilities. As an advocate for Social Security from inside government, he cultivated personal relationships with an extraordinary number of politicians from both parties, and sought to construct policies that would help them gain the support of their constituents.[15]

Educating the Public as a Prelude to Social Reforms Dorothea Dix was one of the most remarkable figures in American social policy history. Overhearing a conversation in 1841 about the treatment of "prisoners and lunatics" in East Cambridge, Massachusetts, she decided to visit the facility. Shocked by the conditions, she visited every jail and almshouse in Massachusetts and accumulated statistics and details that she presented in a "Memorial" to the state legislature. She included many personal cases; for example, she reported that, in the almshouse at Danvers, she saw

> a young woman exhibiting a condition of neglect and misery blotting out the faintest idea of comfort . . . there she stood, clinging to, or beating upon, the bars of her caged apartment . . . the unwashed frame invested with fragments of unclean garments; the air so extremely offensive . . . that it was not possible to remain beyond a few moments . . . irritation of the body, produced by utter filth and exposure, incited her to the horrid process of tearing off her skin by inches, her face, neck, and person were thus disfigured to hideousness.[16]

Her first Memorial had an enormous impact and prompted angry denunciations of her as a liar and sensationalist. Community leaders rallied to her side as they confirmed her findings, and a rising tide of public indignation forced the hand of the state's legislators, who funded space for 200 insane persons in the mental asylum in Worcester. She followed the same course in about twenty other states. In one three-year period, she traveled 10,000 miles by horseback, carriage, and steamboat and visited 300 county jails and 500 almshouses. She not only presented Memorials, but also got to know legislators; she had influential people bring them to her room or alcove in the state capitol, where she talked to 15 or 20 at a time. Realizing that many states lacked revenues to fund mental institutions, she often had to persuade legislators to enact taxes, as well. In 1854, she persuaded both chambers of Congress to enact legislation that would grant the proceeds from land sales to the states for the construction of mental institutions, only to have President Pierce veto the legislation.

Electing Reform-Oriented Candidates to Office Realizing that it would lose its tax-exempt status as a not-for-profit organization if it participated directly in partisan politics, the National Association of Social Workers (NASW) formed PACE in 1975. Funded by contributions from NASW's membership and with its accounts separate from NASW, PACE asks political candidates in state and federal elections to respond to a questionnaire that probes their positions on social issues. Those candidates that PACE approves receive contributions for their campaigns.

Many reformers have taken positions in the campaigns of specific candidates or have worked in local campaign offices on tasks such as media relations, outreach to voters, or fund raising. Beginning with Jane Addams's work in helping to form the Progressive party in 1912, many social reformers have worked for political parties, at the national or state level. Some social workers have sought elective office; for example, Democrat Ron Dellums has been regularly reelected to the House of Representatives from the Eighth District in Berkeley, California.

Influencing Policy from Organizational Settings Often working with advocacy groups

and professional associations, social workers have sought to influence the policies of legislative bodies from their positions in specific agencies. The situation for rape victims was bleak in the early 1970s, when they were commonly assumed to have incited attacks by their clothing or demeanor. Hospital staff often treated them with contempt in emergency rooms and failed even to collect evidence in a manner that could be used by the District Attorney. Rules of evidence in court often allowed the accused offender to place the woman on trial; for example, his attorney could question her about her prior sexual liaisons. Nor did rape victims receive monetary compensation from the state, even though other crime victims were often remunerated for injuries and lost time from work. Concerned that Los Angeles county failed to provide humane services for victims of rape, Gail Abarbanel, a social worker who directs the social work department at Santa Monica Hospital, developed a coalition that proceeded to pressure hospitals, the police department, and the district attorney to put in place new policies for treating rape victims and prosecuting offenders.

Whistleblowers The progressive reformer Homer Folks illustrates how some reformers have sought policy reforms in the agencies and institutions that implement social policies. He was astonished to find, in the early 20th century, that mental institutions in New York State were riddled with corruption and hired staff on the basis of personal friendships. Working from outside the institutions, he mobilized pressure to force the state governor to implement a variety of reforms.

In some cases, social workers have obtained changes of agency policies while holding positions within them. Many of these reforms occur in low-conflict and undramatic fashion—for example, when a staff member alerts his or her supervisor to a dysfunctional policy or inadequate implementation of a meritorious policy. Staff sometimes believe that serious wrongdoing occurs in their agencies, but find that they cannot challenge the unethical practices through ordinary channels for fear that they will lose their jobs. In these rare cases—and only after considerable contemplation—social workers can divulge their concerns to outside agencies or professional organizations.

Seeking Partnerships Within a New Nationalism

We have argued that the nation needs a large, continuing welfare state to address an array of social problems. While conservatives have assertively sought to devolve federal policy roles to states, localities, and the private sector, only the federal government possesses the resources to fund the welfare state; it currently spends roughly twice the resources of all local and state governments combined.[17] Only federal authorities can devise strategies for social problems that cut across states' boundaries—for example, the economic uncertainty that stems from global economic competition or threats to the nation's health such as the AIDS epidemic. Some analysts have begun to speak of the need for a *new nationalism*—that is, for national direction and funding of social programs.[18] By supporting national advocacy groups and linking them to local ones, social reformers can fight efforts to cut federal funding or to devolve policies excessively to local entities.

Yet federal guidance and funding does not mean that state and local governments, not-for-profits, communities, and corporations should not possess substantial roles in social policy. Take the example of the Children's Planning Council established in 1995 in Los Angeles County. Traditional children's programs had proved insufficient to address a range of problems. Schools, child welfare departments, public health programs, and children's mental-health programs had rarely coordinated their activities, much less acted jointly to secure additional funds from the county, the state, or the federal government. The Children's Planning Council is headed by Jacqueline McCroskey, a faculty member of the School of Social Work at the University of Southern California. The County Board of Supervisors ordered its various departments to help build a grass-roots decision-making system to analyze current priorities; to reallocate public funds to new, coordinated programs; and to build partnerships with an array of not-for-profit agencies such as child guidance clinics and child care centers. With representatives from local communities as well as social agencies, the Children's Planning Council would play a central role in forging partnerships between communities, not-for-profits, and public agencies. For example, the Council hoped to establish partnerships that would coordinate preventive programs, which are currently provided in piecemeal fashion by county hospitals, public health nurses in schools, Medicaid authorities, and private hospitals. Far from contradicting the need for a new nationalism, such local partnerships ought to be nested within a national welfare state that provides resources to sustain innovative programs but cedes considerable decision making to local officials and communities.

Social reformers should also realize that some programs need to be funded *and* planned centrally. The states lack the resources to fund antipoverty programs and may discriminate against poor people, who lack political clout and are easily stigmatized. No matter what the short-term outcome of battles between President Clinton and the Republican Congress in 1996 may be, the federal government should continue to fund such programs as Food Stamps, SSI, Medicaid, and Medicare and should not devolve them to the states. We can conceptualize the welfare state as an array of programs on a continuum extending from sole federal funding and implementation (for example, Food Stamps) to sole local funding and implementation (for example, local recreation programs and considerable portions of secondary education). Between these two poles, we can imagine many permutations, with varying degrees of funding and guidance from federal authorities.[19]

As we study the history of social welfare policies, we come to understand the conditions in which Americans lived in eras, such as the Gilded Age, when social policy barely existed. In so doing, we are sensitized to the needs of citizens who experience poverty or other social problems and made aware of our ability to work for reform. By participating in the shaping of contemporary policies, we join reforming pioneers of the past, as we add our strands to a tapestry that is beautiful to behold, but never finished.

NOTES

1. Marvin Olasky, *The Tragedy of American Compassion* (Lanham, Md.: Regnery Gateway, 1992).

2. Joseph Castrovinci, "Prelude to Welfare Capitalism: The Role of Business in the Enactment of Workmen's Compensation Legislation in Illinois, 1905–1912," *Social Service Review,* 50 (March 1976), 277.

3. Michael Fabricant and Stephen Burghardt, *The Welfare Crisis and the Transformation of Social Service Work* (Armonk, N.Y.: Sharpe, 1992).

4. Kevin Phillips, *The Politics of Rich and Poor: Wealth and the American Electorate in the Reagan Aftermath* (New York: Harper Perennial, 1990).

5. Lester Salamon, "The Marketization of Welfare: Changing Nonprofit and For-Profit Roles in the American Welfare State," *Social Service Review* (March 1993), 16–39.

6. Michael Kingsley, "The Ultimate Block Grant," *New Yorker* (May 29, 1995), 36–40.

7. *New York Times* (October 22, 1995), xiii-NJ, 11.

8. Olasky, *The Tragedy of American Compassion,* pp. 35–42.

9. Chester Pach and Elmo Richardson, *The Presidency of Dwight D. Eisenhower* (Lawrence, Kans.: University of Kansas Press, 1991), pp. 229–230.

10. Herbert McClosky and John Zaller, *The American Ethos: Public Attitudes Toward Capitalism and Democracy* (Cambridge, Mass.: Harvard University Press, 1984), pp. 162, 291–292; Arthur M. Schlesinger, *The Cycles of History* (Boston: Houghton Mifflin, 1986), pp. 23–48.

11. Clarke Chambers, *Seedtime of Reform: American Social Service and Social Action, 1918–1933* (Minneapolis, Minn.: University of Minnesota Press, 1963), pp. 29–58, 153–182; Sidney Fine, *Laissez-Faire and the General Welfare State: A Study of Conflict in America, 1865–1901* (Ann Arbor: University of Michigan Press, 1956), pp. 259–369.

12. Everett Ladd, "The Reagan Phenomenon and Public Attitudes Toward Government." In Lester Salamon and Michael Lund, eds., *The Reagan Presidency and the Governing of America* (Washington, D.C.: Urban Institute, 1985), pp. 221–249.

13. David Stockman, *The Triumph of Politics: Why the Reagan Revolution Failed* (New York: Harper & Row, 1986), pp. 376–411.

14. Rick Bragg, "Big Holes Where the Dignity Used To Be," *New York Times,* (March 5, 1996), part A, 8.

15. Edward Berkowitz, *Mr. Social Security: The Life of Wilbur Cohen* (Lawrence, Kans.: University of Kansas Press, 1995).

16. Francis Tiffany, *Life of Dorothea Lynde Dix* (Boston: Houghton, Mifflin, 1891), pp. 78–79.

17. Alice Rivlin, *Reviving the American Dream* (Washington, D.C.: Brookings Institution, 1992), p. 86.

18. Bruce Jansson and Susan Smith, "Articulating a 'New Nationalism' in American Social Policy," *Social Work* (September 1996), in press.

19. For a discussion of eight criteria that may be used to determine where, on this continuum, particular programs should be placed, see Jansson and Smith, "Articulating a 'New Nationalism.'"

Name Index

Subject Index

AAA. *See* Agricultural Adjustment Agency
AARP. *See* American Association of Retired Persons
AB. *See* Aid to the Blind
Abolitionist movement
  Civil War and, 92
  emancipation of slaves and, 20, 95
  women's involvement in, 77–78, 98–99
Abortion
  Clinton era opposition to, 343
  conservative opposition to, 6, 256, 294–295
  disallowal of Medicaid for, 256, 283, 294
  ethical analysis of, 23
  Roe v. *Wade* decision on, 23, 256, 262, 294
ACCD. *See* American Coalition of Citizens with Disabilities
ACLU. *See* American Civil Liberties Union
Acquired immunodeficiency syndrome (AIDS), 282, 292–293, 376–377
Action for Mental Health report, 211
ADC. *See* Aid to Dependent Children
Adolescent Family Life Act, 294
Adoption Assistance and Child Welfare Act (1980), 16, 255, 261, 295, 296, 300, 387
Advertising industry, 149
Advocacy organizations, 387
AFDC. *See* Aid to Families with Dependent Children
Affirmative action
  Civil Rights Act of 1991 and, 299
  Clinton era opposition to, 341–342
  conservative opposition to, 4, 302
  liberal support for, 6
  numerical quotas in, 255, 268
  white backlash against, 250, 268
  women and, 227, 249
AFL. *See* American Federation of Labor
African Americans
  abolitionist racism and, 92

African Americans *(continued)*
  AIDS epidemic and, 292
  attack on racist policies by, 204
  in Civilian Conservation Corps, 161
  civil rights movement and, 207–210
  Clinton era racism against, 340–342
  desegregation policies for, 214
  emancipation from slavery of, 92–94, 354
  employment in 1920s for, 149–150
  Head Start program and, 20
  lynching laws protecting, 176
  militant movement among, 223
  as New Deal era outgroup, 185–187
  post-emancipation conditions for, 94–98
  as progressive era outgroup, 131–135
  as Reagan-Bush era outgroup, 291
  settlement houses and, 123
  as slaves in colonial America, 47–50
  societal disadvantages of, 354
African slaves, 47–50
Aftercare services, 124
Age Discrimination Act (1967), 262
Agrarian society
  colonial America as, 52
  pre–Civil War America as, 60
Agricultural Adjustment Agency (AAA), 163–164
AICP. *See* Association for Improving the Condition of the Poor
AIDS. *See* Acquired immunodeficiency syndrome
Aid to Dependent Children (ADC), 175, 178, 188, 193
Aid to Families with Dependent Children (AFDC)
  block grant proposal for, 327, 332–335, 340
  child welfare and, 335, 340, 342–343
  deterrent policies and, 382
  inadequacy of, 204
  increase in numbers receiving, 211, 219–221
  Medicaid and, 217
  opposition to, 7, 219–221, 244

Aid to Families with Dependent Children (AFDC) *(continued)*
  origin of, 175
  Reagan's cuts in, 276, 278, 283
  societal benefits of, 374
  work requirement for, 220–221
Aid to the Blind (AB), 175, 179, 245
Alcatraz Island, 231
Alcoholism
  in colonial America, 43
  of Irish immigrants, 76
  in nineteenth-century America, 62, 63
  temperance movement and, 65–66
Alien Land Laws, 132–133
Almshouses, 63, 67, 70
Alzheimer's disease, 297, 375
AMA. *See* American Medical Association
American Association for Organizing Charity, 191
American Association of Old Age Security, 151
American Association of Retired Persons (AARP), 15, 261, 297, 314, 336
American Association of Social Workers, 191
American Civil Liberties Union (ACLU), 229
American Coalition of Citizens with Disabilities (ACCD), 261
American Enterprise Institute, 270
American Federation of Labor (AFL), 127, 156, 183
American Freedmen's Inquiry Commission, 93
American Indians. *See* Native Americans
American Life Lobby, 292
American Medical Association (AMA), 14, 122, 142, 176, 210, 217, 336, 378
American Political party, 76
American Psychiatric Association, 229
American Revolution, 37–38
American Social Science Association, 140

Photo Credits

Chapter 1: 3, (*left*) © Scott Stewart/UPI/Bettmann; (*center*) UPI/Bettmann; (*right*) © Gutierrez/UPI/Bettmann. **Chapter 2: 19,** (*left*) © David Weintraub/Photo Researchers, Inc.; (*right*) © Gerd Ludwig/Woodfin Camp & Associates; **Chapter 3: 44,** Bettmann Archive. **Chapter 4: 62,** courtesy of YMCA of the USA Archives, University of Minnesota Libraries. **Chapter 5: 102,** © Lewis Hines/Bettmann. **Chapter 6: 111,** © Rogers/Monkmeyer; **138,** Corbis-Bettmann. **Chapter 7: 153,** The Bettmann Archive. **Chapter 8: 174,** UPI/Bettmann. **Chapter 9: 208,** UPI/Bettmann. **Chapter 10: 260,** © Ron Bennett/UPI/Bettmann. **Chapter 11: 298,** (*left*) © Bernard Wolf/Monkmeyer; (*right*) © 1986 Andy Levin/Photo Researchers, Inc. **Chapter 12: 339,** © Wilfredo Lee/AP/Wide World. **Chapter 13: 365,** © Tim Clary/UPI/Bettmann. **Chapter 14: 384,** American Heritage Library/Forbes, Inc.

TO THE OWNER OF THIS BOOK:

We hope that you have found *The Reluctant Welfare State: American Social Welfare Policies—Past, Present, and Future*, Third Edition, useful. So that this book can be improved in a future edition, would you take the time to complete this sheet and return it? Thank you.

School and address: _____

Department: _____

Instructor's name: _____

1. What I like most about this book is: _____

_____

_____

2. What I like least about this book is: _____

_____

_____

3. My general reaction to this book is: _____

_____

4. The name of the course in which I used this book is: _____

_____

5. Were all of the chapters of the book assigned for you to read? _____

   If not, which ones weren't? _____

6. In the space below, or on a separate sheet of paper, please write specific suggestions for improving this book and anything else you'd care to share about your experience in using the book.

_____

_____

_____

_____

_____

Optional:

Your name: _____ Date: _____

May Brooks/Cole quote you, either in promotion for *The Reluctant Welfare State: American Social Welfare Policies—Past, Present, and Future*, Third Edition, or in future publishing ventures?

Yes: _____ No: _____

Sincerely,

Bruce S. Jansson

FOLD HERE

- -

BUSINESS REPLY MAIL

FIRST CLASS   PERMIT NO. 358   PACIFIC GROVE, CA

POSTAGE WILL BE PAID BY ADDRESSEE

ATT: *Bruce S. Jansson* _____

**Brooks/Cole Publishing Company
511 Forest Lodge Road
Pacific Grove, California 93950-9968**

FOLD HERE

Brooks/Cole is dedicated to publishing quality books for the helping professions. If you would like to learn more about our publications, please use this mailer to request our catalogue.

Name: _____

Street Address: _____

City, State, and Zip: _____

FOLD HERE

FOLD HERE